THE DOROTHY DUNNETT COMPANION

VOLUME II

THE DOROTHY DUNNETT COMPANION

VOLUME II

ELSPETH MORRISON

FOREWORD BY DOROTHY DUNNETT

MICHAEL JOSEPH
an imprint of
PENGUIN BOOKS

MICHAEL JOSEPH

Published by the Penguin Group
Penguin Books Ltd, 80 Strand, London WC2R 0RL, England
Penguin Putnam Inc., 375 Hudson Street, New York, New York 10014, USA
Penguin Books Australia Ltd, 250 Camberwell Road,
Camberwell, Victoria 3124, Australia
Penguin Books Canada Ltd, 10 Alcorn Avenue, Toronto, Ontario, Canada M4V 3B2
Penguin Books India (P) Ltd, 11 Community Centre,
Panchsheel Park, New Delhi - 110 017, India
Penguin Books (NZ) Ltd, Cnr Rosedale and Airborne Roads,
Albany, Auckland, New Zealand
Penguin Books (South Africa) (Pty) Ltd, 24 Sturdee Avenue,
Rosebank 2196, South Africa

Penguin Books Ltd, Registered Offices: 80 Strand, London WC2R 0RL, England

www.penguin.com

First published in the United States of America by Vintage 2002
First published in Great Britain by Michael Joseph 2002
1

Printed in Great Britain by Clays Ltd, St Ives plc

A CIP catalogue record for this book is available from the British Library

ISBN 0-718-14546-1

In Memory of Dorothy Dunnett
1923–2001

What brought us both here? A joyous adventure.

The Unicorn Hunt, Chapter 23

Nec scire fas est omnia

Contents

Foreword

This, like the first *Companion*, is a treasure chest of historical facts. There is no fiction in it. It deals with jokes and paintings and poetry, with wars and sea battles and tournaments, with flamboyant rogues and explorers, with pioneers in trade and invention, with men of faith and women of power and character, all of whom lived within the span of one hundred years – from the middle of the fifteenth to the middle of the sixteenth century – while Europe and the lands on its fringes were experiencing the great explosion of art and culture and learning known as the Renaissance. They all have a place here because they make up the worlds of Lymond and Niccolò, the two fictitious men whose story, after forty years, has just drawn to a close.

The character of Francis Crawford of Lymond, an international mercenary leader and a Scot, was created in 1960, and his life over ten years was detailed in six long, linked novels. The next series, by contrast, dealt with Nicholas vander Poele or de Fleury, a dyeyard apprentice in Flemish Burgundy, and eight consecutive volumes followed his developing merchant career in countries ranging from Cyprus to Iceland to Persia. Fictionally and historically, the two series are connected and form a cycle of fourteen books.

Elspeth Morrison devised the initial *Companion* to satisfy the curiosity of all those who wished to trace or have translated the quotations and allusions in the novels, and to affirm the real historical base for the story. She dealt with the six books of the *Lymond Chronicles* and those five *House of Niccolò* novels then published, avoiding, with tact, any historical fact that might give away the line of the plot, and the final resolution of the entire work.

The intention was to confine this second *Companion* to the final three *Niccolò* novels, which are substantial. Then it seemed only fair to provide some of the historical links between the two series: to show how Lymond's Ivan the Terrible was the grandson of Nicholas's Ivan the Great, how Nostradamus in one was the grandsire of Nostradamus the prophet in the other; how the family of Lennox and Aubigny descended through the missing years between the two tales.

It then struck us both that there was a great deal in the *Lymond* and early *Niccolò* books that had escaped the first volume, and ought to be packed in. It was packed in. Next, a decision was made which has made this volume rather different from the first, and perhaps different from most of its kind.

Great historical figures become the subject of books and monographs and appear in international biographies. Others are not so lucky. There are either no biographies for them at all, or those that exist may be published in foreign documents and periodicals, and can be contradictory.

The *Niccolò* novels in particular are about a cross-section of society. Much of the latter part of the story takes place in Scotland, among the genuine merchants of Berwick and Edinburgh, the skippers of Leith, the burgesses and workmen of the towns and the foreigners who settled there or competed with them. In the case of such little-known men and women, the research has been my own. Hence, among the wealth of Elspeth's enticing entries, I have been allowed to intrude the more leisurely life stories of Anselm Adorne and Wattie Bertram and Paúel Benecke, of the Sinclairs and the Prestons and the Berecrofts family, which have played such a large part in the novels.

This volume also possesses, at the end, a special bibliography. This lists most of the books and records which provided material for the *Lymond* and *Niccolò* novels and for the entries in the two *Companions*. It doesn't pretend to be a comprehensive bibliography for the period – that can be found elsewhere. Instead, it dwells on those areas, both wider and narrower than the Renaissance, which the fourteen novels explore. Many of the books are from my own library. The earliest and maybe the most charming is the small compilation of Psalms printed at Geneva in 1569.

Richenda Todd, once again, has been the gifted and spirited editor of this work, as she was of the novels. But it is Elspeth to whom tribute is due for the *Companion* as it stands – a longer, denser, more challenging book, by the nature of things, than the first. That, I would have said, could not be surpassed. This more than equals it. I am immensely grateful to her for providing the novels with such a lively, thoughtful and finely tailored companion.

DOROTHY DUNNETT
Edinburgh, July 2001

Author's Note

THE purpose of this *Companion* is to enhance the reader's appreciation and enjoyment of the novels of Dorothy Dunnett. Arranged alphabetically, it aims to provide an easily accessible but solidly researched background to the historical characters, allusions and references which underpin the fiction of the *Lymond Chronicles* and the *House of Niccolò* series. As with Volume I, the *Companion* does not attempt to analyse aspects of the Renaissance which are outwith the novels.

What has been most rewarding has been the opportunity to follow events and individuals from the latter half of the fifteenth century to the mid-sixteenth and to see how closely woven are the bloodlines of the major families. Historic characters who make an appearance in the *House of Niccolò* often turn out to have descendants who interact with the fictional Crawford of Lymond. In addition to new maps, this volume includes select genealogies of the important families who feature in both series. Dorothy Dunnett's novels are unlike anything else I have ever read, and her characters are as vibrant and alive as the descriptions of the period they inhabit. The reason is undoubtedly the extensive and meticulous research which has gone into their creation. There has not been time to trace every reference and allusion, but for the first time what has been created, in consultation with Dorothy Dunnett, is a bibliography of the sources consulted for both the *Lymond* and *Niccolò* series. From general histories to the most exacting of primary sources, those readers who wish to understand more about the politics, economics, literature or music of the novels than can be distilled within these pages may be encouraged to do research of their own, knowing that in the calendars of state papers, or the collections of poetry, they may find one of Lymond's allusions or quotes, or one of Niccolò's schemes, which Dorothy had plucked from obscurity, and which has been hanging in the air ever since.

The layout and style of the *Companion* is similar to that of Volume I. Cross references to other items within the book are emboldened; cross references to items appearing in Volume I are asterisked, and the two volumes are best kept side by side. Quotations and phrases in foreign languages are indexed under their first words as they appear in the novels; references and allusions are indexed under their main subject. The names of characters who appear in the *dramatis personae* of the novels are capitalised at the head of their biographies, but historic or mythic individuals who are only alluded to are given in lower case. As with its predecessor, one-word titles have been allocated to each of the novels, and a key to these abbreviations has been included. Two new abbreviations, HN and LC, indicate that the subject of the entry may be of importance throughout both series of novels, rather than the entry referring to a comment or event in a particular chapter of a particular novel. Again as before, part and chapter numbers are given with the book references, rather than page numbers. Where the subject of an entry appears several times, then the book reference only is given. When characters or subjects appear in more than one book, the one in which they are first mentioned is listed. Unless otherwise indicated, all translations are by Dorothy Dunnett. Biographies and other entries contributed by Dorothy Dunnett are indicated by her initials.

This *Companion* has been hard work, but tremendous fun to research and compile. However, the project would not have been possible had it not been for the full co-operation and participation of Dorothy Dunnett, who has allowed me unlimited access to her library and research notes. She has contributed many of the biographies, representing the formulation of decades of research; and in addition to these, her light touch on other entries from *Herpestes Ichneumon* to puffins has made this book what it is.

Sadly, Dorothy fell ill shortly after completing work on this volume, and she died on 9 November 2001.

She is sorely missed.

ELSPETH MORRISON
Edinburgh, January 2002

Acknowledgements

Thanks, first and foremost, must go to Dorothy,
whose intelligence, humour and generous spirit
have made this book a labour of love.
Thanks also to Richenda, who has
helped make sense of it all.

Abbreviations

The novels of Dorothy Dunnett are abbreviated thus in the A–Z:

The House of Niccolò HN

Niccolò Rising RISING

The Spring of the Ram RAM

Race of Scorpions SCORPIONS

Scales of Gold SCALES

The Unicorn Hunt UNICORN

To Lie with Lions LIONS

Caprice and Rondo RONDO

Gemini GEMINI

The Lymond Chronicles LC

The Game of Kings KINGS

Queens' Play QUEENS

The Disorderly Knights KNIGHTS

Pawn in Frankincense PAWN

The Ringed Castle CASTLE

Checkmate CHECKMATE

Bold type (e.g. **Lauder Bridge**) indicates an entry in this volume. Asterisk (e.g. Bishop Kennedy*) indicates an entry in Volume I. Bold type plus asterisk (e.g. **William Knollys***) indicates entries in both volumes.

b. born

c. *circa*

ch. chapter

d. died

(D.D.) entry by Dorothy Dunnett

ed., eds editor, edited, editors

edn edition

fl. *floruit*, flourished

intro. introduction

n.d. no date

no. number

pub. published

trans., tr. translator, translated

vol., vols volume, volumes

THE DOROTHY DUNNETT COMPANION

VOLUME II

A

A coat of arms . . . with a fish in it . . . and a tree and a ring?: LIONS, 22: The reference is to the armorial bearings of the city of Glasgow, which famously incorporates an oak tree proper, the stem at the base surmounted by a salmon on its back, also proper, with a signet ring in its mouth. It signifies an incident in the life of St Mungo. The Queen of his day being rash, she had confided her marital gift-ring to a soldier. The King, observing it on the sleeping man's hand, flung it into the river and went to his Queen, pretending he wished her to show it to him. When she turned to the saint in despair, Mungo advised that a fishing-line be cast into the Clyde, assuring her that the first fish to be caught would have the ring in its mouth or its stomach. He was right. Repossessing the ring, the Queen was able to confound her jealous husband by producing it. The story fails to mention the fate of the soldier. (D. D.)

A Dead Sea apple: KINGS, IV, 2: Mandeville* describes the fruit of the trees on the shore of the Dead Sea in *The Travels of Sir John Mandeville*:

> By the side of this sea grow trees that bear apples fine of colour and delightful to look at; but when they are broken or cut, only ashes and dust and cinders are found inside, as a token of the vengeance that God took on those five cities and the countryside round about, burning them with the fires of Hell.

A good lord, so brave, so sweet, so very debonair: CHECKMATE, V, 8: Spoken of a man lying ill, but in fact the lord is Christ, and the writer Henry Plantagenet, Duke of Lancaster. 'Sweet and debonair' was a favourite phrase of the time, also used of the lover in the French poem, 'The Romaunt of the Rose'. *Jésus, ce prophète debonaire* makes an appearance in French **Mystery Plays.** (D. D.)

A large reporter of his owne Acts: CHECKMATE, I, 5: Quoted from one of the books in the collection of the character the Dame de Doubtance, the description also appears in the *Christian Astrology* (1647) of William Lilly (1602–1681) as the characteristics of those ruled by the planet Mars (extract):

Nature:	He is a Masculine, Nocturnall Planet, in nature hot and dry, cholerick and fiery, the lesser Infortune, author of Quarrels, Strifes, Contentions.
Manners when well dignified:	In feats of Warre and Courage invincibel, scorning any should exceed him, subject to no Reason, Bold, Confident, Immoveable, Contentious, challenging all Honour to themselves, Valiant, lovers of Warre and things pertaining thereunto, hazarding himselfe to all Perils, willingly will obey no body, or submit to any; a large Reporter of his owne Acts, one that slights all things in comparison of Victory, and yet of prudent behaviour in his owne affaires.

Those governed by Mars are prone to "The Gall, the left Eare, tertian Feavers, pestilent burning Feavers, Megrams in the Head . . . and such other Diseases as arise by abundance of too much Choller, Anger or Passion".

***A! mohrioh* [*morior*]:** GEMINI, 9: '*A morior, a morior, a morior, dum, quod amem, cogor et non amor!*' From '*Sic Mea Fata*', a fairly perfunctory Latin love song, in which the swain protests that he would die happy, if he could only sleep just once (literally, '*dormiero*' . . .) with his beloved. The following is the first verse:

Sic mea fata canendo solor,
ut nece proxima facit olor.
blandus heret meo cor de dolor,
roseus effugit ore color.
cura crescente, labore vigente,
vigore labente, miser morior;
tam male pectora multat amor.
a morior, a morior,
dum, quod amem, cogor et non amor!

> By singing, I ease my fate as does the swan near death. An agreeable sorrow clings to my heart, the rosy colour has fled from my face. From increasing care, lively pain, and declining vigour, miserably I die, so badly does love punish my breast. Ah, I die, ah, I die, ah, I die, because I must love and am not loved!

As can be seen, it presents difficulties to one who cannot wholly pronounce the letter 'R'. (D. D.)

A nasty bite for the ass called Brunellus: LIONS, 17: From a popular twelfth-century satire, the *Speculum Stultorum*, which tells how the ass called Brunellus set off through Europe in search of a longer tail, like a monk wishing to better himself. On the way it tried to pick up some learning, and made an abrasive study of all the existing religious orders, meaning to join one. Finding none to its taste, it had decided to found one itself, when its master reclaimed it. So it was brought back to become a plain beast of burden, required to be content with the natural order of things. (D. D.)

A woman is a worthy thing; they do the wash and do the wring: KINGS, IV, 1: From the early lyric 'In Praise of Women':

I am lyght as any roe
To preyse wemen wher that I goo.

To onpreyse wemen yt were a shame,
For a woman was thy dame;
Our blessyd lady beryth the name
of all women wher that they goo.

A woman ys a worthy thyng -
they do the washe and do the wrynge;
'lullay, lullay,' she dothe the synge,
And yet she hath but care and woo.

A woman ys a worthy wyght,
she seruyth a man both daye and nyght,
therto she puttyth all her myght,
And yet she hathe bot care and woo.

***Abboccamento*: See The *abboccamento*. The *impalmamento*. The *ductio*.**

ACCIAJUOLI, Nicholai Giorgio de': See **Greek with the Wooden Leg, The.**

Ad unum mollis opus: PAWN, 8: The lines are from Horace: '*Epodes, Inachiam ter nocte potes, mihi semper ad unum mollis opus*', or: 'Epodes, you may manage to please Inachia three times a night but me, I only ever aspire to one tender deed'.

Adieu, mon compère. Dieu vous doint bonne vie et longue: CHECKMATE, V, 9: In old French: 'Farewell, my friend. May God give you a good life, and a long one'.

Addorsed: RONDO, 39: In heraldry, lions placed back-to-back are termed 'addorsed'.

Adoremus: RONDO, 6: As invoked by **Ludovico de Severi da Bologna*** this was shorthand for the usual formula, *Adoremus Patrem et Filium et Spiritum Sanctum.* The triple *Parcia* which followed was, simply, *Benedicte, parcite nobis, Amen.* Recitations were often resorted to in monasteries as a method of culinary timing (see UNICORN, 42). In the quoted instance, the Patriarch was encouraging the crisping of a piece of roast hare. (D. D.)

ADORNE, Anselm:* HN: (1424–1483) The death of Anselm Adorne in Scotland in 1483 is the historical climax of the *House of Niccolò* novels. From his appearance in the first pages of RISING, he has illustrated through his career the changing fortunes of Europe in his time, and in the final years of the story, not only his life but those of all the other great protagonists – **Edward IV*** of England, **Louis XI*** of France, **Charles, Duke of Burgundy,*** Sultan **Mehmet II*** of Turkey, **Uzum Hasan*** of Persia, Sigismond* and Eleanor of the Tyrol – now draw to a close. Even the reign of **King James III*** of Scotland, although he has some years to live, has entered the channel which will inevitably lead to its end. If a line can be drawn between one age and another, it asks to be drawn here. Shortly, the world will shrink, and the entire power game in Europe will change in the years between the eras described in the *House of Niccolò* and the *Lymond Chronicles.*

Meanwhile, the abilities which had carried Adorne through his complex responsibilities towards Burgundy, Scotland and his own extended family were to be called upon on his return in April 1471 from his year-long journey round the Mediterranean and beyond (described in Volume I). On the way back, he had visited the grave of a brother in a monastery at Montello, near Venice, and had called on Sigismond of the Tyrol, married to a Scottish princess, the Duchess Eleanor, aunt to James III. Home in Bruges,* he found his master Duke Charles now favouring the Yorkist side in the English civil war later known as the Wars of the Roses. It was politic therefore to usher from Bruges (with ducal endorsement) the **Princess Mary** of Scotland, who had been evicted from that country with her husband for political reasons, and had spent the last year in Adorne's house, the Hôtel Jerusalem.

Originally, Scotland, like France, had been of Lancastrian (anti-Yorkist) persuasion, and might be expected to take the unfortunate family back, especially as it included the King's sister and her two Bruges-born children. Yet when Anselm Adorne and his wife tried to promote a reconciliation, leaving for Scotland from Calais in October 1471, they were only partially successful. Despite the urging of Duke Charles, his own second cousin, James III refused to admit the Princess's husband **Thomas Boyd,*** Earl of Arran, or Lord Boyd his father. They remained in England, while the Princess and her children settled in Scotland, where Adorne and his wife were to remain for a year.

During that time, the King showed his appreciation for Adorne's care of his sister, and for his advice on trade between Flanders and Scotland. He was probably impressed by the presentation volume on the family's pilgrimage, dedicated to King James by the Adornes' oldest son **Jan.** None of Adorne's sons is known to have accompanied his parents on this visit, although the town of Perth had registered the existence, in February 1472, of 'Anselm Adorne of Cortachy, knight, burgess and guildsman, and his son Anselm'. This looks like a mistake. The young Anselm Adorne is usually identified with the son who enrolled in **Rhodes** as a Knight of the Order of St. John.* The junior Anselm of Perth is more likely to have been Adorne's sister's son and energetic trader, **Anselm Sersanders**, who passed much of his life in Scotland. To qualify as a burgess, Adorne must have owned a house in Perth, which was not a long ride from Cortachy, and which was then a port, shipping direct to Bruges's port of Sluys.

In June 1472, Adorne received letters patent appointing him consul or Conservator of Scots Privileges in all the states of the Duke of Burgundy, his salary to be raised by a tax on each sack of wool, skins or other. Traditionally, this required him to pursue, procure, request or defend the goods of Scots merchants, and to uphold the standing of Scotland in Flanders. Over the years, he was to serve the Scots King in other ways, arranging for the export of lances to Scotland, and the reception and training of John Brown, a man of the King's household, in the art of playing the lute.

Presumably for his own maintenance, and as a further recompense for Adorne's trouble in habouring the King's sister for so long (his papers, bringing the Princess from Calais, had allowed for a train of up to a hundred, with luggage and jewellery and silver), Adorne was also given in April 1472 'for his worthy and faithful service' some of the lands forfeited by Lord Boyd and his son in the barony of Teling, Forfar, and land in Polgavy, Perthshire, including the mill. The gift was to Adorne and his heirs, and witnesses to the gift included **Thomas Spens**, Bishop of Aberdeen; William Tulloch, Bishop of Orkney; **James, Lord Hamilton** (in two years to marry the Princess Mary) and **William Monypenny.**

The Maxwell family retained some interest in both Teling and Polgavy which remained undisturbed. Despite its heritable nature, the portion which passed to the Boyds and then to Adorne was to be removed from Adorne in October 1482, and returned, for life, to the Princess Mary, whose second marriage had ended, and whose son, James Boyd, had sided with Albany in a recent revolt. No reason was given. The gift also included Boyd land which had not passed to Adorne, and was followed by a separate donation of the lands and castle of Kilmarnock, and other holdings in Ayrshire.

Adorne had already received from James III his greatest honour, the Collar of the Order of the Unicorn,* seen today on his effigy in Bruges.

Paradoxically, the King of England also presented an honour, but to Adorne's wife. The windows of their church in Bruges, painted long after her death, show Margriet's coat of arms encircled with the sun and rose collar of March, a badge given by Edward IV to men and women who had given him service. Among other recipients were a married pair, one of whom (Thomas Colt) had helped negotiate the marriage of **Margaret of York**, Duchess of Burgundy, Edward's sister. The collar may have come to Adorne's wife through the Duchess, who had acted as godmother to the son born to Thomas Boyd and the Scots Princess Mary when they were staying, in Adorne's absence, at the Hôtel Jerusalem in Bruges. It may also represent the goodwill of the Duchess's mother, the Dowager Cecily, whom one of Margriet's daughters seems to have served. Or perhaps Lord Boyd, whom England was courting, suggested an honour for his late hostess. In trade and diplomacy, the influence of Anselm Adorne was worth having, as was that of his friend Louis de Gruuthuse* of Bruges, whom England had made Earl of Winchester for playing host, in parallel style, to the refugee Edward of York.

Margriet van der Banck, Adorne's wife, may not have enjoyed her honour for long. The date of her death is disputed, but the novels place it at Bruges at the end of 1473, soon after her return with her husband from Scotland: her possessions were shared out by the following January. The cause of her death is unknown, and the novels' account of her illness and pregnancy has no basis in history. The couple had many children – estimates run from twelve to sixteen, since the birth of the first in 1444 – and must have been married for something like thirty years. Had her husband died first, the gold ring specially set aside for 'his dear wife' was inscribed *'Hope Gheest kracht'*, 'Hope Gives Courage'.

There followed Adorne's last and potentially most important ducal mission, which was also perhaps one he was glad to undertake after his loss. He was to lead a solemn embassy to Persia for Duke Charles, to persuade its most powerful prince, Uzum Hasan, to help in the western war against Turkey, then as much a threat to fellow-Muslims in Persia as to the Christian nations vowed to crusade, and in danger from Turkish expansion. This Adorne was well fitted to handle, as his Genoese kinsmen were long established in the trading and alum-quarrying areas of the east Mediterranean, and he had recently visited these parts himself. Indeed, returning through Venice* in February 1471, he had met there a large delegation from the same Uzum Hasan, present to discover Christian plans to make war on the Sultan, and to appeal for gunners and founders. Its leaders, by then familiar to the West, were among those once bear-led by the Friar **Ludovico de Severi da Bologna.***

The other object of Adorne's mission was to seek the return of an altarpiece, *The Last Judgement* by **Hans Memling**, painted in Bruges by order of Angelo Tani,* a former manager of the local branch of the powerful Medici bankers of Florence. Dispatched to Florence aboard one of two Burgundian galleys operated by the Medici, it disappeared with the rest of the cargo when the ship was captured by the **Danzig** pirate **Paúel Benecke** in the spring of 1473. Although the ship was insured, the current Medici representative in

Bruges, Tommaso Portinari,* used all his corporate power to try to enforce the return of the vessel and at least part of its cargo. In this, he was (nominally at least) backed by Duke Charles, 'whose flag had been insulted', and possessed the temperate support of the Pope, Sixtus IV.*

Despite badgering, the **Hanseatic League** had expressed itself sadly unable to influence Danzig, and Danzig itself had responded with a flurry of counter-accusations which verged on the cynical. Adorne, whose route would take him through the Hanse towns and Poland, was intended to make the Duke's displeasure known to the Danzig authorities and the Polish King. Knowledgeable himself about paintings – he had willed to his daughters in 1470 two panels by Jan van Eyck* which exist today – he was an excellent choice for the quest. He possibly felt, in addition, that he owed some personal, rather than ducal, responsibility to the Italian banking community in Bruges.

Unfortunately, as later documents showed, the Hanse towns, the pirates and Poland all believed that, if nothing was done, eventually the complaint would be dropped. Adorne obtained no satisfaction travelling through Hamburg and Lübeck, Wisenar, Rostock and Stralsund. He was not helped by the fact that the Duke of Burgundy, spiritually vulnerable during an abortive meeting with the Holy Roman Emperor at Trèves (at which Charles had failed to gain a crown from **Frederick III**), had been accosted by Europe's favourite itinerant, Ludovico da Bologna, Patriarch of Antioch, and had appointed the Patriarch as his second envoy to Persia. The two, Adorne and the Patriarch, joined forces in Germany and thereafter travelled together, arriving at Danzig a little after Easter, in April 1474. There, Adorne was fêted by merchants (most of them German) whom he had encountered often at Bruges, but who showed no signs of taking him seriously.

The Patriarch, a regular traveller to Persia, was full of zeal to reach Uzum Hasan, and not in the least interested in Hans Memling's *Last Judgement*. Adorne found himself foiled by the Danzigers and evaded by the King, **Casimir IV**, who, when found celebrating Pentecost at **Thorn**, simply refused, upon one excuse or another, to receive Baron Cortachy in audience, while at the same time the Patriarch was being made surreptitiously welcome. Finally, Adorne turned back in anger to Danzig, where he compelled from the Governor and council a properly witnessed legal document to attest that he had been there, and had attempted to complete his mission.

The document survives, and also a trace of what seems to have been a summons from Duke Charles demanding that Adorne return home, without proceeding to Persia. The Duke's reasons were probably complex. When Adorne's mission began, the Hanse nations were at last, with Burgundian help, moving towards the peace with England which was partially sealed by the Treaty of Utrecht in February 1474, although negotiations went on until September. It was not the moment to upset the Hanse representatives by taking too subjective a stance over past piracy, as was also evinced, perhaps, by the Polish King's tactical reticence.

Adorne himself appears to have blamed his recall on the Venetians, traditional trading rivals of his Genoese kinsmen in the east. He may have been partly right. The Venetian envoy, **Caterino Zeno**,* had just completed a long stay with Uzum Hasan. It is not known whether he actually met Adorne on his way home, but it is not unlikely that both Zeno and the Patriarch, for different reasons, had come to doubt the tactical value of using Adorne.

There were other reasons to be wary of Venice. Arms intended for Uzum had become detained in Cyprus, and although subsequently put to some use (see **Zacco, King of Cyprus**), Venice gave no further help to Uzum, but moved into peace talks with the Sultan, which lasted ten months. Suspecting as much, the Duke might well have decided not to waste one of his high-ranking fund-raisers on Persia. Hence it was the Patriarch who was to make the journey to Uzum alone, and Adorne who had to return to face the Duke's ill-managed problems.

Adorne's visit to Poland was noted by the exiled Italian **Callimachus** (Filippo Buonaccorsi), who was living there, and he returned by way of Lübeck and Bremen, which he reached in July 1474. He was home shortly afterwards, having been absent from Bruges for six months. Neither he nor anyone else ever recovered the Memling, although the artist, thirteen years later, was to paint a portrait of Adorne's granddaughter, Agnes.

There is no proof, incidentally, that Adorne was accompanied to Poland by his niece Katelijne and her husband, as the novels suggest. Nor, in earlier years, did he equip a ship and send it with his nephew and niece to Iceland, in competition with Paúel Benecke, the pirate who was to capture the Memling. It is not known whether Adorne met Benecke in Poland.

He returned to find Burgundy embarked on a series of blunders. Having emerged from Trèves in September of the previous year as the laughing-stock of Europe, Duke Charles was plunging towards a war with the Swiss Confederation and the Holy Roman Emperor which was to threaten the dismemberment of Burgundy and infuriate England, which had expected him to attack France. Instead, the following spring France took the chance to invade Picardy, and the young Duke René of Lorraine, grandson of King René,* finally joined the Duke's enemies. Officially, the Confederation war ended in June 1475, after a profitless Burgundian siege which Charles was compelled to lift after eight months.

Unhappily, the Duke was still intent on pursuing his displeasure with Lorraine, and although the French were again on the attack, showed no enthusiasm for joining the great English expedition which landed to fight them, and to place the Duke's brother-in-law (perhaps) on the French throne. Eventually, after a lavish outlay of gifts, pensions and compensations for undue expenses, France negotiated a truce with King Edward, who went away, leaving Charles exposed to France, and Lorraine, and the Swiss. The Duke decided, in September, to invade Lorraine.

This was the situation that faced Adorne after Poland. His duty was not in the field, but to represent Charles at home. His personal life, to begin with, seemed unaffected. The commissioning of the triptych for Scotland from **Hugo van der Goes** must have been put in hand, with Adorne's help, before his trip, and the continuing peace between England and Scotland would have helped his Conservatorship. Soon after his return, he was appointed burgomaster of Bruges, as his grandfather had been; and also became Guardian of Bruges leper house, an asylum outside the walls. Perhaps encouraged by Adorne's friends in the Glove-makers' Guild (see guilds*), the city provided the lepers with gloves with which to conceal their hands.

The town accounts record various official trips. Some were doubtless routine, but three at least, by Adorne to Ghent in the spring of 1476, were ominous signs of the Duke's urgent need for a war chest. The Neuss siege alone had cost one hundred thousand florins, and many lives. The towns of the Low Countries, at first pleased by the prospect of peace after Neuss, were aghast to find themselves once more being battened upon.

In Bruges, a personal harangue by the Duke brought the reply that the Estates had already paid to the limit for Neuss, and for the defence of their coast. In spite of their regard for Duke Charles, it was not their concern to help patch up other countries, nor had Duke Philip the Good* his father ever expected it. They refused point-blank to mobilise, pointing out that most of their people were not soldiers but artisans, merchants and fishermen, and that to ruin their trade would remove the Duke's source of funds for the future.

Similarly, that summer, the Estates of Flanders at Ghent not only rejected all the demands of the Chancellor Hugonet, but proposed to reduce the army's allotment, on the grounds that the army no longer existed. A September appeal by the Duchess failed to induce Ghent to supply men or money. The Duke, now fighting over the key town of Nancy, refused to abandon the war against Lorraine, which he saw as a vital link between north and south Burgundy. The Swiss equally refused to make peace without including Duke René. The unrest in Flanders increased.

The widening schism between the mercantile towns and those they regarded as intimates of the Duke may have prompted James III, that spring of 1476, to revoke Adorne's appointment as Scottish Conservator. It was one of many cancelled when the King came into his twenty-fifth year, and was explained as having been made 'before the King had reached years of discretion', and because Adorne was an alien. The post was given instead to 'the King's familiar servant' **Andrew Wodman**, and may have been meant to be temporary. However, the Duke's death in battle at Nancy in January 1477 brought to a head all the seething unrest in Flanders. The disaffected Flemish towns, Bruges among them, seized the chance to demand a return to their ancient privileges, and put their claims to the Dowager Duchess Margaret of York, sister of Edward of England and stepmother of the girl **Marie of Burgundy**, the Duke's sole heir.

Warned of trouble in Bruges, the Dowager placed the town at first under four captains: Louis de Gruuthuse, his son John, Anselm Adorne and Jean Breydel. Finally, after intervention by Gruuthuse, she sanctioned an edict that restored the town's former rights. She had indeed no choice, if she wanted Flemish help against fresh threats to Burgundian frontiers. The new mood in Ghent and Bruges, however, demanded also the humiliation and punishment of the burgomasters and treasurers who had oppressed them with taxes, they believed, on behalf of the late Duke. In Ghent, the violence ran out of control, and despite the hysterical pleas of the young Duchess, men of high office were hanged, including the brother of Cardinal Hugonet, Jan Adorne's employer in Rome. In Bruges, a select group of such men were accused and imprisoned on the general charge of the misuse of public funds. Anselm Adorne was among them.

It is unclear how long the persecution went on, or the degree to which torture was applied. Appeal to the highest authority was evidently useless, in view of the greater need to pacify and unite the land against France. At least one man was tortured and condemned, and some days later three magistrates, Adorne, Jean de Baenst and Paul van Overtweldt, appeared before the tribunal, and were found guilty. That they survived was apparently due to the representations of the Deans of the Guilds, with whom Adorne must have had a close business and personal friendship, especially with those connected with skins and leather-making, which was a family interest in Genoa. The Provost of the Guild of Glove-makers had been mentioned in 1470 in his will, as one who was to pray for Adorne if his own chaplain was absent. Despite that, however, the three accused were now punished: the last two by confiscation of all they had, and confinement for life in a convent. Adorne suffered in other ways. Besides being paraded in public dressed in mourning, he was excluded from public office for life.

This clearly ended his public career in Bruges, and also his chances of ever again representing Scotland there. He left for Scotland, where he had land to support him, a nephew already in trade and the goodwill of the King, which Burgundy needed. And although the Dowager and the young Duchess had been unable to save him, they made sure he departed in honour, unless the saviour was Louis de Gruuthuse, to whose house Duchess Marie had fled after near-imprisonment in the old castle of Ghent. At any rate, Adorne left for Scotland as her accredited envoy for Burgundy: a post he was to hold until her death, and which was not apparently affected by the marriage of the Duchess Marie that same year to **Maximilian** of Austria, son of the Emperor.

He had other reasons to go. A niece, Katelijne Sersanders (see **Berecrofts**), had married, or was about to marry, into a well-placed Scottish family, one of whose members was the Abbot of **Holyrood**, a monastery at the gates of **Edinburgh** greatly favoured by the King. And Adorne himself had formed a liaison in Scotland which was to result in the birth, only recently recognised, of a daughter named Euphemia (see **Euphemia Adorne**).

From the summer of 1477 until his death in February 1483 Adorne was to live in Scotland and serve James Stewart through some of the most difficult and dangerous years of his reign. To the existing circle of advisers he brought his judicial and negotiating skills, his experience as a captain in the management and protection of towns, and what he had learned of the military strategies of the two Dukes under whom he had served. He was a fiscal expert: his father had been Receiver-General of Flanders, and Bruges had been a mint of the Counts of Flanders since the twelfth century. He had friends or relatives everywhere. He knew the opportunities, in detail, for international trade, and how to utilise to the full the power of the crusading Orders, and of Rome. In this last he was not, either, wholly cynical. His life and his family church are both testimony to his faith.

He was put to work right away. The signs are that the Conservatorship, if not returned to him fully, may have become a joint operation between Adorne and Wodman, who could pass freely to Bruges. Certainly, Adorne was regarded as Conservator at his end. As another sign of favour – although perhaps, as in Venice, a nominal one – he was made one of the **Lords of Council in Civil Causes.** The records, at this time defective, show him sitting in council only once. About the same time he received the right, transferred from one Thomas Spens, very possibly the Bishop of Aberdeen of the same name, to collect the dues, worth ten pounds a year, for the use of the herbage and meadows of the palace of **Linlithgow**, which presumably related to a franchise for grazing and hay harvesting.

This was probably connected with Adorne's most significant appointment, which created him Captain, Keeper and Governor of Linlithgow Palace. This great building, which still exists, was a defensible fortress on a lake, lying between the castles of Stirling and Edinburgh, and offering nearby escape by water to both. It was traditionally part of the Queen's dowry, and as such had belonged to the King's mother, Mary of Gueldres, the cousin of the late Duke of Burgundy. Similarly, in 1282, it was the dowry portion of Margaret, wife of Alexander III (King of Scotland 1249–1286), and herself daughter of Guy de Dampierre, Count of Flanders, whose emblem was a unicorn, and who was associated at Ghent with Obizzo Adorno, the first of the Genoese line to settle in Flanders. More recently, on the marriage of King James III, Linlithgow Palace had been promised to his bride, **Margaret of Denmark.** Being then age twelve, she did not take immediate possession.

In the year 1478, however, along with the castles of Doune, Stirling and Threave, the lordship of Galloway and other elements of her dowry, the Crown gave to the Queen the lordship of Linlithgowshire with the palace, lake and ward of Linlithgow, the customs and fermes of the burgh, justice and chamberlain ayres, and the right of patronage of all benefices and churches within these lands. And it was within that context that Anselm Adorne became its Captain, a position of trust, with the duty to defend it at need, or to use it as a base for attack. According to one Flemish account, the building and restoration work in the palace was also in his care. Supremely, too, it was an important lodge for the royal family, when escaping from pestilence, or hunting, or entertaining royal visitors. Henry VI (King of England 1422–1461, 1470–1471) and his Queen had stayed there during the recent English civil war.

Because of this, it carried various privileges, which varied from reign to reign. The herbage franchise was probably one of them. Another was a grant of twenty-three pounds' worth of lands and crofts about Linlithgow, and the use of the King's colliery nearby. On his own behalf, Adorne also seems to have acquired property in Kirkgate, Linlithgow, in addition to houses in Edinburgh whose situation is unknown. He presumably divided his time between Linlithgow and the trading quarters in Edinburgh or the Canongate with which his family were connected.

Apart from his links with the Crawfords, his own connections were irreproachable. The royal family were all well known to him, as were their advisers. The Bishop of Aberdeen, together with James, Lord Hamilton – now married to the Princess Mary and father of her final two children – sat as he did on the Council in Civil Causes. In another concession, Adorne was permitted to build a mill to the east of Linlithgow, which opened towards the palace's port and protection, **Blackness.** Mill construction was normally an expensive but lucrative privilege, and the fact that Adorne later destroyed his own mill is hard to explain, unless to deny food to potential invaders during the English sea attacks of 1480. At the same time, Adorne was given occupation of a tile-roofed house built in Blackness itself for the use of the King, whether as a harbour lodging, or a secure house for possessions. Close at hand there seemed to be a small number of merchants' houses and storerooms, as well as the strong, rock-based castle, which in peacetime was frequently used for high-ranking prisoners, such as **Alexander Home.** It also offered an escape route by water to Stirling Castle, or the north side of the Firth, or to Leith and the sea.

Some events in Adorne's family are known from the first period of this, his last stay in Scotland. In 1479, Adorne's son Arnaud lost his wife, and their baby son Aerendtken lived for only a year. Arnaud confided to friends his small daughter Agnes (later to be painted by Memling), and retired to spend the rest of his life in a **Carthusian** monastery. Jan, the eldest son, became a canon in 1479, and the following year left Rome for Bruges, where he spent some time with a brother, who could have been either Arnaud in his retreat, or Antoon, a canon of Lille. Antoon Adorne is on record as possessing a prebendry in the diocese of Aberdeen, which he resigned in 1482 to his brother Jan. There is no sign that either Jan or Antoon ever lived in Scotland. The appointments may have been set in train by Bishop Spens of Aberdeen, and maintained by his successor, Robert Blackadder, to compensate both young men for the absence from Bruges of their father. Or Antoon may have been simply keeping the post warm for Jan.

Somewhere in this period also must have occurred the birth of Adorne's illegitimate daughter, but the date and place are not known. If, as is suggested elsewhere, this placed Adorne in a relationship with the Dunbar and Sinclair families, it also opened a network of priceless trade contacts which stretched to the Orkneys. This is reinforced by the archives of the time, which show Adorne's nephew Anselm Sersanders frequently involved in trade or property transactions in Scotland, as was the family of his married niece Katelijne in Edinburgh.

Between the time of Adorne's arrival in Scotland, and the autumn before his death, he appears nowhere else on any Scottish record discovered so far. Part of the reason may be that many records are missing. Of the entire reign of James III, only one year (1473–1474) has survived of the audited accounts of the Lords High Treasurer of Scotland, usually the richest source of information about the daily life of the King and his friends; and between July 1480 and the spring of 1483 – the vital time in Adorne's story – the Acts of the Lords of Council in Civil Causes have been lost. Even so, the prolific historians of the next hundred years do not mention Anselm Adorne, among the dozens of named persons who took part in events. To them, possibly he was irrelevant: he had no heirs in Scotland to flatter; there was no lesson to be drawn from his career that fitted the historians' purpose, which was to influence men of their own time, not to lay bare, for its own sake, an accurate picture of a reign. During Adorne's stay of five years, Scotland and England went to war, and the King's brother revolted against him in events as disturbing, on a different scale, as those in Burgundy, yet we do not know what precise part, if any, Adorne played, except by inference.

To be a judge, to be the Captain of Linlithgow and hold a base at Blackness, meant that Adorne did play a part in public life, and also meant that, to the end, he was trusted by the King and Queen, and by the King's loyal advisers. In the disputes which now arose between the King and his two brothers and sisters, Adorne must have stood by the King, as the oldest brother, **Alexander, Duke of Albany,*** seemed to draw the rest to his side. The Princess Mary, who owed Adorne so much, made sure she repossessed his land, although there was some excuse: she may have needed an income for her earlier children, and his royal appointments must have compensated for the loss. Whether she was ever attended by Adorne's niece is conjecture.

Of Adorne's love of music, there can be no doubt. In Bruges, he was a leading organiser, as his uncle had been, of the religious Confraternity of the **Dry Tree**, which specialised in the most sophisticated forms of liturgy. He had found a teacher for a Scots lutenist; he had been entrusted with the sale of two silver trumpets for the Guild of Crossbowmen of St George. Yet there is no indication that Adorne ever met or encouraged **William Roger**, or pursued music in Scotland; although one might expect an interest in the organ of **Trinity Chapel**, commemorated in the triptych by Hugo van der Goes. There is no record of a **Nativity Play**, as imagined in the novels.

Adorne was not used on any English mission, nor is there any reference to him among all the fragments relating to the rebellion of the King's brother

Alexander in 1479, and the subsequent death of the King's younger brother **John of Mar;** he is not mentioned when an English war fleet sailed into the estuary of the Forth and landed at Blackness. Only the reference to Adorne burning his mill may be relevant, and the hurried business precautions taken by Anselm Sersanders.

When, in 1482, after another sea attack and an indecisive shuffling of French, English and Burgundian alliances, the English sent a vast army north, bringing Albany with it on promise of ousting his brother, Adorne is again missing from the histories. And when the King, marching south to confront his enemy, is halted by his own men and forced back to Edinburgh, Adorne's name is not among the long, muddled lists made by later historians who blame the King's unworthy friends for misleading him, and who believe them to have died, in varying numbers, at **Lauder Bridge.** As an envoy, however nominal, of Burgundy, he could not be regarded as low-born, at least. And since Burgundy was involved, it was perhaps considered best not to proclaim which side, if any, Adorne favoured. Or, as hinted by Flemish writers, he may have offered advice, but deliberately abstained from the wars between the King and his brother and the English.

In the event, the English army retreated, and the King's brother remained, alternately bargaining and threatening. After an uneasy Christmas at Court, Albany retreated to his castle at Dunbar, from where he began again to plot, and to solicit the help of the English. The King, fearing a personal attack, called for help. And Adorne, say Flemish reports, fearing bloodshed and disliking the hatred between brothers, offered to mediate.

Thus Anselm Adorne emerges into historical light for the last time just before this, the ultimate Christmas of his life. The records, conflicting and half incomprehensible, are mainly from a work on Anselm Adorne's travels published in Ghent in 1881 by a descendant, Limburg-Stirum, who had access to family papers. Other sources are few, and Scotland has nothing but some posthumous records of property. But Limburg-Stirum quotes fragments from a will written by Adorne on 7 December 1482, the day before his fifty-eighth birthday, which sheds some light on his death.

Adorne had drawn up a testament, as was customary, before he made his 1470 pilgrimage to the Holy Land. Its details are known. An adjustment is assumed to have been necessary, perhaps about 1475, consequent on his wife's death. This, the Scottish will of 1482, was made because there was now a child, Euphemia, to provide for, and because he feared to be murdered, he said, while trying to fulfil his task. He declared his willingness to die for his King, dedicating his suffering to the Lord who had once suffered for him.

The will was practical. Letters were to go to his children abroad, and arrangements made with his brothers and sisters. To his daughter Efemie, he left 'the houses he had bought in Edinburgh, and the property he had owned in Scotland'. And charged to obey his last orders were his nephew Anselm Sersanders, and 'his friend and servant Lepeliers' (see **Dr Andreas**).

He was murdered the following month, on 23 January 1483, having offered to approach the King's brother and try to effect a reconciliation, with the help of 'the Scots Bishop Lachacensis' (see under **Prosper de Camulio***). The accounts of the killing are either bald or suspiciously graphic. The place is uncertain. By one account, Adorne made a pilgrimage on foot 'to the Virgin of Obserdleton by **North Berwick**, in the **Cistercian** convent of Coldstream'. Obserdleton is unknown. Coldstream is not near North Berwick, and quite some distance from Edinburgh. It is near Berwick-upon-Tweed.* It is also close to **Upsettlington** (Obserdleton?), a well-known frontier meeting-point on the River Tweed, but too far away and too close to the enemy for a neutral rendezvous.

There was, however, a Cistercian nunnery at North Berwick, dedicated to the Virgin, and reasonably sited between Edinburgh and Albany's fort at Dunbar. There was also, just over four miles away, the church of **Whitekirk**, famed for its shrine to St Mary since the future Pope Pius* walked there barefoot years before. (Perhaps some of the confusion may be explained by the fact that there was close to Upsettlington another well-known but later-built church, Ladykirk, dedicated to the Virgin.) That the killing took place by North Berwick is likeliest, especially as the church of Whitekirk was already a recognised place of mediation, the open courts of the regality of Broughton (see **Barony and Regality**) being held there, under the Abbot of Holyrood.

Mixed Flemish accounts, put together, think that Adorne stayed the night at the convent, meaning to leave the following morning after Mass. But after supper, at eight in the evening, a troop of eighteen horse and two hundred foot surrounded the monastery. The servants were forced under threat to tell where Adorne was. Adorne, instead of escaping, came before the assailants, and asked only that they should spare the convent. They shouted 'Kill him!' as soon as they saw him. He then fell, pierced with blows: one above the shoulder blade to underneath the heart, one to his leg and the third on his head, splitting his brains. Then they left him, robbed of the Collar of the King's Order, his jewels and his robes.

Who were the killers? Flemish writers suggest high-born Scots, suspicious of the King's foreign friend, his access to troops and his efforts to mediate with the royal brother. As a possible assassin they offer one name, Sander Gartin. Sander is Scots for Alexander. Gartin is not Scots, but might represent Jardine or Gordon. Of all the possible candidates, the likeliest seems to be one Alexander Jardine of Applegarth, who had family connections near Upsettlington, and reasons to destroy the King. Certainly, it was in the interests of many, including Albany's own supporters, that the Duke should not be brought back to the fold.

Because there was no arraignment, and no report of the affray at home or abroad, it seems very likely that Adorne did try to meet the King's rebel brother on neutral ground, and that something went wrong. The delicacy of the power situation at that moment, involving England, France, Burgundy and the wilful, unstable Albany, would dictate a policy of secrecy, as at Lauder. If no one was ever prosecuted for the killing of Adorne, it may have been because the killers did not survive, and it would serve no purpose, at the time, to indict their masters. The supporters of young **James IV**, when he ousted his father, showed the same favour to Anselm Sersanders as their opponents had done to his uncle. The danger that Adorne had foreseen was no more, very likely, than Albany himself and his undisciplined followers. And Albany by then was dead.

Adorne's wishes, as expressed in his will, were carried out. After a service at North Berwick, his body was taken for burial to the Church of **St Michael** in Linlithgow, and his heart was sent to the Jerusalemkirk* in Bruges, to lie by his wife in the monumental mortuary monument which can be seen there today, with their effigies on the lid. The work of the Bruges stone-mason Cornelis Tieleman, the tomb was finished that year, and shows the only known representation of the chain of the Order of the Unicorn laid on Adorne's shoulders. A service was held there a month after his death, so that some of the ceremony proposed in his 1470 will may have been carried out after all.

The post of Conservator, vacated officially by his death, was given to the wealthy Scots merchant **Thomas Swift.** Among the Conservators who succeeded him were three generations of **van Borselens**: Paul van Borselen, son of the King's uncle-by-marriage Wolfaert, and Paul's son and grandson, both named Henry. Anselm Sersanders was appointed Captain of Linlithgow in his uncle's place, became guardian to Efemie Adorne, and seems to have stayed and worked in Scotland so long as she lived. Katelijne and her husband also remained. Adorne's freeholding of the lands of Cortachy returned to the Crown, and probably to the Ogilvy family, which already had claims in the area.

Although there were Genoese Adornes all over Europe, descent through the inbred male line failed in Flanders, where Anselm Adorne's vast family managed no surviving sons, but gave him only his granddaughter Agnes, who died in 1527. She married twice, and the name was sustained when one of her eight children, her heir Jan de la Coste, changed his name in 1512 to Adorne, and became, in time, burgomaster of Bruges and adviser to the Emperor Charles V.*

At a service on Passion Sunday, 1990, a plaque from the Heraldry Society of Scotland commemorating Anselm Adorne was placed in St Michael's Church, Linlithgow, and dedicated in the presence of Adorne's descendants, the late Count Henri de Limburg-Stirum and his son Maximilian. Dorothy Dunnett and her husband were also present. The plaque read as follows:

Remember Anselm Adornes
merchant, diplomat and friend of Scotland.
Ambassador of Charles, Duke of Burgundy
to the Court of King James III.

Conservator of the privileges of Scottish merchants in Flanders.
Born in Bruges 1424, killed in Scotland 1483
and buried near this place.

(D. D.)

ADORNE, Euphemia: GEMINI: (*c.* 1477–d. by 1499) That **Anselm Adorne*** possessed a daughter born out of wedlock in Scotland was a well-kept secret until research for the *House of Niccolò* novels began. During the next fourteen years, helped by the enthusiasm and interest of a number of historians, the following picture has emerged.

The existence of Euphemia Adorne came to light on careful reading of a nineteenth-century family history which quoted a will made in Scotland by Adorne in 1482, a month before he was killed. In it, he left to his daughter 'Efemie' the 'houses he had bought in **Edinburgh** and the property he owned in Scotland'. The rest of his will clearly referred to his existing family of sons and daughters born in Flanders, the oldest of whom was thirty-eight. None of them was left Scottish property. To carry out all his instructions, he named his sister's son **Anselm Sersanders**, who was living and working in Scotland, and a friend and servant called Lepeliers (see **Dr Andreas**).

In a long, fruitful marriage, Anselm Adorne and Margriet his wife achieved something like sixteen children. Not all survived, but most were named in a will made by Adorne in 1470. The name Euphemia does not appear there, and is not a family name among the Flemish Adornes.

Margriet is thought to have died at the end of 1473. Prior to that, Adorne had been absent on a pilgrimage to the Holy Land and elsewhere for over a year. On his return, he and his wife went to Scotland, and enjoyed the favour of the Court there for a year, before their return to Bruges* and Margriet's death. If they had a child in this period none is known, although a fictitious stillbirth is suggested in the novels.

In all the scattered records dealing with Anselm Adorne, no irregularities in his prolific marriage have ever been noticed, nor do there appear any of those talented natural sons which many families paraded with pride. It seems likeliest therefore that this unknown child was conceived after Adorne lost his wife. The gift of Scottish property suggests that the mother was Scots, and so does the exceptionally Scottish name Efemie, short for Euphemia.

In the fifteenth century, names ran in families. The Greek name Euphemia is an old one, although its saintly credentials are not very strong. The most endearing tradition appertains to Euphemia, one of the four concubines of Agrippa the Prefect, who were converted and died for their chastity. In Scotland, for some reason, the name had a long history among noble families until it began to slide down the social scale. It was still popular in the country up to a century ago, when every village had its Lizzie, its Bella, its Effie.

This, however, was not a village affair, since the child had been named in a will, and left property. Rents would pay for its keep in a convent, and would argue that the mother was no longer alive, or that Adorne wished to be seen assuming his charge. He did not, however, name the mother or provide for her separately. The probability was that the mother was a woman of standing, and that either she or the child's godmother was called Euphemia. It was also possible that she did not survive.

There were quite a few Euphemias with the right qualifications, but the wrong dates. Euphemia, Prioress of **Eccles** in 1444, was a half-sister of Bishop Kennedy* who, with his nephew **Patrick Graham**, was a friend of Anselm Adorne. Euphemia Crichton was married to Lord Malcolm **Fleming**, another Kennedy adherent, and there were other candidates with Kennedy connections: Euphemia Dunbar of Cumnock, Euphemia Maxwell, whose family also had an interest in Teling, and Euphemia Scougal, whose family had contributed a son, as had Adorne, to the Knights of St John.*

There were Euphemias connected with Cortachy, from which Adorne drew his title. Over time, several descendants of Euphemia, Countess of Ross, owned that land, largely because it kept returning by forfeit into the royal gift. In the same family line, Euphemia Graham and her second husband owned between them Teling and Polgavy, both of which came to Anselm Adorne. All of these proving void, as said above, through impossible dates, there were tempting Euphemias among the families of Hepburn, Haliburton, Lundy and Stirling of Keir, although also unconvincing in date. There was, a genuine possibility, a Euphemia Scot, the wife of John Arnot of Arnot and the mother of David Arnot (see **Henry Arnot**).

But the likeliest contender was **Euphemia Dunbar**, a well-born unmarried woman whose father, George Dunbar, Eleventh Earl of March, had forfeited his possessions two reigns before and fled to England, dying by 1463. Euphemia, although not apparently in full holy orders, lived in the **Cistercian** Priory of **Haddington**, east of Edinburgh, a place connected with both the King's sisters and with Dr Andreas, and hence well known to Adorne. Although there is no hint of a child, the regular payments for Euphemia stopped in the year before July 1477, and there is no trace of her subsequently.

It is postulated in *Gemini* that the child Euphemia was conceived in 1476 and born to Euphemia (Phemie) Dunbar in Scotland in 1477, when Adorne was in prison in Bruges and unaware of the pregnancy. It is further proposed that her mother did not survive her birth. Working with these few possibilities, research produced a few fragments more.

On the negative side, nothing is known of Efemie's character or appearance, or where she was brought up. That she was Adorne's natural daughter seemed to be publicly known. Her deafness is fictitious, but for some reason she never married, although in that age, bastardy was not a disadvantage if allied to good blood and a dowry. She seemed to be well provided for, as her father had wished: her cousin Anselm Sersanders was duly made her legal guardian, and property in **Linlithgow**, although oddly recorded, was held in her name even after **James III**'s* death in June 1488. Reassuringly, under **James IV**,* Anselm Sersanders remained at work and in favour, as one of the bailies of Linlithgow.

The **tenements** (land-holdings) Euphemia is known to have owned were all in the Kirkgate, the most prestigious passageway of Linlithgow, which still rises steeply up from the High Street to the gates of the palace. Her neighbours seem to have been churchmen, suppliers and craftsmen, and presumably officials in attendance on the palace, and concerned with its restoration and maintenance. Perhaps the captains, including her father and cousin, had premises there, for themselves or their servants. The three holdings owned by Euphemia in the final years of her life passed to her on the deaths of their previous holders, who might have leased them from Adorne.

Of her three predecessors, two were alive in 1487, when they and Anselm Sersanders, Captain of the Palace of Linlithgow, witnessed the same Linlithgow charter. One of these, John French, bears a surname often given to incomers, but could be identified with one of two men. There was a John French, chaplain and notary, who witnessed two charters with David Arnot in 1477. There was a master mason of the same name, the first of three generations to work at Linlithgow and Falkland Palaces, and St Machar's Cathedral, Aberdeen. He was the father of the architect Thomas French whose touch can be seen, it is said, in the famous church lantern-spires of the period made of groined stone in the shape of a crown. One can still be seen at St Giles,* Edinburgh. Others adorned **St Michael's**, Linlithgow, King's College, Aberdeen, and possibly Haddington Parish Church, and none are found further south than the church of St Nicholas, Newcastle, where the pattern may have begun.

Thomas's father, John French, was buried in the north aisle of St Michael's, Linlithgow, in 1489, and it is not hard to wish that his was the tenement in the Kirkgate that passed to the daughter of Anselm Adorne, whose Italian connections and taste may have given the palace some of its particular grace.

By 1499, Euphemia Adorne was dead, and all her holdings returned to the King, who reallocated part of them as a gift. On 2 September 1499, a yard, land and tenement lying in the Kirkgate in the burgh of Linlithgow, and formerly hers, was given by James IV to Sir David Arnot, Provost of Bothwell, then at the start of his career. David Arnot was related to Henry Arnot, and to the musician who would be called Robert Carver.* He was the future Abbot of **Cambuskenneth** and the future Bishop of the **Chapel Royal, William Roger**'s* dream. Again, it was a fitting transition.

There remains Efemie's life with her cousin and guardian, which can only be glimpsed. So can the edge of a story which was to continue for a hundred years more. Immediately after Adorne's death, Sersanders and two other men were in dispute with a fourth. The cause is unknown, but had possibly to do with parkland in Linlithgow. The point is that the two men on Sersanders's side were 'Andreas Lepeldok', elsewhere proposed to be the former royal physician Dr Andreas, and one John McCailze, or McCalzean.

Five years later, in the new reign, John McCailze and his wife Janet Brice protest in court because Anselm Sersanders has failed to come to a pre-arranged meeting. It is not clear which is the primary litigant, but Sersanders is alluded to as 'Anselm Cessanders, guardian to Ewfame Adornes, daughter of the late Anselm Adornes of Cortoquhy, knight', which suggests that the meeting is about some aspect of his guardianship. The case vanishes, but a glance at the McCailze family reveals a large litigious group operating in Linlithgow and, later, in Edinburgh. John, burgess of Linlithgow, is himself presently accused of non-appearance by an angry Glaswegian. James and John, perhaps sons, are Edinburgh burgesses.

In years to come James, a goldsmith, is hauled up for illegally buying and selling newly minted gold coins, shaving the King's money, and kidnapping a woman and her daughter from England. (It is perhaps fair to say that the woman, Mariota Frog, seems to have been related to John MacCailze's wife, Janet Brice, and the daughter's detention may have concerned rights of guardianship.) Notwithstanding, by 1508, James is in the thick of a remarkable battle over stolen knives among goldsmiths. The scrap involved the Dean of the Guild* and the famous goldsmith William Lorimer, alias the Halfpennyman (because he coined the halfpence for James III which were soon worth half their original value; see also **Swift, Thomas**). During the fight someone is gouged in the mouth by a file, and another slashed by his own knife on the hand. A few years later, Robert McCalzean is on the run from the law for coin-filing and -clipping, and for illicitly smuggling the King's gold abroad from his mines.

It would seem the family were redeemed when, in the second half of the sixteenth century, it produced Master Thomas McCalzean of Cliftonhall (beside Ratho), an eminent lawyer who became both Provost of Edinburgh, and one of the Queen's well-beloved (but not necessarily popular) Senators of the College of Justice. Thomas McCalzean had no sons, but an only daughter and heiress, Euphemia. She married an advocate, and was burned alive on Castle Hill, Edinburgh, for consorting with the Prince of Darkness at North Berwick Kirk.

The date was 1591. There were several others accused, and confessions were extracted by torture. Among her other failings, Effie the late Senator's daughter had allegedly planned with one Barbara Napier to injure the King by roasting wax pictures, and seeking some of His Highness's underclothes, 'to do the turn with'. She also raised the storm, it was claimed, which might have drowned Anne of Denmark on her way to the royal marriage bed. The King, who was James VI and I (ruled 1567–1625), took a passionate interest in the trial, being about to write a book on demonology.

One of Effie McCalzean's daughters, Euphemia, married Henry Sinclair of Whitekirk. Another, named Martha, became the wife of David, grandson of Lord Ogilvy of Airlie, the owner of Cortachy.

Euphemia Adorne, says the Privy Seal record for 1499, died bastard, without lawful heirs of her body. How she died, it does not say. She must have been about twenty. As soon as she died, Anselm Sersanders dropped from history. There had been no trace, for a long time, of Dr Andreas. **Jan Adorne**, Efemie's oldest half-brother in Flanders, was dead. Katelijne Sersanders was living, but there are no registered exchanges connecting the two. The signs are that Efemie lived all her life in a convent, sustained by the rents from the rich Linlithgow property managed by her cousin and the McCalzeans, to whom she became, perhaps, part of a legend. (D. D.)

ADORNE, Jan: RISING: (1444–1511) As the eldest son of **Anselm Adorne**,* Jan never seems to have properly grasped the brilliant opportunities put in his way by his father. His education was expensive: an MA from the University of Paris, which he left in 1465, followed by five years at the Italian University of Pavia, where he studied under first-class professors of civil law and notarial practice, several of whom gave him lodging. Graduating from there, he left immediately with his father in 1471 on a prestigious tour of the Mediterranean, ostensibly a pilgrimage, but actually a fact-finding mission in which Adorne represented both Scotland and Burgundy, and which had much to do, very likely, with plans for a papal crusade.

That year, Jan met many of the most eminent men of the Mediterranean world, and revived his own knowledge of Adorno colonies in places such as Chios.* And best of all, for his father at least, there was a private audience with Pope Paul II* in Rome at which Adorne received communion from the Pope's hand, and double plenary indulgences for himself, his wife and his twelve living children, in life and in death. And for Jan, there was an offer of a future post with the Holy See which must have delighted Adorne, but which Jan himself later viewed with misgiving. His father wanted a career for him in Rome, but perhaps the only inducement for Jan was the prospect of another journey like this, with a papal fleet instead of his father.

Meanwhile, taking laborious notes, he made the most of his tour. Some of the experiences were exotic. Staying at the Genoese fondaco in Tunis, he and his father were presented to the ruler, who owned the island of Djerba, retaken since Antoniotto Adorno captured it. The King also possessed (noted Jan) six hundred concubines. In Alexandria, Egypt, they saw Turkish ships celebrating the Negroponte victory. There is an account of the Nilometer* ceremony, to celebrate the coming of the Nile flood in Cairo, for which their arrival was carefully timed. And there was the journey across the desert from Cairo to the monastery of St Catherine's at **Mount Sinai*** and beyond, helped by Brother Lorenzo, who acted as interpreter, and 'deployed his insinuating eloquence with the greatest success', unlike the Arab 'steeped in cunning and crime', who tried to steal from them later. Adorne was taken ill on this journey and Jan went to some trouble to care for him.

Both he and his father left their signatures scratched – with many others – on an arcade of the refectory of St Catherine's. This, too, is the journey on which Jan mentions eating raw gerbils. But they were lucky to be alive at all: on the way to North Africa, four of their company died and close to fifty in total were lost on board a Venetian Ascension Day galley taking pilgrims* to Jaffa. Jan and the others escaped because Adorne had taken places on a Genoese vessel sailing to Tunis.

For Adorne, this tour was a circuit of honour. Jan watched his father become a Knight of the Holy Sepulchre at Jerusalem, and receive the Order of the Sword* from one of the rulers of Cyprus. In **Rhodes**, he was fêted with his father by the Grand Master of the Knights Hospitaller, (Knights of St. John*) and in Genoa by his Adorno kinsmen and his godfather, Paul Doria. Prosper Adorno, just ousted as Doge of Genoa, met Jan and his father in Milan, and Tommaso Portinari's* brother gave them a feast, while several times they went hunting with leopards with the Duke himself ('that figure of rapacity, luxury, perfidy', according to one writer), Galeazzo Maria.

They were received by Ferrante, King of Naples.* Travelling north, Jan was enchanted by the girls of Ferrara, 'the most joyous city of Italy'. Pleasing, cultured and lovely, fashioned to bring joy to those who were sad, the ladies leaned at their windows, turning smiling faces upon all who passed by. Whether or not Jan passed by, he does not say. Plunged into the festivities of Venice* in carnival, the Adornes met the families Bembo and Contarini,* and the visiting Persian envoy, **Hadji Mehmet.** Leaving, Jan accompanied his father to the monastery of Sant' Andrea al Bosco del Montello, where one of his uncles was buried. On his way home, he and his father stopped to confer with Duke Sigismond* and his wife, a Scottish princess, in the Tyrol, where the Venetians were digging for alum. They reached Flanders in April 1471.

It was six years since Jan Adorne had last seen his home in Bruges,* which he describes wistfully as *'in urbe orbis humanissima'*, 'the most agreeable town in the world'. He stayed for only six months, during which, on his father's instructions, he prepared an account, in aberrant French-influenced Latin, of his pilgrimage, dedicated to the Scots King **James III**,* and omitting the more personal details about girls. This, Anselm Adorne was to carry to Scotland that autumn. Jan himself clearly longed to accompany his ambitious *chef d'oeuvre*, but his father had decreed that he must begin his career. Although warmly invited by the **Princess Mary** herself, who was returning to Scotland with his parents, Jan was forced to say farewell to his mother and father at Calais and, turning back, make his way miserably to Rome.

By then he, and his parents, must have known that Pope Paul had died, the prospects of a flamboyant crusade were now nil, and the promised sinecure had probably vanished. Jan travelled with a Scots party, that of **Patrick Graham**, the penurious and eccentric Bishop of St Andrews, and arrived in the new Rome of Pope Sixtus IV.* His pilgrim's beard shaved, he sought first to enter the service of the late Pope's nephew, the Cardinal of San Marco, but found him unfortunately absent. Free of an admonishing father, Jan abandoned Rome, and treated himself to a vacation in Genoa in the house of one Giuliano Alamanni, whose wife Robineta came from Amiens. Joyous and merry by nature (the diary records), she turned Jan's mind from his worries with her pretty French songs.

Eventually, he took himself back to Rome, lodging in the French nation's hospice whose other guests he despised for their frivolity. In the end, he took a stop-gap appointment with Bishop Graham (who was already wildly in debt to the tune of over three thousand gold florins) until the Pope's new batch of cardinals was announced. Blessedly, this turned out to include Philibert Hugonet, brother to **Charles, Duke of Burgundy**'s* Chancellor, and the very man to give employment to an Adorne. In the household of Cardinal Hugonet, Jan Adorne was to remain in exile from his home for eight years.

He would not be short of information, in the Curia, of events further west. The changing team of Scots protonotaries, including **Henry Arnot** and the future Bishop of Aberdeen, Robert Blackadder, would be well known to him, especially as his father was now Conservator of Scots Privileges in Bruges. He would meet the envoys, known to his father, of many nations. He would be familiar with Cardinal Bessarion,* and with the Genoese papal agent **Prosper de Camulio**,* future Bishop of Caithness, Scotland. Nor was he tied to Rome. When the Cardinal travelled on papal business to Tuscany and the Papal States, Jan travelled with him.

In the Papal Jubilee Year of 1475, Jan was sent by the Cardinal to Naples on his one solo mission. This was to take papers to King Ferrante, who was entertaining a Burgundian envoy, the Grand Bastard Anthony, Duke Charles's very able half-brother. The Bastard's purpose was no doubt to discuss the common plans of Naples, Burgundy and the Pope, and to mention that (to the delight of the merchants of Flanders) the Duke was about to renew his peace treaty with France.

The Bastard was also, as it happened, about to collect a substantial troop of Italian mercenaries for his brother. With these, Duke Charles planned to win his current war against Lorraine and the Swiss and thereafter, secure from interference, turn his whole power against France, regardless of treaties. Jan's notes say nothing of this. He did, however, commend the magnificent tournament staged by Ferrante's 26-year-old son, the Duke of Calabria. Jan, two years older, and the son of a jouster, may have envied him.

It all came to a halt in 1480, when Jan simply came home. His writings do not say why. He had not come three years before, when his father was put on trial and might have been executed. He did not come when the people of Ghent killed Chancellor Hugonet, brother to Jan's employer in Rome. He did not come to follow his father to Scotland when Anselm Adorne, spurned by the regime in Bruges, had gone to live in a country where he had an income, a barony and the friendship of the King. He also had a Scottish love-child, a daughter, whose presence perhaps explained Jan's delay.

One can guess at some other reasons. There would be no income for him in Flanders in the turmoil which sent his father away. His future in Rome was at the moment secure if dull, but the Burgundian Cardinal his master was ageing – he would die in 1484 – and was already compromised, perhaps, by the execution of his brother. Jan took the step of applying for a canonry in the capital of French Flanders, Lille, and by the end of 1479 was offered a vacancy in the **collegiate church** of St Peter's where his employer Cardinal Hugonet had also held a canonry, as did Jan's youngest brother Antoon.

None of this was surprising, as St Peter's was directly under the Duke of Burgundy's patronage, and its office-holders were largely his choice. Even after Duke Charles's death, the rule seemed to apply with one precaution: because of the hostility towards France, new applications tended to be sequestered and required special acceptance. Jan became a canon in 1479, and in 1480 returned to Flanders, but not to Lille. He stayed for some months with a brother, who may have been Antoon, or Arnaud, who had gone into retreat after the death of his wife. Eventually, Jan moved to the paternal mansion, the Hôtel Jerusalem, Bruges, where he was to pass several years.

But meanwhile, he had followed Antoon in obtaining a Scottish canonry and prebend in the church of Aberdeen. This must have been arranged in his father's lifetime, with the help and goodwill of at least one of the Bishops of Aberdeen: **Thomas Spens** and Blackadder (whom Jan had known in Rome), and/or Prosper Camulio, now holding the Scots bishopric of Caithness. Accordingly, in March 1482 Rome announced that to John Adournes, a canon of Aberdeen, Licenciate of Laws and Master of Arts, was being provided a canonry and prebend of Aberdeen, void by the resignation of Anthony Adournes, and allowed despite the fact that John held a canonry and prebend of the church of St Peter's, Lille, diocese of Tournai, worth forty pounds.

There is no sign that Jan Adorne ever visited Scotland. He has left nothing to show what he felt, two years after his return, on hearing of the brutal assassination of his father in Scotland. He must, however, have arranged the funeral service for Anselm Adorne, held in his church just one month after his death, and the tomb enshrining his heart which was built that same year. Jan lived in his late father's house until 1488, the date when James III of Scotland died. Then, after an uprising which sent him temporarily to Ghent, Jan left Bruges for good, making his way west of Ghent to the place where he was to spend the rest of a long life: in the famous church of St Peter's of Lille, founded in 1270 by Margaret, Countess of Flanders, and cherished by all the Dukes of Burgundy since.

It must have been a comfortable life. Canons built their own houses in the cloister area, on land which the chapter provided. There were married clerics. Men of Jan's rank were highly lettered, and taught as professors or regents in the college of the church of St Peter's, where the setting for divine worship, it was said, surpassed in splendour that of many a cathedral. But Jan Adorne, by all accounts, withdrew from the world, and therefore cannot have brought the family love of music or art to the brilliant church festivities, or the **Mystery Plays** for which Lille was famous, and to which St Peter's contributed so much. Nor does his name appear in the lively trade that plied between Lille and Scotland and Bruges, where the church of St Donatien had shared interests and even shared provostships, as exemplified by the famous Dean Peter Bogart of Bruges, once provost at Lille. It is a Martin of Lille who trades with Jan's cousin **Anselm Sersanders**, not Jan.

His family inheritance must have brought him some wealth. His past had left him with a wish to spread the cult of St Catherine. During his life he paid to restore various artefacts, and gave money towards the building of Gilleson's great new 1507 library by the gallery cloister. In his will, he left provision for a retable for the altar of St Catherine, or Katherine, to hold a three-panel Jean de Gand painting of the Blessed Katherine, with shutters, for the price of fifty-six pounds, less a fee for his executors. One of his sorrows, noted down in 1500, was that of the six sisters and six brothers who had received the Pope's blessing, 'only one canon and one feeble infant remained'.

He died in 1511, aged sixty-six, and was buried not in the Jerusalemkirk* beside his parents, but in St Peter's own chapel of St Jean, in a fine tomb bearing his name: 'the venerable and noble person Messire Jehan Adornes, licenciate in law, seigneur of Ronsale and de Vive, canon of this church'.

He might have liked to know that in 1545 one Gabriel de la Coste, descendant of Arnaud Adorne, visited Scotland as one of two delegates to discuss Scottish trade at the **Staple** for Flanders. Gabriel might even have met Robert Crawford of **Berecrofts**, his kinsman.

There is an addendum. Whatever severed Jan Adorne from his father, his love and respect for Anselm Adorne found expression once at least, in two lines from the diary of his memorable pilgrimage, where he sets down his gratitude to '*le seigneur mon père*' for the grace of that journey, and for the abundance of gifts for which a son's thanks were due. Then he adds:

> *Ipse ego dum vivam et post dura fata sepultus*
> *Serviet officio spiritus ipse tuo*

which has been rendered into French, Jan's own preferred language, as follows:

> *Tant que je vivrai, je me consacrerai à ton service*
> *et lorsque je serai dans ma tombe,*
> *après l'accomplissement d'un dur destin,*
> *c'est mon âme qui s'en chargera.*

Or in English:

So long as I live, I shall devote myself to thy will.
And even when I lie, worn by toil, in my tomb,
Still my spirit will serve thee.
(D. D.)

Agaric: GEMINI, 18: *Amanita muscaria,* the red-capped, white-spotted mushroom also called fly agaric, takes its name from its use when steeped in milk to stupefy flies. When ingested, the hallucinogenic compounds contained in the mushrooms can induce visions, stimulate the nerves and cause exaggerated responses to minor stimuli. In large quantities it will cause disassociation, severe derangement, dizziness, convulsions, amnesia, respiratory paralysis, coma and ultimately death. Agaric can also aggravate mental illness. If the caps are boiled and taken in soup, nausea is almost immediate, and other side effects, such as sweating, dizziness, enhanced aural perception and excessive salivation, will follow within half an hour. **Anselm Adorne**'s* kinswoman who is said to have indulged in the mushroom was Caterina Fieschi-Adorno (1447–1510), canonised as St Catherine of Genoa. She was married at age sixteen to Giuliano Adorno, a Genoese nobleman. A marriage of financial convenience, it was far from happy: Adorno had a mistress and child and was bankrupt; Catherine subsequently suffered from acute depression and illness. She devoted herself to helping the poor and sick, a task in which she was joined by her husband in 1478. Her life of chastity and poverty was accompanied by periods of fasting. She mortified her body, and her biography notes that food she did eat was deliberately adulterated so as to destroy any pleasure she may have taken in its taste, namely by adding unpleasant-tasting ingredients such as 'hepatic aloe and ground agaric'. She experienced trances in which she felt mystic communion and saw visions of angels. Her only desire was for Holy Communion.

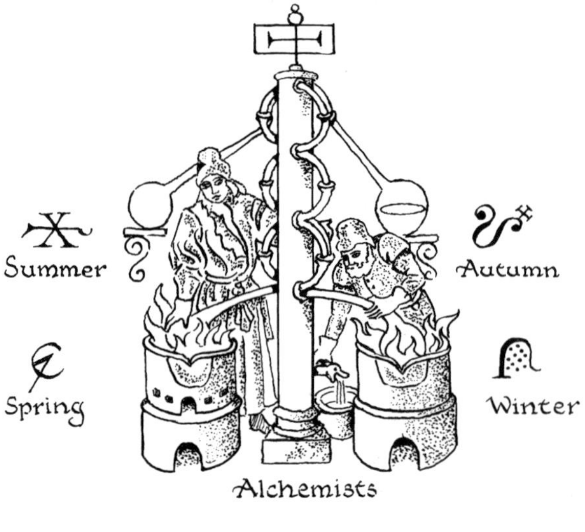

Agrippa's dog: KINGS, II, 2: The 1621 treatise *The Anatomy of Melancholy* by Robert Burton (1577–1640) discusses the portable and adhesive qualities of malignant familiars, including that of Cornelius Agrippa (1486–1535), the German alchemist, who was accompanied wherever he went by the devil: 'As Agrippa's dog had a devil tied to his collar; some think that Paracelsus (or else Erastus belies him) had one confined to his sword pummel; others wear them in rings'.

Ah! I die: See ***A! mohrioh.***

Ahasuerus: RONDO, 36: The name traditionally given to the Wandering Jew.

Ainsi je frappe*:** LIONS, 46: Jousting device of **Charles, Duke of Burgundy: 'Thus I strike'.

***Ainsi soit-il*:** UNICORN, 37: 'So be it'; or, simply, 'Amen'.

ALBANY, Alexander, Duke of:* RISING: (1454–1485) Younger brother of **James III*** of Scotland, his childhood and life before his indictment for treason have already been outlined in Volume I. The records of his adult political career indicate his rapid and violent opposition to the pro-English policies of his brother's government, particularly the English marriage alliance and Treaty of 1474 (see **Cecilia**). As Admiral of Scotland and Warden of the Marches, Albany's southern estates linked him with those border landowners who relied upon bad relations with England. They thrived in the lawless territories between the two countries; not only would rapprochement between Scotland and England damage their power base and authority, but, as they saw it, it was not in the interests of the nation. Such anti-English sentiment was epitomised in ***The Wallace.*** It was as early as 1475 that the Duke of Milan's ambassador in Burgundy began hearing rumours that the King's brother may have tried to poison the King. They were only rumours (this threat of an anti-English pretender to the throne maybe even spread by **Louis XI*** days before an Anglo-French peace treaty) but probably indicate the growing disharmony between the brothers. Albany was indicted for treason in October 1479, for provisioning Dunbar Castle against the King, assisting known rebels and deliberately causing trouble on the border between Scotland and England, in violation of the truce between the two countries, thus abusing his position of March Warden. Prior to the provisioning of Dunbar, Albany had been held prisoner by James III in **Edinburgh** Castle, probably for his forays in the borders, about which **Edward IV*** had already had cause to complain.

Albany escaped from Edinburgh, went first to his castle of Dunbar, then fled to France, where his second marriage to Anne de la Tour took place in 1480. (His first, to Catherine **Sinclair**, had been dissolved in 1478.) In his absence, Albany's companions from Dunbar were forfeited in the October

1479 Parliament, their lands and property escheated to the Crown. Albany was not forfeited, but summoned to answer to the charges laid against him.

Receiving no army from France to overthrow James III, in May 1482 Albany arrived in England, declaring himself king. In June 1482, at Fotheringhay castle (signing himself 'Alexander R'), he agreed to do homage to Edward IV on receipt of the Scottish throne. He also promised to destroy the alliance between Scotland and France and surrender James's pride and joy, Berwick-upon-Tweed,* to the English. Louis XI was only too happy to oblige: allowing Albany to go to England kept Edward occupied and away from France and Burgundy. In receiving Albany from France, Edward had the opportunity to launch a full-scale invasion of Scotland, and the English army marched north under **Richard, Duke of Gloucester.** However, Albany's show of force was not supported by the mass of the Scottish nobility, therefore he accepted that his best bet would be to accept a reconciliation with the King, in return for a full pardon, the title of his deceased brother **John of Mar**, and, most importantly, the post of Lieutenant-General of Scotland. This compromise, making Albany the second most powerful man in the country, in charge of the armed forces, was agreed by Parliament, in the knowledge that it could be – and subsequently was – withheld by James, who was alone in having the power to grant the title. Meanwhile the English army took Berwick, agreed terms with the burghers of Edinburgh and returned south.

The public reconciliation between Albany and James took place, but by Christmas the truce between the brothers was over. Albany once more retired to Dunbar Castle, accompanied by **Archibald Douglas**, Earl of Angus, the **Earl of Buchan, Sir James Liddell of Halkerston** and **Alexander Home**, to begin plotting against the King and renewing the terms of the Fotheringhay treaty with the English. A plot was uncovered to seize the King, but this time Albany could not rely on an English army to support him. He was again forced to flee.

In 1484 his brother James renewed the Franco-Scottish Treaty, which coincided with Albany's last failed attempt to seize power in Scotland. He crossed the border from England in July, accompanied by **James, Ninth Earl of Douglas**, but they were defeated at Lochmaben. Douglas was taken prisoner, while Albany escaped to France, where in 1485, at a tournament between the Duke of Orleans and a knight, he was fatally injured by a splintered lance.

Alexander's reputation was rescued by chroniclers in the sixteenth century (often at the expense of that of his brother the King), partly as a means of justifying the return to Scotland of his son by his French wife, **John Stewart, Second Duke of Albany**, as Regent in the minority of James V* after the battle of **Flodden.** A daughter of Alexander by his first wife Catherine Sinclair, also called Catherine, married Sir Patrick Hamilton of Kincavel (one of **James, Lord Hamilton**'s illegitimate sons). Their son, Patrick Hamilton (1504–1528) was a Lutheran preacher, tried for heresy, found guilty and burned at St

Andrews. His martyrdom served only to spread reforming doctrine in Scotland. Another of their sons was responsible for bringing down James V's favourite, James Hamilton of Finnart (see **Fynnart, Jimmie of**).

In addition to his three children by Catherine Sinclair, Albany, by the time he was twenty-four, already had two illegitimate sons of mother or mothers unknown. History is vague about one, but the other, Alexander, entered the Church and became Dean of Dunbar in 1504. He was also Prior of Whithorn, Abbot of Inchaffray and Scone, and finally Bishop of Moray in 1527. He in turn had three natural children: two sons and a daughter, whose second husband was Colin Campbell of Glenorchy. Of Albany's sons by Catherine, one died young, but the other studied in St Andrews with Alexander, and is shown as visiting France in 1502 and 1506 – perhaps to see his other half-brother. He also accompanied King **James IV*** on a Scottish tour in 1504, but seems otherwise to have led a subdued life.

Albany, John Stewart, Second Duke of: CHECKMATE, II, 5: (1481–1536) Regent of Scotland from 1515 to 1524 in the minority of James V,* son of **Alexander, Duke of Albany*** and his French bride Anne, Duchess of Boulogne (who was the daughter of Bertrand, comte d'Auvergne et de Lauraguez, seigneur de la Tour, de Donzenac and de Brios). He succeeded to the title in 1485 after his father's death, and remained in France with his mother (who was remarried in 1487 to Louis, comte de la Chambre and vicomte de Maurienne. His mother died in 1512, his stepfather in 1517). In 1505 he had married his cousin, Anne de la Tour (eldest child of his mother's brother, Jehan, third comte d'Auvergne). The same year her sister Madeleine became the wife of Lorenzo de' Medici, Duke of Urbino.

In the wake of the battle of **Flodden**, with the death of **James IV*** and the accession of a new child-king, a large faction of the surviving nobility petitioned Albany to come to Scotland and assume the role of Governor of Scotland. At this time, Albany was High Admiral of France. Albany remained in France after the death of Louis XII in 1515 and the crowning of his successor and cousin Francis I.* However, the hasty marriage of Margaret Tudor, James IV's widow, to Archibald Douglas, Sixth Earl of Angus,* and the interest that Henry VIII (King of England, 1509–1547) was paying to his two young Scottish nephews – James V and his brother, who was born posthumously and who died before he was two – perhaps obliged Albany to head for Scotland; although, French by birth and inclination, it was the interests of France that he would serve abroad. Francis I wished to rekindle the French alliance with the Scots and therefore promised Scotland that if England were to attack, France would aid them with money and troops. Albany duly arrived in Scotland in May 1515, and was proclaimed Governor of Scotland in **Edinburgh**, to retain the post until the young King attained his majority of eighteen (in 1530). He was recognised by Parliament as next in line to the throne after

James V and his brother. Albany found Scotland lawless and quarrelsome, united only in its dislike of a foreign Regent.

His first task was to loosen Margaret Tudor and her new husband's control over the young King. Margaret was invited to return to England by her brother King Henry, and it was there that she gave birth to a daughter, Lady Margaret Douglas,* later to be the wife of Matthew Stewart, Earl of Lennox.* Margaret and Angus did their best to attenuate his regency.

Unfortunately, Albany's regency was weak, undermined as it was by Anglo-French diplomatic rapprochement and the pro-English party's hostility to France. As the principal advocate of a Franco-Scots alliance, Albany spent most of his time in France (1517–1521 and 1521–1523), concluding the Treaty of Rouen, a mutually defensive pact between Scotland and France, and arranging the marriage of James V to a daughter of Francis I. He was obliged to stay in France when that country renewed her peace treaty with England, returning to Scotland only when worsening relations with England saw him support two combined Franco-Scottish attacks on Henry's kingdom. But fear of defeat, and the Scots' dislike of being caught up in a battle which was not of their making (a bitter lesson learned from Flodden) meant the Scots were content to observe from the sidelines as the French and English fought.

Albany forfeited the regency of Scotland in 1524 and returned to his French homeland. He was not to return to Scotland again, probably to his great relief. In the same year his wife died. She was not survived by any of their three children, all of whom had died young. Albany continued to serve the French king during his campaigns in Italy (1524–1525) where Francis was taken prisoner at Pavia, although Albany was not captured. In 1530 he became French ambassador at Rome, where he helped arrange the divorce of Margaret Tudor from the Earl of Angus. He also helped negotiate the marriage of his young orphaned niece, Catherine de Médicis* to Henri II* of France and escorted her back to France for her wedding. Albany retired to his estate in Auvergne and died in 1536, bequeathing his estate to his niece, Catherine.

***Aleci rubei*:** LIONS, 22: In early times, salted fish were called white herring, and smoked fish, because of their colour, were called red. *Alecis* was the Latin attempt to translate 'hareng', and *aleci rubei*, strictly speaking, was red herring in the form of a thick red fish sauce. Although utilised here, the phrase 'red herring', meaning a deliberate diversion, had not yet been invented. In the time of **James III**,* herring supplied to the Crown from the Clyde were of a standard size known as the assize herring. (D. D.)

Alexander, Duke of Albany: See **Albany, Alexander, Duke of.**

Alexandria, great poet-librarian of: RONDO, 12: Kallimachos: see **Mouseion of Alexandria.**

All sutty, blakk and unclene: CHECKMATE, V, 7: From the middle English romance, *Octavian*, when the young Florent tries on his father's old armour and weapons in preparation to fighting a giant and proving his strength and manliness. The armour is hardly up to the job:

For sorowe Clementys herte nye braste [nearly broke]
When he on Florent hacton [padded jacket] caste;
The chylde was bolde and kene.
An hawkberke above he let fall,
Rowsty were the naylys [rivets] all
And hys atyre bedeene.
Clement broght forthe schylde [shield] and spere
That were uncomely for to were:
All sutty, blakk and unclene.
A swyrde [sword] he broght the chylde beforne
That sevyn yere afore was not borne [carried to battle],
Ne drawe [nor drawn] – and that was seene [obvious].

The comic effect is heightened when his adopted father Clement attempts to draw the tight-fitting sword from its scabbard. Clement has to pull so hard that, when the sword eventually comes unstuck, he falls backwards and knocks himself unconscious.

Alphonse V of Portugal and African Discoveries: RONDO, 42: (reigned 1438–1481) King of Portugal. Like his predecessor Prince Henry the Navigator (1394–1460), he encouraged Portuguese naval exploration of the coast of Africa, leasing the coast of Guinea to Ferñao Gomes on the condition that one hundred miles of coastline were discovered yearly. Alphonse's conquest of Tangier led to his soubriquet 'the African'.

He was the maternal uncle of Joanna, daughter of Henry IV, King of Castile (1454–1474). Civil war erupted on Henry's death over whether his daughter Joanna or his surviving sister Isabella (married to Ferdinand of Aragon) should succeed to the throne. Alphonse supported his niece and attempted to invade Castile on her behalf, but was defeated in 1476 at Toro. Ultimately a series of treaties handed Castile to Isabella, but Portuguese possessions in Africa were safeguarded. Joanna retired to a convent, and Isabella and her husband Ferdinand were to rule over Spain from 1474 until her death in 1504.

Alphonse's life was cut short by plague. He was succeeded by his son John (João) II (reigned 1481–1495) who ceded much of the New World territories to Spain. The lucrative African routes remained in the hands of Portugal, of vital importance to trade following the circumnavigation of Africa in 1487 by Bartholomeu Diaz, which opened up the sea route to the Indies. (see **Antwerp**)

Amiable as a girl: lively as a fawn: PAWN, 25: A description of Sultan Ismail I (1487–1524) given by an early-sixteenth-century merchant who spent eight years and eight months in Persia:

> His beard is shaved, and he only wears a moustache, not appearing to be a very hairy man. He is amiable as a girl, left-handed by nature, is as lively as a fawn; and stronger than any of his lords.

The Sultan was the grandson of **Uzum Hasan*** by the marriage of Uzum's eldest daughter by his Christian wife, Martha, to Secheaidare (Sheikh Heyder) and ruled from 1501. He was crowned at Tabriz and became the first shah of the Shi'ite New Persian Empire which endured for more than two centuries, despite attacks from the Ottoman Empire, which considered the Shi'ite sect as dangerously heretical. In his campaign to destroy them, the Turkish ruler Selim I (Sultan 1512–1520) conquered Ismail's followers at the battle of Chaldiran in 1514, but failed to crush them totally when the Janissaries* refused to pursue Ismail further than Tabriz. By this campaign Selim acquired Diyarbekir and Mardin from the Shah; territories which had passed from the Black Sheep Turcomans to the White Sheep and thence to Persia.

Amiens: GEMINI, 28: **Louis XI*** was a frequent visitor to the shrine at Amiens; by sending a medal and promising to visit in person, **James III*** was angling for a meeting with the monarch who was doing so much to manipulate the fate of Scotland. This medal, made in gold at Berwick-upon-Tweed* in 1480, was a clear indication of the wealth of Berwick and the King's pride in its goldsmiths. It weighed nearly 2⅓ ounces and was 23" in diameter. On its obverse was the image of a beardless king with long hair, enthroned and holding a naked sword in one hand and a shield with the arms of Scotland in the other. On the canopy above the throne was the legend IN MY DEFENS in Gothic letters and, above it, VILLA BERWICI. On the reverse of the coin was St Andrew. Unfortunately the medal was stolen during the French Revolution.

An accident of the soul: UNICORN, 4: Changes in a person's mental state might be attributed to accidents of the soul. In the same usage in France, *accidents de maladie* were bouts of sickness. (D. D.)

And al was conscience and tendre herte: KINGS, IV, 2: The Prioress in *The Canterbury Tales* of Geoffrey Chaucer (*c.* 1343–1400), General Prologue, line 150.

An eek the buttokes of hem faren as it were the hyndre part of a she-ape in the full of the moone: CHECKMATE, I, 6: 'The Parson's Tale', in *The Canterbury Tales* by Geoffrey Chaucer (*c.* 1343–1400); the passage refers to vanity in clothing, particularly the unseemly exhibition of the nether regions exposed by short upper garments and striped hose.

And Harald went with his host out to Jerusalem-land: CHECKMATE, V, 13: From the Icelandic 'Saga of Harald the Hard-redy' in the collection of sagas by Snorri Sturluson (1179–1241) entitled the *Heimskringla* (*c.* 1220, chapter XII):

Harald went with his host out to Jerusalem-land, and sithence up to Jerusalem-town; but wheresoever he fared over Jerusalem-land all towns and castles were given up to his wielding. So says Stuf the Skald, who had heard the king himself tell these tidings:

> The edge-bold stout-heart farèd
> Jerusalem to conquer,
> The upper land was friendly
> To the Greeks and slaughter wreaker.
> By might enow the land came
> Unburned into the handling
> Of the hardener of the battle.

ANDREAS, Dr: UNICORN: (*fl.* 1470s) A physician and astrologer of this name appears fleetingly in both Scots and Flemish records, and would appear to be the same man. The novels propose that he might be a natural son of the well-known astrologer, John of Wesalia.

The historic John of Wesalia, who died in 1472, was an astrologer and the town doctor of Brussels. He was the son of Peter or Everard Wyting, a native of Wesel in the Hanse. After studying in Pavia, he taught medicine in Louvain* from 1429, and later also taught maths and astronomy. He was Rector of Louvain three times in the 1430s, and was there when the Scottish King's cousin, the future Bishop Kennedy,* was a student. The doctor altered his status from German to Brabantine, changed his name from Wyting to van Wesele, and adopted the Wesel blazon of three weasels.

From 1443–1447 John of Wesalia served at the court of Burgundy, and after a brief return to Louvain, settled in Brussels as a physician. He married twice, having five children by his first wife, and two by his second. In due course his son Everard qualified as a doctor, and took his father's place as physician to the young Duchess **Marie of Burgundy.** Everard predeceased his father, who eventually retired to teach at Louvain again. There, he may have worked with the famous rector, the physician and astrologer John Spierinck, under whom **William Scheves** must have studied two decades before. Astrologers from the Low Countries carried great influence at this particular period, and John of Wesalia was noted for his predictions, one of them being inspired by the comet (in Scots, a fiery besom) of January 1472. He was known for uncompromising omens unfavourable to rulers.

This was also true of Dr Andreas, who was said to have had a 'great reputation' in the Low Countries as a soothsayer. In his fictive persona, he is credited with studying medicine and astrology at Louvain; historically, he appears fully qualified in Scotland between 1470 and 1471, and in 1471 he had received his first annual fee of ten pounds, paid through the customs of the town of **Haddington.** Other royal payments from the same source were concerned with the expenses of **Princess Margaret**, King **James III**'s* younger sister, then being reared by the Prioress Elizabeth at the large **Cistercian** priory in Haddington. The customs income also supplied the Prioress with regular payments for two of her residents: Elizabeth **Sinclair** and **Euphemia Dunbar.**

The doctor's remit is not clear. It was a royal appointment, and he may have had the care of all five of the royal siblings, including Margaret and her entourage at Haddington. It was certainly believed that he made prophecies, and that he predicted that the King would die at the hand of a kinsman, but this may be a later invention of George Buchanan, the sixteenth-century Scottish historian. Buchanan describes him as a Flemish astrologer called Andrews who came to the attention of the King when he accurately predicted the demise of **Charles, Duke of Burgundy.***

In Scottish records, Andreas is next noticed in 1474, when he received four ells of French black for a gown, at thirty-six shillings an ell. There are no further notices in Scotland relating to him, and his payments through Haddington ceased, although from 1479 there are fees to another physician, Master Conrad. It is impossible to tell whether Dr Andreas left the country or stayed, as the novels suggest, to be paid from less public funds. There is however one reference in the records of Bruges for the period. The wealthy of that town were apt to face punitive special taxes for war. In 1475, **Anselm Adorne**'s* son Arnaud paid forty pounds, and 'M. André of Jerusalem' was required to pay ten pounds. The Jerusalem church,* built and maintained by the Adornes, had its own chaplain, and so had the guilds* with which Adorne was connected. There seems a place for a house physician in such an arrangement, and it is not unlikely that Dr André and Andreas are the same.

The wording of Adorne's second will suggests that Dr Andreas was in Scotland when Adorne died, and was one of those he expected to fulfil his wishes. Again, the records are confusing, and suggest the usual problems of translation between Adorne's Flemish archives and the Scots. In fact, the will names as executors Adorne's nephew **Anselm Sersanders**, and his 'friend and servant Lepeliers'. At first sight this suggests a friend from the Skinners' Guild in Edinburgh or Bruges. The names Lepelkin, Lescueillier and La Compagne Lesellier are all on record in Bruges.

In Scotland, on the other hand, five months after Adorne's own death, the *Acta Dominorum Concilii* (Acts of the **Lords of Council in Civil Causes**) record a dispute involving one Andrew Lepeldok, who appears on the same side as Anselm Sersanders and a **Linlithgow** burgess called John McCalzie, known to be involved in the care of **Euphemia Adorne.** There is room to wonder if both Lepeliers and Andrew Lepeldok might turn out to be Dr Andreas of Vesalia, servant to both the Scots King and Adorne.

What became of Andreas after that is not known. There is no further mention of him in Scottish records, nor is there any trace of a marriage or family. The mistress and daughter attributed to him in the novels are invented, as is his connection with the Loire.

Other royal Scottish physicians are known: to have a stable of doctors and astrologers was as important to a ruling house as menageries were to become. Ill-understood illnesses were frightening, and so was poison, and so was the necessity to choose the correct day for a contract, or a battle. The Scottish royal family of the day must however have presented a frightening challenge to the profession, and one could not blame them for retreating into private service. (D. D.)

ANGUS, Earl of: See **Douglas, Archibald.**

Anselm: HN; GEMINI, 5: The name appears in the novels connected with **Anselm Adorne*** and his nephew **Anselm Sersanders.** A very early mention of the name Sersanders occurs in Flemish archives of 1369, which mentions one 'Symoene f. ser Sanders of Ghent'. Two years later, there is a Daniel sher Sanders and a Pierre sher Symoens, men of the feudal court of the Abbot of St Pierre-les-Ghent. Sanders being a common Scots version of the name Alexander, it is tempting to see the name as a development of 'x, son of Alexander'. This might account for the uncertainty which led clerks to refer to him as both Sersanders and Adorne. In Bruges, in 1486, he is called Ancelmus Shersanders.

The name Anselm seems to have come to England first in the eleventh century with the Lombard Anselm, Archbishop of Canterbury. Anselm Sersanders presumably bore it in honour of his mother's brother, whose godson he probably was. In the novels, Anselm Sersanders is referred to for convenience as Saunders, but the abbreviation of Anselm is sometimes given in Flemish records as Mer Ancelmus, or Anceaulme. This, reduced to Ceaulme, with the Flemish diminutive of 'kin', seems to account for the Scottish scribes' entries for 'Sallykin'. (Seaulme is used in the novels for Adorne himself). The Sallykin/Anselm Sersanders entries deal with identical clients, and similar goods.

Anselm was not a usual Scottish name, but one or two Anselms who could be the godchildren of colleagues of friends are recorded about or just after the time of Sersanders and his uncle. These include an Anselm Robieson who was concerned with the lands of Portarside, Linlithgow, in 1494, and another Anselm, perhaps the same, who was sub-chanter of Ross in 1504, when Linlithgow lands contributed to the cathedral of Ross. Robieson or Robertson was the surname of the **Edinburgh** custodian of the burgh customs money who carried (and lost) a coffer of money in 1482 at **Lauder Bridge**, and also of a bailie of **Linlithgow** and a chaplain connected with Cortachy. But the Adorne influence, if it existed, was short-lived, and the name did not persist. (D. D.)

Antioch: HN: Once the capital of the Greek Kings of Syria, Antioch flourished as a city of half a million people under the Romans, and later became one of the earliest missionary seats of Christianity, until its fall to the Persians in the fifth century. Conquered next by the Saracens, it was briefly redeemed in 1098 by the Crusaders, who finally lost it to the Sultan of Egypt. It was to remain part of Syria, although the Latin church continued to appoint so-called Patriarchs of Antioch, among whom **Ludovico de Severi da Bologna*** was one. By the fifteenth century, however, it had forgotten the days of its glory when men called it 'Antioch the Beautiful' and the 'Crown of the East'. It was known to the Syrians, because it rained all the time, as '*Le Pissoir*' (LIONS, 16). (D. D.)

Antiphonal chants: See **Responsorial chants.**

Antwerp: UNICORN, 16: Leading the development of the Atlantic economy for most of the sixteenth century, the city of Antwerp relied on shipping, trade, industry and credit to secure her greatness. Lacking her own fleet and run largely by foreign merchants, she shared similarities with Bruges* (whose future came to an end when her port silted up) as an entrepôt for the consumers of spices and pepper. Initially her harbour was much less impressive than that of Veere (which was able to take ships of up to six hundred tons, as opposed to Antwerp's quay, which could berth only ten ships). However, her dominance began as the commercial centre of Europe shifted from the Mediterranean to the North Sea. With Portuguese ships, goods arrived in Antwerp directly from Africa, instead of going via Venice, checking the traditional Levantine route of the spice trade. The circumnavigation of the southernmost tip of Africa (1487), followed by the discovery of the sea route to India (1498) by the Portuguese, gave Antwerp the opportunity to capitalise on its location as the new bring-and-buy capital of the north, monopolising amongst other expensive commodities the pepper market, pushing out Venice completely. In 1504, when the Venetian galleys arrived in Alexandria in Egypt, they found not a single sack of pepper waiting for them. Antwerp financed what Portugal could deliver; this situation prevailed until at least the middle of the sixteenth century.

Apostolic Chamber: HN: The Chancery and the Camera formed the two departments of the Papal Curia at Rome. The Camera Apostolica was originally simply the department that administered the Papal Domains, collecting taxes and customs, and paying for defence, public order and public works etc. Gradually the work of the Chamber expanded as monasteries and churches, and later large landowners and new states, sought papal protection in return for an annual sum to the Camerlengo (the Governor of the City of Rome). (D. D.)

ARGYLL, Earl of: UNICORN: (d. 1493) Colin Campbell, Second Lord Campbell and Lord of Argyll. The powerful West Highland clan chiefs had held the title of Lords of Argyll since 1445, and in 1457 Campbell achieved the earldom of Argyll, the only territorial (as opposed to honorific) earldom created by James II.* He was also sole Lord Justiciar of Scotland south of the Forth. In 1470 he received from **James III*** the lordship of Lorne, and in May the following year the King named Argyll as Justiciar within the bounds of Lorne. It is possible to chart the rise of this hardworking and ambitious man through the reigns of James II* and James III. He was a constant attender at Parliament in both reigns, and in his many duties combined the roles of magnate administrator, lawyer-diplomat, soldier and powerful clan chief, serving the Crown faithfully until 1488. He acted as exchequer auditor in 1462, was a royal councillor, Master of the Royal Household from 1465 to 1482, Chancellor from 1483 to 1488 and again at the beginning of **James IV**'s* reign. Loyal to the monarchy, he represents a new class of noble, who flung himself wholeheartedly into the career of the man of Court. A man of action as well as the ideal administrator, his lands in the west served as the perfect springboard for operations against the troublesome John, Earl of Ross and Lord of the Isles. Argyll was one of the main architects of the 1474 treaty with **Edward IV**,* sent to agree terms for the marriage of **Cecilia** to the King's eldest son.

His name (along with that of **Andrew Stewart, Lord Avandale**, Chancellor for twenty-two years) disappears from the records following the events at **Lauder Bridge** in 1482, but Argyll was appointed as Lord High Chancellor in 1483 after the death of Bishop Livingston on 28 August. In 1484 he led the embassy to England to negotiate a new Anglo-Scottish peace, by which a three-year truce was indeed agreed, but the Scots never recovered Berwick-upon-Tweed.* He was dismissed from the Chancellorship in 1488, and **David Lindsay**, Earl of Crawford, replaced him as Justiciar. Not actually present when the King lost his life, Argyll was in England on an embassy to Henry VII (King of England 1485–1509). He was restored to the role of Lord High Chancellor under James IV. He died in 1493.

He was married to Isabel Stewart, heiress and eldest daughter of John, Third Earl of Lorne, and they had two sons and seven daughters. His son Archibald, Second Earl of Argyll, was the subject of a Scottish-Irish poem extolling his duty to rise up against English oppression, 'Let us make harsh and mighty warfare against the English, I tell you, before they have taken our native land; let us not give up our country, but anxiously watch over our patrimony just like the Gael of Ireland . . . Burn their bad coarse women, burn their uncouth offspring, and burn their sooty houses, and rid us of the reproach of them'. The anonymous poem, dated before the battle of **Flodden** in 1513 where Archibald lost his life, addresses the Second Earl, and also treats us to a genealogy of the family:

Remember, O cheek like the strawberry, that we have had from the English tyranny and spite in your time, by which the English rule has spread.
Remember Colin, your own father, remember Archibald too, remember Duncan before them, the kindly man who loved hounds.
Remember the other Colin, remember Archibald of Arran, and Colin of the Headsa, whose frame was great, by whom the stake was won . . .
Push against the English in their own home, awake, MacCailéin! Too much sleep is not good for a man of war, you of the golden hair . . .

ARNOT, Henry, and family: LIONS: The family of Henry Arnot, Abbot of Cambuskenneth, took its name from Arnot, Kinross-shire, where it was known from the twelfth century, and was soon connected with the lands round Lochore and Lochleven. Spreading in Fife, they became linked with the local families of Lundy and Largo, including that of **Sir Andrew Wood**, the famous seaman, and the family of Browns which in 1486 contained George Brown, Bishop of Dunkeld. In 1472, Lucas Arnot was Official of the cathedral church of Dunblane. There were also Ayrshire Arnots, who intermarried with the **Colvilles** and with the **Semples** of Renfrewshire in the first half of the sixteenth century.

The Arnots produced able negotiators, churchmen and lawyers and served the Crown well in the period covering the *House of Niccolò* books, where – except for their physical appearance, which is not known – they maintain a strong historical presence, based on actual records.

Henry Arnot first comes to light in 1471, when he was sent to the Roman Curia as procurator for the Scots King, **James III.*** His mission was probably complex, but would reflect the King's wish to limit the papal power over appointments in Scotland. Returning, he seems to have become increasingly employed in public affairs requiring judgement and energy, a task he fulfilled through two reigns. In October 1478 he took his place, for the first of many times, as one of the **Lords of Council in Civil Causes.**

After the death of James III in 1488, it might have been expected that the son who had opposed him at Sauchieburn would have discarded the Abbot who had remained loyal to his father. Instead, the bond between the Crown and Cambuskenneth continued, perhaps fostered by the young King **James IV**'s* remorse. In 1488, Henry received a gift from the King of £138, and later of £100, both considerable sums at that time. Traces of financial dealings with the Crown were to continue: in 1490 a further £100 was paid to the Abbot, in recognition of a loan made to the King 'when he was a prince'.

Henry also went to law that same year in his capacity as factor to the Prior of Inchmahome, the monastery on the Lake of Menteith where the child Mary Queen of Scots* was to make a brief stay. The lawsuit – claiming unpaid dues from a local landowner, John Haldane of Gleneagles–was unsuccessful, and the Prior was advised by the court to claim redress, if he wished, against the Abbot. Henry, used to employing the law, and perennially involved in counter-claims about Forth fishing rights with the community of Stirling, was no doubt undisturbed.

From 1492 until 1495 Henry Arnot followed **William Knollys*** and **Archibald Crawford** as Treasurer to the King. Even after he demitted office, Arnot was clearly holding reserves and handling money for the Crown, and perhaps even helpfully lending the Crown what was not his. In 1501 a furious Alexander, Lord Gordon, demanded the return of a large sum of money wrongfully detained by the venerable father in God, Henry, Abbot of Cambuskenneth. Henry admitted the whole thing at once, and arranged for due recompense: the money, or much of it, had been sent in a box to the King.

Shipbuilding also received the Abbot's attention. Royal boats were built and repaired at Dumbarton, and in 1494 Lord Bothwell gave a mast to the yard, while Abbot Henry provided three sails. It cost the Crown forty-five shillings, paid to a carter, for the 'tursing' (baling) of a great sail, three 'bonnets' given by the Abbot of Cambuskenneth, and such necessities as a barrel of tar.

In 1497 Abbot Henry bought from William, Lord Ruthven, three portions of a piece of land outside Edinburgh and close to **Newbattle** called Cousland. Parts of Cousland had also been held under the **Sinclairs** by **Thomas Cochrane** and his relative **Thomas Preston**, who were both hanged at **Lauder Bridge** for their loyalty to James III. The land-holdings may have been used by the Crown, with the Sinclairs' consent, to provide an extra income for far-travelled servants, or to keep them in age, as in similar gifts to their nurses.

The remaining entries are slight. There is one concerned with ten marks advanced by the Abbot for building work somewhere at Stirling. And in 1496 the King was pleased, one November day, to sanction a tip of four shillings to the Abbot of Cambuskenneth's man, who had brought wild fowls to the King. It seemed to be a kindly relationship that endured to the end.

The novels fabricate very little. There is nothing to connect Cambuskenneth directly with guns, but much to indicate a friendship with the young prince at Stirling, and hence the Queen, whose seneschal was Robert Colville. The one remarkable historical fact which linked Abbot Henry with the novels came to light by pure chance, when the last book was being compiled. Over a century, Edinburgh street names had changed. But the authentic house of Mungo Tennant,* as featured in the first chapter of the first book of the *Lymond Chronicles*, was actually occupied, a century before, by Henry, Abbot of Cambuskenneth.

David Arnot, who was to succeed Henry Arnot as Abbot of Cambuskenneth in 1508, may not have belonged to the same branch of Arnots, and his relationship with Henry is not clear. What is important is his connection to

Robert Carver,* who was to become one of the greatest musicians in Scottish history, and is regarded as either his natural son, or his protégé. David Arnot has no direct role to play in the novels, unless to provide, through his cultivation of music, a link between the Burgundian court of Adorne, and the world which was to greet Lymond. He also embodies a touching extension to the story of **Anselm Adorne.*** It was David Arnot who, in 1499, received in gift from the King a **tenement**, land and yard in the burgh of **Linlithgow**, being in the King's hands through the death of **Euphemia**, Adorne's young orphaned love-child. (D. D.)

***Aspettate e odiate*:** RONDO, 5: 'Wait and hate': Latin motto of revenge. Honoré de Balzac (1799–1850), in 'About Catherine de Medici' connects the saying, reversed (*Odiate e aspettate*), with the powerful family de Guise. Others felt the same about the de Guises, as a little contemporary rhyme explains:

Le peuple excuse Henri
Maudit Montmorency
Haï Diane
Surtout ceux de Guise aussi.

(The people excuse Henry, curse Montmorency, loathe Diane and the de Guises most of all.) (D. D.)

Assassins: RONDO, 27: A slight overstatement of the anomalous dialogue between Christian nations and the Assassins of Persia, a thirteenth-century Islamic sect led by the Old Man of the Mountains* who extorted blackmail from Christians and Muslims alike. Everyone paid up with the exception of the crusading orders of the Knights Templar and the Knights [Hospitaller] of St John,* who reversed the procedure, and exacted tribute from the Old Man. The sect itself apparently continued to flourish. (D. D.)

ATHOLL, Earl of: UNICORN: (*c.* 1440–1512) Sir John Stewart of Balveny, first Earl of Atholl, was the eldest son of Sir James Stewart, the Black Knight of Lorne, by Joan Beaufort, the Queen Dowager of James I, King of Scotland (1406–1437). The Black Knight had colluded with the powerful **Black Douglases** to overthrow the governor of Scotland, Sir Alexander Livingstone. Sir James and his brother William were imprisoned, although accounts differ as to whether they were, as the Auchinleck Chronicler stated, put in pits and boiled, or whether they were later released and given safe conducts (along with Atholl) to travel in England and abroad. In 1475 Atholl was appointed, together with **David Lindsay**, Fifth Earl of Crawford to command the land and naval forces sent to reduce the Earl of Ross, who surrendered before the military might reached him. Five years later Atholl assisted in subjugating Angus of the Isles. In 1482, after the murders of the King's followers at **Lauder**

Bridge, he and the other royal uncles, including his younger brother 'Hearty James', the **Earl of Buchan**, acted as royal 'guardians' of **James III*** while he was imprisoned in **Edinburgh** Castle. In 1488, when James III once again faced his rebellious nobility at Sauchieburn, Atholl was on the side of the monarch against the rebels with the young Prince James as their leader. This loyalty led to his imprisonment for a time in Dunbar Castle after the death of James III.

He married twice; he had two daughters by his first wife who was Margaret, the Dowager Countess of Douglas, known as 'the Fair Maid of Galloway' and the only daughter of Archibald Douglas, Fifth **Earl of Douglas.** His second marriage was to Eleanora **Sinclair**, one of the many daughters of Sir William Sinclair, Third Earl of Orkney and First Earl of Caithness. From this second marriage there were two sons, the eldest of whom, John, became the Second Earl of Atholl, and fell at **Flodden** in 1513. Of the nine daughters the couple also produced, one was Anne, the mother of Matthew Stewart, Fourth **Earl of Lennox** (Matthew Lennox).*

AUBIGNY, Lords of: HN; LC: The Stuarts (the French version of their surname) of Aubigny were descended from Duncan Stewart, Eighth **Earl of Lennox**, who was executed in 1425 (see family tree, p. 442). The dynasty proper in France began with the first John Stuart 'de Darnellé et de Concressault', Constable of the Scots Guard of Charles VI of France (ruled 1380–1422), who, in the last year of his life, made Stewart the hereditary seigneur of Aubigny-sur-Nère, south of Orléans. The previous year, Sir John had won himself the crown of Thomas, Duke of Clarence, brother of Henry V (King of England 1413–1422), killed in the battle of Baugé between the English and French during the Hundred Years' War.

This was the war in which the Fourth Earl of Douglas was to earn himself the title, in 1424, of the Duke of Touraine, with the grant of the town and castle of Chinon. The valley of the Loire was full of Scots soldiers fighting for France, to the extent that King Charles was smitten with *le mal de Fiacre*, a form of piles, after allegedly offending the saint with his anti-Scots cry: '*Je ne puis aller nulle part sans trouver devant ma barbe des Écossais morts ou vifs!*' (Wherever I go, there are Scots dead or alive in front of my beard).

In 1429, after the death of Sir John, and his burial in Orléans Cathedral, the title went not to Alan, his oldest son (who was to be killed by Sir Thomas Boyd), nor to his brother Alexander (who was to kill Boyd in revenge: see under **John Stewart, Lord Darnley**). The second Lord d'Aubigny was Alan's younger brother John Stewart. Alan's line, which was prolific, was to produce generations of fraternal Stewarts who split between them the lands and titles of Aubigny in France and Lennox in Scotland. John's line ended after a promising start.

Sir John, the second seigneur of Aubigny, commanded a hundred Scots men-at-arms for the French King **Louis XI**,* and was a chevalier of the Order of St Michael.* He died in 1482. His son Bernard (Bérault, *c.* 1447–1508) was born to John's French wife Beatrice, one of the ladies of Bonne de Berry, comtesse d'Armagnac, and embarked on a well-documented public career as third Lord d'Aubigny, becoming a captain of lances under the King. He was in Scotland in 1484 on a diplomatic errand from the new King Charles VIII (ruled 1483–1498) to **James III**,* and returned with a party that included his third cousin **Andrew Stewart, Lord Avandale**, and also possibly a band of Scots mercenaries for the use of France against England.

Bernard's nearest relatives in Scotland at the time were Chancellor Avandale, and Sir John Stewart of Darnley, his first cousin. Bernard returned to England the following year to take part with French and Scots troops in the battle of Bosworth, in which King Richard III (formerly **Duke of Gloucester**) was killed, and the French-supported Henry Tudor became the next English King.

Bernard covered himself with glory fighting for France in the Italian wars, and went on to become Viceroy of Naples and Constable of Sicily, and captain of the Scottish Guard in France (1493–1508). Sent to Scotland in 1508 to lead a spectacular mission of friendship from Charles VIII's successor Louis XII (King of France 1498–1515), Bernard died suddenly in the midst of the elaborate festivities. He had been staying at Corstorphine with his friend Sir John Forrester, whose ancestor Sir William Forrester had been taken prisoner in France with the first John Stewart of Aubigny in 1423. Dying, Bernard asked that his heart should be sent to the shrine of St Ninian, Galloway, where the King had planned to take him in person as he had vowed a pilgrimage when he had won his battles in Italy. Court poet William Dunbar (*c.* 1460–1520) wrote, in quick succession, both a welcome poem and the elegy for Stewart, 'The Ballad of Lord Bernard Stewart' and 'Elegy on the Death of Bernard Stewart, Lord of Aubigny', in which the noble is called 'the flour of chevelrie'. From the latter comes the verse:

> O duilfull death! O dragon dolorous!
> Quhy hes thow done so dulfullie devoir [duty]
> The proince of knychtheid, nobill and chevilrous,
> The witt of weiris [wars], of armes and honour,
> The crop of curage, the strenth of armes in stour,
> The fame of France, the fame of Lumbardy,
> The choiss of chiftanes, most awful in armour,
> The charbunckell, cheif of every chevelrie!

Bernard's face, pleasantly confident, double-chinned and Punch-nosed, can be seen in a drawing extant today.

Bernard Stewart married twice. He had no sons, but his daughter Anne by his second wife married her second cousin Robert Stewart (the grandson of Alan), who served for a while under his own brother William (who became a captain of the Scots Guards) and Bernard. Robert Stewart inherited the title of Aubigny from his father-in-law and became a Marshal of France during the Italian wars, in which he fought with distinction, taking part in the battle of Marignano in 1515, by which Francis I* reconquered Milan, defeating the Swiss.

Since Robert had no direct heirs, the titles of Lennox and Aubigny passed to the grandsons of Matthew, Second (or Tenth) Earl of Lennox, who was Robert's elder brother. Matthew was killed at **Flodden**, but left offspring, including a son John by his second wife Elizabeth **Hamilton**, daughter of the Scots **Princess Mary.** Matthew's son, John Stewart, Third (or Eleventh) Earl of Lennox, married a descendant of the **Earl of Atholl**, one of James III's half-uncles, and by her had three sons and a daughter.

The eldest sons of the third earl, Matthew and his brother John,* had been sent to France in 1527 to be placed under the care of their great-uncle Robert Stewart, fourth seigneur d'Aubigny and captain of the Scottish Guard in France. The brothers entered into military service under Robert, and saw service in Francis I's campaign against the Emperor Charles V* in Provence. John Stewart was adopted as his great-uncle's heir and married Anne de la Quelle, while his brother acted as Francis's ambassador to Scotland, until his defection to England and the subsequent marriage to Margaret Douglas* in 1544. Furious at this act of treason, Francis I had John Stewart flung into prison. He was only released in 1547 when Henri II* came to the throne. John became Lord d'Aubigny during the reign of Henri II, when the child Mary Queen of Scots* was in France, and the target of a historic poison plot (QUEENS). John Stewart continued to lead a company of men-at-arms, and fought in the Italian wars. At the battle of St Quentin in 1557, when the French were routed by the army of Philip II,* d'Aubigny was taken prisoner. He asked that his brother pay the full ransom requested by his captor, but Matthew contributed only two hundred crowns, rejected by his brother as not enough. Following the assistance of the Count of Feria,* d'Aubigny's ransom was eventually provided.

John Stewart was an enthusiastic supporter of his brother's scheme to have young Henry Darnley married to Mary Queen of Scots; like his brother, he survived to see the marriage, then the murder of his nephew. John's son Esmé became a favourite of his cousin, Mary and Darnley's son, King James VI (ruled 1567–1625).

AUCHTERHOUSE, James Stewart of: See **Buchan, Earl of.**

Augustinian canons: HN: Priests who lived in a community like monks, emulating the communal discipline of their monastic counterparts. As they were ordained, Augustinians often reached out to the laity in the surrounding community, and they usually had a close relationship to the churches that were provided for them. The Augustinian Abbey of **Holyrood** is a good example of a community with close links with the Canongate and its residents. (See **Barony and regality.**)

Aunty's wool: LIONS, 34: The reference is to a thirteenth-century French lampoon, *'La Laine à ma Tante'*. The 'aunty' is England, and the poet is ostensibly her nephew, attempting to wring payment for wool out of Arras burghers. An Artois phrase of about the same time refers to 'carrying wool to England' in the same sense as 'taking coals to Newcastle'. (D. D.)

AVANDALE, Andrew Stewart, Lord: UNICORN: (d. 1488) Scottish, illegitimate, royal: Andrew Stewart, first lord of Avandale, was one of the small group of discreet men whose careers spanned two reigns, and who until the end of their lives privately steered, cajoled and shoved their masters in the way they thought best for the kingdom and for themselves.

One of seven illegitimate sons, Andrew Stewart was probably brought up in exile in England for the first two decades of his life, and he and a younger brother received English knighthoods. Andrew's paternal grandfather and maternal great-grandfather had both been executed for treason. His father was one or other of two Stewart brothers, both great-nephews of King Robert III (*c.* 1337–1406), and both suspected of disloyalty to the throne. One of these, Lord James Stewart, had fled to Ireland, and was said to have raised an illegitimate family with a mistress named McDonald.

A conflicting story claims that Andrew and his brothers were the progeny of an insecure marriage between Lord James's brother Walter Stewart (executed in 1425) and a daughter of Campbell of Lochawe, ancestor of the Campbell Earls of **Argyll.** Of the illegitimacy there is no doubt, as Andrew and two of his brothers later took steps to obtain **dispensation.** There were also two legitimate brothers, one of whom would become Avandale's heir when he died childless by his only known marriage.

When the child King James II* came to the throne in 1437 on the sudden death of his father, Sir Andrew Stewart (as he then was) entered public life in Scotland, and by 1440 he was a member of the ten-year-old King's general council in Stirling. Much of this decade was occupied with the diplomatic moves necessary to marry off the King's many sisters. Within Scotland, the fall of the **Black Douglases** and the rise of the Chancellor, Sir William Crichton, and later of Bishop Kennedy* occupied the political scene. Joan, the English Dowager Queen, who had rashly remarried in a bid for control, died sheltering in Dunbar Castle in 1445, leaving three Stewart sons who were to become the half-uncles of King **James III:*** the **Earl of Atholl**, the **Earl of Buchan** and **Andrew Stewart**, the Bishop of Moray.

In 1449 King James II himself married the Duke of Burgundy's niece, Mary of Gueldres, who was to become a strong presence in the kingdom for fourteen years. In 1456, Stewart was granted the lands of Avandale, where the ruins of his castle still stand by the present Strathaven in Lanarkshire. The property had been forfeited to the Crown after the killing of William Douglas, Eighth Earl of Douglas in 1452. For that, Andrew Stewart was held partly responsible, which earned him the enmity of the family Ker, but the further favour of the King, who next appointed him Warden of the West Marches, and Keeper of the south-western forces of Lochmaben Castle, a vital post to be held in the next reign by the young **Alexander, Duke of Albany.*** In 1460, now Lord Avandale, Andrew Stewart became Chancellor of Scotland, a position he was to hold for twenty-two years.

On the King's sudden death later that year at the age of twenty-nine, Avandale became for a time one of the Lords of Regency to his eight-year-old son King James III and continued as Chancellor by command of the boy's mother Mary of Gueldres. Holding office with Avandale were Colin, **Earl of Argyll**, Master of the Royal Household, and Secretary **Archibald Whitelaw. John Stewart, Lord Darnley**, and Treasurer Guthrie also served. When the Queen Dowager died in 1463, she left the power in the hands of the young King's 'uncle' Bishop Kennedy, who survived her by less than two years. Avandale and his colleagues were with Kennedy and the twelve-year-old King when he made his three-month royal progress to the north in 1464.

For several years more, complicated by the English civil war between Lancaster and York, Scotland was buffeted by a struggle for supremacy between leading families marked by the rise to power of the family of **Boyd.** Between 1466 and 1467, Chancellor Avandale became Keeper of the castle of Stirling, which served to deny the use of the castle to Lord Boyd, the head of the faction. The other chief officers of state also managed to retain their positions of trust, although Boyd was sufficiently confident to marry his son Thomas Boyd to the King's sister **Princess Mary.** In 1468 Avandale was accompanied by Thomas Boyd when he sailed to Denmark to complete the negotiation by which the King would take to wife **Margaret of Denmark**, daughter of King **Christian I.**

Avandale had been one of the prime movers in this slow-maturing scheme, which had for one of its objectives the transfer to King James of the islands of Orkney and Shetland. The subsequent marriage of the King, with all its desirable benefits, coincided with the disappearance of the Boyds, who had had no noticeable support from Lord Avandale. This had perhaps influenced his enemies the Kers, who were now accused not only of conspiring to help Lord Boyd and bring back the forfeited **James, Ninth Earl of Douglas**, but of trying to poison Lord Avandale.

He bore, if not a charmed life, an exceptionally well-organised one. He had a claim, through his grandmother Isabella, to the earldom of **Lennox.** In 1471, against the counter-claims of several rivals, notably of Darnley, Haldane of Gleneagles and Napier of Merchiston, Avandale succeeded in obtaining from the Crown (which had no right to give it) not the earldom, but the rents of the earldom for life. The fact that he retained them, and that despite continuing complaints, the other claimants continued to work with him for the benefit of the kingdom, perhaps suggests that what he had to offer was worth the fee. And the King, to keep the peace, suggested in 1473 to the tenants of Lennox that they should obey Darnley as Earl, even though Avandale was drawing the life-rent.

The service Avandale was providing represented above all security for the royal family. In 1473 the Queen's first child was born, and would spend most of its youth in or about Stirling Castle at the edge of the Chancellor's Lennox. Since 1472, the Constable of the Castle had been Avandale's own procurator **Malcolm McClery**, a Stirling burgess and lawyer with **Sinclair** connections. The young Queen's marischal was **Sir Robert Colville** of Ochiltree, of a family of hereditary royal stewards who had served the previous King; and the Captain and Keeper of Stirling, once Avandale's own position, was **Sir James Shaw of Sauchie.**

Of increasing concern to all of them was the unruly behaviour of the King's two younger brothers, of whom the elder, Alexander, Duke of Albany, was warded in Edinburgh Castle in 1479 after a series of provocative raids into England which ran counter to the Crown's desire to maintain the peace. When, after he escaped or was allowed to escape, Albany barricaded himself into his castle of Dunbar and refused to negotiate, it was Avandale who invested the castle on behalf of the King. Whether he meant to use force is not known, but Albany certainly turned his guns on the besiegers, killing two of Avandale's supporters from the west, one of whom was another man from the Lennox, **Sir John Colquhoun of Luss.**

Albany then fled to France, and the country prepared for the war with England which followed. When Albany returned in 1482 with an English army led by **Richard, Duke of Gloucester**, the high officers of state seem to have resolved to stand aside from the actions, which halted the King's advance to battle, and the implication of Avandale, suggested by a sixteenth-century historian, Pitscottie, has been discounted. According to the available archives, Avandale, Whitelaw, **William Scheves** and Argyll ceased to take part in public business about the time the English army reached York, a month before the confrontation at **Lauder Bridge.** After that, the band which restrained the King in **Edinburgh** Castle was captained by Lord Darnley, who was Avandale's third cousin. Then, when the English halted their advance and talks were proposed, it was Avandale, Scheves and Argyll who helped guide the negotiation that ended with the retreat of the invading army at a price which included the loss of Berwick-upon-Tweed* to England.

Albany remained, on promises of advancement, and with Avandale and the same two companions, seems to have presented himself at Stirling Castle to hold talks with the Queen. As a result, it would appear, steps were next taken to set up a face-saving procedure to release the King from his imprisonment in Edinburgh Castle. This was done over several weeks in a combined effort by Albany and the leading citizens of Edinburgh which had all the appearance of a genuine siege, to which the castle eventually submitted with grace. By the time the King emerged to effect a dramatic reconciliation with his brother, Avandale and his colleagues had withdrawn, and Avandale had given up his Chancellorship. It may have been meant as a temporary gesture, since the office was taken in turn by two ailing men who both died within the next year. In fact, it eventually went to Colin, Earl of Argyll, probably to encourage his support.

Albany stayed in Scotland with growing disenchantment for the rest of the year, and the three negotiators were absent from the December Parliament, which was conciliatory to the Duke. When the situation finally broke down, they returned to the Parliament of March 1483 which finally pronounced Albany's forfeiture. By then, the Duke had again retired to Dunbar and summoned English help to oust his brother the King.

Although no longer Chancellor, Avandale remained in public life, attending Parliament, and sitting as one of the **Lords of Council in Civil Causes**, and as one of the **Lords Auditor of Causes and Complaints.** In 1484, he was one of the Scottish envoys appointed by the King to return to France with Bernard Stewart, **Lord d'Aubigny**, who had successfully concluded a pact of friendship with James on behalf of the young Charles VIII (King of France 1483–1498). This was the precise time when the disgraced Albany, with some English help, was to make his last bid to oust James by attacking the castle of Lochmaben, after which he would return to end his life in France. Avandale's inclusion in the peace-making visit to France may have come about because Bernard, 'flower of chivalry', was his third cousin, or because it was rumoured that a detachment of troops was sent with the embassy, such as he had already commanded on one occasion against Albany at Dunbar.

It was an example of the extent of Avandale's family connections, which were exceptional, even for his time. Through his grandmother Isabella, Countess of Lennox and Duchess of Albany, he was related to the Menteiths of Rusky, the Crambies of Pitcairn and the Stewarts of Darnley, and through their later marriages to the Napiers of Merchiston and the Haldanes of Gleneagles. One aunt had married a Campbell of Lochawe, and another, Buchanan of that Ilk of Stirling. On the side of Isabella's husband Murdoch Stewart, Duke of Albany, Andrew was related to all the Stewart kings. His great-aunt had married Malcolm **Fleming** of Biggar, progenitor of Robert, Lord Fleming, and all his family. And finally, Avandale's illegitimate sister had married William Edmonston of Duntreath, Lennox, the Keeper of Doune Castle in 1482, from whom connections with the families Forrester and French and Shaw would emerge.

Andrew Stewart, Lord Avandale, returned from France to his usual occupations, signing his last charter in March 1488, just before the events which led to the death of James III, which he may not have lived to see. Certainly he was dead by the following July, when James IV paid for a mass for his soul in the church of Stirling. (D. D.)

Aztec mask: QUEENS, II, 3: Pirates who had earned themselves a reasonable living in the English Channel during the fifteenth century would have been envious of the dazzling fortunes to be made from vessels crossing the Atlantic to Europe from the New World in the decades ahead. In 1521, a fleet from Dieppe, in the north of France, set out for the Azores just after Hernán Cortés (1485–1547) had taken Peru, and managed to capture a Spanish ship full of treasure. Amongst its cargo was an emerald as large as the palm of a hand, gold and silver vases and cups, idols, and jewelled masks in mosaic with gold ears and bone teeth. The commander of the Dieppe corsairs, in a ship of three hundred tons, was one Jean de Fleury. (D. D.)

B

Bad luck at sea: GEMINI, 32: Pigs were considered very unlucky animals by fishermen. They should not even be mentioned, let alone seen before a journey was undertaken, presaging a poor catch or a storm on the way. It was also considered ill-fated to whistle at sea, as it would raise a storm.

Baker of Ferrara: KINGS, II, 3: Victim of a delusional state caused by an imbalance of the humours, as described by Robert Burton (1577–1640) in his witty and informative treatise *The Anatomy of Melancholy* (1621): 'A baker in Ferrara, that thought he was composed of butter, and durst not sit in the sun or come near the fire for fear of being melted.'

Baldur: LIONS, 29: The hero Baldur the White was the most beautiful of the Aesir, the Nordic gods, and was the son of Odin, their leader. His home was at Breidablik, which was later transformed into the zodiacal house we now know as Gemini. Some legends say he himself was a twin, his brother being Hodur, the blind god of war.

When Baldur dreamed of approaching death, his mother took an oath from everything in nature that it would not harm him. The jealous dwarf-blooded Loki discovered that the mistletoe alone had been forgotten, and during some sport of the gods, placed a bough in the hands of blind Hodur, and directed it towards Hodur's own twin. Baldur fell, pierced to the heart.

The gods were bereft, and Hermod the Nimble raced Odin's eight-footed grey horse Sleipnir to Hades to beg the goddess Hel to release Baldur. She consented, provided all things in the world, both living and lifeless, wept for him. With this hope, Baldur gave Hermod the ring which had been placed on his funeral pyre to take back to Odin. But not all things did weep: Loki's step-daughter, the witch Thaukt, abstained, which meant that Baldur could not return, but had to remain lost until the end of the world.

The death of Baldur, the best and wisest of the Aesir, brought about the doom of the gods. The great catastrophe of Ragnarok followed, with the seven Fimbul winters of bitter frost and harsh winds, followed by the terrible waves of disasters: the axe age, the sword age, the storm age, the wolf age. Locked in war, the gods and the frost-giants all perished until, finally, the sun had a daughter, and Baldur the Beautiful returned to the world, bringing happiness and peace once again.

The story is told in the Lay of Vegtam the Wanderer, one of the Eddas, or source-books of Nordic myth. It holds the traces of many legends, and is thought by some to embody a folk memory of an early ice age.

The lines in the novel come from the mysterious oracle of the prophetess Völva, and are as follows:

All ills shall cease	*böls mân alls batna*
Baldur shall come	*Baldur mon koma*
And dwell with Hauthr	*búua their Hauthr*
In Hropt's abodes.	*Hropts sig tóptir.*

Bale-fires: HN; LC: In a hilly country like Scotland, bale-fires were the natural signal for raising the alarm and mustering troops. The codes varied, but in 1455 fires lit on Hume, **Haddington**, Dunbar, Dalkeith, Eggerhope, **Edinburgh** Castle and north to Stirling and beyond could bring all Scotland under arms (that is, able to defend itself locally) in two hours. By the code of that time, one bale-fire meant that the English army was on the move; two that it was advancing, and four in a row that it was coming in strength. Men living west of Edinburgh mustered at the Borough muir, and those living to the east gathered at Haddington. To warn of approaching enemy fleets, Edinburgh Castle used cannon. (D. D.)

Balingers: LIONS, 15: Small craft, about fifty tons or less, as are barges and crayers. Balingers have a crew of between twelve and fourteen, barges have larger crews of thirty-four or so, in case they needed to row.

Baltic drinking: RONDO: Beer varied in composition and quality, as it does today. Polish beer in the fifteenth century was thick, and there was little standardisation of measures in beer (or rye) bought in bulk from, say, **Danzig** or Cracow. In Danzig, one last of frothless beer equalled 2,760 litres of frothing beer, or 2,264 litres of wine, and one average ship could carry fifty lasts. Danzig was the chief distribution centre to the eastern **Hanseatic League** countries for imported Rhenish wine, and wine from Portugal and Aquitaine.

In Holland the last drink, the *Schlaffdruncke* or sleeping-cup, was placed in a pot on the table. Toasts were announced with the hat off. German beer was made in Bremen and Hamburg. (D. D.)

BARBARO, Josaphat: RONDO: (1413–1494) Venetian merchant who spent sixteen years in Persia as an ambassador and representative of Venice. He was consul in Tana until 1460 and an official in Dalmatia, during which time he had lived and traded amongst the **Crim Tartars** of the Lower Don. Barbaro was sent as an ambassador to the court of **Uzum Hasan**.* The memoirs of his travels written in 1487 show him as a tolerant and observant diplomat, who was frequently blessed with more patience and fortune than his fellow Venetian, **Ambrogio Contarini**. Barbaro visited Uzum Hasan's palace at Tabriz which he described in full, commenting in particular on the garden in the centre of the palace where Uzum received his visitors; a green garden 'like a meadowe full of trufles', complete with running water. The palace was built in the centre of a large and beautiful garden, called ***Hesht Behesht*** or Eight Paradises. Present at the audience was a Prince of India, who brought gifts of gems and a menagerie as tribute. Barbaro relates how he was shown some of Uzum's tribute gems: ancient turquoise, porcelain vases, pearls, diamonds and a string of balas rubies, the size of olives, each stone weighing between fifty and eighty carats. Tabriz was, after all, on the lucrative silk route. Whilst travelling, Barbaro's translator died, and failing to find another, Barbaro had to translate for himself for the rest of his stay. He noted many wonders on his travels, as Marco Polo* before him who had travelled in the same region, like Baku on the Caspian Sea, 'where there gushes a stream of oil in such abundance that a thousand camels may load there at once'. The oil is not good to drink, but burns well, and acts as a salve for men or camels with a scab or an itch (RONDO, 29). Barbaro remained with Uzum Hasan for over four years, only leaving after the death of the Persian King in 1478 and arriving back in Venice in 1479.

Barbary ram: QUEENS, II, 1: The Barbary ram, with its long plaited tail, was a novelty in France, where it was imported and sold as a curiosity. A troop of sixteenth-century medical students from Montpellier on a trip to Marseilles went to watch the galleys unload in the harbour. As well as the rams, they had brought ostriches, coral, and a Negro weight-lifter. (D. D.)

Barony and regality: HN: In Scotland, a barony is a large freehold estate, held free of duties except those which are due to the King. In feudal terms, a baron was a tenant-in-chief to the Crown, but in Scotland the holding of such an estate did not necessarily carry with it the title or rank of baron. One tenant could hold several baronies. The Crown would, on occasion, create baronies in regality (or burghs of barony, as they were usually called at this period), which gave the tenant-in-chief the right to hold a market, an annual fair, and a legal court. Their trading centre was the burgh (or town) of barony. The lord was thus granted the right of civil and criminal jurisdiction over all their tenants (excluding only the crime of treason). A grant of regality to a barony gave the holder the authority to deal with crimes which were normally the reserve of the justiciar courts, and entitled them to preside over cases of murder, arson, rape and violent robbery, and to execute the guilty. If tenants of the regality were accused of a crime they could not be tried by the justiciar court, but only in their regality (subject only to Parliament and the King). This made the lord a 'little king' within his own realm; those who were indicted before the King's justiciars would have to be returned to their regality to receive a hearing.

The lands of all the important **monasteries** were regalities, as the Canongate, outside the city walls of **Edinburgh**, was the regality of the Abbey of **Holyrood**. It was a burgh, which meant that it was an urban dwelling (or town) where citizens held their lands or **tenements** for a certain annual rent which was payable to the tenant-in-chief to the Crown. The landlord could be an individual, or an institution, like the Church. In the case of the Canongate, the burgh was one of several which belonged to the **Augustinian** monastery of Holyrood and was granted to the Abbey probably at the time of its foundation in 1128. Monasteries of second rank, such as Crossragruel, **Newbattle** and Kinloss, also held baronies. Baronies making up a regality need not be next to one another, and could represent parcels of property over a large area. Thus monasteries which owned tracts of land over large areas were unable to administer and carry out the legal duties in their regalities and baronies. It proved convenient for them to appoint a lay bailie from a respected and powerful family who would have the respect and prestige necessary to control the regality on their behalf. This office increasingly came to be hereditary and was often concomitant with an increase in status and land ownership, and it was a prize worth fighting for, as did the **Home family** when it came to **Coldingham.** See also **Whitekirk.**

Beaver, self-defence of: KINGS, IV, 2: Robert Burton (1577–1640), author of *The Anatomy of Melancholy* (1621), outlined the causes of and potential treatments for the condition from which he also suffered. Burton wrote that one can prepare for misfortune in advance be removing the cause, and therefore avoiding the effect, as one removes a tooth to stop a toothache. The example of the male beaver, hunted for his musk, is similar:

Ut vivat castor, sibi testes amputat ipse;
Tu quoque, siqua nocent, abjice, tutus eris.

The beaver bites off's stones to save the rest:
Do thou the like with that thou art opprest.

Because it spouts sweet venom in their ears . . . : KINGS, I, 7: From Bellenden's (*c.* 1492–*c.* 1550) political preface to his translation of the Latin *History of Scotland* by Hector Boece (*c.* 1465–1536). The whole verse runs as below:

Show now what kind of soundis musical
Is maist seemand to valiant chivaliers;
As thunderan blast of trumpet bellical
The spreits of men to hardy courage steers,

So singing, fiddling, and piping not affeirs [is unbecoming]
For men of honour, nor of high estate;
Because it spouts sweet venom in their ears,
And makes their mindis all effeminate.

Bee stings: RONDO, 37: Although fatal in large doses and to those with an allergic reaction, Russian folk medicine exhorted the positive benefits of bee-sting therapy for rheumatism and arthritis. It was also a treatment for gout. According to Richard Eden,* the sixteenth-century biographer of the travels of Chancellor* and his contemporaries, in Russia the bees did not live in hives, but in hollow trees. There was no need to call them together or charm them, since the boughs were laden with them. The trees produced massive honeycombs and the Duke of Milan's papal ambassador told the story of a Russian husbandman who stepped up to his chest in a lake of honey and was trapped for two days, surviving off the honey until he was found, and drawn out clinging to a bear.

Bell the Cat: See **Douglas, Archibald.**

BENECKE, Paúel: LIONS: (*c.* 1430–d. by 1477): A splendid piratical figure in the northern seas of the fifteenth century, nick-named '*der harte Seevogels*', or Tough Seabird, Paúel Benecke or Pawel Beneke of **Danzig** (Gdánsk) was born about 1430. According to legend, he was abandoned as a child, and cared for by well-known freebooter Kurt Bokelmann, who presumably taught him his trade. A Danzig skipper of the same time named Michal Benecke might have been a relative.

The highest points in Paúel's career as a privateer and sea captain occurred during the last eight years of his life, beginning in 1469 when he first 'covered himself with glory' (by one account) by hurling himself into the war of the **Hanseatic League**'s towns against England. He was said to be a lucky man, and the opportunities which came his way bear this out. The first of his two famous exploits occurred in 1471, when he went to sea with two ships, the *Madlene von Dieppe* and the *Schwan von Caen*, and there overcame and took captive two important English travellers. One has been called simply John of Salisbury, and might have been John Neville, brother of the Earl of Warwick (1428–1471) and third son of the late Richard Neville, Earl of Salisbury (d. 1460).

The other, boldly described as 'the Mayor of London, Thomas Kriegk', turns out to be the sad person of Sir Thomas Cooke, a wealthy draper from Suffolk who came to flourish initially under King **Edward IV**,* owning ships and a vast foreign trade, as well as brew-houses, taverns, fishing weirs, manors and properties in London, Surrey, Essex and Kent. Unfortunately, as a Yorkist married to a Lancastrian, he was not as adept as others in steering a cautious way among the changes of power between Lancaster and York, and at various times found himself in the Tower of London, impeached for treason, or his lands or effects seized for one reason or another. He incurred the special displeasure of King Edward's brother-in-law **Earl Rivers**.

When, eventually, King Edward came back to power, Sir Thomas and his son had the wisdom to take ship and flee, only to be captured at sea by Paúel Benecke. It must have seemed the last straw. Cooke was bundled to Flanders, flung into prison, and eventually returned, inescapably, to face the ire of King Edward. He survived, living seven years more, but his sufferings were quoted, in later times, as proof of the cruelty of York. In fact, the Tough Seabird provided good propaganda for King Richard III (formerly **Duke of Gloucester**).

All Paúel Benecke's latter history is closely bound with his vessel, the great *Peter von Danzig*, one of the largest European ships of the time. Originally French, and known as the *St Pierre de La Rochelle*, she was a caravel,* a huge three-master with a smooth hull of edge-to-edge planks, instead of the traditional **clinker** (or overlapping) construction. Fast, and of enormous cargo capacity, the type had begun to appear mid-century in Mediterranean and Atlantic ports and this, a very large specimen indeed, had been fitted out and armed as a privateer by the town of Danzig.

It was an act of inspired opportunism. The ship had been laid up in Danzig since 1462, when she had been struck and damaged in harbour by lightning, and abandoned by her skipper, who had been delivering salt. When its French owner died without heirs, the ship was claimed by the French Crown. The hard-headed Danzigers refused to return it without compensation for outlay on repairs. The case escalated, and finally became the excuse upon which **Louis XI*** declared war on the Hanse.

The first known commander of the renovated *St Pierre*, now renamed *Der Grote Kraweel* (*The Great Caravel*), was the Danzig town councillor Bernd Pawest, who in 1471 took her across the North Sea and down the English Channel, raiding as far as Camaret in France, south of Brest and north of the ship's original port of La Rochelle.

It was not a successful voyage. Held up by the weather, poor port facilities, shortages of supplies and a surprising lack of co-operation in Bruges,* Pawest had to return to the River Elbe after only nine weeks of effective fighting at sea. He hesitated. The French fleet were uncomfortably active, and he suffered a shortage of crew, **Charles, Duke of Burgundy*** having forbidden his subjects to serve with the privateers. Finally, with a damaged ship and a mutiny on his hands, Pawest left the caravel stranded in the River Zwyn, beside Bruges, where she stayed until the spring of 1473, when she was recommissioned under Paúel Benecke.

It was another instance of Benecke's luck. With the Hanse war declining, Danzig had withdrawn her armed ships from the fray. Unofficially, one was still active: the *Peter von Danzig*, now solemnly sold to a private syndicate of merchants, members of the Confrérie of St George of the Church of Our Lady in Danzig, and operating on a strictly co-operative basis. The *Peter* was not the handiest fighting ship on the ocean, but she was alarmingly huge. And on the second Tuesday after Easter, 1473, she was hovering in the English Channel when two Flemish galleys appeared off Gravelines. They had been freighted by the Medici factor in Bruges, Tommaso Portinari,* and were on their way south to Italy, pausing only to drop off Tolfa alum* from their previous voyage, and take on English wool at Southampton. Approaching the English cliffs, they were attacked by Paúel Benecke.

A wiser man might not have attempted it. The ships belonged to Burgundy, and had been built for Duke Philip the Good* in 1464 for an abortive crusade. Since they could not be sold, the Duke chartered them to the Florentine banking firm of the Medici, who had advanced the money to build them. From 1467 they sailed under the Burgundian banner on regular trips between the Low Countries and Pisa (the port of Florence), and occasionally from Pisa to Constantinople. That spring, having come late from Pisa and spent the winter at Flushing, the ships picked up Bruges cargo and set out on their return trip to Italy with a freight of woollens, linens, tapestries, gold brocades, crimson velvets, satin, furs and two altar-pieces. One of the altar-pieces was the great *Last Judgement* of **Hans Memling**, commissioned by Angelo di Jacopo Tani,* former Medici agent in Bruges, and destined for the church of the Badia Fiesolana in Florence. The altar-pieces were valued at 360 gold florins, and the value of the whole cargo was sixty thousand pounds.

These were the ships that the *Peter von Danzig* attacked. In the fight, one galley escaped, but the other, the *San Matteo*, crewed by Italians and under the command of Francesco do Messer Tedaldi, was boarded and taken. Reports said that 'of the many' Florentine merchants on board, eight were killed during the assault. The galley was then brought, as an English prize, into the Baltic, and the diplomatic storm broke.

Every side had a different story. The *Peter von Danzig*'s syndicate claimed the *San Matteo* was in English waters, but the victims denied it. The Medici claimed that despite the Hanse war, no one could steal cargo not intended for England, and, with the Duke, claimed the ship back. The ship was at least partly insured, one of the underwriters being the firm of Cambi of Florence, but the Medici were still intent on recovering the galley and at least some of the cargo. The alum alone was worth forty thousand gold florins.

Meanwhile, Benecke had taken the cargo and landed it near the mouth of the Elbe, beside Hamburg, after which it was taken overland across Pomerania to where it was received with great pomp at the abbey of Oliva, a few miles west of Danzig. There, in due course, it was shared out according to custom. Of 400 shares, some were of 100 marks, some of 80, while every man got 21 marks of prize money. The Memling altar-piece, now in the hands of Sidinghusen, Valandt and Niederhof, the merchant-owners of Benecke's ship, is thought to have been presented by them to the altar of their Confrérie of St George in the Marienkirche, the Church of St Mary in Danzig.

The lawyers then went to work. Duke Charles, supporting the Medici, ordered the seizure of all Hanse goods in Flanders, but nothing happened, as was to be expected, since the merchants of Bruges had no wish to see the Hanse merchants leave. Burgundian representations were made to the Hanseatic towns, and Florentine letters were sent to the Kings of Poland and Hungary, the Duke of Cleves, and the Bishops of Bremen and Munster, without effect. Magistrates of the Hanse urged Danzig, in a dilatory way, to return the Medici cargo, and promised, in a dilatory way, to forbid the sale of the stolen goods in their cities. Nothing happened. Nothing happened when **Anselm Adorne*** turned up in the Hanse towns and Poland in 1474, asking for redress. Portinari did doggedly pursue his case through the law courts, and the last of a series of indemnities was paid forty years later.

Nothing quite so spectacular ever happened to Paúel Benecke again. He seems to have continued to captain the *Peter*, and was with her on what seems to have been her last voyage, in 1475, when she sailed from Danzig in a fleet of twenty-eight big ships, bound for Brouage. There, that same year, she suffered shipwreck and sank. No details are known, and although he lived for another two years, Paúel Benecke does not appear again on the records of Danzig. Perhaps he decided it was time to give up the sea. Or perhaps, somewhere, he enjoyed his last fight.

He was married. His wife's name was probably Margaret, since that was the name given to her god-daughter, Margaret Herzberg. Paúel Benecke had one daughter, Elzbieta, about whom there is no information.

His life in Danzig as portrayed in the novels is conjecture, and it is not known whether or not he met Anselm Adorne. There is no record either of a visit to Iceland in the spring of 1472. The first authenticated Danzig voyage to Iceland ended badly, in 1479, with the loss of its one ship off the Kattegat. But the Memling painting, *The Last Judgement*, remains to this day in Gdańsk, where it occupies a room in the Museum Naradowe; while in the Polish Maritime Museum, Gdańsk, is a beautiful scale model of Benecke's ship, the *Peter von Danzig*. (D. D.)

BERECROFTS: UNICORN: Robert Crawford of Berecrofts (referred to in the *House of Niccolò* novels as Robin) was the son and heir of Archibald Crawford of Berecrofts, who died between 1494 and 1500. He in turn was a son of William Crawford of Berecrofts, who had died by 1494, and who was almost certainly the brother of **Archibald Crawford**, abbot of **Holyrood**. Archibald, father of Robert, may have had a brother, William Crawford, whose son, another Archibald, held land in **Linlithgow**, having married one Janet Amisfield. A probable relation, James Amisfield, was a goldsmith who was witnessing Canongate charters in 1504.

The Berecrofts family had property in the Canongate, **Edinburgh**; in **Leith**; and in Berecrofts, a fertile stretch of land in the country west of Edinburgh on the River Avon, beside what is now Grangemouth. Berecrofts (a

Paúel Benecke's ship ~ 'Peter von Danzig'

farmlands name – bere was an early form of the cereal barley) was then under the jurisdiction of the barony of Kerse, the regality of Broughton and the sheriffdom of Stirling (see **Barony and regality**). Broughton, now a suburb of Edinburgh, lay on the old road to North Leith and was then (as were North Leith and the Canongate) under the rule of the Abbot of Holyrood. During the tenure of Abbot Archibald, naturally all of his family flourished. The novels assume that the family also possessed land close to their ancestral origins in Lanarkshire, but there is no proof of this, and the site of the west-country property (although carefully chosen) is fictitious. Migration to the west is however very likely, as the Berecrofts land did not remain in the hands of the Crawfords, but by 1615 had fallen, like much of the area, into the possession of Sir John Hamilton, who also held lands by the Grange stream and across the river in Culross.

The detailed records of the Crawfords of Berecrofts are late, being contained in a register of minor property deals and litigation from 1485 to 1515, and which was not publicly accessible until 1952. The family had a presence on both sides of the high street of the Canongate, but their original town house appears to have been at the head of Leith Wynd. They also held in North Leith and in Berecrofts. Shortly before his own death, Robert's father Archibald Crawford had acquisitions on both sides of the Canongate, for which his procurator was John Ramsay.

The name of Katherine **Sersanders**, Robert's wife, (a niece of **Anselm Adorne*** of Bruges) is first mentioned together with his in 1503, when the family had tenants on the south side of the Canongate. Then in 1508 Robert Crawford of Berecrofts and 'Katherine Cessanderis his spouse' resigned to bailie Richard Faffinton the rent for the lands and tenants of John Forester of Barnton, lying on the south side of the high street of the Canongate, thus permitting the holding to be transferred to another John Forester, probably a son.

In 1505 there is a dispute over the foreland of the **tenement** of Robert Crawford of Berecrofts on the north side of the high street of the Canongate, at the head of Leith Wynd. In 1506 there is reference to rents he drew from the lands of the dead Hector Meldrum in the same area, which also included the land of the late Patrick Crawford. In the same year, Robert Crawford of Berecrofts resigned to George Crichton, Abbot of Holyrood, his waste land in North Leith. He also resigned to the bailie of the Canongate (Richard Faffington, who was also procurator to Robert) further rents from the east side of Leith Wynd, including property leased to Sir John Crawford, Treasurer of the **Chapel Royal**. (These transactions were often a simple formality, marking the transfer of the land to an heir.)

In the Canongate, their neighbours were bailies, goldsmiths, fleshers, tanners, merchants, masons, skinners, dyers, court officials and cooks, and there were butchers' stalls in the road. They grazed animals behind their houses, and brewers and fleshers kept geese to fatten. There were kilns. There must have been dyevats and ovens and furnaces as well. The noise and the smells would presumably pass quite unnoticed.

The dates of death of Robert Crawford and Katherine his wife are not known, although they were both still alive in 1508. There is proof, however, that the family survived in Berecrofts for at least two more generations before the land ownership fell, as noted above, to the Hamiltons. In 1525 Robert Crawford, son and heir of the late Robert Crawford, handed Berecrofts in turn to his own son of the same name, keeping only the life-rent. The formality was negotiated on his behalf by John Hamilton of Torrance, who had married the daughter of George Parkle, of the family that had succeed Anselm Adorne, the uncle of Katelijne Sersanders, as Captain of Linlithgow Palace. In 1530, Robert Crawford squashed an attempt by Robert Cairncross, the lord Abbot of Holyrood, to pass a holding in Berecrofts to one William Cairncross. That same year, Robert applied for retrospect dispensation for his marriage to an Elizabeth Brown, which had taken place in ignorance of a family relationship. John Hamilton again acted on his behalf, as did a Mr Henry Lauder.

Nothing is known of the lives of Robert and Katherine Crawford of Berecrofts beyond the disposition of their property. At least one son, Robert, is recorded: the novels give them two further fictitious children. It is not known how many they actually had. Robert's share in the battle of Nancy and his injuries are fictitious, as is his visit to Iceland with Katelijne and **Anselm Sersanders**, and Katelijne's inclusion in the pilgrimage of Anselm Adorne and his son, which included **Mount Sinai**.* The novels assume that Katelijne was sister to Anselm Sersanders, rather than a less likely daughter. (D. D.)

Bergenfahrer: RONDO, 2: *Fahrer* meant seagoing merchants. This was the name of one of their clubs, based in Lübeck, and consisting of merchants of the **Hanseatic League** sailing to Bergen.

Berserker: LIONS, 26: These were originally god-endowed wrestlers, trained by Odin in the magical arts. Later, the name became attached to terrifying, half-mythical warriors who fought, primed with drink or with drugs, as if crazed and who appear in the Icelandic sagas. Called 'bear shirts' and 'wolfskins', these men goad themselves into a violent frenzy; they identified themselves with the animal from which they took their names, and probably wore their pelts. There are glaring berserkers, their teeth sunk in the rim of their shields, among the famous sets of thirteenth-century Scandinavian walrus-tusk chessmen found in 1831 in north-west Scotland in the island of Lewis, which was ruled by Norway until 1266. The pieces are now spread between the British Museum and the Museum of Scotland. (D. D.)

BERTRAM, Walter: UNICORN: (d. by 1496) Married to Elizabeth **Cant** and brother-in-law of Margaret **Preston** of Craigmillar, Walter Bertram brought to the council table of **Edinburgh** the support of men – and women – from the wealthiest burgess families in the city, whose trading forged valuable connections overseas, and provided King **James III*** with the money he needed in crisis. It was during Bertram's leadership of the merchants, as Provost of Edinburgh, that the English invasion of Scotland in 1482 was halted and turned back.

He belonged to a family that had deeper native roots than the vivid incomers from Normandy, Brittany and Flanders who surged into Scotland with the early Stewart kings. The Bertrams, first noticed in Fife, Scotland, in 1296, may have originated somewhere between south-east Scotland and northern England, and came to establish themselves on the Continent as merchants from Scotland: there was a Robert Bertram living in Bruges* in the second half of the fifteenth century. Before that, they appear as burgesses and merchants in Edinburgh and its immediate surroundings, although they came to have interests in the Crawfordmuir lands of the west and in Berwickshire, where the vicar of Swinton was an uncle of Walter's. Walter himself was to possess a house in Berwick-upon-Tweed* (near that of **Sir John Colquhoun of Luss**), and in 1478 would control the customs of the port in partnership with **Thomas Yare**, who was also housed locally, as was **William Scheves**, the future Archbishop of St Andrews.

The Bertrams were best represented, however, in Edinburgh. There, the lucrative rights in the Butter Tron, the weigh-house for butter and cheese in the Upper Bow, just short of the castle, were owned in 1458 by Margaret Bertram, while Laurence Bertram, possibly their brother, lived in the Canongate next to the Bishop of Orkney and seemed to have shipping interests.

So also did Walter himself, who had a safe conduct to England in 1464, and was importing cloth for King James by 1473, supplying such items as four ells of French black (through James Homyll) for a royal side-gown. He had property, unsurprisingly, in the port of **Leith**, beside that of Marion Bonkle (daughter of Alexander Bonkle* of Bruges and Middleburg), who married into the family of the future provost Robert Logan of Coatfield, a branch of the Logans of Restalrig.

Walter's Edinburgh dwelling house, and that of James Bertram, were on the north side of the Canongate, not far from Leith Wynd and the property owned by the Crawfords of **Berecrofts**. Walter also held waste Napier land between the High Street and the Cowgate of Edinburgh. Among the witnesses to deals involving his property or his immediate neighbours' were the mason John Merlion, the Moffat family and the brothers Archibald and William Crawford of Berecrofts. Walter also held twenty-five acres of land in St Giles Grange by the burgh muir under Alexander, the son of David **Crawford**. Andrew and David Crawford were sailing with Walter in 1474 on the trading ship *Mary*, along with **Henry Cant** and Alexander Turing. The *Mary*, which sailed with Thomas Cant the following year, carried salmon as well as general goods.

At the same time, the family kept an educated connection with the Church. A charter of 1497 by the Abbot and convent of **Holyrood** mentions Sir James Bertram, a chaplain and occasional co-witness with the Bishop of Orkney. As early as 1470, Walter Bertram was witness, along with George Bertram (later a burgess) to a gift from Leith and Restalrig land to the altar of **St Catherine** in St Giles,* under the seal of Logan of Restalrig. He later witnessed a similar gift to St Ninian's altar (which had its equivalent in Bruges).

Walter himself was to be generous to St Giles, although he also founded a chaplainry there for which he obtained feus from the Abbot of Dunfermline in 1472. In 1478, however, he made a donation to the altar of St Francis, consisting of dues from Leith and Edinburgh and Restalrig land which adjoined that of his fellow-merchants **Thomas Swift** and **Thomas Spens**, Logan and Napier, and citing Alexander and John Bonkle as witnesses. He made another donation when his wife died, giving to the altar of St Laurence and St Francis the returns from **tenements** in Edinburgh, the Canongate, Barnton and Leith, some of it relating to property of the late **Thomas Preston**. He also gave to the Edinburgh Franciscan of the **Observatine** reform, a sect he noticeably favoured, perhaps because of its association with the late Queen Mary of Gueldres, her son and her grandson; with Flanders; and with his associates, the family Bonkle.

The Preston connection arose from the marriage of Walter's brother and heir, Andrew Bertram, to the sister of Sir Simon Preston of Craigmillar. This brought Andrew, a booth-owner, bailie and fish-pricer (as was Thomas Yare), into touch with families such as Napier, Ramsay and Cumming, many of them with positions in the royal household as well as in the control of the city.

Even before the climax of the trouble between the King and **Alexander, Duke of Albany**,* his brother, Bertram was being courted by both parties. In 1475, Albany made a gift at Dunbar to Walter Bertram and his wife of Berwickshire land resigned by David Haliburton: the charter was witnessed by **Alexander Home**, Robert Lauder, and **John Ellem of Butterdene**. The following year, **David Lindsay**, Earl of Crawford (and future Duke of Montrose) sold land in the **barony** of Crawford-Lindsay, Lanarkshire, to Walter Bertram. Alexander Bonkle, John Napier and Henry Cant were among the witnesses.

In 1482, the Duke of Albany returned to Scotland from France as part of an English invasion under **Richard, Duke of Gloucester**, which was to end in the taking of the port of Berwick-upon-Tweed.* As Provost of Edinburgh, Bertram seems to have played no active part in the abortive march south of the army under James III, which turned back at **Lauder Bridge**.

The customar of Edinburgh was however present in the person of George Robison, who carried into the field for the King's use the sum of £146, which was taken from him at Lauder by one Alexander Lauder and never returned, so that the King had to ask the Exchequer to reimburse Robison and hound Lauder for the sum. Then, after Gloucester and Albany had come to parley, the English army was persuaded to return south after two agreements had been made: one with the men of the King's inner council, and one with Provost Bertram and the merchants, burgesses and community of Edinburgh, who promised to refund all the eight thousand marks' dowry money paid by the English King for his daughter **Cecilia**'s future marriage in Scotland, if the marriage fell through.

Since it was a foregone conclusion that the marriage would fail to take place, the burgh was committed to pay, every year, a vast sum as the price of that peace. It was not a new procedure. The town had already delved into its pockets when James I (King of Scotland 1406–1437) was to be ransomed from England.

Bertram was no longer Provost during the last phase of that episode, when the citizens surrounded Edinburgh Castle until their King was released, and he was not named in the royal donation of November 1482 which thanked those who took part, although he was one of the four burgh commissioners who attended Parliament that December. As Albany was then in the ascendancy, it is of interest that Bertram was chosen, at that same Parliament, to go to France to complain about Scottish goods being detained there. It seems likely that, in the end, he did not go. Certainly, by December it was apparent that Albany was not likely to be reconciled to the King, and eventually he himself returned to France. A few years later, King James himself met his death, having arranged, that same year of 1488, to pay Walter Bertram and his wife an annual pension of forty pounds from the Edinburgh customs to compensate for the expenditure, damage and loss of goods suffered 'because of the late Duke of Albany and his accomplices'. The gift was made at a time when the King needed popular support.

The transition from the reign of James III to that of his son found the Bertram family still adroitly placed, although a John Bertram took part in the 1489 revolt at Dumbarton Castle against some elements of the new regime.

Walter seems, however, to have taken appropriate steps, and a year or two later **James IV*** confirmed a charter by Walter and his wife who, for the soul of the late King, presented the Franciscans of Edinburgh with dues from land beside Niddrie's Wynd. Two years later, for the soul of the King and also of his late uncle, the vicar of Swinton, Walter made a similar gift from some of his tenements in Leith and Restalrig and Haddington to the altar of St Clement in the church of the Franciscans in Haddington (home of John Yare), with John Bonkle and David Crawford among his witnesses. Andrew's name also appears as witness to a charter of **Robert Colville**'s involving Cowgate land.

Elizabeth Cant, Walter's wife, died, seemingly childless, before 1495, and Walter did not live long after, as his brother Andrew resigned to the Crawfords in 1496 fifteen acres of his late brother's lands in St Giles Grange. By 1497 the whole twenty-five acres had passed (leaving the life-rent with David Crawford) to the burgess Thomas Cant, and after him, to John Cant his heir. Thus it seemed that the Bertram inheritance devolved to the family Cant, through Walter's wife and her namesake, who had married William Simpson, a squire of James III. But Walter had already made his mark on history in the previous reign. (D. D.)

Besse: LIONS, 26: To do something 'by leave of Besse' was an Icelandic way of indicating that no permission had been asked for or obtained. Besse/Bersi was a he-bear, and Bera/Birna the female. Siberian Mongols referred to the great white bear as Ese, or as Monseigneur or Grandfather.

White bear-cubs were much esteemed gifts: about 1054, the first native Bishop of **Iceland**, Isleifr, son of Gizur the White of Mosfel, took one as a gift to the Holy Roman Emperor Henry at Goslar. The exiled Italian **Callimachus** flattered Lorenzo de' Medici* with a less volatile gift of white bearskins. Early Icelandic laws mention polar bears as pets, probably imported from Greenland, although adult bears would occasionally arrive on the drift ice. Pets or not, they undoubtedly became an inconvenience, as they nosed about snowy farm-steadings, and occasionally fell through the roof. (D. D.)

Betise: KINGS, I, 7: A piece of stupidity.

Bien plaintive de tous biens: UNICORN, 47: From a critic's pronouncement, summing up Cyprus as: '*mout riche et bone et bien plaintive de tous biens*' or 'well-doing, and wealthy, and always complaining of something'.

Billon: LIONS, 40: Alloy with a very low silver content used for the striking of pennies and halfpennies. Inflation during the reign of **James III*** made it necessary to have a billon coin larger than a penny. These four-pence coins were called placks, from the Flemish *placke* or *plecke*, a coin of Brabant and Flanders. See also **Coining**.

Birleyman: UNICORN, 19: In Scotland, the man in charge of a country birlie- or byrlaw-court, a form of community law in which every holder of a local freedom had a say. Its purpose was broadly to settle local disputes, to determine the number of cattle each burgess should pasture on the common, to decide on the sharing of farm labour, and to estimate the value of crops. The birleyman, one of themselves, was the court's appointed arbiter, and the meetings were not known for their reticence. The name, also found in medieval England, derives originally from *byjarlog*, law of a *by* or township. (D. D.)

Bishop's Buss: LIONS, 26: A 140-ton flat-bottomed boat with three sets of sails which was to prove important for the development of North Sea fishing, as it could spend a week or more in the herring grounds, being large enough to carry supplies for many days' fishing, and sufficient salt to preserve the catch, necessarily greater after the longer time spent at sea. In the fourteenth century, when trade with Bergen was brisk, William, Bishop of Skálholt, travelled back and forth from Iceland in a boat built by himself, which was appropriately (to modern ears) called the Bishop's Buss. Less appropriately, buss (QUEENS, IV, 6) is the ancient Scots word for a kiss. (D. D.)

Black Douglases: HN: See **Douglas, Earls of**. The byname originated with Sir James Douglas (*c.* 1286–1330), son of Sir William Douglas (d. 1298) and champion of Robert the Bruce (Robert I of Scotland 1306–1329). Before his death in 1329 Bruce asked Sir James to take his heart to the Holy Land in fulfilment of his crusading vow; Douglas set out the following year, together with Sir William **Sinclair** of Roslin, but both died in Spain fighting against the Moors. (See also **Red Douglases**.)

Black money: LIONS, 40: Used here as a generic term to describe both **billon** and base-metal coinage used as small change, both of which were prevalent in the reign of **James III***. It was stamped with crowns, mullets (a star with a hole in the centre, used on coins since the reign of Alexander III, 1249–1286) and thistles (groats struck in Scotland from 1471 to 1483 have thistles for the first time). Shortage of bullion (or rather, an increase in the price of silver) in the reign of James III created long-term economic problems in fifteenth-century Scotland, worsened by the exportation of large reserves of currency which had left Scotland to pay for the ransoms during the reigns of King David II (1329–1371) and then James I (1406–1437). Scotland exported basic commodities, such as wool, hides, fish and timber, but an increasing taste for luxury goods and the necessity of importing manufactured items could see gold and silver reserves leaking abroad. James III enacted statutes similar to those of James II,* banning the export of bullion. Devaluation of the coinage (base billon coins) and the minting of coins purely in base metal served in part to make what bullion there was go further. This led to the creation of a new coinage in copper, the first time that a completely base metal had been used for coins. Used for small change, copper farthings were struck in Edinburgh from about 1466 and again from 1470. They were also known as 'money of the poor' and may also have been minted at St Andrews. See **Coining.**

Black soup: GEMINI, 18: See **Agaric**.

Blackfriars: UNICORN: The Friars Preachers or Black Friars of the Order of St Dominic were, like the **Franciscan Friars**, an order dedicated to preaching in the vernacular. They were licensed to hear confessions, and to bury the laity in their graveyard. The Dominicans arrived in **Edinburgh** in 1230 and were granted a manor on the south side of the Cowgate, with a vennel leading to the High Street, known as Blackfriars Wynd. The **Sinclair** family also had property here. Amongst the monastic buildings, which became known as Blackfriars, was an upper and lower hall and apartments which were used as a royal guest-house, by arrangement with the King. The estates of Parliament, Councils and the Court of the Exchequer also met there.

It was damaged by fire in 1528, and plundered by the Duke of Somerset in 1547 after the battle of Pinkie. The church attached to it and the **monastery** were destroyed by the Reformers in 1559.

Blackness: GEMINI, 29: Just over three miles from **Linlithgow**, the castle stronghold of Blackness was probably built about 1449 by the local baron Sir George Crichton, Earl of Caithness, Admiral of Scotland and sheriff of Linlithgow, possibly to replace a tower just destroyed by the **Black Douglases**. This Crichton was a cousin of Sir William Crichton, Chancellor to King James II,* and grandfather of the future lover of the King's daughter, **Princess Margaret**. In 1453 the family relinquished Blackness to the Crown, and it became a royal fortress, providing the monarchy with an excellent strategic position on the south of the Forth estuary, an important counterpoint to the **Red Douglas** strongholds of Inveravon and Abercorn.

Built on a spit of rock and cut off on the marshy landward side by a ditch, the castle was surrounded by walls: its resemblance to a long narrow vessel led to its being called 'the ship that never sailed'. The courtyard contained a central tower with three storeys and an attic over a vaulted basement, and there were extra residential buildings, including a great hall, built along the curtain walls. It was used by the Stewart kings as a high-ranking state prison, and also as a garrison fortress protecting the anchorage and harbour that served Linlithgow Palace, whose maintenance the lucrative Blackness great custom would help to underwrite. A north tower later provided extra service and other accommodation and stowed the humbler prisoners in its dungeons, which the tide slopped out twice a day. The Captain was often the sheriff of Linlithgow. When the fortifications were strengthened a century later, the architect was the illegitimate Sir James Hamilton of Finnart (see **Fynnart, Jimmie of**), eldest of the nineteen children of the husband of **Princess Mary**, the sister of Margaret. The resulting fortress of the water's edge can still be visited, and remained in military service until the second decade of the twentieth century.

Its small cove formed a natural harbour on the south side of the Forth which had been in use since the twelfth century, and the site had a long military history. It was attacked by an English fleet under John, Lord Howard, in 1480, and under its loyal Captain, **Sir John Ross of Hawkhead**, harboured **James III*** and his nobles when they met just before the fatal battle of Sauchieburn in 1488. (Ross was to be followed as Captain by **William Knollys.***) In the following century, its vessels were again burned by an English admiral, and in 1548 it was garrisoned by a French force under the commander d'Essé.

For the village which grew up to serve the needs of the Crown and the merchants using the harbour, see under **Anselm Adorne*** (the Captain of Linlithgow) and Sir John Ross. It seems very likely that the premises used by Adorne and the Landells family may have housed a mint. Coins of James I (ruled 1406–1437) were minted at Linlithgow, and the moneyer's accounts for the mint of Linlithgow of 1435 mention the minting of both gold and silver. It is said that the silver was found locally and minted in a house on the west side of the marketplace, known as the Cunyie Neuk.

Blind Harry: GEMINI: (*fl.* 1470–1492) Poet, blind (although perhaps not from birth, as related by John Major 1470–1550). He was certainly at the Scottish Court from 1490 to 1492, where his name appears in the accounts of the Lord High Treasurer as having received some small payments. His greatest work was ***The Wallace***, intended to warn the Scots against an alliance with England.

Blue Blanket: KNIGHTS, III, 17: Also known as the 'Banner of the Holy Ghost', this is the familiar name given to the historic flag or standard of **Edinburgh**, presented to the town by **James III*** and emblematic of the privileges granted to the town in 1483 when the burgesses supported the King, imprisoned in Edinburgh Castle after the incident at **Lauder Bridge**. It accompanied the Scots army to **Flodden**. See also **Henry Cant** and Mungo Tennant.*

Bóg: RONDO, 9: Samarto-Iranian term for God (mother of God being Bógomater). Perun* (RONDO, 23) was one of the ancient Gods of the Sarmatians and Scythians, along with Bóg and Triglav, the three-headed one. In the fourteenth century the proudly pagan empire of Lithuania put their trust in Perun, the God of the Thunderclap. Lithuania finally converted to Christianity when their king, Jogaila, became the first king of Poland of the **Jagellonian dynasty** in 1385, taking the name Wladyslaw (Ladislaus)-Jagiello. The Samartians invaded the Slav culture of what is now Poland in the second century B.C.; Samartia became the Latin name for Poland.

The Samartian term for God is not to be confused with the Christian Bogomil heresy of Persian origin that first appeared in tenth-century Bulgaria and spread across Europe, which took its name from a Bulgarian Paulician monk, Bogomil. This heresy, which spread like wildfire over the next three centuries, was founded on the dualist belief that the spiritual world was God's domain, but the physical world was made by the devil, therefore all material things are corrupt. The heretics were also known as Poblicani, Cathari, Albigenses or Bougres (RONDO, 6). Numerous crusades were undertaken to deal with them. By the thirteenth century, Bosnia had become the centre of the heresy. Hungarian kings, including **Mathias Corvinus**, led military crusades against them. When the Ottoman Empire conquered Bosnia in 1463, there was a whole-scale conversion of the Bogomils to Islam.

BOLOGNA, Ludovico de Severi da: See **Ludovico de Severi da Bologna**.

Boon companion: RONDO, 29: The quoted extract comes from *Seyasat-nameh*, or *The Book of Government*, a volume of wise advice addressed to governors, envoys and kings, written by Nizam al-Mulk (1018/9–1092), a cultured Persian vizier to the Seljuk court of Sultan Malikshah. The sections of the book deal with wide-ranging subjects. One begins: 'Spies must constantly go out to the limits of the kingdom in the guise of merchants, travellers, sufis, pedlars and mendicants, and bring back reports . . .' Another starts: 'It is the King's duty to enquire into the condition of his peasantry and army, both far and near . . . If he does not do this he is at fault, and the people will charge him with negligence, laziness and tyranny.' Nizam al-Mulk's master was lazy, and for thirty years the vizier governed the land for his lord, introducing reforms and founding institutions of learning, while writing and revising his book. An unwise addendum naming the enemies of the state led to his assassination by one of them. (D. D.)

Bougre: RONDO, 6: See **Bóg**.

Bourbon, House of: HN; LC: 'The Bourbons, who learn nothing and forget nothing.' A princely family which, by judicious marriages, spread through the courts of Europe in the fifteenth and sixteenth centuries, and was to introduce a new dynasty to follow Henri III (ruled 1574–1589) and the House of Valois in France.

Philip the Bold, Duke of Burgundy 1363–1404, married his niece Marie de Berry to John I, Duke of Bourbon 1410–1434. His brother, Charles V, King of France 1364–1380, had also married a Bourbon of the ducal house, Jeanne. In 1428 the son of Duke John I, Louis de Bourbon, comte de Montpensier (d. 1486), married Jeanne, only daughter of the Dauphin of Auvergne. When she died in 1436, Louis de Bourbon married her cousin and heiress Gabrielle, daughter of Bertrand VI de la Tour. Their daughter Charlotte de Bourbon in

1468 married Wolfaert **van Borselen**, widower of the Princess Mary of Scotland, sister of King James II.* Anna, the daughter of Charlotte and Wolfaert, went on to marry the son of the Bastard Anthony, natural son of Philip the Bold's grandson, the Third Duke of Burgundy, Philip the Good.*

Duke Philip the Good died in 1467, leaving fourteen bastards and one legitimate son, the future **Charles, Duke of Burgundy**.* In 1454, Duke Charles had married Isabelle de Bourbon, daughter of Charles I Duke of Bourbon 1434–1456, his cousin. By her he had one daughter, **Marie of Burgundy**, who became the wife in due course of **Maximilian** of Austria. Marie de Bourbon, the Duchess Isabelle's sister, married John, Duke of Calabria (d. 1470), the son of King René of Anjou.* John's nephew, René II (d. 1508), was to lead an army against Duke Charles at the battle of Nancy in 1477, when the Duke lost his life.

Charlotte's brother (and Wolfaert's brother-in-law) Gilbert de Bourbon, comte de Montpensier (d. 1496), became viceroy of Naples. A lazy man (he never rose before noon), he left most of the work to his renowned Scottish commander, Robert Stewart of **Aubigny**. Gilbert married Claire Gonzaga of Mantua, and of their children Renée (d. 1539) married Antoine, Duke of Lorraine, and Louise (d. 1561) married Louis de Bourbon, lord of Roche-sur-Yon.

A second batch of Bourbons had meanwhile descended from Duke Philip's sister Agnes, who married Charles I, Duke of Bourbon. A magnificent athlete ('an Absolom, another Trojan Paris', breathed his contemporaries), Charles de Bourbon owned his own private military troop, including several companies of the notorious *Écorcheurs* (Flayers): freebooters who were not above roasting peasants over slow fires to make them give up their goods. The Dauphin Louis (the future **Louis XI***) during his period at the Burgundian court, found Charles a useful ally. By her marriage to Charles, Agnes of Burgundy had a large family, which included Louis of Bourbon, the Prince-bishop of Liége, who in 1553 (at the age of fourteen) became Provost of St Donatien, Bruges,* and, at the age of sixteen, was also made Provost of St Pierre, Lille. (Disliked as representing Burgundian influence in French Flanders, the Bishop was killed in the end, in 1482, by the Wild Boar of the Ardennes, William de la Marck.) Of Agnes's other children, her son Charles de Bourbon (*c.* 1434–1488) became first Archbishop of Lyon and later (1476) a Cardinal, while Isabelle de Bourbon (d. 1465), as mentioned above, married her cousin Duke Charles the Bold.

Agnes of Burgundy also had a son John, who became John II, Duke of Bourbon 1456–1488, and another daughter, Catherine de Bourbon, who became the wife of Adolf, Duke of Gueldres. Adolf was the brother of Mary of Gueldres, who married James II* of Scotland and became Queen-Regent and mother of **James III**,* **Alexander, Duke of Albany**,* the **Princesses Mary** and **Margaret** and **John of Mar**. There was also a natural brother, Louis, Bastard of Bourbon and Admiral of France, who married Jeanne, a natural half-sister of King Louis XI.

In all of this, the above Alexander Stewart, Duke of Albany, brother of James III of Scotland, had some part also to play. Albany, having fallen out with his brother, fled to France, where (having dissolved his first marriage) he was given as second wife Anne de la Tour de Boulogne, whose mother happened to be Louise de la Trémouille, of the family connected with Gabrielle de Bourbon, Wolfaert van Borselen's sister-in-law. By Anne, Alexander of Albany had one son, **John Stewart**, Second Duke of Albany, who became briefly Regent of Scotland. John married his cousin, Anne de la Tour d'Auvergne (see **Chinchins, Les**).

The Second Duke of Albany was well equipped with cousins. One was Diane de Poitiers,* the legendary royal mistress, who was descended from John's mother's aunt. Another was Queen Catherine de Médicis,* daughter of Lorenzo de' Medici, Duke of Urbino and Madeleine de la Tour d'Auvergne. This meant that John was a kinsman of Pope Clement VII,* Lorenzo's brother. It was a family worth marrying into twice over.

Mention should also be made of Charles de Bourbon, duc de Vendôme, (1515–1537), whose gallant sons, the Sieur d'Enghien and the hunchbacked Prince de Condé* among them, were prominent courtiers of the mid-sixteenth century. Their aunt was Antoinette de Bourbon (d. 1584), whose daughter (their cousin) was Mary de Guise,* sister of the famous de Guise* brethren, and mother of Mary Queen of Scots* (who would, of course, marry the Dauphin Francis, the future Francis II,* son of Catherine de Médicis).

Returning full circle, it might be recorded that the second wife of King Janus of Cyprus, the grandmother of **Zacco**'s half-sister Carlotta, was a Charlotte de Bourbon, who died in 1422.

Traces of the Bourbons can be seen everywhere, but especially in Paris, where they had a spectacular presence. In 1318 the Duke of Bourbon bought property with a large garden in the rue de St Antoine which passed eventually, as 'le petit Bourbon', to two royal mistresses, the Duchess d'Étampes (Francis I*) and Diane de Poitiers (Henri II*). Its principal entry was off the rue des Célestins, and its gardens abutted on to the **rue de la Cerisaye**. It was sold in 1554 to become a monastery, still showing, they say, the yellow paint with which the building was stigmatised after the disgrace of the Constable (a Bourbon) at the Battle of Pavia (1525). Elsewhere, the family possessed at least three other houses of pleasure in Paris, with gardens, granges and vineyards which supplied them with wine and with grain.

They were a remarkable dynasty. Presumably the incessant marriages between cousins was a reason for the erratic fertility of some of the lines. Fortunately, the wrong side of the blanket was generally fruitful. (D. D.)

Bouton: LIONS, 1: 'Flower-bud'. A suitable pet name for a child called de Fleury. Another, for any young child, might be *broquette:* a small nail with a large head.

BOYD, James: GEMINI: (1470–1487) Born in 1470 in Bruges,* Flanders, in the home of **Anselm Adorne**,* James Boyd was the godson of **Margaret of York**, Duchess of Burgundy, sister of the English King **Edward IV**.* It established a connection with England perhaps reinforced by the permanent exile in that country of his grandfather, Robert, Lord Boyd, an English pensioner and opponent of James's uncle, King **James III*** of Scotland. The boy's fortunes then followed those of his mother, the **Princess Mary**.

Since his father, **Thomas Boyd**,* had also been repudiated by the King, James Boyd and Margaret his sister were without status or lands, since all those belonging to Boyd had been confiscated and redistributed. The Queen had received the **barony** of Kilmarnock, and Anselm Adorne, who was eventually to settle in Scotland, had been given land in Teling and Polgavy, two areas in Forfar and Perth. A new marriage arranged for the Princess Mary re-established her standing as the lady of **James, Lord Hamilton**, in 1474, but Hamilton was a widower with an existing large family of legitimate and illegitimate children, to whom the Princess Mary now bore an additional son and daughter, legitimate rivals to her previous brood.

When Lord Hamilton died, in the same year that **Alexander, Duke of Albany**,* James's uncle, had clashed with the King and then fled to France, James was nine years old. The following year, war broke out with England, and Albany, now with English support, returned with an army in the summer of 1482 to oust his brother the King, or force him (as it turned out) to offer him fulsome reinstatement if he remained. When the English left, the bounty showered upon Albany was shared by Mary his sister and her son James, now old enough to attach himself to his uncle. When news came of the death of his grandfather, still an English pensioner, the boy took the title of Lord Boyd.

The lands the Boyds now received came from James's Queen **Margaret of Denmark**, and from Anselm Adorne, and were part of those the Boyds had originally forfeited. The deal, presumably managed by Albany, supports the impression that he and his sisters, none of them especially able, were united in their resentment of the King. James clearly shared this view, and when the reconciliation came to an end, and Albany fled to defend his castle of Dunbar and recall the English, young James – perhaps not for the first time – went with him.

When Albany's effort failed and he escaped from Dunbar, James does not appear in any of the events of that year, which closed with Albany's departure. James remained in Scotland and was not sentenced at law, although in April of 1484, he and his mother were required to return the barony of Kilmarnock to the Queen, and all the other lands they received during the courting of Albany. For their sustenance, they were presumably now dependent on the Hamilton family of capable brothers. Three years later, James was killed, aged seventeen, by Hugh Montgomery of Eglinton, in the course of a long-running dispute.

Princess Mary his mother died the following year. With the death of James, unmarried, the earldom of Arran had already reverted to the Crown.

James Boyd's sister Margaret married twice. Her first husband, Alexander, Lord Forbes, died before 1491, leaving her with a son and heir, Arthur. Her next marriage, in 1509, was to David, Lord Kennedy, later to become the Earl of Cassillis. It completed a circuit half begun over forty years previously, when her father Thomas Boyd had been contracted to marry another Kennedy, the niece of Bishop Kennedy,* but had instead managed to marry a princess.

Between her two marriages, Margaret Boyd was sustained by her cousin **James IV**,* who arranged for her to have an annual allowance from 1493 to 1509, just as he paid for his unfortunate aunt the **Princess Margaret** until the end of her life. Indeed, his last known allotment to the Princess, in 1503, was made through her niece Margaret Boyd, Lady Forbes, who must have cared for her latterly.

Cassillis died at **Flodden**, and Margaret Boyd is last heard of in 1516, staying with her stepfather's family, the Hamiltons. She was alive therefore when the new Regent of Scotland arrived: the half-French son of James's failed hero, the Duke of Albany. (D. D.)

BOYD, Mary: See **Mary, Princess**.

BOYD, Thomas: UNICORN: (d. *c.* 1474) Thomas Boyd, Earl of Arran, first husband of **Princess Mary**. He and his father Robert, Lord Boyd, disappeared from the Scottish scene after their fall from power in 1469. Lord Boyd was in receipt of an English pension according to the Patent Rolls of 1474, and his son spent time in London and on the continent after his forfeiture, but the date of Thomas Boyd's death is unrecorded, and even the place is in dispute. One sixteenth-century writer, the Piedmontese Ferrerius, says that 'he was slain in Tuscany, by a gentleman whose wife he had attempted to debauch'. Writing at about the same time, the historian George Buchanan, who was Scottish, has a nobler but equally dubious story. According to this, Thomas Boyd, rejected by **Louis XI**,* bravely fought for **Charles, Duke of Burgundy**,* and died in 1469 in Antwerp, where the Duke built him a magnificent tomb. There is no trace of the tomb, and Thomas Boyd was still alive in 1471, when he left Bruges with his father and **Anselm Adorne**.*

The politics of the time also cast doubt on this tale. England prudently retained Lord Boyd on a pension, but there was now a Yorkist King on the throne, and Scotland, which, like Burgundy, had once favoured Lancaster, immediately turned towards a marriage alliance with York. The Duke of Burgundy, married to the English King's sister, also made friends with **Edward IV*** whom he needed against the depredations of France.

Naturally France and Anjou would have less time for a powerless Thomas

Boyd, with a father owing allegiance to England. It would have been equally unwise of Burgundy to show him great favour. Then, by the beginning of 1474, Princess Mary was married to someone else, and Boyd was divorced, dead or conveniently inaccessible. When, at the end of the decade, war broke out between England and Scotland and Lord Boyd came at last into play as an English pawn, with young Albany, there was no word of Thomas Boyd. Lord Boyd was definitely dead by 1482, when his short-lived grandson **James Boyd** is referred to as Lord Boyd. Thomas's younger brother Alexander was restored to a portion of the Boyd estate in 1492, but was not given the title Lord Boyd. Alexander's eldest son was made Lord Boyd in 1536. (D. D.)

Brittany, planned Scottish invasion of: LIONS, 30: **James III**'s* claim to Brittany stemmed from his aunt, the Duchess of Brittany (see **James II's sisters**). His hopes to reclaim it were probably encouraged by **Louis XI**,* who sent **William Monypenny**, to Scotland in 1472 to offer Brittany to James in return for the services of a Scottish army. The request before Parliament was for a levy of five thousand pounds and an army of six thousand men. What was most controversial was James's aspiration to lead the army himself. Parliament was not in favour of the levy; firstly because of the amount requested; secondly the risk of the King leaving the country when peace with England was not assured; and thirdly the prospect of the nation being without an heir if James should die abroad. He was forced to delay, and ultimately abandon his invasion. The Duke of Brittany was concerned enough to ask **Edward IV*** for six thousand archers in case of Scottish attack. These were not forthcoming, but **Earl Rivers** (later proposed as a husband for **Princess Margaret**) was sent with a small force and a few ships.

Broquette: LIONS, 14: See ***Bouton***.

Brunellus: See **A nasty bite for the ass called Brunellus.**

BUCHAN, Earl of: UNICORN: (d. *c.* 1499) James Stewart of Auchterhouse, half-uncle of **James III*** from the marriage of Joan Beaufort (James I's widow) to James Stewart, the Black Knight of Lorne. He was the younger brother of John, **Earl of Atholl**, born of the same marriage. On the fall of the Boyds (1469) he was made Chamberlain in place of Robert Boyd,* and was then granted the title Earl of Buchan. He was made Chamberlain once more after the crisis at **Lauder Bridge**. Buchan was Warden of the Middle Marches, notably including the Lauder area, therefore it was likely that he was one of those who was behind the seizure of the King and his incarceration in **Edinburgh** Castle. With the forfeiture of **Alexander, Duke of Albany**,* in 1483, Buchan was found to be in discussion with both Albany and **Edward IV**,* and was exiled for three years. He was obliged to resign the office of Chamberlain and his wardenship of the Middle Marches, but when he returned, with his brother, he took the side of James III in 1488 against the future **James IV.***

BUONACCORSI, Filippo: See **Callimachus**.

BURGUNDY, Dukes of: see **Charles, Duke of Burgundy***; Philip the Bold.*

Burnt Njall: See **Njall's story.**

Buss: See **Bishop's Buss**.

Buza: RONDO, 18: Turkish and Persian beer.

C

Caeculus no longer: RONDO, 2: From the Latin *caecus*, meaning blind, Caeculus was the name of the Roman god who caused blindness. It was also the nickname of Filippo Buonaccorsi or **Callimachus**, given to him by his fellow academicians on account of his myopia. One of his fellows (Giovanni Antonio Campano d. 1477) described him thus:

Callimachi quamvis lippi videantur ocelli,
Sitque minor stella pupula Cantaridis,
Plura videt, quam linx, vigili nec cesserit Argo,
Noctem vel media perspicit ille die,
Clarus erit caelo, quamvis Sol aspicit umbras,
Sitque serena dies, tota videt nebulam.
Cumque alii videant, que sunt tantum modo, suevit
Quaeque etiam non sunt, cernere Callimachus.
Quodque magis stupeas, oculis non spectat apertis,
Ut videat, claudit lumina Callimachus.

'Although Callimachus's little eyes seem blind, with pupils smaller than those of a Spanish fly, he sees more than a lynx and yields nothing to the vigilant Argus whether midnight or noon, he sees the same. Although the sun beholds shadows the sky will be bright to him, and though the day may be clear he can yet discern a cloud. And when others see only those things that are, Callimachus can see even those things that are not. What may astound you more, Callimachus does not see with his eyes open; in order to see, he shuts his eyes'.

Cafaggiolo: LIONS, 10: A distinguished villa built in 1451 by the Florentine architect and sculptor Michelozzo (1396–1472) for Cosimo de' Medici* in the Mugello, a mountainous district to the east of Florence where the family had its origins. Built (no expense spared) on the lines of a fortified farmhouse and furnished for comfort, it was provided with towers and battlemented arches, and set in groves and fountains and gardens which included a moat. The place was a favourite hunting estate of the Medici, and also the centre of their agricultural holdings, which supplied grain, hay and wine to the city of Florence. (D. D.)

Caieta: LIONS, 2: The revered nurse of Virgil's hero pious Aeneas (the name also enjoyed by Pope Pius II*). She was buried in the town named after her.

Calcio: LIONS, 11: Among the many pursuits – tournaments, chariot races – which took place in the Piazza Santa Croce in Florence from the fourteenth century onwards was the town's famous fast ball game called the *Calcio.* It was played by twenty-seven men a side, all young nobles richly dressed in doublet, hose and cap in silk or velvet or even cloth of silver or gold, in team colours. The players marched to the field accompanied by standards, trumpets and drummers, referees and a ball-thrower. The square was palisaded, and contained stands for high-ranking spectators and umpires, tents and uniformed halberdiers. Of the 27 players, 15 runners or *corridori* stood in front of 5 *sconciatori,* or spoilers, who were there to mark the opposite runners. The spoilers were supported by 7 hitters (4 front and 3 back). Unlike the spoilers, the hitters were allowed the use of their hands.

The game began on the third blast of a trumpet, when the ball was hurled at a marble wall-tablet and bounded back to the runners, who had to steer it past the spoilers and hitters and into the opposite goal. Success was proclaimed by the shout *Colpito!* – a strike.

In modern times, a reconstruction of the *Calcio* has been played out in sixteenth-century costume during St John's Week in Florence, with teams representing the four *quartiere* of the city: San Giovanni, Santa Croce, Santa Maria Novella and San Spirito. It is generally achieved (says one guidebook) 'with few rules and considerable violence'. (D. D.)

CALLIMACHUS: RONDO: (1437–1496) Filippo Buonaccorsi, the humanist statesman, scholar and writer. Originally from San Gimignano, halfway between Florence and Siena, it was there he began his academic career, studying poetry with Mattia Lupi (1380–1486). In 1460 he moved to Venice, which had developed a reputation as a centre for Greek studies even before the fall of Constantinople. It was probably in Venice that he developed his lifelong interest in the esoteric sciences, particularly astrology. He then moved to Rome, where he joined the elitist and hedonistic humanist academy run by **Maestro Laetus.** The members emulated their Roman forebears, wearing Roman costume and calling each other by classical nicknames (see **Caeculus no longer**); it was probably at this time that Buonaccorsi adopted his pen name Callimachus (see **Mouseion of Alexandria**). The academy's discussions of archaeology, philosophy, poetry, art and philology were somewhat undermined by its members' reputation for libertine sexual behavior and Epicurean over-indulgence.

In 1468, Callimachus and his academicians became involved in a plot to murder Pope Paul II* and other members of the Curia, for their hostility towards humanism. The plot was discovered and Callimachus, whilst protesting his innocence, was forced to flee, via Sicily, Cyprus, then Chios* in the summer of 1469, where he was implicated in a further plot to hand the island over to the Turk. Reaching Constantinople, he met a distant relative, Jacopo Tedaldi (who was acting as an advisor to Mehmet II*). The Tedaldi family in Poland enjoyed good relations with **Gregory of Sanok**, and when Callimachus arrived in Poland he stayed at Gregory's palace at Dunajow. His plight as a fugitive caught the Polish scholar's imagination: his strongly held dislike of papal interference meant that despite pleas from papal envoys and the agreement of the Polish Diet to surrender Callimachus to the Pope in 1470, Gregory and another politician (Dersław of Rytwiany) thwarted them.

When Paul II died in 1471, he was succeeded by Sixtus IV,* who was well disposed to humanism and allowed the re-establishment of the Accademia Romana. Callimachus was therefore free from fear of arrest and able to leave the intellectual haven provided for him at Dunajow, but he had by this time decided to make his life in Poland, where he became a royal secretary and counsellor. He returned to Italy only as a diplomatic envoy of the Polish Crown. His main work was the *Consilia* of 1490, written some twenty years before *The Prince* (1513) of Niccolò Machiavelli (1469–1527) but similar in that it offers advice for a ruler on how to govern his realm and increase its strength. Callimachus believed that magnates should be politically subdued in favour of a strong centralised monarchy and the papacy should not interfere in national policy. Developing a prosperous indigenous bourgeoisie was also important, and democracy should not be limited by political power remaining solely in the hands of the privileged aristocracy. Unsurprisingly, his work was greatly disliked by the local Polish nobility. He was fundamentally a practical politician: the art of ciphers and encoding messages was introduced to Poland by Callimachus. While there he called himself Callimachus Experiens, Callimachus the Experienced, or Active (RONDO, 19).

In his self-imposed and romantic exile, Callimachus continued to correspond with leading humanists, such as Marsilio Ficino* and Giovanni Pico della Mirandola (1463–1494). He maintained his friendships, often giving expensive gifts: in one of his letters to Lattanzio Tedaldi (probably written from Venice where he stayed at Murano whilst on a diplomatic visit), he reminds Lattanzio of a stone seal for letters that he had asked to be prepared so he could have it made into a ring for Arnolfo Tedaldi. His generosity was often reciprocated. When he lost all his writings and his books in a fire in 1487, his Italian correspondents hastened to make good the losses to his library. A lifelong Epicurean, he composed the first poetry written in Poland on erotic themes. He was appointed as tutor to **Casimir IV**'s sons; however, his philosophy of enjoying life to the full, which he passed on to his pupils, including the future King Jan Olbracht, is said to have led to the King's addiction to sensual pleasures. This weakened Jan Olbracht's constitution to such an extent that he was undermined by disease when his country needed him most.

Callimachus died of a haemorrhage on 1 November 1496 and was buried in Cracow, in the Church of the Holy Trinity.

CHIOS ~ PORT & TOWN

Cambuskenneth: LIONS, 15: Of which **Henry Arnot** became Abbot, was a fine twelfth-century Abbey built on the left bank of the Forth, opposite Stirling Castle. Founded by David I (King of Scotland 1124–1153) in 1140, and colonised from Arrouase in France (although relations with the mother house lapsed after 1470), it was enriched and favoured by successive kings, and served by vigorous abbots who in turn were employed by the Crown on state affairs of the highest importance. Parliaments met within its walls, and it housed the assembly of nobles who, in 1308, swore before the High Altar to defend the claim of Robert the Bruce to the Scots Crown. Both **James III*** and his Queen, **Margaret of Denmark**, were buried before the same altar, although successive waves of destruction almost demolished the buildings, the royal relics were exhumed in 1864, and a cast was made of the King's skull which had been found in his ancient oak coffin. (The remains were reinterred on the site of the altar.) The large slab of blue stone covering the relics is the only fragment of a royal tomb which remains in Scotland. Similarly unique is the sixty-seven-foot bell tower, detached from the rest of the church buildings. It is the only campanile of its type in Scotland.

CAMPBELL, Colin: See **Argyll, Earl of.**

CAMULIO, Prosper Schiaffino de, de' Medici:* RISING: (fl. 1450–1480) After the election of his compatriot Francesco della Rovere to the papacy in 1471,

Prosper de Camulio became Apostolic Protonatory to the new **Pope Sixtus IV**,* and embarked with his usual slightly disoriented vigour on that portion of his career which was to provide him, naturally, with a bishopric in Scotland.

It began with the success of his 1474 visit to England, made necessary, in the Pope's view, because the income from Peter's Pence (the traditional annual tribute to the Roman see from wealthier households) had greatly diminished through the negligence of the Collectors of the Camera, and through refusals to pay. Master Prosper de Camulio, clerk of Genoa, was appointed Collector of the Apostolic Camera and Nuncio in England, and sent off to set things right, collecting by compulsion if need be. John, Bishop of Lincoln, for example, was to be dunned for the money and goods he had received but not passed on for the crusade, and a former Collector made to cough up his receipts. Prosper was so successful that the following year he was appointed permanent Collector, and his office extended to include Scotland and Ireland, all other collectors and sub-collectors being revoked.

Behind this, one suspects, was the papal distrust of Milan, and an escalating web of alliances and counter-alliances concerning Genoa, France and the Medici, hastened by the murder of Duke Galeazzo Maria of Milan in 1476, which left Milan a regency with a seven-year-old Duke. (See Sforza, Francesco, Duke of Milan.*) Camulio, a patriotic Genoese violently opposed to occupation by other powers, must have seemed useful.

In May 1477, his activities seem to have caught up with him when, after a papal mission to Scotland, details unknown, he was arrested and detained at Chiaravi by Milanese officials, and sent to Milan for questioning about anti-Milanese activities among Genoese exiles. The time was just after the death of **Charles, Duke of Burgundy**,* and the consequent confusion. Camulio's claim to be travelling as an ambassador of **James III*** of Scotland, or alternatively, as a councillor of **Louis XI*** of France, was disbelieved by Giovanni Simonetto, the young Duke's secretary.

Giovanni Simonetto was not a man enamoured of Scotland, which he had been known to refer to as '*il quale se pò dire in culo mundi*', or politely, 'the end of the world'. (The occasion had been a rather brash Scottish offer of a royal marriage.) Giovanni, a historian, had followed his uncle Angelo and brother Cecco (or Cicco, i.e. Francesco) in serving the great Duke Francesco Sforza. Cecco was currently in conflict with the Ghibelline nobles of Milan, and opposed to the Pope. Nevertheless, after a few months, Camulio was freed, probably as a result of pressure from his brother and sister, as well as from Sixtus himself. He was then deftly dispatched out of Italy by the Pope and King Ferrante I of Naples,* ostensibly to settle a quarrel between two claimants to the see of Constance, but in fact to drum up Western help for a war against Milan.

It was not wholly successful. Beginning in Switzerland, Camulio met with frustration at the courts of Sigismond, Duke of the Tyrol,* and the Emperor

Frederick III, where he was designated by the Milanese ambassador as a '*fonticho di puzza*', or 'stinker'. The Emperor did, however, name him consul of the German Nation of Genoa.

Whether he returned there is not known. By April 1479, when he was again sent to the west, affairs in Italy were moving fast. Following the relative failure of the 1478 attack on the Medici, the Pope and Naples were about to combine forces against Florence, while Cecco planned to send a Milanese army to help the Medici (see **Pazzi Conspiracy**). The Milanese nobles did the opposite, and backed Naples. Naples then persuaded Prosper Adorno, Doge of Genoa, to throw off Milanese supremacy, and a Milanese army sent by Cecco to subdue Genoa was crushed. By 1479 Cecco, realising that Genoa could not be held, persuaded Milan to recognise Genoa's independence, and engineered peace with King Ferrante and the Pope.

Camulio, diligently quartering Europe, carried out his orders as best he could, as indeed did the bane of his life, the Milanese foreign envoys, who gleefully brewed up trouble before Camulio even reached Louis of France, his last call. Their plan was to spread a rumor in France that Camulio had warned the Emperor not to trust the word of the French, but to hasten to recruit all the Swiss mercenary bands that he could, to deny them to Louis. It may have worked. Camulio received his audience in France from the King, and duly urged him to force Milan to honour the King's outstanding claims. The King made no discernible promises.

This was probably Camulio's last political mission, as indeed it was the end for the brothers Simonetto, as it transpired. After a revolt against Cecco, he and his brother were sent to prison in Pavia, where Cecco, aged seventy, was executed. Giovanni, after some years in Vercelli, was allowed back to Milan.

For Camulio, it was time to receive the Pope's gratitude, in a fashion that would cause no offence, waste no valuable vacancy and adjust the balance of favours at an appropriate level. Camulio's visit to Scotland in 1477 had been better than most: the following year, the Cardinal of Pavia had written to King James III expressing thanks for his support for the Nuncio, who was by then perhaps out of prison. The Bishopric of Caithness, with its seat at Dornoch, in the far north of Scotland (*culus mundi*), had fallen vacant, and it was the Pope's nephew the Cardinal of San Pietro ad Vinculi who proposed his friend Prosper de Camulio, employing that special procedure in consistory which handled posts for the Pope's friends and kinsmen, free of costs. By July 1478, Camulio's procurator had received the bulls providing the Apostolic Protonotary to the church of Caithness, and by May 1480 had paid the 650 florins necessary to validate them. In September 1481, the King of Scotland recorded that, having received his sworn oath, he had admitted Prosper *Episcopus Cathanensi* to his temporalities.

Camulio's movements in Scotland after 1477 have never been traced. Assuming he came, as Bishop-elect or eventually Bishop, he must have been on familiar terms with **Anselm Adorne**,* who had a son **Jan** at the Curia in

Rome who had read law at Pavia, and shared vital interests in Genoese politics, in alum,* in Chios,* which must have brought them together already in Bruges.* Adorne, his elder son and Camulio might have met during Adorne's earlier visits to Genoa and Rome. The prebends enjoyed by Adorne's sons were not in this Bishop's diocese, but he may have helped bring them about. He would certainly have known Robert Blackadder, Bishop of Aberdeen, during his stay in Rome, and perhaps even **Henry Arnot** of **Cambuskenneth** before that.

The actions and appearance of Camulio in the novels are therefore mostly fictitious, especially as regards his presence in Scotland. There is some ground, however, for placing him there in the months that led up to Adorne's death, which took place in Scotland in January 1483. Confused Flemish accounts suggest that Adorne, in his efforts to reconcile the two princes, James III and his brother, went on pilgrimage with 'the Bishop of *Lachacensis*'. No such bishopric is known. This might be an attempt to name Bishop Blackadder. Or it might be the Bishop of *Chatenensis*. Of the two, it seems perhaps likelier that for this ultimate purpose, Adorne would have chosen a compatriot, and that Camulio was his companion.

It was the last trace of Camulio. By the following year he had gone, and the record for 26 May 1484 announces that John **Sinclair** (Oliver's brother) had been provided to the church of Caithness, void by cession of Prosper de Camulio, Bishop of Caithness. It was another mark in the long history of foreign church appointments in Scotland, and the presence in Scotland of the individuals, the trading vessels and occasionally war fleets of Genoa, that adventurous city. (D. D.)

Cannon, the name of a: RONDO, 39: Guns, like jewels and bells, carried names. Typical of those made in Mons in the period were Mad Martha, Dulle Griet (Furious Margaret) and Mons Meg. Others were called after wild beasts or birds. Pope Pius II* named two cannon after himself: Enea, and Silvia; and a third, Vittoria, after his mother. (D. D.)

Canongate: UNICORN: See **Barony and regality.**

CANT, Henry: GEMINI: (d. 1492) Henry Cant, merchant, was the natural son of Thomas, an **Edinburgh** burgess, and a member of a family which was present in Scotland in 1376, but which originated most likely in Ghent, spreading from there to settle elsewhere in Flanders and in Scotland. Men and women called Cant – Baudoin, Lisbette, Simon, 'Henricus dictus Cant Picart' – had rents in Bruges from 1228 onwards, mixed up with surnames spelled 'de Gand' and 'Kante'.

In Scotland, the name proliferated from the early fifteenth century. Records show an Edinburgh bailie, a dean of guild,* and two Scottish merchants trading in England. Adam Cant had an Edinburgh booth in 1458, and was surety for another for Alan Brown. The family name is also found in the East Scottish port of Montrose, where Alexander Cant appears as the name of Provost or burgess through several generations. In 1493 John Cant of Muraystreet was rector of the church of Logie-Montrose, and burgess Walter Cant also had a **tenement** in the town, where he had witnessed a 1483 charter for Walter Ogilvy. In 1461, Alan Cant was rector of the Hospital of **Soutra**, having graduated, like George, James and John, at St Andrews University. Further north, a family of Cants leased land from the Abbey of Coupar-Angus, where **William Roger** the musician may have been a tenant in 1473, and where at least one of the sons of the Queen (**Margaret of Denmark**) was born. (It was the scene, in 1479, of a violent and unexplained raid upon the monks' possessions by the heir to **David Lindsay**, Fifth Earl of Crawford.)

In Fife, Katerina Cant was the wife of James of Balbirnie, in 1451, and she held Balbirnie with her sons John and Patrick after her husband died. Another Cant daughter, Elizabeth, was married by 1486 to William **Simpson** of Lathrisk, one of the squires of King **James III**.* In 1474 a gift to St Salvador's, St Andrews, mentioned land south of St Andrews belonging to the late John Cant and the late Andrew Simpson. Another John Cant, chaplain, witnessed a charter of the consuls of Inverkeithing in 1484, and earlier, in 1464, George Cant and Robert Bonkle* were witnesses to a Wemyss, Fife, charter involving two of the King's half-uncles.

The connection with Flanders was maintained. In 1416, Paton Cant was one of a large group of merchants from Edinburgh who went to complain to Duke John of Burgundy (1371–1419) over the detention at Sluys of three of their ships, containing goods owned by another Robert Bonkle of the same Scottish–Bruges family. And in 1621, when John Porterfield, Master of Conciergery House, died at Veere (home of the **van Borselen** family in Zeeland), his hospice for Scottish merchants continued under his widow, Elizabeth Cant, who by 1624 had married again, to the merchant David Peebles.

The fullest record of the family occurs, however, in relations to **Leith** and Edinburgh, where the Cants were part of the active merchant community, further integrated by the marriage of another Elizabeth Cant (d. by 1495) to the burgess and one-time Provost **Walter Bertram**. As early as the 1450s Patrick Cant with Walter Carruthers sailed from Leith in a ship of two hundred tons, while Alexander Cant took the merchandise of the Abbot of **Melrose** and other merchants on the *Antony*. By 1474 and 1475 Thomas and Henry Cant were using the *Mary* to transport salmon and other goods of Andrew and David **Crawford**, Walter Bertram and Alexander Turing among others.

Thomas, son of Adam Cant, was a burgess of Edinburgh whose two illegitimate sons, Henry and John, were to inherit from both the Bertram and Cant families. The family tenement in Edinburgh, with lower cellar and upper booth, lay on the south side of the High Street, beside that of Alexander Tweedy. Henry Cant, William **Preston** of Craigmillar and Alexander Tweedy were witnesses together in 1477 to a charter of Archibald Dundas, lord of Barnton, outside Edinburgh.

Henry Cant became a councillor in the 1470s, and then a member of Parliament from 1473 to 1493. He was also a burgess **Lord Auditor of Causes and Complaints** along with John Napier and Richard Lawson. As with most other merchants of Edinburgh, he is not named as taking part in the King's march south to **Lauder Bridge** in 1482 to counter the invasion of his brother **Alexander, Duke of Albany,*** and **Richard, Duke of Gloucester.** Henry was, however present at the subsequent siege of Edinburgh Castle by the new Provost Patrick Barron of Spittalfield (by Inverkeithing), accompanied by Patrick Balbirnie of Balbirnie (son of Katerina Cant), David Crawford of St Giles Grange (Walter Bertram's landlord), and Archibald Todrik as bailies; with **Thomas Yare**, Treasurer, and councillors including John Napier, William Rind, Robert Bonkle, William **Sinclair** and Robert Folkart. In November of that year Henry Cant and the others received the royal grant of the customs of Leith and the banner of the Holy Ghost, or the **Blue Blanket**, in thanks for the King's release from the castle.

In 1490, Henry Cant resigned to Alexander Lauder of Haltoun his lands of Brownisfield (now Bruntsfield) in Edinburgh. For a short time he also rented the bellhouse loft in the **Tolbooth** (for forty shillings a year), and this later passed to Henry Preston, whose relative Margaret was married to Walter Bertram's brother. Henry Cant, Thomas's natural son, had died a bastard without legitimate heirs by 1492, and his property passed to Richard Lawson. In 1504 another Henry Cant, burgess in the Canongate, was procurator for Edward **Spens**, the grandson of Thomas Preston, while by 1501 Elizabeth Cant, now a widow, was renting her house to William Cumming, Marchmont Herald, who had married a Preston. Still perpetuating relationships, John Cant became a councillor in 1484 along with Ninian Peebles, presumably an ancestor of David Peebles of Veere.

There were other Edinburgh Cants, usually surrounded by fellow-merchants, as in 1495, when Walter Cant appeared as a councillor along with Thomas Homyll, John Lauder and John Brown. A Nicholas Cant in 1505 was a witness to a charter involving Robin Crawford of **Berecrofts** and Richard Ramsay. Fourteen years before, David Ramsay had lived next to William and Archibald Crawford of Berecrofts and was possibly connected to the dazzling careerist John Ramsay (son of a Napier), who had played a part as a youth at Lauder Bridge, and who by 1484 was married to Isobel Cant, the widow of Thomas of Dumbarton.

Less usually, from 1477 onwards the name of Cant – Alexander, then David – appeared on the roll of Archers* of the French royal guard, traditionally drawn from the old Franco-Scots families, but now acquiring for the first time a Lauder, a Ross or a Haliburton. It was probably good for trade.

There is a Cant's Close in Edinburgh, now within a hotel on the south side of the High Street just before it joins the Canongate, and above where Blackfriars Wynd leads down to the Cowgate. It was said to be named first for Adam Cant, the Edinburgh customar of 1456, but by 1514 was known as Alexander Cant's Close. There was also a Cant's Land, now Fisher's Close, in the Lawnmarket, close to the site of the Butter Tron. (D. D.)

Carroccio: LIONS, 14: Italian war chariot which became symbolic of the independence and military power of the Italian communes in the medieval and renaissance period. Loss of the *carroccio* in battle was seen as the ultimate humiliation, similar to the loss of the standard or ensign. In peacetime the *carroccio* also served as a decorated float for processions or plays.

Carthusians: RONDO, 14: Members of the most austere of monastic orders, they combined the spirit of monasticism with the hermetic life of the early Christians. Founded by St Bruno in 1084 they took their name from Cartusia, later the town of Chartreuse, near Grenoble in south-eastern France (the English form 'Charterhouse' being a corruption of Chartreuse). The Carthusian life was extremely strict; their members claimed that theirs was the only order which did not need to be reformed, as it had never deviated from its original spirit. Charterhouses were built for multiples of twelve choir monks in units of twelve self-contained small houses. A silent order, the monks would spend most of their time in isolation, in their individual cells grouped round a large cloister. Each monk would have access to running water and their own small garden. Their meals would be served through a hatch, allowing no visual contact with the lay brethen who worked for the order. In addition to private contemplation and prayer, on Sundays and special feast days some level of communal activity was permitted. The Grand Chartreuse maintained control over the meticulously regulated way of life of the monks. Carthusian houses were always Priories, never Abbeys, and thus the head of a Carthusian house was always a Prior, not an Abbot.

James I (King of Scotland 1406–1437), on his return to Scotland in 1424, had seen the rapid spread of the order in the south, and was anxious to encourage the order and its spirit of simplicity in Scotland. In 1429 the Charterhouse at St John's Town of Perth was founded. The first community arrived from the continent, and the first intake of monks to the 'Vale of Virtue' at Perth included at least one Scot. **Anselm Adorne*** and his family fostered the Scottish interest in the order, and also supported the Duke of Ferrara's Certosa at Montello (RONDO, 15). The second Prior at Perth was a Scot and Scottish recruits began at once to enter the noviciate. The Charterhouse's links with mainland Europe, particularly Flanders, remained strong. Martin of Ghent (d. 1455) was Prior, and his son Dean William of Ghent was a monk at the Charterhouse. Nor was the order divorced from the culture of Scotland outside the confines of the Charterhouse; Prior Ramsay (from 1497) borrowed books to have them copied, organising the transcription of *The Bruce* (1376) by John Barbour (*c.* 1320–1395) and **Blind Harry's *The Wallace*.** The

Charterhouse was sacked and destroyed in May 1559 by the Reformers and the Priory was extinct by 1602, when it was totally suppressed.

Ca' d'Oro: RONDO, 29: Called the House of Gold (the Casa d'Oro) from its once-gilded carvings, this mansion of the **Contarini** family, begun near the Rialto Bridge in 1425, is the most beautiful Gothic palace in Venice. The first owner, Marino Contarini, was Procurator of the Basilica of San Marco, and his patrician clan, which by the fourteenth century ran to sixty-eight families, was one of those upon which Venice drew for her statesmen and doges. The building was designed by Marco d'Amadio and erected and decorated by Lombard and Venetian stone-masons, supervised by Matteo Reverti and Giovanni Bon, and taking nearly ten years to complete. It stood on the site of a former Veneto-Byzantine building, and the glorious traceried façade, said to resemble an oriental carpet, derives from these cultures. The main courtyard has a handsome wellhead, and within, the two principal floors have richly decorated rooms with fine ceilings and, on the first floor, a loggia overlooking the Grand Canal. (D. D.)

Casimir IV: RONDO: (1427–1492) Casimir, although Lithuanian, became one of Poland's greatest kings. His marriage to Elizabeth of Habsburg secured peace with Hungary and Bohemia, and the succession of their children to the newly acquired thrones. He was elected at age thirteen to the Dukedom of Lithuania while his elder brother Władysław (1424–1444) ruled in Poland (1434–1444). After Władysław was killed in a campaign against the Turks near Varna, the Lithuanians agreed to Casimir's election to the Polish throne in 1447 on the condition that Lithuania's territorial integrity and political autonomy were respected. Basing himself in Poland, Casimir's neglect of Lithuanian affairs led to bitter territorial disputes and violence (including an attempted assassination in 1481 and several threats to place a new Grand Duke on Lithuania's throne). Casimir, probably the last Grand Duke to speak Lithuanian, saw the polonisation of Lithuania in the fifteenth century, with its population comprising Polish-speaking nobility and Lithuanian-speaking peasantry.

Casimir had six sons (and seven daughters), four of whom became kings: Władysław (1456–1510), King of Bohemia from 1471 and King of Hungary from 1490; Jan Olbracht (1459–1501), King of Poland from 1492; Aleksander (1461–1506), Grand Duke of Lithuania from 1492 and King of Poland from 1501; and Zygmunt the Elder (1467–1548), Grand Duke of Lithuania and King of Poland from 1506. His other two sons were Frederick (1468–1503), Bishop of Cracow, **Archbishop of Gniezno** and Cardinal; and Kasimierz (1458–1484), the second eldest son who became patron saint of Lithuania. The Lithuanian and Polish territories of Casimir and his sons were undermined by the encroaching power of **Ivan III**, and there was war between Lithuania and Muscovy between 1500 and 1513.

Casimir's education had been purposely neglected, since the Lithuanian magnates believed that with uneducated kings it was easier to realise their own plans. It is indeed remarkable that a monarch who was unable to read and write should have left behind him such highly educated sons whose mentors included Jan Długosz, **Jan Ostróróg** and **Callimachus**.

C'aurait dû être Bertrand: QUEENS, IV, 3: 'That must have been Bertrand'.

C'est un bachique!: LIONS, 8: 'Here's a wild laddie!'

C'est une belle, mais frigide . . . Pas frigide du tout!: QUEENS: IV, 2: 'It's a beauty, but cold . . . No, not cold in the least!'

Cecilia: GEMINI, 8: An embassy of Scottish ambassadors arrived in England in 1474, initially to discuss the terms regarding spoliation of the ***St Salvator***, but their main task was to negotiate a marriage between **Edward IV**'s* daughter Cecilia and Prince James of Scotland, eldest son of **James III**.* The final negotiations and settlement took place in **Edinburgh** in October 1474 and the betrothal was solemnised in **Blackfriars.** As Prince James and Princess Cecilia, the prospective groom and bride, were respectively aged one and five, they took no part in the ceremony: **David Lindsay**, Earl of Crawford, and Lord Scrope stood in as proxies. The treaty of October 1474 brought James III much-needed finance. The dowry for the Princess was fixed at twenty thousand marks of English money, paid in instalments of two thousand marks a year for the first three years, and thereafter at a rate of one thousand per year. Payments were to begin on 3 February 1475 in St Giles,* Edinburgh. The profitable prospect for James was the assurance that if his son or Cecilia died before they reached marriageable age, the dowry was to be retained by James, to the value of 2,500 marks. The treaty was intended to bind England and Scotland together in everlasting friendship; and although the peace was not perpetual, it at least lasted for five years. James was proving that for once, he was not at the beck and call of **Louis XI**,* and, as he remarked to **Charles, Duke of Burgundy**,* he had made peace with the only King who made war on him. A policy of peace with England (and an end to English piracy) helped the burgesses, merchants and traders of the realm, even if it did engender violent opposition from some quarters.

Following the English invasion of 1482, the burgesses of Edinburgh, led by their Provost **Walter Bertram**, were obliged to promise that if the wedding between Cecilia and Prince James were not to take place, the money paid by Edward was to be paid back in yearly instalments, in the same way as it was paid out to King James. By October, Edward decided that he would rather have a refund of the cash than the wedding. Although James's attempts to revive the marriage were unsuccessful, he maintained a pro-English policy for the last five years of his reign. He also managed to retain eight thousand marks of the dowry money.

Chapel royal: LIONS, 10: A chapel constructed for the private worship of the royal family. In fifteenth-century Scotland the phrase is occasionally used to describe the **collegiate church** of Restalrig under **James III**,* but more often refers to St Mary on the Rock, St Andrews, and later to denote the collegiate chapel of Stirling during the reign of **James IV**.* In James III's day, the designated chapel royal probably moved from St Andrews to Restalrig, much closer to the King's preferred base of **Edinburgh**, being only two miles from **Holyrood.** The elaborate chapel of Restalrig was under construction from 1486. There was definitely not a chapel royal at St Andrews by 1501, when Stirling's chapel royal was erected under James IV. Work on the chapel royal at Stirling may have begun as early as 1485, as mention is made in the accounts of the Lord High Commissioner of Scotland on James III's resolve to increase the choir, the cost of which would be met by suppressing **Coldingham**.

CHARLES, Duke of Burgundy:* RISING: (1433–1477) The territorial war with **Louis XI*** of France cost Charles the Bold his dukedom and his life. His dynastic ambitions to restore the old kingdom of Burgundy led him to reconquer Lorraine, Provence, Dauphiné and Switzerland. War raged between France and Burgundy till 1475 (see under **Anselm Adorne***), when Charles turned anew to his favourite scheme of conquest, and soon made himself master of Lorraine. Invading Switzerland he stormed Grandson and hanged and drowned the garrison, but was humiliatingly defeated by the Swiss on 1 March 1476 (see **Jewels with a name**). Charles then besieged Morat, but sustained an even greater defeat (22 June). The news that Duke René* was trying to recover his territories roused him once more to action, and he laid siege to Nancy. His army was small, however, and his chances of victory were destroyed by the treason of his Italian mercenaries under Nicolò de Montfort/Gambatesta, Count of Campobasso, who went over to the enemy. Charles fought with all his wonted recklessness, and perished in the battle.

Chien d'attache: See **Leashed dogs.**

Chinchins, Les: LIONS, 2: In the novel, the name of a troupe performing a comedy interlude in a passion play in Angers, France. (King René* attended a similar **Mystery** performance in Angers in 1471.) The name was also given (fictitiously) to a ship from Hull taking part in the fifteenth-century cod war in **Iceland.** A group of entertainers called the Chinchins are on record in performances of passion plays at Mons at the end of the fifteenth century. Even a Scottish Regent was treated to one: in 1516 **John Stewart, Second Duke of Albany**, who had married Anne de la Tour d'Auvergne, was presented by the

Auvergnats with a theatrical play as part of his Grand Entry to Montferrand. (D. D.)

Chinsing-iron: LIONS, 16: A caulker's tool: an instrument for pressing sealing-material between planks.

Choose the trussell or the pile: KINGS, Gambit: Heads or tails: see **Coining**. (See also **Face or pellet?**)

Christian I: UNICORN: (1426–1481) Father of **Margaret of Denmark**, Queen of **James III*** of Scotland, Christian was elected to the throne of Denmark in 1448 in succession to his distant kinsman Christopher of Bavaria, the great-nephew of the intrepid **Margaret of Norway** who united the three Scandinavian countries in 1389. Originally Count Christian of Oldenburg, the new King was nephew of the Duke of Schleswig, and was elected Duke of Schleswig-Holstein in 1460. Although Norway eventually recognised the new King's right to the throne, Sweden insisted on electing its own Regent, and when Christian attempted to use force, he was beaten in a battle near Stockholm in 1471.

Under his rule, Norwegian trade in timber and cod was badly hampered by the monopolies of the **Hanseatic League**, despite Christian's much-improved fleet, and Greenland was neglected. Money was tight, and Christian sought means of obtaining it by renewing Norwegian claims for payment of past Scottish debts. With France as the earliest mediator, this became converted into a contract of marriage between Christian's young daughter Margaret and King James III of Scotland. The marriage took place in 1469, and resulted in the acquisition by Scotland of the islands of Orkney and Shetland as security for part of her dowry, which Christian was unable to pay (see **Orkney dowry**). Christian, facing continuing problems with the Swedes in his own country, as well as with England and the Hanse, was glad thereafter to have Scotland's aid in consolidating an alliance with France in 1472. A possible marriage between Christian's son and the daughter of **Louis XI*** of France came to nothing, however, and the Prince married Kristina, the daughter of Ernest of Saxony in 1478.

Christian made several state journeys with some religious intent, perhaps combined with political need, and some vanity. He was believed to be moved by a prophecy that a northern ruler would conquer the Turks. Because of this, and perhaps the strength of his fleet, he had the Pontiff's endorsement, and sought to urge other rulers to join the Pope against Turkey. When in 1474 he made a solemn journey to Rome, he made an impact on those who saw him: a grave man, with a long grey beard, and an entourage of 150 with strange, pale-coloured skin and hair, and pilgrims' staves embroidered on their horse-clothes. The entire papal court emerged to escort the King to St Peter's, and thence to the hospitality of a palace formerly occupied by the Emperor **Frederick III.**

He stayed for three weeks, during which time he was overwhelmed with gifts from Pope Sixtus,* including a portion of the true Cross, a portable altar, a valuable ring and a splendid mule with a bridle studded with gold. To the Cardinals, who had also been generous, Christian returned beautiful furs. On Easter Sunday, the King was given the Golden Rose, an annual symbol, representing Christ the Redeemer, presented by the Pope as a pledge of his benevolence to a monarch or ruler whom he held in esteem. James III received a rose in 1486 from Innocent VIII (Pope 1484–1492), and his son James, Christian's grandson, was also given one in 1491. When King Christian left the papal city, all the Cardinals escorted him to the gate, and members of the Sacred College accompanied him as far as the frontier. Indeed, the visit pleased Christian so much that he had a medal struck to commemorate it.

Other favours were exchanged. The Pope agreed to promulgate certain bulls, and the ground was laid for the foundation of the University of Copenhagen the following year. There were political niceties to be discussed. The Sforza* family of Milan wished a royal crown. Within Christian's own family, a marriage had been proposed between his half-Scottish grandson, aged one, and a daughter of Galeazzo Maria Sforza (1444–1476), Duke of Milan. This, Louis of France was anxious to promote, since it would prevent another, much more dangerous marriage alliance between England and Scotland. James of Scotland had in fact attempted to come to Rome that same year, perhaps to call at Milan, since war with England seemed not unlikely. In the event, the Duke of Milan diplomatically refused to consider the marriage, English relations improved, and the infant James was promptly contracted to **Cecilia** of England.

While in Rome, Christian had the opportunity, also, of meeting others connected with Scotland. **Jan Adorne** was then in the city, and envoys of James III such as the future Bishop Blackadder, concerned with the destiny of Archbishop **Patrick Graham.** En route, Christian may also have encountered **Ludovico de Severi da Bologna,*** who had visited the King in Denmark in 1468, and who was travelling to Lübeck on his way to Poland at that time. Certainly, King Christian stopped at Bologna, where he conferred a knighthood upon Annibale, the five-year-old son of Giovanni Bentivoglio, whose mother would later receive an Italian biography of Christian's daughter. He also created a legend in the duchy of Milan, where he was heard to describe the Duke's treasure as 'unbefitting a true and generous prince'. The Duke, undisturbed, played his host at Pavia and sent him off to the delights of Milan in a chariot drawn by four white ducal horses. On his return journey from Rome, Christian again enjoyed the hospitality of Galeazzo Maria when passing through Parma, Piacenza and Cremona, and finally vanished beyond the frontiers of the despised duchy, having borrowed ten thousand ducats from the Duke.

From Italy, Christian travelled (without a coach and white horses) to Augsburg, where he stayed until June with the Holy Roman Emperor, after which he went back to Holstein. The King's final expedition that year was to the great camp of **Charles, Duke of Burgundy**,* who had begun a siege against Neuss, which was to last for two years. The camp, built like a city with commercial streets and two markets, had many eminent visitors who were received in two richly decorated pavilions. The Duke lived in a collapsible timber hut before which musicians sang every morning, and the whole so impressed the Venetian ambassador that he commissioned an artist to paint it. (Sadly, the resulting picture was no luckier than **Hans Memling**'s *Last Judgement.* On its way home to Venice, it was intercepted and kept by Duke Sigismond* of the Tyrol.)

Christian of Denmark arrived before Neuss with a splendid suite, including a brother, a nephew, the three Dukes of Saxe-Laurenbourg, Mecklembourg and Brunswick, and two hundred knights. His stated aim was to reconcile the Emperor, Burgundy and France, and bring them into the field against the Turk. He set up house in a village nearby where he held talks with officials, and his first ducal audience, when it came, took place not in a pavilion, but upon a flotilla of boats on the Rhine, where the Duke of Burgundy appeared in a pearled tunic worth a hundred thousand florins. There followed a series of rural banquets for Christian, one of them situated as far off as Düsseldorf. Finally, the King packed up and went home, leaving the Duke's plans quite unaltered. From here, no combined army was to set out against the Turk.

Christian died in 1481, leaving a troubled heritage to his son Hans (or John, 1455–1513). The new King was accepted by Norway and Denmark, but shared Schleswig-Holstein with Frederick, his brother, who in 1481 was briefly contracted to marry an English princess. King John ruled until 1513 and maintained his father's strong fleet, although not always wisely. He also suffered reverses with the Swedes and with the Hanse, as his father had done. In 1486, after the death of Queen Margaret, King James of Scotland asked the Pope, through his Archbishop's embassy, to confirm the settlement reached by James and the late King Christian over the donation of Orkney and Shetland, almost as if it had been challenged. There was set on foot, at about the same time, an effort by James III to canonise the late Queen, John's sister.

It is unclear what share, if any, John of Denmark took in that; but he seems to have reached the conclusion that the friendship of King James's son was going to be worth more than that of James himself. He and the Prince exchanged letters when reports spread that Queen Margaret had been killed with her husband's connivance, poisoned by John Ramsay. Soon after, a fleet from Denmark, sent by John, arrived at **Leith** outside **Edinburgh** just about the time of the final battle which led to the death of the King. The fleet commander remained in Scotland all winter at the expense of the new young King **James IV**,* departing with a gift of five hundred pounds. A lavish exchange of letters and gifts between John and his nephew then began, building towards a treaty of alliance with Scotland which eventually took place in 1492, and was to lead in 1502 to a Scottish expedition to help John's son in Norway. It is perhaps worth noting, as an interesting footnote, that Sir David **Sinclair**, son of the last Earl of Orkney, had interests in both Shetland and Norway, where he received a knighthood from John of Denmark, and was for a time governor of Bergen Castle. There is an unconfirmed report that Sir David took part in the 1502 expedition, accompanied by 'Sir Oliver Sinclair', presumably his half-brother. (D. D.)

Christus, Petrus: LIONS, 19: (*c.* 1420–1473) Flemish painter, born in Baerle, Brabant, who became a master in Bruges* in 1444. Believed to have been the pupil or assistant of Jan van Eyck,* he reputedly introduced geometric perspective into the Lowlands. (See also **Dry Tree.**)

Cirkelselschop: RONDO, 2: This was the name of an exclusive 'Circle' society in Lübeck, the largest town in north Germany after Cologne. In style, it was probably much the same as the White Bear Society* in Bruges, and represented the elite end of a wide network of merchant confraternities which contained in its lower reaches clubs such as the **Bergenfahrer** for cod merchants from Lübeck. Members of the Cirkelselschop intermarried only with one another, or with wealthy foreigners. They also commissioned and presented plays, as many such groups did. Such performances were initially religious, but often changed in character over the years, causing the disaffected to observe that many brotherhoods had become little more than drinking clubs. At their height, they could admit their members to valuable privileges, such as storage monopolies.

The Artushof in **Danzig**, originally the headquarters of the Brotherhood of St George, performed a similar office for international merchants and shipowners, who were allowed to congregate there in the absence, as yet, of any long-term consular system. Admission could however be selective, as English merchants found, when they had to beg for reinstatement after some perceived national shortcomings. (D. D.)

Cistercians: HN: Also known as the White Monks, a reformed order based on social isolation founded by St Robert of Molesme (*c.* 1027–1111) at Cîteaux in 1098. Its greatest period of influence was during the period when St Bernard of Clairvaux (1090–1153) joined the order in the early twelfth century. After 1134, all Cistercian churches were dedicated to the Blessed Virgin Mary. They deliberately sought a harder way of life than the established orders of the time, basing their monastic communities in the 'wilderness', making the order ideally suited to the border lands between Scotland and England, and Yorkshire. Their desire for self-sufficiency meant they became particularly adept at transforming wilderness into profitably cultivated farming and arable land. The order was brought to Scotland by David I (King of

Scotland 1124–1153) who introduced the order to **Melrose**; a 'daughter' house was soon founded at **Newbattle** and another at Kinloss (see Bishop Reid of Orkney*), which in turn founded Culross (with its commercial scriptorium) and Deer. The 'family' relationship between houses was very strong, with 'daughter' houses obliged to attend regular General Chapters. A specialty of the Cistercians was wool-farming, particularly at Melrose, which sold its wool in the Low Countries as early as the twelfth century. As the largest producers, they exported the wool themselves. Smaller houses would sell the wool to foreign merchants at the point of production, rather than incur the expense and organisation of export themselves, via Berwick-upon-Tweed,* until it was lost to the English. Melrose, as the 'mother' house of Cistercian **monasteries** in Scotland, collected the wool from the smaller houses to export also. It became the largest single producer of wool in Scotland.

Cito, cito, cito: UNICORN, 46: 'Quick, quick, quick'. When written, it usually preceded '*pro re ducali*' on ducal mail.

Clacquedent . . . Punto tirato . . . Molar merletti: LIONS, 14: A series of wild puns to do with threats to draw a musician's teeth. *Clacquedent* (rattle-teeth) is a common French nick-name. *Punto tirato* refers to embroidery, and is drawn-thread work. *Molar merletti* implies teeth gapped like the machiolations of a citadel. *Embouchure* is the muscular circle of a trumpeter's lips, and the Order of the Garter appears as orderly garters. Tuscany/Tuskany drawn-thread work is embroidery.

Clerk-register: HN: The official in charge of public records in Scotland. When the **Lords Auditor of Causes and Complaints** met in session, a clerk-register attended to record the causes.

Clinker-built: LIONS, 21: Ships of the Atlantic and North Sea were built with overlapping planks fastened with copper nails, as opposed to flush planking with no overlap to be found on galley* and carvel-built boats.

COCHRANE, Thomas: UNICORN: (d. 1482) Early writers picked out Thomas Cochrane, mason to King **James III*** of Scotland, and made a myth of him, almost within his own lifetime. When he was killed, no one was punished.

The legend, even yet not fully dissected, made of Thomas (or mistakenly Robert) Cochrane a brash base-born mason's apprentice who rose from unknown origins to flatter a weak King, ruining the kingdom by issuing worthless money, and seizing the earldom of Mar when the King's young brother died, perhaps through his agency. Witchcraft is mentioned. He met his fate at **Lauder Bridge** when the King marched south by way of **Soutra**, against an advancing English army, and Cochrane, heavily bejewelled (says the story), swaggered up to a meeting of conspiring nobles who hanged him, with all the rest of the King's low-born playfellows, from the bridge.

Some of it is true. He is unlikely to have been legitimate. He was a mason. But the Cochranes were not an unknown family. They were so numerous indeed that the confusion between Thomas and Robert Cochrane was understandable.

The surname Cochrane first came to light in the thirteenth century in lands of that name in Renfrewshire, on the west side of Scotland, and remained strongly based there. In 1493 Robert Cochrane of that Ilk (i.e., head of the family) was concerned in a law case over his mill on the river called the Black Cart. He was probably the same man who witnessed the founding by John, Lord **Semple**, in Renfrewshire of a **collegiate church** on the pattern of **Edinburgh**'s **Trinity Chapel.** The names of Cochranes, Semples and Lennox appear commonly together in public records.

Other Cochranes scattered widely, as did the Renfrewshire Stewarts and their associates, who traditionally held land in the **barony** of Bathgate, close to **Linlithgow.** George, William, James and Rankin Cochrane were important enough to witness charters connected with Fife, Perth, **Roslin** and Stirling between the reigns of James I (1406–1437) and **James IV**;* and 'George Cochrane' appears several times in connection with the hospital at Soutra, which had property in the Cowgate, where he lived in 1481, adjacent to the late Thomas of Soutra. Other Cochranes now surfacing in Edinburgh include a burgess and lawyer, Robert Cochrane, in 1496 and a mason, John Cochrane, important enough to appear several times, and be linked with the master mason William Merlion, whose family worked on the **Sinclair** family's Ravenscraig Castle.

In 1487, Agnes Cochrane appears as the wife of William Charteris of Cagnor, knight, a man connected with **Cuthilgurdy**, who had a presence in Perth, and held widely in Lumphannan and other places in Aberdeenshire, where the names of Cochrane, Charteris and Ogilvy (owners of **Anselm Adorne**'s* Cortachy) appear amicably on the same charters. In Fife, there was a John Cochrane active in 1510, and a chaplain Andrew Cochrane at the same time. Abroad, 'John Cochrane the Saxon' was an Archer in the French Royal Guard under Patrick Flockhart in 1449 (see Scottish Archers*).

There were at least two Thomas Cochranes during the reign of James III.* One was the son of the sheriff depute of Renfrewshire, who did not die until 1488. The other is the man of the novels, whose parentage is a mystery, but who fits well into the family of a Mariota Cochrane who held land in Lanarkshire, but also in Grugfoot, Linlithgow, which she resigned in 1468 to her son Alan Cochrane and his wife Alison Russell. Alan is last on record in 1473, but his widow may be the Alison who then married one Thomas Preston and had a son, Archibald Preston, who inherited some of his late father's rights.

The **Prestons** of **Craigmillar Castle**, by Edinburgh, were royal adherents: one of them was nurse to the young Prince. They were also closely connected with the Sinclairs, whose surrender of the earldom of Orkney had been a component of the King's marriage arrangements and who had equally supplied the royal family with nursing and tutelage care. Other associated houses included that of Cumming of **Culter** in Aberdeenshire, one of whose members was Marchmont Herald, and later Lord Lyon King of Arms; and the family of Hector Meldrum, the royal macer. The Sinclairs and their close allies the **Dunbars** were in turn linked by marriage with **Sir John Colquhoun of Luss**, who was killed in May 1479 by a shot fired from Dunbar Castle by the men of **Alexander, Duke of Albany.***

Sir John Colquhoun had been the King's Household Controller, and was still in his household as Usher of the King's Chamber Door. His wife, Elizabeth Dunbar, was Countess of Moray by a previous husband, and had once been betrothed to the Earl of Huntly. As sheriff of the port of Dumbarton, Sir John had trading concerns of his own, including his own ship. He also possessed (like **Thomas Yare, Walter Bertram** and Bishop **William Scheves**) a house in Berwick-upon-Tweed.* When he died, he left a credit of sixty pounds, owed him by four men, which went not to his heirs but to Thomas Cochrane, by decree of the **Lords of Council in Civil Causes**, one of whom was Bishop **Thomas Spens** of Aberdeen. This has the look of a business debt, incurred by a consortium. All four men were from the north-east. Two were Cummings of the family of Marchmont Herald, and two were extremely well-known Nairn men, the Thane of Cawdor and Hugh Ross of Kilravock. The implication is that Cochrane had performed a service or acted as agent for Sir John Colquhoun in some royal transaction (probably in salmon) for which he was now being paid.

This happened just before the death of **John of Mar**, and just after the flight of the Duke of Albany to France, and is the first appearance on record of Thomas Cochrane. The next, in 1481, might indicate a lack of rapport between Cochrane and the absent Albany. In that year, Parliament instructed Thomas Cochrane to obtain and hand back to Dick of Rowlis (Richard Roule) a brown horse Cochrane had allowed to pass to Edward and David Sinclair. This may have been a plain dispute over horse-dealing – Alan Cochrane had been involved in a complaint about horses five years before. Or it might have to do with the fact that *John* Roule was Albany's steward, and that Catherine Sinclair was Albany's just-divorced wife. The law was harsher on Richard Roule in the next reign, when he was accused of stealing horses, oxen and farm goods from an Edinburgh burgess, John Wilson, who seems to have been the stepfather of the young royalist of Lauder, John Ramsay.

These episodes show Cochrane as perhaps a supplier or an agent. The north-eastern consortium does more, in linking him to an area where he operated as a builder. On unwritten evidence, now accepted by historians, the massive Ogilvy castle of Auchindoun, crowning a rock above the River Fiddich in Banffshire, and defended on all sides by river and moat, was rebuilt on an earlier foundation by Thomas Cochrane. Apart from the castle's defences –

it was on the road leading from Elgin into Aberdeenshire – its most striking feature was the great hall occupying the middle floor, its vaulted roof upheld by fluted pillars and groined and ribbed in two bays, unlike the barrel vault of Craigmillar Castle. Its walls were ten feet thick.

The style of Auchindoun is that of the mid-fifteenth century, but there are no dates, and great gaps in the records. Cochrane might have built on another man's work, or worked in partnership. His training is unknown, and that given him in the novels is fictitious. There is a clue perhaps in his next recorded appearance twenty miles from Auchindoun in the much greater role of Constable of Kildrummy Castle, the chief castle of Mar, and one of the largest in Scotland, occupying a three-acre site on a rock flanked by two ravines. Once a seat of the Kings of Scotland, it controlled the whole district of Garioch and Mar. The post of Constable, meaning governor of a royal castle, was a military one, suggesting that Cochrane's speciality was fortification rather than domestic building.

Like Linlithgow, Kildrummy had once belonged to Queen Mary of Gueldres. Following the death of the last Earl of Mar, John, her son, war had broken out between England and Scotland, and the revenues of Mar were in limbo. Since the King did not apparently receive them, they may have been used for such building works. From this no doubt rose the later tales that credited Cochrane with Mar's title and wealth. The earldom seems to have been held back until, after Cochrane's death, it was accepted as a temporary bribe by the Duke of Albany. Later it passed, for loyal service, to the Earl of Huntly, who was Keeper of Kildrummy by 1486.

This was after Cochrane's death. There are many different versions of the events of July 1482. The English army marched north, under **Richard, Duke of Gloucester**, the future Richard III, to take Berwick-upon-Tweed and try to put Alexander, Duke of Albany on his brother's throne. With a much smaller army, King James set off south to confront them. At Lauder, a small town about twenty-five miles south of Edinburgh and halfway to the frontier with England, the march stopped, either because the army rebelled, or because wise counsel prevailed. The headstrong King was constrained to turn and go back, and was then detained in Edinburgh Castle in the custody of his half-uncles until negotiating time had been bought.

Later accounts excused the treasonable handling of the King as a necessity, cleansing the royal entourage as it did of base-born jumped-up favourites, led by the high-handed Thomas Cochrane. Writers of the next century saw in Cochrane a spoiled favourite who could be blamed for the kingdom's monetary problems. His activities in the north were equated to his assumption of the earldom of Mar. (See also under **William Knollys.***) Reports claimed that during the incident all the favourites were killed, commonly specifying that it was done by hanging them from Lauder Bridge.

Of the long and imaginative list of those who died, only three appear to be genuine victims. One was Cochrane, one was the eminent musician **William**

Roger, and one was a **Preston** related to Cochrane. It is hard to see why these men should have suffered. They were not young or base-born. Cochrane and Roger were experts in their own line. There is no evidence of exploitation or influence – the **black money** had been circulating long before this. There were always grudges and private vendettas, especially where money was involved. It is true, however, that Cochrane and Roger were among those most likely to have been swept up by the King's passionate war fever. Marching armies needed guns and munitions, and music. And there is here the last hint that Cochrane, in the multiskilled fashion of the times, was not simply a dealer, or a merchant, or a builder, but supplied, as masons and carpenters did, the materials of war: the cannon balls and the gunpowder and the artillery carriages, and the organisational skills to handle and transport them. One account specifically says that at Lauder, Cochrane had charge of the artillery train.

In the long run, he may simply have wanted to march on and fire at the English, just as the King did; and his kinsman and Roger may have supported him. He had the guns. In the panic, the antiwar faction may have taken the only way they saw open to stop him.

Whatever happened, it must have been over before the army had fully collected. It might never have happened at all, had **John Stewart, Lord Darnley**, been there, or been there in time. It was he and a special light troop who occupied Edinburgh Castle at the same time as the King was secured there, and Darnley may have escorted the monarch from Lauder. There were three Cochranes from Renfrewshire – John, William and Edward – in Darnley's troop.

The aftermath gives some last, fragmentary substance to this potentially appealing and certainly obstinate man. His goods were forfeited, thus conveniently implying that he had committed some serious crime, and that his killing was justified. In the faulty records, there is no sign of a legal process concerning his crime. But the forfeiture reveals that Cochrane possessed tenant's rights in a piece of land called Cousland, close to **Newbattle** Abbey, which was owned by the Sinclairs – most recently by William, Oliver, and then Henry. The land had several occupants, one of whom was Dr Conrad, who had come as a physician in 1472 and was to serve this royal household and the next for nearly twenty years. In later times, **Henry Arnot**, Abbot of **Cambuskenneth**, was also to become a tenant.

After the hanging at Lauder, a claim to his father's share in the same land of Cousland was made by Archibald Preston, son of the Thomas Preston who died at Cochrane's side. This was possibly what led George Buchanan, the sixteenth-century historian, to assume that Cochrane was Thomas Preston's son-in-law. But there is no sign that Cochrane was ever married, and Archibald's claims came very late – ten to fifteen years after his father's death, suggesting that he was not of age when that happened. It seems likelier that his mother Alison had first married a brother of Cochrane's, and inherited some Cousland rights on the death of Thomas Cochrane.

In the event, the Cousland land associated with both Lauder victims went to William, Lord Ruthven. So also, in 1482, did Thomas Preston's land at Middle Pitcairn, in the barony of Ruthven, Perth, which had also been owned by the Sinclairs. Ruthven already had land in the area, and received the forfeited land from the King – and later a lordship – to ensure his loyalty in the last six years of his reign. The same man, acting shrewdly, survived a bumpy ride at the start of the following reign, on the assurance that he 'kept a good part to the King that dead is, and gave no partial counsel against the King that now is'.

Because of the singular circumstances of his death, the life of Thomas Cochrane survived as a series of picturesque dramas, confined by very few facts. There is no proof that he was connected with fortifications and artillery, or was an importer and supplier of war goods. There is a tenuous connection with other masons, and with the Sinclairs, although the scenes in the novels associating him with building in **Roslin** and elsewhere are fictitious. It seems very likely that a mason's training and a talent for management led his career into a path which the missing records would have shown to be very like that of the gunners, the purveyors, the furnishers, the timber experts, the smiths and the masters of work who ran the practical side of the kingdom. He was perhaps too enthusiastic. (D. D.)

Cod: See **Stockfish.**

Coeur, Jacques de: LIONS, 3: (*c.* 1395–1456) Keeper of the Purse of King Charles VII* of France, Jacques de Coeur was one of the greatest merchants of his time, with a fleet which made him a fortune in Mediterranean trade. His annual income was vaunted to be as much as that of all the other merchants of France put together, and his motto, '*À vaillans coeurs rien impossible*' ('to valiant hearts nothing is impossible') must have seemed true at the time – the King was deeply in his debt, and it was de Coeur's money which had financed the conquest of Normandy. He was, however, rash enough to lend money and help at the same time to the King's hated son and heir, the Dauphin Louis (later **Louis XI***), and the King, when he found out, took his revenge. In 1453 Charles had de Coeur accused of treason (in fact, accused of poisoning the King's mistress, Agnès Sorel), fined him four hundred thousand crowns, seized his goods, and sent him to prison for life. Escaping after a year, the merchant sought help from the Pope Callixtus III,* and died on the island of Chios* in November 1456, while leading a fleet against the Turks. His great palace at Bourges (of which his son was at one time Archbishop) can still be seen, together with the holes in the attics which served his army of carrier-pigeons, the fast courier service of the day. (D. D.)

Coffee: See under Qahveh* in Volume I. An early rival to coffee in the Levant was known as *salep*, and made from *bassarin*, a liquid derived from the dried tubers of orchids. Still used today, especially in Istanbul, as a flavouring for ices, its flavour is said to be reminiscent of wild mushrooms and damp goat.

Coffins à roupies: QUEENS, II, 4: Women's riding veils, such as the French *touret,* stiffened and shaped to conceal the nose and the chin. Irreverently known, no doubt accurately, as 'containers for the rheum'.

Coining: LIONS, 14: The actual process of coining changed little in the fifteenth and sixteenth centuries, regardless of which metal was used: gold, silver, **billon** or copper. The metal was first cast in bars, and beaten out to the required thinness by hammers. It was then cut into squares of the same diameter as the future coin, flattened, annealed, rounded and made the correct weight. After further shaping, annealing and blenching (cleaning and chemically treating the surface preparatory to striking), the blanks were ready to be turned into coins. The blank (or flan) would be placed on top of the obverse mould of the coin, a highly polished steel die known as the pile. With the blank piece of metal in the middle, the upper die, or trussel, was held by the coiner in his left hand on top of the flan as he brought the hammer down on the die (hence, 'choose the trussel or the pile'). If the impression was not satisfactory, the procedure would have to be repeated, taking great care to align the coin and the dies exactly as before to avoid any doubling, which would render the impression illegible. Coiners therefore had to have good hand-to-eye coordination, confidence and a significant degree of upper body strength to wield the hammer precisely (skills still required in the hand-hallmarking industry in the present day). This perhaps accounts for the popularity of coiners and hammermen in fifteenth-century jousts. (GEMINI, 8).

Master moneyers of **James III**'s* time were **William Goldsmith** (1466), Alexander Tod at Perth (1467), Alexander Livingston (1476–1488) and Thomas Todd (1476–1487), whilst wardens of the mint included George Grinlaw (1467), who was warden in the absence of Alexander Tod, and James Crichton (1488). The warden was in charge of the bullion, assaying, care of money minted and of the coining dies, whilst the master moneyer was presumably in charge of the actual process, that is, the coining and the design and manufacture of dies. The 1434 constitution of the mint stated that goldsmiths were not to be employed by the mint unless no other could be found: either to avoid giving them access to the equipment and encouraging their forgery; or to encourage them to fulfill what their training had enabled them to do, make objects not coins; also perhaps because of the goldsmith's traditional role as banker. Great care was taken to avoid the dies used from falling into the wrong hands, and to prevent forgery. Several mints existed in fifteenth-century Scotland, principally to allow coins to be struck locally to aid distribution. Mints are recorded during James III's reign in **Edinburgh**, St Andrews, Berwick-upon-Tweed* (see **Amiens**) and Aberdeen.

Coining was a source of revenue for the King, who would take approximately two to three per cent of the amount of bullion struck in duty. Bullion came from dues imposed on merchants who exported commodities (the export of jewels, gold and silver, coined or uncoined, was prohibited by Parliament in 1436 and again in 1466 when a penalty of ten pounds was imposed on anyone attempting to take money out of the kingdom); from melting down foreign currency and plate; and from local mines. Thus Scotland's bullion came both from imported and native supplies, although more bullion seemed to leave the country than arrive. Crawfordmuir provided a large amount of gold bullion in the early sixteenth century; miners came to Scotland from Germany, Lorraine and England to extract it. During the minority of James VI, when Regent Morton ruled (1572–1578), a gold basin of the capacity of four English quarts, and filled with coins called unicorns, was presented to the

King of France: both basin and contents were native Scottish gold. The 1539 regalia of Scotland was also made from native gold. (See also **Black money;** Coinage;* **Lion; Thomas Swift.**)

Coldingham: LIONS, 9: A Benedictine Priory, ten miles north of Berwick-upon-Tweed,* founded as a gift of lands to Durham in 1098, perhaps on the ruins of the double monastery of both monks and nuns founded by Ebba, daughter of King Ethelfred of Northumbria, in 664 and destroyed by the Danes in the ninth century. By 1140 a regular monastery existed at Coldingham, which was until 1462 a dependency of Durham. The Scots then took advantage of the English civil wars to eject the English monks. The Priory soon became the centre of a purely local struggle between members of the Scottish baronial **Home family.** Patrick Home, Archdeacon of Teviotdale, attempted to obtain the Priory in commendam (meaning that he would hold the benefice and its revenues) in 1461, but his claims were thrust aside by Sir Alexander Home, who as bailie of Coldingham since 1442 wanted his son John appointed as Prior so that his family could continue to enjoy the revenues of the Priory.

In 1464 John Home was duly provided to Coldingham and his position was unchallenged until the Prior of Durham petitioned **James III*** to allow English monks to reoccupy the Priory. Ignoring the pleas of the Home family and of Durham, James III took the opportunity to petition Sixtus IV* to suppress the Priory and allow him to use the funds for his own **chapel royal.** As part of a compromise plan, in 1473 the Pope agreed to the suppression and also that part of the funds of Coldingham should go to James's chapel royal, but the residue should go towards the erection of Coldingham as a **collegiate church** with dean and prebendaries, making Patrick Home the dean. John Home appealed to the Pope, who recognised his superior claim, and Patrick was forced to resign as dean, although he was allowed to take part of the revenues for himself. Patrick died in 1478. James III had never recognised John Home as the rightful Prior, and the political crisis of 1482–1483 gave the Homes the opportunity they had been waiting for to take advantage of the situation and have the suppression of the Priory and the allocation of the funds to the King's chapel royal overturned. **Alexander Home** had broken allegiance to warn the King of a plot **Alexander, Duke of Albany,*** was hatching against him; perhaps Alexander had expected in reward the return of the Priory to his cousin John, but the King did not oblige. The chapel was partially erected when John Home went to the new Pope, Innocent VIII, in 1484, on the understanding that he would arrange for the erection of additional prebends. He misused his royal letters of revocation and instead achieved the suppression of the collegiate church at Coldingham, meaning all the revenues of the Priory now came to the Home family. Parliament demanded that the Pope overturn his decision, and in 1486 it was agreed by the Pope to return to the compromise agreement of 1473 with the continuation of the collegiate plan and the suppression of the Priory. James's next step was to remove the Homes altogether; in 1488 he set up a parliamentary enquiry which found it a treasonable offence to attempt to suppress the collegiate church of Coldingham. The Home family was incensed at royal interference in a matter which they considered to be their personal family inheritance. The dispute alienated the Homes and their allies the Hepburns to the point that they were foremost among the rebels who stood against the King in 1488. Matters were somewhat resolved after James's death in 1488; the collegiate church was abolished, the Priory reinstated, and John Home remained as Prior until at least 1500.

Not much remains of the original Priory; it suffered in the 1540s from English attack, especially in 1544, when it was stormed by the English and converted into a garrison for Irish troops. Garrisoned by the Scots the following year, it was retaken by the English and in 1549 a band of Spanish mercenaries under the command of Julian Romero, quartered in the village of Coldingham, were slaughtered by the Scots, who took them unawares. The remains of the Priory are incorporated into the church. The monastic choir, dating from the later twelfth century, still remains, and there is evidence of the monastic buildings of the Priory to the south of the choir.

Collegiate Churches: GEMINI: Colleges were communities of clerics (not monks), called chaplains, canons or prebendaries, under the control of a provost or dean, similar to the structure of a cathedral staff, but funded by their founder or benefactor rather than from a specific religious order. Their duties included saying prayers for their benefactor, in perpetuity: votive masses which would lessen the time spent by the donor in Purgatory. Cheaper to found than a monastery, the smallest Scottish collegiate chapels, such as Maybole, had as few as three priests; the largest, such as **James IV**'s* **chapel royal** in Stirling Castle, under the Bishop of Galloway, had as many as twenty-eight priests and a dozen or more singing clerks or choristers. Depending on the resources of the founder, as long as there was a large enough endowment to say prayers for all time, the size of the structure could be as grand or as modest as funds would allow. A small chapel for the collegiate services could be added to the parish church, or the church itself could be wholly rebuilt. The collegiate aisle at Restalrig dates from the period of **James III**,* a hexagon of two storeys, similar in design to a polygonal chapterhouse. Many of the buildings survived the Reformation; extant collegiate chapels of note are at **Roslin**, and the truncated remains of **Trinity Chapel** in **Edinburgh.** Attached to many collegiate churches and cathedrals of Scotland were 'Sang Schools' (choir schools), expressing a revived interest in church music.

Colpito*!:** LIONS, 11: 'A hit!' Or, 'A goal!' A genuine term in the Florentine game of football, ***Calcio.

COLQUHOUN, Sir John, of Luss: GEMINI: (d. 1479) The surname comes from lands in the western lowlands of Scotland first held in the thirteenth century by an Unfridus de Kilpatrick. By 1259 there was a Robert de Colquhoun in Dumbarton, a rock fortress on the River Clyde in the same area. A hundred years later, Sir Robert de Colquhoun married the heiress of Humphrey de Luss, on the western shore of Loch Lomond, and the future lords of Colquhoun and Luss had a seat at Rossdhu Castle, on a promontory on the loch, as well as at Dumbarton and at Dunglass, two miles upriver.

In 1440, an early Sir John Colquhoun of Luss was killed in an affray with Islesmen near Inchmurrin, Loch Lomond, the seat of the Lennox family. The next Sir John, who was to be a loyal adherent of **James III**,* increased his lands after 1455 by marrying Elizabeth **Dunbar**, the daughter of James Dunbar, Earl of Moray, and the widow of Archibald **Douglas**, Earl of Moray, brother of Earl William Douglas, killed in 1452 by King James II.* He was supported by the future Lords **Darnley** and **Avandale.** By this means Sir John held Luss, Colquhoun, Dumbarton and part of Sauchie in Stirlingshire.

In 1464, Sir John became the Household Controller of the young King James III, and in 1466 was witness, with Colin Campbell, **Earl of Argyll**, and **Archibald Whitelaw**, to bonds concerning the King's tutelage, involving Robert, Lord **Fleming**, and Robert, Lord **Boyd.*** After the downfall of the Boyds, Sir John became lessee of the island of Arran. By 1471, Sir John was sheriff of Dumbarton, as he was Keeper for a time, of Dumbarton Castle, and also customar of Dumbarton. In 1474 he was one of the group, which included **Sir James Shaw of Sauchie** and Bishop **Thomas Spens**, appointed to arrange a marriage between the child prince James and **Cecilia**, daughter of King **Edward IV*** of England.

By 1477, Sir John Colquhoun was still one of the King's familiars (now, formally, Usher of the King's Chamber Door), and seemed to be acting for the King much as he had over ten years before, when he was Controller of the Royal Household, although on a more personal basis. As well as other duties, an Usher might receive rents and collect money and pass over funds to the King, and keep an eye on his outlays and borrowings, as well as carry letters and bring people he wanted to see.

Colquhoun had a house and, no doubt, trading concerns in Berwick-upon-Tweed,* where his neighbours included **Thomas Yare, Walter Bertram, William Scheves**, Robert Inglis and Lauder of the Bass. By this time, with sea outlets at both Dumbarton and Berwick, he possessed at least one merchant ship – the *Star of Bethelehem* – which was also perhaps used for other purposes: in 1475, Edward of England had to make restitution for a vessel of Colquhoun's captured by Lord Grey. The King was also trading through his own ships, and Dumbarton was a lively centre for the building and outfitting of vessels.

The end of Sir John's life came unexpectedly in 1479 when the King's brother, **Alexander, Duke of Albany**,* garrisoned his castle of Dunbar against the King, whose attempts to maintain peace with England were being put under threat by Albany and his friends. When the King sent a force under his kinsman, Andrew Stewart, Lord Avandale, to lie before the castle, apparently in the hope of a peaceful resolution, Albany had his guns fire on Avandale's camp, killing both Sir John Colquhoun of Luss and Sir William Wallace of Craigie, Ayrshire, very likely by accident. Paradoxically, it had been Wallace's information, it was said, which contributed to the great anti-English poem about the historical hero William Wallace, ***The Wallace.***

The death of Sir John left his widow and son to battle furiously through the courts for a variety of rights, during which Humphrey disputed with both Robert, Lord Fleming, and his grandson. The Berwick house was lost to the English, and the family's property in south **Leith** was rented to Walter Haliburton, but Humphrey kept the tenement on the north side of the Canongate, and continued to trade. His formidable mother died by 1488, and Humphrey himself had died by 1494, leaving four sons and a daughter. There is no trace of Colquhoun participation in the events in 1482 which saw the King taken captive to Edinburgh Castle, and there were no Colquhouns in the castle garrison captained by Darnley. A posthumous debt owed Sir John and paid instead to **Thomas Cochrane**, one of the victims of **Lauder Bridge**, was thought to indicate that Cochrane had usurped Sir John's position at Court, but was more likely to represent a trading commitment.

It was different, however, in 1489, a year after the young **James IV*** had taken the throne, when eight Colquhouns joined the rising against his mentors, and held out in Dumbarton Castle under Matthew Stewart, the son of the same Darnley, now the **Earl of Lennox.** Their complaints eventually prevailed, and the Parliament they were demanding was called, with no punishment meted to those who had taken part in the rebellion.

As a consequence of their family connections, if nothing else, the Colquhouns of Luss were bound to exert influence on the monarchy. Because Sir John's wife was a niece of the Earl of March, she was associated with all the great **Sinclair** family into which that Earl had married. Her sister Janet Dunbar had married the eldest son of Chancellor William Crichton, and hence Humphrey Colquhoun was first cousin to **William, Third Lord Crichton**, the father of **Princess Margaret**'s child. A brother, Robert Colquhoun, was Bishop of Argyll, and Sir John and his son held property in Fife as tenants of Colin Campbell, Earl of Argyll. Humphrey's daughter Isabella was to marry the son of Sir Alexander Cunningham of Polmaise, with whom **Anselm Sersanders** was assiduously doing business in 1494.

What value the Colquhouns placed on the monarchy must be deduced from their actions. A more decorative picture of government is presented in 'The Buke of the Howlat'* written by **Richard Holland**, secretary to Archibald Douglas, Earl of Moray, and dedicated to Archibald's wife Elizabeth, later Lady of Luss. Three years afterwards, Holland's patrons the **Black Douglases** lost their power, Archibald and his brother Hugh were killed, and the **Ninth Earl of Douglas** was forfeited. As a eulogy of the Douglases, the poem must have become a millstone to its dedicatee and her second spouse. (D. D.)

COLVILLE, Sir Robert: GEMINI: (d. by 1489). Seneschal to **Margaret of Denmark**, Queen of **James III.*** The Colvilles of Ochiltree in Ayrshire were hereditary royal stewards or seneschals, controlling the formal administration of the royal household, as the original immigrant Stewarts did for their kings. The Colvilles were in fact Normans, emanating from Coleville, between Caen and Bayeux. The Colvilles also supported **Newbattle** Abbey, as did many Scots of Norman origin.

In Scotland, they flourished. Sir Robert Colville (d. by 1466) was steward to King James II,* personally trading by sea in 1446 when he and colleagues from Ayrshire were captured and then released by a Bremen ship from the **Hanseatic League**. By 1451, Sir Robert was married to Christina Crichton of Sanquhar, who later went on to marry Alexander, the son and heir of Thomas, Lord Erskine. Alexander Erskine subsequently went to law to claim a share in the **barony** and bailery of Ochiltree.

The Colvilles were opponents of the **Black Douglases**, and in 1449, a Douglas follower, Sir James Auchinleck, was killed by a Richard Colville, who himself was later slain by William, Eighth **Earl of Douglas.** The situation was eventually improved, despite further litigation, by the marriage of a Colville daughter to a William Auchinleck of Bellsbank, which led to an even more productive union between their son James Auchinleck and Egidia, daughter of **Sir John Ross of Hawkhead.**

Queen Margaret's steward, also called Sir Robert Colville of Ochiltree, was married to Margaret Logan (*fl.* 1483), who was possibly from the family of Logan of Restalrig, distant cousins of the King, and highly placed in **Edinburgh** and **Leith.** By other family marriages, Colville was connected to most of the families loyal to the Queen in Stirling, Renfrewshire and **Linlithgow**, and would work closely with the Keeper of Stirling Castle, **Sir James Shaw of Sauchie**, and the Stirling lawyer **Malcolm McClery**, its Constable. As well as inheriting substantial Ayrshire lands, he kept the family's rich Tweed fishing at Oxnam.

The Colvilles were not named in the events that led up to or followed **Lauder Bridge** in 1482, but the following year, after **Alexander, Duke of Albany**,* had left Scotland, the King, 'at the special request of Queen Margaret', gave the land of Hilton, Clackmannan, for singular favour to Sir Robert Colville, seneschal of the Queen, and his wife Margaret Logan, for faithful service to the King, the Queen and their son.

The gift may have been for general loyalty. It might also refer to some part played by the family at the castle of Crichton in 1482 when, in the diplomatic resistance to the King's will, the building 'was stuffed against him', an act for which the garrison was subsequently summoned individually to answer. Since there is no mention of fighting, it would appear that the King was simply denied entrance to the castle, either to use as a base or as a source of manpower and weapons with which to prosecute the English war. **William, Lord Crichton** (**Princess Margaret**'s lover) was not in the castle, but his two brothers were, and five other Crichtons, as well as two men named Logan and another whose connections form a link with Sir Robert Colville, son of a Crichton. The possibility at least exists that as at Edinburgh, the Queen was privy to a policy which had more to do with checking the King's impetuous advance than any fondness for Albany. It was said that, although forfeited and banished for three years, Lord Crichton was later to meet the King in Inverness.

The Queen died in 1486, and two years later her young son was released by Sir James Shaw of Sauchie to take the part of the faction against his own father. The bond implied in the gift of Clackmannan land must still have been valid, however. When the reign of James III came to its sudden end in 1488, one of the new King's first acts was to appoint Sir Robert Colville as his Director of Chancery for the remaining months of Colville's life, and to give him the house and properties in the Cowgate, Edinburgh, that had once belonged to Albany's steward **Sir James Liddell** of Halkelston and, after him, to John Ramsay.

By Margaret Logan, Sir Robert had several children. His son, Sir William Colville of Ochiltree, became seneschal in his turn, and by 1509 had died serving **James IV**.* William's sister Margaret married Sir John **Semple** of Lochwinnoch and Renfrew Castle, whose second wife, after 1500, was to be Dame Margaret Crichton. Sir John Semple's son by his first (Colville) wife would marry an **Arnot** by 1523, while his other son, Gabriel, was the ancestor of the Semples of Cathcart.

Robert Colville of the next generation held both Ochiltree and rights in **Sinclair**'s Ravenscraig, as well as Oxnam and Hilton. In time he also claimed his share in those parts of Cleish which once belonged to Elizabeth Shaw and Christina **Preston.** The Tweedside possessions may explain why, out of proximity rather than friendship, Colville of Ochiltree appears on the same charter as Alexander Jardine of Applegarth, whose father attacked **Anselm Adorne**.* The family loyalty extended through to King James V,* to whom James Colville of Ochiltree acted as Director of Chancery and Keeper of the Great Seal until discharged in 1526. (D. D.)

Come dance with me in Ireland: KINGS, I, Gambit: A fragment of fourteenth-century verse:

Ich am of Irlaunde,
ant of the holy londe
of irlande.
Gode sire, pray ich þe,
for of saynte charite,
come ant daunce wyt me
In irlaunde.

Commynes, Philippe de: LIONS, 37: (*c.* 1445–1511) French statesman and historian, famous for his *Mémoires* (1524). He served Burgundy from 1463, but after nine years turned his allegiance to follow **Louis XI**,* becoming one of the King's most trusted advisors. Louis made him his Chamberlain and Commynes served him as a political advisor. After Louis's death in 1483, Commynes did not fare as well, enduring physical and economic hardship, but after several years was returned to a degree of favour under Charles VIII (1470–1498), accompanying the King on his Italian expedition (1494), where he met the Italian statesman and writer Machiavelli (1469–1527).

Compass: LIONS, 29: In use from the thirteenth/fourteenth centuries, the magnetic compass was sometimes unreliable in the north, where local magnetic anomalies caused seamen to believe that their compasses were bewitched. Housed in a lead-covered binnacle, the compass was employed with the lead-line to sail a direct course across moderate open spaces such as the Bay of Biscay, when sailing from Finisterre to Bristol and the English Channel. It made possible other long journeys, so that a ship could travel from north-west Ireland in a north-north-westerly direction for seven hundred miles. An improved compass with a thirty-two-point 'rose of the winds' had been in use in the Mediterranean from the fourteenth century, but northern navigators at first preferred to keep the suspended iron needle, magnetised when required by rubbing with a lodestone. The permanently magnetised needle with its direction card followed by the second half of the fifteenth century.

Another aid to navigation was the hour-glass, to time the length of the tacks. It was said to be the bad sea-keeping of the Lancastrian adherents of Henry VI (King of England 1422–1461, 1470–1471) that persuaded the merchants to support his rival of York. (D. D.)

Concessum: GEMINI, 20: 'Agreed'.

Confiteor: GEMINI, 53: 'I admit it all'.

Consanguinity and dispensations: SCALES, 40: It was of fundamental importance that not only was marriage one of the sacraments of the Church, it was also a legally binding contract. A public declaration meant that neither party could claim that the union did not exist, to the detriment of the spouse or potential heirs, and it also ensured (by the reading of the banns) that both parties were free to marry, and that there were no impediments to the marriage. In Scotland, however, the localised custom of 'handfasting', marriage by habit and betrothal, was still considered an acceptable form of marriage, requiring no clergy. The church thus had to deal both with the legitimation of children born before marriage, or of children considered to have been legitimate and then found to be the product of an invalid relationship. Such relationships were superseded by Church laws enacted by James II,* and subsequent children from such relationships were bastardised.

In addition to these problems, the greatest challenge the Church faced in terms of marriages was the issue of consanguinity. Leviticus 18: 16–18 was the guideline for the medieval Church and, according to the Lateran Council of 1215, marriages between people who were related up to and including the fourth degree were not allowed unless papal dispensation had been granted. This covered relations who were the grandchildren of first cousins (by blood or by marriage) and those related by the sacraments of baptism and confirmation (godfather and goddaughter). Given the complications of the laws, and the relative size of the Scottish nobility, one Archbishop of St Andrews complained to the Pope that it was impossible for anyone of any social standing in Scotland to marry at all. However, there were nearly always dispensations to be had from Rome, for marriage and its dissolution. Church rules could thus be used to negate or adjust contracts.

The precision of the law meant that marriages could be dissolved more easily than one would imagine: impediments such as interrelationships between families could be concealed at the time of the marriage, meaning papal dispensation could justifiably be given for divorce and the relationship could be annulled. The legitimacy of marriage and offspring was of paramount importance when it came to inheritance; without legitimation, lands and estates would fall back to the Crown. Marriage alliances bound families together in feudal Scotland and were indicative of a political allegiance, not a personal one. A 'love-match' was not the intention; marriage was a legal contract between individuals and families, allying their property and inheritance rights, formalised or dissolved by the Church as convenience and dispensations would allow.

Conservator of Scots Privileges: See under individual Conservators: **Anselm Adorne,*** **Thomas Swift, Andrew Wodman** and **Wolfaert van Borselen.**

Considerably more than doth the nightingale: KINGS, I, 3: The General Prologue to *The Canterbury Tales* by Geoffrey Chaucer (*c.* 1343–1400) says of the squire:

> He could songes make and well endite,
> Joust and eek dance, and well portray and write.
> So hot he loved that by night at all
> He sleep no more than doth a nightingale.

During the mating season the nightingale was believed to sing all through the night and not to sleep at all.

CONTARINI, Ambrogio: RONDO: (*c.* 1429–1496) Born in Venice, a less than lucky traveller, Contarini was the Venetian ambassador to **Uzum Hasan**,* sent to encourage him to wage war on the Turk, who spent nearly four years on his mission to the East. He left a detailed account of his journey from Venice, to Poland and then on to Lower Russia. He very soon found himself out of step with the Russians, as he had no stomach for strong drink and no patience with drinkers. He also had no fond feeling for the Tartars, who (he stated) stank so badly of horseflesh that he could not stand next to them. To smooth their passage to Caffa, his interpreter persuaded the Tartars that he was Genoese, not Venetian.

Contarini described his welcome from the Tartars:

> Travelling with my guide, we lodged, in the evening, in the open air among some Tartar carts with their skin covering. Many of the Tartars immediately surrounded us and wished to know who we were: on hearing from our guide that I was a Genoese, they presented me with sour milk.

Even a well-meaning gesture is portrayed by Contarini as a slight. His terror of being discovered by the Genoese meant he spent nearly all his time in Caffa hiding indoors. He then travelled via Georgia, where he found the people as mad as the Mingrelians, much of the food inedible and the guides inordinately expensive. He was again contemptuous of the drunken habits of his hosts. Avoiding 'thieving Turcomans', he finally arrived at Tabriz, in Armenia, the land of Uzum Hasan, only to find that after his arduous journey, he had missed Uzum, who was on his way north to quash his rebellious son at Shiraz. Contarini received an audience with one of his sons instead, but did not see the fabled riches that his fellow Venetian ambassador **Josaphat Barbaro** mentioned. Contarini accompanied a Cadi Lasker to meet with Uzum at Shiraz, but was forced to stop for two weeks because of illness. Arriving at the town of Spaan, he met up with Barbaro. His description of Persia for once is favourable; the people are 'well behaved and of gentle manners . . . While in Persia we did not suffer a single outrage'. While at Uzum Hasan's Court,

Contarini was to meet the ubiquitous **Ludovico de Severi da Bologna**,* who was also visiting the court in 1475. Uzum Hasan (tall and thin with a slight Tartar countenance, as Contarini described him) promised that he would make war on the Ottoman Turks, and the ambassador was treated to a full display of the Tartar soldiery, comprising thousand upon thousand of foot and horse. (Barbaro doubted that this display of force would ever be put to Venetian ends.) Contarini was told to leave Uzum's Court, but Barbaro was invited to stay on.

On Contarini's return journey to Caffa, he learned that it had fallen to the Turk and was thus forced on a tortuous journey that eventually ended when he and Marco Rosso (**Ivan III**'s envoy to Persia) arrived in Moscow, deep in debt. He was obliged to stay in Moscow until his priest, Stephano, sent to Venice from Moscow, returned with enough money to repay the moneylenders he was obliged to borrow from. Having lost patience utterly with his troublesome and ever-complaining companion, Marco Rosso offloaded Contarini onto **Rudolfo Fioravanti**, but his stay there was short, as he was soon ordered 'in the Duke's name, to leave this house' and new lodgings were found for him and his servants. It would seem that everyone by this stage wanted Contarini to go home: Grand Duke Ivan even offered to pay the debts on Contarini's behalf. Eventually a banquet was held to celebrate his departure, at which, once again, the ambassador's inability to stomach strong drink became an issue. Ludovico da Bologna, also in Moscow at this time, declined to leave with him. Contarini arrived home in Venice in April 1477. Because of the deaths of Uzum Hasan and **Mehmet II*** he was the last Venetian ambassador to be sent to Uzum Hasan. (See also **Ca' d'Oro**.)

Contra Nando* [*navigando*] *Incrementum: GEMINI, 9: 'Against the stream we multiply' – the motto in 1153 of the Scottish town of Peebles, whose coat of arms (gules, three salmon proper) denoted a thriving salmon fishery on the River Tweed. The motto implied that for every fish that struggled upstream to spawn, two would come back. Or that faith, perseverance and obstinacy could sometimes pay off. (D. D.)

Copernicus: RONDO, 9: (1473–1543) Nicholas Copernicus, the renowned astronomer and mathematician who published his heliocentric theory of the universe in 1543. His father, Mikołaj Kopernik, a Germanised Slav originally from a settlement called Koperniki in Silesia, was a burger of Cracow, and a copper broker for Slovakian copper. He visited **Danzig** on business in 1454, and four years later came to live in nearby **Thorn**. He married Barbara Watzenrode, and their fourth son, Mikołaj (or Nicholas), was born in the town in 1473 (in the house described in the novel). He was brought up mostly by his maternal uncle, the Prince Bishop of Ermeland, and studied mathematics, optics and perspectives at the University of Cracow, then canon law at Bologna and Ferrara, and medicine at Padua. He spent most of his life as a canon of the

Warmian Chapter at Frauenberg, and as a secular canon he served as bailiff, military governor, tax collector, vicar general, judge, physician and reformer of the coinage. Perhaps his most famous achievement as an astronomer came in 1530 when he proved the sun to be at the centre of the universe; his theory was published in the treatise *De revolutionibus orbuim coelestium* ('On the Revolutions of the Celestial Spheres') in 1543, just before he died.

Coquet seals: LIONS, 20: Appended to the stamped customs receipt issued by officials confirming that all goods carried by a ship had been entered on the bill of lading, and that duty had been paid. Seals in general were supposed to authenticate parcels or letters, but could be forged or exchanged. Experts used horses' urine to detach them, and fixed them elsewhere with hot wax. Missives with truly grand seals were treated with the reverence due to their senders: when honoured with a royal letter, a man showed his respect to the courier by removing his hat before accepting and reading it. If he was not wearing a hat, it was enough for him to rise to his feet. (D. D.)

Corbie and doo on the ane twig: KINGS, IV, 2: 'Crow and dove on the same twig'; Scots expression similar to 'chalk and cheese'.

Corvinus, Mathias: See **Mathias Corvinus**.

Coulanges: LIONS: 1: A village in the valley of the River Cisse, a few miles to the south-west of Blois and close to the ruins of the thirteenth-century abbey of **La Guiche** and to Chouzy, which stands at the confluence of the Cisse and the River Loire. Perhaps a rather dull place, it became the butt of a joke: to go to Coulanges meant to vanish off the face of the earth. Speaking of fruit, you could say: 'The apricots ripened badly this year: they've gone to Coulanges'. The patron saint is St Denis, to whom people come to pray against fear. (D. D.)

Coup . . . de foudre: GEMINI, 37: A *coup* means 'a triumph'; when *de foudre* is added the phrase as a whole means 'a thunderbolt'.

Courtibaut: LIONS, 9: French patois for 'little man', and hence appropriate for a child (from *court* meaning 'short').

Craigmillar Castle: GEMINI, 18: The castle was built on the outskirts of **Edinburgh** in the early fifteenth century by the **Preston** family, Lairds of Craigmillar. The inner curtain wall and the tower are fifteenth century, and its strong defences made the castle an ideal retreat for royalty and the Court.

The L-shaped tower house stood within a stout curtain wall with corner towers, and contained a third-floor hall over two lower storeys, with side chambers and a loft overhead. The view from its roof, as it stood on its rocky eminence, made it an important watchtower. Built as it was on the edge of a steep drop, access could be permitted only if a wooden bridge were placed over the chasm; the drop was filled in during the sixteenth century when a second external curtain wall protected the castle. The entrance above both the inner wall and doorway of the tower display the Preston coat of arms: three unicorns.* The great hall on the first floor of the tower, with its eleven-foot fireplace, has been restored, and access is still possible to the roof.

CRAWFORD, Archibald: UNICORN: (b. before 1418–1483) Archibald Crawford, Abbot of **Holyrood**, was the son of Sir William Crawford, a West Lothian landowner, and was probably the brother of William Crawford of **Berecrofts.** The family home was Haining (later Almond) Castle, a keep near to Polmont, newly built by the Crawfords in the reign of King **James III**,* but lost by the next century to the Livingstone family. Archibald was born before 1418, and by 1433 was attending the University of St Andrews, where his fellow students included the future Bishop of Aberdeen **Thomas Spens**, Henry Parkle, whose family would provide a future Keeper of the Palace of **Linlithgow**, and William Semple of Renfrewshire.

By 1446, Archibald was procurator to James, Abbot-elect of Holyrood. In 1450, now Abbot himself, Crawford travelled to England as a Commissioner to broker an English truce, and again in 1474 to arrange for a marriage between the Princess **Cecilia** and the son of King James. Soon afterwards he was appointed Lord Treasurer of Scotland, a post he held until his death in 1483. While at Holyrood, he was responsible for extensive building in the Abbey church, adding buttresses to the walls of the north and south aisles, and possibly the ornate doorway to the north aisle. His personal arms – a fesse ermine with a star of five points in chief, plus an abbot's mitre on a pastoral staff – appears more than thirty times in the church's interior carvings.

Archibald had at least two brothers: Patrick Crawford of the Canongate, and William Crawford, presumably the same man who possessed property in the Canongate and in Berecrofts, West Lothian. There was also at least one nephew, a brother's son called Robert (or sometimes Robin) Crawford, who in 1473 was given a livery collar of the King's to recompense him for his own, valued at fifteen pounds eight shillings and fourpence, which had been handed by the King, in a burst of generosity, to a visiting envoy of his wife's father, King **Christian I** of Denmark. The following year, the Prior of the Abbey was asked by the King to disemburse a shilling to 'the meikle long man that had the white doublet' who was staying with Robin Crawford. This Robin Crawford (not Robert of Berecrofts) had a son, Archibald Crawford of Haining, and was probably also the father of one Gelis (Egidia) Crawford.

Holyrood Abbey, like other stone-built religious houses, appeared to act from time to time as a royal bank and place of deposit, although at least some of the Abbey's treasure was held for safety within **Edinburgh**'s walls in the house of Abbot Archibald's chaplain, Sir Walter **Swift.** A life which encompassed the religious duties of the abbacy, the control of the Abbey's important regalities, the building activities inside and outside the cloisters, the maintenance of a royal residence and the relatively new office of Treasurer to the kingdom, in addition to fulfilling a mitred Abbot's commitments to Parliament and its working committees, would seem to indicate that Archibald Crawford was a man of exceptional vigour in body and mind. (D. D.)

Crawford, Fifth Earl of: See **Lindsay, David.**

CRAWFORD Family: UNICORN: The surname dates back to the twelfth century, and was originally simply 'of Crawford', a place in Lanarkshire, in the western Lowlands of Scotland. From the earliest times, the family has been associated with the surname of **Fleming**, and seems to have arrived in Scotland as part of the influx of settlers from Flanders in the train of Maud de Senlis, the Flemish Queen of David I, King of Scotland 1124–1153. The first Crawford may have been John, the stepson of Sheriff Baldwin of Biggar, whose own family may have come from near Ghent.

The families from Crawford proliferated and spread to the east, where they appear in the fifteenth century as merchants. One of the best known was Andrew Crawford, who in the 1450s procured a camel for King James II.* Among his other services to the Crown, he entertained sixty Frenchmen for one day in his **Edinburgh** house, and put up a heraldic envoy from Austria for eleven weeks. Towards the end of the reign, an Englishman called William Bertram, with nine families, was sent to live with him for a week 'drinking Rhenish wine to the success of an unspecified enterprise', according to a contemporary document.

Andrew's sons were probably Alexander Crawford, Clerk of the King's Chapel, who died by 1490, and David, burgess of Edinburgh and one of **Thomas Yare**'s team of fish-pricers. Andrew's 'son' Richard, mentioned in the *House of Niccolò* novels, is fictitious, although Richard Crawford was a name historically connected with **Linlithgow**, and the burgess Richard Crawford who lived there until the late 1490s was probably a nephew of Robert Crawford of **Berecrofts**. An Arthur Crawford, living in Linlithgow in 1541, was a sub-prior of **Newbattle** Abbey, which employed several officers named Crawford over the years, having Abbey lands of their own in the west. In the mid-sixteenth century one John Crawford was the Abbey's bailie for the Monklands in Lanarkshire, and also a bailie of Crawfordmuir.

The Crawford family, owning land in many areas, also established, by chance, links which led to an association with **Princess Mary** and the **Boyd** family. As far back as 1423, the Ayrshire lands of Trarynzeane had been owned by a Crawford. Later, part or all of the lordship seems to have fallen to Euphemia Graham, Countess of Douglas, whose second husband **James, Lord Hamilton**, was to divorce her in order to marry the King's sister Mary. This, as it turned out, was Euphemia's second misfortune, as her share of Trarynzeane had already been prised from her and given, in 1467, to the same Princess Mary and her first husband Thomas Boyd. By the following year, the Countess Euphemia appeared to be dead. Part of the lordship resigned by Euphemia was by 1476 in the hands of George Campbell, the sheriff of Ayr, but actually found its way back to the Crawfords through a fortuitous marriage. In 1512, William Crawford of Lefnoriis and de Beax was able to give his heir part of the lands of Trarynzeane.

Crawfords, as well as being landowners, often held office as bailies or customs officers. In 1492/1493 another Alexander Crawford was deputy to Thomas Yare, customar. In the 1460s, William de Crawford and John Muir were responsible for the customs of Linlithgow, and their names appear again in 1480. The surnames were still linked forty years later, when Alexander Muir had followed John Moffat, who was Conservator of the **Staple** at Bergen-ap-Zoom, and Jasper Crawford was proposed as his successor. By 1600 a Patrick and a James Crawford were serving the Staple at Veere, which had already, of course, sent a stream of conservators to Scotland bearing the name of **van Borselen.**

The name Rankin Crawford appears first in Scottish records in 1446, and may well represent, with its Flemish 'kin', a shortened Flemish forename. It occurs also in 1454, in a West Lothian petition from the people of Manuel, and Rankin de Crawford, their nobleman and temporal lord. A Robert Crawford (doubtless of Haining) still held Manuel in 1477. There is a Rankin Crawford involved with a court case in 1493, and it is not altogether surprising to find a Rankin Muir in a Wigton charter of 1482. One greets, however, with furtive delight the discovery that a John Muir, associated with a Berecrofts Canongate property, handed it down to another Muir called Egidia.

The Crawfords were also men of arms. Sir William Crawford was killed at the battle of Crevant in 1423, and Guille Craffort served with the French King's men-at-arms in 1448, at a time when the corps also included a Ramsay, a Haliburton and a Spens. Crawfords named James, John, David, William and Thomas served through the succeeding decades, including the period when **David Simpson** and **Andrew Wodman** were in the French guard of Scottish Archers.* Both David and William Crawford fought in the Italian wars of 1494. The family also sent its sons to St Andrews University, where Archibald, John and Patrick Crawford studied between 1430 and 1476.

The family branches which appear most often in the novels are those of Robin Crawford (see Berecrofts) and **Archibald Crawford.** The earldom of Crawford was a title held by the **Lindsay** family, not the Crawfords.

On a personal note, Alastair M. Dunnett was descended, on his West Highland side, from a Crawford. (D. D.)

Crichton, William, Third Lord: GEMINI: See **Margaret, Princess.**

Crim Tartars: See **Mengli-Girey.**

Crions, chantons . . . Bien vienne: RONDO, 41: Two lines from a song offered to the bride following the marriage in Bruges* in 1468 of **Charles, Duke of Burgundy*** and his Duchess, **Margaret of York.** The song is translated elsewhere in full: see *Bien vienne la belle bergére.**

Croatia: RONDO: See **Mathias Corvinus.**

Crowing like the cocks of Cramond: KINGS, I, 3: A reference to the Scots fairy tale of the Gyre-Carling, a witch that lived off the flesh of Christians. Besieged by the elfs and the King of Faery she changed into a sow, fled Scotland via the Greek Sea, became Queen of the Jews and married Mahoun. Not everyone was happy to see her leave:

> Sensyne [since then] the cokkis of Crawmound crew nevir a day,
> For dule [sorrow] of that devillisch deme [dame] wes with Mahoun mareit [married],
> And the hennis [hens] of Hadingtoun sensyne wald nocht lay,
> For this wild wilroun [wild witch] wich [who] thame widlit sa and wareit [troubled and worried].

Culdees: LIONS, 25: See **Iceland.**

Culter: LC: Of the two areas called Culter in Scotland, both have a similar early history, and both are said to be connected with the Knights Templar, the religious order which was suppressed in Scotland in 1312 when their estates were taken over by the Order of the Knights Hospitaller of St John.*

Culter in Lanarkshire is a country area bounded on one side by the Culter water, a tributary of the River Clyde, and on another by the high hills of Culter Fells. It is just under three miles south of the small town of Biggar, home of the **Flemings** of Boghall Castle, and Crawford lies further off to the west and south. At Wolfclyde there is a Flemish motte-hill, and there is the trace of a Roman road at Causewayend.

There has been a church (now rebuilt) on the eastern bank of the Culter burn since the time of William the Lyon, King of Scotland 1165–1214, and its earliest charters carry the Norman/Flemish names of Hugh, Walter and Radulphus. The connection with the Templars rests on a charter of about 1221, granted by Walter Bisset, in which the parson Richard of Culter promised Abbot Herbert and the chapter of **Kelso** to ensure that the proper liberties of their church of Culter would not be lost because of a building he, Richard, had erected for the Templars in the vicinity. Today, at Chapelhill on the other side of the water, there are traces of a building which might belong to a chapel, and there is a site not far away now called 'Temple'. Recent opinion, however, considers that the Kelso charter is more likely to refer to the well-known Templar site at Maryculter, Aberdeen, which is sometimes called simply Culter.

More recent records for the church at Culter show that one of its eminent rectors was George Schoriswood, chaplain to King James II* and Chancellor of Scotland from 1456 to 1460. Also, between 1482 and 1484 William Halkerston was presented to the benefice by Elizabeth, Countess of Ross, daughter of James, Lord Livingstone. In 1496, it was held by one Thomas Baillie.

The land of Culter was owned in the thirteenth century by 'Alexander of Culter', presumably an incomer who simply took his name from the place. From the time of David II (King of Scotland 1329–1371), Culter was divided between several lords, some of them bearing the Norman names of Bisset and Menzies. In 1369, Sir Archibald Douglas held half the barony; and part was held by William, **Earl of Douglas**, in 1449. In 1431, half was held by David Menzies, and in 1458 by James, first Lord Livingston, the father of Elizabeth, Countess of Ross, who obtained the advowson (the right to patronage or presentation of a benefice) of the church. The record then jumps to 1479, when two parts of the barony were in the King's gift, and the remaining third belonged to Marion, the wife of James Tweedy. John Brown of Culter appears at an inquest of gentlemen of the shire in 1492. By then, Nesbit and Culter Mains had each become a separate tenure.

The connection made in the novels between Culter and a family named Crawford is fictitious. It is not known what property, if any, the Crawfords of **Berecrofts** had in the west, but many of those who first adopted the place as their surname seem to have retained some ancestral links with that part of Scotland. The coat of arms of the fictitious Crawfords was a play on the name of culter, meaning the blade of a ploughshare. The place-name is thought to have come from the Welsh *culdir*, signifying a narrow stretch of land. If, on the other hand, the name was transplanted from the north-east, it is more likely to derive from the Gaelic *cul-tir*, the lying-back land.

Maryculter in north-east Scotland takes its name from a chapelry in the lands of Culter dedicated to St Mary, and dependent on the church of St Peter Culter, now Peterculter, a few miles to the south and west of Aberdeen. If the Culter charter refers to this district, then Maryculter was granted to the Knights Templar by Walter Bisset, lord of Aboyne before 1239, while reserving the rights of the monks of Kelso. (By marrying in 1233 the sister of Alan of Galloway, Walter had inherited a great deal of Irish and Scots land.) In 1312 Maryculter was transferred to the Order of St John. Henry Livingstone was Preceptor of the Order of St John from 1449 to 1462, which explains the Livingstone interest in both regions. By 1547 the lands of Maryculter were held in **regality** by Sir James Sandilands,* Lord St John and Preceptor of **Torphichen.**

The Menzies family acquired the estate of Maryculter early in the fourteenth century. The area is also connected with the Comyns (from Comines, by Lille), who were benefactors of Kelso and ambitious for power in Scotland, one of them becoming Earl of Buchan by marriage. Robert Menzies and Walter Bisset were part of the group who opposed them before 1242. Although the family failed in its objectives, their descendants, now Cummings, retained their interests in the northeast, where the River Dee provided rich fishing in salmon. Men of note included the future Lord Lyon, William Cumming, and his kinsmen Thomas and Alexander Cumming of Culter who, in 1480, were to owe money to **Thomas Cochrane**, who died at **Lauder Bridge.** (See also **Preston family** and **William Knollys.***) (D. D.)

Cursing: GEMINI, 8: Until the end of the sixteenth century, witch-hunts as such did not figure largely in the social scene, although witches would be invoked, in a cursory way, to explain or justify the killing of the Duke of Clarence (1449–1478), or **John of Mar** (both of whom, the chroniclers claim, consorted with witches in their efforts to oppose their brothers, **Edward IV*** and **James III*** respectively). When it came down to annoying or blasphemous behaviour, a process of correction did exist. In 1492 Sir John Crichton of Cairns escaped a summons over rents because Margaret Semple, who issued it, was under sentence of cursing. She appeared to be his mother-in-law.

There was a similar hiatus in a case in 1466 between Margaret **Preston** and Archibald Melville over a tenant-holding in **Linlithgow.** Since Margaret was at the time under process and sentence of cursing, the case could not be resolved until she had received absolution. (D. D.)

Cuthilgurdy: SCALES: A **barony** in Perthshire, Scotland, owned in the fifteenth century by the Dunbarrow family, which derived from a region to the north-east of Perth, near Forfar and just short of Cortachy. Alexander Dunbarrow held the lands of the barony in 1443, but the family resigned their rights in 1471 when Cuthilgurdy passed from John de Dunbarrow to the Provost of Perth, Andrew Charteris.

The Charteris family, in origin from Chartres in France, had first appeared in Scotland in the thirteenth century, although legend links one of its ancestors, a pirate called Thomas de Longueville, with William Wallace (*c.* 1270–1305), who made him into a friend and an ally after capturing him at sea. Robert the Bruce (1274–1329) is said to have presented him with the lands of Kinfauns on Tayside, six miles from Perth, which had power of admiralty over the Tay. Now named Charteris, the family became established as local lords in several areas, one of them being Amisfield in Dumfriesshire; and by 1478 Sir William Charteris of Kinfauns and Cagnor had married a niece of **Andrew Stewart, Lord Avandale**.

The Charteris family of Cuthilgurdy had a distinguished presence in Perth. Andrew Charteris was both Provost and sheriff in 1469; between 1465 and 1500 he was Provost of Perth fourteen times; and in 1471 and 1473 he also sat with the **Lords Auditor of Causes and Complaints.** He must have been well known to the Burgundian **Anselm Adorne**,* Baron Cortachy, who was a burgess of Perth in 1472. Andrew was followed by two nephews, John and Andrew Charteris of Cuthilgurdy. A brother, Gilbert, was eight times elected a bailie of Perth between 1480 and 1500, and bailies of the same name continued in the records until at least 1543.

Through the years, there was some friction with the family of Ruthven, who claimed the rights of hereditary sheriffs. In 1493 Andrew Charteris of Cuthilgurdy was engaged in a dispute over mills with William, Lord Ruthven, and his son, and in the next century John Charteris of Cuthilgurdy, then Provost, faced opposition in 1544 when he was proposed as sheriff in place of William, Second Lord Ruthven, who had succeeded his grandfather about 1528. It was Patrick, the eldest son of this Lord Ruthven, who was involved in 1566 in the murder of David Rizzio, the secretary of Mary Queen of Scots.* (D. D.)

King James IV gold unicorn

D

Dame Trotula of Salerno: See **Trotula, Dame, of Salerno.**

Danzig: RONDO, 1: This port, now known as Gdańsk, on the left bank of the mouth of the River **Vistula** was seized by the **Teutonic Knights** in 1308 and held by them until 1454, when it became a free city under the control of King **Casimir IV** of Poland. Its merchants continued to play an important role in the **Hanseatic League.** Amongst its medieval buildings is the Marienkirche, the church of St Mary, begun in the mid-fourteenth century (1343–1502) which housed **Hans Memling**'s *Last Judgement*, stolen by the pirate **Paúel Benecke** and never returned, despite the entreaties of **Anselm Adorne.*** There is also the fourteenth-century church of St Catherine (1326–1330).

The Teutonic Knights used Danzig as their chief emporium, building the **Ordensmuehle**, the great mill of the town which served the entire population. The knights charged poundage on all exports by sea, but after the Polish towns defeated the Order at Grunwald in 1410 merchants petitioned for the removal of the export tax. The Order stopped it occasionally, but, despite the complaints of the Danzigers in particular, the unpopular tax remained; the towns retained one-third of the tax, and the Order took the rest. This damaged trade between the Hanseatic merchants and the Order, as no Baltic ports not under Teutonic control charged poundage. During the Thirteen Years War (1454–1466), Danzig eventually broke the Knights' control. Freedom from the Teutonic Order and increased liberty to trade gave Danzig special privileges: the town was self-governing, raised its own finances and minted its own currency.

Danzig was the main port for Polish grain, which arrived at the coast from the heart of the Polish countryside via the Vistula, as did other heavy goods, such as wood, difficult, slow and expensive to transport by land. Foreign entrepreneurs would arrive in Danzig for the season on spring tides in March or April and leave in October before winter storms. In later centuries, many settled in the town, including Danes, Flemings and Scots, as in Bruges* and **Antwerp.** Foreigners came to dominate banking, credit and commercial transactions (as they had the ships, resources and the foreign contacts). Its lucrative export of grain was matched by imports; the town exported wool, flax, leather, timber and metals, and imported salt, wine, coal and fish, bringing great wealth to the developing city.

Darnley, John Stewart, Lord: GEMINI: (d. 1495) Destined to be the first Lord Darnley, John Stewart was a great-grandson of Duncan Stewart, the Eighth Earl of Lennox, and inherited land in the lordship of Annandale, in south-west Scotland, from his grandfather, Sir John Stewart of Darnley, who had married Duncan's daughter Elizabeth, and was killed in 1429 fighting against the English in France at the siege of Orléans. John's father Alan also met a violent end, being killed at **Linlithgow** in 1439 by Sir Thomas **Boyd.** (Sir Thomas, whose grandson of the same name was to marry the **Princess Mary**, was later done to death in retaliation by Alexander 'Bucktooth,' Alan Stewart's brother – an act which appeared to end the blood feud, for the sons were soon found acting together against the Douglases.)

In 1438, while still under age, John Stewart of Darnley married Margaret, eldest daughter of Alexander Montgomery, Lord of Ardrossan in Ayrshire; and went on to father ten children. He was created a lord of Parliament as Lord Darnley after the death of James II* in 1460, and about the same time began to pursue his claim to a share in the earldom of Lennox (see **Lennox inheritance**), which had become vacant. In 1465 he was appointed Keeper of Rothesay Castle on the island of Bute until the new King should become fifteen, and in 1466 inherited some of his grandfather's lands by Strathaven, in Clydesdale. When King **James III*** was twenty-five, Lord Darnley's appointment to Rothesay was reaffirmed.

By 1471, his kinsman the Chancellor, **Andrew Stewart, Lord Avandale,** possessed the life-rent of the whole of the **barony** of Lennox, while the claims of his relations by marriage, Napier and Haldane, were in temporary abeyance. In 1473, the King briefly conferred on Darnley the title of Earl of Lennox, and confirmed his lands in Renfrewshire and Ayrshire. Two years later, when the Earl of Ross was forfeited for his rebellion in the west and the north, Darnley was given a commission of lieutenancy for the sheriffdoms of Renfrew, Ayr and Wigtown, the Stewartry of Kirkcudbright, part of Clydesdale, and the islands of Arran and Bute, which had been wasted by Ross. In 1476, Darnley lost his title of Lennox again, but became Keeper of Dingwall Castle, retaken by Huntley after Ross's treason.

When, after the outbreak of war, Parliament met in the spring of 1482 to plan its defence against England, Lord Darnley was appointed Warden of the West Marches, which had Lochmaben Castle as its chief base. At least one account of the time suggests that Darnley was at **Lauder Bridge** when the King was stopped on his way to confront the larger English army under **Richard, Duke of Gloucester** and **Alexander, Duke of Albany,*** the King's brother. As Warden of the West Marches, Darnley may well have brought his force over from Annandale on learning that the English advance was confined to the south-east. Certainly, he was at the castle in **Edinburgh** at the time of the King's enforced imprisonment, with a band of sixty-six men including six Stewarts, three Cochranes, three Maxwells, two Campbells, three Douglases, one **Semple**, one Brown and one **Fleming.** And Rothesay

Herald, the officer-at-arms who served his lord and his Duke, the latter being the child heir to the throne (the future **James IV**).*

Officially, the King was being held by his three half-uncles, but Darnley's presence – and complaisance – suggests that he agreed with those who wished to avoid an armed confrontation. **Margaret of Denmark** was custodian of Edinburgh Castle, and had been for five years: there passed between the Queen and Darnley that year the large sum of over ninety-five pounds due to its Keeper. It was Queen Margaret who interviewed Albany after the English troops had retreated, and who, helped by the King's royal officials, may have made it possible for the King to emerge from confinement, as he did, and engage in a brief reconciliation with Albany. Before leaving the castle himself, Darnley was armed first with a missive from the King, addressing Darnley as cousin, and ordering him to deliver the castle to the King's dearest **eme**, his half-uncle of **Atholl.** A fortnight later another useful letter arrived, proclaiming Darnley innocent in respect of his monarch's detention, and thanking him for his secret care and protection at a time when the King feared for his life. Without access to the Privy Seal of Scotland, the letter was sealed with James's signet ring portraying a unicorn,* bearing the legend *'Tout a Une'* (GEMINI, 46).

In 1484, Darnley was appointed Keeper of Bute, continuing an association which may have brought him into regular touch with the King's son and heir, the Earl of Carrick and Duke of Rothesay. The Queen died in 1486. Thereafter, like **Sir James Shaw of Sauchie**, Darnley seemed to lose faith in the King, and, with his own son and heir, Matthew, began to cultivate the young Prince. By the start of 1488, a party, which included Matthew, the **Earl of Argyll** and Robert Blackadder, was prepared to ask English help for Prince James. When the climax came, and the King lost his life, Darnley took the earldom of Lennox (Avandale having died), and was appointed Keeper of Dumbarton Castle by the young James IV.*

The transition to the new king was, however, badly managed. The Earl of Lennox and Matthew his eldest son were among those who, in 1489, rebelled against the administration, although not the King. Returning from the north to reinforce Dumbarton, which was held by Matthew's force of well over a hundred (including seventeen Stewarts, eight Colquhouns, eleven Flemings, eight Lindsays, five Crawfords but no Campbells or Cochranes or Browns), Lennox was captured and the castle was taken, besieged by Argyll for the King. Lennox and Matthew were forfeited. They were not, however, left in the wilderness long. The forfeitures were rescinded, and soon the King was addressing them both as his 'trusty and well-beloved cousins and counsellors'. Very soon, the rival claims to the earldom had also been settled, and when he died in 1495, John Stewart, Earl of Lennox, was well positioned in the new reign.

At least four of Lennox's sons were to live and work in France. His four daughters all made excellent marriages, largely into families with contiguous lands who were also close to James III. Elizabeth married Archibald, son and heir of Colin Campbell, Earl of Argyll. Marion married Robert Crichton of Kinnoull, first Lord Crichton of Sanquhar. Janet married Ninian, Third Lord **Ross of Hawkhead**, and Elizabeth married John, son and heir of Humphrey **Colquhoun of Luss.**

John Stewart's eldest son Matthew became Second (or Tenth) Earl of Lennox after his father. Matthew's younger brother Robert (*c.* 1470–1543) took service in France and was titled seigneur d'Aubigny. (See under **Lords of Aubigny.**) Along with Archibald, Second Earl of Argyll, Matthew commanded the right wing of the Scots army at **Flodden** in 1513, where he, Argyll and most of their followers were killed. His second marriage had been to Elizabeth, daughter of **James, Lord Hamilton**, and **Princess Mary**, and their son was John Stewart (d. 1526), Third (or Eleventh) Earl of Lennox. The title then passed to John's eldest son, Matthew Lennox (b. 1516),* the fourth earl, the great-grandson of John Stewart of Darnley and the husband of Margaret Douglas.* Exiled for being an English agent, he was allowed to return to Scotland in 1564, but left for England after the murder of his son, Henry Darnley (1545–1567), Mary Queen of Scots'* husband. He returned to Scotland to become Regent in the minority of James VI (1566–1625), but was shot and killed in an affray in Stirling in 1571 when Lord Huntly and Lord Claud Hamilton led an attack on the Parliament in session there. (D. D.)

Dates: HN, LC: Particular care should be taken when reading fifteenth-century primary sources because of the confusion which can be caused by not appreciating when the calendar year changed. January the first does not signify the start of the new year in the medieval and early modern Christian world, but it can be hard to pinpoint exactly which day does: the Chronicler Bede (*c.* 673–735) and other thirteenth-century sources date the year of grace as starting on Christmas Day, but a calendar which reckoned the year began with the moveable feast of Easter was also used, from the late-twelfth to the early-thirteenth century. (Easter was eventually fixed as taking place on the Sunday following the first full moon on or after 21 March.) Commonly used was Lady Day, the Feast of the Annunciation: 25 March. This means that a document which in the English calendar appears as 20 March 1450, is actually 1451 if we use our modern year as starting on 1 January. To complicate matters further, in Pisa until 1750 the feast of the *previous year* signifies the start of the year, so Pisa was a year ahead! Elsewhere, the feast date was of the date *after* Christmas: that is to say, the anniversary of the Annunciation rather than counting forward from the Annunciation itself. This method was spread by the Cistercians (and probably originated in the Abbey of Fleury, in the eleventh century), and was used in England until 1752. Again causing confusion was the fact that in the period contiguous with the *House of Niccolò* and the *Lymond Chronicles*, Genoa's new year began on 1 March.

We now of course take the historical year as beginning on 1 January (like the Roman civil year). In Scotland it was the official beginning of the year from 1600 (31 December 1599); in England and Ireland the change occurred in 1751 when after 31 December the year changed to 1752.

Dominant in both periods of the novels would be the old-style Julian calendar. The new-style Gregorian (introduced by Pope Gregory XIII in 1582) aimed to correct the divergence between the calendar and the solar year (see **Eke-week**), a discrepancy of ten days by 1582, but was not universally adopted until the sixteenth century in Catholic states, the eighteenth century in Protestant states and the twentieth century in Russia, Greece and the Balkans. For the sake of clarity, months and dates within the novels have been deliberately standardised to the modern calendar.

De ce côté-ci du Pô/Tous sont fils de Niccolò: LIONS 14: 'Across the land, from here to Pô / Are none but sons of Niccolò'. Satirical verse referring to Nicolas d'Este, the Marquis of Ferrara in the time of Philip the Good, Duke of Burgundy,* whom he outmatched in the matter of bastards. Ferrara sired sixty-six. Duke Philip was slightly less prolific, perhaps bearing in mind his chivalric pledge to his half-Portuguese, half-English bride: *Aultra n'aray; Dame Isabeau tant que je vivray.* Or, in increasingly familiar translation: 'Long as I live, I shall have none other than Isabeau'. A near winner in the fertility stakes was his near-contemporary John II, Duke of Cleves, who had sixty-three bastards, and was known as the Kinder-maeker. (See also **Ferrara wedding.**) (D. D.)

De foudre: See ***Coup . . . de foudre.***

Deals under carts: LIONS, 17: 'Low deals under carts' was the common phrase for what would now be called black-market trading. Scots suspected of nefarious plotting were said to be meeting 'in hiddilles', or huddles.

Deceit deceiveth and shall be deceived: KINGS, I, 2: Moral poem: as ye sow so shall ye reap.

> Dysceyt disceyueth, and shal be diceyved;
> ffor by disceyt, who that is diceyvable,
> Thouh his disceyt be nat out parceyved [perceived],
> To a disceyvour disceyt is retournable.
> ffraude quyt with fraude is guerdone [reward] covenable,
> ffor who with fraude fraudulent is founde,
> To such defraudour fraude wele ay rebounde.

Delay . . . : GEMINI, 8: The last lines of this the lyric poem '*Procurans Odium*'. This is the whole song:

> Averting ill will
> by its own effect

scarcely satisfies
the intent of detractors.
The bond of hearts
is separation itself.
So, against the enemy
I do not know,
this provision is made here,
happy condition
of lovers in this situation.
The insults of such people
I feel to be useful; the occasion of relieving boredom
has passed.
Delay,
By perverse intent,
holds joy in suspense
but increases longing.
By such a remedy,
from the thorns of enemies,
I harvest grapes.

Diabetica passione: RONDO, 7: A fifteenth-century term for an excessive flow of urine.

Dìreach air a shùil: GEMINI, 33: 'Just so!' 'Precisely!'

Disdain me not without desert: KINGS, I, 2: Poem by Sir Thomas Wyatt:*

Disdain me not without desert!
Nor leave me not so suddenly!
Since well ye wot that in my heart
I mean ye not but honesty.

Refuse me not without cause why!
For think me not to be unjust!
Since that by lot of fantasy
This careful knot needs knit I must.

Mistrust me not! though some there be
That fain would spoil my steadfastness,
Believe them not! since that ye see
The proof is not as they express.

Forsake me not till I deserve!
Nor hate me not till I offend!

Destroy me not till that I swerve,
But since ye know what I intend!

Disdain me not that am your own!
Refuse me not that am so true!
Mistrust me not till all be known!
Forsake me not now for no new!

Dispensations: See **Consanguinity and dispensations.**

Diwan: GEMINI, 48: A medical *diwan*, in Arabic, is more or less the same as a guild.*

Doc-Doc: LIONS, 17: A French nickname, *Docque-Doque*, applied to an individual who is both adroit and subtle.

Dominicans: See **Blackfriars.**

Donna di governo: LIONS, 42: A managing woman.

DOUGLAS, Archibald: GEMINI: (*c.* 1449–1513) Fifth Earl of Angus and heir of the **Red Douglas** family, he received his nick-name 'Bell the Cat' as a consequence of what were said to be his actions at **Lauder Bridge** when – in the depiction of the later chroniclers – the low-born favourites of **James III*** were removed. The legend relates that as the nobles gathered to complain about the King's favourites, their situation was compared to the assembly of mice who all agreed that the cat would be much easier to live with if only it wore a bell round its neck. When the question arose, 'Who will bell the cat?' Angus is said to have volunteered. The deaths of **Thomas Cochrane, Thomas Preston** and **William Roger** followed.

It is likely that Angus's assessment of the 1474 marriage treaty with England was similar to that of **Alexander, Duke of Albany,*** and the anti-English tone of ***The Wallace***, and in 1480, as the peace between Scotland and England was breaking down, he laid waste to parts of Northumberland. However, his role at Lauder was probably not that which the chroniclers gave him, as he did not have control over the King when he returned to **Edinburgh.**

His marriage to Elizabeth, sister of **Thomas Boyd**, just before the fall of the family may not have endeared him to James; he certainly did not rise rapidly to high office under the King. Douglas supported Albany between 1482 and 1483: in February 1483, he, Lord Gray and **Sir James Liddell of Halkerston** renounced their allegiance to Scotland and became the liegemen of England. These same three were subsequently involved in Albany's attempt to revive the Fotheringay treaty of 1482, and Angus went on to side against James III in 1488. Under **James IV,*** he was in favour until 1491, when he was found to have treasonable dealings with England. James IV besieged his castle of Tantallon, and Douglas lost the lordship of Liddesdale. Reconciliation with the King in 1492/1493 was consolidated by the fact that the King's first mistress was Douglas's niece, Marion Boyd. He was appointed Chancellor from 1493 to 1497 and made Warden of the Middle Marches. In 1496 he received the lordship of Crawford Lindsay with the castle of Crawford in Lanarkshire. By 1501/1502 he was once more out of favour. Too old to fight, but still able to give advice, he advised James IV against the battle of **Flodden**, but two of his sons, including his heir, followed the King into battle and were killed. A third son survived: Gavin Douglas, churchman and poet.

Archibald was succeeded by his grandson, Archibald Douglas,* Sixth Earl of Angus (*c.* 1489–1557), who in 1514 married Margaret Tudor (1489–1541), widowed after the death of James IV at Flodden. They were the parents of Margaret Lennox.*

DOUGLAS, Earls of: HN: This branch of the Douglas family, known as the **Black Douglases**, were extremely powerful in the earlier part of the fifteenth century. Descendants of Sir William, Lord of Douglas (d. 1298) and Robert III (King of Scotland 1394–1406), they were the greatest landholders in Scotland, second only to the King. The Earls were lords of Galloway, Annandale, Ettrick, Lauderdale, Eskdale and Teviotdale, as well as holding lands in the north. Famed for their warlike valour, they could easily raise an army from those who lived on their estates. This strength and wealth made them a potential rival to the monarchy.

In the minority of James II,* the King's guardians, Sir William Crichton and Sir Alexander Livingston, plotted the murder of William, Sixth Earl of Douglas (b. *c.* 1425). In 1440 he was invited to **Edinburgh** Castle and murdered: an occasion described as the Black Dinner. The killers were aided by the Earl's great-uncle, James the Gross (d. 1443), who, after inheriting the Douglas title and lands, took no part in avenging the death of his great-nephew. James was succeeded by his son, another William, Eighth Earl of Douglas, who broke the alliance between Crichton and Livingstone and was proclaimed Lieutenant-General of Scotland. On achieving his majority, the King's principal adviser was Bishop Kennedy,* who was keen to limit the power of the Scottish barons, and focused his attention on the powerful house of Douglas. William and his brothers Archibald, Hugh and John between them held three of Scotland's eight earldoms (Douglas, Moray and Ormond respectively, while John was Lord of Balvenie). Archibald's twin brother James (the elder of the two) was Bishop of St Andrews.

William was considered a threat because of a bond of alliance he had made in 1444 with John, Lord of the Isles and Earl of Ross, and Alexander **Lindsay**, Fourth Earl of Crawford. The bond between these three has not survived, but provided the King with the justification to suppress a magnate who was potentially creating a treasonable league. William returned in 1451 from a mission to Rome to find that his authority in his own domains had been undermined by the King. In the Earl's absence, the King had invaded his territories, besieged his castles and slain many of his tenants. The dispute was temporarily resolved by Parliament, which in October confirmed the Earl's many territories, but in the following year, 1452, William was summoned by the King to appear at Stirling Castle, perhaps in reaction to an attack that he had made on Chancellor Crichton in Edinburgh. Aware his safety was threatened, William demanded a safe conduct from the King, which was duly granted. At the meeting James ordered him to renounce his bond with Ross and Crawford. William refused, and in a fit of rage, the King is said to have stabbed him. The Earl was stabbed a further twenty-six times by James's courtiers.

After his murder, William's brother, the Bishop James, became **Ninth Earl of Douglas**, and sought to avenge his brother's death by gathering his followers and burning Stirling in retribution, although the Douglases submitted to the authority of the King after a Parliament in Edinburgh. James was granted a **dispensation** to marry his dead brother's widow, Margaret, the Fair Maid of Galloway (who was also his cousin), which meant he could inherit all of his brother's lands. Peace, however, was only temporary, as by 1455 the King was using artillery to batter the Earl's castle strongholds into submission, and diplomacy to woo the Earl's potential allies in the south-west away from the Douglases. Those who were encouraged to aid the King included their own kin, the **Red Douglases.** The cause of renewed aggression is not clear: perhaps the Earl had been dealing with the Yorkists in England when the monarchy still supported the Lancastrian side. James fled to England, leaving his brothers in Scotland, defeated in battle in May 1455. John, Lord of Balvenie, escaped, but Archibald, Earl of Moray, was slain in battle, and Hugh, Earl of Ormond, was executed. The Douglases were found guilty of treason and the family's estates were forfeited to the Crown. In the Scottish Parliament of May 1455 it was decreed that anyone who assisted survivors of the family would incur the penalty of treason and forfeit their life, lands and goods, and that no descendants of the Black Douglases would ever be allowed to inherit their property in Scotland.

DOUGLAS, James, Ninth Earl of: GEMINI, 39: (1426–d. by 1491) Of the fated **Black Douglases**, James was the brother of William the Eighth Earl, killed by James II* at Stirling Castle in 1452. In an attempt to avenge the death of his brother, James made open war on the King but was forced to flee to England in 1455 when his allies changed sides and supported the monarchy. Nor could the Douglases even rely upon their own family for support: their cousin, George, Fourth Earl of Angus, assisted in their downfall, described as the **Red Douglas** (Angus) bringing down the Black. James's brothers were forfeited and killed, including his twin Archibald, Earl of Moray and patron of **Richard Holland.** James found favour in England as a staunch supporter of **Edward IV*** of York at a time when Scotland was still supporting the rival Lancaster claim, and became the first Scot to be made a member of the Order of the Garter.*

When James was in England he sided with **Alexander, Duke of Albany,*** and was with him when the Duke attempted his final abortive invasion of Scotland in July 1484. He was captured at the resulting battle of Lochmaben and James III had him confined to the Abbey of Lindores in Fife, where he spent the last years of his life.

Dry Tree: LIONS, 14: While music in the fifteenth century was one of the statutory indulgences of wealthy courts, it was also available to the affluent burgesses of lower rank through certain religious societies, two of which flourished in Bruges* in Burgundian Flanders. One of these was the Ghilde van Onzer Lieve Vrauwe van den Droghen Boome, the Marian Confraternity of the Dry Tree. (The Dry Tree was a symbol of the Immaculate Conception, LIONS, 18). This was a society established about 1396 by merchants mostly native to Florence, in a chapel within the convent of the **Franciscan** friars on the Braemberch, Bruges.

The church and its chapels, which also served the guild* of the Archers of St Sebastian, had the support of the town, the Dukes of Burgundy and the local nobility, and most particularly of the Florentine and Castilian merchant communities. Nobles and merchants treated the confraternity in its earlier days as a club, which might admit such foreign members as Sir Henry Percy of Northumberland (1364–1403). By 1469, its leading organizers included **Anselm Adorne*** (following his uncle, Jacques), Giovanni Arnolfini (of Jan van Eyck's* marriage portrait), Paul van Overweldt (Dean), Jan van Nieuwenhove, **Petrus Christus** and Tommaso Portinari.* Among the remaining two hundred were Philip the Good* and the Duchess Isabella of Portugal, their son **Charles***, the future **Duke of Burgundy**, Louis de Gruuthuse,* the Bastard Anthony, and the wealthy unmarried daughters of the Abbey of the Rich Clares. Other women were also admitted, and so were children.

The Friars Minor were paid to sing regular masses, some specified to be in descant. Soon, the Confraternity began to hire singers from outside, and to lure performers and even an organist from St Donatiens.* Three ducal singers are named, and four city minstrels played on special occasions. There were two organist-members, and an organ-builder was retained to look after maintenance. Polyphonic music was a speciality of the society, and some of their Lady Masses may be found in the great Lucca choir book written in Bruges about 1470, and presented by the above Giovanni Arnolfini to the Cathedral of Lucca. None of their other music has survived, save for a few leaves of an **antiphonal.**

The Confraternity changed its composition when the Duchess Isabella and her successor **Margaret of York** developed a preference for the reformed branch of the Franciscans, the **Observatine Friars**, of which **Ludovico de Severi da Bologna*** was a well-known representative. A new convent and church for the Observatines was sited outside the Ezelpoort on land presented by Tommaso Portinari, and this eventually overtook the old church in popularity. In 1518, the two houses were merged.

It appears that the Confraternity of the Dry Tree fostered art as well as international music (and, presumable, trade). A copy by Petrus Christus of a painting of St Francis, made by van Eyck for the Duchess Isabella, may have led to Adorne's acquisition of the two pictures he bequeathed to his daughters.

Many of the members of the Dry Tree also supported the musical Confraternity of Our Lady of the Snow, named for the popular basilica of Santa Maria Maggiore in Rome. Founded before 1450 by the Tailors' Guild, this Confraternity met in the **collegiate church** of Our Lady in Bruges, and came to include among its members – which numbered nearly a thousand – the Duchess Isabella and Duke Charles of Burgundy; painters such as **Hans Memling** and Christus; Michele Arnolfini; some members of the Gruuthuse* family; and Alexander Bonkle of Scotland and Bruges, whose kinsman Edward Bonkle* was painted by **Hugo van der Goes.**

Adorne is not named as a member, but the Bonkle connection perhaps explains why the collegiate church of **Trinity Chapel, Edinburgh**, of which Edward Bonkle was first Provost, unusually enjoined the regular use of polyphonic music in its earliest statutes. The Confraternity was a lively one: apart from its magnificent religious ceremonies with choirs and hired singers, it sponsored several annual feasts, including a banquet in the guild-house of the tailors for which a new play was performed almost every year. The Church of Our Lady in Bruges was also known for its polyphonic masses for St Catherine of Alexandria and **Mount Sinai**,* one being specifically endowed by the ducal councillor Paul van Overtweldt, who was to be imprisoned with Adorne after the death of Duke Charles in 1477. Again, such links with merchants in Bruges may partly explain the reverence for this saint in Edinburgh. (D. D.)

Dubia: LIONS, 17: Lists of subjects selected for disputation exercises. Here applied to ledger items open to question.

Dufay of the north: LIONS, 10: (*c.* 1400–1474) Guillaume Dufay was one of the most famous composers of his time. One of his best-known works was his version of a *Missa l'homme Armé*, one of the many masses composed around the well-known French recruiting song *'L'homme armé'*,* *'Beware the Armed Man'*. His music was not always spiritual or literally martial: he also composed the piece *'Donnés l'assault á la fortresse'* (*'Storm my sweet lady's defences'*). (D. D.)

Dunajow: RONDO, 16: See **Gregory of Sanok.**

DUNBAR, Euphemia: UNICORN: Study of the life of **Anselm Adorne*** suggests that the mother of his acknowledged natural daughter Efemie (**Euphemia**

Adorne) was Euphemia Dunbar, daughter of George Dunbar, Earl of March (d. by 1463), and niece of William **Sinclair**, Earl of Orkney and Caithness, who died between 1479 and 1480. Her own birth-date is unknown.

An illegitimate child was commonly named after the mother, and of the many Euphemias in Scotland in the fifteenth century, Euphemia Dunbar (called 'Phemie' in the novels) was a person of the right age and standing, whom written record placed at **Haddington** Priory, where the King's sister **Princess Margaret** was reared from 1464 until 1477, after which date Margaret had an illegitimate child of her own.

Links exist between Adorne and Princess Margaret, and between Adorne and Haddington Priory, seventeen miles east of **Edinburgh**, which was the largest and wealthiest foundation in Scotland for **Cistercian** nuns, and played a large part in public affairs. The **Princess Mary**, Margaret's sister, had lived and borne two of her children in Adorne's home in Bruges* before returning to Scotland. Also, the Prioress of Haddington was charged by the King with paying from the Haddington customs fees to a number of persons in the King's favour who would be known to Adorne. As well as handling the expenses for the Princess and the nun, Dame Alice or Elizabeth Maitland, who looked after her, Elizabeth, Prioress of Haddington, paid the fees of **Dr Andreas**, the royal physician associated with Adorne, and Dr Conrad, who arrived a year later than Andreas, and eventually succeeded him. There was an annual fee to Elizabeth Sinclair (widow of Patrick Dunbar and daughter of William Sinclair), who had cared for the Princess Mary when young. And from 1460, there was an annual royal payment to Elizabeth Sinclair's cousin Euphemia Dunbar.

Euphemia Dunbar was paid the comfortable sum of ten marks a year, half as much as her cousin and Dr Andreas, but double the fee for Dame Alice the nun. Her religious standing is hard to decipher, and it is not clear what her employment within the Priory might be, or how much freedom of movement she had. The indications are that she had been placed there after her father was forced by the greed of James I (King of Scotland 1406–1437) to forfeit his earldom, which had been in the family for three hundred years. (Despite this, the brother of the dispossessed Earl remained loyal, and was later injured when pursuing the assassins who murdered the King.) Sensible of an injustice perhaps, the later Stewart Kings seem to have contributed towards Euphemia's expenses, and she may have eked this out by teaching. Her Sinclair mother (name unknown) was presumably dead. The situation continued until July 1477, when Cristiane Dunbar, probably a sister, was paid the sum of five pounds to the credit of 'the late Euphamie of Dunbar'. Elizabeth Sinclair and Dame Alice were still there.

That is all that is known. The novels predicate a friendship with Adorne during his penultimate visit to Scotland, with his wife, in 1471. It further invents a reason for Euphemia to have visited Bruges,* but there is no evidence for this. There is none either for her appearance or character, or the manner and place of her death. All that can be done is to build up a picture of her family, which places her in the centre of a network of landed families with a strong interest in trade.

Her name appears to have come from her maternal, Sinclair side. Her cousin Elizabeth (Betha in the novels) had three daughters, of whom one, Euphemia, was an heiress in Ayrshire. One of Betha's sisters was Euphemia Sinclair.

Her father, George Dunbar, retired after his forfeiture to Kinconquhar in Fife, where as it happened the nuns of **North Berwick** had their hospice, and his earldom passed to the Crown, and eventually to **Alexander, Duke of Albany,*** **James III**'s* brother. This particular earldom, spread as it was down the east coast of Scotland towards the Marches (or frontier with England), was of supreme strategic importance, and always subject to turbulence. It had been forfeited intermittently in the time of Earl George's father, who lost it a second time to James I.

It had also produced some remarkable women, as did the Dunbars of the earldom of Moray, who were cousins. In 1338, Black Agnes Dunbar of Moray, the swarthy wife of Patrick, Eleventh Earl of Dunbar and Second of March, held Dunbar Castle against an English force for five months, taunting her foes by sending out silken-clad maids with clean handkerchiefs to flick the cannon balls' marks from her walls. It impelled the besieger (history claims) to burst into immortal verse:

Came I early, came I late
I found Agnes at the gate.

Agnes Dunbar's eldest daughter, of the same name, became the mistress of King David II (b. 1324) and would have been Queen had he not died suddenly in 1371. Her sister, Agnes's daughter Elizabeth, married Sir John Maitland of Lethington, ancestor of the Dukes of Lauderdale (see **Mount Sinai***) and perhaps also of Dame Alice Maitland, the nun of Haddington Priory. Black Agnes's grandson George, Fourth Earl of March, was brother to Columba Dunbar, Bishop of Moray, who restored Elgin Cathedral, and was buried in the Dunbar Aisle. Euphemia's father was the last Dunbar to hold the earldom of March.

Meanwhile, however, Euphemia's uncle, James Dunbar, possessed the earldom of Moray and founded the castle of Elgin. Of Earl James's daughters (Euphemia's cousins), Janet married James Crichton, the eldest son of Chancellor William Crichton, and their son, **William, Third Lord Crichton**, became the young lover of the King's sister Margaret. The other, Janet's sister Elizabeth Dunbar, Countess of Moray, married twice: once to Archibald Douglas, briefly Earl of Moray, who was forfeited (See **Earls of Douglas**); and then (as the Lady of Luss) to **Sir John Colquhoun of Luss**, who managed the customs of Moray and Mar, and in 1471 was sheriff of Dumbarton, before being killed when camped before Albany's castle of Dunbar in 1479.

Euphemia appeared to have at least two brothers and one sister. The sister, assumed to be the Cristiane who accepted her back pay, was the wife of Alexander Innes of Innes, eldest son of James of that Ilk who held land in Banffshire, and owned important salmon fisheries on the River Spey. James III was still addressing him as his familiar servant a few months before his death.

There remained her mother's family, the Sinclairs, whose connections were even more prodigious. Her mother's brother William, First Lord Sinclair, Earl of Orkney and Caithness, died between 1479 and 1480, having weathered the complex transaction whereby he exchanged his earldom of Orkney for other benefits, after the deal that brought James III his Danish Queen. Her mother's sister, Beatrix Sinclair, married James, Seventh Earl of Douglas, whose daughter Janet became the bride of Robert Lord **Fleming.**

Whatever else she was not, Euphemia Dunbar was a walking almanac of the more effective Scottish nobility of the second half of the fifteenth century. On the facts that remain, it would seem to be quite appropriate for her to have married Anselm Adorne, Baron Cortachy, Knight of the Unicorn, Captain and Governor of **Linlithgow** Palace, if she were the mother of his child. Perhaps it was prevented, as the novels suggest, by Adorne's incarceration in Bruges at the time of her death. Or there may have been other political factors involved. It is interesting to speculate on what would have happened had they married, and had the child been a son, entering the reign of **James IV.*** (D. D.)

Durfermline, the young man from: See **Henryson, Robert.**

dwór: RONDO, 1: Polish name for a country manor: more likely than not a one-storeyed timber building, steep-roofed, with low eaves and surrounded by similarly built domestic outbuildings. The nobility's preference for building in wood meant that in Poland stone was used for fortifications, not homes.

E

Eccles: RONDO, 31: The **Cistercian** Priory of St Mary's, founded on the Scottish Border at Eccles in 1155, was particularly vulnerable to English invasion, being situated on rich arable land only two miles from the frontier on the River Tweed, five from Kelso, and six from Coldstream. In 1543 its corn was burned, and in 1544 the church was won by assault and eighty men slain in the Priory and the town. In 1545 the Priory was said to be razed, although there was a Prioress called Marion Hamilton in possession between 1548 and 1566 (a period of apparent rivalry between Prioresses), when leases of some of the convent's land at Eccles and Bothkennar were given to Sir Alexander Hamilton of Innerwick. In 1566 the Priory was granted to Isobel Home, and on her demission before 1575 it passed to James Home, second son of Sir James Home, after which it was erected into a temporal lordship for Sir George Home in 1609.

In 1444, the Prioress of Eccles was Euphemia Graham, granddaughter of King Robert III (ruled 1390–1406) and half-sister of James Kennedy,* Bishop of St Andrews. Bishop Kennedy, like herself, was first cousin of King James II,* whose young son **Alexander, Duke of Albany**,* he had once escorted to Bruges.* The date of Euphemia's birth is unknown, but the novel assumes that, if she lived to her mother's age, she might be Prioress still in 1481 when the Duke's brother, King **James III**,* confirmed all his ancestors' gifts to the Priory, with the affirmation of the Archbishop of St Andrews, **William Scheves.** The novels suggest that when the English invasion threatened the following year, the Prioress of Eccles took refuge at the Cistercian Priory of **North Berwick**, which had been supported by the Kennedy family at least to the time of Bishop Kennedy's grandfather.

North Berwick, on the estuary of the River Forth, was also within easy reach of the church of Bothkennar, of which the Prioress and convent of Eccles were patrons. Bothkennar (now Skinflats) in Stirlingshire lay in rich carse land a few miles west of the home of Crawford of **Berecrofts**, whose heir, Robert Crawford, was connected by marriage to **Anselm Adorne**,* the Genoese–Burgundian nobleman who lost his life at North Berwick in 1483. Berecrofts also passed in the mid-sixteenth century into Hamilton hands.

Nothing more about the Prioress Euphemia is known, although fragments of her Priory at Eccles are still to be seen. There might be some warrant for

the contemporary belief that the monks and nuns of the Borders hedged their bets, on occasion, by informing on the combatants of both sides. (D. D.)

Edinburgh: HN; LC: Perched on the outcrop of an extinct volcano, the town of Edinburgh was in effect the capital of Scotland under **James III,*** as it became the chief residence of his Court. It was to dominate the political and economic development of Scotland in the early modern period. In early times the justice and Parliament of Scotland had been peripatetic, but increasingly centred on the town. The area encompassing the castle had been a centre of habitation since the Bronze Age, and developed into a defensive fortress. It was in the twelfth century that Edinburgh was made a royal burgh by David I (King of Scotland 1124–1153), who also founded the Abbey of **Holyrood**, which in time was to provide more luxurious accommodation for the monarchs of Scotland: a palace replaced the modest hunting lodge and guest accommodation provided by the Augustinians in their burgh outside the town, the **Canongate.** In 1400 the inner town of Edinburgh consisted of four hundred houses, growing steadily over the next two centuries. By the mid-fifteenth century records suggest a population of between 7,500 and 13,500 for those living within the walls of the town, excluding the Canongate and **Leith** (the latter, still described as a village, had a population estimated at four thousand during this time). Edinburgh's first census at the close of the sixteenth century found a total of 8,003 adults living to the north and south of the High Street.

Edinburgh dominated Scotland's export trade. The loss of Berwick-upon-Tweed* to the English (although briefly back in Scottish hands under James III) meant that there was no east coast town to rival Edinburgh from the English border to the Tay. Edinburgh came to monopolize Scotland's trade in wool and hides, exported from the nearby port of Leith. By 1500 there were already fourteen distinct **markets** in Edinburgh. As the population expanded, Edinburgh spread eastwards, down from the castle. To the north and south of the high ridge (known today as the Royal Mile), were homes and enclosed gardens; on the north side they spread to the shore of the **Nor' Loch**, and to the south down the parallel slope to the Cowgate. The town remained physically compact: by the mid-sixteenth century it was still only approximately half a mile long and the same distance wide. To defend the city there were the walls, built in 1450 and extended in 1514 the year after the battle of **Flodden.**

St. Giles ~ the Norman Doorway ~ destroyed at the end of the eighteenth century

See also **Blackfriars, Blue Blanket, Greyfriars, Halkerston's Wynd,** St Giles,* **Trinity Chapel** and **Tolbooth.**

Education: See **Learning and deportment.**

EDWARD IV:* RISING: (1442–1483) After the rebellion which forced Edward into brief exile in Bruges,* he regained the throne of England in 1471 and reigned for the next twelve years. His sister **Margaret of York**'s marriage to **Charles, Duke of Burgundy,*** allied the two against **Louis XI*** of France, who had supported the Lancastrian claim against York, although in 1475 Edward was shrewd enough to accept the private offer of a French pension in return for peace with France. Peace abroad allowed England's trade with the **Hanseatic League**, France and Burgundy to flourish, thus increasing the revenues of the Crown. Increased prosperity enabled Edward to take an interest in the arts, as a patron of Caxton* and collector of illuminated manuscripts, probably encouraged by the Duchess Margaret's interest in the same field.

Having come to terms with overseas enemies, Edward faced dissent and rebellion from his own family; chiefly from the Duke of Clarence, who had schemed to marry the daughter of **Marie of Burgundy** and was infamously executed for treason in 1478 by being drowned in a butt of Malmsey. Yet the threat to Edward's heirs was ultimately to come from another brother, **Richard, Duke of Gloucester.**

To end France's ongoing war with Burgundy, the Treaty of Arras in 1482 saw France turn against England once again, and Louis withdrew Edward's lucrative pension. Edward's daughter Elizabeth had been promised as a bride to Louis's son, the Dauphin, but Louis broke the agreement and promised the Dauphin instead to Marie of Burgundy's daughter, Marguerite. This betrayal incensed Edward, but, already failing physically, he was unable to respond against France with a show of force. He was once tall, handsome and physically impressive, but a life of excess had led to a creeping corpulence, which undermined his health. He died suddenly in 1483 at the age of forty and was survived by seven of his children, five daughters and two sons: Edward, Prince of Wales and his brother Richard, Duke of York. Placed in the Tower of London for their supposed safety, the children were murdered on the orders of their uncle and protector, Richard of Gloucester, who was then crowned as Richard III. Richard's brief rule ended with the battle of Bosworth Field in 1485. After his defeat, the houses of Lancaster and York were united with the marriage of Edward IV's daughter Elizabeth to the victor of Bosworth, Henry VII (1485–1509).

Eh bien, c'est M. JeMoi . . . Comme tu est gros: LIONS, 5: Teasing rebuke to an importunate child: 'Well, well, here he is, Master Me-me-me-me . . . Aren't you getting big'.

Eke-week: LIONS, 40: Occurring every six to seven years, this was a bonus week made up from left-over days in the early calendar, which did not otherwise end the year tidily. A heathen week in the north had five days, but Christian Iceland eventually acknowledged seven, including Lauger-Dagr, bath-day. It was a Saturday.

ELLEM, John, of Butterdene: GEMINI, 22: The Ellem family had owned upland farming land in Butterdene from the thirteenth century. West of the parish of **Coldingham**, it formed part of the property of the **nunnery** of Abbey St Bathans. John Ellem was one of **Alexander, Duke of Albany**'s* followers, and was witness to a charter in January 1477 in which Albany granted various lands to **Alexander Home**, heir apparent to Alexander, Lord Home, for his loyalty, and for services done and (ominously) to be done. Ellem of Butterdene was forfeited in 1482 for holding the castle of Dunbar for Albany. His lands were conferred on his son, George.

Eme: GEMINI, 1: Scots for 'grandfather'.

En seguida: KINGS, 1, 5: 'Pronto'.

Endeclocken: GEMINI, 53: Mourning-bells.

Endymion: RONDO, 12: In classical lore, the handsome shepherd boy who obtained the promise of Jupiter that he would stay always young and – the present point – would be able to sleep as much as he wished. The question is whether, in the human world, a pregnant woman given a sleeping draught would give birth to an Endymion. (D. D.)

Enfants de la Mate: KNIGHTS, III, 17: Thieves and cut-throats in sixteenth-century Paris. A tale survives of a grand ball at which the host secretly arranged for the *enfants de la Mate,* dressed as lackeys, to mingle with and steal from their guests. The booty, when displayed triumphantly at the end to the horror-struck victims, included purses of money, pearls and expensive caps, and was worth three thousand écus in all. It was returned to the owners. (A sly man is a *matois.*) (D. D.)

Entre cuir et chair: LION, 6: 'Secretly', or, literally, 'between skin and flesh'. Said here, rather eerily, of knowledge privily stored.

Esota: RISING; GEMINI, 26: This is a version of the old name Isolde. Tristan (Trystram or Trysting) and Isolde were the supreme medieval exponents of adulterous love. Tristan, an orphan whose name means 'sorrowful' (his mother died giving birth to him, and he lost his father in infancy), was knighted by his uncle, King Mark of Cornwall, became one of King Arthur's Knights of the Round Table and married Isolde of the White Hands, daughter of Howell, King of Brittany. However, he fell in love with another Isolde, the wife of his uncle Mark, Isolde the Fair, daughter of Anguish, King of Ireland. She was trapped in a loveless marriage, and hated her husband as much as she loved Tristan. The couple eloped, spending three years at Joyous Guard Castle, Carlisle, before she returned to her husband where, according to one version of the tale, Tristan was stabbed in the back and killed by King Mark. The tale of Isolde the Fair and the magic potion that made Tristan her lover was perennially popular, and Tristan winning Isolde a favourite theme for exhibition jousts between gallant knights.

Est conformis precedenti: KNIGHTS, III, 15: 'It follows precedent'.

Et non est qui adjuvat: BONDO, 12: 'And there is no one to help'.

Et tu ne vois au pied de ton rempart: PAWN, 3: From a poem by Pierre de Ronsard (1524–1585), which uses the Trojan war to consider his own condition. Cassandra is the daughter of the King of Troy, Myrmidones and Dolopes are peoples hostile to Troy, and Philoctetes was the archer who killed Paris, Cassandra's brother, using the arrows of Hercules. In the novel, the last line was changed to suit the dialogue:

Je ne suis point, ma guerrière Cassandre,
Ni Myrmidon ni Dolope soudart
Ni cet Archer, don't l'homicide dard
Tue ton frère et mit ta ville en cendre.

Un camp armé pour esclave te rendre,
Du port d'Aulide en ma faveur ne part,
Et tu ne vois au pied de ton rempart
Pour t'enlever mille barques descendre.

I am not, my warrior maid Cassandra,
A tool of Myrmidon or Dolopes, thy foes
Nor that cruel murderer whose barb
Thy brother slew, and set thy Troy ablaze.

No army will embark, in cause of mine,
From Aulis port to render thee their slave,
Nor need thou fear to find beneath thy walls
A thousand boats to ravish thee away.

(D. D.)

Etiquette: hospitality and conduct in public: In 1434, the city magistrates of Bern were thanked by the visiting Emperor Sigismond (Holy Roman Emperor 1410–1437) for allowing him and his attendants to make free use of their brothel for three days (RONDO, 7). Similarly, it was a courtesy in **Iceland** for the eldest daughter of the household to remove the clothes of an honoured guest. Lapps* were equally generous. On non-sexual affairs, it was not considered seemly in Poland to blow the nose through the fingers, or into the hat like a peasant (although into the coat was permitted), or to urinate on the hangings or staircase.

Other nations dealt with the same problems differently. At the dinner table, a sudden departure was acceptable 'if the guest had a nose-bleed'. The Parliament of Paris, which in 1316 preferred to sit early, from the hour of the first Mass until noon, did not expect members to absent themselves unless *pour necessité corporelle.*

Spitting was another social liability. It was rude to spit into the fire, instead of under the table, or against the wall. Fruit stones must not be spat out, but removed from the mouth with two fingers. Spitting in France was given a special entry in the *Babees' Book*, an early compendium of advice for young nobles about to serve a great lord:

> *Ne craîche par dessus la table*
> *Car c'est chose desconvenable.*
>
> To spit on the table
> Is considered distasteful.

Table manners varied from country to country. It was correct to take salt with the point of the knife, and knives were passed round by the point, after wiping. A napkin, if offered, was supposed to lie on the shoulder or arm. It was wrong to blow on the dishes to cool them, but amiable to offer superfluous titbits to the servants. One didn't drink from the dish, or eat bread before the meat had appeared.

A glimpse of early Russian manners appears in the *Domostroi*, a book on household management long attributed to a priest Silvester (CASTLE, I, 3) who served Tsar Ivan IV* (Ivan, the Terrible). Discipline and punishments had their place, but in moderation: those about to beat pregnant women and children were advised to use only the lash. There were instructions on how to make mead and brew beer, but sobriety was also enjoined: 'A drunk man is bad, but a drunk woman is not fit to be on earth'.

The book's attitudes to womanhood were chiefly drawn from the Bible ('whatever her husband orders, she must accept with love; she must fulfil his every command') and – considering the history of the times – perhaps represents wishful thinking rather than an accurate picture of Ivan's household, at least.

Etiquette: language: In Poland, it was usual to *Waszmość* acquaintances, i.e., address them formally in the third person, employing *Wasz-*, Your Love, or *Waćpan*, as in *Wasza Miłość, Panie.* This was the equivalent of using *Usted* in Spain. The formality extended to the family; it was also usual for children to *Waszmość* their parents. Formal behavior extended elsewhere: in Poland, sons saluted their parents on one knee; daughters on both, and an independent lady might find herself called Herod-baba, wild woman. In France, the second person singular ('thou') was used in familiar language to close friends and children, and to do so was termed to *tutoyer* someone (RONDO, 20). To call a nobleman 'thou' in Poland was correct only when he was about to be hanged.

Etiquette, letters: The florid style, when prince addressed prince, might appear unduly familiar, but was generally intended to invoke a relationship which was real if obscure. That is, policy changes being what they were, most European rulers ended up being related to one another, which was sometimes worth mentioning. When King **James III*** of Scotland addressed **Edward IV*** of England as 'richt hie and michty prince, and dearest brother and cousin', it could be because his sister was about to marry the King's brother-in-law, his son was about to marry the King's daughter and King Edward's sister was married to the **Charles, Duke of Burgundy**,* who was a cousin to King James's late mother.

In Flanders at this time, knights could use M'her or Mer before their names. Wives of knights were called dames, and wives of gentlemen, demoiselles. (D. D.)

Exchequer: LIONS, 40: The Scottish Exchequer audit took place only once a year, usually in June and in **Edinburgh.** The auditors, who were chosen by the King, received, heard (hence audit) and read the accounts presented to them by all the accountants and official receivers of royal funds, and checked that the charges were in order. They also had power to remit funds to the Crown. One of the problems with the system was that the King could not bypass the exchequer if he needed funds, and the lack of a tally system meant that the churchmen and counsellors appointed by the King had to take the receipts given to them at face value. Incompetence or corruption could be difficult to detect. Unlike England, fifteenth-century Scotland did not have a permanent accounting staff directly responsible to the Crown. To by-pass the system, James directed his crown revenues directly into the household accounting system through his comptrollers and treasurers. He also leased crown lands to raise money and, despite the warnings of Parliament, like his father and grandfather, sold **remissions.** To overcome the financial difficulties of the monarchy (caused in part by Parliament's lack of trust in him and consequent refusal to vote him taxes), James also borrowed money from Edinburgh merchants, such as **Walter Bertram.**

F

Fa me indovino, et iou te davo dinare: LIONS, 2: 'Tell my fortune, and I'll pay you'.

Face or pellet?: LIONS, 30: 'Heads or tail', a generic term not specific to the **Lion** of **James III***, which had the lion on one side and St Andrew on the reverse with fleur de lis and crowns. Pellets (little round balls, generally in groups of three) appeared on the reverse of the Scottish silver groat in James II's* reign, which has the King's face on one side and crowns and pellets on the other. James III's groats have mullets (stars with holes in the centre) and pellets on the reverse, minted between 1467 and 1475; a later debased silver groat *c.*1470 has the King on one side and, for the first time, thistles on the reverse. See also **Coining.**

Faire, faire!: GEMINI, 22: The equivalent, more or less, of 'Dear me!'

Faith has a fair name, but falsheid faris bettir: CHECKMATE I, 1: From the poem 'The Tretis of the Tua Mariit Wemen and the Wedo' by Scottish poet and priest William Dunbar (*c.* 1460–1520), in which the widow gives the impression of being the pious devoted griever, but takes as many lovers as she can find.

Falsing the doom: CASTLE, III, 13: The Scottish legal system's right of appeal on sentencing. Complaints could be laid against an erring or corrupt local judge by those who considered they had been inappropriately dealt with; the litigant had to pronounce immediately that the sentence was 'false, stinking and rotten'. He could then submit to arbitration, or proceed with his appeal to the Parliamentary Committee that heard falsed dooms.

Fate *plus mal que morte:* KINGS, I, 1: 'A fate worse than death'.

Fatiste: LIONS, 4: Author of **Mystery Plays.**

Favouzat, cavouzat: CHECKMATE, IV, 1: Abacadabra. Gossiping about the French court in the second half of the sixteenth century, the diarist Abbé de Brantôme (*c.* 1540–1614) writes of a sycophant who lined his pockets in secret, 'making the King's money jump into his own coffer by saying favouzat cavouzat, as Maître Gonnin does with his passe-passe (sleight of hand)'. Brantôme does not say who the conjurer is. (D. D.)

Ferrara wedding: RONDO, 9: Even the preliminaries were dazzling in this wedding of 1473 between Eleanora, eldest daughter of King Ferrante of Naples*, and Ercole 'Divus' d'Este, Duke of Ferrara (*fils* of the prolific Niccolò, see ***De ce côté-ci du Pô*** . . . The ubiquitous Sabadino (see Queen **Margaret of Denmark**) has left some idea of the extravagance of the rulers of the time. Top of the league was the Papal Court, led by the Cardinals Pietro Riario and Giuliano della Rovere. These, the favourite nephews of Pope Sixtus IV*, elected to startle the world when they entertained the bride Eleanora on her way north to her wedding with a train of 1,400, including Ercole's brothers, an entourage of nobles from Naples and Ferrara, and her own considerable household.

A vast timber palace, painted like stone, was built for her in one of Rome's central squares, with sleeping accommodation for her personal entourage, and a shaded courtyard with fountains and flower-wreathed pillars. Within, the walls, floors and ceilings of the public rooms were hidden behind gold-embroidered arras and carpets, and there were magnificent displays of silk flowers from France, while the stage was draped in white velvet. For the feast given for Eleanora on Whit Monday, the banqueting hall was kept cool by three invisible bellows, which directed streams of air over banks of snow from the mountains. There were four tablecloths to each table, one being drawn at the end of each course, while the stewards changed dress to match. The twelve-shelf sideboard held massed silver plate. Guests were welcomed with sweetmeats and malvoisie, after which trumpets and fifes ushered them to their tables. During the six hours of the banquet, forty-four dishes were served, including stags roasted whole in their skins, and ending with a bear with a staff in its jaws. The groom's name was celebrated in a life-sized representation in sugar of the labours of Hercules. Ten confectionery ships then sailed into the hall, bearing sugared almonds shaped like the acorns on the Rovere arms. After the performance of allegories and singing, classical heroes with their mistresses performed a ballet, interrupted by Centaurs, who were vanquished by Hercules.

The lady stayed until June. (D. D.)

Ffarewell Carboncle chosen chief: CHECKMATE III, 1: The line comes from the fifteenth-century lyric in the courtly love tradition, 'A Lover's Farewell to His Mistress'. This long goodbye of a poem (comprising thirty-four verses) compares the mistress's many attributes to precious gems, a carbuncle being a cabouchon gem (extract):

> ffarewell Carboncle chosen chief;
> ffarewell gloriouse as gold y-grave [engraved],

ffarewell pured [very fine] principall in prees,
ffarewell graciouse, god you save!
ffarewell derworth [beloved] of dignite,
ffarewell grace of gouernance,
how-euer y fare, ffarewell ye!
ffarewell prymerose, my plesaunce.

Ficino, Marsilio:* See **God in his Ipseity.**

FIORAVANTI, Rudolfo, degli Alberti: RONDO: (1415–1486) Bolognese architect, military engineer, bronze founder and mathematician, also called 'Aristotele'. He became known first in Rome, where he performed the prodigious feat of moving huge monolithic columns to the court of the Vatican from the Piazza Minerva, the site of the ancient Temple of Minerva. Returning to his native Bologna, Fioravanti brought his experience to the post of engineer of the commune, and increased his reputation in 1455 by managing to shift for thirty-five feet, without damage, one of the great towers of the city, of which there were at one time no less than 180, mostly family-owned. This specimen, known as 'della Mazione', was thirty-six feet in height. The operation so impressed the then papal legate, Cardinal Bessarion,* that he presented Fioravanti with fifty florins. In Bologna, the architect would certainly have known the friar **Ludovico de Severi da Bologna,*** and probably the future Pope, Francesco della Rovere, who studied at the University of Bologna, the oldest in Italy, where Fioravanti had learned his mathematics. (The town, greatly gratified, was to dispatch a magnificent embassy to Rome in 1471 to congratulate their former student on his election as Sixtus IV.*)

Fioravanti was by then much in demand. From Bologna he moved to Naples, and then to Duke Francesco Sforza* in the duchy of Milan. **Mathias Corvinus** asked the Reggimento for him on loan, in 1465, and he went to Buda in 1467, where he had access to architectural treatises by both Alberti and Filarete, and where he was admired as an engineer with the intellectual mastery of an architect. He made a second visit to Rome, where Pope Paul II* wished him to move from the south side of his basilica an 82-foot granite obelisk from Heliopolis, placed by Caligula (AD 12–41) on the spine of what became Nero's Circus. This was one task Fioravanti did not perform. A hundred years later, it was done by command of Sixtus V (Pope 1585–1590), with the help of 900 men, 150 horses and 47 cranes.

News of his skills as a designer of fortifications spread to Russia and Turkey, and invitations reached him from both countries. In the event, he turned down the Sultan **Mehmet*** in favour of **Ivan III**, Grand Prince of Muscovy, whose wife **Zoe Paleologina** had been brought up under the roof of the Cardinal Bessarion, and who summoned him to Moscow in 1474. Fioravanti went, taking Andrea his son, and his pupil Pietro.

The work for which he was to be remembered, however, was his artistic rather than his military achievements, and particularly his rebuilding of the great Moscow Cathedral of the Dormition, or the Assumption, on the Kremlin. The original cathedral had been built 150 years earlier by Ivan Kalita and the Metropolitan Petre and had fallen into decay. Ivan III had authorised the construction of a new cathedral by builders Miskin and Krivtsov, but two years after they began rebuilding, the walls collapsed. Initially the blame was laid on an earth tremor, but a team of troubleshooters brought from Pskov blamed poorly mixed mortar. The Pskov engineers declined to rebuild the cathedral, so Ivan sent for Fioravanti to design and build a replacement. Before starting this task, he was sent to study other early Russian churches, most notably the twelfth-century buildings of Vladimir, as well as Susdal and **Novgorod**. He taught new techniques, such as how to fire brick that remained strong and not friable; how to mix high-quality mortar; and how to use an infill of brick and cement instead of gravel and sand. He introduced new methods of hoisting and stone-cutting and, unusual in Muscovy, he made use of drawings. The cathedral was begun in 1475 and dedicated in 1479. Rather than reflecting the Renaissance, the cathedral was self-consciously in the Byzantine style. Within, the iconostasis was painted by Dionysius and his associates in 1481 in the tradition of the school of Andrei Rublev,* and the church, as the most important in Muscovy, was furnished with the finest of icons. Some fragments of the frescoes remain.

Fioravanti was also a gunsmith, and is credited with bringing to Russia the ability to cast bronze pieces, less likely to rupture than iron. The casting of lead and then iron cannon balls was introduced, and the making of gun-carriages. Before his time, guns were little use on campaign because of the lack of good roads, and of structures strong enough to sustain them. In 1477, during the activity that preceded the final siege of Novgorod, to the awe of spectators, Fioravanti built a pontoon bridge over the River Volkhov which actually remained afloat and carried traffic. He brought artillery to the Kazan campaign of 1482, and cannon and other firearms against Tver in 1485.

He kept in touch with Milan, in 1476 sending his son with a gift of hunting falcons to the Duke Galeazzo Maria, who responded with money and fabrics. Anxious for even more profitable contact, the Duke sent back with Andrea two Italian falconers, with offers of rich cloth in return for more birds. The exchange was closed, a few months later, by the assassination of the Duke of Milan.

While in Moscow, Fioravanti would certainly have renewed his acquaintance with Ludovico de Severi da Bologna during his stay after the fall of the Genoese colony in **Caffa**, in what is now the Ukraine. During frequent bouts of diplomatic activity, the architect was forced in 1476 to offer temporary hospitality to the Venetian envoy **Ambrogio Contarini**, who found it convenient to share a house so near the ducal palace. In 1479, Bologna tried to reclaim his services, but Fioravanti did not go back, although disturbed by the Grand Prince's excesses, and sometimes tempted to flee. The opportunity and the challenge were both, perhaps, too compelling. He died in Russia. (D. D.)

Fish, Gilbert: GEMINI, 17: (d. by 1503): Gilbert Fish (Gibbie in the novels) was a goldsmith and a bellfounder who became a burgess of **Edinburgh**, perhaps following William Fish, burgess in 1423.

Gilbert was engaged in royal trade, and appears in 1474, supplying **James III*** with a pair of bag harnesses (metal mountings). By 1484 Fish was engaged in the kind of transaction which permitted him to sue a burgess of Perth for twenty-four barrels of salmon, 'full red and sweet', or equivalent, as per his written promise. In a reversal the following year, Fish and one Thomas Tod were reckoned to owe George Robieson £110 in gold and silver 'at the rate of the time of the **black money**'. The dispute concerned a royal order of over twenty-one stones of copper delivered to Robieson, and iron 'prented' by Fish. Robieson was Treasurer to the burgh of Edinburgh, and Tod presumably belonged to the family of Alexander Tod, who was a coiner in Stirling from 1443 until the late 1460s.

The change between James III and **James IV*** had no visible effect on Fish's business: in one of the first acts of the new reign, Gilbert Fish was given twenty pounds from the treasury for life, for faithful service. In the same year, 1488, he was paid for gilding a basin, a ewer and a salt-cellar for the King, and that December was given £33s for royal work, including making a bell. In 1490 Fish was claiming from Sir Thomas Tod the sum of two hundred marks, the residue of five hundred marks he had owed, perhaps for another metal transaction. In 1491 he witnessed at **Linlithgow** a charter concerning Laurence, Lord Oliphant.

Gilbert Fish was a coiner too, operating probably in the reign of James III, when he may have made the **Amiens** medal at Berwick-upon-Tweed.* He was certainly a master moneyer before 1493, when Parliament discussed the problem caused by cracked money, and the diversity of coins struck by different moneyers. An edict was made that all coins should be accepted, 'whether of the strike of Gilbert Fish, called Berwick groats', or of the late Livingston and John Currour. Coins in dispute were to be brought into the office. Berwick fell to the English in 1482, and Alexander Livingston was a practising moneyer in the 1470s and 1480s, so that the coinage in question was minted in the reign of James III. The 'Berwick groats' might even represent the ghosts of the 'Cochrane placks' which supposedly made **Thomas Cochrane** so unpopular that he was hanged the year that Berwick was taken.

Unlike **William Goldsmith**, Fish was not one of the group which sealed itself off in Crichton Castle after the disturbance of **Lauder Bridge** in 1482, but he was the beneficiary, with **Thomas Yare**, when **William, Third Lord Crichton**, died and left Easter Hailes in the **regality** of Musselburgh to them both, under a reversion. Because of Crichton's subsequent forfeiture, Easter Hailes in fact went to the King. Part of it had been owned by Gilbert Fish since 1483, and in 1485 he had been supported by **Sir Robert Colville**, the Queen's steward, in a **sasine** case concerning Thomas Cockburn and Robert Ramsay of Cockpen in Hailes.

Gilbert's work continued, and in 1496 he was busy on a stop lid of the King's, using five ounces of silver. By 1503 he had died. He had a house on the south side of the **Canongate**, Edinburgh, next to the land of **Archibald Crawford.** Thomas, Gilbert's son and heir, was also a goldsmith and burgess, and the following year employed Matthew Auchinleck, goldsmith, as his assignee over the reversion to Gilbert during his lifetime of **tenements** on the south side of the highway, between John Barker and the late Nicholas Wright (probably Nicholas the goldsmith). Yet another goldsmith, James Amisfield (from whom **Anselm Sersanders** once claimed money), was one of the witnesses. (D. D.)

Fisher's Ring: GEMINI, 16: To be Under the Fisher Ring implies a solemn missive sealed by the Pope.

FLEMING family: HN; LC: Men from Flanders who settled in Scotland in the twelfth century took a variety of names, but some of them simply adopted the soubriquet Fleming. Many of these came in the train of Maud of Lens, the Flemish wife of David I, King of Scotland 1124–1153, and among them was Baldwin the Fleming of Biggar, who married the widow of Reginald, son of Alan, Earl of Richmond, England. Baldwin's stepson, the widow's son John, acquired land in Lanarkshire in what later came to be called Crawfordjohn, and was the earliest properly recorded member of the family **Crawford.** (This was the same area colonised at the end of the century by William de **Lindsay**, of separate origins, whose family later became Earls of Crawford.) The descendants of Baldwin became the Earls of Wigton and (of greater consequence) Lords Fleming of Biggar and Cumbernauld, with their seat at Boghall Castle, Biggar, Lanarkshire.

Under King Alexander III (ruled 1249–1286), a Sir Malcolm Fleming was sheriff of Dumbarton, and another Malcolm, about 1327, gifted land near Dumbarton to **Newbattle** Abbey. But by the turn of the century yet another Malcolm Fleming has appeared as the husband of Elizabeth Stewart, Lady of Biggar, a first cousin of King James I (ruled 1406–1437) and sister of Sir Murdoch Stewart, who married Isabella Stewart, Countess of Lennox. As well as Biggar, this Sir Malcolm's family also owned Cumbernauld, with its castle and forest and the lands, **barony** and mills of Monycabo in Aberdeenshire, which included fishing rights on the River Don, and was to be the cause of endless disputes with the Huntly family.

One of Malcolm Fleming's two sons lived in England for five years as hostage for his mother's cousin James I, being freed to return in 1432. Events, however, blighted any ensuing atmosphere of goodwill. After James II* came to the throne in 1437, Malcolm Fleming of Biggar and Cumbernauld found himself implicated in the quarrel between the King and the **Black Douglases**, and was executed with the Sixth **Earl of Douglas** and his brother at the notorious Black Dinner at Edinburgh Castle in 1440.

Malcolm Fleming's son of the same name died early, but his other son, Robert, who was to live until 1491, was allowed to succeed to his father's forfeited lands, and maintain his father's claim to Panmure, Forfar and leases at Cousland, close to Newbattle, which Henry, Lord **Sinclair**, was later to claim. Robert was even given land in the barony of Kinghorn, Fife, all to compensate for his father's execution. Importantly, he was also permitted to marry Janet, a daughter of James, the new Seventh Earl of Douglas. (He later took as second wife Margaret, daughter of Lord Lindsay.) He became steward of the King's household. In 1451 Biggar was made a burgh of barony, and the following year Robert became the First Lord Fleming, one of a group of eight new lords of Parliament that included **John Stewart, Lord Darnley**, and Sir Alexander Boyd.

Although of no very great political influence, Robert Fleming seems to have been a rumbustious character sought out by others and soon led, like his father, into dubious partnerships. He was adopted as an ally by the **Boyd*** family during the minority of the next young King, **James III**,* but survived the débâcle which followed their attempt to capture and then influence the King. Through the late sixties, seventies and eighties, he sat as one of the **Lords Auditor of Causes and Complaints** along with **Henry Arnot**, Abbot of **Cambuskenneth, William Knollys*** and **Henry Cant** among others.

By his Douglas marriage Robert had two daughters and two sons, Malcolm and Robert. Malcolm seems to have been an able man who held a number of public offices. In 1471 he was sheriff of Stirling, where he had a house; and in 1474 was appointed a commissioner to treat of the English Princess **Cecilia**'s wedding to the future **James IV.*** Unfortunately he predeceased his father, as his namesake had done, leaving Robert to roar through his remaining years 'guilty', as one report says, 'of many outrages: furious, profuse and insane'. The records, overflowing with litigation over unpaid debts, disputed grazing rights, wrongful occupation of lands, appropriation of cattle and withholding of rents, tend to bear out the description. In 1480, although the old man was still alive, the lands at Biggar, Cumbernauld and Monycabo and the Stirling house tenancy were resigned into the safer hands of his elder grandson David, one of Malcolm's two sons; and when David soon died, to his brother, Robert's other grandson, John Fleming.

This was another stroke of bad luck, since John Fleming displayed more than a few of his grandfather's traits. For his behaviour as a youth in 1482 at the time of the army's muster to march with the King to **Lauder Bridge**, he had been dispatched briefly to prison. Later, he joined **Archibald Douglas**, Earl of Angus and Alexander **Home**, and turned fully against James III in 1488 in support of the young Prince James. When his grandfather Robert finally died in 1491, John became the Second Lord Fleming. One of his marriages, to Eufemia Drummond, appears to have been orthodox, but he created a scandal by kidnapping the **Princess Mary**'s small granddaughter Margaret Stewart, daughter of Elizabeth **Hamilton** and Matthew, Second

Earl of Lennox, and demanding a **dispensation** to allow him to marry her in 1509. Castigated as a dissolute and turbulent man, John Fleming met a violent death in 1524, killed by John Tweedie of Drummelzier.

Four years later his widow Agnes, daughter of Sir John Somerville, was to take as second husband the much-married George, Fourth Earl of Rothes,* who had already had two sons and a daughter by Margaret Crichton, the love-child of the **Princess Margaret**, sister to the Princess Mary above. Agnes gave Rothes an additional three sons and four daughters and died in 1542, after which Rothes married the widow of **David Lindsay**, Eighth Earl of Crawford, in between giving Margaret Crichton another five children.

Semiroyal marriages were in the air. John Fleming's son Malcolm, Third Lord Fleming, was born in 1494, and married Janet Stewart, the natural daughter of King James IV. Taken prisoner at the rout of Solway Moss in 1542, Malcolm was tried and acquitted in 1545 of treasonable collaboration with the enemy. He died fighting against the English at the battle of Pinkie in 1547.

In 1548 Malcolm's eldest son James, Fourth Baron Fleming,* helped escort the five-year-old Mary Queen of Scots* to France, where in due course she was to marry the Dauphin. Her governess was James's widowed mother, Lady Fleming,* who won her way into the bed of the French King, Henri II,* and triumphantly bore him a son. James's sister Mary Fleming was the most sprightly of the Queen's four maids of honour called Mary, and grew up to wed William Maitland of Lethington (1525–1573), son of the poet Sir Richard (see **Mount Sinai** and CASTLE, III, 5).

In 1549, James Fleming returned to visit France with the Queen Dowager, Mary de Guise,* and in 1553 was made Great Chamberlain of Scotland for life, as well as becoming guardian of the East and Middle Marches. In 1557/1558 he was one of the eight commissioners appointed to attend the wedding in France of Queen Mary, now fifteen. There was friction over the marriage agreement, and the fatal illness which overcame four of the commissioners, including James Fleming, was thought to be induced by poison. Three of the Scots – the Earl of Cassilis,* Robert Reid, the Bishop of Orkney,* and George, Earl of Rothes (the fervent family man who married John Fleming's widow) – died when embarking for home from Dieppe. James, in the hope of a cure, managed to travel to Paris, but succumbed there. The culprits were never found. (D. D.)

Flemish painter . . . in Urbino: See **Justus of Ghent.**

Flodden: GEMINI, 43: The 'great national victory' ironically alluded to in the chapter is that of Flodden Field, September 1513, where the Scots led by **James IV*** met the English and were utterly defeated. It is estimated that ten thousand Scots lost their lives, including the King and many of Scotland's greatest earls and nobles.

A renewal of the Auld Alliance with Louis XII (King of France 1498–1515) drew Scotland into the complex machinations of the Holy League which united the papacy and England against France. Scotland and France agreed in 1512 that if either country were to go to war with England, the other was committed to help by declaring war on England also. However, prior to this in 1502, Scotland had made the Treaty of Perpetual Peace with England, sealed with the marriage of Margaret Tudor (daughter of Henry VII, King of England 1485–1509) and James IV in 1503. This peace, sealed with papal approval, had been renewed in 1509. The Auld Alliance placed James between England and France, promised to both sides. When Henry VIII came to the throne, his antagonism to France placed James in an untenable position. As his peace with England and the subsequent marriage had been given express papal sanction, in 1513 the newly elected Pope Leo X threatened James IV with excommunication if he were to break it. Yet, when Henry VIII invaded France, James had no choice but to send the Scottish fleet, with the best of his artillery, to France's aid. James then amassed his army and, at its head, marched into England.

The Scots army of twenty thousand men is considered the largest ever to have entered England. The initial position taken by the Scots was a favourable one, on Flodden Hill. As the English army (of equivalent size) under the Earl of Surrey forded the River Till and effectively blocked the Scots' path back to Scotland, the Scots changed position first to Branxton Hill, where the superior English artillery (lighter and more manoeuvrable than the Scottish culverins) picked off the Scots in their defensive position, and forced them down the hill to the muddy field below. The Scottish gunners could not find the range of their English enemy. The main Scottish army was armed with long pikes, spears seventeen and a half feet long, useless when fighting the English hand-to-hand, being too long and much more unwieldy than the English short halberd, only nine feet long with a combined spear and axe-head. Nor were the Scots' long swords an effective weapon in the circumstances. The Scots' forces were routed. Amongst the dead was King James IV, whose demise once again placed a child on to the throne of Scotland. James V's* mother briefly acted as Regent, but her hasty marriage to Archibald Douglas,* Sixth Earl of Angus, saw her lose the position, which then fell to **John Stewart, Second Duke of Albany.**

Fly agaric: GEMINI, 18: See **Agaric.**

Foghnaidh salann salach air im roineagach: GEMINI, 45: 'Dirty salt will suffice for hairy butter': Gaelic saying.

Fokke-deck: LIONS, 24: In Hanse nautical language, *Fuk* meant fore, from *fiuka*, to drive, and was used as an adjective or a noun. In Denmark, *fok* meant a foresail, and *fukke* included both mast and yard. A ship in 1460 might have two fuksails and one mizzen. The cokswain (modern coxwain) was in charge of the ship's boat or pinnace.

Fonticho di puzza: GEMINI, 23: See **Camulio, Prosper Schiaffino de, de' Medici.***

Food: See **Frozen food.** On a warmer note, an Italian dish with a long history was ravioli. In the fifteenth century it signified a packet of chopped herbs and pork mixed with cream cheese, in an envelope made from egg-white and flour. This was then fried and eaten powdered with sugar. When forbidden to serve too many courses at once, the Florentines devised a giant, multipurpose filled pasty featuring ham ravioli. It also contained sausages, chickens and pork; salt and onions; parsley, dates, almonds, spices, saffron, cheese, eggs and sugar in appropriate layers. No dessert was necessary. (D. D.)

For in this country be many white elephants without number, and of unicorns and of lions of many manners: CASTLE: III, 12: Mandeville,* chapter thirty-two of *The Travels of Sir John Mandeville:* the animals of the wilderness in the empire of Prester John.*

For it is full of serpents, of dragons, of cockodrills, that no man dare dwell there: CHECKMATE: I, 5: The uninhabitable wastes of Ceylon, as depicted by Mandeville,* chapter twenty-one.

For to give good smell and odour to the Emperor . . . : QUEENS, III, 6: Description of the twelve vessels of balm, lit in the bedchamber of Prester John,* according to Mandeville,* chapter thirty.

Forgive! and never will I aft tresspass: CHECKMATE; I, 4: The last line of the poem 'Health' by Thomas Hoccleve (*c.* 1369–1426):

> O God, O Health, unto thine ordinance
> Wealeful [prosperous] lord, meekly submit I me!
> I am contrite, and of full repentance
> That e'er I swimmed in such nicety
> As was displeasant to thy deity:
> Now kythe [make known] on me thy mercy and thy grace!
> It fits a God of his gracé free;
> Forgive! and never will I aft trespáss.

Formulating with passion various astronomical equations: UNICORN, 46: Said of one of the great eleventh-century mathematicians of Andalusia, Spain. His full name was al-Hasan ibn Muhammad ibn al-Hasan ibn Hayy al-Tajibi, and he came from the capital city of Córdoba. His knowledge of geometry and astronomy enabled him to draw up astronomical tables and he was much in demand, moving from Andalusia to Egypt to the Yemen, where he was lavishly treated, and sent as an envoy to Baghdad. He died in the Yemen about 1064.

Four-eyebrowed beauty: PAWN, 13: Refers to a youth whose moustache has just begun to grow, but it also appears in a poem by Mesíhí (d. 1512) entitled 'Ode on Spring' where each of the lines represents an eyebrow (extract):

> Fain I hope, Mesíhí, fame may dwell with this my foursome lay;
> May these four-eyebrowed beauties bide, my keepsake with the gay.
> Wander 'mong the roseate faces, nightingale so sweet o'say.
> Drink, be gay; for soon will vanish, biding not, the days o' spring!

Frae vulgar prose to flowand Latin: KINGS, I, 1: In the novel, a reversal of a line by John Bellenden (*c.* 1492–*c.* 1550). It appears in the political preface to his translation of the Latin *History of Scotland* by Hector Boece (*c.* 1465–1536):

> When busy Ceres with her plough and harrows
> Has filled her granges full of every corn;
> And stormy Chiron with his bow and arrows
> Has all the cloudis of the heavenis shorn,
> And schill Tryton with his windy horn
> Ourewhelmèd all the flowand ocean
> And Phoebus turnèd under Capricorn,
> The samen greis [degrees] where I first began.
>
> Sen thou art drawen sae compendius
> Frae flowand Latin into vulgar prose,
> Show now what princes been maist vicious,
> And wha has been of chivalry the rose.

Franciscan Friars: See **Observatine Friars.**

Frederick III: LIONS, 46: (1415–1493) Frederick, son of Duke Ernest of Austria, was elected King of Germany in 1440 and Holy Roman Emperor in 1452; he was the last Emperor to be crowned in Rome by the Pope. Yet more important to Frederick than the governance of his territories was his overwhelming desire to launch a crusade. The fall of Constantinople to the Ottoman Empire in 1453 and the collapse of the Byzantine Empire made Frederick's Holy Roman Empire the greatest Christian power in the world. But it was never wealthy enough to mount a crusade, nor powerful enough to keep the Ottomans from attacking its eastern borders.

Frederick married Eleanor of Portugal; their son, the future **Maximilian I**, was born in 1459. Aware of the wealth and potential power of Burgundy, Frederick avoided the conclusion of a marriage between Maximilian and **Marie of Burgundy** (during her father **Charles, Duke of Burgundy**'s* lifetime), in return for which the Duke expected to obtain the coveted title of King of the Romans. In anger at his failure to secure the marriage and the title, Charles waged war against the Swiss Confederation allied to Frederick's empire, with disastrous results (see **Adorne, Anselm***).

While Frederick undoubtedly neglected the management of the empire as he pursued his more pressing interest in alchemy, astrology and botany, the territories under the familial control of the Habsburgs nevertheless grew with the eventual marriage of Maximilian to Marie, making Frederick's monogram AEIOU (*Austriae est imperare orbi universo*, or *Alles Erdreich ist Oesterreich unterthan*) a reality. The Habsburgs who followed him were to dominate central Europe for centuries to come.

Freya: LIONS, 26: A powerful goddess of Nordic legend who watched over lovers and women in labour, and had some powers over the dead. One of the twin children of Njord, she travelled in a chariot drawn by cats, and wept tears of red-gold when her husband Od left her. On the other hand, scandal accused her of love-dealings with her own twin brother Freyr, and of taking all the gods and elves as her lovers. There is a story of how she obtained her famous necklace by sleeping in turn with each of the four dwarves who forged it. Odin and Freya were worshipped in Iceland for longer than most of their fellow-gods. See **I will not serve an idle log.**

Frozen food: RONDO, 34; CASTLE II, 4: Cold weather in the north, such as in **Iceland** and Russia, made it easy to preserve food. Animals were chopped up in the markets of Moscow, where the meat would keep for three months. In Iceland, a barrel of sour whey mixed with water could keep for several years, and rancid cow or sheep butter (poor, white and full of hairs) would last for twenty. If scarce, it was replaced by lumps of tallow. A sauce of melted tallow was eaten with baked mutton, for example. Cheese, made late in the season, was of poorish quality. Sheeps' heads were kept in sorrel juice, or fermented sour milk.

Other kinds of food were preserved by hanging in wind-houses: wind-dried cod was eaten uncooked. Wind-hung sharks took three months to mature. Cultivated from necessity, a taste for sour food appeared to be widespread, even far south in Scotland, where connoisseurs of the mouth-wringing recommended Corstorphine cream.

Also on the menu, of course, would be seaweed, birds' eggs, and the popular standby, a cauldron of soup with an auk in it. Auks were deemed to mean guillemots or razorbills, but might also include the odd **poffin.** In the right season, there would be a good variety of fresh fish and fowl: the fish included cod, salmon, plaice, ling, herring and halibut. (Halibut were not simply for eating: Shetlanders used them as pads over which to haul up their boats.) The climate being unsuited for corn, bread was expensive and rare. Unsurprisingly, there was a name for Icelandic scurvy, which translates as 'corpse-pang'. (D. D.)

Fynnart, Jimme of: KINGS, II, 1: James Hamilton of Finnart, reputed or actual Master of Works at **Linlithgow** Palace (he also worked on Falkland, Edinburgh and Stirling) and favourite of James V* who had been executed in 1540 following charges of heresy and plotting against the King, although James's detractors and later historians have asserted that the allegations were based on nothing more than the acquisitive King's desire to seize Hamilton's riches. (See also **Hamilton, James, Lord**, and **Albany, Alexander Duke of.***)

G

Gaineth me no garland of green, but it ben of withies wrought: KNIGHTS, III, 16: Fragment of an early-fourteenth-century song found in *The Red Book of Ossory*, a collection of Latin songs to be sung to the tune of earlier secular lyrics. The couplet (which was either the opening lines of the song or the refrain) indicates the familiar tune to which the Latin poem was to be sung.

Galabiya: UNICORN, 36: Full-length Arab garment, either loose, with wide sleeves and a low, round neck, or tailored, with a high buttoned neck and cuffed sleeves.

Galley argot: PAWN, 3: Built chiefly for war and trade in the seas of the Levant, the galleys of the fifteenth and sixteenth centuries used crews of many nationalities. At sea or in harbour, they obeyed the silver whistle of the boatswain, known as *le comite*, and addressed as '*notre homme*', 'our man'. The master who commanded the boatswain used a language based on French but created especially to be understood by the Italians, Danes, Greeks, Turks, Arabs and Moors who also occupied the rowing benches. It was used also by the great corsairs like Barbarossa* and Dragut Rais.*

Most oarsmen were criminals, and were treated as such. They spent their lives shackled, even at night, when they slept on their own benches, made of wood covered with worn wool and cowhide. They worked stripped to the waist, heads and beards shaven and legs and feet bare, and more died of cold than of injuries. Punishment was by the lash, and sometimes by the sword. Travelling, they spent more time under sail than under oar, although the ceremony of entering and leaving harbour required a rigorously drilled display of fast oarsmanship. An order to row *tout avant* was a direction to employ the full *chiourme*, or body of slaves. To row backwards was *scier* ('*La scie!*'), and forwards was *voguer*. To row *à outrance* meant to row at the uppermost limit of speed, which in calm weather was something like four and a half nautical miles an hour, requiring twenty-six blade strokes a minute – spectacular, but too exhausting to keep up for long.

In its most extreme form, in war, this speed was attained by rowing *à toucher le banc* (literally 'touching the bench'). This meant that all the oarsmen stood upright, one foot forward, oars aligned, and then the oars were plunged in the water as each slave lifted the end he was holding, braced his free foot on the top of the bench in front, and after striking the water, threw himself back on the bench, head turned to the prow. To increase the pace even more, it was possible to lower the oar in the process to touch the bench where the rower's foot rested. It could not be sustained for very long.

Leaving harbour (the sheep were last on board), the boatswain would receive the commands: '*Avertissez que nous allons partir; que le canon soit leste pour tirer le coup de partance!*' ('Ready to leave! Prepare to fire the parting salute!'). '*Boute-feu!*'('Fire!'). '*Leva lengue!*' ('Quiet!'). '*Tout le monde fore du coursier, et tout le monde à sa poste!*' ('Clear the gangway; men to their stations!'). When under sail, the commands for the helmsman and mariners were also unique. To pay off, or bear away from the wind, the order was '*Pouge!*', from Poggia, leeward; and to sail close-hauled, the Levantine order was '*Orse!*' (from Orza, windward, rather than the usual French '*Loffe!*'. '*Mettre la galère à la trinque*' (the trinketum was the sail of the prow) meant to bring the vessel into the wind, deliberately losing seaway in order to perform a manoeuvre. '*Forté*' was the order to belay and hold firm.

The anchor (there were four) was simply known as *le fer*, the iron; and the anchor cable was *la gume*, which fell down into the equivalent of the modern chain-locker. The cable below deck was referred to as *le mort* (the dead portion), and that emerging to drop to the water was *vif* (alive). Hence the command '*Hâte le vif! Recouvre le mort!*' was an order to heave up the anchor cable, and pay it out quickly.

It was the boatswain's job to identify the strong oarsmen and place them effectively, since a weak *bancade* (benchful of oarsmen) could break the rhythm, and kill other rowers. The vital positions were those of the *vogue avants* or bow-oars, each of whom was responsible for engaging the end of his oar, rowing and also directing it. Of these the finest – usually Turks – were placed at the back, in the *banc* (bench) *des espalles*, where they set the stroke for the rest of the *chiourme*. *L'espalle* was the staging reached by some steps next to the poop, and the place where all boarders first set foot on the vessel. Only the slaves, they said, regularly came in by the poop but left feet first (i.e., dead) by the prow. (D. D.)

Galoppini: RONDO, 41: Literally, 'the fast lads': the name given to court runners. In the novel, it is elevated to mean that the cavalry have arrived.

Garden of Balm: See **Matariya.**

Geese, fishing with: GEMINI, 36: An ancient ploy among farmers living close to the Lake of Menteith, the only stretch of water in Scotland to bear the name Lake instead of Loch. They are said to have resorted to geese to help them catch its rich store of pike. Baited lines, two or three feet in length, were tied to the legs of the farmers' own geese, which were then driven into the lake and left to swim their way home. Naturally, the bait was soon swallowed, and, says one report, 'a violent and often tedious struggle ensued, in which, however, the geese at length prevailed, though often much exhausted before they reached shore'. The goose-owners, it is assumed, claimed the fish brought back by their birds. The Lake of Menteith is also home to three islands, on the largest of which are the ruins of Inchmahome Priory, where the young Mary Queen of Scots* was kept safe shortly before her journey to France (KINGS I, 3). (D. D.)

Gel, gel, gel: LIONS, 8; PAWN, 21: To a well-trained camel, a command to hurry.

Geysir cooking: LIONS, 27: The fictitious cooking experiment described in the novels was, astonishingly, repeated four hundred years later by another visitor to **Iceland**, a naval commander called Forbes. In his case, having dispatched his companion to purchase a bottle of corn-brandy and some coffee from a neighbouring farmer, the commander took his reserve flannel shirt and packed a breast of mutton securely in the body, and a ptarmigan in each sleeve. Then he piled forty minutes' worth of turf into the geysir called the Strokr, and added the shirt. In due course (in fact seven minutes late) there was a tremendous eruption and, surrounded by steam and turf-clods, he beheld his shirt in mid-air, arms extended, like a head- and tail-less trunk. It fell lifeless by the brink and, when retrieved, proved to contain the mutton done to a turn, although the ptarmigan, sadly, were in threads. The shirt was none the worse, except that the colour had all been scalded out of it. (D. D.)

Giovane di lingua: LIONS, 16: 'Interpreter'.

GLOUCESTER, Richard, Duke of: GEMINI: (1452–1485) The Duke, brother to **Edward IV*** commanded the army that marched on Scotland in 1482, comprising a force of twenty thousand men paid for four weeks, and an additional force of 1,700 men for an additional two weeks (to lay siege to Berwick-upon-Tweed*). It was the largest English force to be seen in the field for over eighty years. King Edward's failure to set **Alexander, Duke of Albany,*** on the throne of Scotland was somewhat offset by the return of Berwick to England; and the English King's future plans for the domination of Scotland were cut short by his death in 1483. Gloucester worked hard to have himself proclaimed Regent, and after the murder of Edward's two surviving sons (who were left in his care after the death of their father), was crowned Richard III in 1483. His reign was to be short. His enemies, led by Henry Tudor, Earl of Richmond (1457–1509), defeated and killed Richard at the Battle of Bosworth Field on 22 August 1485. Richmond was proclaimed Henry VII and a three-year truce was agreed between Scotland and England in September 1488.

Gniezno, Archbishop of: RONDO, 7: One of the wealthiest magnates in late-fifteenth-century Poland. The Archbishop of Gniezno at the beginning of the sixteenth century held title to 230 villages and 13 towns, 10 times the amount of his nearest secular rival. From 1462 the Archbishop also held the title Duke of Łowicz. In the later-fifteenth century and early-sixteenth century the position was held by Frederick, one of the sons of **Casimir IV**, King of Poland.

God at his eye-window knows: GEMINI, 14: From a fourteenth-century religious work, describing how David, God's prophet, lost his heart – 'My heart has fled from me' – and how, when he blesses himself, it returns. 'How did so holy a man let it escape from him? And where did it break out from? Where? God knows, at his eye-window'. For humans, on the other hand, 'eye-windows' were equated with 'harm windows', as St Bernard held, lecturing on the dangers of the unchaste eye: '*Sicut mors per peccatum in orbem, ita per has fenestras intrat in mentem*'. ('just as Death entered the world by means of sin, so through these windows it may enter the soul'.) (D. D.)

God in his Ipseity: GEMINI, 28: from *ipse*, self. Ipseity in modern terms generally means personal identity. In a Christian religious context, it concerns the relations of the Persons in the Trinity. Trinitarian dogma was something which greatly exercised philosophers such as Marsilio Ficino* (1433–1499), a protégé of the Medici in Florence and a leading member of their Platonic Academy, which developed ideas newly revealed to the West by Ficino's translations. A key argument rested on a passage in the Epistle to the Romans, which the Vulgate took to refer to the Father, the Son and the Holy Spirit. For all his questioning, however, Ficino was a priest who revered and followed 'the divine footsteps' of Augustine. Described by gossip as a little, dapper fellow and a great hypochondriac 'who reached no higher than the girdle of an average man', Ficino lived to be nearly seventy, and established his name as one of the founders of neo-Platonism.

The word in question had a different meaning for Turks, who (it was noted) had no truck with the Trinity, but praised God for His Ipseity and His Unparticularisedness. (D. D.)

Goes, Van Der, Hugo: See **Van der Goes, Hugo.**

Golden Horde: RONDO, 10: The Tartar khanate of the Golden Horde was the westernmost section of the great Mongol empire of Genghis Khan (*c.* 1162–1227). The empire was vast, stretching to be the size of the former USSR, but after Genghis's death, the empire split into four sections. Under Genghis's grandson Batu (who conquered Hungary in 1241; d. *c.* 1255), the Golden Horde settled on the Volga at Saray, which became the centre of their empire. The Horde were also known as the Tartars, a corruption of *tatar,* from the biblical Tartarus, meaning mountains. From Saray, they ruled over Russia and the eastern Slavs. In 1382 they captured Moscow, forcing tribute from the Russians until **Ivan III** finally broke free and ceased payment in 1480.

The Horde was in decline in the fifteenth century and were further weakened by internal divisions. The khanate of Kazan defected in 1438, the Crim khanate followed in 1441 (see **Mengli-Girey**) and Astrakhan separated in 1466. While still a suzerainty of the Golden Horde, the Crim Tartars became a vassal state to the Ottoman Empire and turned against the Horde, destroying their capital, Saray, in 1502. The Golden Horde then ceased to exist as a territorial empire.

Goldsmith, William: GEMINI, 33: See under **Adorne, Euphemia** for an explanation of his nickname 'the Halfpenny Man'. See also **Coining; Fish, Gilbert; Swift, Thomas.**

Golf: UNICORN, 2: The game of golf was particularly popular in Scotland from the second quarter of the fifteenth century, to the extent that it was beginning to interfere with more traditional recreations, such as archery. The first written reference to the sport comes in the parliamentary statute of 1457 which condemns the game:

> ye fut bawe and ye golf be uterly cryt done and not usyt and at ye bowe markes be maid at all parochkirkes apair of buttes and schuting be usyt ilk sunday . . .

This indicates that, along with football, it was considered an unsuitable urban pastime for the masses; compared to archery, golf did not have potential military uses. Those who did not comply with the act's exhortation to shoot six arrows at the targets every Sunday were subject to a fine of two pennies, which would go towards buying drink for those who had practised their archery skills. The prohibitions against golf were reiterated by the Parliaments of **James III*** in 1471 and of **James IV*** in 1491.

Other than the fact that the game was played with a ball and stick, and was very popular, the early rules or structure of the game have not survived. Games with balls and clubs were popular across Europe, but the specific game of golf would appear to have two main ancestors. The first was known in the Low Countries in the fourteenth century; in it a club called a *kolf* was used to drive a ball across the ground at a target. In the other variation, popular in Scotland, the aim was to hit the ball into a hole in the ground. The game was well suited to being played on links, common open ground often close to the coast (such as **Leith** Links, although there were links, such as Bruntsfield in **Edinburgh**, to the south of the castle and not adjacent to the coast where golf has been played since the sixteenth century). These areas (if too poor quality for common grazing) were general recreation grounds, used for horse racing, football and archery.

The game became a favourite of the royal family: the Lord High Treasurer's Accounts of 1503 list the golf balls and clubs bought by James IV, and the fact that he spent 3 February playing golf with the Earl of Bothwell. There is evidence to suggest that the King unsuccessfully gambled on the outcome of the game, as the day cost him three French crowns. James played golf while staying in Edinburgh, Perth and probably St Andrews. In 1502 James paid fourteen shillings for clubs from a *bowar* or bowmaker of St Johnston (Perth), and a 1506 entry in the Treasurer's Accounts indicate that his clubs cost a shilling each, and the balls were three for a shilling. The balls were probably imported from the Low Countries, by the barrel. The early balls were likely to have been made of boxwood (which would float, important in the Low Countries' version of the game, which was often played on ice), and the clubs in two pieces with a flexible shaft and hardwood head.

Golf became popular in England in the early sixteenth century, possibly following James IV's marriage to Margaret Tudor. It remained popular with Scottish royalty, particularly Mary Queen of Scots,* who is recorded by her enemies as playing golf in East Lothian (in the grounds of Seytoun) very shortly after the murder of her husband Henry Darnley in 1567.

GRAHAM, Patrick : UNICORN: (*c.* 1435–1478) Grandson of Mary, daughter of Robert III (ruled 1390–1406), and nephew of Bishop Kennedy*, Graham was set for a meteoric rise through the Scottish Church, and an equally speedy decline. In 1463, he was provided to the see of Brechin, probably at the instigation of his uncle. On Kennedy's death in 1465, Graham was made Bishop of St Andrews at only thirty years old, at the expense of other more experienced bishops, much better suited to the task. Unfortunately for Graham, his appointment was made in the minority of **James III*** and when the King attained his majority in 1469, his government acted to strengthen the power of the Scottish Church at the expense of the Pope, challenging the Pontiff's authority. Bishop Graham was caught in the middle of the argument between the Pope and the King, and was set on interfering to aggrandise his own position, to the detriment of his fellow clerics. The Bishopric of St Andrews was to be granted immunity and independence from the control of the papacy, meaning the provision of candidates to monastic houses was to be decided locally, not by the Pope. It cut papal patronage out of the appointment to eleven Scottish Abbeys and four Priories.

In an effort to come to an understanding about the situation in St Andrews, in June 1471 James appointed **Henry Arnot**, Abbot of **Cambuskenneth**, to act as his procurator on a mission to the Roman Curia, to sort out the issue of provisions. However, Patrick Graham (without permission from the King even to leave Scotland) reached Rome before Arnot and gained favour with the new Pope Sixtus IV,* and got him to come to an agreement that suited Graham's greed rather than the monarchy or the Scottish Church (in addition to securing for himself a raft of other titles and privileges). **Jan Adorne** accompanied Graham to Rome and worked for him. In 1472 Pope Sixtus IV erected St Andrews into an archiepiscopal see, making Graham Scotland's first Metropolitan. The other twelve bishops of Scotland were now to be suffragans, owing obedience to the new Archbishop. His promotion earned Graham the wrath of the Church's Scottish hierarchy. Prior to this, Scottish bishops with local disputes could appeal directly to Rome rather than having to refer pleas to a local metropolitan; the lack of a metropolitan in Scotland also meant that the King could resist papal claims more effectively. An intransigent locally based primate could undermine the local authority and independence of the other bishops, and interfere with political decisions by using his position to impose papal policy on the monarchy.

It was an appointment inevitably rejected by both the King and the other bishops, unified in their dislike of Graham. He put off his return to Scotland until the autumn of 1473, but it was simply delaying the inevitable. James seized the temporality of St Andrews, and acted quickly on Graham's arrival to have him removed from office on the basis of incompetence and clear signs of mental instability. He was subsequently found guilty of both heresy and simony. The charges against him included maladministration of the archbishopric, oppression of his subjects, blasphemy and his claim that he was a Pope, elected by God and crowned by an angel with the task of reforming the Church. He was imprisoned in Inchcolm, then at the castle of Lochleven until his death. James had won against the Pope, and retained the title of Archbishop to confer on **William Scheves** in 1478, the man whom Graham had opposed as a candidate for Archdeacon of St Andrews.

Grandson: See **Jewels with a name.**

Grant, John le: RAM: Johannes Grant first appears in 1453, as a member of a seven-hundred-strong company of soldiers from Genoa, Chios* and **Rhodes,** fighting to hold Constantinople against the Turks side by side with the Venetians, their traditional rivals and enemies. The Genoese, skilled at defending walled cities, were led by a youngish soldier called Giovanni from the famous family of the Giustiniani, cousins of the Doria. John le Grant, a trained engineer, was set to counter the infiltration of Turkish miners. This he did by digging an opposing tunnel, entering that of the Turks, and burning the wooden props so that the roof caved in, burying the enemy. During the siege, Grant was recruited by the Greek commander Lucas Notaras to dig counter-mines, smoking the enemy out of caverns, and flooding the mines from the ditch-cisterns. When Turkish prisoners later disclosed where individual mines had been laid, Grant was able to seek out and destroy them one by one. The fall of Constantinople that year and the death of Giustiniani presumably ended this phase of his career.

Johannes Grant was thought to be German, but later opinion considered him to be a Scottish adventurer who had worked his way through Germany to the Levant. Le Grant, or 'le Grand' in French, simply meant a big man, and the le Grants of Scotland were originally a Norman family which first settled in Nottinghamshire, England, and appeared in the north-east of Scotland in the thirteenth century. A hundred years later, there are several references to their connection with the Knights Hospitaller of St John of Jerusalem,* which would make it seem likely that the John le Grant who fought in Constantinople with soldiers from Rhodes, the home of the Knights, was from Aberdeen. For example, in 1379, the layman Robert Grant of the diocese of Moray was Administrator of the Order's property in Scotland, with the consent of the Prior in England. Part of his job was to ensure that leaseholders paid their proper dues to Rhodes. He himself, or a man of the same name, was in the same year given the land of **Culter** in Aberdeenshire by the Grand Prior. The parish church of Culter was dependent on the Order's Scottish base at **Torphichen.** Annual dues from Torphichen to Rhodes were sent to Bruges,* and were thereafter handled by the Society of the Medici at Florence. In 1445, the sum paid to Bruges amounted to five hundred Venetian ducats.

It seems likely that there existed a link between the Aberdonian Grants and John le Grant, the mining expert of the Levant: he could have been a grandson of the Administrator Robert. But from his first appearance as Red Johannes in Florence, all his career in the novels is fictitious. (D. D.)

Grata ingluvies: GEMINI, 32: Roman description of the agreeable taste of the oyster: roughly, 'the divine mouthful'.

Great Margaret: GEMINI, 25: See **Margaret of Norway.**

Great Seal: RAM, Overture: See **Greek with the wooden leg, the.**

GREEK WITH THE WOODEN LEG, THE: RISING: Nicholai Giorgio de'Acciajuoli: The importance of the real Acciajuoli family* is explained in Volume I. As described in the *House of Niccolò*, virtually all the story of Nicholai Giorgio is fictitious, and his relationship to the alum* farmer Bartolomeo Zorzi* is guesswork. His name has been assumed to be that of a real Greek who visited Scotland in 1459, having lost all his goods upon the fall of Constantinople, and whose name Scottish scribes rendered as Nicholai Georgei de Arcossoune, *Greci cum pede ligneo* (the Greek with the wooden leg).

His visit was no doubt meant to encourage the Scottish King to support a crusade to recover Constantinople. His personal objective, however, was to raise funds for the ransom of his brother (unnamed), who had been captured when that city fell to the Turks. The King, James II,* gave him his sympathy, and issued letters of protection to allow the Greek to stay and ask alms 'from the Scottish people'. It is not clear whether this was to be done through public funds, or by personal supplication, say, to the churches. Since royal sanction was needed, the King's decision appears in the Register of the Great Seal of Scotland, which held all the decrees requiring the ratification of the King's seal, such as the confirmation of titles of land or offices already granted by the monarchy.

The Greek probably did not stay long. He may have been one of two 'knights of Greece' who received fifteen pounds from the customs of **Edinburgh** in 1460, or the Greek who, with a German, was paid four pounds by the King's order in 1459 from his Stirling accounts. There were many such well-born refugees travelling through Europe at the time, and rulers were generous, being no doubt uncomfortably conscious of their unfulfilled vows. There was already a historical connection between Eastern alum and Scotland. Had the Greek then travelled to supplicate in Bruges,* or in Veere, he would almost certainly have shared the company of both the King's cousin, Bishop Kennedy,* and the King's half-brother, the future **Earl of Buchan**, who was at that time visiting his sister, married to Wolfaert **van Borselen** of Veere.

It is not known whether Acciajuoli married. His subsequent travels, and his connection with Violante of Naxos* and the boy Nerio, are fictitious. So also is the strain of cynical mysticism with which he is associated throughout. (D. D.)

Gregory of Sanok: RONDO, 16: (1407–1477) One of those entrusted with the education of King **Casimir IV** of Poland's children, Archbishop Gregory was renowned for the learned circles who gathered at his residence near the River Dunajec, where he had built a small town, palace and fortified castle, called Dunajow. His palace became a humanist 'salon' where, amongst others, he played host to **Callimachus:** it was the exiled Italian who wrote his biography. Under the influence of Gregory and his humanist contemporaries, Poland's renaissance of literature and learning flourished. He also reformed the state of his clergy and the finances of the bishopric. He was willing to buttress the power of the King at the expense of the magnates, and he also wished to free Poland from papal policies and politics, which interfered with the country's ability to rule itself. His defence of Polish national interests manifested itself in a dislike of the **Teutonic Order** as an ally and tool of the papacy.

Greyfriars: UNICORN, 5: This Franciscan **monastery** was founded by James I (King of Scotland 1406–1437) and situated at the south side of the Grassmarket in **Edinburgh**, almost opposite the West Bow. A grand building, it was the temporary residence of Mary of Gueldres on her arrival to Scotland in 1449. From 1461 to 1464 it provided refuge for Henry VI and his Lancastrian family, forced to flee England. The monastery was utterly destroyed by the Reformers in 1558; its grounds provided the new sixteenth-century burial ground of Edinburgh when that of St Giles* had become overcrowded. See also **Observatine Friars.**

Gunpowder: LIONS, 25: Not made in Scotland in bulk in early times, although a few licences for manufacture were issued to private individuals. The ingredients – such as sulphur from **Iceland** – were much sought after. The Arsenal in Venice,* which produced gunpowder in bulk, had workshops for preparing saltpetre, and storehouses for powder, charcoal and sulphur, with protective lead roofs for the powder houses. Gunpowder served purposes other than warfare: masons used it for clearing building sites, and **Mystery Plays** (for example) required saltpetre, sulphur and charcoal for Hell. On board ship, the primitive state of the cannon meant that powder charges had to be weak, and massive ship-to-ship bombardment was impossible. The main seagoing gun was the serpentine, referred to morosely as 'merely a man-killer'. (D. D.)

H

Ha! Meschant homme, qu'as tu fait/ Fors ordure et sterilité!: LIONS, 2: 'Ah, wicked man! What hast thou brought, but ordure and sterility?' Spoken by God in the script of a French **Mystery Play**, probably performed in Mons about 1501.

Haddington: UNICORN, 4: Royal burgh, founded in 1130, on the left bank of the River Tyne. Lying in the direct route of English invaders from the south, the town was burned by forces from across the border in 1216 and again in 1244. It is the site of the largest of the **Cistercian** houses of Scotland (the second largest was probably **North Berwick**), founded in 1159 by Ada, Countess of Northumberland and Huntingdon. In records for April 1461 it was said to have twenty-four nuns, and in 1560 there were eighteen. In common with many other Cistercian nunneries in Scotland, its strategic location on the border between Scotland and England meant it, like the town, was in danger of attack when there were hostilities between the two countries. It was burned by the English in 1336 and again in the mid-sixteenth century. It was greatly supported by the Hepburn family.

Hag on the post: CHECKMATE, V, 12: The phrase 'stryk ane hag [notch] into the post' appears in Sir David Lindsay's* *Satire of the Three Estates*, in the interlude of Folie and Diligence, meaning a notch made to mark an unusual event. In the play it refers to a bishop coming to preach in Fife. The term is used by Lindsay lightly, but in any context indicates a simple mark made to commemorate something of moment.

Halkerston's Wynd: LIONS, 14: The main access from the High Street of **Edinburgh** to the foot of the **Nor' Loch**, leading to **Trinity Chapel** and hospital, it probably took its name from the architect of the **collegiate church**, John Halkerston.

HAMILTON, James, Lord: UNICORN: (d. 1479) James was created a Lord of Parliament in 1445 and all his estates were united into the lordship of Hamilton. He remained a member of the **Lords of Council in Civil Causes** until his death. He was allied to the **Black Douglas** family through his marriage in 1441 to Lady Euphemia Graham, eldest daughter of the Earl of Strathearn and Lady Euphemia Stewart, granddaughter of Robert II (King of Scotland 1371–1390). Euphemia Graham was the widow of Archibald, Fifth **Earl of Douglas.** In 1452 he accompanied William, Eighth Earl of Douglas, to Stirling, where the Earl was subsequently murdered by King James II.* Hamilton's allegiance initially lay with the Douglas family but, encouraged by Bishop Kennedy,* he changed his allegiance in 1454 to follow the King rather than avenge the death of the Earl. He was rewarded with the hereditary sheriffdom of Lanark, previously held by the Black Douglases, the survivors of which fled to England. (See also **James, Ninth Earl of Douglas.**)

His first wife died in 1468, and his second marriage, rewarding Hamilton for his service and loyalty, was in 1474 to **Princess Mary.** In addition to a number of illegitimate offspring, by his first wife he had two daughters: Elizabeth, married to **David Lindsay**, Earl of Crawford (who became Duke of Montrose) and Agnes, married to Sir James Hamilton of Preston. By the second marriage to Princess Mary, he had a son and a daughter, James and Elizabeth. James (*c.* 1475–1529) was created Earl of Arran in 1503, a title previously held by **Thomas Boyd** and granted to James probably in recognition for his involvement in the negotiations between Scotland and England culminating in the marriage of Margaret Tudor to **James IV.*** He was also the father of several illegitimate children, and had a mistress *en titre* called Janet Calderwood. One of the Earl's illegitimate sons was Sir James Hamilton of Finnart, favourite of James V* of Scotland (see **Fynnart, Jimmie of**). The Earl's heir, James, who gained the title Second Earl of Arran,* became Regent of Scotland on the death of James V, and was declared heir presumptive to the throne. Until the reign of James VI (1567–1625), a Hamilton was either the direct heir to the Crown, or heir next to a royal child.

Elizabeth (the daughter of Lord Hamilton and Princess Mary) married Matthew, Second **Earl of Lennox** and it was through this union that the Lennox family claimed their place in the royal succession. Their grandson, the fourth earl, was Matthew Lennox.*

Hamundarson, Gunnar: LIONS, 29: The best friend of Njall, the fated hero of **Njall's story**, the Icelandic saga of the thirteenth century. He is described thus:

> He was a tall powerful man, outstandingly skilful with arms. He could strike or throw with either hand, and his sword-strokes were so fast that he seemed to be brandishing three swords at once. He was excellent at archery, and his arrows never missed their mark. He could jump more than his own height in full armour, and just as far backwards as forwards. He could swim like a seal. There was no sport at which anyone could

even attempt to compete with him. It has been said that there has never been his equal.

A long-running family feud led Gunnar to kill two men sent to attack him. The judgement of the Icelandic Parliament, the Althing, was that he must leave **Iceland** (see **How lovely the slopes are**). Refusing to do so, Gunnar was eventually defeated when his enemies removed the roof from his house to get at him (and his wife Hallgerd refused to help him by making him a bowstring of her hair). After his death, the saga relates that verses were heard being chanted from the inside of his burial mound, a portent witnessed by his son and a son of Njall; his message to them being that he would 'rather die than yield' to his enemies, obliging them to revenge his murder.

Hanged in irons within the floodmarks of thy pride: QUEENS, IV, 3: The punishment for pirates, captured and found guilty in London. Their fate was to be hanged in irons at the low-water mark at Wapping.

Hanged with clooth of gold, and nat with sarge: CHECKMATE, IV, 2: From *The Canterbury Tales* of Geoffrey Chaucer (*c.* 1343–1400). 'The Knight's Tale', a shortened version of the *Teseida* of Boccaccio (1313–1375), tells the story of Palamon and Arcite, rivals in love, who compete in a tournament in Athens. The city is arrayed in splendour as they ride to the lists (extract):

> Up goon the trompes and the melodye,
> And to the lystes rit the compaignye,
> By ordinance, thurghout the citee large,
> Hanged with cloth of gold, and nat with sarge.

Hanseatic League: RONDO: The *hanse*, meaning a group or company, was an early association of merchants with ships; trading and bartering goods throughout northern Europe. In 1356 the network formed the Hanseatic League, centred on the German town of Lübeck, and began to establish trading posts and agencies across Europe. The League's treaties with foreign governments protected their posts (*Kontors*); their trading privileges were assured by their political and economic strength, backed by the protection of the **Teutonic Knights.** Unlike the trade of Venice,* the Hanseatic League concentrated on barter rather than credit and bills of exchange, trading such basic commodities as wine, wood, grain, honey, cloth, furs, wax and fish.

The high point for the Hanseatic League was the late fourteenth century. In the late fifteenth century their strength was compromised by a fall in value of their exported goods, as compared with manufactured or industrial products; their raw materials were no longer in such high demand; silk replaced their furs, honey was replaced by sugar. Also, since they relied on the Teutonic

Knights for safety on their trade routes across the Baltic, when the Knights no longer supported and protected them, the way was left clear for others to muscle in: namely the English and ships from Holland and Zeeland. The League's monopoly in the Baltic and its control of the salt and fishing trade were disputed by its neighbours: England, Scandinavia, France and the Netherlands. Its dispute with the Netherlands caused the league to move its *Kontor* from Bruges* to Dordrecht (in the time of Philip the Bold*), but Philip acquired Holland in 1433; the league could not afford to ban trade with the whole Netherlands. Loss of its trade monopolies (as at **Novgorod**) further weakened the League.

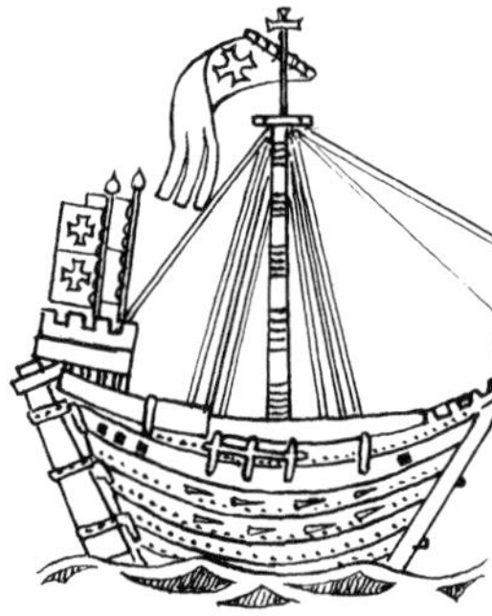

Hansa cog ~
from the city seal of Elbing

Harry, Blind: See **Blind Harry.**

HASAN, UZUM: See **Uzum Hasan.**

He's twice the size of common men . . . : KINGS, IV, 2: From the early ballad, 'The Marriage of Sir Gawaine':

Hee's twyce the size of common men,
Wi' thewes, and sinewes stronge,
And on his backe he bears a clubbe,
That is both thicke and longe.

This grimme barone 'twas our harde happe,
But yester morne to see;
When to his bowre he bore my love,
And sore misused me . . .

The hero of the ballad, King Arthur, cannot defeat the Baron in battle, and must return in a year's time with the answer to the Baron's question: 'What is it that women desire?' A hideously misshapen woman promises she will tell him the secret if Arthur brings her a husband. All women, she tells him, 'will have their wille, This is their chief desyre'. The misshapen woman turns out to be the Baron's sister. As the answer is correct, Arthur does not have to forfeit his life or lands, but can return home as the Baron swears to wreak revenge on his sister. Guinevere greets her husband:

> What newes! what newes! thou noble king,
>   Howe, Arthur, has thou sped?
> Where hast thou hung the carlish knighte?
>   And where bestow'd his head?

Arthur explains that to learn the answer to the Baron's question he promised to find a young and courtly knight to marry the Baron's hideous sister. Sir Gawain, Arthur's nephew, nobly volunteers. His bride tells him she can either be beautiful by day or night, but not by both; which would he rather have? Gawain initially answers that he would prefer to have her beautiful by night, but as she points out, this would mean she could never be seen in company with him. Gawain yields, and says, 'Because thou art mine owne ladye, Thou shalt have all thy wille'. The enchantment upon her is broken by Gawain for letting her have her way and now his bride will be beautiful both day and night, and her brother, the Baron, will also be freed from being a 'carlish boore'.

Heel naturlijk: UNICORN, 36: 'Very true to nature' (in Flemish).

Hekla: LIONS, 22: Most famous of **Iceland**'s volcanoes. Situated seventy miles east of Reykjavik, Hekla stands 4,829 feet above sea level. In the Middle Ages it was considered to be the **Mouth of Hell ('crapault'** LIONS, III) and the portal to the world of the damned. The first recorded eruption was in 1104, and it has erupted at least sixteen times; the average eruption lasts between six months to a year, with violent explosions typifying the early stages of eruption.

Helga Bok: LIONS: 28: Icelandic for the Holy Book on which oaths were sworn. In the thirteenth century, because of the difficulty of preserving such a delicate and expensive object, the *Helga Bok* in everyday use was sometimes simply a block made of wood, or a casting painted to look like a book. (D. D.)

Henryson, Robert: GEMINI, 33: (*c.* 1452–*c.* 1506) Scottish poet and canon lawyer who probably lectured at Glasgow University in 1462. After Glasgow he is thought to have studied in Paris (before 1465), in which case he is likely to have met **Jan Adorne.** By 1477 he was a public notary and most likely a priest in Dunfermline, where he witnessed several deeds for the Abbot, and may have been master of the Abbey's grammar school. He had an earthy caustic humour in life, which showed itself both gracefully and abrasively in his poetry, of which a good deal remains. He is mentioned also in the powerful elegy, the 'Lament for the Makaris' by his fellow poet William Dunbar (*c.* 1460–1520). Henryson's greatest poem is perhaps his *Testament of Cresseid*, following Chaucer (*c.* 1343–1400). Among his other works are *Sum Practysis of Medecyne, Robene and Makyne* and a collection of fables under the title *The Moral Fables of Aesop*. He uses the fables to comment obliquely on the monarch (**James III***), the nobles and the commons of Scotland, and on the failings, as he sees them, of the courts of justice and of diocesan officials. His exact meaning still divides current opinion. Here is an extract from one of his less controversial poems, the love story of Makyne, who in the course of sixteen verses throws herself at the boy's head, becomes annoyed at his resistance and walks off just as he has begun to become eager:

Robene sat on good green hill,
Keepand a flock of fie [sheep or cattle],
Merry Makyne said him till,
'Robene, thou rew [pity] on me;
I have thee loved lowd and still [openly and secretly],
Thir yearis two or three;
My dule in dern [sorrow in secret] but gif thou dill [unless thou share],
Doubtless but dread I die.
(D. D.)

Her se Gud: LIONS, 25: Icelandic for 'May God be in this place'.

Here maun I lie, here maun I die: KINGS, II, 3: From *Hardyknute*, a Scots poem describing the battle of Largs in 1263, fought between the Scots and the Norwegians:

And he has ridden o'er muir and moss,
O'er hills and mony a glen,
When he came to a wounded knight
Making a heavy mane;
'Here maun I lye, here maun I dye,
By treacherie's false guiles;
Witless I was that e'er gave faith
To wicked woman's smiles'.

See also **To horse, to horse, my royal liege.**

Hermes, Graceful as: RONDO, 39: The Greek god Hermes, patron of merchants and messengers, was identified by the Latins as their swift and mischievous Mercury,* of the winged cap and feet. The symbol of the divine messenger's power was the herald's wand called the caduceus, which he received from Apollo himself. Early bronze sculpture shows the youth Mercury poised, lithe and amused, with one arm lightly enfolding Apollo's rod twisted with snakes. (D. D.)

Herod-baba: RONDO, 4: Polish for 'wild woman'; see **Etiquette: language.**

Herpestes Ichneumon: PAWN, 16: The Egyptian mongoose. Venerated by the ancients and easily domesticated, this animal is larger than a cat. Its body is elongated and brownish grey, its paws and muzzle black, its face small-eared and sharp. It feeds on eggs, insects, crabs, lizards, and birds up to guinea-fowl size. It also eats rats, making it an acceptable member of Near Eastern households, in the same way that its cousins in India are kept to kill venomous snakes. (Herpestes can kill snakes as well.) It swims well, and picks its teeth with its foreclaws. It is not cute. (D. D.)

Hesht Behest: RONDO, 29: 'The Eight Paradises', the title given to a history of the first eight Ottoman Sultans written by the Persian Monlá Idrís (d. 1554); it was also the name given to **Uzum Hasan**'s* palace garden at Tabriz, as described by **Josaphat Barbaro.**

His mind is on fleshly lusts and his treasure: KINGS, Gambit: The observation of the character of Death in the medieval morality play *Everyman* (*c.* 1509–1519) on the preoccupation of the central character:

> Lo, yonder I see Everyman walking.
> Full little he thinketh on my coming;
> His mind is on fleshly lusts and his treasure,
> And great pain it shall cause him to endure
> Before the Lord, Heaven King.

Hoast: GEMINI, 48: A Scots cough. Not to be confused with a host, which is an army or assembly. To be confined to bed with a hoast refers to the former definition.

Hocket: GEMINI, 9: Or *hoquetus.* Literally a hiccup, but not the kind treated in QUEENS, I, 6 by sucking the far rim of a cup. A hocket is a musical device dating back to the thirteenth century. It happens when the melodic line is tossed quickly between different voices or instruments, creating a hiatus within the individual parts, but a continuous stream of sound to the ear. (D. D.)

Holland, Richard: GEMINI, 22: (d. 1482) Scottish poet in the reign of James II.* Richard Holland was a priest of the see of Moray in the north of Scotland, rector of Halkirk parish, Caithness, and secretary to Archibald **Douglas**, Earl of Moray, before the latter's forfeiture and eventual death in 1455, following the murder of his brother William, Eighth Earl of Douglas, in 1452 by James II. Holland is chiefly remembered for his alliterative poem *The Buke of the Howlat,** probably written in the spring of 1450 and dedicated to his patron's wife Elizabeth **Dunbar**, daughter of James Dunbar, Earl of Moray. *The Buke* owes something to both *The Bruce* (1376), a verse chronicle of over 13,000 lines by Scottish poet John Barbour (*c.* 1320–1395), and *The Parliament of Fowls*, the 699-line dream-poem written between 1372 and 1386 by Geoffrey Chaucer (*c.* 1343–1400). Holland's poem tells of the dilemma of the humble howlat, or owl, in a gaudy array of birds representing nobles, clergy and civilians, with the Pope as a peacock. Above all, however, it celebrates the past deeds of the family Douglas. See **O Dowglass, O Dowglass, Tender and Trewe!**

With the **Black Douglases** banished or dead, the earldom of Moray was taken into the Crown, and Holland's future must have seemed uncertain, not least because his former benefactress next married **Sir John Colquhoun of Luss**, who was to die a loyal servant of **James III.*** On the other hand, Earl Archibald's sister had been married to William **Sinclair**, the last Earl of Orkney before it was transferred, with Shetland, into the possession of James III on the occasion of his marriage in 1469 to **Margaret of Denmark**. Under the auspices of Earl William, it is possible that Holland stayed on for some time in the north, and can be identified with the Richard Holland who was vicar of Ronaldsay, Orkney, in 1467.

Holland's later movements are difficult to trace, but the main branch of the family seems to have moved to Berwick-upon-Tweed* after its recovery from the English in 1461. It is unlikely, however, that men favouring the Black Douglases or those strongly predisposed to England would have been welcome there upon the outbreak of the English war in 1480, and the subsequent moves to recapture the town. There are signs that, between 1479 and 1480, Holland was already in England and being used, with the exiled **James, Ninth Earl of Douglas**, to carry messages north of the Border. In the spring of 1482, a year before the murder of **Anselm Adorne**,* the King issued an offer of prize money for the capture of certain men. For the taking of the traitor, Earl James, twin of Holland's past employer Archibald, the King was prepared to pay the immense sum of one thousand marks. For his traitorous friends, the King offered twenty pounds for those of gentle blood, down to ten pounds for a yeoman.

To any man helping the Douglas who would defect back to the King within twenty-four days, pardon was extended, excepting only those who were sworn Englishmen staying in England, and four who were specifically named. One of these was Earl James himself. One was Patrick Haliburton, a chaplain in English pay who had been used to foment trouble among the disaffected Scots in the north-west. One was Alexander Jardine of Applegarth, who had not left Scotland for long if at all, for he was to spearhead the attack on Anselm Adorne. And one was Sir Richard Holland, the unwise poet and secretary of the wanted man's twin – perhaps now the secretary of the Ninth Earl himself.

He was never caught. (D. D.)

Holyrood: LIONS, 17: The medieval Abbey at the foot of Edinburgh's Royal Mile, founded by David I (King of Scotland 1124–1153) in 1128 for the **Augustinian canons** and largely rebuilt in the thirteenth and fourteenth centuries. The thirteenth-century nave still remains, as does evidence of **Archibald Crawford**'s rebuilding work when he was Abbot between 1450 and 1483; including supporting buttresses along the sides of the nave; a new doorway and the rare survival of a screen at the entrance of the transept from the north aisle, separating the sections of the church used by the laity from those used by the canons. It has a central doorway and clearly visible in a roundel are the arms of the Abbot.

The royal residence attached to the Abbey grew in time to become the palace of Holyroodhouse, **James IV*** being responsible for much of the palace building. It became the home of **John Stewart, Second Duke of Albany**, when he arrived in Scotland in 1515 to undertake the role of Regent and he continued the building work of his cousin. The palace was to outlast the Abbey, which was badly damaged by the English and then the Reformers in the sixteenth century.

Seal of St. Giles

Seal of Holyrood Abbey

HOME, Alexander: GEMINI, 49: (d. 1506) Alexander Home of that Ilk (pronounced 'Hume'), was grandson of the first Lord Home. In December 1482, **Alexander, Duke of Albany,*** granted to Home a portion of land in the town and territory of Letham, lying within the earldom of March and the sheriffdom of Berwick, for faithful service done and to be done, witnessed by **John Ellem of Butterdene**. Instead of supporting Albany in the plan to kidnap **James III,*** Home rode to Edinburgh and informed the King of the plot. Between December 1482 and March 1483 Albany retaliated by arresting Home and other members of his family, claiming they were sent by the King to kill him. After the forfeiture of Albany, the granted lands were reconfirmed by James III, but it did not quell the family's animosity towards the king over the **Coldingham** affair, and Home sided with the rebels in 1488 when James III was killed. Alexander succeeded his grandfather as Lord Home in 1491, and became Chamberlain for life, Keeper of Stirling Castle and guardian of John, **James IV**'s* younger brother. The revenues of the earldom of Mar and Garioch were assigned to him from 1490, and he held the post of Warden of the East Marches from 1489 to 1496.

Home family: HN; LC: The Home, or Hume, family occupy a prominent place in the history of the East Marches of Scotland and in the fight over the priory of **Coldingham**. Patrick Home, graduate of St Andrews, Archdeacon of Teviotdale, had claim to the Priory but was rivalled by John Home, second son of Alexander Home of Dunglass and cousin of **Alexander Home**. John did eventually succeed as Prior of Coldingham, holding the title until at least 1500. Over eighty of the family fell at **Flodden**, and the estates passed to David Home, the second son of the third laird of Wedderburn. Initially in favour of **John Stewart, Second Duke of Albany** as the new Regent of Scotland, the family soon turned against him. In 1515 the family, headed by Alexander, Lord Chamberlain of Scotland, supported Angus* and Arran* in a failed revolt against the Regent. Angus fled to England and Arran was forgiven when his mother **Princess Mary** (Albany's aunt) interceded on his behalf, but Alexander Home and his brother William, Prior of Coldingham, were seized, found guilty of treason and rebellion against the Regent and were duly executed. In Albany's absence from Scotland, the Home family under their kinsman David Home of Wedderburn later revenged themselves on Albany's fellow Frenchman Anthony D'Arcy, seigneur de la Bastie, made Warden of the East Marches after Alexander Home's execution. Bastie (or Sir de la Beautie as the ballads of the incident title him) was pursued and beheaded outside Duns by the Homes. The family were declared traitors, but came to terms with the Regent and received some of their family estates back, including Home or Hume Castle. The castle was defended by Lady Home ('that senile idiot', KINGS, I, 4) against the English, but taken by Protector Somerset* in 1547.

David Home was killed in 1524 and was succeeded by Alexander, Fifth Baron Home (d. 1575), who entertained Mary Queen of Scots* and her husband Darnley in 1565/1566. He supported Bothwell and Mary at the battle of Langside after their defeat, but was later restored to his estates under the Protestant regime.

Hooks and Cods: RONDO, 39: The opposing political parties in Holland, under the lordship of Burgundy. Duke Philip the Good's* representative at the Hague, Lalaing,* was a Hook, and Franck **van Borselen**, husband of Jacqueline, Countess of Holland, was a Cod.

Hosanna to thee, suffering Africa: SCALES, 19: Amended for the purposes of the novel, the original quote is 'Hosanna to thee, suffering Italy: now wilt thou be envied of all'. The words are those of Dante Alighieri (1265–1321) in 1310, welcoming the advent of Henry VII, Holy Roman Emperor (1308–1313), to support the Ghibelline cause in the Italian Guelph and Ghibelline conflict. (D. D.)

How lovely the slopes are: LIONS, 29: The Icelandic saga **Njall's story** tells how **Gunnar Hamundarson** killed two men who set out to ambush him. The Icelandic law tribunal the Althing judged the matter and agreed that Gunnar was to pay compensation to the families of his victims, and that he must leave **Iceland** for three years. If he did not leave, his life would become forfeit to the kinsmen of his enemies. With all his belongings packed, accompanied by his friend Kolskegg (similarly banished), he made his way to the harbour:

> They rode down toward Markar River. Just then Gunnar's horse stumbled, and he had to leap from the saddle. He happened to glance up towards his home and the slopes of Hlidarend.
>
> 'How lovely the slopes are,' he said, 'more lovely than they have ever seemed to me before, golden cornfields and new-mown hay. I am going back home, and I will not go away.'

By thus breaking the settlement agreed at the Althing, Gunnar was declared an outlaw and his tragic fate sealed.

Howard, John, Lord: GEMINI, 31: (1430–1485) English naval commander who led the ships which attacked the east coast of Scotland prior to **Richard Duke of Gloucester**'s invasion. In 1466 he was the vice admiral for Norfolk, and was Treasurer of the King's Household from 1467 to 1474. In 1470, when Henry VI briefly returned to power, Howard was made a baron, but remained loyal to **Edward IV**,* proclaiming him King on his return in 1471. With the death of Edward in 1483, Howard allied himself to the Duke of Gloucester, and persuaded Edward's widow to allow her younger son the Duke of York to be placed with his brother in the Tower of London. He acted as high steward at the coronation of the Duke of Gloucester as Richard III. In 1485 when the Earl of Richmond (the future Henry VII 1485–1509) landed in England, Howard remained loyal to Richard III and was killed at the battle of Bosworth.

Hugh of Lincoln, the murdered: QUEENS, IV, 5: The reference is to the victim in a popular folk tale, a child supposedly murdered by the Jews in Lincoln in the thirteenth century. The child, 'Sir Hugh,' is lured into a house by the Jew's daughter, stabbed, wrapped in lead and flung down a well. His mother, 'Lady Helen,' calls for him and the child (although murdered) answers loud and clear, leading to the discovery of the body. There are at least eighteen subsequent versions of the ballad, from Valladolid to Cracow. A similar tale appears in *The Canterbury Tales* by Geoffrey Chaucer (*c.* 1343–1400) as 'The Prioress's Tale,' and in the Scots ballad, "The Jew's Daughter'.

Hume: See **Home family.**

Hungary: See **Jagiellonian dynasty.**

Hurley-hackit: KINGS, I, 7: Tobogganing, Scottish style. Applied in folklore to an old game in which children (allegedly) raced each other down a steep snowy slope, riding on deer skulls. (D. D.)

Hyacinth of Cracow: RONDO, 12: A Polish saint born of a fighting family, Hyacinth (Jacek, or Iaccho) (1185–1257) was descended from the Counts of Oldrovans in Silesia. His grandfather, a general, made his name in armed conflict against Tartars, while Yvo his uncle became a statesman and Chancellor of Poland. Hyacinth studied in Cracow, Prague and Bologna, where he became a doctor of laws and divinity. When Yvo was made Bishop of Cracow, he took his nephew Hyacinth with him to Rome, where in 1218 he encountered St Dominic, and was persuaded to enter his convent. From there Hyacinth issued to travel and preach in Austria and Silesia and Poland, where he founded **Dominican** convents in the principal cities. Thence he travelled to Scandinavia and Muscovy, converting Greek schismatics and Muslims and establishing **monasteries.** When his life ended at Cracow he had penetrated, it was said, as far as Tibet and Cathay, and had several times executed the miracle of walking on water when crossing the Rivers Vistula and Dnieper. He was canonised as St Hyacinth by Pope Clement VIII in 1594. (D. D.)

Hypophrygian mode: See **Spondaic rhythm.**

I

I am Arnaut who gathers the wind: SCORPIONS, 44:

I am Arnaut who gathers the wind	*Ieu sui Arnautz qu'amas l'aura,*
And hunts the hare with the ox	*E chatz la lebre ab lo bou*
And swims against the incoming tide.	*E nadi contra suberna.*

Reminiscent of the motto of Peebles (see ***Contra Nando* [*navigando*] *Incrementum***), this was the work of one of the greatest of the twelfth-century troubadors, the poet-knight Arnaut Daniel (*c.* 1180–1200). A gentleman by birth, he abandoned his learning to take to the road with his songs, and wrote these lines for a noble (married) lady of Gascony, who had refused him her favours. Another troubadour is quoted as calling him 'Arnaut the scholar, who is ruined by dice and backgammon, and goes about like a penitent, poor in clothes and money.' He is supposed to have taken part in a poetic competition at the court of Richard the Lionheart (1157–1199). Eighteen of his songs have survived, and among those who have admired and tried to imitate his poems are Dante Alighieri(1265–1321) and Petrarch (1304–1374), who called him 'the Great Master of Love'.

Arnault is alluded to in the novels because of his home, which was the castle of Ribérac, now demolished, on the banks of the River Dronne, fifty miles north-west of Bordeaux. Built by the counts of Périgord in the tenth century, it was the seat of a viscount. A fictitious character in the *House of Niccolò*, Jordan de Ribérac, is placed there. (D. D.)

I am as I am, and so I will be: KINGS, I, 2: Sir Thomas Wyatt,* 'The Re-Cured Lover Exulteth in His Freedom':

I am as I am, and so will I be;
But how that I am none knoweth truly.
Be it evil, be it well, be I bond, be I free,
I am as I am, and so will I be.

I lead my life indifferently,
I mean no thing but honesty;

And though folks judge full diversely,
I am as I am, and so will I die . . .

Praying you all that this do read
To trust it as you do your creed;
And not to think I change my weed,
For I am as I am, however I speed.

But how that is, I leave to you;
Judge as ye list, false or true,
Ye know no more than afore ye knew;
Yet I am as I am, whatever ensue.

And from this mind I will not flee;
But to you all that misjudge me
I do protest, as ye may see,
That I am as I am, and so will be.

I am in love-desire: CHECKMATE, V, 13: *Hewá*, which translates as 'love-desire'; 'Thou hast cast me into Love Desire' is an image from 'Joseph and Zelikhá' by the Ottoman poet Hamdí (*c.* 1448–1509).

I be lightly drunken, as the man said, and have but little appetite to meat: CASTLE, III, 7: Mandeville* described the inhabitants of Ethiopia thus: 'And the folk of that contree ben lyghtly dronken and han but litille appetyt to mete. And thei han comounly the flux of the wombe, and they lyuen not longe' (*The Travels of Sir John Mandeville*, chapter seventeen).

I can't sit on anything green: LIONS, 40: Said of the turtledove which, on losing its mate, will not perch (they say) upon anything of that colour. Green was forbidden to Christians in Muslim countries, where it was reserved for the use of Mohammed's kinsmen and men of religion. A Christian wearing green shoe strings would be beaten by cudgels. (D. D.)

I've been a joyless jeweller: KINGS, IV, 2: From *Pearl* (*c.* 1375–1400), the medieval English dream-poem in which the poet mourns the death of his infant daughter, his precious jewel:

'O pearl,' said I, 'in pearls of price,
Are you my pearl come back again,
Lost and lamented with desolate sighs
In darkest night, alone and in vain?
Since you slipped to ground where grasses rise
I wander pensive, oppressed with pain,

And you in the bliss of Paradise,
Beyond all passion and strife and strain.
What fate removed you from earth's domain
And left me hapless and heartsick there?
Since parting was set between us twain
I have been a joyless jeweler.'

I pray thee, for the love of God . . . : PAWN, 29: A couplet written by Nejátí, the great lyric poet of the Ottoman Empire who died in Constantinople in 1509. The verse appeared on his tomb:

I pray you for the love of God go build Nejátí's tomb
Of marble, for he died of parting from a stony heart.

I shall harness thee a chariot of lapis-lazuli and gold: CHECKMATE, IV, 9: From a poem in Babylonian mythology dealing with the exploits of the hero Gilgamesh. The words are attributed to the cruel Babylonian goddess Ishtar or Astarte, the Lady of Battles and the divine manifestation of the star Venus, who drives a chariot drawn by seven lions. Dazzled by the beauty of Gilgamesh, she addresses him:

Come, Gilgamesh, be my lover!
Be my husband and I shall be thy wife!
I shall harness thee a chariot of lapis-lazuli and gold.
Come into our dwelling, in the perfume of the cedars.

When he rebuffs her, knowing too well how she treats her lovers ('Thou has loved the lion, mighty in strength, and thou has dug for him seven and seven pits. Thou hast loved the steed, proud in battle, and destined him for the halter, the goad and the whip') she vows vengeance. Gilgamesh is saved by his great hero-friend Enkidu, but Ishtar punishes Enkidu with a mortal illness, and he dies in Gilgamesh's arms. (D. D.)

I shall sink my anvil further into the flesh of your heart; I shall install my forge in a deeper place: PAWN, 24: This continues: 'until I have heard the words; until I have learned from you the magic words.' It comes from the great Finnish epic the *Kalevala*, assembled from ancient songs about 1828, and eventually comprising twelve thousand verses. This episode relates how the hero Väinämöinen has arrived in the underworld seeking the three missing words that will allow him to finish building his ship. There he finds the giant Antero Vipunen, lying under the earth with his songs, a poplar tree growing from his shoulders, an alder from his cheeks, a willow from his beard, a fir from his forehead, and a wild pine between his teeth. When nearly vanquished in the ensuing fight, Väinämöinen turns himself into a blacksmith and smites the giant, shouting his challenge. Cowed, Vipunen yields, and opens 'the coffer full of words; the coffer full of songs' to the hero. Väinämöinen tears out the magical chant and, returning, completes his ship. (D. D.)

I take my refuge . . . : GEMINI, 20: This verse, which is meant to be spoken, is from the opening chapters of the Koran under the heading of 'The Drum'. It is followed by another headed 'The People':

> I take my refuge in the Lord of the people,
> the King of the people,
> the God of the people,
> from the evil of the furtive whisperer
> who whispers in the breasts of the people,
> of the genies and of the people.

I was to be driven into the nets since, unlike the beaver . . . : see **Beaver, self-defence of.**

I will not serve an idle log . . . : LIONS, 26: A verse composed by Hjalti Skeggjason which appears in the Icelandic **Njall's story.** From AD 980 as the first millennium loomed, Christian missionaries came to **Iceland** to encourage the inhabitants to turn from their pagan gods and embrace Christianity. The missionary Thangbrand converted many of the island's powerful families, but he too had his enemies (see **Sorceror-Hedin**). Hjalti's poem was blasphemous to the traditional gods ('**Freya** is a bitch'), and in AD 999 he was outlawed by the Icelandic parliament, the Althing. The following year, AD 1000, the Althing officially proclaimed Christianity as the religion of Iceland.

I wish to rule, and I will not let anyone pick my nose: RONDO, 4: Comment most famously made by Stephen Bathory, Prince of Transylvania, who ruled Poland from 1575 to 1586 as its most successful King when the republic was in anarchy. **Danzig** was in revolt, Ivan IV* (Ivan the Terrible) was encroaching on his territory and a hundred thousand Tartars ravaged the country in the first year of his reign. The comment relates to an incident described by his chronicler and fervent admirer, Reinhold Heidenstein, where the members of the Sejm of **Thorn** (the Assembly or Senate) kept pestering him to explain his intentions:

> 'I was not born in a pig sty,' he said. 'I was born a free man . . . I love my freedom and intend to guard it. By God's will, it was you who elected me King. It was at your request that I came here. It was you who placed the crown on my brow. So I am your King. But I will not be a fashioned or a painted one [*non fictus neque pictus*]. I wish to rule, and will not let anyone pick my nose. It is agreed that you be guardians of your own free-

dom. But I will not allow you to act like schoolmasters over me and my senators. Watch for your freedom, but lay off any pranks'.

Stephen Bathory waged war against the Grand Duchy of Moscow under Ivan the Terrible, a matter of survival rather than merely principle, as the Duchy was laying claim to and swallowing up territories it had no right to control. War with Muscovy lasted until 1582, when, eventually, Ivan's army was forced to withdraw completely from Livonia. Bathory died in 1586.

I Wot a Tree: PAWN, 3: From a rhyme about the days, weeks and months of the year:

> I Wot [know] a tre [tree] XII bowys betake,
> LII nestys beþe þat up ymad [be there that aloft are];
> In euery nest beþ bryddys [be there birds] VII.
> I-thankyd be þe God of heuene [heaven]
> And euery bryd wyth selcouth [uncommon] name.

Iceland: LIONS: Known as Ultima Thule (LIONS, 22) after the term used by the ancient Greeks and Romans to denote the most remote northern portion of the world. Colonised by Norsemen (Vikings) from AD 870 onwards, settlers came to the fertile but isolated island from Scandinavia and the Norse colonies in Ireland, Scotland, Orkney and Shetland. Before the Norsemen, Irish monks (Culdees, LIONS, 25) had arrived on the island and lived a hermetic life but they left when the settlers arrived, as they would not live with pagans.

Famous for having the oldest recorded national General Assembly, the Althing, its annual Parliaments are well described in the sagas dating from the thirteenth century and relate the lives of Iceland's tenth- and eleventh-century heroes. Iceland was Christianised in 1000, by decree of the Althing, following a Christian mission from 980.

In the Middle Ages, Iceland suffered from increasing poverty and political weakness as the Church and tenant farmers carved up the island between them. The internal power struggles lost Iceland her independence, giving the Norwegian throne the opportunity to take control in 1262, when the Althing agreed to pay tax and give allegiance to the Norwegian Crown. In 1380, when Norway and Denmark united under one King, Iceland came under their authority.

The population in the early modern period is estimated at being between thirty and seventy thousand. The island was ravaged by plague from 1402 to 1404, which killed between thirty and sixty per cent of the population. It struck again in 1494–1495, sparing only the population of the Western Fjords.

The outstanding natural feature of the island is its volcanoes (see **Hekla**), which have been active roughly every five years in the last few centuries. Many different types are present; ice-covered volcanoes such as **Katla** explode and cause tremendous floods, *jökulhlaup*. Earthquakes are also common. The numerous spouting hot springs known as *geysirs* take their name from Geysir, in Haukadalur, formerly spouting water up to a height of sixty metres.

From the thirteenth century, the principle export of Iceland was its home-spun cloth, *vaomál*, and as the **Hanseatic League** began to control the export markets of Norway in the fourteenth century, **stockfish** and fish-oil began to feature as Iceland's chief exports in return for essential supplies. From around 1400, German and English fishermen started to come to Iceland directly to fish and trade for themselves, making great profits, but rivalries between the merchants could lead to conflict, and even war.

The Colonial Governor's residence at Bessastadir

Icelandic harridan: LIONS, 30: This was Ólöf Loftsdóttir, wife of the Governor of **Iceland.** When her husband, Bjorn the Mighty, was killed by the English in 1467, his body thrown into the sea, his son taken for ransom and his house of Skard emptied and burned, she collected men, put on a shirt of mail under her dress and set out to avenge him. The Englishmen she did not kill were put to work on her farm. (D. D.)

Ichneumon: See ***Herpestes ichneumon.***

Ignaures: GEMINI, 12: A reference to 'Ignaures the well-beloved: a lover, and jovial', given in *Tirant lo Blanc*. This Catalan romance of chivalry was begun *c.* 1460 by Joanot Martorell (*c.* 1420–1470) and completed after his death by Martí Joan de Galba.

Il sale, il zucchero e le puttane: RONDO, 9: From the proverb which says that in Cyprus, three things are good and cheap: the salt, the sugar and the whores. Another saying holds that Italians are mad twice a year, at Shrovetide and Lent.

In articulo mortis: KINGS, IV, 3: 'On the point of death'.

In culo mundi: GEMINI, 23: See **Camulio, Prosper Schiaffino de, de' Medici.**

In manners well dignified. In feats of warre and courage invincible . . . : CHECKMATE, V, 12: See **A large reporter of his owne Acts.** Both the quotes refer to the horoscope for Scorpio.

Interest: See **Usury.**

Io son fatta da Dio, sua merce, tale . . . : KINGS, IV, 2: From the *Divine Comedy* of Dante Alighieri (1265–1321), Part I, Inferno. Canto II. The words of Beatrice, untouched by the fires of Hell surrounding her and the damned.

Io son mercatante e non filosofo: KINGS, 12: From *The Decameron*, the collection of one hundred tales by the Florentine writer, scholar and humanist Giovanni Boccaccio (1313–1375). This was a period when the growth of humanism was opposed by some who feared a reversion to the pagan world associated with the classics. Here, the character Bernabò of Genoa, speaking to his fellow merchants, is careful to proclaim: 'I am a merchant, not a philosopher', adding, '*e come mercatante rispondero*' ('and it is as a merchant that I shall answer you'. (D. D.)

Irene and the Emperor Leo: CHECKMATE, I, 5: Leo IV (ruled 775–780), son of Constantine V (Emperor of Constantinople 741–775), was physically and mentally enfeebled. Constantine V chose his son's wife, Irene who, according to Gibbon's *Decline and Fall of the Roman Empire*, was 'an Athenian virgin, an orphan seventeen years old, whose sole fortune must have consisted in her personal accomplishments'. After Leo's death she was declared the Empress Guardian of the Roman world, and of their son Constantine VI. He ruled (780–797) but rebelled against his mother, who took the throne and had her son's eyes put out. She ruled from 797 until 802 until the patriciate rebelled against her and put the Tyrant treasurer Nicephorus (ruled 802–811) on the throne instead. Irene was exiled to Lesbos, where she died in 803, and was subsequently canonised by the Greek church.

Iron-beaked ravens: LIONS, 29: A reference to the saga **Njall's story**, to an incident which occurred off Orkney on the boats of the apostate Brodir, who had been consecrated a deacon but abandoned the Christian religion to make sacrifices to heathen spirits and use magic. The tale gives an impression of the effects of volcanic eruption:

> One night a terrible clamour broke out above Brodir and his men. They all awoke and jumped up, and put on their clothes. At the same time, boiling blood reigned down on them. They tried to protect themselves with their shields, but several of them were scalded. This phenomenon lasted until dawn, and one man on each ship was killed. The others slept all that day.

Next night the clamour came again, and they all jumped up once more. Their swords leapt from the sheaths, and axes and spears flew into the air and fought of their own accord. The weapons attacked the men so fiercely that they were forced to protect themselves, but several of them were wounded and one man on each ship was killed. This lasted until dawn. Then they slept again during the day.

The third night the same clamour was heard. Ravens came flying at them with beaks and talons that seemed made of iron. The ravens attacked them violently, but they defended themselves with swords and sheltered behind their shields. This lasted until dawn, and once more one man on each ship lost his life. Then the others slept for a while. Brodir's brother Ospak interpreted the events to him, 'The blood reigning down on you signifies that you shall shed much blood, your own as well as other people's. The great clamour you heard signifies the rupture of the world: you shall all die soon. The weapons attacking you signify battle, and the ravens which attacked you signify the demons which you once believed in and which shall drag you down to the torments of Hell'.

Is it for this thou wast created?: CHECKMATE, V, 12: According to legend, the voice of the Unseen as heard by the Central Asian mystic Ibráhíim ibn-Edhem (or Adham, d. *c.* 780) while he was out hunting. He abandoned the wealth of his father, forsook earthly pleasures and became a poor wandering dervish.

It is another disease that grieveth me: KINGS, II, 3: From *Everyman*, the popular 921-line morality play of *c.* 1508–1519. Destined to face death and judgement, the character of Everyman seeks a friend and advisor to accompany him to the next world, and calls upon the character of Worldly Goods, but Goods excuses himself:

GOODS: Who calleth me? Everyman? What!
hast thou haste?
I lie here in corners, trussed and piled so high,
And in chests I am locked so fast,
Also sacked in bags. Thou mayst see with thine eye
I cannot stir; in packs low I lie.
What would ye have? Lightly [quickly] me say.

EVERYMAN: Come hither, Good, in all the haste thou may,
For of counsel I must desire thee.

GOODS: Sir, and ye in the world have sorrow or adversity,
That I can help you to remedy shortly.

EVERYMAN: It is another disease that grieveth me;
In this world it is not. I tell thee so.
I am sent for, another way to go,
To give a strait count general
Before the highest Jupiter of all;
And all my life I have had joy and pleasure in thee,
Therefore, I pray thee, go with me;
For, peradventure, thou mayst before God Almighty
My reckoning help to clean and purify;
For it is said ever among
That money maketh all right that is wrong.

GOODS: Nay, Everyman, I sing another song.
I follow no man in such voyages;
For, and [if] I went with thee,
Thou shouldst fare much the worse for me;
For because on me thou did set thy mind,
Thy reckoning I have made blotted and blind,
That thine account thou cannot make truly;
And that hast thou for the love of me.

EVERYMAN: That would grieve me full sore,
When I should come to that fearful answer.
Up, let us go thither together.

GOODS: Nay, not so! I am too brittle, I may not endure;
I will follow no man one foot, be ye sure.

IVAN III: RONDO: (1440–1505). Nicknamed *Grozny*, or awesome (which in the case of his grandson became translated as Ivan the Terrible*), Ivan Vasilievich became Grand Duke of Muscovy in 1462. He was a cautious, calculating man who was to use these qualities to push back the frontiers of his domain, and who owed at least some of his style to his dynastic marriage in 1472 to **Zoe Palaeologina**, niece of the last Emperor of Constantinople.

Up to that point, Ivan (or the more European Ioann, which he preferred) had concerned himself with countering and harassing Tartars where he could, sending his boyars and provincial levies on campaign against Kazan and its outposts. At the same time, he exerted guile. In Moscow, where the Tartars of the **Golden Horde** held him in vassaldom, he continued to hand over the annual tribute to them, while cultivating **Mengli-Girey**, the Khan of the Crim Tartars, a disaffected offshoot of the Horde situated at Qirq-yer in the Crimean Peninsula. He avoided trouble with Turkey, even while his churchmen reminded him that his was the only surviving independent Greek Orthodox state.

Marriage to Zoe, daughter of Caesars, introduced a new element. It was not Ivan's first contact with Byzantium: his aunt had been the first wife of the Emperor John (VIII) Palaeologus. Nevertheless it gave Ivan (and his successors) added title to consider his Moscow as the Third Rome; a city which, unlike Constantinople (the second), would survive to spread Orthodox Christianity. The concept of the Duchy as the Third Rome was formulated by the Pskov monk Philotheus (Filofei) in the sixteenth century in a letter to Vasily III, Grand Prince of Moscow 1505–1533, declaring, 'Two Romes have fallen, but the third stands, and fourth there will not be' (CASTLE, I, 3).

The marriage also gave him Zoe's driving ambition to see re-created the Byzantine world of her forefathers. Ivan adopted the two-headed eagle as the symbol of Muscovy's succession to the Byzantine Empire. The result, however, was less to sharpen Ivan's attitude towards Ottoman Turkey than to redirect his interest towards consolidating his own domains. His aim was to recover the lands of Lithuania which had once belonged to the Kievan Russian state, and which threatened his frontiers to the west. To help him do so, he sought to reduce the smaller dukedoms, principalities and cities which might become the allies of **Casimir IV**, Grand Duke of Lithuania and King of Poland.

This he succeeded in doing, while fighting sometimes with, and sometimes against the surrounding Tartars. **Novgorod** the Great was finally annexed in 1478, allowing Ivan to confiscate vast tracts of land for his supporters. The next mission was against the Golden Horde, the children of Ahmed, the remnants of the Mongol invaders, now based at Saray on the Volga. In fact the Horde, having disintegrated into the separate khanates of Kazan, Astrakhan and the Crimea, were proving less and less able to impose their will upon Moscow, despite the encouragement of Casimir IV. Thus, when Khan Akhmat of Saray invaded in 1480 and Ivan fled from the field (having dispatched his treasure and Zoe to Beloozero), the Horde still lost the fight, largely because Casimir failed to come to their aid while the Crim Tartars were blocking their way. When Khan Akhmat was murdered, the Horde's dominion over Moscow vanished for good.

The consolidation went on. Tver was conquered in 1485. In 1491, Ivan mobilised his army to aid his ally, the Khan of the Crimea, against the Tartars of the southern steppe. In 1497 he agreed to a plan with King John of Denmark (ruled 1481–1513) reminiscent of one proposed by John's father **Christian I** more than twenty years previously. Both were to help Denmark subdue Sweden. In the first, Christian had hoped to involve **James III*** of Scotland, husband of **Margaret of Denmark**, Christian's daughter. This time, Ivan launched his troops against Finland, permitting King John to invade western Sweden, and assert his rights there. (It was successful, at first.) Meanwhile, in 1493, Ivan had turned his attention at last to his chief enemy. He conquered the heart of Kievan Rus, and by annexing Smolensk and Chernigov in 1500, changed the whole Lithuanian frontier.

Throughout, the future of Muscovy remained of paramount importance to the West. While waiting for Ivan to aspire to the imperial crown of Byzantium, Venice* spent the mid 1470s negotiating with the Golden Horde in hope of launching them against Constantinople via the Black Sea and Wallachia. Poland, although charmed by any plan to attack Turkey, was averse to becoming a highway for two hundred thousand Tartar horsemen en route, and sent **Callimachus** to Rome in 1477, via Venice, to say so. In much the same way, Ivan weighed his putative Byzantine crown against the benefits of nonaggression with Turkey, and acted accordingly.

After the fall of Caffa in the Crimea (1475) and during the final alignment of the Crim Tartars under Ottoman rule, Moscow was visited by a sequence of envoys, among them **Ambrogio Contarini** and **Ludovico de Severi da Bologna**.* Most were sent to engage the interest of Muscovy in an alliance against the Polish dynasty of the **Jagiellonians.** Before the end of the reign, there arrived a singularly inept emissary, one Nicolas Poppel, from the Holy Roman Emperor **Frederick III** and two from his son **Maximilian**, one of them ostensibly seeking the hand of a daughter. Maximilian later called off the proposed union: there had been, he said, some mistake. (In fact he married a sister of the Duke of Milan.) In 1492 Sigismond of Austria,* Archduke of the Tyrol, sent a Master Snups, who wanted to learn the language and advance his knowledge of science by exploring north to the Ob, in which ambition he did not succeed.

There was also an influx of military and architectural advisers – engineers, armourers, cannon-founders, silver-workers and miners, mostly from Italy. By 1488, a cannon-casting works stood inside Moscow, and Paolo Dubosis entered the record books with a rupture-resistant brass cannon weighing 3,600 pounds. The Cathedral of the Assumption was rebuilt by **Rudolfo Fioravanti** of Bologna, who brought his military engineering to the Kazan and Tver campaigns. Among other northern Italian builders, the Milanese architect Pietro Antonio Solari was responsible for the Facets Palace inside the Kremlin, the Grand Duchess's Golden Apartments and the Granovitaya Palace (see CASTLE, II, 1). By the end of Ivan's reign, there were brick walls round the Kremlin, modelled on those built for the Sforza Castello in Milan. Their features included the St Nicholas Tower, with its fine mosaic over the entrance; the Water Tower, with its machinery for drawing up water; the Tower of Secrets, with its underground passage to the river; and the Tocsin Tower, with its bell to warn against Tartar attacks.

Autocratic to the end, the Grand Prince of Muscovy assumed the unquestioned right to choose his successor. Ivan III had taken as first wife (in 1452) Maria, daughter of Boris Alexandrovich (1425–1461), Prince of the (then) independent republic of Tver. Maria (d. 1467) had given him a single son, Ivan, while – after two daughters – Zoe had borne him no less than five sons: Gabriel, Dmitri, George, Simeon and Andrew. When Maria's son Ivan died (amid rumours of poisoning) in 1490, leaving a six-year-old boy, Dmitri

Ivanovich, the Grand Prince designated Dmitri as his successor, bypassing his oldest son by Zoe, to her displeasure. Her son, even more displeased, listened to low-ranking friends and rebelled overtly, which led to their execution and his disgrace. Redemption followed. Dmitri's mother Helen fell out of favour. Her son, also reviled, was imprisoned by Zoe's son Gabriel, and Gabriel, now renamed Vasily, or Basil, was chosen as the Grand Prince's successor instead.

Vasily III (1479–1533) was to inherit (in 1505) a Muscovy quadrupled in size; a country which included Novgorod, Tver, Jaroslavl, Rostov, and about a third of all Lithuania, and which extended from Novgorod on the west to the Urals on the east; and from Tula in the south to the Barents Sea in the north. He also inherited the title of the sovereign of all the Russias, which his father had assumed in 1472, even though it implied possessions which were not entirely his. Wily, vigilant, ruthless, Ivan himself had learned the style of a Byzantine despot, lacking consideration for his subjects or family, but deploying the strength of his boyars to conquer and defend. For all the increasing size and efficiency of his army, he was a strategist who seldom went personally to war. According to the Palatine of Moldavia, Ivan III increased his dominion 'while asleep drunk at the table at home'. There may have been some truth in this, but not much. However it happened, he and Zoe between them changed Russia.

The son of Vasily III was **Ivan IV*** the Terrible (1530–1584), who was the first to assume the title of Tsar. Ivan IV subdued Kazan and Astrakhan and annexed Siberia, but his murderous temper destroyed a reign which might have brought real rapprochement at last with the West. He died of sorrow, it was said, for his son whom he had murdered in a fit of rage. (D. D.)

J

Jagiellonian dynasty: RONDO, 9: Pertaining to the Grand Duke of Lithuania, a recent Christian convert, Jogaila, or Jagiełło in Polish, (*c.* 1351–1434), who was elected to the throne of Poland in 1386 after marrying the heir to the Polish throne Jadwiga, daughter of Louis the Great (King of Hungary 1370–1382). Jogaila ruled until he was eighty-three, uniting Poland and Lithuania under his successors for the next 186 years until 1572. He is remembered for having encouraged the powers of the nobility and the growth of the church, and revitalising the university of Cracow, which now bears his name.

The dynasty ruled the republic of Poland – Lithuania (1386–1572); Hungary (1440–1444; 1490–1526); and Bohemia (1471–1526). The Jagiellonians also controlled vassal states in the Balkans. Control over the Hungarian throne began with Jogaila's son Władisław VI and I (1440–1444), killed at the Battle of Varna (1444). Hungary was then ruled by Ladislas V Posthumous (1444–1457) (who was the son of the Holy Roman Emperor and Habsburg ruler Albert V). Ladislas ruled mostly in name only, as he was predominantly based in Prague. He was succeeded by **Mathias Corvinus**, (elected in 1458), who died without legitimate issue, giving the Jagiellionians the opportunity to return to the throne in 1490 with Władisław II (1456–1516), son of **Casimir IV** of Poland. Władisław was King of Hungary (1490–1516) and Bohemia (1471–1516), followed by Louis II. A subsequent pact of mutual succession with the Habsburgs allowed the descendants of the Emperor **Frederick III** to control the parts of Hungary not overrun by the Ottomans after the battle of Mohacs in 1526 at which Louis II was killed and his feudal army destroyed. Hungary was split between the Ottomans and the Habsburgs.

James II, King of Cyprus: See **Zacco, King of Cyprus.**

James II's sisters: HN: James II* was blessed with six sisters: Margaret, Isabella, Joanna (or Joan), Eleanor, Mary and Annabella. James I intended them to marry abroad, to the diplomatic and economic advantage of Scotland. Margaret, the first and eldest of the daughters, was in 1436 betrothed to the Dauphin of France, later to become **Louis XI**,* but the marriage was neither happy nor productive. There were rumours of her close relationships with her private circle of handsome poets and she was also accused of deliberately preventing successful pregnancy using a combination of vinegar and green apples (RISING, 34). She died childless in 1445. Mary was next to marry, in 1444, taking as her husband Wolfaert **van Borselen.** They had one son, Charles, who died in adolescence, and Mary herself died in 1468. In 1445 two more of the sisters, Joanna and Eleanor, journeyed to France to see their sister and take their places in the dynastic marriage market, accompanied by **Thomas Spens.** Hard upon the death of their mother, Joan Beaufort, when they arrived they were informed that their sister Margaret had also just died. Charles VII,* King of France, took it upon himself to arrange a match for Eleanor, the cleverest and most able of the daughters. He initially hoped to receive a papal dispensation to allow Eleanor to marry the Dauphin, but it was not forthcoming. Instead, in 1447 she was betrothed to Sigismond of Austria* whom she married the following year. Despite his profligacy elsewhere, the couple remained childless and she remained with him until her death in 1480.

In 1441 Isabella had been proposed as a potential bride for Francis, comte de Montfort, son and heir of John, Duke of Brittany. Esteemed for her beauty and her health (assessed as likely to produce an heir), she seldom spoke and there were doubts as to her intelligence. Far from presenting a problem, Duke John positively revelled in the idea of a less-than-bright daughter-in-law, and reputedly answered her detractors saying:

> My friends, return to Scotland and bring her hither: she is just such a person as I wish for my son. Knowledge or cleverness does a woman more hurt than good; upon my soul I shall have no other. By the body of St Nicholas, I esteem a woman wise enough when she can make a distinction between her husband's shirt and his doublet.

The marriage took place in 1450 and Isabella presented her husband with two daughters: Margaret married her cousin Francis, Duke of Brittany, and the younger daughter married John, vicomte de Rohan. Isabella outlived her husband, and survived several more Dukes of Brittany, dying only in 1494.

James II had written to Charles VII to ask his assistance in finding suitable spouses for the remaining sisters Joanna and Annabella, as well as a bride for himself (James was to marry Mary of Gueldres, the niece of Philip the Good, Duke of Burgundy,* in 1449). However, Joanna remained in the French Court, unmarried (GEMINI, 21), perhaps on account of fears that her deafness was hereditary. Returning eventually to Scotland with Bishop Kennedy,* she married James Douglas, Earl of Morton, in 1458, and died before 1490. Their son, the Second Earl of Morton, had two daughters: Margaret, who was to marry Sir Patrick Hepburn of Hailes, and Janet, who married Thomas, Lord Erskine.

Annabella, the youngest of the daughters, was at the age of eight (in 1444) betrothed to Louis, Count of Geneva, but the marriage was broken off when, as an adult, she arrived in Savoy. Like Joanna, she returned to Scotland, where she married George, Master of Huntly. They had a large family of four sons and six daughters; one of their daughters became the bride of Perkin Warbeck (*c.* 1474–1499), the Pretender to the throne of England supported by **Margaret of York.**

James III:* UNICORN: (1452–1488) Later chroniclers of his reign have depicted James as an inadequate monarch whose rule was characterised purely by his acquisitiveness, favouritism, manipulation of the coinage and the judiciary and criticised his tendency to stay in **Edinburgh** rather than administer justice and good government throughout his kingdom. But the chronicles tell only part of the story. James III could have been a moderately successful monarch had his kingdom not been riven by a chronic lack of funds and many of his contemporaries' perennial antipathy towards England. His rule may have shown signs of weakness compared to that of **Louis XI*** or **Edward IV**,* but, given his economic limitations, James did attempt to expand the territorial boundaries of Scotland. He obtained **Orkney** and Shetland through his marriage to **Margaret of Denmark**, but his desire to invade Brittany and acquire both the Duchy of Gueldres and the French county of Santoigne were frustrated not by his own apathy, but the refusal of Parliament to grant him funds and leave to go abroad. His imperial and dynastic ambitions were thwarted by the nobility and his own family. His rapprochement with England and proposed marriage alliances (see **Cecilia**) did not sit well with his brothers **Alexander, Duke of Albany*** and **John of Mar**, nor with many of the border nobility who, putting local loyalties above national interest, would rather hark back to the period encapsulated in ***The Wallace*** than make peace with the Auld Enemy England. The affair at **Lauder Bridge** and the English invasion of 1482 were the lowest points in James's reign. Caught between the French and English monarchs, James was outclassed, outmanoeuvred and undermined. Maintaining peace with England and attempting to rekindle the Auld Alliance with France were the mutually exclusive foreign policies that were alternatively to dominate Scottish foreign policy for the next eighty years.

The novels portray a monarch who was simply not capable of dealing with the circumstances and the problems that beset late-fifteenth-century Scotland. In reality, at Lauder Bridge in 1482, his own counsellors and family acted to remove him from power. It happened again in 1488, when his reign came to an abrupt end. A rebel force using James's eldest son as their figurehead met with the King at Sauchieburn near Stirling. So close to the site of the battle of Bannockburn, James is said to have carried the sword of Robert the Bruce (1274–1329) into battle in an attempt to emulate the hero king. Failing to come to terms with the nobles, James, as relayed in Parliament the following year, 'happinnit to be slane', probably killed in a skirmish on the battlefield. No one was tried for his murder. He was succeeded by his son **James IV**,* leader of the rebel force. The new King's brother James Stewart, Marquis of Ormond, Duke of Ross, was Archbishop of St Andrews between 1475 and

1504; and John Stewart obtained his uncle's title, Earl of Mar, in 1479. He died in 1503.

King James III ~ base silver groat ~ showing two thistles ~ the first time the plant was used to symbolize Scotland

James IV:* GEMINI: (1473–1513) Recognised as the new King of Scotland following the death of his father at Sauchieburn in 1488, James IV attempted a conciliatory policy towards the rebels rather than one of revenge; however, in private penance as recognition of his involvement in the death of his father, James is said to have worn an iron belt under his clothing for the rest of his life (details are found in the household accounts of the worsted fabric used to cover it and prevent it from chafing his skin). He also spent a great deal of time with the strict **Observantine Friars** in Stirling. More popular and successful than his father, James IV fostered the arts, law and sciences. He made it compulsory for men of substance to have their sons educated in the arts and law (1496) and introduced the printing press to Scotland (1507 or 1508). During his reign and that of his son, vernacular prose flourished, as did building work at the height of the renaissance in Scotland, particularly at Stirling, Falkland and **Linlithgow.**

His attempts to consolidate friendship with England led in 1503 to his marriage to Margaret Tudor (1489–1541); the union of the Thistle and the Rose thus cemented the Treaty of Perpetual Peace between Scotland and England which had been sealed with papal approval in 1502. But when France and England went to war under England's bellicose new monarch Henry VIII (king of England 1509–1547), the renewal of the Auld Alliance between Scotland and France obliged James to make war against England. The Scottish army under the monarch took the field against the English at the battle of **Flodden**, 1513, and were slaughtered. Among the dead were King James and the greater part of the nobility. The heir to the throne was only a child. The pattern of child monarchs in Scotland had begun with the murder of James I in 1437, and until 1625, every monarch ruling Scotland came to the throne as a child. The powerful nobility of Scotland, as in generations past, once again vied with one another for power and control over the young King James V.*

Jelita: RONDO, 12: Authentic noble Polish family or clan name, clan heraldry being different in Poland than Scotland or England, in that coats of arms were not held by individual nobles, but the heraldic symbols (blazons, motto and devices) were held in common with many others, not all of whom were related. The membership system may have been based on patronage and ties of loyalty if not strictly familial. Jelita (bowel) is said to originate in 1331 from the battlefield of Plowe, when the King of Poland found Florian Szarzy disembowelled by three spears from the **Teutonic Knights.** In recognition of the unfortunate knight's heroism, the Jelita clan was formed, using the three spears as its heraldic device. The fifteenth-century historian Jan Długosz noted 139 clans in Poland. The devices stayed simple: because they were held in common, there was no need to modify them to delineate succession, inheritance or marriage. Each clan simply had one motto, one device and one coat of arms.

Arms of the Medici Popes

Jewels with a name: LIONS, 37; 46: Only important jewels were given a name, and the most staggering list of such gems comes from a battlefield: the treasure found by the Swiss in 1476 in the abandoned camp of **Charles, Duke of Burgundy**,* outside Grandson, where he had been waging war against the Swiss. The total booty, including horses and arms, pavilions and equipment (and two thousand girls) was valued at hundreds of millions of marks. The golden seat of the Duke was taken, and his hat sewn with jewels (in which he had mounted one of the largest diamonds in the world), and his diamonds. The regalia of the ducal chapel was also lost, including a reliquary of gold inlaid with gems and containing eighty separate relics, and three to four hundredweight of silver, gold and silver gilt. The great sword of state, encrusted with rubies, pearls and diamonds, went too.

The finest jewel, a yellow diamond of 139 carats set in gold and pearls, was called the 'Grand Duke of Tuscany', at the start of its career. It was picked up by a lad from Zoug, who flung it away, then changed his mind and took it to a foot soldier, who bought it for a florin or two. The soldier handed it to the authorities, who paid him three francs. It was then officially valued at twenty thousand florins, but no suitable buyer was forthcoming until 1492, when one Bartholemy May (a name well known in Bruges)* bought the jewel for five thousand florins. From there it went to a Genoese dealer who sold it to Ludovic the Moor, Duke of Milan (1452–1508), for double the price. The next owner was Pope Julius II (Pope 1503–1513), who acquired it for twenty thousand ducats. From Julius it passed to Pope Leo X,* and hence to the Medici family, changing its name for that reason to 'The Florentine.' Next the stone arrived at the court of Vienna and entered the Habsburg collection, where it remained until 1918. The last Emperor of Austria carried it into exile, and it was put up for sale in 1929, but no buyer was found until 1955, when it went to an American. By 1977, it had disappeared without trace. The second finest, '*Le Sancy*', of one hundred carats, reappeared in the French crown jewels in the eighteenth century, and then was bought by a Maharaja. The '*Federlin*', of 5 balas rubies, 4 diamonds and 69 pearls, was fixed on a hat. The '*Gurtelin*', the badge of the Order of the Garter, was bought by the Emperor **Maximilian I** for eight thousand florins, and the '*Three Brothers*', three balas rubies of seventy carats, supposedly went to King Henry VIII, but vanished after the execution of King Charles I in 1649. The '*Rose Blanche*' was a spinel surrounded by petals in white enamel. Among the jewels which were never traced were two large pearls: '*Non Pareille*', and '*La Ramasse* of Flandres'.

Other avid jewel collectors of the period included Pope Paul II* (a handsome man, who had to be dissuaded from taking the title '*Formosus*'). Smitten early by the coin-hunting mania which then rampaged without scruple through Italy, Paul also specialised in antique cameos and engraved jewels, medals and bronzes. Some of the pieces were mounted on silver-gilt tablets with his name; one, an amethyst called '*Abundance*', was set as a seal with his arms under the gem. He was respected, however, for fair dealing; his offer for a cameo owned by the town of Toulouse included building a bridge for them. An inspection on his death in 1471 revealed a treasure valued at a million ducats, among which were fifty-four silver shells filled with pearls, worth three hundred thousand ducats. These were set aside, to be used for the war against Turkey. By December 1471 Pope Sixtus IV* had sold many of the late Pope's jewels, some to the Medici. Others went to the King of Naples as security for a loan.

The great banking families of the Medici and, later, the Fugger were probably the ultimate beneficiaries of it all. (D. D.)

John of Stobo: See **This officer but doubt is callit Deid.**

Jökulár: LIONS, 29: In Iceland there are ice-rivers, fast-flowing streams born under a *Vatnajökull*, a glacier, as part of the greatest ice-cap in Europe. These debris-ridden glacier rivers were dangerous and variable and far from jocular in any sense: a river current could reach eight m.p.h. In colour, a *jökull* would be a cold greenish blue. (D. D.)

Joy plays the organ and Memory works the bellows . . . : LIONS, 17: Taken from the action of an early French **Passion Play** featuring allegorical figures: Love, Good Counsel, Diligence, Equity, Humanity, Understanding etc. The players in all such performances were a mixture of workmen, noblemen, bourgeois or priests (whose special task it was to teach the boys playing girls how to walk). When retiring to eat during rehearsals, the cast beguilingly disposed itself according to temporary status: God the Father, Lazarus, the Magdalene and a score of others would resort to one inn, St John the Baptist and his crew to another, and Lucifer and the Pharisees to a third. (D. D.)

Justification: GEMINI, 20: The Roman sense is salvation. In early Scots usage, it meant to be punished with death.

Justus of Ghent: LIONS, 7: (*c.* 1435/1440–*c.* 1480) Also known as Joos van Wassenhoven, or in Italy as Giusto da Guanto. A member of the Antwerp guild* of painters in 1460, Joos had moved to Ghent by 1464 and may have taught **Hugo van der Goes**, whom he sponsored that year to enter the Painters' Guild in Ghent. He and Hugo were both guarantors in a similar way when the artist Sanders Bening turned Master. Bening's wife was Catherine van der Goes, and his daughter Cornelia was married to the Scot Andrew Haliburton. Hugo, who was to have his own Scottish clients, lent money to Joos in the late 60s or early 70s when Joos left to travel to Rome, and then to work at the wealthy Italian court of the Count of Urbino.*

His well-known work there, the main panel for a Last Supper altar-piece, was painted by chance. The predella panels had already been completed by a Florentine painter, Paolo Uccello (1397–1475). The large central painting, ten feet square, was offered to Piero della Francesca (*c.* 1410/1420–1492), who had to refuse the commission. It was therefore confided to Joos, who worked on it between 1472 and 1474. Although initiated by a confraternity, the Corpus Domini, the altar-piece had received a generous contribution from Federigo da Montefeltro, created Duke of Urbino in 1474. As a result, the painting contains portraits of the Duke and his baby and late wife Battista Sforza, as well as two leading courtiers, and a turbanned and bearded figure usually described as an ambassador of the Shah of Persia who came to Urbino to urge Federigo to launch a Turkish crusade.

One source identifies the Persian envoy as a richly dressed Jew and Christian convert called Isaac. It is likely however that he may have been Hadji Mehmet, the far-travelled envoy of the leading Turcoman prince **Uzum Hasan.*** Hadji Mehmet called at Urbino in 1471 on his way to Rome from Venice, where he may have met **Anselm Adorne.*** During the campaigns against Turkey, the Turcoman agent was a longtime ally of the Franciscan friar **Ludovico de Severi da Bologna**,* and in 1461 he had visited Ghent with da Bologna as part of an embassy which had started in Rome, in the company of Bianca Visconti, wife of Duke Francesco Sforza* of Milan. Hadji Mehmet was also well known to **Caterino Zeno**,* the Venetian envoy, whose wife Violante was related to Uzum's Christian wife.

This painting by Joos, *The Communion of the Apostles*, is in the Galleria Nazionale delle Marche, Urbino. Other possible pictures by Joos also exist in Urbino and Paris, but their attribution has been difficult to prove. He seems to have stopped working by 1480, by which time the Flemish method of painting in oils was attracting increasing attention in Italy. (D. D.)

K

Kanclerz: RONDO, 7: 'Chancellor,' one of the sixteen officers of state in Poland chosen by the King for the senate.

Katla: LIONS, 26: The Icelandic volcano hidden beneath the ice cover of Mýrdalsjökull has erupted at least seventeen times since **Iceland** was first colonised. See also **Hekla.**

Kelso: GEMINI, 41: Immensely wealthy Tironensian Abbey. Monks from the Order of Tiron, established in 1109 by St Bernard of Poitiers and originally from Thiron-Gardais in south-east Normandy, first settled in Scotland at Lindean, near Selkirk, in 1113, but in 1128 David I (King of Scotland 1124–1153) moved the order to Kelso. Like the other border Abbeys, it was in a precarious position when Scotland and England were at war, as it was only a mile or so from Roxburgh Castle, under English occupation until the siege of 1460 (at which James II* lost his life). In 1462 it was home to seventeen or eighteen monks, but in its heyday it had between thirty and forty monks. In the mid-sixteenth century it was attacked and burned by the English (in 1532, 1542, 1544 and 1545) and it was further reduced and ultimately suppressed by the Reformers in 1560, by which time only a dozen monks remained.

King of the Sea: GEMINI, 10: As part of the Mayday celebrations in the port of **Leith**, there was an annual competition which involved boat-jousting. The winner was titled 'King'. The pynours, porters or labourers of the port were responsible for the celebrations.

Kiss any arm you cannot break: UNICORN, 39: A saying which continues: 'And pray God to break it'.

Knights of St John:* See **Knollys, William;* Rhodes.**

KNOLLYS, William:* UNICORN: (d. 1510) The financial expertise and management skills of William Knollys, for forty-four years Preceptor in Scotland of the Knights Hospitaller of the Order of St John of Jerusalem (see Knights of St

John*), left their stamp on the reign of **James III*** and afterwards, through the adroit transition managed by himself for himself, on the first years of the reign of his son.

The Scottish Preceptor's base was at Torphichen, which in Gaelic means 'Ravens' Hill'. The only certain house of the Hospitallers in Scotland was four miles from **Linlithgow** and fifteen miles from **Edinburgh;** but the headquarters of the Order was nominally at Clerkenwell, Middlesex. As with the Knights Templar, who came to Scotland in 1128 and whose home was at the Temple in London, the early Scottish preceptory was usually staffed with English Knights. Torphichen, founded in 1153, was supposedly granted to the Knights of St John by David I (King of Scotland 1124–1153). Given their special allegiance, it was not surprising that both the Knights and the Templars supported the English King Edward I (ruled 1272–1307) during his wars against Scotland.

In 1298, the Scottish patriot William Wallace (*c.* 1270–1305) briefly occupied Torphichen. The Order later returned, wary of popular opinion, and ready to fly to Linlithgow peel tower if assailed. English Kings continued to use both the military orders. The Templars were expected to supply Edward II (ruled 1307–1327) with men and cattle for the continuing war against Scotland, and later monarchs looked to them for money. The Order found it necessary to acquire a system of lawyers and bribes to protect itself.

In 1312, when the Knights Templar were suppressed, Torphichen was transferred to the Hospitallers, together with the Templars' estates, which lay in nearly every county of Scotland, and especially where the first Norman, Breton and Flemish incomers had settled. These great fiefdoms were what the Preceptor controlled through a system of bailies, ordering their trade and transmitting their dues to the 'Convent' or home of the Order, at this time in **Rhodes.** At the height of its spiritual power, Torphichen was a sacred building, a head court of justice and, as the home of a Sovereign Order, a place of refuge for all seeking immunity. Its community was a mixture of laymen and clerics. Its great cruciform church had a bell tower, and a nave over a hundred feet long. A post-Reformation church is on the site of the nave, but the fifteenth-century vaulted transepts and tower remain.

The clerical aspect of the Order in Scotland declined. After a mild revival of crusading ardour following the fall of Constantinople in 1453, the organisation of the Servants of God's Poor and the Pope's Dear Children in Scotland developed into a complex land-management and trading operation involving a tax-raising structure not unlike that of Rome. Under the systems laid down abroad, workers cared for the lands and its beasts; cured the fish; cut the peat; made the malt and the salt. There were mills, fishing and hunting rights. Free tenants held leases of different lengths, and supplied movable stock in return. Horses were raised. The bailies traded. Money payment was made through Italian bankers. In 1417 the Order was conveying at Bruges* every year all the fruits due from its house to the Society of the Medici of Florence. By 1445 Brother Andrew Meldrum, prior of Maryculter (see **Culter**) and Lord of Liston, was lodging five hundred Venetian ducats annually at Bruges from the Religion in Scotland. His priest and chaplain was John of Kinloch.*

In 1467, William Knollys became confirmed Preceptor, Prior or Master of Torphichen for life by a special dispensation which absolved him from serving the mandatory three prior years at Rhodes, and five in the Order. He was not a warrior monk: his military skills were not why he was wanted. His family were almost certainly Norman: possibly (like the **Preston family**) connected with the Malherbes, the undertenants of Roger de Courcelles, who held Somerset land after the Norman Conquest at Knowle. They were also associated with Leighton Buzzard, a town lying to the south of the Northampton lands of King David I, where St Giles was also revered. One branch of the Malherbes, arriving in East Lothian, Scotland, in the twelfth century, changed their name to that of their new home, Moreville, and by 1200, Morehams were witnessing a charter in the Cortachy area to the benefit of **Newbattle** Abbey.

The Preceptor's connections were also in the north-east of Scotland, and place him in the branch of the family Knollys (or Knox) which came from Deer, Aberdeen. One of those who installed him was the Archbishop of Arles, the French seaport in Provence which served Venice,* Genoa and the Holy Land, and the place which may have later acquired for William Preston the precious bone of St Giles* for the town church of Edinburgh. The Grand Priory of St Giles, just outside Arles, controlled fifty of the Order's Commanderies, and had been the Order's first foothold in Europe.

Knollys seems to have had two brothers. One, Patrick Knollys de Eodem, head of the family, held land in Berwickshire and was the overlord, in **Alexander, Duke of Albany**'s* earldom of March, of John of Scougal, of a well-known Hospitaller family, who was viciously killed in 1479 by the same Duke of Albany. The reason was never disclosed, but between William Knollys and Conventual Brother Patrick Scougal there was a long-running legal battle which began in 1466 and was still continuing in 1492 over Scougal's right to the Preceptorship. John, the Preceptor's other brother, was a burgess of Aberdeen, and also the Order's Aberdeen bailie. One of John's two sons stayed in Aberdeen. The other married the granddaughter of Alexander Haliburton, possibly related to his own grandmother, who seems to have been a daughter of John Haliburton, sheriff of Berwick-upon-Tweed* in 1449, thus establishing a useful trading connection.

The Preceptor William Knollys himself had four illegitimate sons, mother or mothers unknown. Two were to be connected with Linlithgow, and one of these, Robert, married before 1503 Libra Parkle, daughter of an illegitimate kinsman of the well-connected George, who had followed **Anselm Sersanders** as Keeper of Linlithgow, immediately preceding the Preceptor himself. All were later legitimised (see **Legitimation**).

Knollys himself appears in 1460 as rector of Whitsome in Berwickshire, close to his brother Patrick's Duns, and in an area long held by the Templars. By 1463 William was in England on a peace mission together with **Thomas Spens**, Bishop of Aberdeen, and one John Knollys, who might be William's father or brother. John, with the same Thomas Spens when Bishop of Galloway, had been in Newcastle nine years before on the same errand. The association with Spens was to be a long one: Knollys was named his executor when the Bishop died in 1480, and long after that death, was taking the Bishop's debtors to law.

In 1469, two years after he became Preceptor, William Knollys briefly held the royal appointment of Lord High Treasurer. In 1471, he was appointed one of the **Lords Auditor of Causes and Complaints**, and took his seat along with the country's chief bishops and abbots, the high officers of state, some nobles and merchants or customars like William of Edmonston and Haliburton. Some years later, John Knollys was to follow him. William also began to go to law on his own behalf, to recover sums of money as large as £450, or release produce or property belonging to, or due to, the Order. (Rules were strict: chickens offered in tribute in France had to be big enough to fly as high as the hub of a cart wheel.) One of his earliest cases was against Andrew and John Bisset over the former Templar property of Liston, now Kirkliston (see Culter).

Some causes seemed to be settled outside court. In 1473 there was a dispute of some kind between the Preceptor and someone called simply Cochrane. Three years later, Robert Cochrane and the Preceptor were at odds in an unresolved case – perhaps the same – to do with a site in Edinburgh 'below the castle wall'. The Order's Edinburgh hospice was then on the south side of the **Canongate**, next to the yard of **Greyfriars** monastery, and close to the ground under the castle wall commonly used for jousting.

Related to all of this may be a curious sixteenth-century tale of a single combat staged in the time of James III between Robert Cochrane and one 'William Tor'. Modern commentators suggest Robert Cochrane is really **Thomas Cochrane**, the legendary King's favourite, who is said to have won the fight because Tor's horse stumbled, 'perhaps because of witchcraft'. The same sixteenth-century source lists among other royal favorites one Torphichen, a fencing or dancing master.

There were in fact two Cochranes, one Thomas, one Robert. It seems likely that Thomas was later attached to events which actually involved Robert, and that both William Tor and Torphichen represented a confusion between a real William Tor and William, lord of Torphichen of the Knights of St John. There is even the strange possibility that the fiscal power and personal ostentation of William Knollys were the true targets of contemporary critics, not the person of Tom Cochrane at all. It is the case that the Cochranes and Knollys may have had an earlier, English common heritage. In 1370 Edward III (King of England 1327–1377) provided safe conducts for John de Cogherane and others, going on the King's service overseas under Sir Robert de Knollis, an Englishman.

In 1477 the Preceptor is found as chaplain to the King's half-uncle James, **Earl of Buchan**, then Chancellor to the King. This might be a relic of an earlier custom whereby the royal household retained a Knight of the Order as almoner. Knollys remained active at law, summoning single noblemen and groups of debtors from Bathgate to Ayrshire and from Aberdeen down to **Leith** for substantial payments of tiends (tithes) – Robert Lord Lyle is ordered to pay the Preceptor nine hundred units of meal owing as fruits of the church of Inchinnan. Knollys took an interest in northern fisheries in the Dee, exporting salmon from his estate at Maryculter; he purchased barrels from the coupars of Aberdeen.

From 1478 William Knollys served in Parliament, sitting either with churchmen as Preceptor of Torphichen, or with the barons, as William, Lord St John of Jerusalem. John of Knollys, burgess of Aberdeen, had preceded him. William also, the same year, became one of the **Lords of Council in Civil Causes**, serving among others with the **Earl of Argyll**, whose kinsman Colin Campbell of Glenorchy allegedly fought with the Knights Hospitaller at Rhodes. Knollys was not present at the one recorded sederunt (court sitting) on 28 November 1478, which included **Anselm Adorne.***

In 1479, Knollys was a witness in the process against the King's brother Alexander, Duke of Albany, called to appear for a list of misdemeanours. Other witnesses included **Thomas Swift**, who was to succeed Anselm Adorne as Scottish Conservator. By 1483 Patrick Knollys also was sitting in Parliament.

About the same time, William Knollys was appointed a customs commissioner. His position may or may not account for an extraordinary series of mounted robberies, by apparently respected and responsible people, which took place on the Preceptor's Lothian possessions before March 1483, the date on which Knollys arraigned the culprits before the Council in Civil Causes. Goods were stolen from four different locations, and ranged from house furnishings to farm produce and a considerable number of beasts. From Torphichen itself, the family of Sir Gilbert Johnstone of Elphinstone and ten others took, among other things, fourteen oxen, a down bed with a bolster, arras, pewter, an iron chimney, coals, peats and twenty stones of cheeses. There were similar abstractions from three other sites in the same area, including Liston (now Kirkliston).

The records lapse before the cases were decided, leaving a mystery. Several of the men involved in the four raids – notably Johnstone of Elphinstone and his family – had interests in other parts of Scotland, but most also held in the areas roughly east of Torphichen. Some were directly connected to Templar or Hospitaller land, and belonged to families who held responsible office, and were found witnessing bailies' charters. Some had names which might suggest connections with Newbattle Abbey. Others were connected by marriage. Most of the same men took part in the two bigger raids, on Torphichen and Liston. It is an open question whether or not this represented a general resentment against heavy-handed tribute-collection and some perceived injustice by Knollys, or whether it had to do with the Preceptor's personal stance over Albany and even the death of Adorne. Certainly, those taking part were from areas between Linlithgow and the east coast most affected by the struggle between the King and his family.

Between the disappearance of Albany and the unrest that ended with the death of the King, Knollys seems to have steered a neutral course almost until the end, when he abandoned James III for the cause of the rebels and the young future King, James's son. The one markedly unpleasant incident occurred in September of 1485, and concerned the interrogation of Sir James Liddell of Halkerston, the loyal steward of the absconded Duke of Albany, accidentally killed that same year in France.

The Liddells favoured the Order of St John. As far back as 1427 a John Liddell, squire of James I (ruled 1406–1437), had been procurator and administrator of the Order in Scotland. Now Sir James, bound and condemned to death in the **Tolbooth** of Edinburgh as a traitor, was put to the question by the Preceptor's bailie, the Edinburgh burgess James Ross, over the rightful possession of Halkerston. This seemed to refer to Liddell's forfeited possessions in Temple Hall, south of Edinburgh. The outcome was inconclusive. Sir James 'could not say', it was recorded, whether Halkerston stood on old heritage lands, or on land owned by the lord St John of Torphichen (if the latter, of course, it had been unjustly withheld from his lordship, and could be plausibly claimed from the King). It seems a somewhat unchristian excuse for badgering a chained man on the eve of his death. Liddell's only sin had been his loyalty to Albany.

In time, a transfer of some kind took place, but not under that King. Six years on, it was ordained that the **barony** of Baltrudo, with the houses of Halkerston belonging to William, Lord of St John, were to be renamed the barony and castle of St John, with all the old privileges and freedoms. It was just the year before William Knolly sued John of Liddell for holding back a gold chain.

King James III died in 1488, to be succeeded by his son, **James IV**,* aged 15. If Knollys took part in the final battle, it was by that time on the side of the young Prince and the rebels, who won. William Knollys immediately became Treasurer for the second time, in succession to David Lichton, Abbot of Arbroath. His first task was to help recover and inventory the previous monarch's boxes of treasure, some of which Lichton had held, and now gave up. The secure places of the military orders in England were commonly used by the Crown to store its war chests, and it is probable that, like **Holyrood**, the Scottish Preceptory also stored royal treasure. On the field of battle itself had been found a box carried there for the King, containing four thousand pounds and the sword of Robert the Bruce.

Now Knollys was also appointed Keeper of **Blackness** Castle and sheriff of Linlithgow. As Treasurer, Knollys attended the first Parliament of October 1488, along with Henry Preston of Edinburgh, the Bishop of Aberdeen, Alexander **Home** of eodem, Angus, Huntly, Errol, Hailes, **Lennox**, Lyle, Oliphant and all the other survivors. John Knollys sat with the Lords of Council in Civil Causes with **Henry Cant**.

William Knollys remained as Preceptor, and was confirmed in his temporal barony by the young King, who granted him customs privileges. John Knollys, one of the customars for Aberdeen, dealt with the eight lasts of salmon owed to the Grand Master at Rhodes by the Preceptor, and salmon in quantities of over twenty-three lasts (a last being a dry weight equivalent to 4000 lbs) at a time passed through the customar's hands, some of it sold custom-free. John, a burgess of Aberdeen (whose wife was a Hay), was also favoured by the new King, being given land in Kincardine, and Aberdeenshire land formerly owned by George, son of William Meldrum.

Further south, money for the King's use was handled by Treasurer Knollys, who also confirmed grants made by the late King to men now being courted, such as the Earl of Argyll, the Earl of Bothwell and some members of the family Home. As early as 1489 he was involved in bitter controversy with **Archibald Douglas**, Earl of Angus, over a missing sum of one thousand pounds in which Colin, Earl of Argyll, and Laurence, Lord Oliphant, were involved, and which at some point threatened actual bodily harm.

The Preceptor's Edinburgh bailie, working from the Order's hospice there, dealt with case after case involving ex-Templar land. **Sinclairs**, Ramsays, Napiers, and Prestons appear in the Treasurer's disputes. Knollys went to law several times against Marchmont Herald, William Cumming, over Fife land claimed by John Knollys. Fifteen years after Albany's death, Knollys was still contriving to retrieve tenanted land of the Duke's on behalf of John Knollys his brother. Not everything necessarily went the Preceptor's way. William, Lord of Torphichen, was pursued more than once by the Abbot of Kinloss for withholding salmon and money due from several churches.

In 1490, Knollys was made Master of the Royal Household, and in 1491 was given custody of the Palace of Linlithgow with the peel, loch, parks, coal, etc., and ten pounds of the King's land of Kincavil, as held by the late Keeper, George Parkle. The Preceptor's son Robert by 1492 had acquired land next to **Thomas Yare** on the north side of the High Street in Edinburgh.

Besides collecting his dues, the Preceptor traded. In 1490, at the town of Leighton Buzzard, Henry VII (King of England 1485–1509) issued a safe conduct for a year, to be delivered for execution at Knolle, England, allowing Sir William Knollys or his factors to import and export to England, using his vessel of eighty tons. Two years later, the King's almoner transmitted permission to trade with a vessel of 160 tons. In Edinburgh, the customars such as Thomas Yare and James Turing dealt with dacres of hides belonging to Lord St John, Master of the hospice.

Although the Preceptor had many more years ahead with the Order, his public life was about to diminish as the King grew out of his minority, and the kingdom came to terms with the change. For a while, Knollys took part in peace missions: in 1492 he was one of a party which met at Coldstream to extend the English truce. Over the following years, Knollys was given several safe conducts to lead parties to England. But in 1492, in response to unrest over the disposition and slow rate of recovery of the late King's fortune, Knollys was removed as both Treasurer and Master of the Royal Household. **Henry Arnot** of **Cambuskenneth** became Treasurer in his place. When, over the next year or two, **Archibald Whitelaw** retired, and the death of Colin, Earl of Argyll, gave the Chancellorship to Archibald, Earl of Angus, the end of the Preceptor's public career was in sight.

Accustomed to ships, he did take part, at the end of 1494, in the planning for a seaborne army to take the King to quell a revolt in the Hebrides. **Sir Andrew Wood** of Largo was one of his associates. Knollys maintained his hold over the Order's estates, and continued to export quantities of salmon as part of his responsions to Rhodes. By 1504, he had become infirm, and for the rest of his life he had the aid of his successor as Preceptor, George Dundas. When William Knollys died in 1510, he left a neglected church but a well-run business, which perhaps had usurped the proper priority required by the kingdom he was also serving. The dual responsibility was probably more than even the most forceful and able of men could comfortably handle, although William Knollys never seemed to have doubts.

After Knollys, possession of the preceptory passed through four pairs of hands, all in dispute, until in 1547, Brother James Sandilands* of Calder was confirmed by the Grand Master de Homedès* as the new Preceptor of Torphichen and took possession (in 1550) of all the Order's temporalities and possessions in Scotland. But by now the Reformed religion had come. Sandilands married. He actually kept the Order's lands until 1564, before taking steps to resign them all to Mary Queen of Scots.* Next, by paying ten thousand crowns, he received them all back, in the form of his own hereditary barony of Torphichen.

It was what William Knollys must have dreamed of. (D. D.)

Kochajmy Się: RONDO, 9: 'Let us love one another', a toast of the Polish nobility, underlining their Christian duty of charity to the rest of society and expressing their ideal of social harmony.

Kolf: UNICORN, 2: See **Golf.**

Kolpak: RONDO, 2: Lithuanian tall fur hat. The traditional trimming and lining material for noble clothing was sable, sold or gifted in *soroki,* bundles of forty skins for winter coats.

L

***La cauza doussana*:** LIONS, 42: *Per far la cauza doussana*, or 'To do the sweet thing', (the act of love) comes from a mischievous troubadour song, in which a gallant lord courts (in vain) a thoroughly sensible peasant girl. Here is some of the dialogue between the two:

'Toza,' fim eu, 'gentils fada
Vos adastret, quan fos nada,
D'una beutat esmerada
Sobre tot' autra vilana;
E seriaus ben doblada
Sim vezi' una vegada
Sobeira e vos sotrana'.

'My dear', he said, 'a good fairy endowed you at birth with a pure beauty beyond all other village maidens, and your looks would be doubly enchanting, if seen by me from above, with you under me'.

'Don, hom coitatz de folatge
Jur' e pliu e promet gatge,
Sim fariatz homenarge,
Senher,' so dis la vilana;
'Mas ges per un pauc d'intratge
No volh de mon piuzelatge
Camjar per nom de putana'.

'Sir, a man in a moment of madness, swears and pledges a gauge. So would you do me homage, my lord,' said the girl. 'But for some small entrance fee, I am not inclined to trade my maidenhood for the name of a prostitute'.

'Toza, tota creatura
Revertis a sa natura.
Parelhar parelhadura
Devem eu e vos, vilana.

A l'abric lonc la pastura:
Que melhs n'estaretz segura
Per far la cauza doussana'.

'My dear, every creature reverts to its nature. We should become equal, you and I, country maiden, in some leafy coign by the pasture. There you can do the sweet thing much more safely'. (D. D.)

La Guiche: HN; LC: An old Abbey, now in ruins, situated just north of Chouzy-sur-Cisse, to the south-west of Blois in France. It was founded in 1268 as a monastery for Clarisse nuns by Jean de Chatillon, comte de Blois, as a thank-offering for his recovery from an illness. According to legend, a mysterious dancing flame led to the discovery of an ancient wooden statue of Our Lady, which was installed in the new altar and, until it disappeared at the Revolution, was venerated by all the neighbouring parishes, and carried in procession at Easter. It is also close to **Coulanges.** (D. D.)

La nourriture passe nature: GEMINI, 54: 'Environment is stronger than heredity'. Lycurgus the Lawgiver, Father of Sparta, conducted a famous experiment with twin dogs, as related by Plutarch (*c.* 46–120). One was brought up as a house dog, and the other as an outdoor hunter. They developed quite differently. (D. D.)

***La quale è molto utile et humile et pretiosa et casta*:** LIONS, 12: From the 'Canticle of the Sun' by St Francis of Assisi (1181/1182–1226), who praised earth and fire and stars, wind and water and air as manifestations of the divine beauty and goodness. It translates 'Which [or in the context of the novel, who] is most useful, and humble, and precious and chaste'.

Lady Better-than-Good: LIONS, 42: Or, more prettily, *Miel-de-Ben.* One of the code names given by troubadours to the anonymous ladies whom they serenaded. Another was 'More than a Friend'. (D. D.)

Laetus, Maestro: RONDO, 9: (1428–1497) Julius Pomponius Laetus (Leto), Italian humanist, was master and founder of Rome's Accademia Romana, a semi-secret society devoted to archaeological and antiquarian interests and the celebration of ancient Roman rites. **Callimachus** was a student there, and, like his master, was 'sadly maligned' for his supposed fondness for young boys. Both Callimachus and Leto were implicated in the plot to assassinate Pope Paul II* in 1468. Before the plot was discovered, Leto had moved to Venice, where his tutoring of two young men led to charges of pederasty. Proclaiming his innocence, he was extradited to Rome on the orders of the Pope, where he was imprisoned in the Castel Sant' Angelo. By May 1469 he and his associates were set free; the academy was re-established after the succession of Sixtus IV* to the papacy in 1471.

Lamb family: UNICORN, 2: A family of **Edinburgh** burgesses long identified with the mercantile and shipping community of **Leith**, Edinburgh's port at the mouth of the River Forth; and with a probable share in the Leith artillery contracts. Simon Lamb, son of the late William Lamb of Leith, burgess of Edinburgh, was given land by the vennel in Leith in 1432 which had been resigned by John Lamb. In 1439, Edinburgh burgess Richard Lamb was one of a group of merchants using the sixty-ton vessel *Giles* out of Leith, one of his colleagues being the well-known royal merchant Andrew **Crawford.** In 1451 the merchant Thomas Lamb was shipping with the one-hundred-ton vessel the *Mary* in partnership with John **Preston**, Alexander Harwood and William Bonar. It seems likely that Bonar was the William Bonar of a long line of gunners who was then the master of artillery at **Linlithgow**, and that Harwood was the forerunner of Robert Harwood, the royal gunner who would replace a later John Lamb as the King's chief gunsmith by 1502.

The merchant John Lamb of the novels was a well-known incumbent in 1468, a Dean of Guild* with a house in south Leith, which was under the lordship of Logan of Restalrig. Lamb's toft (homestead) was next to that of William Bell, and near to the family Turing, which imported iron for the royal cannon. John was probably the John Lamb who was a customar at the port of Dunbar in 1474 along with George Edwardson, who was himself trading by sea in 1486. Another relation was Matthew Lamb, who married William Bell's niece Janet Brown. The Browns were a north Leith family who had premises next to the goldsmith Matthew Auchinleck in the **Canongate**, then a popular quarter among importing merchants. A claim put forward in 1493 by the Harwood family to Matthew Auchinleck's land brought a representation by Archibald Crawford of **Berecrofts**, who had property in the same area. Matthew Lamb had died by 1508, but had a son John who followed him. An Andrew Lamb also stayed in south Leith, dying before 1502.

Another Richard Lamb owned property in southern Leith somewhere before 1495, and had a home also in Edinburgh, where he was a neighbour of the Swift burgess family, one of whose members, **Thomas Swift**, became Conservator of Scots Privileges in the Low Countries after **Anselm Adorne.*** William Lamb's land in Edinburgh was next to that of Thomas's niece (and Henry Swift's daughter) Elizabeth Swift, who had died by 1475. Another Lamb in the Canongate was James, who had a house on the north side by 1507, and could have been the man of that name who joined the raiding party against **William Knollys*** in 1483. Ten years or so later, James Lamb is found acting as witness for Prioress Alison Home of the **Cistercian** Priory of **North Berwick**, a small ferry port which interestingly supplied another raider against Knollys. A successful and industrious clan, the Lambs seemed to be typical of the multiskilled merchants of Stewart Edinburgh and its port.

A house in south Leith known as Andrew Lamb's house is still there, although it dates only to the early seventeenth century, and has been converted to other purposes. Lamb property through the generations was probably in the same area near the river wharves in south Leith, built on the narrow tofts laid out in the time of David I (King of Scotland 1124–1153). John Lamb, **James IV**'s* chief Scottish gunsmith, had a house in Leith, several storeys high and very narrow. It was built to the rear of the plot, fronting onto Rotten Row (from *rattan*, referring to undressed wood; the original barns and sheds in the area would have been traditional log-cabin-style construction). The front of his strip of land looking onto the shore would have been occupied by a warehouse. (D. D.)

Lauder Bridge: GEMINI, 42: Approximately twenty-five miles from **Edinburgh** on the Leader Water. Facts are scarce when it comes to analysing what actually happened there in July 1482; little actual documentary evidence remains other than the apocryphal legend of **Archibald Douglas**, 'Bell the Cat', and the sixteenth-century chroniclers' tales of the hanging of **James III**'s* low-born favourites. Recent historical research has diverted attention away from the death of the supposed 'favourites' and on to the seizure of the King, where his half-uncles acted as the King's jailors. The danger at Lauder came from the massive English army advancing north. If James and his masons had managed to take the guns further south, they would probably have been killed. In an effort to avert outright civil war by James facing his brother on the battlefield, the King was removed to Edinburgh and terms were reached by which Albany (with the King's agreement) was to be titled Lieutenant General of the Realm, second only in power to the King, and in control of the army. Albany's plan of supplanting his brother floundered due to lack of widespread support.

As for the victims who were hanged at the bridge, recent historians now consider that they were not low-born 'favourites' or counsellors deluding the King or suggesting widescale demoniterisation of the coinage, nor were they the King's administrators; they were members of his household staff. James III's choice and patronage of counsellors was not behind the affair at Lauder Bridge. For an assessment of their position and how they came to be at Lauder, see under **Thomas Cochrane, William Roger** and **Thomas Preston.**

Lawburrows: KNIGHTS, III, 10: A writ, binding a person to give security against doing physical violence to another.

Laws of Oléron: LIONS, 40: Just south of the great medieval French port of La Rochelle, the Île d'Oléron is the largest of the islands of the west coast of France. Like the rest of the area, the island was for a while in the possession of England as part of the dowry of Eleanor of Aquitaine (*c.* 1122–1204). It was she who established the Rôles d'Oléron, articles which established the basic rules of maritime law, down to a code for the paying of mariners. It appeared in all early pilot books, and by the fourteenth century had been accepted by the English Court of Admiralty (created in 1340). It also became the foundation of all subsequent French naval statutes. Oléron itself reverted to France in 1370.

Fifteenth-century sea rules required two servings of 'kitchens' (cuisine) a day, meaning cooked meat or fish. It suggests a disarming French-based origin for the old-fashioned Scots use of 'kitchen' as shorthand for a proper knife-and-fork meal. (D. D.)

Le crapault d'Enfer: LIONS, 2: See **Hekla; Mouth of Hell.**

Le feu épure l'or: LIONS, 14: 'Fire purifies gold'. Normally meaning that suffering may bring spiritual benefits.

Learning and deportment: HN; LC: In fourteenth-century mercantile Florence no book learning was expected of girls, but merchants' daughters were taught 'to walk well; to dance without jumping and without showing their legs; to laugh prettily, and to cry without making too much noise'. They also learned how to cook, spin and sew.

The education of sons was a different matter. Taking as typical a friend of Filippo Strozzi,* a Florentine nobleman in the mid-fifteenth century might have a large family, legitimate and other, all of whom would be privately tutored at home until the age of eighteen. They would be introduced to reading at four, and become familiar with holy works through the family chaplain. There would also be a resident agent and notary. The father, absent from home, would still direct his boys' studies by letter. Older sons, already matriculated, would also help supervise. Leaving home, a youth would take his tutor to university with him, to coach him and to arrange for his food. (D. D.)

Leashed dogs: QUEENS, II, 2: Or *chiens d'attache.* Dogs of this kind were usually kept on leash, and bred to attack the most dangerous beasts.

Legitimation: GEMINI, 45: Legitimations were granted in common chancery to children from all classes of society, without which they would not be allowed to legally inherit property. If legitimations were not procured, the parents' estate would be escheated to the Crown. See also **Consanguinity and dispensations.**

Leith: UNICORN, 2: Two miles from **Edinburgh**, the chief port for the town was founded in the twelfth century when David I (King of Scotland 1124–1153) established a harbour for himself on the south side of the river inlet on the shores of the Forth. Land on the north side of the inlet (the Water of Leith) was granted to the Abbey of **Holyrood** at its foundation in 1128. In 1329 Robert the Bruce (King of Scotland 1306–1329) granted the royal harbour to the burghers of Edinburgh, and a town gradually grew up on both sides of the river inlet. A bridge was built in the fifteenth century, replacing the ferry service which linked north and south Leith, owned and operated by the Abbey of Holyrood, which collected tolls from its users.

James I (King of Scotland 1406–1437) built up the port, in 1428 granting Edinburgh a charter to collect dues on imported goods and vessels arriving at the port: 'haven silver'. James I and James II's* interest in armaments led to Leith in the fifteenth century becoming a specialised centre of weapons manufacture. James I also constructed a storehouse and arsenal in south Leith, the King's Wark: a tower house with apartments for royal visitors. Ordnance and skilled gunsmiths were imported from the Low Countries, as were specialised skills in shipbuilding. James II extended the King's Wark by the construction of a long low building, probably as an arsenal for his ordnance. Workshops and storehouses were built behind the wark after 1463, and in the floor of one of the sheds was discovered a hoard of mostly Scottish pennies dating from the reigns of James II and **James III**;* it perhaps represents someone's savings hurriedly buried when English ships appeared off the east coast in 1481 (GEMINI, 31, 34).

The port grew in the sixteenth century, and its shallow harbour, suitable for the construction and arrival of small ships, was superseded by the construction of a new port in an area to the west of north Leith, on land acquired from Holyrood Abbey. Newhaven, as the harbour was to become known, was used for the building of **James IV**'s* flagship, the *Great Michael*, later captained by the loyal captain **Andrew Wood.** Taking six years to build, this ship, the largest of its kind to have been built in Scotland, is said to have been 240 feet long and 36 feet wide, and had a crew of 300.

Under the regency of Mary de Guise,* the port was further expanded and fortified, as it provided a lucrative target for the hostile English forces. Leith was burnt by the English fleet in the spring of 1544 under the Earl of Hertford, and again in 1547 under the Duke of Somerset.* In 1548 the port was garrisoned by French troops, as the young Mary Queen of Scots* escaped to France. The fortifications were designed by Piero Strozzi,* who constructed a star fortress, enclosing the whole of inhabited north and south Leith. The stone-faced defences and ramparts were rendered indefensible in peacetime, but refortified in 1559 when John Knox* and the Protestant reformers occupied Edinburgh. Leith was garrisoned by French troops and remained loyal to Mary de Guise until her death in 1560, when the fortifications were once more made ineffective.

Leith's chief income came from fishing and trade, but Edinburgh forbade the inhabitants of Leith from trading imported goods in their own port. Heavy low-cost items, such as wood, would be sold at Leith (at the Timber Bush, a corruption of *bourse*), but Edinburgh reserved the right to most of the trade goods for her own **markets** within the town, once duty had been fully enumerated in the **Tolbooth.** With the loss of Berwick-upon-Tweed,* Leith came to dominate east-coast trade, but the burghers of Edinburgh kept close control over its trade. The jurisdiction of the town could be avoided only if a skipper resided or stored his goods in north Leith in the lands owned by Holyrood Abbey, as did the real **Crawfords** of Bonnington and fictional characters in the *House of Niccolò* (UNICORN, 3). The other way to avoid the tolls and duties was to smuggle the goods into Leith and then to Edinburgh over the **Nor'Loch** by cover of night. (KINGS, Gambit)

Lennox, The: GEMINI: From the Gaelic *Levenach:* a rich and beautiful tract of land in south-west Scotland containing both the River Leven and the whole of Loch Lomond, once named Loch Leven. In early times the Lennox stretched north from Dumbarton on the River Clyde to include the whole of that county, as well as a large part of Stirlingshire and a portion of today's Perth and Renfrew. Its original *caput* lay on Loch Lomond, in the island castle of Inchmurrin.

The first earldom of Lennox was created about 1174 by William the Lyon, King of Scotland 1165–1214, for his brother David, Earl of Huntingdon, in England. A line of Celtic earls followed. In the next century, Malcolm, Earl of Lennox, supported Robert the Bruce (1274–1329) against Sir Alexander Menteith, Governor of Dumbarton Castle and sheriff of Dunbartonshire and the captor of William Wallace (*c.* 1270–1305). In 1424 the Eighth Earl of Lennox, Duncan Stewart, shared the downfall of his son-in-law, Murdoch Stewart, Regent for the imprisoned James I (ruled 1406–1437), and was executed with him. The **Lennox inheritance**, after the death in 1459 of Duncan's daughter Isabella, fell to the offspring of her sisters Margaret and Elizabeth, and was to be a cause of dispute for most of the century.

Lennox, Earls of: See **Darnley, John Stewart, Lord.**

Lennox inheritance: GEMINI, 38: Created Lord **Darnley** in 1460, John Stewart did not finally became Earl of Lennox until after the death of **James III*** in 1488. He first laid claim to a share of the earldom of Lennox in 1460, after the death of Isabella, Duchess of Albany. She and her two younger sisters Elizabeth and Margaret were the daughters of Duncan, Eighth Earl of Lennox. John Stewart Lord Darnley was descended from Elizabeth. He claimed half of the estate; the other half to be split between the other claimants descended from Duncan's daughter Margaret; these were Agnes Menteith (married to Sir John Haldane of Gleneagles) and her sister Elizabeth Menteith (married to John Napier of Merchiston). The matter came before the Lord Chancellor, **Andrew Stewart, Lord Avandale**, who was himself the grandson of the recently deceased Isabella, and thus had a strong claim to the earldom. Therefore, Avandale took no action to aid John Stewart's petition and Stewart did not take possession of his half of the Lennox estate. The dispute over the

Lennox title continued; in 1471 Avandale was granted the life-rent of the entire earldom of Lennox, to which Darnley objected, asserting his right not only to the earldom but also to the title itself. He attempted to convince the Menteith sisters to give up their rights to their share; Elizabeth Menteith agreed but agreement could not be reached with Agnes and her husband Sir John Haldane. In 1473 Stewart came to an agreement with Avandale that he would not contest his right to the life-rent; in return Darnley received the right to half the lands, and the title. Conveniently, Haldane was in Denmark on a diplomatic mission. On his return in 1475 he disputed the arrangement on the grounds that Agnes and Elizabeth's mother had been the elder daughter after Isabella, not the youngest, therefore they had a better claim than Stewart and should receive half of the estate, not just a quarter. Stewart attempted to dispute the legitimacy of Agnes, but in 1476 Haldane was recognised as a senior co-heir, and Stewart was stopped from using the title. Avandale, however, still held the life-rent.

The disputed title did not, as has been mentioned (see **John Stewart, Lord Darnley**, and **Margaret of Denmark**) seem to prevent the litigants from co-operating in the running of the kingdom. After the affair at **Lauder Bridge**, when Darnley had remained loyal to the King and acted as his protector in Edinburgh Castle, he was in a position of suitable power and favour to finally come to suitable terms with Haldane and Napier, who then received a quarter share of the Lennox estate each, but Darnley only used the title 'Earl of Lennox' once more, in 1488, after the deaths of Avandale and James III.

Les Chinchins: See **Chinchins, Les.**

Li beaus, li blonz: CHECKMATE, I, 6: 'The beautiful, the fair', from *Aucassin and Nicolette.**

LIDDELL, Sir James, of Halkerston: See **KNOLLYS, William.**

Lindsay, David: UNICORN, (1440–1495) David Lindsay, the politically ambitious Fifth Earl of Crawford, did not come into his own until the downfall of the **Boyd*** family in 1469; indeed, he was one of the judges who presided over their fate. He was a constant attender at Parliament and acted as charter witness and ambassador to **James III.*** He received the lordship of Brechin, was Keeper of Berwick from 1473 to 1476, was Master of the Household from 1482 to 1483, Chamberlain in 1483, and became Duke of Montrose in 1488, the first time the title had been awarded to anyone outside the royal family. In comparison to the treatment of the **Earl of Argyll** and **Andrew Stewart, Lord Avandale**, Crawford was amply rewarded by the King for his loyalty and good counsel, and kept the rewards till the end of the reign. Unlike Argyll, Crawford remained on the King's side and was severely wounded at Sauchieburn in 1488 before being taken prisoner. He was ransomed, but under **James IV***

he was deprived of his offices and surrendered his hereditary sheriffdom of Angus.

Linlithgow: UNICORN, 8: Sixteen miles to the west of **Edinburgh**, and halfway between the capital and Stirling, the burgh of Linlithgow was founded by David I (King of Scotland 1124–1153) in the twelfth century; there was a royal manor house there in the thirteenth century, which provided a base and fortified garrison for Edward I (King of England 1272–1307) when he arrived in Scotland to promote the claim of John Baliol to the throne. After the battle of Bannockburn in 1314, it reverted to Scottish control. Fire swept though Linlithgow in 1424 and gave James I (King of Scotland 1406–1437) the opportunity to build anew, starting work on the church of **St Michael** and constructing the east quarter of the palace and the north and south sections. His coat of arms can still be seen on the original entry to the palace in the east section. In 1461 it was one of the many residences used by Henry VI (King of England 1422–1461 and 1470–1471), the Lancastrian claimant then supported by Scotland. The burgh was a standard dower gift from the monarch of Scotland to his bride. James II* was more interested in military fortifications than domestic architecture, but under his son, **James III**,* prior to his marriage to **Margaret of Denmark**, a great deal of work went into getting the palace ready for the new Queen. The south quarter was continued, ending in a rectangular tower, and the southernmost part of the west quarter was begun. Under **James IV**,* the enclosed courtyard was completed, By this time, the former manor house had been transformed into Scotland's foremost Renaissance palace, consisting of a quadrangular courtyard with four gabled towers. Born in the palace, James V* created a new entrance to the south and, as a wedding present for his bride Mary de Guise,* commissioned the massive courtyard fountain which ran with wine for their wedding. Their daughter, Mary Queen of Scots,* was also born at the palace.

The north range was reconstructed in the seventeenth century for James VI (ruled 1567–1625), but the palace was somewhat neglected when the Stewart monarchy moved to England in 1603. Remains of the great hall, 30 feet wide and 100 feet long, are still worth seeing, although roofless and open to the elements, the great fireplace that could burn whole tree trunks is still present. Amongst the Keepers of the palace were **Anselm Adorne*** and **Anselm Sersanders.** As successor to Sersanders at Linlithgow, James IV and his councillors had the wisdom to choose another who had also been loyal to the previous King, and whom they clearly felt they could trust in the new reign. George Parkle, familiar squire of James III, became George Parkle, familiar squire of his son, being constituted in June 1488 captain, custodian and Governor of the Palace of Linlithgow with its lake, park and meadow, etc., which was treated as if it had been held in the name of Anselm Adorne ever since his death five years before. Hence Parkle, whose family had long held in Linlithgow, came into possession, for the expenses of service, of ten pounds of the land of Kincavil, and the acres and crofts round the burgh of Linlithgow which Anselm Adorne first held and occupied, plus the coalheugh of the King at Ardengaith, near Linlithgow.

His tenure was for seven years, but he lived less than three, leaving two daughters by his wife Margaret Napier (putative aunt to John Ramsay). Also related was the illegitimate Patrick Parkle, whose daughter Libra married Robert Knollys, believed to be the natural son of **William Knollys,*** Preceptor of the House of St John of Jerusalem, Torphichen. It seemed that the Parkle family, like that of the Crawfords, was ousted from its traditional land by the Hamiltons. In 1529, John Hamilton in Parkle is found in a charter of Robert, son of Robert (Robin) Crawford of **Berecrofts.**

Again, custody of Linlithgow Palace was granted to someone who had given loyal service through both reigns. The keeper after George Parkle was William Knollys, the Preceptor himself, Treasurer, Keeper of Blackness and sheriff of Linlithgow to the new King.

Lion: LIONS, 30: Also known as a *demy*, a gold coin of James II's* reign in circulation from 1436 to 1451, showing a lion rampant on the obverse and a small St Andrew's cross with fleur-de-lis on the reverse. In **James III**'s* reign, the first gold coinage issued in 1460 had the lion rampant of Scotland on its obverse and a larger portrait of the saint on the reverse; these coins were known as lions or Scottish crowns. Two new gold coins appeared in the reign of James III, the rider (with an equestrian portrait of the King on the obverse), and the unicorn, which replaced it in circulation in 1484 (with a unicorn on the obverse and a wavy star on the reverse). Gold coins of this period were of fine (pure) gold. See also **Coining.**

Coins of King James III

Gold rider Gold half-unicorn

Lion sans vilainie: LIONS, 39: A heraldic term for the upper half of the Lion Rampant: the beast with his 'villainy' (i.e., member and testicles) absent. (The times were not prudish in these matters: the scholar Filefo (1398–1481) was nicknamed *triorchos*, or triple-testicled [UNICORN, 36]). The Privy Seals were embossed with wax lions. (D. D.)

Lions: LIONS: A popular emblem with the leading houses in Europe in the fifteenth century. One who wished to lie with a lion could choose one or all of eight bedfellows: it appeared on the flag, badge or insignia of René of Anjou,* Eleanor of the Tyrol, and the rulers of Burgundy, Venice,* Scotland, England, Cyprus and Denmark. (D. D.)

Lippi, Fra Filippo: LIONS, 19: (*c.* 1406–1469) Religious painter, born the son of a butcher in Florence, pupil of Masaccio (1401–*c.* 1428): he led a highly controversial life. Captured by Barbary pirates off Ancona, he was kept in chains and then freed. Although variously described as a drunkard, a lecher, a whoremonger, a scavenger and a fraud, he was so esteemed by Cosimo de' Medici that he possessed a studio of his own in the Medici Palace in Florence. In 1456 he (a monk) eloped with Lucrezia Buti (a nun); she became the model for many of his Madonnas. Later Pope Pius II* released him from his vows so that he could marry her. Their son was the equally celebrated artist Filippino Lippi (*c.* 1475–1504). (D. D.)

Lithuania, Grand Duchy of: RONDO: Lithuania united with Poland under the **Jagiellonian dynasty.** See **Casimir IV; Whoever is unsupported by the Mystery of Love.**

Lords Auditor of Causes and Complaints: HN: This small legal council, which was the final appeal court, was elected in and by Parliament, and sat only when Parliament was in session, except for an occasional continuation. The cases handled were accordingly limited. Members were drawn from the Church, the barons and the burgesses, and included such men as **Henry Arnot**, Abbot of **Cambuskenneth, William Knollys,*** the Preceptor of Torphichen, and John Napier.

Lords of Council in Civil Causes: HN: Another legal council, larger than that of the **Lords Auditor of Causes and Complaints**, was that of the Civil Causes, which **Anselm Adorne*** once attended. This included members from the same three estates as the Causes and Complaints, and also the King's familiars and the officers of state such as the King's secretary (**Archibald Whitelaw**) and the Chancellor (**Andrew Stewart, Lord Avandale**) and the Treasurer (**Archibald Crawford**). Archbishop **William Scheves** also attended. It met more often than the Auditors, sitting for six full days a week and hearing seven causes a day. It entertained a wide variety of appeals, especially those involving the Crown, and dealt with some of the overflow from the Auditors.

Louis XI: RAM: (1423–1483) For details of the early career of the King of France, see Volume I. After encouraging Swiss and Flemish revolt against **Charles, Duke of Burgundy,*** Louis could sit back and wait as Charles the

Bold flung himself against Lorraine, dying at Nancy in 1477. His death gave Louis the opportunity to claim that Burgundy was a vacant fief for the taking. He was, however, resisted by **Marie of Burgundy** and her new husband **Maximilian**, who were forced to cede Artois and Burgundy to France, although they retained prosperous Flanders. Having thus undermined the strength of the duchy, Louis acted to weaken the strong commercial and political links between England and Burgundy. This he could do by publicising his truce with England in 1480 (showing **Edward IV**'s* double-dealing and proving that he would not be coming to Marie and Maximilian's aid), and destroying the cordiality that had developed between Scotland and England. The arrival of **Alexander, Duke of Albany**,* in France gave Louis the ideal opportunity to encourage him to go to England, where Edward IV used him in his plans against Scotland, which saw England mobilise the largest army to be seen in the field for eighty years. The death of Edward IV on 9 April 1483 and the murder of his sons, probably in August, by **Richard, Duke of Gloucester**, was followed by the death of Louis at the end of the same month, too ill to enjoy his victory to the full. His scheming, manipulation and great intelligence set in progress the development of the modern, absolutist state. He alone could state 'I am France'.

Louis XI was succeeded first by his son Charles VIII (d. 1498) and then by Louis XII of Orleans (d. 1515), who laid claim to the Kingdom of Naples (as a descendant of the Angevins) and to Milan (as the nephew of Valentina Visconti). The French invaded Italy in 1500 and with great speed secured the conquest of Milan and Genoa which had been under Milanese overlordship since 1488. In 1511, Julius II (Pope 1503–1513), with Spain, Venice and Switzerland, joined by Maximilian and Henry VIII (King of England 1509–1547), formed the Holy League to liberate Italy from France. France made haste to encourage Scotland, under **James IV**,* to attack England: the consequence for Scotland was the battle of **Flodden.** Louis XII was forced to vacate Milan, which was, however, later regained by his successor Francis I* (King of France 1515–1547).

When Charles V* came to the throne of Spain in 1516, he would not recognise France's rights in Italy. Both were rivals for the German Imperial Crown, which fell to Charles in 1519. Constant struggle between the Habsburgs and France over Italy led to war between Spain and France throughout the first half of the sixteenth century (1521–1526; 1528–1529; 1536; 1542–1544). In 1525, Francis I was taken prisoner in the Italian wars, although he freed himself and left as hostages his two sons, Charles and Henri (see M. d'Orleans, a large round face who does nothing but give blows.*) Henri was to succeed his father as Henri II.* Charles V abdicated in 1556, and died two years later. His brother Ferdinand became Emperor, and Charles's son Philip II* inherited the Spanish throne, promoting the Habsburg alliance with England in the marriage treaty between himself and Mary Tudor.*

LUDOVICO de Severi da Bologna:* HN: (b. *c.* 1410) Volume I describes Father Ludovico's career. Now, in the last decade of his extraordinary life, the Patriarch of **Antioch** is about to tread the same path, for a while, as **Anselm Adorne**,* one of the other fascinating unexplored figures of fifteenth-century Europe. But first, in the autumn of 1473, newly back from yet another papal mission to Persia and the Levant, and the death of **Zacco, King of Cyprus**, the Patriarch hurled himself into Trèves, a day's ride from Luxembourg. There he proposed to confront the two great Western lords meeting there – Frederick III, the Holy Roman Emperor, and **Charles, Duke of Burgundy** – and demand that they support **Uzum Hasan**,* Prince of Persia, in his war against Turkey.

Considering the massive distrust that existed between Duke Charles and the Emperor, the prospects for collecting war-aid would seem poor, particularly when this meeting collapsed in sly discord. The Patriarch did nevertheless emerge from Trèves with travel expenses of 405 livres, and a remit, as Burgundian counsellor and envoy, to go and discuss 'certain secret matters' with Uzum Hasan, described by a French contemporary as '*Hugon Assain, le plus grant des Machomettes*'. The Patriarch was also a legate of the Holy See.

This expedition coincided with a similar journey by the Bruges* nobleman Anselm Adorne, Baron Cortachy, also representing Duke Charles. Joining forces in Germany, Adorne and the Patriarch reached **Danzig** with their respective parties after Easter 1474, and from there travelled to **Thorn**, eighty-five miles south of the Baltic, to seek audience of King **Casimir IV** of Poland at Pentecost. Whereas Adorne then unexpectedly left Thorn for home, Father Ludovico continued, accompanied by five or six horsemen, on the long journey to Persia.

Uzum Hasan, the greatest power in Persia, had been in prolonged negotiations with Western Christian countries to obtain their help to fight off the Sultan of Turkey, **Mehmet II**,* but was apt to receive nothing but promises. At the same time, Western countries wished him to continue the war, which distracted the Sultan from Europe. To this end, one Russian and two eager Venetian envoys were already installed in the Persian camp when the Patriarch made his approach, fifteen miles out of Tauris (Tabriz) that May of 1475. One of the Venetians, the less talented **Ambrogio Contarini**, apparently took it upon himself to introduce the Patriarch favourably to Uzum, although privately persuaded that he might be an impostor, rather than the **Franciscan** who, these fifteen years and more, must have embodied the busiest one-man shuttle service between Uzum Hasan and the West.

At the priest's ceremonial reception next day (wrote Contarini, still unimpressed), the Patriarch followed this by presenting the Prince with nine robes, three of cloth of gold, three of crimson velvet and three of violet material, after which he made a long speech offering the services of Burgundy, which 'seemed to have little effect on the Shah'. The speech, at least, sounds familiar, even though it is hard to credit the rough-living Franciscan with bringing such priceless parcels intact across Europe. (Perhaps he had packing advice from Adorne.)

Sadly, nothing appeared to have much effect on the 'Shah' although, as ever, the situation was left open to hope. One report says that the Prince announced flatly at Ecbatane that he wouldn't attack the Turks. Another version says that in Tauris the following month, the Prince dismissed the Patriarch, Contarini and the Russian envoy, Marco Rosso, with the message that he was 'on the point of making war with the Turks'. Each of the three was given money, horses and light robes, and further presents when, after travelling part-way in consort with Uzum Hasan, they finally took their leave. **Josaphat Barbaro**, the second Venetian envoy and a personal friend of Uzum's, stayed behind.

The Patriarch and his party continued north through Armenia and Mingrelia, crossing the Tigris and travelling via Tiflis (Tiblisi) to Fasso (now Poti), on the southern coast of the Black Sea, being entertained on the way by King Pancrazio of Georgia. It was then July. At Fasso, they learned that Caffa (now Feodosiya), the Genoese colony in the north-east of the Crimea, on the opposite shore of the Black Sea, had fallen to the Turks. This meant an abrupt change of route. According to Contarini's indignant account, the Patriarch, who was familiar with the region, proposed to continue alone, aiming to reach Muscovy by way of 'Circassia and Tartary'. Reminded of his own past insistence on travelling in convoy, the Patriarch (says Contarini) merely offered the 'strange and iniquitous reply' that it was time for each to care for his own safety. He then departed, taking only his own attendants and the envoy allotted him by Uzum Hasan; while the Russian party, and Contarini and his Venetians, went their separate ways for the winter.

They were all to meet up again. By January, Contarini heard that Father Ludovico's party had been robbed at Avogasia of all it possessed, to the anger of Uzum's envoy, who had blamed Father Ludovico for the losses and returned forthwith to his master in Persia. The Patriarch and his servants then proceeded to Moscow, where Duke **Ivan III** put him in prison, on the advice of Marco Rosso, the Russian agent. Contarini, arriving in Moscow by sledge, was successful (a triumph) in freeing the Patriarch, but not in persuading him to leave Muscovy with him. It seems likely, reading between the lines, that the imprisonment was diplomatic, and that both the Patriarch and the Duke had business still to transact, away from Venetian eyes. Equally, one wonders whether, in a land full of fleeing Latin refugees, the Patriarch might have found a good use for his cargo of statutory gifts to Duke Ivan, however he accounted to his lords for their loss.

It is perhaps noteworthy that Father Ludovico tended to represent himself on this journey as ambassador of the Duke of Burgundy rather than as Papal Legate. Part of the general confusion may have been caused by the fact that there was at the same time a titular Patriarch of Antioch of another name. From 1457 to 1470, this post was held by Guillaume de La Tour. Under Sixtus IV* (Pope 1471–1484), the title of Patriarch of Antioch was used in Rome to refer to Lorenzo Zeno, a papal legate with the papal army, and treasurer and personal friend of the previous Pope, Paul II*.

Ludovico da Bologna left Moscow at last in 1477. At the end of that year, another safe conduct was prepared by Pope Sixtus to permit the Patriarch and his company to travel among the princes of the West to invite their help with an expedition against 'the perfidious Turks'. This appeared to conflict with another project, sanctioned the previous month, which would have sent Father Ludovico back to Uzum Hasan. Commentators think the Patriarch may possibly have made this final visit to Persia. In autumn 1477 the Turk invaded Venetian territory, and in the middle of that year, a papal envoy was received by Uzum, and was able to discuss strategic plans. More might have come of it, but in 1478 Uzum Hasan died, and the Patriarch resumed his work in the West.

There is not much more on record. He visited the Holy Roman Emperor, Frederick III, to persuade him to release Cesare Malvezzi, a nobleman of Bologna imprisoned in Germany. This was recorded in May 1479, but may have taken place some time before. The impetus appeared to come from the Pope, who wished to gain credit with powerful silk merchants who owed debts abroad. Finally, in a magnificent collection of royal letters, there is in March 1479 a trace of the Patriarch in France, in a typical encounter with authority. Writing from Les Forges at that time, King **Louis XI*** sent an instruction to Tours, commanding his Chancellor to interview someone he calls simply 'this Patriarch', and to drag from him the secret message he carries from the Emperor to the King. The King (Louis makes plain) does not wish to speak to the Patriarch. A note sent with the letter revealed that the envoy was the Patriarch of *Antioch*, but his name is not given.

A modern footnote proposes that this Patriarch of Antioch was one Laurent Zane (Lorenzo Zeno, see above), Bishop of Brescia and Patriarch before 1478,

who died in 1485. But the Patriarch of the letter came from the Emperor. And Louis wised to escape an encounter. It sounds like someone else.

Ludovico da Bologna was a man by then close to seventy or more, who had travelled long and hard all his life, and fought without compromise for his beliefs. The final paragraph of his first entry in Volume I sums up his life. The scenes in the novel *Gemini* which show him, now failing, in Germany are supposition, but cannot be far off the truth. One hopes that, as the novel suggests, he expended the last of his strength and his courage on a journey that was not for his own earthly masters, but for the other he served, and himself. (D. D.)

Lupins: UNICORN, 36: Not quite today's garden flowers, but an early version grown for fodder in the warmer parts of Europe. Rotation of crops was standard practice in Italy, where the fields would be sown with beans or lupins, wheat, barley or spelt, or another fodder plant like lucerne. (D. D.)

M

McClery, Malcolm: GEMINI: (*fl.* 1463) An attorney and a burgess of Stirling with undoubted Gaelic connections (his name means 'son of the cleric'), Malcolm McClery was already well known to the inner Council when the boy king **James III*** came to the throne in 1460. He was to spend the latter part of his life in the Stirling entourage of James's young Queen.

Within the first five years of the reign James, aged thirteen, confirmed a land gift made two years previously by one of his regents, William **Sinclair**, Earl of Orkney, to his squire Malcolm McClery. The lands were in Garden-Sinclair (originally Gartane) in the earldom of Menteith, and nearby Mye, in the earldom of **Lennox.** Both places were in an area west of Stirling and south of the Lake of Menteith. The Earl's gift, ratified by the Crown, perpetuated a Sinclair attachment to the royal household in Stirlingshire, where Sinclair's daughter had helped rear the King's older sister, the **Princess Mary**, and where his son Oliver was later to hold considerable lands.

McClery's right to Garden-Sinclair was confirmed yet again in 1471, after the King's marriage to **Margaret of Denmark**, whose settlement was to include Doune Castle and Menteith, the earldom in which these lands lay. A year after that, Malcolm McClery of Garden-Sinclair and Mye appears several times as attorney in local land cases for the Franco-Scot **William Monypenny**, and for **Andrew Stewart, Lord Avandale**, Chancellor of Scotland and owner of the life-rent to Lennox, who was himself a distant cousin of the King's. Also in 1472, Malcolm received land from John Haldane of Gleneagles, the second cousin of Lord Avandale (and very likely the father of Oliver Sinclair's third wife). That same year, McClery is referred to as Constable of Stirling Castle, and hence responsible for the military defence of the castle, as well as being the royal family's adviser in local law.

In 1473, when the Queen's first son was born, it was evidently decided formally to make over to her these considerable parcels of land in the Stirling area which had been promised her on her marriage and in this, Malcolm McClery acted as her attorney. For the rest of that decade, he worked on various legal cases for different parties. In 1478 he was enfeoffed with land by the Provost and bailies of Stirling, and in the same year James III gave him land worth forty pounds and the mill of Drummond, by Stirling, in consideration of his office at Stirling Castle.

The King had already endorsed McClery's possession of lands and fishing rights on the Clyde formerly held by a Nigel McClery, relationship unknown. By this time too, McClery, with Gilles Maclehose, was receiving a fee for the upkeep of the royal park and gardens of Stirling, in a composition which also mentions Lord Avandale as Captain and Keeper of Stirling Castle, and James Homyll as the King's servant. In the 1480s, the Keeper of Doune Castle, with its fishing rights and mill, was Avandale's brother-in-law William Edmonston, who presently received, with McClery, the right to work for iron in Duchray, in Buchanan country to the west. McClery already held a sub-tenancy, with William Stewart, in the Queen's lands of Balquhidder, where there were also iron reserves, and where Colin, **Earl of Argyll**, held an adjacent tenancy.

Favoured by both the King and Queen, Malcolm McClery may have performed his chief service to the Crown with his position of trust at Stirling Castle, as Constable to **Sir James Shaw of Sauchie**'s office as Keeper. In 1482 neither he nor Avandale was present when the King was forcibly brought back from **Lauder Bridge** to **Edinburgh** Castle. Their duty was, presumably, to protect the Queen and the Princes in Stirling. It was also a diplomatic action which kept open the avenues for negotiation, and bought time, at least, until **Alexander, Duke of Albany**,* fled the kingdom the following year. The novel assumes that McClery took part in these talks, but there is no later mention of his name. His personal life is not easy to distinguish. He was twice married, and his eldest son by his first wife is mentioned in 1477. His second son, also a Malcolm, appears in a 1472 Lennox land agreement involving the Haldanes, kinsmen to Lord Avandale.

It is not known whether Malcolm McClery outlived either James III or the Queen, but the fact that the land of Garden-Sinclair was in the possession of a Walter McClery until 1496 would imply that the family kept the friendship of the young Prince, as well as his parents. (D. D.)

Machiniste: LIONS, 4: In **Mystery Plays**, the operator of the 'secrets'; i.e., the technician in charge of the special effects, such as the mechanism for the Ascension, or the Wheel of the Damned, or the trap (*secret de terre*) for the Deluge in Noah's Ark. (D. D.)

Magnet: See **Compass.**

Maitland family: See **Sinai, Mount.**

Manhood but prudence is a fury blind: KINGS, 1, 1: From a political homily by priest, scholar and poet John Bellenden (*c.* 1492–*c.* 1550) introducing his translation of the Latin *History of Scotland* by Hector Boece (*c.* 1465–1536). The verse continues:

Manhead but [without] prudence is ane fury blind,
And brings a man to shame and indigence;
Prudence but manhood comis oft behind,
Howbeit it have nae less intelligence
Of things to come than gone by sapience.
Therefore, when wit and manhood doth concur,
The honour rises with magnificence,
For glore to nobles is ane grounden spur [sharp stimulus].

Manna, the land of: UNICORN, 42: 'Sweeter than anything else in the world' is how the fifteenth-century traveller Felix Fabri described the substance he discovered on the bushes and stones of the approach to **Mount Sinai,*** and which he believed to be the life-saving food of the Israelites: the manna that sustained them during their Biblical wanderings. Falling by night through each August and September, he says, the liquid hangs like dew where it drops, until, by day, it has congealed and is collected by Arabs, who then sell it to pilgrims. To the ancients, he continues, dew was the child of the moon and the air. Carried by bees to the comb, it changed into sweet honey; and when it fell into sea-shells, it became precious pearls.

More prosaically, the origin of the manna seems to be a local bush of the tamarisk type, which exudes a reddish syrup when punctured by insects. Spread on bread, it was eaten like honey by the monks of Mount Sinai. (D. D.)

Manus loquacissimae: KINGS, IV, 1: 'Most eloquent hands'.

MAR, John of: LIONS: (*c.* 1456–1479): Little is known about the death of John Stewart, Earl of Mar; again the legends and enhancements popularised by sixteenth-century chroniclers have obscured potential connections between Mar and the rebellion of **Alexander, Duke of Albany,*** against **James III.*** What is known is that he last appeared in Parliament in March 1479, but by July of 1480 he is described in the pages of the exchequer as dead and his earldom forfeited.

The reasons for his imprisonment in **Craigmillar Castle** and his removal to the **Canongate** are also subject to conjecture. A near contemporary chronicle claimed that Mar was executed for his involvement with witches and warlocks. Abell's history (1533) claims it was on the advice of 'ane trucur called **Cochrane**'; Bellenden (1530s) and Pitscottie (1576–1579) both claim that he was killed in a bath vat, but do not give a reason, other than that it echoes the execution of the English King **Edward IV**'s* brother, George, Duke of Clarence, in 1478. Other late-sixteenth-century sources such as Buchanan, Ferri and Lesley unite the witchcraft charges against Mar with his execution in the Canongate, claiming he was using sorcery to conspire against James III and was executed by having his veins opened. All the sources indicate he was executed; only Pitscottie claimed it was murder, yet nothing concerning a trial or sentence survives in the parliamentary records.

It was not until the mid-seventeenth century that the potential for accidental death was raised; William Drummond of Hawthornden, apparently working from the records of Bishop William Elphinstone (a statesman contemporary with James III), claimed that Mar was involved with witches and had been implicated in a plan against the King. He was committed to Craigmillar, where he developed a fever, believing himself to be in prison. The King's physicians attempted to bleed him, but Mar lost consciousness and died.

The novels' portrayal of Mar's mental instability and suicide are fictional, but it is likely that there was distrust between James III and Mar, and that he was, like Albany, against the pro-English policy of the King. After the death of Mar his title was granted to his brother Alexander, Duke of Albany, and when Albany was forfeited the title passed in 1486 to the youngest son of James III, John Stewart (1479/1480–1503) who held it until his death.

Margaret of Denmark: UNICORN: (1457–1486) From the age of three, this daughter of the House of Oldenburg must have been taught that one day, she was to cross the sea to Scotland and marry its King. Her father, splendour-loving King **Christian I** of Norway, Sweden and Denmark, lord of Schleswig-Holstein, had been elected in 1460 to rule over kingdoms only recently united and still shaken with dissent. To help his coffers and obtain an ally, King Christian immediately set about trying to revive an early Norwegian treaty which required an annual payment from Scotland for the acquisition of the former Norse isles to the west.

From this developed the final deal whereby the fee was replaced by a new financial and territorial arrangement dependent on the marriage of the King's daughter to the son of James II.* Steps towards this had already been taken in the summer of 1459, when King Charles VII* of France acted as arbiter. The sudden death of James II in 1460, and later the deaths of his widow and closest adviser, all interrupted the scheme. Finally, pushed through by the late Regent's advisers and by the latest family of powerful magnates, the **Boyds,*** the arrangement was ratified in Denmark, and Margaret, aged twelve, arrived in July 1469 for her wedding in Edinburgh to **James III,*** aged seventeen. She brought with her the Norwegian rights to the islands of **Orkney** and Shetland and received the promise of a dowry which included one-third of the Scottish Crown's property and income for life, the palace of **Linlithgow**, and the castles of Stirling and Doune.

Much of James's childhood had been spent in Stirling Castle, or Doune, or the lodge at Falkland, all used by his father for hunting. After his father's death he had been for three years in the care of his mother, Mary of Gueldres, of whom he seems to have been fond. During those years, his brother **Alexander, Duke of Albany,*** was absent in Flanders. In the time between the return of his brother and his marriage, James and his Court moved restlessly all over Scotland, hunting in Balquhidder; visiting Perth, Stirling, Falkland, Jedburgh, Peebles and Kirkcudbright. When in **Edinburgh**, the young King stayed in the royal apartments at the Abbey of **Holyrood**, or in the royal lodgings in David's Tower at the Castle. Linlithgow Palace was not often used, except briefly, for hunting, or to avoid threat of pestilence. The King did, however, arrange for some refurbishment just before the wedding.

James must have been well briefed in what to expect when he welcomed his bride. He had just had a triumph – the magnates of the Boyd family who had taken over his life had been banished at last – but with them had gone the **Princess Mary**, his elder sister, who had married Thomas Boyd against the King's wishes. On the other hand – another triumph – clever negotiations over the marriage had brought him the islands of Orkney and Shetland, once the possession of Norway (see **Orkney dowry**), and he could boast of ruling his land from the Shetland Islands in the north to Berwick-upon-Tweed* in the south. For him, young and enthusiastic and not over-sensible, it must have seemed like the first step towards an expanding future.

To Margaret, the court must have been not unlike that at home. The language was different. She would have heard Scots in Copenhagen, where there was a small Scottish colony, and a constant stream of incoming ships, and where the delegates arranging her marriage had stayed for the better part of a year. There would be Latin for formal exchanges. And she would have the services of William Tulloch, Bishop of Orkney, who spoke her tongue, and had served both her husband's family and her father. She might even have found Danish speakers in the household of the **Sinclairs**, the lordly family who had given up the earldom of Orkney when her marriage was arranged.

The summer after her marriage, the King took his bride on a two-month royal progress through the north. They stayed at Inverness for four weeks, and visited his lords in Aberdeen, Fyvie and Banff. They may even have met churchmen and merchants who spoke her language. That summer, when she was thirteen, her eighteen-year-old husband made her the gift of a free **barony** in Kilmarnock in south-west Scotland, which had belonged to the disgraced family Boyd whose lands he had annexed.

The disposition had not in fact been agreed to by Parliament, which had intended this and all the other vast lands of the Boyds to be reserved for the King's first-born son. Instead, James gave Kilmarnock to Margaret for life, 'to pay for her gowns and the ornaments of her head'. Perhaps the marriage had been consummated. Perhaps she lacked the resources to dress royally for grand tours and state occasions. Perhaps it was a sop, to cover the fact that the lands promised her in the marriage settlement had not so far materialised. And that in turn might indicate an act prudently deferred until the first son had appeared. Parliament did, however, solemnly ratify other elements of the marriage treaty – the necessary adjustments to Margaret's dowry if she outlived the King, and the offer to return Orkney to Norway in part-payment of returnable dowry if she elected to leave Scotland and settle elsewhere. Provided, that is, she didn't marry the King of England or one of his subjects.

In fact, three years later, in March 1473, James, Prince and Steward of Scotland, Duke of Rothesay, Earl of Carrick and lord of Cunningham, was born, and seven months after the birth the Queen received part at least of her dues: those lands in and about Stirling Castle where the royal young would be brought up. Among these were Stirling Castle itself, the customs of St John's town of Perth, the King's lordship of Menteith, Stirlingshire and Tillicoultry, and lands at and around Balquhidder to the north. It must have been the first time she had extra money to spend. Between that year and the next, Margaret deployed over £757 on clothes and other expenses.

That July (of 1474), she went on pilgrimage to the shrine of St Ninian in Whithorn, Galloway, where **Thomas Spens** had once held the bishopric. There was a Scottish altar to St Ninian in Copenhagen, as there was one in Bruges,* its chaplain appointed by the Bishops of Galloway. Whithorn, in the extreme south-west of Scotland, was also the French-founded mother-abbey of the church at Fearn beside Tain in Ross, much farther away to the north. The Tain shrine to St Duthac, revered by her husband, was also to be supported by her son. It is possible that King James took her to Whithorn which in any case was to be part of her dowry, and whose tributes could pay for their stay.

It is also possible, now that she had attained maturity, that Margaret had discovered that the marriage bed was rougher than she had expected, and both her faith and her sense of duty were being tried. Writing about the Queen just after her death, an Italian biographer (of whom more below) included carnal abstinence as one of her virtues:

> Margaret was a woman of such chastity and modesty that she would have no relations with her husband except for the procreation of children, behaving towards him in such a way that, when she knew conception had occurred, she declined relations until after the birth, despite his demands, curbing his unseemly desire by good sense and restraint.

It was in the interests of both Scotland and Denmark, however, that the marriage should continue. This, 1474, was the year when, according to Russian history, Christian of Denmark (who also visited Rome) vainly attempted to persuade both the Grand Prince **Ivan III** of Muscovy and James III of Scotland to help him subdue Sweden by invading from either side, after which the Scots were to move in and form colonies there. King Christian at least wanted the goodwill of Scotland. Hence Margaret's marriage continued, and she gave her husband the sons that he needed. The next child, James, Marquis of Ormond, was born in March 1476.

The birth of two sons and the near-completion of the first decade of marriage brought, at last, the rest of the Queen's dower settlement in the course of a spate of re-grants made by the King at the start of 1478. This placed in the possession of the Queen the lordship of Galloway, including the castle of Threave and the burghs of Kirkcudbright and Wigtown, with their wealthy wine-importing trade. She also received the lordships of Ettrick and Strathearn, and of Kinclaven and Methven and the castle of Methven, and the lordship of Linlithgowshire, with the palace, lake and ward of Linlithgow, and the customs and patronage rights of the burgh. Here, her Captain, Keeper and Governor was **Anselm Adorne.*** Confirmed in addition were the lands the Queen already had, including the castles of Stirling and Doune, and the lordships of Menteith, Strathgartney and Balquhidder.

As would appear wise, the Queen and her children seemed to spend the years after 1480 in the safety of Stirling Castle, and the boys were reared in and about Stirling. The heir, James, had for Governor **Sir James Shaw of Sauchie**, Keeper of Stirling Castle, while the second son was trained by another Shaw – George, Abbot of Paisley and future Lord High Treasurer. Their cousin Andrew, one of the discarded Sinclair sons of her brother-in-law Albany, studied with them.

Sir James Shaw, together with **Andrew Stewart, Lord Avandale** the Chancellor, **Robert Colville** her steward, **Malcolm McClery** the Constable of Stirling Castle and Colin, **Earl of Argyll**, the Master of the Royal Household, had formed by now a regular group of advisers who both controlled the dower lands where she lived with her children, and possessed lands which could raise men or offer refuge and a means of escape to the west or the north. In addition, the Queen could rely on **Henry Arnot**, the Abbot of nearby **Cambuskenneth**, as well as the Adorne uncle and nephew at Linlithgow, and **Sir John Ross of Hawkhead** at **Blackness.** When war came, all this would be vital. Meanwhile, she and the King went hunting at Falkland in Fife (where her horses and his were both stabled), and eventually between 1479 and 1480 a third son, John, was safely born in a religious house, outside the Castle, just as the peace with England was finally broken.

With the increasing problems brought by the war and the King's brother Albany, the Queen emerges for the first time as a discernible figure in government. Albany's first strenuous clash with the King took place in 1479, when Lord Avandale took command of the siege of Dunbar Castle which ended with Albany's flight to France. The death of **John of Mar**, his young brother, followed. When Albany returned with English support in 1482, the Queen seems to have been kept well advised of the events at **Lauder Bridge** in July which halted the King's advance to meet a superior English army, and resulted in his enforced return to Edinburgh Castle, where he was held by his own three half-uncles, and served by a Lennox man, **John Stewart, Lord Darnley**, with a company of men from about his own region.

This time, none of the chief royal advisers took part in the action. Some at least would have the duty to protect the Queen and her children in Stirling. All would at least retain some kind of neutrality which enabled them to meet the invaders and negotiate an agreement, with the help of the burghers of Edinburgh. As a result, the English army turned back for a consideration, while Albany, coaxed apart from his English sponsors, remained in Scotland with high expectations.

That the Queen endorsed their plan seems certain. The King was still immured in Edinburgh Castle. When Albany came to Stirling to visit his sister-in-law and the young heir his nephew, she received him. He meant to persuade her, no doubt, to give the crown to her son, under his governorship. Instead, he seems to have accepted at face value a more subtle plan. Immediately after he left, there began the long, gentle siege of the Castle by the Provost and leading burghers of Edinburgh, who had already committed themselves financially to encourage **Richard, Duke of Gloucester**, to leave. A month later, on 29 September, her husband King James was released and there was a carefully public and joyful reconciliation between the King and his brother. So that no ill will might remain, the King framed a letter for Darnley declaring him innocent of any crime at the castle, and thanking him for agreeing to stay at the King's request to protect him. In fact, for five years the Queen had been custodian of Edinburgh Castle, and a large sum of money, as Keeper's fee, passed between her and Darnley that year. Also, among the men of his band was her own son's Rothesay Herald.

During the final three months of 1482, every effort was made to please Albany, always excepting his final investment as royal Lieutenant-General and Warden of the East and West Marches – a potentially explosive appointment which was efficiently passed by Parliament and thereafter hovered, awaiting ratification by the King. All the other signs were reassuring. The royal officers changed, and Avandale was no longer Chancellor. Albany became Earl of Mar and the Garioch, the honour possessed by his late brother, and land was given to the Princess Mary his sister, who was a widow again. The gifts to Mary and her son came from the Queen – her barony of Kilmarnock – and from the land in Teling and Polgavy, some of which had been presented to Anselm Adorne. All of it had been confiscasted in 1469 from the Boyds. It would seem that the King's younger siblings had drawn together against him, and that the Queen's advisers recognised that conciliation must extend to them, too.

The whole precarious situation was to collapse at the turn of the year, and for a time, Margaret must have feared for her husband's life, as plots and counter-plots of assassination and poison were rumoured, and Albany locked himself into his castle of Dunbar, along with his sister's young son, and summoned English troops for his garrison. Even then, negotiations continued. Adorne was killed in the first of several efforts at reconciliation, a loss which must have seemed shocking to the Queen, whose Linlithgow Captain he was. Then the English King, **Edward IV** died, (necessitating for his tomb the delivery from the Low Countries of thirty-three casks of touchstone, or black marble, which endorsed the fashion sense of **Thomas Yare**). Gloucester had to leave his northern post for the south, and Albany's rebellion slowly came to a halt.

By the following spring, the familiar faces had come back to Court, and the Queen ended the farce, or the tragedy, by unsentimentally applying to Parliament to call back from young James Boyd and his mother those lands she had allowed to be given them which were, in fact, part of the inheritance of the heir to the throne. Parliament agreed. Kilmarnock was to go to Margaret at once, and to her son James, Duke of Rothesay, when he was of age.

The Prince himself was still at Stirling with the Queen and his small brothers when, in the end of the year 1484, Albany failed in his last coup and left Scotland for an uncertain future in France, where there was a new young King, Charles VIII (1483–1498), friendly towards Scotland. England, about to change Kings at Bosworth Field, was not likely to renew Scottish hostilities. There was no direct challenge now to the Scottish throne, but some unease over the King's conduct which affected both the Queen and her son. Margaret's father had died in 1481, to be succeeded by her brother John (King of Denmark 1481–1513). If James her husband were to perish or abdicate, Margaret would be left to rule with a regency council, unless she decided to leave Scotland altogether, in which case part of her dowry would return to her brother, on a shaky and penurious throne.

She remained. She had money to spend. The records tell of her travelling gear: panniers, saddlebags, stirrup irons covered in velvet, a gilded saddle, a riding gown and livery gowns for six ladies of the chamber. A **Leith** smith made a chimney for the Queen's closet. There were sheets to wrap the Queen's bath vat; collars, tippets, a tiring bonnet. A dozen gloves from a skinner, and foot socks and satin stomachers and a long gown for Parliament. Clothes for the infant: ermine to line the scarlet cot; white for a night cot; petticoats and sarks and lawn mutches for the child, and a cloth of gold gown. Clothes for the nurse. The Queen's household was busy, and probably not solely on domestic matters in these last years. Only guesswork is possible. But the fondness her son was to show her memory suggests that he endorsed whatever she did, both then and during the Albany crisis. She and her advisers might have brought the King safely through the ultimate challenge of 1488 except that she died, cause unknown, in July 1486, and was buried in the Abbey of Cambuskenneth. She was not yet thirty.

Before the next year was out, an embassy including Archbishop **William Scheves** had visited the Pope with a mission to discuss, among other things, the canonisation of the late Queen. Shortly afterwards, early in 1488, the fifteen-year-old Prince James was allowed to leave the custody of Sir James Shaw at Stirling and join the party which opposed his father's policies. That spring, his uncle John wrote him from Denmark, repeating a claim (by the same opposing party) that his mother had died of poison given her by John Ramsay, in collusion with the King. Later, a Danish fleet was dispatched to Leith under Count Gerhard of Oldenburg, King John's uncle.

Whatever it intended to do, it evidently played no part in the climax of that year, when James III of Scotland was killed in a short, confused battle against the men who had drawn off his son. The son, now James IV, or his advisers, paid the Count of Oldenburg five hundred pounds and lodged him in Scotland for the winter. The following year, a clerk in the Bentivoglio household, Italy, began writing a biography of Queen Margaret which portrayed her as a saint, partnered by a weak and vindictive King James.

It is hard, now, to distinguish the truth among the confusion of political motives. The canonisation came to nothing, but had been sponsored presumably by James III in the belief that his own reputation would be unharmed. The Pope, Innocent VIII (1484–1492), did actually appoint a commission consisting of the Primate of Scotland, the Bishop of Glasgow, the Bishop-Elect of Aberdeen and the Abbot of **Holyrood** 'to enquire into the Queen's virtues and miracles, with a view to her canonisation'. Such propositions were not uncommon, and their objectives were often a mixture of the spiritual, the political and the commercial. The Calendar of Saints' Days at the King's favourite shrine and occasional treasure-house at Tain seems to show an entry for Margaret, as if the canonisation had taken place. Indeed, this ancient Premonstratensian house, sanctuary of **Princess Margaret**'s lover, **William, Third Lord Crichton**, might have supported the initial canonisation attempt, which took place in the year when it was itself created a **collegiate church** under the earldom, later the dukedom of Ross. Magnus McCulloch, one of its canons, and possibly a 1477 graduate of Louvain,* was a familiar clerk of Archbishop Scheves, and between 1481 and 1484 worked for him at Edinburgh Castle on the text of the Scottish historical work, the *Scotichronicon*. There were other royal connections with the monastery of Fearn, beside Tain, which, as early as 1436, had been lavishly provided with furnishings, an organ and vestments from Flanders. The hand which entered the Calendar date for 'St Margaret' also registered the death, in 1501, of Andrew Stewart, Bishop of Moray, one of James III's half-uncles. And when he came to reign, James IV displayed a continuing devotion to the shrine of St Duthac at Tain.

A final view of Margaret of Denmark comes from a strange source: a work compiled abroad by that prolific writer, courtier and notary Giovanni Sabadino degli Arienti, the son of a Bolognese barber. After a period as chamberlain with Ercole d'Este at Ferrara, Sabadino was for twenty years secretary to Conte Andrea of the Bentivoglio family of Bologna. By 1483 he had published his most famous work, a collection of gallant tales about the baths at **Porretta.** This later book, begun in 1489, was dedicated in 1492 to Ginevra Sforza, niece of the Duke of Milan, mother of sixteen and wife of Giovanni, the successor to Sante Bentivoglio (SCORPIONS, 1), to whom she had also been married. In it were essays on thirty-two worthy women, only two of whom were not Italian – Joan of Arc and Margaret of Denmark, Queen of Scotland, who had died six years before. Her biography is next to that of Elisa Sforza, mother of the condottiere Roberto da San Severino, whose account of the Garden of Balm at **Matariya** compares with that of **Jan Adorne.**

The reasons for the biography are unclear. It may simply have emerged as a timely tribute to the daughter of Christian of Denmark, who had conferred a knighthood on Ginevra's five-year-old son Annibale Bentivoglio on his way south to Rome in 1474. Its ecstatic praise of Margaret ('a woman of lofty and wonderful virtue . . . a beauty, a modesty and a prudence unequalled in their glory and splendour . . . Much more loved and revered by the people than was the King . . . She governed the people . . . with justice and integrity, as though she were a Numa Pompilius . . .') might have come from the canonisation proposals, and indeed the piece ends: 'In life and in death she was considered saintly.'

On the other hand, Sabadino roundly condemns James III in the same manner as the conflicting tales put about after Margaret's death. ('The more . . . love she showed to her husband, encouraging him to live the upright life of a true King, the more anguish she received from him'). She was hated by the King, Sabadino explains, who blamed her for his imprisonment in Edinburgh Castle, and kept her thirty miles from his presence for three years, although he allowed her to rear her three children until she died from poison, 'it was said'. Her dying exhortation to her son is quoted at length and verbatim, in terms which the same son, by then King James IV, would much appreciate. Once, as an infant, he had been turned down as a possible husband for the daughter of the Duke of Milan. The result of Sabadino's work, interestingly, linked the Prince with his saintly mother and restored his position as a possible player in the marital game. Ginevra did have seven living daughters, even if not all were available, and one had killed her husband with her own hand.

The essay also includes detail about the arrest and release of James III and the machinations of Albany, which has much in common, in its inaccuracy, with the surviving tales accounting for the gift to James III of the Golden Rose, a papal honour personal to the King which reached him just before Margaret died, and which Sabadino does not mention. For what he does mention, S. B. Chandler suggests as one of his sources a William Baillie, a Scots doctor trained in Bologna. There are many other possible informants (GEMINI, 24). Milan would certainly be conversant with Scottish affairs, through its network of envoys and men like **Prosper de Camulio.*** There were many Scots at the papal court. Dorothea of Brandenburg, Queen of Denmark, stayed in Ferrara at the magnificent Palazzo Schifanoia of the family d'Este on her way south in 1488, the year after the Bentivoglio heir married Lucrezia d'Este, and the year before the adulatory essay was begun. Finally, there was the Patriarch **Ludovico de Severi da Bologna,*** who had visited King Christian in Denmark in 1468, and was a longtime acquaintance and travelling-companion of Anselm Adorne, who knew Scotland well. The Patriarch's first cousin Severo was Chancellor and Secretary to the Duke of Ferrara.

Giovanni Sabadino's information on Scotland was probably excellent, but his biography of Margaret of Denmark was shaped to the requirements of patronage. It has to take its place, therefore, among the other unverifiable fragments that, fitted together, hint at all anyone can know of her life. It must have been a comfort to the new King of Scotland, rehearsing the weaknesses of his father, and affirming the worth of his mother and himself. (D. D.)

Margaret of Norway: GEMINI 25: (1353–1412) Potential role-model for **Margaret of Denmark**, Queen of Scotland. Daughter of Valdemar IV Atterdag, King of Denmark (1340–1375), this forceful lady married the Scandinavian ruler Haakon VI, King of Norway (1343–1380), the son of Magnus Ericsson of Sweden. On the death of her father there were no male heirs, so Margaret was offered the crown by the Danish nobility to hold in trust for her infant son Olaf. On the death of Haakon, she also ruled Norway on behalf of her son. He died in 1387, and two years later, Margaret and her army invaded and conquered Sweden, thus making her ruler of Denmark, Norway and Sweden. Her grand-nephew Eric of Pomerania was crowned king of the three Scandinavian kingdoms in 1396, but the actual power remained in Margaret's hands. The following year, by the Union of Calmar, the three kingdoms were united under one monarch, each kingdom retaining its own laws. Margaret died in 1412, having united the three Scandinavian kingdoms and opposed German supremacy in the Baltic, but leaving behind her an uneasy legacy of dissent among the countries she had subjected to Denmark.

Margaret of York: UNICORN: (1446–1503) Sister of **Edward IV*** of England and the bride of **Charles, Duke of Burgundy**,* she was fifteen when her brother was crowned, but had to wait until she was twenty-two until a suitable marriage was arranged for her. Charles of Burgundy opposed his father Philip the Good's* friendship with France and, on succeeding to the dukedom, sought to strengthen links with England to avoid a Franco-English alliance at the expense of Burgundy and its territories. (**Louis XI*** attempted to thwart any developing alliance between England and Burgundy, but failed.) Negotiations began as soon as Charles's first wife Isabelle of **Bourbon** died in September 1465; he was a widower on the marriage market. There was only one surviving child of his marriage to Isabelle, an eight-year-old daughter, **Marie of Burgundy.** Charles needed more heirs and quickly, and neither he nor his father Duke Philip had been tempted by the offer of Louis XI's four-year-old daughter Anne: to Charles, a long betrothal meant too long a time to wait to gain an heir.

Hostilities between France and Burgundy also encouraged Charles's hopes for an alliance with England. It made sense in terms of their territorial ambitions, and would help trade between the two countries, especially the English export of unfinished cloth and wool to the dyers and cloth-finishers of the Low

Countries. France also sent good offers to England for Margaret's hand, but not as good as Burgundy.

After two years of negotiations, the death of Duke Philip in 1467 secured her marriage, which took place in 1468; the ceremonial was largely organised by the ducal chamberlain Olivier de la Marche (see *Bien vienne la belle bergére**), and the wedding and entry to Bruges were an ostentatious display of wealth (SCALES, 41). The marriage, despite a lack of potential heirs, seemed to be amiable. Infertility rather than bad marital relations seems to have been the cause of the couple's lack of children. (Despite the fact that Margaret was one of seven healthy surviving children, her infertility was probably inherited from her York and Mortimer antecedents.)

Margaret seemed to have been genuinely fond of her eleven-year-old stepdaughter Marie, and they developed a close relationship over the years. Following the marriage, Margaret spent much of the next nine years with her, and they went on pilgrimage together. Marie's asset as heir to Burgundy meant she remained unmarried through her father's lifetime, although she was a valuable bargaining tool to use with the Emperor **Frederick III** in Charles's attempt to secure for himself the title of King of the Romans, and the right of succession to the Empire. She was not short of suitors. After the death of Charles at Nancy in 1477, it was up to Margaret to ensure that the marriage to **Maximilian** (uniting Habsburg with Valois, protecting the Duchy of Burgundy from Louis XI) went ahead.

The Anglo-Burgundian alliance secured by Margaret's marriage was thoroughly undermined at every opportunity by Louis XI. The wealth of Burgundy was immense; Philip the Good had left a personal treasure of four hundred thousand crowns. In attempting to support the cohesion of the various possessions which made up the duchy, the Valois towns were of paramount importance; Ghent and Bruges were rich through commerce and banking, but each stressed its independent privileges often at the expense of the Duke. Margaret's role as Duchess was a practical one; she aided the Duke as an administrator and his representative in the vast territories of the duchy.

During their first seven years of marriage Margaret and Charles spent less than a year in each other's company; they did not meet at all after July 1475. They were restricted by their duties in the government of the duchy, the subsequent military campaigns of the Duke and the fact that few locations could cater for their combined households. Both Margaret and her husband were often on the move; Margaret undertook twenty-eight major journeys in her eight and a half years as duchess, concentrating on imposing the will and taxation of the Duke on the towns of Burgundy.

Following the death of Charles, Margaret attempted to conciliate the Flemish towns, resentful of the loss of their privileges (which she was obliged to restore) and the cost in men and taxation of the Duke's 'foreign' campaigns. Added to this were Louis XI's efforts to reclaim and conquer Burgundy as soon as the Duke was dead, claiming that in default of a male heir, Burgundy passed back to France. When Margaret was forced to leave Ghent, the town's anger turned on the officials who remained, seeing them as responsible for enforcing the harsh taxation imposed by the Duke. Ghent hanged many of the former Duke's officials, including Chancellor Hugonet. Marie and Margaret put their hopes in the long-promised imperial marriage to Maximilian. The Empire was the only power they saw that could protect them from France. Louis's further attacks on Burgundian soil (especially in the Low Countries) served only to increase support for the marriage.

As Dowager Duchess of Burgundy, Margaret was one of the wealthiest widows in Europe. She was also an important figure in Burgundy's attempt to keep England interested in her future, particularly with respect to protecting her rights and dower territories with an English army. This in turn encouraged Louis to keep paying Edward IV's annuity. She visited England only once after her widowhood, in 1480, and stayed for three months, attempting to gain English support for Maximilian and Burgundy against France, either direct military assistance for Maximilian in the form of English archers, or, at the very least, a firm friendship which Maximilian could use as a weapon to coerce a realistic peace with France. Edward, however, was very fond of his French annuity and used Margaret's visit as an opportunity to strengthen his own position. Edward's daughter Elizabeth was promised in marriage to the Dauphin of France; a match was arranged between Maximilian and Marie's son Philip and Edward's daughter Anne of York. Edward would agree to invade France only if Burgundy undertook to replace the French annuity with a similar amount, and if no dowry were required for Anne's marriage, which was to take place in six years' time. In the meanwhile, Maximilian did his best to pacify France, but neither that attempt, nor the good relationship with England, was to last.

The death of Edward in 1483, the usurpation of **Richard, Duke of Gloucester**, then the accession of Henry VII in 1485 (supported by France and therefore not a friend to Burgundy) meant that Margaret lost her trading rights granted by Edward, which is probably why she supported the pretenders Lambert Simnel (posing as the Earl of Warwick) and Perkin Warbeck (posing as Richard, Duke of York) against Henry. Burgundy's support of Warbeck in particular, for which Henry put the blame clearly on Margaret's shoulders, for harbouring such long-term malice against him, led to an economic war between England and Burgundy from 1493 to 1496, stopped only when Philip the Fair (1478–1506, Marie's son) was made to understand by the Flemish towns that if he continued to support Warbeck's Yorkist invasion at the expense of Flemish merchants' interests, there would be full-scale internal rebellion. Warbeck's attempted invasion in 1495 failed, and he sought refuge in Scotland at the court of James IV of Scotland, marrying a cousin of the king, Lady Catherine Gordon (daughter of Annabella, **James II's sister**) and staying for two years until he attempted another failed invasion in the south-west of England.

Margaret never remarried; as her Scottish namesake's fecundity prior to marriage ended any possible marriage alliances, so Margaret of York's noted barrenness prevented any hope of dynastic succession for potential suitors; also, who could hope to match the status and wealth of her former husband? Scotland was most certainly not in the running, despite **James III**'s hasty proposal of 1477 to have the widowed duchess married to **Alexander, Duke of Albany.*** Instead, as an accomplished administrator and organiser, Margaret helped govern and advise in the reign of her step-daughter Marie and then, after Marie's death in 1482, that of her godson Philip the Fair. Her direct and efficient tone with her officials is summed up by one of her favourite phrases used in letters to her staff, '*toutes excusacions cessans*', 'no more excuses'.

She was an avid collector of books, and a patron and employer of Caxton;* he had entered Margaret's service by March 1471, as her commercial and financial adviser. She became his patron in his translation of Lefevre's *Recueil des Histories de Troie*, which he had started in 1469. Her interest in books sat well with that of the Burgundian court; Philip the Good's library comprised some nine hundred volumes, on all subjects from romances to religion. At Nancy, Charles had with him suitably martial literature: Xenophon translated by Lucena and histories of Hannibal and Alexander. The majority of Margaret's books were on religious subjects. Their example encouraged Edward IV to collect illuminated manuscripts.

The Dowager Duchess spent her later years at Malines and at Binche. She did not retire, although her public appearances were curtailed by illness. Pious and devout, she was actively involved in the reform of the church (supporting the **Augustinians**, Poor Claires, **Observatine** Franciscans and the **Carthusians**, especially their charterhouse at Louvain). She spent her last months at Malines, and died in 1503 just as celebrations were under way for her step-grandson Philip's return to the Low Countries after a year-long absence in Spain, claiming his title to the Spanish throne.

MARGARET, Princess: UNICORN: (d. by 1546) Sister of **James III.*** Born just before the death of her father in 1460, Margaret was the youngest of the five surviving children of King James II* of Scotland. Her first nurse was a Mariota Darrauch, not the traditional **Sinclair**, who cared for her in 1462 at the hunting lodge which is now Falkland Palace. The following year, she was staying at Stirling Castle with her elder sister and brother **John of Mar.** Finally, when aged about four, she was sent to be reared at the **Cistercian** Priory at **Haddington**, beside **Edinburgh**, where she became the special charge of one of the nuns, Alice or Elizabeth Maitland, whose family were associated with the Priory, and upon whom was settled in 1477 an annual payment for life for her services, past and future, as a guardian and servant to Margaret. The last payment was made in 1480.

Also present in the Priory during the years of Margaret's attendance were the widowed Elizabeth Sinclair, who had cared for Margaret's much older sister the **Princess Mary**, and **Euphemia Dunbar**, who may have been the mother of **Anselm Adorne**'s* natural daughter **Euphemia Adorne.** The Prioress, Elizabeth, was allowed to draw twenty marks a year from the customs of Haddington for Margaret's expenses, and also paid in the same way the annual fees of the physicians **Dr Andreas** and Conrad. (Conrad received twenty pounds and the feed for two horses.) Robert Lisouris the 'carpenter' was also paid by this means.

By 1478 the Lady Margaret had left the Priory, having already been allowed to spend some time intermittently at Court. The records show consignments of dresses arriving for 'my lady in Haddington, the King's sister' for special occasions such as the opening of Parliament, and the betrothal of her infant nephew, the future **James IV*** (see **Cecilia**).

She was proffered initially by her brother James III as a bride to George, Duke of Clarence (1449–1478), brother of **Edward IV;*** James also proposed to marry his brother Albany to **Margaret of Burgundy**, the recently widowed Duchess of Burgundy, Edward's sister. This plan was rejected by Edward (the reason given that both his brother and sister were too recently bereaved), and in 1478 it was agreed between Scotland and England that she should instead marry the English King's brother-in-law, **Earl Rivers.** The marriage was agreed in January 1479. Instead of providing a cash dowry (the Scottish Parliament did not seem to trust their King enough to vote him the large sum of money he requested, perhaps believing he would use the amount for some foreign expedition or scheme) Margaret's dowry was to be subtracted from the dowry payments already being made by England to Scotland for Cecilia. Safe conducts were issued twice in 1479 for Margaret to go down to England and marry, but she did not leave Scotland.

The reason is assumed to be the fact that it was now obvious she was about to have an illegitimate child. The father was young and already married – William, Third Lord Crichton, the grandson of the Chancellor of the same name, and husband of Marion Livingston of an equally eminent family. The circumstances of the liaison are unknown, but Crichton's aunt on his mother's side was Elizabeth Dunbar, Countess of Moray, whose second husband was **Sir John Colquhoun of Luss.** Elizabeth was related to both Euphemia Dunbar and Elizabeth Sinclair of Haddington Priory. Taken along with the death of Mar, the defection of Albany and the collapse of Anglo-Scottish relations, Margaret's illegitimate offspring ended any likelihood of her being offered abroad as a spouse.

The Princess's child, a daughter named Margaret, was born about 1479, not very long after Adorne's natural daughter Euphemia, who might have been her father's second cousin. The Princess herself did not marry, and seems to have spent most of the rest of her life in the Cistercian Priory at Elcho, outside Perth. James III died in 1488, succeeded by his son James IV, who was generous to his aunt: the accounts show sums of money he sent to her, or paid to her man to buy 'kerchiefs, sarks or other small gear'. A large bill for dresses was entered for her in the year of the young King's accession, next to the items of clothing for himself and his brothers; and Margaret's dress money continued to feature all through her years in the Priory. The King also funded his aunt's living expenses, paying the Prioress of Elcho a hundred marks every year through his steward in Fife.

The arrangement lasted until about 1503, when Margaret moved from the Priory to Hamilton, perhaps to the home of her late sister Mary's son James, second Lord **Hamilton**, the new Earl of Arran. The last recorded payment for the Princess was made that year to her widowed niece Margaret **Boyd**, Lord Hamilton's half-sister, whose first husband Lord Forbes had died in 1491. After that, nothing more appears in the records about James III's sister Margaret. Her appearance and nick-name in the novels are both invented, but not her character, which seems to have been not unlike that of her sister. As it turned out, she outlived all her siblings.

Margaret Crichton, her illegitimate daughter, seems to have possessed all the talent and hard business head of Chancellor Crichton, her great-grandfather, and was likely to have been a willing collaborator, if not the instigator of the shrewd marriages through which she ordered her life. A ledger entry about 1495 for 'dress for my lady Margaret's daughter' might indicate her first wedding. This was to William Todrik, from a well-established Edinburgh burgess family – twenty years before William Todrik had been offered five pounds for helping to rescue the King's ship the *Yellow Caravel* when she was in trouble, captained by John Barton, off **North Berwick.** Now, Margaret's groom was fortunate enough to receive certain exemptions from custom for his goods and merchandise, 'in consideration of his marriage with the King's cousin'. Todrik did not survive beyond 1503. Margaret married next another well-connected Edinburgh burgess called George Halkerston, who, with his new wife, was also endowed with a customs exemption of exports and imports worth a hundred pounds a year. Very soon, along with his fellow Customar Sir Alexander Lauder of Blyth (Berwickshire), Provost of Edinburgh, George was taking credit for supplying the King with provisions and wine worth £1,387.

It ended at the battle of **Flodden**, where Halkerston and Lauder both seem to have fought and died. In 1514 their widows, Margaret Crichton and Janet Paterson, together rendered the account for the customs of Edinburgh. Two years later, Margaret Crichton alone supplied the account for one month. She was followed by Robert Barton, son of John and colleague and agent of George Leslie, Earl of Rothes,* whom Margaret in 1517 made her third husband. Her connections with other royal Stewarts remained strong; in 1516 she entertained her cousin **John Stewart, Second Duke of Albany**, in Edinburgh, where the records indicate that five and a quarter bottles of claret were consumed, for which she was to be recompensed.

The Leslies, originally of Flemish extraction, had long been established in the north-east, and Rothes lay on Speyside, beside Banff and Elgin in Moray, where both James III and IV broke their journeys to Tain. The family were doubly connected by marriage to the Sinclairs (and hence by marriage, to Margaret's uncle, **Alexander, Duke of Albany***). Christian Leslie, the aunt of Earl George, was actually the mother of Henry, Third Lord Sinclair, who was to die also at Flodden. During Margaret Crichton's marriage to Rothes, Barton acted on her behalf in disentangling inheritance rights from her union to Halkerston, a friend of Barton's since both men bought naval supplies for James IV.

In 1520, Earl George divorced Margaret, who had given him two sons and a daughter in quick order. Some twenty years later he had the decision reduced and remarried her, notwithstanding the fact that in the interval he had married two if not three other women, beginning with Elizabeth Grey, Countess of Huntly (a family already related by marriage to the Crichtons), and Agnes Somerville, widow of John, second Lord **Fleming**, who bore Rothes three sons and four daughters. When Agnes died in 1542, Earl George is found marrying his next wife, Isobel Lundy, the widow of **David Lindsay**, Earl of Crawford.

Margaret Crichton, already the mother of three of Earl George's children, is said to have given him another son and four daughters from what, in view of her age, must have been a long-standing relationship outside marriage. Rothes also had at least four illegitimate children. His offspring must have totalled just under twenty when he died in Dieppe in 1558, supposedly poisoned with James Fleming and others after attending Mary Queen of Scots's* wedding in France.

Margaret Crichton died in 1545. Neither she nor her mother the Princess appear, from existing records, to have had any association with William Crichton after the birth of his child. In 1484, Crichton was outlawed for his activities during the Duke of Albany's rebellion, although he was absent when his two younger brothers and others held Crichton Castle against the King's men at that time. He escaped capture by slipping north ahead of the law, and taking sanctuary in the vicar's house within the garth of the monastery of Fearn, by Tain in Moray, where a macer was sent in December 1483 to stand at the market cross in Tain and summon him to answer to Parliament for treasonable correspondence with England. Failing to go, he was outlawed and forfeited the following February. St Duthac's was a favourite shrine of the King's, and one account says that he and Crichton later met at nearby Inverness and effected a partial reconciliation. The plan to canonise Princess Margaret's sister-in-law the late Queen **Margaret of Denmark** may even have occasioned the visit, as the monastery seemed to support it. Lord Crichton is believed to have lived there for the rest of his life. He died in 1498.

On the whole, the Crichton family and its branches were prominent as supporters rather than adversaries of the reigning royal family. One of William Crichton's aunts on his father's side had married Alexander, First Earl of Huntly, whose son George was to marry the Princess Annabella, one of the King's six aunts, on her return from Savoy (see **James II's sisters**).

In 1484, when Albany launched an attack on the Lochmaben area, the Crichtons of Sanquhar were rewarded for fighting against him. A James Crichton was Provost of Edinburgh in 1478, and James de Crichton of Ruthvendean was an Officer of the Mint in 1488. The Crichtons were associated with the Napiers. The wife of Sir Simon **Preston** of Craigmillar in 1491 was a Crichton, and so was the Abbot of **Newbattle** Abbey between 1474 and 1482. David Crichton of Cranston in 1474 was involved in a land deal with Robert Lauder of Edrington and Lord Crichton's cousin, Sir John Colquhoun of Luss, who was killed by Albany's guns. William Crichton's own career was blighted at the start, but some of the family talents seem to have descended to his daughter. It was probably fortunate that she was not a son. (D. D.)

MARIE of Burgundy: RONDO: (1457–1482) The daughter of **Charles, Duke of Burgundy,*** and Isabelle of **Bourbon**, Marie lost her mother when she was only eight. Three years later (1468), her father remarried **Margaret of York**; Marie, by all accounts, proved a loving and devoted step-daughter.

As the sole heir to the Burgundian empire, she was destined to remain single while her father was alive, as he used her as a bargaining tool to achieve the strongest and most advantageous alliance. In 1477 the death of Duke Charles at Nancy left Burgundy open to piecemeal destruction by France. In addition to external threats, Marie was facing internal rebellion from the towns of Flanders, which she was unable to control (she is said to have run into the street to try to prevent the execution of her Chancellor, Hugonet). Aided by the Dowager Duchess Margaret, Marie strong-mindedly pursued the proposal of marriage to **Maximilian:** since **Louis XI*** had pensioned off **Edward IV*** of England, only the empire of the Germanies was strong enough to hold France at bay.

Maximilian's arrival was delayed by the time it took for the impoverished Emperor to raise the necessary money to outfit him properly, and then when he arrived he was unable to speak to Marie in her own language (the Dowager Duchess took it upon herself to teach him). However, Marie and Maximilian were married in August 1477, and went on to have three children: Philip (1478–1506, later to become Archduke Philip the Fair), Marguerite (1480–1530) and Francis, the youngest, who died in infancy. Marguerite was to spend most of her childhood in France, as a result of the Treaty of Arras, by which she was betrothed to Louis XI's son, the future Charles VIII (King of France 1483–1498). Philip was to become heir to Castile, Aragon and the Habsburg Empire.

Marie's life was cut short by a fall from her horse when falcon-hunting in the spring of 1482. After her death, her stepmother the Dowager Duchess and her widower Maximilian helped govern and advise the Low Countries in the minority of Philip. On reaching adulthood he was to marry Joanna 'the Mad' (1479–1555, daughter of Ferdinand of Aragon and Isabella of Castile) by proxy in 1495. She came to the Low Countries the following year, but mental instability marred her life. Their children were to include Emperor Charles V* (the father of Philip II of Spain*) and Ferdinand I (emperor after Charles). At the same proxy ceremony Philip's sister Marguerite was betrothed to Joanna's brother, Don Juan, heir to the Spanish throne (Charles VIII having repudiated her in 1491). She left for Spain in January 1497, but Don Juan was dead within the year. Marguerite returned home in 1499, and in 1501 married Philibert II, Duke of Savoy. He too died only three years later. Marguerite never married again.

Through his wife and brother-in-law, Philip was now heir to the kingdoms of Spain. His son Charles V thus inherited Spain, the Low Countries and the German Empire. After the death of Philip, his sister Marguerite governed the Low Countries for her nephew Charles V, as Margaret of York had done for Philip. She was to inherit her godmother's library, and even her staff was largely the descendants of Margaret's own retainers. Reflecting her misfortune in marriage, amongst the lyrics on one of her poetry books is the verse *tant que je vive.**

Markets in Edinburgh: HN: Urban markets were closely regulated in medieval Europe, in terms of where, what and when it was permissible to sell. Edinburgh had fourteen markets spread throughout the town in the fifteenth century. An extract from the burgh records of Edinburgh for October 1477 lists the locations at which produce could be offered for sale on market days, fair days, 'and all vther dayis neidfull' (the markets for the various types of produce were ordained to occupy their traditional, unchanging locations, unlike the shifting uncertainty of modern supermarket aisles):

> In the first the merket of haye, stragers, and hors mete to be vsit and haldin in the Cowgate, fra Forestaris Wynd doun to Peblis Wynd; alsa the fisch merket fra the Frere Wynde to the Netherbow on baith the sidis of oure commoun strete; alsa the salt merket to hald fra Nudreis Wynde; alsa the cramys of chepmen to be set fra the Belhous doun to the Trone, on the north side of oure saide strete; alsa the hatmakars and skynnaris fornent thame on the south side of the saymn; alsa the wod and tymmer merket fra Dalrimpill yarde to the Grey freris and Westirmart; also the scho merket of cordenaris fra Forestaris Wynde end westwart to Dalrimpill west yarde dike; alsa the rede barkit ledder with thame; alsa the nolt merket of carcagis and mutoune about the Trone, and sa doun throuch to the Frere Wynde, and nocht on the wolke day; alsa all partikis, pluuaris, capons, conyngis, chekinnis, and all vther wyld fowlis and tame to be vsit and sald about the merket croce, and in na vther place; alsa all qwyk bestis, ky, oxon nocht to be brocht in the tovne bot vnder the wll fer west at oure stable; alsa the mele merket of all grane and cornes fra the Tolbuth vp to Libertons Wynde; alsa fra thine vpart to the

treves the merkett of all cottone claith, quhite, gray, and allvthir claith quhitis within vj quartaris, and al lynnyng claith to be sald thare and in na vther place; alsa all buttir, cheis, woll ans sic like gudis that suld be weyit to be vsit at the Ouer Bow, and a trone set thare and nocht to be opinyt quhil the hour of nyne forow none; alsa all irne werk belanging cutleris, smethys, lorymaris, lokmakaris, and all sic werkmen to be vsit beneath the Netherbow, before and abowt Sanct Mary Wynde; alsa all graith and geir to be vsit and sauld in the Friday merket before the Gray freris, lyke as is vsit in vther cuntries.

The reality of life in a town with so much activity could be less than pleasant. William Dunbar (*c.* 1460–1520) in his poem 'To the Merchantis of Edinburgh', decried the markets and the impression that the sights and smells of the traders made upon visitors to the town:

May nane pas thow your principall gaittis
For stink of haddockis and of scattis,
For cryis of carlingis [old women] and debaittis,
For fensum flyttingis [slanderous cries] of defame:
  Think ye not schame,
Befoir strangeris of all estaittis
That sic dishonour hurt your name!

Your stinkand Style [buildings round the Tolbooth], that standis dirk,
Haldis the lycht fra your parroche kirk [St Giles];
Your foirstairis makis your housis mirk,
Lyk na cuntray bot heir at hame:
  Think ye not schame,
Sa litil polesie to wirk
In hurt and sklander of your name!

Marriage: See **Consanguinity and dispensations.**

MARY, Princess: UNICORN: (1451–1488) The first surviving child of James II* and Mary of Gueldres, the lady Mary Stewart was early placed in the care of Elizabeth **Sinclair**, a married daughter of William, Earl of Orkney, and probably spent her childhood, like her sister, in Stirling and Falkland as her mother gave regular birth to her brothers and sisters until 1460, when the King died. He was succeeded by Mary's younger brother **James III**,* who took the throne at the age of eight, with Mary of Gueldres and his father's cousin Bishop Kennedy* to advise. Six years later, the Dowager and the Bishop were both dead, his brother **Alexander, Duke of Albany**,* had returned from Flanders and England, and the kingdom was being rent by the ambitions of the family Boyd to exercise power over the young King. By February 1467 Robert,

Lord Boyd, had become the King's official Keeper, and Mary had entered into an arranged marriage with **Thomas Boyd**,* his son. She was still only fifteen.

The young King James III later wrote that he wept for shame over the wedding. Mary's own feelings were clearly different. When, after little more than one year of marriage, Thomas (now Earl of Arran) left as part of an embassy to Denmark, the Princess waited faithfully for his return a year later with her brother's new Queen, **Margaret of Denmark.** That year, with the absence of Thomas and the departure of his father in 1469 on business to England, saw the beginning of the counter-attack against the family Boyd. It also saw the first formal visit to Scotland of **Anselm Adorne**,* as an emissary of **Charles, Duke of Burgundy*** and of Bruges.* Adorne had returned to Bruges by the time the Danish embassy returned with the future Queen Margaret, but the revulsion against the Boyds had now reached its peak, as was to be clear when Lord Boyd and his son were formally arraigned for treasonable crimes that October, for which their lives, lands, rents, possessions, offices and goods were all forfeit.

They did not answer the summons. Lord Boyd, foreseeing trouble, had prudently failed to return from his mission in England, and Thomas had been warned off by his wife, who fled with him from Scotland the moment he came back that summer. Early historians have produced colourful and conflicting accounts of how this was done, and also which (politically improbable) countries Thomas visited in his subsequent wanderings. What happened to Princess Mary is never mentioned. A legend (see **Nólsoy**) suggests that they touched down initially in the Faroe Islands, sufficiently quiet and obscure to avoid compromising their overlord, Denmark.

No early history mentions Anselm Adorne. Historically, there is no doubt whatever that in 1470 and 1471 Princess Mary was living in the Hôtel Jerusalem, Bruges, the home of Adorne, then absent on pilgrimage, or that her husband Thomas was with her for at least part of that time, since her two children James and Margaret were born there between March 1470 and September 1471. In fact James, the elder, was a godchild of **Margaret of Burgundy**, the English wife of Duke Charles, who was cousin to the Princess's mother, and whose help Mary must have invoked. While in Bruges, Mary was also joined by Robert, Lord Boyd, Thomas's father. In October 1471, the entire family recrossed the Channel in the hope of reconciliation with James, already urged to it by the beleaguered Duke of Burgundy, who was also indirectly housing his wife's two Yorkist brothers. Adorne and his wife accompanied the Boyd party, and their son **Jan**, who escorted them as far as Calais, reports how the Princess tried to persuade him to come with her to Scotland, but his father made him refuse.

In Scotland, James remained adamant that he would receive no one but the princess and her children and Adorne's party. Mary parted from her husband and his father in England, where Lord Boyd would eventually end his days. In returning to Scotland, Mary perhaps hoped her brother would later relent. More likely, by now, her concern was for the future of her children. Before he left Scotland in spring 1472, Anselm Adorne received the forfeited Boyd lands of Teling and Polgavy, no doubt in part-recompense for his hospitality. Other lands which might have been Mary's had understandably gone to reward those who had helped bring the Boyds down. Mary was given the lands of Bothwell by the King, and the customs records for 1473 show that cloth was being supplied to her. Further details may have been lost with the records.

In 1473 Queen Margaret gave birth to a son, thus establishing a direct royal line, and negotiations would soon begin to contract the infant in marriage to an English Princess. James III, unforgiving, complained to England about their harbouring of Robert, Lord Boyd, in the Northumbrian town of Alnwick. Boyd, who had joined **James, Ninth Earl of Douglas**, as a troublemaker in exile, was receiving two hundred marks annually from the English King.

In the spring of 1474, while James III was concluding the lucrative English contract to marry his infant son to **Cecilia** of England, the lady Mary remarried, this time to **James, Lord Hamilton** of Cadzow, one of the party which had helped with the overthrow of the Boyds. She was twenty-three. Hamilton was a widower with a grown family. The status of Mary, his new wife, whether a divorcee or a widow, has never been entirely clear, since the fate of Thomas Boyd is not known.

While her husband was becoming a grandfather, Mary gave him a new son and a daughter, James (born about 1475) and later, Elizabeth. There was a problem with their legitimacy, since the marriage was still subject to a canonical bar. Dispensation had to be sought (and was given in 1478), since Lord Hamilton's first wife was related to Mary through their common descent from Robert II (King of Scotland 1371–1390; see **Consanguinity and dispensations**). This failed to address the belief that Hamilton's philandering had included ladies related to the Princess. While the Princess was married, the King gave the **barony** of Kilmarnock, once Lord Boyd's, to Queen Margaret, and she also began to acquire all the remaining lands due to her as her dowry. In March 1478, the Duke of Albany obtained a divorce from his Sinclair wife on terms which removed his children from the possible succession. When Lord Hamilton died in November 1479, Mary was left with four children including two sons, James Boyd, now aged nine, and James Hamilton, four. **John of Mar** was dead. Her other brother, Albany, had now fled to France. Mary's two sons remained, each of which could claim royal blood and perhaps a royal inheritance provided the two royal Princes, both also called James, were out of the way.

The Hamiltons would stay loyal to the Crown, and would look after their own. It was inevitable, then, that Mary should want to secure the future of her two children by her first marriage, and that the boy, **James Boyd**, should see the return of his uncle Albany in force in 1482 as a promise of eventual power.

When the English army turned back, and Albany remained, showered with promises by the King, the same good fortune seemed to have come to his sister Mary, who was given the barony of Kilmarnock and its castle, the barony of Dalry and other Ayrshire lands which had once belonged to Lord Boyd and his son Thomas, and had since been held by the Queen. Mary was given liferent of the lands, while her son James was to hold them in feu. Teling and Polgavy, part of which had been held by Anselm Adorne, were also returned to Boyd hands. Unfortunately, the honeymoon lasted only a season. By December, Albany had stormed from the Court to his fortress at Dunbar, where young James joined him and his followers in a hopeless gesture of defiance which dragged on from the start of 1483. In the course of it, Anselm Adorne was killed.

It is hard to believe that the Princess Mary or James her son would have wished the death of this man they knew well, in whose home the boy had been born. Nevertheless, Adorne, who had been back in Scotland since 1477, had been bound, by his service to the King, to attempt a reconciliation between Albany and his brother which the extremists did not want. When the rebellion failed and Albany left for France in 1484, the future of the fourteen-year-old James must have been of deadly concern to his mother. In April of that year their possessions in Kilmarnock were taken from them and returned to the Queen. James however was not touched by the law. Instead, he lost his life in a personal feud in 1487, when he was aged only seventeen. One year later, Mary Stewart herself died, only in her thirties, just before the battle that ended the life of her brother the King. As she probably would have resented, her immortality eventually came, not through the children of Thomas Boyd, but through her children by Lord Hamilton. Of her son and daughter to Hamilton, her daughter married Matthew, Second **Earl of Lennox**, who fell at **Flodden** in 1513. Matthew, the Fourth Earl of Lennox,* was the husband of Margaret Lennox,* and they were the parents of Henry Darnley, Mary Queen of Scots's* second husband.

Princess Mary's son became Earl of Arran (d. 1529) and her grandson, James Hamilton, Second Earl of Arran,* was Governor of Scotland and after **John Stewart, Second Duke of Albany**'s death in 1536, next in line to the throne after Mary Queen of Scots. He was prevailed upon to resign the regency of Scotland in 1554 in favour of Mary de Guise.* (D. D.)

Maryculter: See **Culter.**

Matariya: UNICORN, 36: Four miles north-east of Cairo, the Garden of Balm (in Arabic, *el-Matarijeh*) grows where sweet water famously sprang from the heels of the baby Jesus when the Holy Family rested there during their flight from Herod's Egypt. The aromatic oil for which the garden was famous is variously said to have dripped miraculously from the bushes where the sacred infant's clothes were laid to dry, or to be a property of plants originally brought by the Queen of Sheba on her visit to King Solomon, and transplanted there.

The Matariya bush is the resinous *Commiphora opobalsamum*, a common basis for perfume. It comes from Southern Arabia, and hence would be known in Yemen, once the home of the Sabaens, from whom 'Sheba' probably came (with or without the single webbed foot attributed to her by Gothic allegory). Being much revered by Christian pilgrims, the Garden of Balm was a miraculous source of revenue for the Sultans of Egypt. By the time – 14 August 1470 – that the Genoese nobleman **Anselm Adorne*** and his son **Jan** trotted on donkey-back into the garden, it had become a leading tourist attraction, as well as a pleasant retreat for the Sultan Qayt Bey* and his Mameluke* court at the height of its season in March.

Surrounded by their stately houses, the gardens with their trees and airy gazebos and terraces formed an oasis in the desert. Pilgrims were allowed to walk among the low, small-leaved resinous shrubs, but forbidden to crush the leaves, far less take cuttings. The finest balm was processed by the Sultan and sent as offerings to fellow potentates. Balm of an inferior kind was allowed to some merchants: Adorne received the gift of a phial, which he carefully consigned home to Bruges* by Venetian galley.* Its quality could be tested, wrote Jan, according to whether a drop on the palm caused the skin to burn when held up to sunlight.

Pilgrims were shown various wonders, including the gnarled and bent fig (*fiscus Pharaonis*) which had stooped to show reverence to Jesus. Christians viewing the marble-edged pool of the Holy Well were told by other Christians, in secret, how the oxen turned the two wooden irrigation wheels, each fixed with a chaplet of pitchers, but stubbornly refused, despite whipping, to work after Vespers on Saturdays, resuming only after Vespers on Sundays. The Adornes also heard of a child, recently supposed drowned in the well, who rose again unharmed and smiling, standing dripping on one of the wheels.

According to the Italian condottiere Roberto da San Severino, who visited the garden twelve years before (see **Margaret of Denmark**), a conduit from the well led to a magnificent bath-house able, Roberto claimed, to accommodate three hundred bathers. Jan omitted to mention it. (D. D.)

Mathias Corvinus: RONDO: (*c.* 1443–1490) Also known as Matija Korvin, he took his name *Corvinus* from the raven (*corvus*) in his coat of arms. He was chosen as King of the Hungarian–Croatian lands in 1458 after the Habsburg Ladislas V (ruled 1444–1457) died without an heir. His reign kept the Habsburg lands united against the Turks, keeping them out of Slavonia (the eastern part of Croatia) for another fifty years after Bosnia fell in 1463, although he did lose the last of the Croatian islands in the Adriatic to Venice* in 1480. From 1467 he was responsible for the creation of one of the first standing armies of Europe, the Black Army, hiring Czech, Polish-German and south Slavic mercenaries, which were used to keep the Turks at bay and to conquer territories for Mathias. After his death, centralised power declined as did control over the army, which descended into brigand units and was disbanded by 1492. Corvinus gained control over Moravia, Bohemia, Silesia and portions of Austria, and saw himself as a candidate for Holy Roman Emperor. He left one illegitimate son, Johannes Corvin, to be ruler in his stead, but from 1490 to 1526 Hungary was ruled by the **Jagiellonian dynasty**, and Croatia was divided between the Turks and the Venetians. The Croats recognised **Maximilian I** of Austria as their king, but the Turks defeated the Croatian army at Krbva in 1493. In 1526 the Hungarians were defeated by Suleiman* at the battle of Mohacs, at which King Louis II was killed. Hungary and Croatia elected Ferdinand of Habsburg as their king in 1527. The Habsburgs remained on the throne for over 385 years.

Maximilian I: RONDO: (1459–1519) Son of Emperor **Frederick III** and Eleanor of Portugal, Maximilian, Archduke of Austria, in turn became King of Germany (1486) then Holy Roman Emperor (1493). His marriage to **Marie of Burgundy** in 1477 followed the death of **Charles, Duke of Burgundy*** at Nancy. Physically striking (tall and blond), but unable to speak the language of his bride, and inept in diplomacy and manipulation when compared to **Louis XI**,* Maximilian attempted to secure peace with France and still retain good relations with England. With the death of Charles and in default of a male heir, Louis claimed inheritance to Burgundy. Although military victory over the French at the Battle of Guinegate (1479) drove them from southern Flanders and peace was made between France and Burgundy in 1480, it was to be short-lived. Louis undermined the long-standing alliance between Burgundy and England with the publication of his secret truce and pension payments to **Edward IV**,* showing the English King's claims that he would come to Burgundy's aid to be duplicitous.

Nor were the burghers of Flanders happy with Maximilian's presence. The terms of Marie and Maximilian's marriage treaty excluded him from the succession, but following the death of Marie in 1482, Maximilian proposed to govern as Regent in the minority of his four-year-old son and heir, Archduke Philip. The estates made it clear that they would prefer a regency council, which Maximilian was forced to accept. Louis XI meanwhile offered a betrothal between Philip's sister Marguerite and the Dauphin, meaning an end to the war with France (on terms which would, naturally, favour France). Continuing rebellion against Maximilian in Utrecht and Gueldres persuaded him that peace with France must be made, so he was obliged to sign the Treaty of Arras (1482), promising to the young Dauphin of France his even-younger daughter Marguerite. This peace deprived Edward IV of his annuity, and of the promised marriage of his daughter Elizabeth to the Dauphin. Marguerite was sent immediately to France, where she remained for most of her childhood, and Edward IV of England, dying, was unable to do anything either to support Burgundy or attack France. Louis XI's death in the same year as Edward (1483) temporarily improved Maximilian's position against France, although he remained unpopular in what remained of Burgundy. Revolts against Maximilian continued in Flanders. In 1488 he was publicly humiliated when he was trapped in Bruges,* his army kept outside the town. Maximilian endured months of imprisonment, forced to watch as his pro-empire advisers and counsellors were tortured to death in the main square of Bruges below his prison. He was released only when the burghers were faced with the combined threat of excommunication by the Pope and Emperor Frederick's German army, despatched to free Maximilian and quell the rebellions in Bruges, Ghent and Ypres by force.

In 1490 he attempted to unite Brittany and Burgundy against France by marrying Anne, Duchess of Brittany, by proxy. This marriage and the Treaty of Arras were ended when, after invading Brittany in 1491, Charles VIII of France married Anne and sent Marguerite back to her father.

With the death of Frederick III in 1493 Maximilian became Emperor, spending the majority of his time in his territories of the empire. His reign had secured Bohemia and Hungary for the Habsburgs, in addition to the Spanish Empire secured through the marriage of his son Philip. Peace within the Low Countries was also obtained – eventually. Maximilian was ultimately forced to hand Burgundy over to France, but kept wealthier Flanders and Franche-Comté, and regained Austria from the occupying **Mathias Corvinus.** He married again in 1494, to Bianca Sforza, the daughter of Galeazzo, Duke of Milan, but the couple had no children. Maximilian was part of the Holy League in 1511 that brought together England, Spain and the Pope against Louis XII (King of France 1498–1515), and, following the invasion of France by Henry VIII (King of England 1509–1547), saw the Scots King **James IV** defend the French alliance against England at the battle of **Flodden.**

May dew or none, my brown and tender diamonds don't engender, they dissolve: KINGS, GAMBIT: In *The Travels of Sir John Mandeville,* Mandeville* described the diamonds found in India, that grow together, both male and female, and are nourished by the dew of heaven: 'Thei engrendren comounly and bryngen forth smale children that multiplyen and growen alle the yeer' (chapter seventeen).

Medicinal plants: See **Agaric; Soutra.**

Mehmet, Hadji: See **Justus of Ghent.**

Mehmet II:* RAM: (1432–1481) See Volume I. The capture of Constantinople in 1453 endowed Mehmet with unparalleled prestige in the Muslim world; his victory over **Uzum Hasan*** twenty years later at Terjan marked an equally important turning point, sealing as it did his domination over Anatolia and the Balkans. In terms of his campaigns against the hostile Christian world, his main objective was the capture of **Rhodes** from the Knights of St John.* In this he failed, but his seizure in the same month of the southern Italian port of Otranto (August 1480) clearly indicated he was still intent on invading Italy in a new attempt to found a world empire. This attempt was brought to an abrupt end by his death in May 1481, but he had laid the foundations for Ottoman rule in Anatolia and south-eastern Europe that would survive for the next four hundred years.

Mehmet was succeeded by his eldest son, Bayezid II (b. 1447/1448), who in turn resigned the throne in 1512 to his son Selim I (1467–1520), or Selim 'The Grim'. Selim had been governor of Trebizond until the abdication of his father. It was Selim who overthrew Shah Ismail of Persia (see **Amiable as a girl: lively as a fawn**), head of the powerful Shi'ite movement. His reign only lasted eight years, but he strengthened and unified the Ottoman Empire, dominating the Mameluke* sultanate of Egypt, Arabia and the former territories of the White Sheep in Persia. The Empire's power was to culminate in his son, Suleiman the Magnificent,* who at the time of his grandfather's abdication was governor of Caffa in the Crimea (see **Mengli-Girey**).

Meine Königin: RONDO, 9: 'My Queen.' Spoken to the Queen of Poland. German was used at her court, and was the official language of Cracow in the period covered by the novel.

Melrose Abbey: HN; LC: Founded by David I (King of Scotland, 1124–1153) in 1136, the Abbey at Melrose was the first **Cistercian** foundation in Scotland, and one of the largest in Britain, originally colonised from Rievaulx Abbey in Yorkshire. Monastic houses were built to a standardised Benedictine plan, with the monastic buildings grouped round the cloisters on the south side of the church (see **Monasteries and nunneries**). In Melrose, however, the cloister and domestic buildings are on the north side of the church. The standard plan was reversed to utilise the River Tweed, flowing to the west of the monastery, dammed and brought through a lade, to run the Abbey mill, and then diverted through a massive drain (now excavated) to supply the pits of the monks' latrines.

Like other Cistercian houses in Scotland, Melrose capitalised on the rich arable land of the Borders. The Abbey pastured three flocks of wedders, each five hundred strong, at **Haddington.** In 1247 they were buying horses – they made the expensive purchase of a stud of horses and brood mares that year from one Patrick of Dunbar.

The monastery was burned in 1322 and 1385, providing the impetus for a rebuilding plan on a grand scale, but further English attacks in 1545 meant that the Abbey was never completed according to the fourteenth-century plans, nor did it fully recover. The upstanding remains of the Abbey date from the late fourteenth to the sixteenth centuries and the layout of the monastic buildings can be clearly examined. The remains of the monastic choir became part of a Protestant church when it was revived in 1618.

MEMLING, Hans: LIONS: (*c.* 1433–1494) One of the great masters of the portrait in Flemish devotional art, Memling was a German by birth. His family name comes from Mömlingen, a village on the river Mömling, a tributary of the Main, and Hans, or Henne, was brought up nearby in the small weaving town of Seligenstadt, close to a fine Benedictine Abbey. Memling seems to have left home young, about 1450, when his parents both died during an outbreak of plague. He may have studied in Germany, but to experts his technique strongly suggests that he spent time as a journeyman in the workshop of the Brussels Master Rogier van der Weyden.

Six months after van der Weyden's death in 1464, Memling is found living as a privileged citizen in the artists' quarter of Bruges,* where he was the leaseholder of a large house on the east side of Sint-Jorisstraat which he later bought. He also occupied two adjoining houses, one of which was called *den Inghel*, the Angel. Together, they formed a complex with a transversal annexe or workshop, and a smaller house opening into Jan Miraelstraat. All are now gone.

There is no record of early trial works by Memling. Sponsored perhaps by van der Weyden, he seems to have found clients immediately in the Burgundian court, and among wealthy members of the Church and the merchant community. Duke Philip the Good's* famous son the Grand Bastard Anthony, already magnificently painted by Weyden, was later to commission a second portrait from Memling. In Bruges, usually, he was known from the start as the Master.

His first identifiable painting, in 1467, was the great triptych *The Last Judgement*, now in Gdansk, whose adventures during the **Hanseatic League**'s war are described under the names of **Paúel Benecke**, who stole it, and Tommaso Portinari,* manager of the Medici Bank in Bruges, who appears in it. For Portinari himself, Memling painted two devotional works, one a Scenes for the Passion and another, possibly a Virgin and Child, to mark Tommaso's wedding in 1470 to Maria Baroncelli. Portraits of proud Tommaso and his sixteen-year-old wife appear in both, as did paintings of the elderly Angelo Tani* and his young bride Caterina Tanagli on the wings of *The Last Judgement*. There exists also a pen-portrait of Caterina in one of the brisk letters of the matriarch Alessandra Macinghi negli Strozzi* of Florence, who had once contemplated the girl as a match for her son Filippo.

Other Memling commissions included a triptych for Abbot Jan Crabbe of the Ten Duinen Abbey. A painting of the Martyrdom of St Sebastian may have been meant for the chapel of the Guild* of St Sebastian, a society of crossbowmen whose premises were first rented to them in 1454 by the father of **Anselm Adorne**,* who himself was a practitioner. The chapel was in the church of Bruges's **Franciscan** monastery. For St John's Hospital, of which the same Pieter Adorne had been Guardian, Memling painted four great works which are there to this day. (One of them contains a dazzling portrait of the famous Bruges crane.) Memling also inserted double portraits in a religious setting for Sir John Donne of Kidwelly, of the English army at Calais, who had bravely underwritten part of the massive ten-thousand-pound Medici loan required by **Edward IV*** to pay for his sister's Burgundian wedding.

After the death of **Charles, Duke of Burgundy**,* and through the consequent turbulence, Memling was forced with the rest to contribute to the cost of the war against France. In 1487 his wife Tanne (Anna) died, leaving him with three children, Hannekin, Neelkin and Claykin, of whom the oldest was still a minor. Among his portraits at this time were those of two nephews of Tommaso Portinari, and one, incorporated in a diptych, of the twenty-three-year-old Maarten van Nieuwenhove, whose burgomaster brother was to be tortured and executed during the rising against the incomer **Maximilian** of Austria.

A branch of this family was also connected with Anselm Adorne in several ways. Nicholas van Nieuwenhove, as Treasurer of Bruges, had subsidised Adorne's wife during his absence in the Holy Land. In 1476 Agnes van Nieuwenhove, the daughter of Nicholas, married Adorne's son Arnaud. The daughter of Arnaud and Agnes, another Agnes, took as second husband the well-known Genoese Andrea della Costa (d. 1542), tax-collector for Maximilian of Austria and orator of the deanery in Bruges. He seems to have commissioned a diptych from Memling, of which only an incomplete copy remains. It shows the Deposition, with a figure of St Andrew on the reverse. The son of this couple, John de la Coste, changed his name to Jan Adorne to honour his great-grandfather.

Hans Memling died in August 1494, and was buried in St Giles's Church, Bruges, which shared with St Giles* in **Edinburgh** the armbones of the saint. His three children kept the houses he had bought (now tiled, and no longer thatched) until 1509. The artist appears as Master Hans in an allegorical ode on the arts (effectively a list of painters) to Marguerite of Austria (1480–1530), written by Jean Lemaire before 1511 (extract):

Il y survint de Bruges maistre Hans
Et de Frankfort, maistre Hughes Martin
Tous deux ouvriers tres clers et triomphans.

From Bruges Master Hans
And from Frankfurt, Master Hughes Martin
Both brilliant and successful craftsmen.

Or, as a later writer put it, in 1534:

Meester Huge, meester Rogier die wonder hebben verziert
Met den Duytschen Hans om te schilderen abusen.

> They painted wonders, Hugo, Rogier – right?
> But German Hans deceived your very sight.
> (D. D.)

Men on Pytan live by the smell of wild apples: KINGS, II, 2: Mandeville's* description of the island:

> . . . where the folk neither plough nor sow the land, and neither eat nor drink. Nevertheless they are a very fair people, well coloured, well shaped, according to their stature; for they are little, like dwarfs, somewhat bigger than the pygmies. This people lives on the smell of wild apples that grow there; and if they go far from home, they take some of these apples with them, for as soon as they lose the smell of them they die. This people is not fully rational; they are very simple, like beasts.

Mengli-Girey: RONDO: (d. 1515) Khan of the Crim Tartars, who had broken from the **Golden Horde** in 1441, Mengli-Girey allowed the Ottomans to overrun Caffa in 1475, in return for which the Genoese were removed from the peninsula. The Crim Tartars were fearsome fighters and spent the later part of the fifteenth century under their leader harassing the East; Kiev was looted and burned in 1482; and Poland and Lithuania were attacked almost annually from 1484. **Casimir IV**, acting on the Venetian maxim of 'set a dog on a dog', encouraged the Golden Horde to attack Mengli-Girey, leading to peace for Poland – Lithuania on the Crimean side (1483–1486), but the Ottoman Sultan Bayezid II (ruled 1481–1512) provoked the Golden Horde to attack the rich **Jagiellonian** lands instead of the Crim Tartars who were vassals of the Turk. Russia similarly encouraged Mengli-Girey to destroy the Golden Horde, and free **Ivan III** from the tribute he paid to them. The Golden Horde were defeated by the Jagiellionians in 1491 (who had made a two-year truce with Turkey), and their capital was destroyed by the Crim Tartars in 1502. The destruction of the horde meant that Mengli-Girey was more able to harass Lithuania. In 1506 he sent his sons with an army of over ten thousand men to devastate Lithuania, but they failed. The Tartars were routed, and later joined with the Jagiellonians against the encroaching power of the Duchy of Moscow, and continued to act as a thorn in the side of the Russians for nearly a further three centuries. The khanate of the Crimea continued until 1783.

Menteith, Lake of: See **Geese, fishing with.**

Merrybuttocks: LIONS, 30: The name of a real English ship, captured by de la Motte, the French ambassador to Scotland, and sold in Leith in 1511. It was bought by John Balyard and Walter Carr of Leith, and probably sold to **James**

IV.* It was sent to Norway in May 1513. Other striking ship-names of the period included the *Jesus of the Tower*, an early-fifteenth-century ship of one thousand tons. The title referred to the Tower of London, home of England's royal defences. Vessels were often also called after their owners' families, and their names might be masculine, feminine or disembodied, as in *The Holy Ghost.*

Meydyns' maryage wolde he spyll . . . : CHECKMATE, III, 3: From the middle English romance *Sir Gowther*, the protagonist of which is half-human child, half-fiend. The preceding verse tells how Gowther and his men had raped a convent of nuns, then locked them in the church and set fire to it. His evil reputation now spreads far and wide:

> *All that ever on Cryst con lefe [believe],*
> *Yong and old, he con hom greve [made them grieve]*
> *In all that he myght doo.*
> *Meydyn's maryage wolde he spyll [ruin]*
> *And take wyffus [wives] ageyn hor wyll,*
> *And sley hor husbondus too.*
> *And make frerus [friars] to leype at kraggus [over cliffs]*
> *And persons forto heng on knaggus,*
> *And odur prestys sloo [priests slayed].*
> *To bren armettys [burn hermits] was in dyssyre [his desire]:*
> *A powre wedow to seyt on fyre,*
> *And werke hom mykyll woo [much woe].*

Minute: LIONS, 2: This is the technical name, in a French **Mystery Play** or a farce, for a rough text for reading aloud. Directions to players would be in the vernacular (referred to as *mi-patois*) or in dog-latin, expressed sometimes as *mi-latin de cuisine* (or cooking-Latin). (D. D.)

Mohacs: KINGS, I, 1: See **Mathias Corvinus.**

Monasteries and nunneries: HN; LC: For reasons of simplicity, as both single-sex devotional lifestyles followed the rule of St Benedict, monasteries and nunneries have been dealt with as one subject. Twelfth-century Scotland under King David I (ruled 1124–1153) saw a period of growth for monasticism, and the monarch personally endowed many new foundations. Most of these continued to grow in wealth and stature until the Reformation appropriated their funds and lands, and the reformers destroyed many of the buildings.

When an established order founded a daughter house, it would have thirteen monks (or nuns); twelve members and their Prior, echoing Jesus and the twelve disciples. Monastic houses were built to a standard Benedictine plan, with the monastic buildings grouped round the cloisters on the south side of the church, making the most of the available light. This square of buildings would consist of the west range, where the outside world met the monastery, beyond which was the courtyard and gatehouse. This was the area where visitors were received and alms distributed and the west wing would contain guest-chambers. Lay brothers working for the community (very common with **Cistercian** houses, owing to the large workforce needed to farm and pasture their tracts of land) would live and eat in the west range. The south range comprised the kitchen, communal warming room and the refectory on the upper floor, echoing Christ's Last Supper in an upstairs room; and the east range consisted of the dormitory upstairs and chapter house (for the reading of the Rule of the Order) and book cupboard downstairs. Entrance was gained to the church from the east range, via the transept. Leading off the east range would be the latrine block, well supplied with running water. Also separate from the monastic cloistral buildings to the east was the infirmary with its own chapel; to the south was the cemetery and to the west, guest-houses. To the west would also lie the bakehouse, stables, workshops and masons' yard, all within the monastery compound's walls and entered through a defensible and impressive gatehouse. All monasteries followed this basic layout of St Benedict; where an exception was made, it would be to maximise access to local resourccs, such as water (see **Melrose.**)

In charge of the monastery would be an Abbot, (or Abbess in the case of a nunnery); his second in command was called a claustral Prior. Large monastic institutions tended to be called Abbeys, those which remained small (or had not become fully independent of their founding 'mother' house, or were cathedral monasteries) were referred to as Priories and at their head would be a claustral Prior, not an Abbot.

Silence was observed for most of the monastic working day, and completely between Compline at nine in the evening and Prime the following day, in the first hour after sunrise. Work or study would stop for regular prayers through the day. Meals would also be taken in silence, hence the logic for the enclosed orders having developed basic sign language as an essential tool for communication.

The work and accumulated wealth of Scotland's monasteries is well known: from the fat Cistercian sheep of the Borders to the scribes of Holy Island and the commercial scriptorium at Culross for the production of manuscripts to the hospital at **Soutra;** as centres of study, prayer and devotional care their reputation remains. They also provided an additional service in the time before banks, acting as a respository for cash and valuables. The nunneries, as portrayed in the novels, also fulfilled the rolls of crèche, nursery and school environment for the nobility and royalty of Scotland.

Monna Donnina: RONDO, 41: 'My lady', in flamboyant terms.

Monypenny, William: RISING: (d. by 1491) William Monypenny, Lord of Concressault, was one of the adroit diplomats of the period, able to serve the dual interests of France and Scotland. From 1439 he was mainly based in France, attached to the Dauphin, but travelled widely between Scotland, France and England. In the 1440s he was involved in the marriage negotiations between Isabella Stewart and the Duke of Brittany's eldest son, and the marriage of Eleanor Stewart to Sigismond of Austria.* (See **James II's sisters.**) In 1456 he was sent by France with proposals for peace between Scotland, France and England.

He received grants of land and titles from both France and Scotland and was elevated to Lord of Parliament. **Louis XI*** further rewarded his loyalty with a pension of 1,200 livres, and he was appointed Seneschal of Saintogne. He was the ambassador sent to Scotland by Louis XI to offer **James III*** part of Brittany in return for an army, the offer James was sadly obliged to decline. From 1474, a Monypenny (either William or a son) was one of Louis's new company of one hundred guardsmen, all of whom had to be of impeccable lineage. His mention in the novels comes from his assignment to **Alexander, Duke of Albany,*** during his first French sojourn. The family tradition of diplomacy and negotiation passed to his descendants; Monypenny's son Alexander also acted as a diplomat and expatriate Scot in the services of the French Crown, while another son, George, who is described as a Doctor of Laws, also served Louis as an ambassador in England in 1470.

Morales: KINGS II, 2: Cristóbal de Morales (*c.* 1500–1553). Spanish composer, born in Seville, whose first post was as *maestro de capilla* in Ávila (1526–1529). He joined the papal choir in Rome (1535), where he remained for ten years. He was subsequently *maestro de capilla* at Toledo Cathedral, and, finally, at Málaga (1551). He composed twenty-one masses; his magnificats were extremely popular and widely reprinted. He also wrote many motets: *Jubilate Deo Omnis Terra* was commissioned by Pope Paul III* to mark the peace treaty between Charles V* and Francis I;* and Palestrina* parodied one for his mass *O sacrum convivium.*

Moss: LIONS, 25: In Iceland, moss (kept in barrels) was eaten after being steeped, pounded and boiled with milk to a jelly. The result was pale green, and inclined to be bitter. As a dish, it was found in many other parts of the world, including the Tyrol. This Russian folk medicine recipe using moss guaranteed to render the patient incapable of drinking alcohol ever again: a particular variety of club moss was boiled in water for twenty minutes. The resulting solution had to be drunk hot by the sober patient, followed by a glass of vodka. Immediate and painful vomiting would follow. The procedure was repeated up to three times. The intolerance to alcohol that resulted was said to last for years.

Mouettes rieuses: LIONS, 32: Black-headed gulls. Literally 'laughing gulls', from the sound of their cry.

Mount Sinai: See **Sinai, Mount.***

Mouseion of Alexandria: UNICORN, 32: Founded for Ptolemy I Soter (*c.* 366–*c.* 283 BC) from the beginning of the third century BC by Demetrius of Phaleron, a follower of Aristotle, the Mouseion contained not only a library but lecture halls, laboratories, observatories, a park and a zoo. The library, its chief wonder, held at one time half a million books, and its librarian, Kallimachos (d. 240 BC), was the director of the whole complex. His fame stems from his work in the library, founded to collect all Greek literature. He compiled a bibliographical guide to the collection, and is regarded as the originator of library science. It was written of him that he mourned his friend, the poet Heraclitus of Halicarnassus, by quoting an epigram he had based on the words of a woman dying in childbirth: 'I left one twin to guide my husband's old age, and took the other to remind me of him'.

As well as serious scientific and literary research, one of the tasks of the specialists at the Mouseion was to respond to commands from the palace. Its poets, astronomers and engineers made war engines and mechanical toys, turned out literary puzzles and jokes – they rewrote the whole of the *Odyssey* once without using the letter 'S' – as well as composing hymns, odes, eulogies, love songs and even cooking and medical recipes. If the Queen lost her hair from the temple to which she had dedicated it, the astronomers sought it for her in a constellation, and the poets wrote an elegy on it.

Under the Ptolemies, during the years of witty exchanges, the Mouseion was at its height. Later, under the Romans, its interests were to turn rather towards philosophy and religion. A fire burned down part of the library during the siege of Alexandria by Julius Caesar. Of the rest, part was destroyed by fanatical Christians in AD 391, and the rest in the Arab conquest of AD 631. Legend says that the books heated the city baths for six months. (D. D.)

Mouth of Hell: LIONS, 22: Often depicted in **Mystery Plays** as a tower, with a hideous dragon's mouth for a door, opening and shutting. The French name was *'le Crapault d'Enfer'*, the Spittle of Hell. See also **Hekla.**

Muggers: GEMINI, 9: Itinerant sellers of earthenware mugs were common on the borders of Scotland, and had a name for gypsy-like thievery and violence at fairs.

Mulier intacta: RONDO, 5: A variant of the proper term, *virgo intacta*, or virgin. *Mulier* in this instance means a married woman, and the request is to return her intact, meaning unravished.

Murrey and plunket: RAM, 3: Murrey comes from the Latin for mulberry, and denotes the dark purple-red of that fruit, or, in heraldic terms, the colour called sanguine. Plunket is a pale greyish blue, from the Latin for lead. Dark red and blue were much in favour for doublets, and were also the colours of the English royal house of York. (D. D.)

Music make[s] men mad: KINGS IV, 2: Robert Burton (1577–1640) relates in *The Anatomy of Melancholy* (1621) how music may do good or harm to those suffering from depression:

> Many men are melancholy by hearing music, but it is a pleasing melancholy that it causeth; and therefore to such as are discontent, in woe, fear, sorrow, or dejected, it is a most present remedy: it expels cares, alters their grieved minds, and easeth in an instant. Otherwise, saith Plutarch, *musica magis dementat quam vinum* [music maddens more than wine]; music makes some men mad as a tiger; like Astolpho's horn in Ariosto, or Mercury's golden wand in Homer, that made some wake, others sleep, it hath divers effects; and Theophrastus right well prophesied that diseases were either procured by music or mitigated.

See also **Spondaic rhythm.**

Music, soothing: See **Spondaic rhythm.**

Music to sound in a high tower . . . So merrily that it was a joy for to hear, and no man should see the craft thereof: KINGS, IV, 2: A reference in Mandeville's* *The Travels of Sir John Mandeville* to one of the subtle tricks used by the leader of the **Assassin** cult to convince new converts that they were listening to the sound of angels in Paradise.

My lyves loy, myn hertes plesance: CHECKMATE, V, 13: See **Right godly fresh flower of womanhood.**

My Sole cleaveth to the Pavement: LIONS, 27: From Psalm 119 which begins,

> Blessed are they that undefil'd,
> And straight are in the way;
> Who in the Lord's most holy law
> Do walk and do not stray.

The phrase in the novel, which refers to a disturbing vibration underfoot, is adapted from verse twenty-five of the psalm. In the original the 'Sole' is the 'soul' and the 'pavement' represents humility. (D. D.)

My tail is plaited like a Barbary Ram: See **Barbary Ram.**

Mystery of Love: See **Whoever is unsupported by the Mystery of Love.**

Mystery Plays: LIONS: By the end of the fourteenth century many European countries had developed a series of dramatic verse pageants or plays based on biblical stories and the lives of the saints. They were immensely colourful and lavish productions, often accompanied by complex stage machinery and special effects. This was not drama for its own sake, but a civic expression of piety with its roots firmly in the liturgical drama of the church. Large-scale performances were undertaken not by professional actors, but by the townspeople themselves, often by the guilds,* who would each perform a separate pageant, hence the term 'Mystery Play', or 'Mystery Cycle', the 'mystery' referring to the guild, the cycle being the individual plays making up the whole, from the Creation to the Resurrection of Christ. The plays were also organised by religious societies or confraternities, town councils, or encouraged by an individual such as René, Duke of Anjou,* who sponsored at least five full-scale Mystery Plays.

The Nativity Play in the novel owes its origins to the surviving texts of miracle and Mystery Plays performed in France and in Burgundy from the mid-fifteenth century, and also to the accounts left by contemporary chroniclers and in archives regarding the arrangements and manner of their performance. Such plays could be performed in a day, or over a series of days, coinciding with the saint's day if the play covered his or her life story, or a particular festival of the Church. They could also be held as a form of thanksgiving by the townspeople for having been spared from some natural disaster or calamity that may have affected another area.

The script for the performance was written or compiled by a *fatiste*, who would call upon the narrative texts available to him, and also might rewrite existing plays to bring local colour and relevance to the drama. A massive undertaking and a great expense, the production would involve many professionals and craftsmen. In addition to a full copy of the text, scribes were employed to copy each actor's part onto narrow strips of parchment four inches wide which would contain all their speeches and cue-lines. These sections were pinned or sewn together and then nailed to a stick or rod, round which the script would be tightly rolled and unfurled as rehearsals proceeded, called *rolles* (hence the name for the part given to the actor, his rôle). (See also ***Minute***.) The director, called the *meneur du jeu* or *Protocolle*, would have a script which showed the first and last lines of the actors' speeches and stage directions. The stage designer (*painctre*) was another professional who could employ further professionals to create the special effects (see ***Machiniste***), such as pyrotechnics, or the noise and smoke of hell (see **Mouth of Hell**). The town's own workmen would be called upon to provide the backgrounds and costumes and supply food for the actors. They would also build the stage: the surviving French examples often make use of a large urban space such as the town square to create a theatre in the round. The staging in the centre would be built specially, as would the seating (see **Nails**), with boxes for dignitaries and terraces for the more humble members of the audience. There would be no naturalistic scene changes; all areas, such as Hell and Heaven, occupied separate areas of the playing area.

The actors were likely to be literate, making it easier for them to learn the script, and there would be rivalry amongst the guild members for the best parts. Rehearsals would begin many months before the date of the performance, and the actors would split into groups (devils in one, disciples in another) to make it easier to rehearse together. Food and drink would be provided for them.

Immensely colourful and lavish productions, the plays seldom made a profit, but they enhanced civic reputations, and those who travelled to the town to see the performance would benefit the local economy. They would also have shared in a common religious experience, creating a sense of community and purpose amongst the audience. The texts of the plays which survive contain both serious and comic elements: farce and humour coexist with the moral or violent aspects. They portray real human action and reaction to events, and elicit from their audience an emotional and spiritual response, emphasising the humanity of the characters and the power of spiritual redemption.

N

Na baba: RONDO, 39: 'You must be joking'.

Naglfar: LIONS, 23: The *Naglfar* was in Norse legend the ship of the Frost Giants, built by a dwarf and held together by the **nails** of dead men. It was smaller than the *Hringhorn*, the ship of **Baldur**, which became his funeral pyre.

Nails: LIONS, 28: The Icelandic for nail is **nagl** (see above). The trick of dismantling an enemy's ship by secretly withdrawing all the nails (LIONS, 24) is recorded as having actually happened. The work of the ironsmith was vital in domestic and agricultural life, in battle and in early shipbuilding, when nails, anchors, rudder-hinges, grappling-irons and spikes were all made of iron. Hence iron – and nails – were of great importance in early times, and therefore a popular subject for story and myth. In this chapter the mention of horseshoes leads to the idea of nails (always carried by Icelanders when riding), and then to the large numbers of nails (costing ten shillings a thousand) required to build the seating and staging for a **Mystery Play.** The nails were often supplied by the cast members or their relatives, and in one version a fish pool was provided in which to plunge **Tubal**, known as the Paralytic.

The posts of Thor's shrine were fastened by *regin-naglar*, Nails of Divinity (LIONS, 30). The papal tithe in Iceland was at one time a single nail, upon a tenth of an ell of wodmal (cloth), the equivalent of two fish. Tartars called the Pole Star the *Selesnicoll*, the iron nail.

Of a different kind of nail: in the world of German drinking the *Nagel Probe*, or nail test, was a grim one. If, when the cup was upturned, there was not enough left to wet the thumbnail, then replenishment was demanded. (D. D.)

Nativity Play: See **Mystery Plays.**

Nay, not so. I am too brittle; I may not endure: KINGS, III, 4: See **It is another disease that grieveth me.**

Nettles in winter: KNIGHTS; III, 1: The chapter takes its title from a verse satirising the perfidity of women. The first verse gives a feeling for the bitterness of the lyric:

> When netilles in wynter bere Rosis rede,
> & thornys bere figges naturally,
> & bromes bere appylles in euery mede,
> & lorelles bere cheris in the croppis so hie,
> & okys bere dates so plenteovsly
> And lekes geve hony in þer superfluens –
> Than put in a woman your trust & confidens.

New gripes of dread then pierce our trembling breasts: CHECKMATE, I, 5: From the translation of Virgil's *Aeneid*, Book II, by the Earl of Surrey (*c.* 1517–1547), describing the death of Laocoön and his two sons, squeezed to death by serpents.

Newbattle: GEMINI, 16: Founded by David I (King of Scotland 1124–1153) in association with his son, Earl Henry in 1140, the **Cistercian** monastery was colonised from **Melrose**, and is one of only two houses in Scotland not to be built along strict Benedictine lines, but expanded to allow the housing of more altars. By the late-fourteenth century, the **monastery**'s income could support eighty monks and seventy lay-brethren, but the destruction of the Abbey by Richard II (King of England 1377–1399) in 1385 meant a total rebuild was necessary. The monastery once again prospered in the fifteenth century. A large amount of restoration and building work was carried out in the time of Abbot John **Crichton** (Abbot from 1474); the masonry was emblazoned with his coat of arms.

Newbattle's wealth came from the great estates it possessed (used for farming and pasture), and its access to mineral resources. The Abbey held estates in six counties (**Edinburgh**, Haddington, **Linlithgow**, Lanark, Peebles and Stirling), much of their Crawford land being granted to the Abbey by their great benefactors the **Lindsays**, providing excellent grazing land for their sheep, as did Abbey lands at Clydesdale and Monklands. It allowed the Abbey to produce some of the finest quality wool in Scotland.

Peat, wood, lead and coal were necessary for their salt-making industry, also carried out on their land. As early as 1316 an old dispute with **Holyrood** had eventually been settled; Newbattle took the church and church lands of Bathcat (Bathgate) in lieu of the rents owed to Newbattle by Holyrood for the rent of the Abbey salt works 'in the carse of Kalentir'. In 1471 Abbot Madowre obtained a decree against James, **Lord Hamilton**, for the despoliation of the Abbey's lead mines; Hamilton was accused of having taken a thousand stone of ore from the Abbey's land.

The monks of Newbattle receive the credit for being the first coal-workers in Scotland, following the coal bank next to the monastery down to the main seam. The deeper the seam became, the more engineering work was needed to stop the shaft from filling up with water.

With the Reformation, Newbattle was erected into a **barony** and the monastery suppressed in 1587. There is now a college on the site of the east range of the monastery; the foundations of the church and other monastic buildings are buried beneath the gardens.

Niacal, fhir mo chridhe: GEMINI, 45: 'Nicol, my dear man,' literally, 'man of my heart'.

Nibal: LIONS, 2: See **Tubal.**

Nickomack: UNICORN, 36: The Arab name taken by the character Nicholas means 'Conqueror of the Enemy'; Aristotle (384–322 BC) was the son of Nicomack of Gerasha.

Nie pozwalam: RONDO, 4: 'I do not allow it'. The phrase used to veto a decision in the Polish Sejm (Assembly of Nobles). Any single dissent from the majority would halt proceedings until the refusal had been debated and resolved.

Nightingales are not born from owls: RONDO, 4: The petty nobility of Poland were obsessive not about their wealth (as they were often little better off than peasants), but about their bloodlines and inheritance. The comment refers to the tolerance of the petty nobility to intermarriage or irregular unions outwith their class. There was no ideological opposition to such dalliances, as long as it was perfectly clear that the issue of such a union could never be considered noble; even if the father were noble, if the mother were of peasant stock, then the child would be similarly tainted by ignobility. They were passionate about their supposed biological superiority and the exclusivity of their birthright. Bastardy similarly barred the way to any claim to nobility: adding a spurious *ski* to one's name made no difference. The quote in which the proverb was captured dates from the 1620s:

> Balsam, when added to tar, ceases to be balsam but turns to tar; and if tares, though sown in the finest field, will not become wheat . . . So, if a noblewoman marries a peasant, she will certainly give birth to an ignoble child. For what purity can come from such impurity, what perfume from such a stench! It's a wise proverb: Nightingales are not born from owls.

Njall's story: LIONS, 29: Late-thirteenth-century popular Icelandic saga, telling the history of Iceland's heroes of three centuries earlier and essentially showing the destructive consequences engendered by the thirst for money, power and revenge. Njall is the hero of the saga, skilled in the law and sought by many for his wise advice. His many attempts to keep a blood feud from destroying his friendship with **Gunnar Hamundarson** and keeping his friends out of trouble tragically lead to his own demise as he and his family are burned alive in their house. Originally an oral tradition, by the thirteenth century formal readings of sagas (from manuscript editions) had developed as a popular form of entertainment.

Noli tangere: LIONS, 42: 'Touch who dares'. Later taken as the motto of the Order of the Thistle in Scotland.

Nólsoy: LIONS, 20: A small Danish island in the Faroes group, three miles by sea from its capital of Tórshavn (Thor's harbour). The precise route taken in 1468 by the Scots **Princess Mary**, fleeing her brother King **James III*** with her unpopular bridegroom **Thomas Boyd**,* has never been clear. All that is certain is that her travels ended in 1470 in the Bruges home of **Anselm Adorne**,* and that her two children by Thomas were born there.

The diversion proposed in the novel derives from a Faroese legend which suggests a romantic connection between Princess Mary and the village of Korndalur (Corn Dale) on Nólsoy. According to John F. West, author of *Faroe: The Emergence of a Nation*, a daughter of 'James II of Scotland' fled to that place when pregnant by a nobleman unacceptable to the King. The Princess and her husband were eventually pardoned, but forbidden to come back to Scotland, and her children, 'two boys and a girl', remained on the islands. The story adds, touchingly, that the Princess drew water from a stream diverted to run within her front door, so that she might obey her father's command never again to show her face in the light of day.

The legend says nothing of **poffins**, but anyone familiar with the Faroes would agree that they are part of the experience. (D. D.)

Non est vivere extra venetiis: SCALES, 38: 'Life outside the Veneto [Venetian territory] just isn't life'.

North Berwick: GEMINI, 50: The Priory of St Mary's at North Berwick was large by Scottish standards; this was a twelfth-century nunnery founded by Duncan I, Earl of Fife, and built nineteen miles east of **Edinburgh**, close to the spot from which pilgrims to the shrine at St Andrews were ferried across the Forth Estuary to Andross (Kilconquhar). The same Earl endowed two hospices at North Berwick and Andross which later passed to the nuns, who were thus obligated to serve needy travellers on both sides of the water. The name Earlsferry on the Fife coast commemorated the crossing. The settlement of

North Berwick itself, developing about the small, exposed harbour, had become by 1373 a burgh of the **Earls of Douglas**, and was so called to distinguish it from the large trading port of Berwick-upon-Tweed* further south. Visible for twenty miles, the cone hill of Berwick Law backed the Priory, and the Bass Rock, equally formidable, rose from the sea on its opposite side.

Although possibly Benedictine in origin, the foundation developed as a Priory for **Cistercian** nuns. In the time of Robert II (King of Scotland 1371–1390), the **barony** in which the Priory stood stretched from the property of the Earls of Fife to that of the Douglases of Tantallon Castle, who paid tiends (tithes) to the Priory. Because of the early patronage of Robert Bruce, Earl of Carrick, the foundation was also supported from the start by West Scotland lords, and the Ayrshire names of Carrick, Kennedy, Cathcart and Maybole appear in early charters, beside those of French-derived nobles of Fife such as Ness of Ramsay; and of Borderers such as Robert of Upsettlington. Elena of Carrick was Prioress in 1386.

Some of these connections persisted. Witnesses to Priory documents of 1463 included William Bell, rector of the church of Upsettlington, and the Prioress's procurator was a David Ramsay. The Priory also owned property. Its tenement in North Berwick itself was in 1477 next to one held by John Gulyng, of a family which (with Sir Gilbert Johnstone) was accused of raiding Sir **William Knollys**'s* goods at Torphichen in 1483. (Sir William was one of the Priory's procurators in 1463.) Among other possessions was property in Leith and Greenside, Edinburgh, gifted by the Lestralrig family, and some close to Berwick-upon-Tweed near the cemetery of St Nicholas. This last may have come through the closure of the Cistercian priory in that area, which suffered from proximity to the English border. The Border Cistercian abbey of **Melrose** probably shared some of the concerns of North Berwick, as it did those of **Haddington**, only eight miles away; and there were close parallels between North Berwick and **Newbattle** Abbey, founded from Melrose, and showing similar Anglo-Norman names in its early charters. The Priory also drew support from the parish church of St Andrew, later linked with notorious witchcraft trials.

In its earliest days, when it retained Benedictine characteristics, the Priory had a sub-Prioress under a male Prior, and at another time, a Prioress but also a master. As the local Maitland family were prominent in Haddington Priory, so the Ramsays and more especially the Formans were patrons at North Berwick. Mariota Ramsay was Prioress in 1463, and when she died in 1474 was succeeded by one of her nuns, Elizabeth Forman. The families were connected, and both were active politically in the years that ended the reign of **James III.*** The Formans had property in Hutton, seven miles west of Berwick-upon-Tweed, and fishings on the Tweed. The name also appeared further north – in 1426 Adam Forman was squire to Archibald Douglas, Earl of Angus, and in 1477 James Forman was a familiar in the inner household of James III.

Nevertheless, a James Dalrymple 'alias Forman' was one of those accused of later holding Crichton Castle to the King's detriment, and in the next reign, **James IV*** formally forgave Sir Adam Forman, John Ramsay and John Liddell (son of **Sir James Liddell of Halkerston**), who had been secretly sent by Henry VII (King of England 1485–1509) with a boatload of munitions to help the rebels at Dumbarton Castle (see **John Stewart, Lord Darnley** and **Sir John Colquhoun of Luss**). Tentative links, through Liddell and others, with the late **Alexander, Duke of Albany**,* are repeated in 1498 when two brothers Forman from Hutton, one a merchant, the other the Prior of May, act as executors in a case involving the late Ellem of Butterdene.

Andrew Forman, the Prior of May, had an illustrious career. In 1491, as James IV's protonotary in Rome, he was appointed by Innocent VIII (Pope 1482–1492) to deliver the Golden Rose to the King. In 1502 he became Bishop of Moray, and he succeeded the King's son (killed at **Flodden**) as Archbishop of St Andrews (1514–1522), as well becoming commendator of Pittenweem and Abbot, for a while, of Dunfermline. As an ambassador of note, treating for the marriage of James IV to Henry VII's daughter Margaret, arranging a truce with the French King Louis XII (ruled 1498–1515) – after which he was made the Archbishop of Bourges in France – he attracted so many benefices that his unpopularity at home became marked. He was even put forward for a cardinalate by his friend the Regent, **John Stewart, Second Duke of Albany**, son of Alexander. Other Formans also flourished. Andrew was followed in Pittenweem by Robert Forman, Dean of Glasgow, and in 1546, Adam Forman was Prior of the Charterhouse, Perth.

Scarcity of records makes it difficult to fit the history of the North Berwick Priory into the wider political pattern. It suffered in the wars between Scotland and England, especially in the fourteenth century and again in the mid-sixteenth century. The reign of James IV benefited the family **Home**, and the Priory reflected their importance for several decades. Alison Home was Prioress, and Alexander Home of Polwarth featured as witness to a charter in about 1493, while in 1525 Isabella Home replaced Alison Home as Prioress. Moving towards the Reformation, there were still more than twenty nuns in the building in 1544, and apart from the Homes of Polwarth and elsewhere, the families of Ramsay and Douglas are still mentioned, along with those of **Crichton** and **Sinclair.**

The Homes, however, were the principal beneficiaries of the secularisation brought about by the Reformation. In 1548, the Prioress Margaret Home sold the convent's chief estate at North Berwick to her brother, and by 1587 all but the purely ecclesiastical possessions of the Priory had been erected into the barony of North Berwick, in favour of Alexander Home, by which time many of the buildings were in a state of disrepair. By 1596 the Priory was reduced to the Prioress Margaret Home and one nun, and the following year it was suppressed. The surviving vestiges are now in the grounds of a home for the elderly. All that remains is an oblong range of conventual buildings to the north which suggest a first-floor hall, a refectory, and a kitchen running east to west over a chain of four barrel-vaulted chambers for storage. There is also extant a fireplace, a staircase and traces of a hoarding or penthouse: a square tower was added when the Priory was already in ruins. Thirteenth-century floor tiles, some of them found in the cellars, may derive from a kiln discovered near the north wall. The tile designs, unusual for Britain, are similar to geometric or zoomorphic moulds then in use in the Rhineland: some are on show in North Berwick Museum, and in the National Museum, Edinburgh.

The Priory is thought to be the site where **Anselm Adorne**,* the Burgundian trader and diplomat of Genoese origins, met his death in 1483, on his way to a rendezvous at **Whitekirk.** Garbled and contradictory records have obscured much of the story, and also the name of the Bishop who accompanied him, who might have been his fellow Genoese **Prosper de Camulio**,* or possibly Bishop Blackadder, a former Abbot of Melrose whose family was intermarried with both the Douglases and the Formans, and who had close connections with Cistercian Culross.

It is also proposed in the novel that, in this era of English invasions, the Prioress of the Border Priory of **Eccles** sought refuge here with her Cistercian sisters. There is no proof of this, but it is not unlikely, given that the lady's half-brother was Bishop Kennedy* of St Andrews, destination of the North Berwick pilgrims, and that he came from a family which had supported the latter Priory from its earliest days. (D. D.)

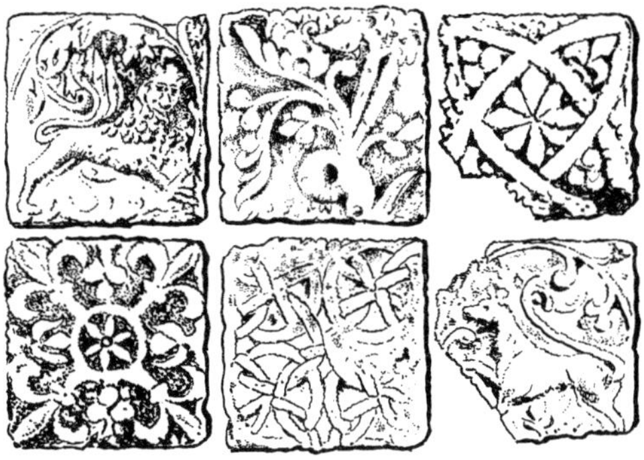

Group of 13th Century floor tiles from North Berwick including rare zoomorphic patterns

Nor' Loch: HN; LC: Lying in the valley below the north face of Edinburgh Castle, the loch has now returned to a pleasance of gardens, as it was in the time of David II (King of Scotland 1329–1371), when tournaments were held in some parts, and others were morass and pools, where wild animals roamed. In 1450, the decision was made to flood the valley to form a permanent defence, joining the loch to the town wall at the east end, where the royal gardens were swamped. The loch was fed by several springs, including that at St David's Well, and was regulated by a dam and sluice situated at the foot of **Halkerston's Wynd.**

The dam also provided a path from the town to the fields to the north and, later, to the slope down to **Leith.** When **Trinity Chapel** was built, it was given the privilege of an eel ark at its door. There was boating for the householders from the ridge, and plentiful rural and maritime bird life: swans and wild ducks, partridge and coots, woodcock and snipe, as well as otters and water rats. Later, a pillar and basin marked the spot where erring women were ducked. The loch was not safe when frozen, and drowning while sliding and skating was not uncommon. Legend had it that foxes kept clear after Candlemas, and if crossing in winter, would stop, ear to the ice, to listen for the spring water below. (D. D.)

Nostalgie de bain: GEMINI, 16: A yearning for the bath. A play on the common phrase *nostalgie de boue*: a yearning for the mud, or self-abasement.

NOSTRADAMUS, Pierre de: LIONS, 2: This was not the better-known physician and astrologer, but a man of three generations before. Historians differ, but the novel presents the popular view that Pierre de Nostradame was a Jewish doctor employed first by John, Duke of Calabria (1427–1470), and then by John's father, René, Duke of Anjou, King of Naples and Sicily* (1409–1480). It also accepts that Pierre was the grandfather of Michael Nostradamus*, the famous prophet (1503–1566) who served Catherine de Médicis* of France. Both Pierre and Michael are said to have converted to the Christian faith.

Before he died, Pierre is said to have given the boy his early training in mathematics, Greek, Latin, Hebrew and celestial studies, after which Michael rejoined his father Jacques de Nostradamus, thought by some to be a notary of St Rémy in Provence. Other historians believe that the link between Pierre and Michael came about through Michael's mother Renée de St Rémy (so named after King René), whose forebears were astrologers, mathematicians and physicians serving both the King and his son.

A more recent theory (by Erika Cheetham) considers that the family came from around Avignon, and that Pierre de Nostradamus was a grain dealer whose son Jacques moved to St Rémy in 1496 and married Reyniere de St Rémy, the granddaughter of a former doctor turned tax collector. This meant that, although Pierre was the grandfather of Michael, the family were not part of 'the illustrious line of Jewish-Italian doctors' at the court of René and his son.

It is hard to distinguish the facts. King René's son John, soldier and composer of delicate poetry, spent most of his life fighting in Italy (where he was briefly governor of Genoa), as well as supporting his father in Provence, the Loire and Lorraine, of which John became Duke, with a residence at Nancy. His death in Barcelona while fighting in Aragon in 1470 was a devastating blow to his father, who elected to leave Anjou and France, and return to his castle of Tarascon in Provence (see **Tarasque**). When René himself died, the whole of Provence fell to France. The Dukedom of Lorraine, held by John, went to his son Nicholas, who died three years later, and then to another young René, cousin of Nicolas and nephew of John of Calabria. It was this René, Duke of Lorraine, who fought at the battle of Nancy in 1477, in which **Charles, Duke of Burgundy**,* died. The Burgundian doctor, Matteo Lope, was Portuguese.

There may or may not have been exotic antecedents for the race of Nostradamus, but it seems safe to assume that Michael Nostradamus was the grandson of Pierre, and it would seem likely that Pierre served René and his son. With reference to the novel: a physician of King René would certainly have attended the court at Angers, but his presence at Trèves is conjecture. (D. D.)

Icon of St. Nicholas ~
Novgorod 14th C.

Novgorod: RONDO, 33: The eastern Russian trading centre second only to Moscow in terms of its wealth, whose independent status made it a target for **Ivan III.** The **Hanseatic League** had seen the potential of the town in the twelfth century, establishing themselves there and focusing on the important Russian trade (notably in furs and salmon). However, strains developed within the city. In 1471 Novgorod had formed an alliance with Poland-Lithuania under **Casimir IV.** This was considered by Ivan to be a betrayal of him and the Orthodox church, as Poland-Lithuania was Catholic. Ivan overran Novgorod, demanding that the inhabitants swear loyalty to Moscow and pay a tribute. Ivan subsequently demanded subservience from the town; it refused and in retaliation he laid siege to the town and demanded its surrender. This second war ended when Novgorod conceded defeat in January 1478. Novgorod ceased to exist as an independent territory, its lands annexed to Moscow. Twelve months later, further signs of resistance from the merchant classes of the town led to their execution or deportation to central Russia. In the years that followed, trade with western Europe via Novgorod ceased, and the colony of German traders were sent home. The *Kontor* of the Hanseatic League was destroyed in 1494. The territorial ambitions of Poland-Lithuania were temporarily reduced, but were to re-emerge at Novgorod in the following century under Ivan IV.* Following the unification of the kingdom of Poland and the Grand Duchy of Lithuania in 1569, letters were forged proving that the Archbishop and Governor of Novgorod had been guilty of treasonable conduct with the Polish king. Ivan the Terrible personally oversaw the torture and slaughter of the town's inhabitants. In five weeks the city was reduced to ashes.

Nunneries: See **Monasteries and nunneries.**

O

***O Dowglass, O Dowglass, Tender and Trewe*!:** GEMINI, 23; KINGS, I, 6: A couplet from Sir **Richard Holland**'s allegorical poem, the *Buke of the Howlat.** The lines are reputedly embroidered on the coat of arms of the pursuivant in the poem.

O God! Thou art all-pardoning, Thou likest pardon, pardon me: RONDO, 44: An early religious text quoted by the seventeenth-century Turkish traveller Evliya Efendi (1611–*c.* 1684) when travelling in Angora in the aftermath of a successful uprising against the Pasha of Amasia. Evliya was enjoining compassion on one of the participants (who, however, remained obdurate). (D.D.)

Observatine Friars: HN: Also known as the Friars Minor and as the Grey Friars. St Francis's collection of like-minded souls, espousing poverty and self-denial, and dedicated to spreading the word, were not organised or structured like their contemporaries the **Dominicans.** Conflict emerged within the order between those who wished to live and preach in absolute poverty, and those who realised the practical need for a base from which to operate; the Observatines and the Conventuals respectively. The asceticism of the Observatines made them attractive to new founders; they had a significant number of new foundations in the second half of the fifteenth century. They were brought to Scotland from Cologne by Mary of Gueldres (*c.* 1477) and were in **Edinburgh** by the mid-fifteenth century. Their monastery at the east side of the Grassmarket (**Greyfriars**) was destroyed by the reformers in the sixteenth century, its yards turned over to be the new extended graveyard for Edinburgh.

Odysseus polymetis: LIONS, 17: Odysseus, the god of wiles.

Of Paradise ne can I not speak properly, for I am not there: KINGS, IV, 1: In chapter thirty-three of *The Travels of Sir John Mandeville*, Mandeville* regrets that of all his fabulous descriptions, here he must stop short.

Of wyne and wax, of gamyn and gle: KINGS, I, 5: A *cantus* (song) of eight lines, preserved in *The Orygynale Cronykil* [Chronicle], *c.* 1420, of Andrew of Wyntoun (*c.* 1350–*c.* 1425), a metrical history of Scotland (in octosyllabics) from the beginning of the world to the accession of James I (1406). This *cantus* describes the devastation to Scotland by English raids following the death of Alexander III in 1286:

> Quhen Alysandyr oure kyng was dede,
> That Scotland led in luüe [law] and lé [quiet],
> Away wes sons [abundance] off ale and brede,
> Off [past] wyne and wax, off gamyn [amusement] and glé:
> Oure gold wes changyd into lede.
> Cryst borne into Vyrgynyté
> Succoure Scotland and remede [help],
> That stad [is in] perplexyté.

Oh Doge, as a flower shall you fall: LIONS, 12: From a grave and noble message to all future Doges of Venice, inscribed near the doorway by which the reigning prince of the Signoria entered the church of St Mark from his palace. In full it read:

> Love justice; give to every man his rights. The poor, the widow, ward and orphan look for a guardian in you. Be pious to all: let not fear, nor hate, nor love, nor gold betray you. As a flower shall you fall, oh Doge, dust shall you be, and as you have acted, so shall you be esteemed after your death. (D. D.)

Ointments: See **Soutra.** An Italian street cry in Renaissance times, '*Unguento per la rogna!*', advertised 'Ointment for the itch!' Because of the prevalence of what was delicately referred to as the Italian itch, early travellers to that country were advised to wear breeches in bed. (D. D.)

Oléron: see **Laws of Oléron.**

Olwen's trefoils: KINGS, I, 6: An image from the tale 'How Culhwch won Olwen' from *The Mabinogion*, a collection of eleven Welsh prose tales written down in the thirteenth century. The tale relates the numerous tasks that Culhwch must undertake to win the beauteous Olwen, whose name means 'white track':

> Olwen came, dressed in a flame-red silk robe, with a torque of red gold round her neck, studded with precious pearls and rubies. Her hair was yellower than broom, her skin whiter than sea-foam, her palms and fingers were whiter than shoots of marsh trefoil against the sand of a welling spring. Neither the eye of a mewed hawk nor the eye of a thrice-mewed falcon was fairer than hers; her breasts were whiter than the breast of a

white swan, her cheeks were redder than the reddest foxgloves, and anyone who saw her would fall deeply in love. Wherever she went four white trefoils appeared behind her, and for that reason she was called Olwen.

Ophites, serpent of the: KINGS, III, 3: From Greek *ophis*, 'serpent', the Ophites* were a gnostic sect who worshipped the serpent Ouroboros, a dragon-like creature portrayed as biting its own tail, a circular symbol of metamorphosis, renewal and eternity.

Or a-t-il bien son temps perdu . . . : LIONS, 6: Jeering Burgundian song aimed at King **Louis XI*** of France. The Yorkist King **Edward IV*** has been successful in taking the throne of England on the death of the Earl of Warwick, to the mortification of Louis, who supported the opposite, Lancastrian side:

> Now you can tell he has wasted his time,
> Wasted his money, which matters much more,
> For Warwick is dead, and his cause in decline
> So Ha! this poor Louis is sore!
> So Frenchies, fine Frenchies,
> Go blubber and bleat,
> For Warwick your hero
> Is beat.

Ordensmuehle: RONDO, 12: The great mill built in Danzig in 1350 by the **Teutonic Knights.** It had no less than eighteen wheels, and was used to produce the wherewithal for brewing and baking. Because of the characteristic noise of the wheels, floating watermills in Poland were called *bzdziety*, or 'farters' – a favourite schoolboy joke, as when guild* members gave one another such nick-names as *Pierdzikrzyczywoł*, 'farting-shouting-ox'. (D. D.)

Order of Teutonic Knights: See **Teutonic Knights.**

Orkney dowry: LIONS: The Western Isles had been transferred to Scotland from Norway in 1266, in return for which Scotland had promised to pay an 'annual' of one hundred merks (marks). The amount had seldom been paid, and in 1460 James II* took advantage of the penury of Denmark – Norway, demanding that the 'annual' be remitted and that a Danish marriage alliance should be arranged. King **Christian IV** of Denmark at first refused, but Scotland's hold over Orkney was already strong. In 1468, negotiations were opened, the Scottish ambassadors including **Andrew Stewart, Lord Avandale**, and **Thomas Boyd;*** the marriage of King Christian's only daughter, **Margaret of Denmark** to **James III*** was arranged. Part of her dowry was the agreement by Christian to cancel the debt of the 'annual', in addition to which he would provide a payment of sixty thousand florins. Scotland also promised an alliance with Christian to help him against any parties other than current allies. A down payment of ten thousand florins was to be paid before the Scottish ambassadors left Denmark, and Scotland would have all the land, rights and revenues currently held by the Norwegian crown in Orkney, until the balance of fifty thousand florins was paid. The Scots offered Margaret a substantial wedding portion: one-third of the lands and revenues of the Scottish Crown. If she outlived her husband, she would lose the dower but receive seventy thousand florins in compensation and Orkney would return to Denmark–Norway. Unfortunately, Christian was so cash-strapped that the initial amount could not be raised, and he had difficulty even raising two thousand of the first ten thousand florins. A compromise was reached in May 1469 by which Christian pawned Orkney to Scotland until the rest of the initial payment could be sent. The agreements made it clear that when King Christian was no longer as financially embarrassed as his war with Sweden and other debts had rendered him, the pledges could be redeemed. Any offer to do so was to fall on deaf Scottish ears. Intended as a temporary measure, Christian was never able to redeem his pledge. James III encouraged Sir William **Sinclair** to resign the Earldom of Orkney (and the dependency of Shetland) to him personally, in return for concessions, one of which was the freedom for life from the responsibility of attending Parliament or holding office. This gave James and the Stewart monarchy direct control and rights over the comital rights and privileges of the islands, and in the Parliament of 1472, Orkney and Shetland were formally annexed to Scotland. The Kings of Norway–Denmark were never given the opportunity to redeem their pledge.

OSTRÓROG, Jan: RONDO, 9: (1436–1501) Humanist-inspired, anti-Vatican, secular, nationalist Polish political writer, he became Wojewoda (Voevoda) of Poznań, and was the first layman to make a serious contribution to literature in Poland. His political views, similar to those of **Archibishop Gregory of Sanok**, anticipated the foundation of the modern state. He declared that one law should apply to all; that Polish should be the language of the official records rather than Latin, and that Polish, not German, should be the language of towns and monasteries, proclaiming, 'Let him who would dwell in Poland learn to speak Polish'. He demanded that the Church in Poland should be free from the interference of the papacy and that Polish clerics should not be exempt from royal taxation. His opinions paved the way for Poland to adopt its own abbots and bishops without reference to Rome (from 1463, confirmed by Leo X in 1513, the year he became Pope). The education of the sons and daughters of **Casimir IV** was entrusted to Ostrórog, along with **Callimachus**, the Nuremburg artist Weit Stoss, the historian Jan Długosz and Archibishop Gregory.

Ótta: LIONS, 28: One of the nine divisions of the Icelandic day, which were: *ótta*, midnight to three a.m. (*hanna-ótta* is cock-crow); *miður-morgun*, three to six a.m.; *dagmál* (day-meal), six to nine a.m.; *hádegi* (high-day), nine to midday; *mið-mundi*, first dog-watch, from noon to one-thirty; *nón*, second dog-watch, from one-thirty to three p.m.; *miðr-aptan* (mid-afternoon), three to six p.m.; *nátt-mál* (night-meal), six to nine p.m.; *mið-nœtti*, nine to midnight. Another version has eight divisions, calculated by dividing the natural horizon into eight equal portions called day-marks. (D. D.)

Out of his Nois the meldrop fast can rin: CHECKMATE, III, 4: Description of Saturn, from **Robert Henryson**'s *The Testament of Cresseid*:

His face fronsit [frostbitten], his lyre was lyke the Leid [lead],
His teith chatterit, and cheverit [shivered] with the Chin,
His Ene [eyes] drowpit, how sonkin in his heid,
Out of his Nois the Meldrop fast can rin,
With lippis bla and cheikis leine and thin;
The Iceschoklis [icicles] that fra his hair doun hang
Was wonder greit, and as ane speir als lang.

Atouir [over] his belt his lyart lokkis [grey-streaked hair] lay
Felterit [clinging] unfair, ouirfret with Froistis [Frost's] hoir,
His garmound [garment] and his gyis [guise] full gay [great] of gray,
His widderit [weathered] weid [dress] fra him the wind out woir [wore];
Ane busteous [powerful] bow within his hand he boir,
Under his girdill ane flasche of felloun flanis [arrows],
Fedderit [feathered] with Ice, and heidit [headed] with hailstanis.

Oysters: GEMINI, 1, 32: The European mollusc *Ostrea edulis* is a hermaphrodite, being first an egg-laying female, and then a sperm-producing male, unlike the *Ostrea virginica* of America, which is separately sexed. The *edulis* reaches maturity in the third or fourth year of life, when it may measure three inches across, and will have acquired certain accomplishments: for example it can recognise the shadow of an approaching boat, and has learned to keep its mouth shut against starfishes.

Dwelling in colonies, within between three and twenty fathoms of water, oysters can be lifted by tongs and rakes, as well as by dredging. Through the sensitive fringe of the mantle, they learn not to open their mouths at low tide, or when travelling. It was believed that a fisherman had to sing to his oysters, to tempt them into the net. The oyster boats were at least full of music: the rowers had their own rhythmic 'dreg song' (now lost), to keep the boat steadily moving. Fishing was done in the winter, with close season from early June to mid August in cold waters. The oysters in *Gemini* which caused such (fictitious) distress to the English were culled at the dubious end of the season.

The oyster-beds or scalps of the Forth were deservedly famous, and the subject of fierce competition. Scalp-mails were the rent paid for fishing-rights.

The pearl within the mantle was poetically known as the Margarita, from its Latin name of Greek origin, and was a term of endearment (GEMINI, 9).

To drink to one's oysters meant to fare accordingly.

Diverging from oysters, it is interesting to follow the parking rules of the crustacean world. For example, a barnacle will eat where it is, but a limpet will come back from lunch, and expect to find the same space for its foot. (D. D.)

P

Palaeologina, Zoe: See **Zoe Palaeologina.**

Panie Bracie: RONDO, 9: 'My Lord Brother'. Formal greeting amongst the Polish nobility.

Paper promises flying over the Alps, expertly sanitising the profits of usury: LIONS, 40: See **Usury.**

Par saint Georges, mes enfants, vous avez fait une belle boucherie!*:** LIONS, 37: 'By St George, children mine, you have made a fine killing!' **Charles, Duke of Burgundy, approvingly to his troops at Nesle (LIONS, 34).

Parchment Bible: RONDO, 8: A bible of parchment not only employed the skins of three hundred sheep, it cost six times the cost of a paper one. Driving a pen across parchment also made great physical demands on the scribes, who had to be extremely fit to work for long periods. Some of their weary remarks are still to be found, as the following written in 1338 by Martino da Trieste at the end of a manuscript of the epic *Pharsalia* by Lucan (Marcus Annaeus Lucanus, AD 39–65):

> *Dextra scriptoris careat gravitate doloris*
> *Detur pro penna scriptori pulcra puella*
>
> I can't feel my hand, my head's in a whirl
> I'd swap you my pen for a beautiful girl

(D. D.)

Parcia*:** See ***Adoremus.

Pardoning crimes: See **Remissions**.

Parrots: HN; LC: Popular in France. Marie of Anjou, Queen of Charles VII,* kept a parrot, and Charles VIII (King of France 1483–1498) had them hatched and reared by a Moor. King **Louis XI*** established an aviary with parrots at Amboise. It was said that after the mortification of his imprisonment at Péronne (October 1468), Louis found on his return that all the parrots had been trained to squawk *Péronne! Péronne!* when he passed (LIONS, 2). He is supposed to have had them all rounded up. In Ottoman poetry the parrot is prized for its bright plumage and its ability to learn and recite. The poet Hafiz (d. 1388) described how parrots were taught to speak. A mirror was placed in front of the parrot, and the trainer stood behind the mirror. When the parrot heard the trainer speak, it was fooled into thinking the sound came from the reflection, which it took to be another parrot, and thus would attempt to reply using the same sounds:

> Parrot-wise, before the mirror do the Fates me hold;
> What the Master of Creation bade me say, I say.

Here is the start of another sweet poem by Hafiz which mentions the parrot in a more sensual context:

> Soft wind, speak grace to that gazelle;
> Give her in her elegance what you have us,
> A taste for the mountain and the wilderness.
> Sugar-seller – may your life be long! – why
> Are you not searching for your sugar-eating parrot?
> Does pride of your beauty, O Rose, not allow you
> To ask for the love-mad nightingale? . . .
> When you sit by your love measuring wine,
> Remember the lovers who measure the winds.

See also: I'd give unto her Indian mole Bokhara town and Samarkand.* (D. D.)

Pate-claith: UNICORN, 19: Scots: head-cloth or wrapping.

Pazzi conspiracy: GEMINI, 16: Rivalry between the Florentine families of the Pazzi and the Medici was worsened by Pope Sixtus IV's* choice of the Pazzi rather than the Medici as his bankers. The choice was in part due to the fact that the Pope's nepotism had been thwarted by Lorenzo de' Medici,* who saw the Pope's acquisition of Imola as a threat to Florentine trade. Florence, Milan and Venice had combined against Naples and the papacy; the Pazzi and Sixtus's nephews retaliated with a plot to kill the Medici brothers Giuliano and Lorenzo at Easter 1478. The brothers were attacked in the cathedral as they attended Mass. Giuliano was killed, but Lorenzo survived. Florence rallied to the Medici and the Pazzi were hanged, as was one of their co-conspirators, the Archbishop of Pisa,* which gave Sixtus the opportunity to excommunicate Lorenzo and begin a war against Florence, lasting until Lorenzo obtained a peace settlement in 1480, restoring the alliance of Naples, Florence and Milan against the papacy and Venice.*

Peely-whatsit on Ossy-whatsit: KINGS III, 3: Spoken by a character with a fine disregard for classical order. The reference is to the mountains Pelion and Ossa in Thessaly, and the mythical wars between the gods and the giants. According to legend, the giants uprooted Ossa, once the home of the Centaurs, and, by dumping it on top of Pelion, contrived a staircase for themselves to the heavens. Now, to pile Ossa on Pelion implies excessive repetition, or overkill. (D. D.)

***Per Robert*:** QUEENS, III, 6: Old pear trees of French extraction were common in Scotland, where the red honey pear could grow fifty feet high, with trunks of nine feet in circumference. Early Scottish varieties bore names such as the 'Grey Gude Wife' and the 'Forrow Cow'. Famous early gardens included that belonging to the Priory at **Haddington**, and the orchards in Paisley owned by the **Semple** family, both of which date back to the reign of James I (1406–1437). The gardens at Kinloss were already famous before before 1540, when the celebrated Dieppe gardener William Lubias was brought to lay out the garden and orchard at Beauly Priory by Bishop Reid of Orkney.* An apple and pear from this garden survived until 1877. Monastery gardens also admitted one variety of thistle: the Blessed Thistle, or *Carduus benedictus*. (It is a powerful laxative.) Secular gardens were said to be common in Midlothian by the time of **James III**,* and he himself made a new one at the foot of the Castle Rock, Stirling.

Permitte divis caetera: PAWN, 9: Horace's *Odes*, I, ix, 9; translated as 'Leave the rest to the Gods'.

Pero–como asi?: KINGS, 1, 5: 'But how did this come about?'

Perth, the Cartusia outside: See **Carthusians.**

Peter's pennies: LIONS, 40: Peter's pence: see **Camulio, Prosper Schiaffino de' Medici.***

Petit mafflu: LIONS, 4: A child with round cheeks.

Pia Mater: KINGS, II, 2: The brain. Literally, 'tender mother', the membrane surrounding the brain.

Picardesque fougousite: LIONS, 8: The ardour attributed to men from Picardy.

Pigs: GEMINI, 8: Pottery jars, pitchers or crocks to hold wine, water, oil, butter, ointment, honey – or poison. Oildolie pigs were produced in **Edinburgh** in 1606, and glue pigs with legs in 1552. In more recent times, earthenware pigs were found in Scots homes as bed warmers, or as money boxes for children. Pig-makers, or piggers, manufactured such coarse crockery in a pig-house, after which it was sold by pig-wives driving carts harnessed to donkeys, or pig-asses. From the pig-merchant's load of assorted objects came the phrase 'gone to pigs and whistles', or rubbished. (D. D.)

Pleasures, as someone said, are best when deferred: LIONS, 6: See **Delay . . .**

Poetic ropes: See **The beards of women, the roots of stones . . .**

Poffins: LIONS, 20: Sea-parrots, or *Fratercula arctica*. Everyone's favourite seabirds, with their dazzling black and white feathers and great red parrot-like beaks. Now referred to as puffins, their Icelandic name is *lundefuglen*. (Lundy is Norse for island of puffins.) In Shetland they are called Tommy Noddy; in Scotland, coulterneb (plough-blade nose); and the French name is *le Macareux Moine* (the puffin-monk).

Twelve inches long and too tubby to fly well in a gale, they are seen riding the seas in great rafts, ducking when trouble appears – but can also appear quite some way from their puffinries. Their homes, mainly in north-west Britain, and especially in Orkney and Shetland, consist of colonies of comfortable burrows (often obligingly vacated by rabbits) on turfy islands or cliff-tops, where the one egg is laid during May. Remarkably calm in the presence of watchers, they feed their young in their own picturesque way, rolling flat-footed up to the burrow with the grotesque beak full of sand eels, expertly laid head to tail. Some fifty thousand annually gather in the **Westmann Islands** off **Iceland.**

Sadly, in hard times they themselves were much sought after for food, especially in deprived medieval communities. From June to August, puffins were traditionally caught in the air with long Y-shaped nets, or were tugged out of their holes by means of a hook at the end of a stick, bringing out three or four, clinging to each other, at once. The birds were eaten broiled, smoked, or in soup (LIONS, 25), or for those of more delicate taste, might be stuffed with raisin pudding and baked. Faroe islanders simply munched the boiled breast and thighs, holding the head and the legs in their fists. Early Inuits stored the bodies in blubber and ate them mature, even raw. The flesh of the young puffin has been compared to tenderest beefsteak, losing its fish taste when cooked.

Nothing of the carcass was wasted. In a timberless land, the head, feet, wings and entrails, dried and mixed with cow-chips, made excellent fuel, and the feathers and down sold for mattresses. (D. D.)

Poland: See **Casimir IV; Jagiellonian dynasty.**

Polar bears: See **Besse.**

Popolo minuto: LIONS, 38: The small or common people. In France, rich and poor were described as *peuple gras* (fat), or *peuple menu* (thin). By the latter were understood artisans, clerks and small traders living in cities; and the peasants of the countryside. (D. D.)

Porphyria: GEMINI: Serious metabolic disorder, transmitted from generation to generation by a genetic mutation. It is a rare condition that interferes with the ability of the body to make the red pigment in blood. Different types are associated with abdominal pain (acute porphyria), skin sensitivity (cutaneous porphyria); or both (mixed or variegate porphyria). With variegate porphyria, there is a one in two chance of the offspring inheriting the condition; up to half of those with the condition will die from the disease.

Symptoms include: attacks of severe abdominal pain; temporary mental disturbance; sensitivity to sunlight; production of very dark urine (GEMINI, 48; see urine glasses);* and peripheral neuropathy, which affects the body's non-conscious functions (heart, intestinal movement, sweating etc.). This causes general muscle weakness, numbness, constipation, difficulty in breathing and swallowing and also leads to profuse sweating, increased heart rate (tachycardia) and high blood pressure; the patient becomes hypersensitive. Not everyone who inherits the agent responsible for the disorder develops the disease and it can skip generations, or be brought on by diet, alcohol or exposure to certain chemicals or drugs. There is no cure.

The recent connection of porphyria with the symptoms and behaviour of George III (King of England 1760–1820) can be perhaps also be traced back to the Stewart royal family: the case has been made for porphyria as the illness responsible for the resigned and sudden death of James V,* for Mary Queen of Scots's* 'colicky' pains and vomiting and for her son James's debilitating illnesses, which were associated with the passing of urine the colour of dark red wine. As it is a hereditary condition, it is possible that it may have its roots even earlier in the Stewart line.

Porretta: SCORPIONS, 1; GEMINI, 24; PAWN, 15: Poets, scholars, soldiers and statesmen patronised the sulphurous baths of Porretta, which long served the ailing and rich both for bathing and drinking. Situated in the Bolognese Appenines, halfway between Florence and Bologna in the north of Italy, they fell within the control of the Bentivoglio family of Bologna, who were themselves keen users of the baths. The 'Magnificent [but illegitimate] Messer Sante', lord of Bologna from 1445, had a famous romance before and after his marriage with the Countess of Porretta, a learned and beautiful young matron called Nicolosa Sanuti, with whom he exchanged sonnets. A contempoary work, *Le Porrettane,* a collection of tales allegedly exchanged at the baths by the cream of Bolognese society, has left an alluring picture of the Countess, sitting on a hillside above the River Reno, wearing a gown of purple silk and a rose-coloured cloak lined with ermine, 'the life and centre of the company'. One of her best-known orations was against the sumptuary edict of Cardinal Bessarion,* which proposed to restrain extravagance in women's dress.

The proverb about the drinking water of Porretta, which 'either cleans you or bursts you', is quoted in PAWN, 15; according to the original Italian: *Che beve l'acqua della Poretta, O che lo spezza, o che lo netta*'. For more about Giovanni Sabadino degli Arienti, the author of *le Porrettane*, see **Margaret of Denmark**, about whom he later compiled a far from frivolous biography. (D. D.)

Porto Santo: SCALES, 10: A Portuguese island, close to Madeira. Its governor was Bartolomeo Perestrello of Portugal, who occupied a modest fief on the island, and so was technically a nobleman. His wife came from a family which had long served the Portuguese Crown. Their daughter, Dona Felipa, entered the history books about 1478 by marrying Christopher Columbus (1451–1506) and, giving him Diego, his only legitimate son. Columbus visited **Iceland** in 1477, some years after the expedition described in LIONS. (D. D.)

Portugal's sea discoveries: HN: Its sailors, cartographers and navigators led the way in the European discovery of Africa and the expansion of trade with that continent. Portugal occupied Madeira in 1420, and headed the rediscovery of the Azores in 1430 and the Cape Verde Islands in 1455. Portugal laid claim to a monopoly of trade with black Africa by the treaty of Alcobaça, signed with Spain in 1479; and the fort of São Jorge da Mina on the coast of Guinea in 1481 secured their monopoly, trading in ivory, malaguetta pepper, gold dust and slaves. Portuguese traders did not export firearms or spirits to Africa, but there were many other nations who would later exploit the scattered tribes and weak infrastructure of the Gold Coast and the potential of slaves for wholesale export. (See also Sagres.*)

PRESTON family: GEMINI: Closely connected with the **Sinclairs**, the Prestons seem to have come from the Continent to England, and settled in Scotland by the start of the thirteenth century, probably following King David (ruled 1124–1153) in one of the secondary waves of Norman – Flemish immigration. Their Scottish surname is thought to have come from their first lands at Preston – priests' tun – between **Haddington** and Dunbar, east of **Edinburgh**, although it is also possible that they brought the name with them, since Preston was not an uncommon place name in England, and there were some with early ties to this family.

The Scottish Preston was the 'priests' town' of the monks of **Newbattle** Abbey, founded in 1140, and was known at one time as the 'Abbot's cottar town of Preston' – a small colony serving the salt-pans. Alured of Preston was established there by 1222, and a later Preston had land in **Linlithgow**, which he gave to Newbattle.

In Scotland, Norman, Flemish and Breton names persist, often in the same groups, from earliest times. Charters of the thirteenth and fourteenth centuries name Prestons along with St Clairs (Sinclairs), Ramsays, Bissets, Melvilles and the family de Vallibus (Vaux), lords of Dirleton. They were also successful. By 1337 Laurence de Preston was sheriff of Lothian and Keeper of Edinburgh Castle, a post many of his descendants were to hold. Very soon after, the name of Governton (Gorton, by Preston) appears when William de Lisouris, lord of Goverton, witnessed a grant to the lord William Sinclair of the Temple Lands of Gorton. Grazings in Gorton were held by the Abbot of Newbattle.

In 1342, King David II (ruled 1329–1371), son of Robert the Bruce, gave Sir John Preston part of the old **barony** of Gorton, which lay on the east bank of the River Esk, continuing the links between Sinclair, Preston and Lisouris. By 1363 a Preston was buying jewels for the Queen of David II; and shortly afterwards, John's son Simon Preston of Gorton is found as sheriff of Edinburgh. Then, in 1374, King Robert II (ruled 1371–1390) granted Sir Simon the lands of Craigmillar, a few miles from Edinburgh Castle, which had been resigned by William de Capella, the Hereditary Usher of the King's *capella*, or Chancery.

Sir George Preston, most likely the grandson of Simon, began the building of **Craigmillar Castle**, which, through many changes, was to become a favourite among royal visitors, not least with Mary Queen of Scots.* The Prestons kept some outlying lands to the east, and especially their salt-panning concerns towards Musselburgh and Prestonpans – the last also famed for its 'Pan-door **oysters**', so called since they lay off the doors of the salt-pans. The Prestons were patrons of the altar of St Ninian in the parish church of St Michael, Musselburgh, and in 1491 supplied its parish clerk. Newbattle, **Holyrood** and **Melrose** Abbeys were among others with interests in the salt works, and some also in the local coal deposits at Inveresk, Prestongrange, Tranent and Pinkie which fuelled them, leading to frequent disputes.

Through the fifteenth century, the Preston line continued to contribute to civic affairs and hold a vigorous place in the merchant community of Edinburgh, where there were two Preston burgesses in 1403. By 1425 there was a branch of the family at Binning, by Linlithgow, which was to produce **Thomas Preston.** George Preston, who held the Linlithgow wool customs in 1455, was probably from the same branch. In 1435, Sir Henry Preston of Craigmillar was sheriff and Provost of Edinburgh, and Governor of Edinburgh Castle. The lands of Gorton and Craigmillar, not completely unified, became so by 1459 when John Preston of Craigmillar died, followed by his wife Cristine Cockburn, and his lands were given by the King to Sir William Preston of Gorton, who then held in both places.

The father of this Sir William, of the same name, was responsible, with Constable Thomas Oliphant, for repairs to the stonework, the woodwork and the roofs of the turrets of Edinburgh Castle. His chief claim to fame, however, was his feat in bringing to Edinburgh from France in the 1450s an armbone of St Giles,* to be placed in the 'mother kirk of St Giles' in the High Street of Edinburgh.

This was a time, following the fall of Constantinople in 1453, when crusading fever was at its height. Between 1454 and 1455, perhaps following the same initial route as Sir William, a priest called Alexander Preston went to fight for a year with several Scottish Archers* under an Italian knight and – he reported proudly – *met infidels* while searching for sweet water off the coasts of Barbary. Sir William acquired his relic by leave of the French King Charles VII* 'and other lords', and it may have come from the tomb of the saint in St Saturnius's church in Toulouse, or possibly from the shrine of St Giles on the pilgrim (and trading) route beside Arles, in Provence. A possible connection with the Knights of St John* is described under **William Knollys**.

Perhaps not by coincidence, another armbone had been presented to the church of St Giles in Bruges* by Guillaume de Grauchet, 'a crusader', and authenticated this time by the Pope. At the height of their consequent glory, the relics in Edinburgh and Bruges were well served by their worshippers. Each 1 September, the day of the Feast of St Giles, there was a procession drummed through the streets in both towns. Edinburgh paraded a canopied life-sized effigy of St Giles in rich vestments hung with jewels, and with a kid, his usual attendant, playfully leaping up to his hand. The pedestal bore the three-towered castle and legend as on the seal of St Giles: '*S. Commone Capti Bti Egidii de Edinburgh*'. The silver arm holding the relic was polished, and the figure kept painted, by the Dean of the Guild.*

Sir William Preston himself was buried in a lair (tomb) of embossed brass in the Lady Aisle, now the south aisle of the choir of St Giles, having stipulated that the relic, when carried, should be borne by a Preston. Sadly, in the next century the 'marmouset idol', as the Reformer John Knox* called the figure, was stolen, drowned in the **Nor' Loch** and finally burned as a heretic. Even so, Edinburgh's hopes, ever green, were resurrected once more when, at the start of the last century, the building of the Thistle Chapel in St Giles revealed an arm in a reliquary. A match with Bruges was triumphantly sought, until it was noticed that both were left arms.

The next William Preston of Craigmillar was favoured, as was his son Simon, by King **James III**.* In 1472 Sir William was given lands in Lauderdale, Berwickshire, to add to his Gorton estate. He was appointed one of the **Lords Auditor of Causes and Complaints**, and in 1478 became a member of Parliament – the last Preston to appear in Parliament until 1487. Craigmillar was by then a substantial castle, although by no means as large as more modern additions have made it. Although its hall measured only thirty-five by just over twenty feet long, it was for both hunting and health reasons a frequent resort for the Court, by now largely settled in Edinburgh, and was presumably surrounded by less permanent lodgings. It was also used as a prison.

The scenes set in Craigmillar Castle in GEMINI are not historical, but reflect the increasing divisions within the royal family, and in particular the unruly conduct of **Alexander, Duke of Albany**,* and **John of Mar.** The fact that Craigmillar is repeatedly mentioned in the dubious tales of the death of Mar, the King's brother, suggest that the castle, and the loyal family within it, may have been used more than once as a safe house: a place where a difficult situation could be worked out in privacy. As an example of the King's personal trust, even the nurse of the future King **James IV*** was a Preston: Agnes, the wife of the important burgess John Turing, probably the son of the John Turing of Bruges, who in 1424 organised the ransom for the King's grandfather James I.

Agnes was one of a formidable array of Preston women who, in their own right and through their remarkable marriages, infiltrated the entire trading system of the times. Seven of them were called Margaret, and two were named Cristiane or Cristina. One of the Cristinas was the second wife of William Cumming of Inverallochy (beside Philorth), Marchmont Herald and future Lord Lyon, whose kinsmen Thomas and Alex Cumming of **Culter** were part of the 1480 consortium who owed money to **Thomas Cochrane**. She may be the same Cristiane who received royal payment in her own right between 1459 and 1462 from the Exchequer Rolls. One Margaret married Andrew Bertram, brother of the famous merchant **Walter Bertram**, who was married to Elizabeth **Cant**. Another married into the Barker family, one of whom, Thomas, was to be bailie of Musselburgh. A further one married Archibald Napier of Merchiston: Alexander Napier was to be procurator to Sir Simon Preston of that Ilk over the question of the barony of Culter.

Margaret, Sir Simon's own sister, was the first wife of John, son of **Sir James Liddell of Halkerston**, whose execution for treason as Albany's steward did not affect the career of his son. One Margaret Preston, perhaps the wife of Barker, in 1466 was under process and sentence of **cursing** (details unknown; GEMINI, 8), and was suspended from a dispute with Archibald Melville over a **tenement** in Linlithgow until her absolution had arrived. And there was Jonet

Preston, sister of one Sir Simon and daughter of another, who married Alan Borthwick and received rents from Alexander Brown's land at Fisherrow, and from lands and buildings in Musselburgh. And Elizabeth Preston married John Williamson, who also had interests in Musselburgh, and who in 1490 was given **Roslin** land by Oliver Sinclair.

The men of the family also married well, and maintained their position through the transition from the reign of James III to his son. Sir Simon Preston's wife in 1503 was Elizabeth Crichton, who could have been related to the current Abbot of Newbattle and even to the lover of **Princess Margaret**. John Preston, who was a burgess and owned Temple land in Edinburgh, was the first husband of Elizabeth, daughter of Sir **William Monypenny**. And by 1500 Robert Preston married as his first wife Gelis Crawford of the family of Crawfords of Haining, which produced Abbot **Archibald Crawford** of **Holyrood**. The union was followed by litigation, as Archibald, the Abbot's great-nephew, tried to retrieve goods passed by his late father to Gelis's husband, including an eight-ounce gold chain worth fifty pounds given to Gelis herself. Archibald Crawford, who made all the fuss, was probably Gelis's brother, and would have been second cousin to Robin Crawford of **Berecrofts.**

At about the same time, William Preston, son of Sir Simon, married Elizabeth Hepburn, perhaps related to Margaret Hepburn who, in 1488, was married to William, third Lord Sinclair. By 1502 Sir Simon Preston was referring to Patrick, Earl of Bothwell, Lord Hailes, as his blood cousin in a matter to do with the district of Gilmerton, next to Craigmillar. In the 1480s Sir Simon also received, in feu for life, part of the lands of Kincavil, worth an annual fee of £13 6s 8d. Another part of Kincavil, worth eight pounds and traditionally the perquisite of the Keeper of Linlithgow Palace, was held at the same time by **Anselm Sersanders.**

Also prominent towards the end of the century was Henry Preston, burgess, sheriff depute and Treasurer of Edinburgh, who shared premises in High Riggs with John Preston, and himself had a son James. In 1482 he was renting the expensive bellhouse loft in Edinburgh **Tolbooth** for his business, at nearly twice the price Hector Meldrum paid for his cellar. Among the many law cases brought for or against him is one in 1483 concerning a band of named men who removed from Henry and handed to someone else eighty ewes and a horse. This followed a dispute over the breakdown of a £300 marriage agreement, and was typical of the turbulent course of Henry's life.

Henry Preston weathered the change after the death of James III, and sat in the first Parliament of James IV with John Knollys of Aberdeen, and John Hepburn of Haddington: William Knollys was Lord High Treasurer. Sir Simon was likewise confirmed under the new reign in his barony, to be called Preston rather than Gorton. A few years later, Sir Simon and friends obtained **remission** after another outbreak of lawlessness over conflicting rights in Gilmerton, Edinburgh.

They were energetic times. The Prestons fought abroad as well as at home. The name of Edward Preston is repeated for 20 years in the lists of Scottish Archers of the French royal bodyguard, and is accompanied for part of the time by that of **Andrew Wodman.** Other familiar names in the same period include those of Archers Spens, Lisouris, Flockhart, Arnot, Brown, Edmonston, Lockhart, Ramsay and Bonar.

They remained important within Edinburgh. Sir Simon Preston (d. 1519), who was laird at the time of GEMINI, had his lands of Craigmillar, including the castle, fortalice and mill, made into a barony by James IV in 1511. The outer curtain walls surrounding the castle date from this time. This Simon Preston was succeeded by his son George in 1520, who twenty-three years later resigned the barony in favour of his son Simon (d. 1575). He served as Lord Provost of Edinburgh and was a supporter of Mary Queen of Scots.* In his Edinburgh house, opposite the High Kirk of St Giles, Mary spent her last night in the city after her defeat at the Battle of Carberry (1567).

The Prestons stayed in Craigmillar Castle for three hundred years. (D. D.)

PRESTON, Thomas: GEMINI: There were three identifiable Thomas Prestons in the Scotland of the second half of the fifteenth century. One, still alive in 1489, was a little-known brother of the head of the family, Sir Simon **Preston** of **Craigmillar Castle, Edinburgh.** A second, Thomas Preston of Binning, by **Linlithgow**, and perhaps from the main family, was slaughtered in a courtroom brawl in Forfar in 1474 (GEMINI, 17). The third (nick-named 'Leithie' in the novel) was not directly connected with the august Craigmillar, but was a sea-going man who lost his life at **Lauder Bridge** in 1482 as the army of King **James III*** set out to face the English army marching north with the King's brother, **Alexander, Duke of Albany.***

Apart from rare identifications, it is hard to separate the lives of the three men called Thomas Preston. Thomas, brother of Sir Simon Preston of Craigmillar, took some part in the continuing public life of the family, and in the early years of the reign of **James IV*** is found in charters in the company of several **Sinclairs**, especially Oliver Sinclair of **Roslin Castle**. Sir Simon's brother may have been the Thomas who in the 1450s was a bailie in Edinburgh under Provost Alexander Napier, and deputy sheriff, then sheriff of the middle ward of Edinburgh and the constabulary of **Haddington**. In 1442 a Thomas Preston helped the first recorded water bailie in **Leith** to raise twopence in custom from each incoming boat; and in 1445 was probably one of a group of Scots merchant-skippers who were sent to settle a **Hanseatic League** quarrel at Bremen.

In 1455 one of the three had rights to win and mow hay in the King's Park in Edinburgh, in which he had some association with **Thomas Swift** and his father John. In 1475 one of the two men still alive was concerned with the Haddington customs, having eighty pounds in his hands. It may have been the same man involved with letters to Mr John Moffat, Official of Dunblane, concerning the 'purgation of a woman by her spouse accused of sorcery'. Disappointingly, nothing else about that is extant. And lastly a Thomas, brother of Sir Simon Preston, is on record in Musselburgh arranging the appointment of a vicar for Inverurie, on the River Don north of Aberdeen.

Thomas, the brother of Sir Simon Preston, had land in the High Street of Edinburgh which contributed to the altar of St Laurence and St Francis in St Giles, and payment from it after Thomas's death was made by **Walter Bertram**, his sister's relation by marriage. This house, which eventually went to Thomas's nephew John Barker, was sited next to other kinsmen by marriage, William and Alexander Napier of Merchiston, **Henry Cant** and Walter Spens, who was perhaps related to **Thomas Spens**, who had royal hay rights at Linlithgow (rather than Edinburgh or Stirling) just before **Anselm Adorne.*** There was also property in the **Canongate.** It was a close-knit community, in which the burgesses and merchants of Edinburgh operated to the benefit of themselves and the King.

The life of the Thomas Preston killed in 1474 is difficult to disentangle from the above, and the obvious alarm caused by his death does not explain the reason behind it, which may have been less than momentous. Violence during local adjudication was not uncommon, and officials were sometimes sent to cancel a potentially dangerous meeting. Others were appointed to act as mediators afterwards, to calm angry barons and prevent a process of revenge. In this case the mediator was **Sir James Shaw of Sauchie**, Governor of Stirling Castle, guardian of the King's year-old son and member of the inner, loyal circle of servants to the King.

In this instance, trouble seems to have been expected at Forfar. Marchmont Herald (William Cumming), who was on tour delivering letters to summon a Parliament, called at Angus with special instructions for the King's half-uncle, James, **Earl of Buchan**, and the Lord Oliphant 'to stanch the gathering for the court of Forfar'.

They were too late. The meeting was held, and Preston was killed. There was an immediate flurry. A courier was sent 'in haste' to Perth, with letters for Oliphant about the slaying of Preston. Next, Marchmond Herald, who was later to marry a Cristiane Preston, was dispatched to summon two men, one Lord Oliphant and the other Sir Lawrence Mercier (who was married to Oliphant's niece). Finally, **David Lindsay**, the Earl of Crawford, who was sheriff of Forfar, was instructed to make a composition with James Shaw and Michael Balfour of Burleigh, a royal official in Fife and once the Keeper of the castle of Falkland. The object was 'the escheat and remission of them that were at the slaughter of Thomas of Preston', and the sum involved was five hundred pounds.

The cause may have been a family feud, or it could have been a simple clash over property between hot-tempered men. Preston may have even been there to support Buchan, whose lands of Auchterhouse were next to Anselm

Adorne's Teling, and a short ride from Forfar. Seventeen years later, a macer was again sent to Perth (at a cost of twenty shillings) to 'cease the gathering' between the Earl of Buchan and Lord Oliphant, which lends colour to the theory of a continuing quarrel. The last legal decision affecting this Thomas Preston was a compound between James Shaw of Sauchie and the laird of Craigmillar for the ward and marriage of the heirs and lands he had left. The 'heirs' were probably the three Preston sisters, Cristiane, Margaret and Katherine, who all made good marriages.

There remains the Thomas Preston who died at the side of **William Roger** and **Thomas Cochrane** at Lauder in 1482. Some of the activities above may be his, and he may be the harbour man who saw to Leith customs, or the merchant who went to settle a problem in Bremen. He is implicated in the killing at Lauder Bridge only in the conflicting tales of later historians, and by the fact that he died at that time. The sixteenth-century historians Buchanan and Ferreri describe him as an innocent royal favourite of good birth. His family was certainly close to the inner family circle of the King, and could be blamed for supporting the King's personal decisions and unpopular policies. The obscure death of the King's brother **John of Mar**, linked to detention of some kind at Craigmillar, could have encouraged the idea that Mar's death was the result of a conspiracy. And Preston, if attending the King on the march to Lauder, may have felt himself bound, as was Cochrane, to reinforce the King's wrongheaded wish to carry an ill-founded army south against the superior English force. Certainly, the Prestons were not consulted over what eventually occurred, which was the enforced return of the King from Lauder to Edinburgh Castle, leaving his army to scatter.

Because of the absence of Treasurers' records from 1474 to the end of the reign, any personal ties between the royal family and this Thomas are unknown. There is a single mention of the sum of ninety pounds earned by Thomas Preston just before he died, when he went to Orkney to bring home an English prize ship full of wine. The circumstances of this are not given, and the explanation in GEMINI is supposition. It fits, however, the opening episode of the war with England, when an English fleet under **John, Lord Howard**, came into the estuary of the Forth and, after raiding several harbours, attempted to make a landing at **Blackness**. The English wine-ship may have been forced, by the wind or the enemy, to fly north in an attempt to escape through the Pentland Firth to the west coast, and might have been waylaid in Orkney, or pursued as suggested by Preston's vessel. There is no proof that Oliver Sinclair sailed with Preston, or that the skipper of the wine-ship was Alexander Brown of Leith and *le James*, although he was known for plying between England and Scotland and was soon to forfeit his life as a traitor.

All that is otherwise known of this Thomas Preston depends on the disposition of his goods after Lauder. These were forfeited to the King, presumably as part of the exercise to remove blame from all the valuable participants of the Lauder events. Preston's lands were redistributed. The land and tenants of Middle Pitcairn, which Thomas had held under William Ruthven in the Perthshire **barony** of Ruthven, were given to Ruthven's son on Christmas Day, 1482, in a grant under the **Great Seal** formally witnessed by, among others, **Archibald Whitelaw**, the Earl of Crawford and the Duke of Albany himself, in his last official act before his sudden flight to Dunbar Castle. The grant was made to ensure Ruthven's loyalty: he was to be made a lord later. Ten years after, in the next reign, Thomas Preston's son and heir Archibald maintained his claim to the land in a case witnessed by Sir Simon Preston of that Ilk, Alexander Napier and Henry Preston.

The Prestons, including Sir Simon of Craigmillar, also held land in Cousland, beside **Newbattle** Abbey, on the way to Haddington and the coal mines of Tranent. The overlords of this barony were the Sinclairs, and their other tenants included Cochrane, who also died at Lauder Bridge, and Conrad the royal physician. Here, Archibald Preston seems to have laid claim to Cochrane's land as part of his inheritance. His claim was apparently allowed, but caused endless disputes as to the nature of his obligation towards Henry, Lord Sinclair, William, Lord Ruthven, and other tenants, and their obligations to him. At one point, John of Halkerstone was appointed to speak for him in an attempt of 1499 to clarify one aspect of the case, which failed, and produced a counteraction by all the others. The rights of the land were still in contention in 1501. Like his parents, Archibald possessed dogged qualities.

The descent of this land led the early historian Buchanan to deduce that Cochrane married an unknown daughter of Preston's, and hence the Cochrane inheritance of Cousland would devolve, if his wife died, on her brother Archibald. There is evidence that, instead, the link was Alison Russell, who married first Alan Cochrane (a probable brother of Thomas), and then Thomas Preston, by whom she had her son Archibald, still young when his father was killed. Alison, Archibald's mother and Thomas Preston's widow, spent a victorious year after his death in reclaiming vast sums, from sixty to two hundred pounds, due to her from marriage arrangements or other deals made with her or with her late husband. Or even deals with the late Thomas Cochrane, since one of Alison's debtors, James Bonar, came from a family connected with artillery, gunners and shipping, especially the export of salmon – the essence of Cochrane's likely pursuits. Indeed, as successful partners in business, Cochrane and Preston might well have aroused contention among their rivals and debtors, which may have added an extra vindictiveness to the happenings at Lauder. (D. D.)

Pretz and Paratge: RONDO, 41: In thirteenth-century France, a term which in Languedoc implied excellence, honour and chivalry, in contrast to humble submission to the stern rule of the Church. (D. D.)

Prince aux trente deniers: GEMINI, 23: King **Louis XI*** of France in 1478 used the term when comparing the Prince of Orange ('the prince of thirty pieces of silver') to Judas. After attempting to poison the King (Louis claimed), the Prince defected to the Duchess **Marie of Burgundy**, where he planned to stir up a revolt against France. The novel places it in the context of the equally malignant defection of Sigismond of the Tyrol.*

There was a lot of it about. In the same year, Louis gave towns, castles and seigneuries to the Bastard Anthony, half-brother of the late **Charles, Duke of Burgundy**,* who had elected to join him. Philippe, the equally prudent son of the Bastard, stayed where he was, married Anna **van Borselen** of Veere, and became councillor and chamberlain to **Maximilian** of Austria, seigneur of Beveron, Veere and Flushing; Governor of Artois, and Admiral and Governor of Flanders. In 1480, Jean, son of Louis de Gruuthuse,* crossed in the opposite direction, and did equally well. (D. D.)

Priors and priories: See **Monasteries and nunneries.**

Protocolle: LIONS, 17: In early French **Mystery Plays**, this was the name of the person who carries the book of a play, and directs it. The modern word 'protocol' has a different meaning.

Pucelle: LIONS, 35: Literally, maiden, or virgin. The *Pucelle d'Orleans* was Joan of Arc (see Charles VII*; *Petite Pucelle** of Ireland). Accordingly, the *pucelle* tradition was a tough one.

Puffins: See **Poffins.**

Purves's clocks: QUEENS, III, 1: William Purves was a burgess and resident of **Edinburgh** and a clockmaker by trade. He was responsible for the new clock supplied to St Mary's Church, Dundee, the details of which appear in the Dundee Council Records:

> Ane sufficient and substantious Knok, justly ganging to strike hour and half hour complete and justlie the 24 hours day and night, with warnings to strike at matins, mass and evensong upon the five bells in the steeple, for the sum of seven score and seventeen pounds, ten shillings. The weight to be fourscore stanes or thereby, and gif it happen that the knok weigh mair or less to be decuted accordingly.

Purves's clock remained in service until 1553, when a replacement was provided by a Dundonian clocksmith.

Putoduli: RONDO, 41: A curt Low Countries term for those who hate themselves.

Pynson: QUEENS II, 3: Richard Pynson (d. 1530) was a printer born in Normandy who practised his trade in England from about 1490. He became printer to Henry VIII (King of England 1509–1547) in 1508 and used the first roman type in England. His *The Art and Craft to Know Well to Dye* was a work on mortality; *memento mori* literature was exceedingly popular; another *Art of Dieing* was produced by Caxton* in 1490. Pynson's title is quoted maliciously by one character in the novel to indicate, by a private pun, that he has penetrated another man's disguise of darkened hair. (D. D.)

Q

Quant compaignons s'en vont juer . . . : KINGS, IV, 3: Song:

When comrades set out to gamble
They can say goodbye to supper –
Juicy rabbits, roast capons –
Once their money has gone . . .

Quanto juniores tanto perspicaciores: LIONS, 11: Quotation from Priscian (sixth-century Latin grammarian born in Caesarea) meaning, roughly, 'The younger the smarter'.

Qu'est que c'est?: LIONS, 10: 'What is it?'

Que pasa . . . ?: KINGS, I, 5: 'What's happening?'

Question me, o doorkeeper. I am a sorceror: QUEENS, II, 1: Taken from the Irish folktales of the Tuatha de Danaan (Peoples of the Goddess Danu), strong, beautiful beings who were greater than the mortals they lived amongst. The tale entitled *The Second Battle of Mag Tured* describes how the warrior Lug Samildanach travels to Tara, the seat of the High Kings of Ireland, where the doorkeeper asks what skills he has, 'as no one without an art enters Tara'. Lug answers the doorkeeper saying, 'Question me, I am a wright'. The doorkeeper says they have no need of a wright as they already have one. Lug then replies, 'Question me, O doorkeeper! I am a smith'. Again the doorkeeper replies that he is not needed as they have a smith already, 'Colum Cualleinech of the three new processes'. Lug continues to repeat the phrase, 'Question me, doorkeeper', enumerating his skills as a champion, harper, hero, poet, historian, sorceror, leech (healer), cupbearer and brazier, but each time entry is refused as there are men within Tara with all the skills. Lug persists:

> He said again, 'Ask the King', said he, 'whether he has a single man who possesses all these arts, and if he has I will not enter Tara'.

Then the doorkeeper went into the palace and declared all to the king. 'A warrior has come before the enclosure', said he. 'His name is Samildanach [many gifted], and all the arts which thy household practises he himself possesses, so that he is the man of each and every art'.

Lug Samildanach was allowed into the enclosure of Tara, and allowed to sit in the sage's seat 'for he was a sage in every art'.

Questo gioco è uno sconio!: LIONS, 12: The reference is to a game of Florentine football (***Calcio***) being played on the walls of the castle in **Edinburgh** and about to get out of hand. Put into the annoyed voice of the young Queen of Scotland (**Margaret of Denmark**), the cry translates as 'This game is a *scandal!*' The original cry, '*Questo libro . . .*' referred to a book. (D. D.)

Qui va piano, va lontano: RONDO, 44: Proverb: 'He will go far, who goes cautiously'.

Qumiz: RONDO, 18: Fermented mare's milk, drunk by the Tartars and considered therapeutic for the treatment of anaemia, chronic bronchitis, respiratory and digestive disorders and general exhaustion. It was seen as responsible for the stamina of the Mongol warriors. It did not keep or travel well but had to be drunk in the place where it had been fermented, and was available only in the foaling season. The Tartars also drank the blood of their horses.

Quoi! Ce n'est pas encore beaucoup d'avoir de mon gosier retiré vostre cou?: KINGS, II, 1: 'What! Isn't it enough to have got your neck out of my gullet?'

Quoi? Quoi donc?: LIONS, 19: 'What? What is it?'

R

Rallentando . . . sforzando: GEMINI, 25: Musical terms. The first implies a gradual slowing down; the second asks that a sound be suddenly pushed into emphasis.

Rankin: See **Crawford Family**.

Ravioli: See **Food**.

Raxing yourselves in Edinburgh killing poor folk as they walked their ain causeway: KNIGHTS, I, 1: Despite the close alliance between Scotland and France through the centuries, occasionally incidents would occur which showed the stresses placed (by misunderstandings) on a country garrisoned by foreign troops. A misapprehension led to bloodshed in **Edinburgh** in 1548 when French troops arrived in Scotland to help in the war against England. After a failed attack on **Haddington**, the French retreated to Edinburgh and were quartered in the **Canongate**, outside the city walls. A French soldier delivered a culverin to the Edinburgh gunsmith George Tod to be restocked. Carrying it through the High Street of Edinburgh, Tod was stopped by another French soldier who claimed that the gun was his property. Tod refused to hand over the gun, and an inevitable scuffle took place, joined by locals and the Provost of Edinburgh, James Hamilton of Stanehouse, who beat back the French and arrested two of their number. These men were being escorted back up past St Giles* from the Mercat Cross to the **Tolbooth**, when they were attacked by sixty or so Frenchmen with drawn swords. The citizens of Edinburgh gallantly defended their Provost and drove the French down the High Street to the Netherbow port when fresh reinforcements arrived on the French side, and outnumbered and overpowered the locals. The Provost, his son and five burghers were killed in the struggle. ('Raxing' is Scots for 'stretching'.)

Red Douglases: HN, LC: The line of the Douglas family which inherited the earldom of Angus, descended (as were the **Black Douglases**) from their common ancestor Sir William, Lord of Douglas (d. 1298). Sir George Douglas, Fourth Earl of Angus and father of **Archibald Douglas**, 'Bell the Cat', Fifth

Earl of Angus, assisted James II* when he crushed the Black Douglases in 1455, forcing **James, Ninth Earl of Douglas**, into exile in England.

Regality: UNICORN, 7: See **Barony and regality**.

R'garde!: LIONS, 5: 'Look at *me!*'

Register of the Great Seal: RAM, Overture: See **Greek with the wooden leg, the**.

Remissions: GEMINI, 17: It was in the King's power to commute the death penalty for certain crimes (excluding arson, rape and treason against the King's person), if an appropriate fine were paid to the monarch. **James III**'s* and his father's apparent willingness to do so was praised by their adherents as merciful, but condemned by their critics as acquisitive. A poem called 'The Harp' (pre 1461) criticises James II* for his casual reversal of justice for financial gain:

> Bot of a thing all gud men mervallis mare [more]:
> Quhen gret consale, with thin awyn [own] consent
> Has ordand strayt Justice, na man to spare
> Wqithin schort tym thou changes thin entent
> Sendand a contre letter in continent,
> Chargeand that of that mater mare be nocht:
> Than all the warld murmuris that thou art bocht [bought].

Parliament constantly reminded James III that justice was undermined by such activities, particularly as his tendency to stay in **Edinburgh** rather than promote law and order by touring his kingdom detached him from the judicial process. For a king branded as obsessed by money, the ability to earn income by forgiving criminals was a potentially lucrative one. This has focused attention on the financial aspect of granting remission rather than its universal use as a political tool to retain the loyalty and talents of followers who had overstepped the mark.

Responsorial chants: GEMINI, 9: Such chants alternate between chorus and soloist, whereas antiphonal chants are sung alternately by two halves of a choir.

Rex hic: GEMINI, 39: 'The King is here'. The formula used for noting the presence of the monarch during the hearing of cases at law – satirically employed in this case.

Rhodes: HN: From 1261, when Constantinople was recaptured by the Byzantines, Rhodes belonged to Byzantium but was ineffectively administered by their Genoese admirals. With the fall of Acre in 1291, the Knights of St John* were looking for a new base; in 1306 the Genoese admiral Vignolo sold Rhodes to the Knights (along with Chios* and Leros). About four hundred Knights would have been stationed on Rhodes at the time of **Mehmet II**'s* attack in 1480, plus chaplains and sergeants. As many Knights again were stationed in Europe in the twenty-five Priories of the Order. Employees and foreign settlers as well as the local inhabitants of the Order worked towards strengthening the base of the Knights.

Annual raids on the island throughout the 1470s intensified from 1476, culminating in a full-scale assault in 1480. The Turks blockaded the island and trained their heavy artillery on the fortifications. The Knights were forewarned of the advancing Turkish forces, which arrived on 23 May, failing to take the island by surprise. The Turks concentrated their efforts on attempting to take St Nicholas's tower, which would give them control of both harbours and make the city and its defensive towers vulnerable to bombardment. St Nicholas's tower was at the end of the pier at the northern harbour of Mandraki, and Philip the Good,* Duke of Burgundy had given ten thousand crowns towards its construction, which took place between 1464 and 1467. Burgundy's coat of arms appears on the tower, as does a sculpture of St Nicholas (although the polygonal bulwark dates from after this period). A force of between 10,000 and 15,000 Turks laid siege to the main city, defended by about 3,500 men. Constant bombardment reduced the west side of the fort to rubble, but it was shored up by a timber stockade. The Turkish attackers concentrated their bombardment on the Wall of the Jews in the Jewish Quarter and the grain windmills to the east of the Great Harbour. Mortar attacks plagued the inhabitants day and night, but the Knights remained firm. The Turks failed to take St Nicholas's tower, and the defenders reinforced the western and southern walls against attack as the Turks built a ramp towards the Wall of the Jews. Despite the fact that nearly all the dwelling houses (and the Grand Master's palace) were destroyed by bombardment, the city repelled the Turkish assault on the nearly destroyed wall. The Knights withstood the entire campaign, and in August the Turkish armada left Rhodes.

The damage caused to the town by Mehmet II was compounded by an earthquake in 1481. Pierre D'Aubusson (Grand Master 1476–1503) repaired the island's defences in anticipation of the further attack Mehmet fully intended to mount the following year, but the sudden death of the Sultan and the resultant power struggle between two of his sons gave the Knights the opportunity to repair the damage done by the siege and the earthquake. Djem, the younger son of Mehmet II, attempted to take the throne from his brother, Bayezid II, and turned to the Knights of St John for help. Djem was imprisoned by the Knights, but Bayezid believed that the Knights would support his brother, and so did not attack Rhodes for fear of the Knights' releasing Djem to raise an army against him. Bayezid was prepared to pay the Knights a handsome annuity to keep him imprisoned, which he did until Djem's death in 1495.

Rhodes remained in the hands of the Order until, in June 1522, Suleiman the Magnificent's* Turkish fleet of 300 ships and 100,000 troops attacked the island. It finally fell after a six-month siege, when the treason of one of the Order's own officials gave Suleiman the victory (and left Chios as the only Western-held island in the Levant). The Knights then moved to Malta.

The island of Rhodes remained in Turkish control until 1912, when it was taken by Italy, which restored the Knights' *castello* and in 1947 ceded it to Greece. The Street of the Knights (with the houses for each of the *langues* or 'tongues' of the Order) still exists. Elsewhere on the island is the Petaloudhes Valley, with its running water, towering trees and natural ponds. During the summer, moths fill the valley, attracted by the large number of storax trees (Greek common name *zidhià*). Deciduous and similar in appearance to plane trees, they can grow nearly fifty feet high. The trunk yields a vanilla-scented resin called melistyrax, used today to make pharmaceutical products and perfumes. It is this which brings the millions of small speckled moths to the valley, where they lie dormant by day, silently smothering the barks and foliage of the trees and the bushes, unless roused by a sharp noise or movement (SCORPIONS, 32).

Richard III: See **Gloucester, Richard, Duke of.**

Right godly fresh flower of womanhood: KNIGHTS, III, 13: A reference to the Virgin Mary from a fifteenth-century lyric praising her in chivalric terms:

> Ryht godely, fressh flour of womanhode,
> My lyues Ioy [joy], myn hertes plesance,
> Example of trouth and rote of godelyhode,
> And verayly my lyues sustenance–
> And, with al þe hool, feythful obeisance
> That seruant can thenk or deuyse,
> To you þat haue myn herte in gvuernance,
> Me recemande in all my best wyse.

Rim-Papa: RAM, 20: An insulting name attached to a Westerner's dog by a member of the Greek Orthodox Church. It meant, more or less, 'Latin priest'. Muslims also used the pejorative term 'dog' for Christians. (D. D.)

Rivers, Earl: GEMINI, 16: (*c.* 1442–1483) Sir Anthony Woodville, Second Earl of Rivers and Baron Scales, originally fought on the Lancastrian side in the English Wars of the Roses, but when it became apparent that the cause of Henry VI (King of England 1422–1461, 1470–1471) was going to fail, he transferred his allegiance to **Edward IV.*** When Rivers's sister Elizabeth married Edward in 1464, her brothers also found favour with the King. Rivers, now in the ascendant, formed part of the embassy that made the final arrangements for the marriage of **Margaret of York** to **Charles, Duke of Burgundy.*** When Edward fled to the Low Countries, Rivers shared his exile, returning to England with him in 1471.

Rivers was a great patron of Caxton,* and his translation of the *Dictes and Sayings of the Philosophers* was the first book printed by Caxton in England, in 1477. Jean de Teonville's French version of the original Latin had been borrowed by Rivers to read when he was making his pilgrimage to Compostella in 1473. During his absence his wife had died, and in 1478 he was proposed as the future husband of **Princess Margaret** of Scotland. Although a safe conduct was issued to Margaret to come to England in August of 1479, she did not go south. When Edward IV died in 1483, to be replaced by **Richard, Duke of Gloucester** as Protector, the family lost their pre-eminence. Rivers and his followers attempted to stop Gloucester from reaching young Edward V (1470–1483), but the Earl was imprisoned on charges of treason and executed on 25 June 1483.

Roger, William:* UNICORN: (d. 1482) The mysteries surrounding this English musician who made his career at the court of **James III*** of Scotland become even deeper towards the end of his life. Although he had resigned, in 1476, whatever income he received from his interest in the lands of Traquair, Peeblesshire, it was not until 1479 that Traquair officially passed into the hands of one of the King's half-uncles, James Stewart, **Earl of Buchan.** The length of Roger's tenure as Master of the Hospital of St Leonard's, by Peebles, is not known, but the early payments through Peebles and **Haddington** customs do not persist. In 1473 a man called William Roger was paying rent on a holding in Coupargrange under the Abbot of the monastery of Coupar-Angus, but might not be the same man. Described as a clerk of the King's chapel in the records, the musician may well have continued to hold that position, the chapel in question being at St Andrews. While Roger must have been involved in the King's efforts to divert funds to Stirling from **Coldingham**, with its prospect of an attached school of music, he did not live to see the outcome.

Tradition has it that Roger met his end in 1482, hanged at **Lauder Bridge** by a group of disaffected Scots nobles when the King and his army were passing south to face the English in battle. There is very little contemporary evidence for what happened, and the graphic but conflicting reports that exist depend on histories written a hundred years later. King James had advanced from **Edinburgh**, against advice, to deal with a powerful English invasion led by **Richard, Duke of Gloucester**, the future King Richard III, who was accompanied by the King of Scotland's own rebel brother, **Alexander, Duke of Albany.*** As the Scots army rested at Lauder, the King was seized by some of his own commanders and forced back to captivity in Edinburgh Castle, while some of his entourage died. The army disbanded.

This has been variously explained. Not all the King's subjects wished war against England. Furthermore, they were being invited to tackle a much greater army, yet to be joined by unknown numbers of Albany's friends. There were other issues. A policy of currency debasement was causing distress, and this and other injustices were attributed (said the legend) to the King's reliance on low-born favourites, who surrounded him even at Lauder. (No reference was made to the King of France, whose favourite ambassador was his barber.)

The list of royal favourites varied both in number and probability, as did the list of those who died at Lauder, whether by lynching, or by hasty trial and immediate disposal. On analysis, the probable total of victims comes down to three: **Thomas Cochrane, Thomas Preston** and William Roger. Cochrane, a carrier of guns, was for several reasons a natural target, and Preston, a kinsman, suffered with him. The killing of Roger seems to the modern view pointless, and was perhaps inadvertent. On the other hand, he was loyal to the King, and as a musician would be part of this army, with a function to escort it to war. It is unlikely that, after so long, his English birth was a factor.

The late William Roger is mentioned in a claim by the canon of **Holyrood** in 1490 concerning property in North **Leith**, which was under the jurisdiction of the Abbot of Holyrood.

Roger's appearance, character and nick-name in the novels are all invented, and so are his compositions, none of which has survived even by name. His place of burial is also a guess, but the manner of his death is an attempt to reconstruct what might have actually happened, in tribute to this shadowy figure, whose work seems to have prepared the ground for the splendid **chapel royal**, which blossomed in Stirling, with David **Arnot** as its bishop, and the genius Robert Carver* to compose for it. (D. D.)

Rolls: LIONS, 17: See **Mystery Plays.**

Romans Idylliques: KINGS, I, 4: Tales of love.

Rose of Bremen: LIONS, 8: This was a royal Scottish ship, put out of action in a battle with pirates. The vessel, from Bremen, had been presented to Scotland by the Bremeners in 1445, together with forty lasts of beer, to compensate for damage to Scots ships during the trade war between Bremen and the combined strength of Burgundy and Brittany. (D. D.)

Roslin Castle: GEMINI, 4: The Midlothian residence of the **Sinclair** family, surrounded by high enclosed walls. The castle was built in the mid-fifteenth century, in the valley below the **collegiate church.** The east side of the castle faced a steep drop to the River Esk; the west side was protected by a wall which ran from a tall gatehouse at the north to a tower house at the south. The castle, chapel and the glen take their name from the Celtic *ross* and *lynn*, meaning rocky promontory and waterfall, both visible if one stands at the entrance to the castle and looks down to the glen below. The castle itself is on the left bank of the River Esk and the ridge is spanned by a bridge; there was possibly a drawbridge in earlier times.

Roslin Chapel: GEMINI, 4: The **collegiate church** dedicated to St Matthew at Roslin, or Rosslyn as it is now known, stands six miles south of **Edinburgh**, near to the ruins of **Roslin Castle** and within walking distance of Roslin village. Both the castle and chapel were the building projects of the powerful **Sinclair** family. The founder of the chapel was William Sinclair, Earl of Orkney and Caithness, who succeeded Lord Crichton as Chancellor in 1454 and was also a beneficiary of the fall of the **Boyds** (1469). Building began in 1446; the chapel was referred to as being collegiate in 1456 and papal confirmation of its status was received in 1477. The intention was to create a cruciform building with a tower at its centre (the foundations for the nave as originally planned show the structure exceeding ninety feet in length), but only the choir was completed, in style a small version of the straight ambulatory of thirteenth-century Glasgow Cathedral, but lavishly enhanced with every sculptural embellishment that there is room for, no expense spared. After the Third Earl's death, the roof of the original choir was completed by his son Oliver Sinclair.

The sacristy may predate the chapel, and the sketch drawings on the wall suggest that it was used as the masons' workshop. Compared to the chapel, it is relatively bare of ornamentation. The many carvings of the chapel (including the famous 'Apprentice Pillar') are almost overwhelming; any piece of masonry that could be carved seems to have been carved. Images range from the wholly Christian (Christ, the Apostles, Angels etc.) to the pagan (there are said to be over a hundred representations of 'green men' in the chapel). There is a detailed representation of plant life both local and from further afield: the depictions of maize and aloe cactus predate the 1492 discovery of America (unless they are, as they have been more recently described, simply stylised asiatic aloe and cuckoo spit). Among the lively carvings are angels with bagpipes, lutes and drums and a fine example of the *danse macabre*.

Over the centuries, mythology and legend have overlaid the architectural detail of the chapel. Interest in Rosslyn now concerns its supposed links with the Knights Templar and the later Masonic connections of the Sinclair family.

Ross, Sir John, of Hawkhead: GEMINI: (d. by 1502) Jouster, poet, Keeper of the royal fortress of **Blackness** and loyal to King **James III*** to the end, John Ross, First Baron Ross of Hawkhead, takes his title from land of the same name just two miles from Paisley in Renfrewshire, and belongs probably not to those named after Ross in the north, but to the family Roos that came to Scotland in the twelfth century as vassals of the Morevilles of Normandy, then friends of King David I (ruled 1124–1153). Two centuries later, under King Robert II (ruled 1371–1390), Sir John Ross of Hawkhead acquired by marriage the **barony** of Melville, originally owned in Midlothian by incomers also from Normandy, and Ross–Melville marriages were still taking place a hundred years later.

The young John Ross, laird of Hawkhead, had been a squire of King James II* for two years when he was picked by the famous jouster James Douglas in 1449 (brother of William, Eighth **Earl of Douglas**,) to support him in a challenge bout against the Burgundian chevalier Jacques Lalaing* and his uncle. (The King halted the fight when James Douglas was thrown to the ground.) During the next year or two, John Ross appears as witness to a **Black Douglas** charter at Threave Castle, and between 1450 and 1451 he accompanied William, Eighth Earl of Douglas, and Adam Auchinleck on a visit to Rome. On his return he is next recorded as *miles*, a knight, receiving gifts of land in Renfrew and Ayr in 1451. Earl William's death at the hands of the King, and the general fall of the Black Douglases by 1455, was followed by the King's own death in 1460, leaving a son aged eight to rule as **James III.*** The Dowager Queen Mary of Gueldres and her advisers seemed content to recognise Ross, who in 1468 was given a quantity of land in the barony of Bathgate, which by a historical quirk came within the sheriffdom of Renfrew.

He then, for some reason, fell into temporary disgrace, but was rescued by King **Christian I** of Denmark, father of King James's future bride, who begged James to restore him to favour. He must have done so, for the sheriffdom of **Linlithgow**, which had been briefly his, was restored, and in 1473 he was appointed sheriff for life, while he began to receive once again his annuity as Keeper of Blackness Castle, paid from the income from Bonnington coal and from the rents of Blackness, the port of the Queen's palace, of Linlithgow.

Part of the hiatus may have been due to a decision taken during the minority of the King to dismantle the castle, reusing the stones for a pier, and releasing local merchants from their obligation to contribute to its costs. However much the suggestion was welcomed, no action was taken, and the rights were withdrawn by 1476. Thereafter it was put to use, like the castles of Dumbarton, Berwick-upon-Tweed* and Lochleven, as a prison for high-born offenders: after his assault on the Abbot and convent of Coupar-Angus, the Master of Lindsay, for example, was ordered in 1479 to enter Blackness Castle at his own expense, and remain until freed by the King. The same year, Thomas Jefferson was dispatched there for seizing royal letters.

Scattered records in the 1470s show Sir John Ross as witness or arbitrator in matters to do with Fife and Ayr, once accompanied by **Sir James Shaw of Sauchie**; and by 1478 he had land-holdings in Linlithgow in the same region as **Thomas Spens**, to the east of the ovens of the burgh. From 1477 onwards, he must have worked closely with **Anselm Adorne**,* the Burgundian Keeper of Linlithgow (and also a jouster), especially when war with England broke out, and Blackness became vulnerable to invasion or attack by sea. For this reason, perhaps, Adorne was given charge of the King's tiled (i.e., fire-resistant) house at Blackness which his predecessors, John and Alan Landells, may well have managed as a royal secure house or even a mint. (In 1453, John Landells was the name of a master moneyer.) When the English naval attack came, led by **John, Lord Howard**, in 1480, the only landing was made at Blackness, where the village was burned, and also a great barge lying beside. The castle was unharmed, and no troops penetrated inland towards Linlithgow.

The next attack was overland from the south in 1482, when an English invasion was persuaded to turn back, in return for certain favours to its leaders, to **Alexander, Duke of Albany**,* the King's brother, who had accompanied them, and to the half-uncles of the King. Sir John Ross of Hawkhead was one of those present that November when one of the uncles, **Andrew Stewart**, bound himself to repay the Provost and burgh of **Edinburgh** at some date for the six thousand gold ducats they were raising through foreign sources to pay for Andrew's promotion to the Archbishopric of St Andrews, 'or any other dignity or privilege'. (**William Scheves**, from whom he planned to take the Archbishopric, received it back smartly as soon as the crisis was over.) There is no word of Ross's movements during the invasion: it is to be supposed that, like that of Adorne, his task would be to guard his territory, and protect the access to the Queen (**Margaret of Denmark**) and Princes at Stirling. When the invasion and its aftermath were over, Ross was one of the commissioners for truce talks who visited England in 1484.

Four years later, it was to John Ross of Hawkhead at Blackness Castle that James III brought his supporters before the obscure sequence of events that led to the foray against his own rebels which would end his life. The Queen by then was dead, as was Anselm Adorne, whose nephew **Anselm Sersanders** had succeeded him as Captain of Linlithgow. Like Sersanders, Ross survived the transition when the King's rebel son became **James IV**,* and lived to be created the First Baron Ross of Hawkhead. No longer young, he lost some ground: his custody of Blackness passed to **William Knollys**,* the Preceptor of Torphichen, who was also to succeed to the Keepership of Linlithgow Palace. Ross's land beside Bathgate was given to Edinburgh burgess David Liddell, probably of the same family which had resigned the land to Ross in the previous reign.

Ross still appeared in public, however, acting as conciliator in a dispute between the **Earl of Lennox** and Lord **Semple** (with both of whom he had connections), and defending cases before the **Lords of Council in Civil Causes**. He kept his Linlithgow property, some of which he passed to his son John Ross of Melville, and after he died, the King confirmed to that same son the land near the burgh of Renfrew as given to John Ross of Hawkhead by the King's royal father and grandfather. The elaborate tomb with the effigies of the first Baron and Marjory Muir, his wife, can still be seen in the parish church of Renfrew. The tomb shows nine coats of arms, all supported by angels, and there are two angel musicians at the ends.

Lord Ross's family continued to make distinguished marriages. His son Robert married the daughter of Thomas Melville, whose son John Ross was killed in 1513 at **Flodden.** Lord Ross's daughter (or, less likely, sister) Elizabeth married Thomas Semple of Elliotstoun, sheriff of Renfrew, and had a son John, first Lord Semple, who married a **Colville** of Ochiltree, and died also at Flodden. Lord Ross's heir, John, the future Second Lord Ross of Hawkhead, married Cristiane Edmonston. Ninian, to be Third Lord Ross of Hawkhead, married into the prodigious family of **James Stewart**, **Lord Darnley**, First Earl of Lennox. Lastly, Lord Ross's daughter Egidia (Gelis) married James, the son of Sir John Auchinleck and nephew of Adam, secretary to William, Earl of Douglas, who had once travelled with Sir John Ross to Rome. The marriage required dispensation, for James's mother Elizabeth was a Melville, and it lasted only until about 1492, when James died, predeceasing his father. By 1501, the Auchinlecks were courting the **Red Douglases**, as Gelis's daughter Elizabeth married Sir William, brother of the poet-Bishop Gavin Douglas and son of **Archibald Douglas**, Fifth Earl of Angus. Two of Archibald's sons, including William, Elizabeth's husband, died at Flodden.

About 1505 the Scots writer William Dunbar (*c.* 1460–1520) composed a poem, 'Lament for the Makaris'. This gave a list of dead Scottish poets, not all of them known to us now. One was James Affleck (an abbreviation of Auchinleck), who was associated with ballads and tragedy. One was **Robert Henryson**. And one was Sir John the Ross, appointed as Dunbar's aide in the witty flyting (scurrilous battle) on paper between Dunbar and another poet, Walter Kennedy (*c.* 1460–1508).

> That scorpion fell hes done infek [infected]
> Maister Johne Clerk, and James Afflek,
> Fra balat making and tragidie;
> *Timor mortis conturbat me* [Fear of death disquiets me].
>
> In Dunfermelyne he hes done roune
> With Maister Robert Henrisoun;
> Schir Johne the Ros enbrast [embraced] hes he;
> *Timor mortis conturbat me.*

Nothing remains that can be attributed to 'John the Ross', and Auchinleck is only tentatively attached to two works, 'The Quare of Jelusy' and 'Lancelot of the Laik'. There is no direct proof of either poet's identity, but Roderick Lyall has painstakingly shown that they might well be Sir John Ross of Hawkhead and his son-in-law, Egidia's husband.

It is appealing to think so. (D. D.)

Rosslyn: see **Roslin.**

Rublev, Andrei: RONDO, 34: (*c.* 1360–1430) Renowned icon painter who adapted the Byzantine style of icon painting, having seen Greek icons brought to Russia from Constantinople in 1422. In Moscow in 1405 he worked with the Greek Theophanes on the old Cathedral of the Annunciation, and in 1425 with Daniel Chorni on the monastery of the Trinity and St Sergius (the Troitsa). There he completed a painting showing the Holy Trinity as three angels seated at Abraham's table, each representing one soul thrice reincarnated, and re-creating the grace and serenity of early Christian catacomb paintings. Rublev was also responsible for the fresco on the west wall of the Cathedral of the Dormition, which the Bolognese architect **Rudolfo Fioravanti** would begin to rebuild nearly fifty years later.

Rue de la Cerisaye: LC: This cul-de-sac in Paris, which plays a part in the plot of *Lymond Chronicles*, was once (but no longer) one of the loveliest streets in Paris, situated on the right bank of the Seine, from which it was divided by the religious buildings of the Célestins. The rue St Catherine and the rue St Pol ran parallel to it, and it was near the Château St-Antoine, now the Bastille. The fictitious house occupied part of the site of an elaborate and beautiful retreat built by the **Bourbons**, and later used as a love-nest by several French Kings. This contained porticoes, galleries and lodgings built around a vast courtyard, and its gardens stretched inland as far as the rue St-Antoine. (D. D.)

S

St Catherine: See **Sinai, Mount**

St Cuthbert's sandals: LIONS, 27: A reference to a legendary medical case at the monastery of Lindisfarne, where the learned physicians failed to help a youth with ascending paralysis. Nevertheless, when the boy asked for the sandals of St Cuthbert to be placed on his feet, he was instantly cured. Modern commentators (Bernard Bachrach and Jerome Kroll of the University of Minnesota) point out that the case is readily ascribable to hysteria, but might be an example of Guillain-Barré Syndrome, a neurological illness probably of viral etiology, with a time-limited course of ascending paralysis and a gradual spontaneous recovery. (D. D.)

St Giles, armbone of: See **Preston family.**

St John's town of Perth: See **Carthusians.**

St Mary's Priory: See **North Berwick.**

St Michael: GEMINI, 53: The church of **Linlithgow** was established when David I, King of Scotland 1124–1153, founded the burgh and the church, the latter being granted to St Andrews Cathedral Priory in a charter of 1138. In 1301, when Edward I (King of England 1272–1307) was garrisoning the manor house that became Linlithgow Palace, he also used the church as a garrison storehouse. After the 1424 fire, parts of the church were rebuilt at the same time as the palace. Three generations of the Frenssh (or France) family of masons worked on the church in the late fifteenth and sixteenth centuries, but it must have been mostly completed by the time that John French was buried in its north aisle in 1489. John French's **tenement** in the Kirkgate, Linlithgow, passed to **Euphemia Adorne** on his death. This may or may not be the John Francis/French who was one of the Conservators of Scots Privileges after **Thomas Swift**. The church was the last resting place of **Anselm Adorne**.*

St Salvator: RISING, 1: Bishop Kennedy's* fine five-hundred-ton barge, used for ceremonial occasions, and by Scottish merchants. In March 1473, the barge sank off Bamburgh and, following the shipwreck, the cargo was seized by James Ker, an Englishman. One of the passengers, the Abbot of Inchcolm Priory, was taken hostage and released only on the payment of eighty pounds. The Scots merchants who had lost their cargo petitioned for over a year for compensation, until a Scottish embassy was sent to England to discuss restitution. Fortunately for the merchants involved, their commonplace case was not the main item on the agenda. The ambassadors were primarily there to discuss the peace treaty between Scotland and England and the marriage proposal of Princess **Cecilia.** Raised under such circumstances, terms were speedily agreed on both items, and in February 1475 the Scots merchants who lost cargoes were offered five hundred merks (marks) in compensation, received on their behalf by Bishop **Thomas Spens.**

Salep: See **Coffee.**

Sang School: KINGS, I, 2: See **Collegiate churches.**

Sanok, Gregory of: See **Gregory of Sanok**

Sasine, to take: GEMINI, 8: In Scots law, the act of taking possession of feudal property, often represented symbolically by a handful of earth, or a piece of rope, or a stone.

***Sauve qui peut!*:** RONDO, 43: 'Save yourselves!'

Sawest not you my oxen . . . : KINGS, I, 5: From the anonymous poem 'My Twelve Oxen':

> I haue XII oxen þat be fayre & brown,
> & they go a-grasynge down by the town.
> with hay, with howe, with hay!
> Sawyste þow not myn oxen, þou litill prety boy.
>
> I haue XII oxen, & they be ffayre & whight,
> & they go a-grasyng down by the dyke.
> with hay, with howe, with hay!
> Sawste not þou myn oxen, þou lytyll prety boy.
>
> I have XII oxen, & they be ffaryre & blak,
> & they go a-grasyng down by the lak.
> with hay, with howe, with hay!
> Sawyste not þou myn oxen, þou lytyll prety boy.

I haue XII oxen, & they be fayre and rede,
& they go a-grasyng down by þe mede.
with hay, with howe, with hay!
Sawiste not þou my oxen, þou litill prety boy.

Scalp-mail: GEMINI, 9: See **Oysters.**

Scheves, William: UNICORN: (*c.* 1439–1497) Bibliophile, scholar, physician and eventually the first Primate in Scotland, William Scheves is another royal servant whose life has been obscured by the poor records of the reign of **James III**,* and by the bias of sixteenth-century writers which led to his being regarded as an obscure charlatan, dabbling in necromancy, and over-promoted by a doting king.

Men of his surname came from Shivas in north-east Scotland, which by 1500 was in the hands of the Gordons. In 1393 John Shivas, scholar, went to Oxford. The name had spread before that to Berwick-upon-Tweed* and to **Soutra.** The father of Archbishop Scheves was probably John Scheves, Clerk Register in the minority of James II,* and probably the same Master John Scheves, doctor in decrees, who in 1429 went to hear English Border complaints twice at Hadden Stank, along with such colleagues as Walter Haliburton of Dirleton, William Crichton, Master Thomas Roulle and Sir John Forrester, Baron of Liberton.

William Scheves attended St Andrews University, and was a determinant at the same time as **Patrick Graham**, whom he was to succeed as Archbishop of St Andrews in 1476. After obtaining his Arts degree in 1454, he became by 1460 a resident master at the university, and his name appeared intermittently as a faculty member for a further ten years, although he went on, after 1465, to enrol as a postgraduate student of the University of Louvain,* Flanders, where he is said to have studied under the physician and astrologer John Spierinck, who was three times its rector.

Louvain had been founded by Pope Martin V (1417–1431) and Duke John IV of Brabant, whose wife Jacqueline of Holland (1401–1436) was to marry Franck **van Borselen** in 1432. The van Borselens were linked by marriage to the Scots royal family, and hence to Bishop Kennedy,* who also studied at Louvain from 1430, and who was the uncle of Patrick Graham.

The family Monypenny, the Tullochs of Caithness and Orkney and Stephen Angus, an early Scots Conservator in Flanders, all attended, as did the physician and astrologer John of Vesalia, who was invited to read mathematics in 1431 (see **Dr Andreas**). Other students included, after 1457, the future King **Louis XI*** of France. Charles, son of Wolfaert van Borselen and a nephew of James II, died there, aged thirteen, in 1464. William Scheves was therefore educated in a tradition that was royal as well as academically sound.

Scheves studied theology, medicine and mathematics, as well as astronomy and possibly astrology. He was certainly interested in this last: a work on astrology would be dedicated to him in 1491 by Jaspar Laet de Borchloen, who published a further work containing predictions for Scotland. Scheves himself emerged from his training as a dedicated collector of books. By 1471 he was in royal service in Scotland, and was paid twenty pounds annually as a royal physician for a form of personal service which went far beyond the routine importing of drugs from Bruges* for the King, and green ginger for the ailing royal servants. Familiar with Low Country trade, and following the practice of Rob Scheves of the Wardrobe, who was no doubt a kinsman, William ordered cloth for the King, paid for his shirts to be sewn, bought him velvet and looked after the silver for the royal harness. In return, he received oats for his horses, cloth for his gown and velvet for his doublet, whether as physician or house-steward.

After 1474, that income was enhanced as he was enabled to move from civil employment to the hierarchy of the Church, being made Archdeacon of St Andrews that year, and also, for four years, Provost of Crichton **collegiate church;** he also became Master of the Hospital at Brechin. From 1475 he began to serve as Auditor of the **Exchequer.** The following year the Pope appointed him co-adjutor of the see of St Andrews, on account of Patrick Graham's excommunication and insanity, and Scheves had the charge of placing Graham in his last place of restraint at Lochleven, where the Keeper, Robert Douglas, was well known to him. Scheves now also served on the Parliamentary committee set up to continue the business of Parliament (including the marriage of the **Princess Margaret**, for which he helped to collect money), and from then until the mid-eighties became a consistently hard-working member of the King's inner council. Twice, acting as notary for Scotland, he departed to England to arrange Princess **Cecilia**'s dowry payments, and for much of the time he worked personally with the King: from 1476 onwards, important royal letters are often signed by them both. In 1479, Scheves was consecrated Archbishop of St Andrews, and appointed Chancellor of the University. He was then about forty years old.

While still Archdeacon, Scheves possessed a **tenement** in the Briggate of Berwick-upon-Tweed,* next to the houses of Lauder of the Bass, custodian of Berwick Castle, and of Alexander Inglis, who was Clerk Register, as Scheves's father seems to have been. Among his other neighbours were **Walter Bertram** and **Thomas Yare**, the officials of Berwick. It seems likely that Scheves's considerable imports for both the King and the Queen passed through this frontier port, in Scottish hands since 1461, and long familiar to men of his name. Even after Berwick was lost, Scheves kept an interest in shipping. His books were imported by Haliburton.

In 1480, James III confirmed the privileges held William Scheves, 'our dear and intimate counsellor', and by the see of St Andrews. At the same time he granted Fife lands to St Salvator's College for Masses to be said for the soul of **John of Mar.** The death of John and the initial rebellion of the King's other brother, **Alexander, Duke of Albany,*** had by then both taken place. In

March 1482, with an English war imminent, the Archbishop sat in the Parliament that met to lay plans. Together with **Andrew Stewart, Lord Avandale, Colin Campbell,** Earl of Argyll, and **Archibald Whitelaw**, he continued with routine government until June, just before Albany brought an English army into the country.

After the crisis at **Lauder Bridge**, when Albany still challenged the throne, Scheves and his colleagues, who seem to have formed, *in absentia*, an unofficial council of regency, met the Duke and the invading **Richard, Duke of Gloucester.** The result was an accommodation which allowed Gloucester to leave with certain concessions, including the permanent loss to Scotland of the town of Berwick-upon-Tweed. Albany stayed, in hopes of something near sovereign power, and Scheves was one of those who accompanied him to Stirling Castle to discuss the future with the Queen, **Margaret of Denmark**, and the young Prince, her son. During the following months Whitelaw remained, but Scheves and his other colleagues withdrew while the administration was adjusted to Albany's liking. During this period Scheves was forced to resign his Archbishopric, which seemed destined for **Andrew Stewart**, the King's youngest uncle, but was able to resume it after Albany fled to his castle of Dunbar. Scheves reappeared in royal charters in January 1483, the month of **Anselm Adorne**'s* death, and he attended the first post-Albany Parliament in March.

The crisis with Albany ended, but the last years of the King's life were less agreeable for the Archbishop. He had some family about him. Rob Scheves, who was illegitimate, died about 1483; but the Archbishop's brother Henry in Fife had a son John of his own, and was procurator, and a steward of regality to William Scheves. He visited France in 1484 as part of the courtly exchanges between James and Charles VIII, the new King of France (1483–1498). Pope Sixtus died that same year, opening the way to possible concessions from a new Pontiff. But as the inner council aged or dispersed and the King's temper changed, there appeared rivals to Scheves, such as Dr John Ireland, a Franco-Scottish doctor of theology who became Archdeacon of St Andrews, and Robert Blackadder, who would eventually wrest the bishopric of Glasgow from under his province.

The latter attended the Curia with Scheves in the winter of 1486–1487, when the Archbishop led the embassy making obedience to the new Pope, Innocent VIII (1484–1492). In Scotland, King James had just received the papal accolade of the Golden Rose, brought by the Bishop of Imola. The Scottish mission had several objectives: to obtain increased control for the King over episcopal promotions; to erect St Andrews into a primatial church; to set afoot the canonisation of Queen Margaret, who had just died; and to confirm the validity of the donation of Orkney and Shetland, made when she married James III (see **Orkney dowry**). The Pope gave immediate approval to all but the canonisation of Margaret, towards which Scheves and Blackadder were to investigate her life, and report to the consistory. The death of the King perhaps ended the effort.

Scheves was again absent from Scotland in the early part of 1488 and so, deliberately or not, was not involved in the events that led up to the battle of Sauchieburn and the death of James III. Blackadder, who had joined the rebels and the future James IV in 1488, was even better placed to gain from the new reign. Scheves attended the young King's first Parliament, but was not appointed one of the Lords of the Articles. Nor was he made, in 1489, one of the inner councillors of the King. When, that same year, the castle of Dumbarton was involved in an insurrection, the Archbishop was summoned to help the King's cause. Afterwards, his stock improved: he became a Lord of the Articles and continued to act as one of the **Lords Auditor of Causes and Complaints.** He was summoned to Rome, where he went to congratulate the new Pope, Alexander VI, upon his election in 1492, and to hear his plans for a crusade. It was perhaps during this trip that Scheves had a portrait medal struck in the Netherlands. The result, now in the National Museum of Scotland, was probably by Flemish artist Quentin Matsys (*c.* 1465–1530), and shows in profile a heavy, quizzical, intelligent face. He also arranged to have sent from Bruges the stone for his tomb in St Andrews Cathedral, to be done to a design of his own.

William Scheves remained Archbishop and Primate until 1497, when he died, leaving his own mark on history as the first Primate of Scotland. He also left a remarkable library, volumes of which still exist, annotated in his own bold hand. One of them embodies his obsessive interest in Scots history, and especially the work of the chronicler John of Fordun (d. after 1384), in whose memory Scheves provided a silver casket, enriched with gold and precious stones for the relics of St Palladius, the fifth-century apostle of Ireland who died at the place called Fordun. The text of Fordun's work is still extant, as copied in Edinburgh for Archbishop Scheves by his clerk Magnus McCulloch, a canon of the church of Fearn in Tain, Rossshire.

To succeed William Scheves as Archbishop, the King appointed his own younger brother James, Marquis of Ormond, Duke of Ross, then about twenty, or five years under canonical age. Until he reached his majority, his revenues would conveniently come to the Crown. The plan may have been known to Archbishop Scheves: from the age of fifteen, the boy prince appeared frequently in his company at the council table or in Parliament. Haliburton, who imported for Scheves, was the youth's business agent, perhaps supplying him with part of his lavish wardrobe: the French black for his night-robe; the gowns of scarlet lined with damask and satin; the red and green satin doublets; the black holland shirts; the shoes, thirty pairs at a time. And also perhaps handling his salmon, one of the assets of Ross.

The training was wasted, for the young man did not survive beyond 1504, and never became an Archbishop. The King's choice for next primate was Alexander, then aged eleven, his own illegitimate son by Marian Boyd.

Through this excellent arrangement, theoretically the King had the use of his son's dues for some fifteen years, during which time Alexander, legitimised, was set to be given the best theological education in the world.

It was a practical system, and it might have succeeded. The boy was sent to study in Pavia, where he was shortly joined by an eight-year-old brother, also illegitimate. He had the good fortune to be taught, in Pavia and in Siena, by Erasmus (1466–1536), who left a delightful description of the youth at his studies. The occasion for the panegyric was however tragic, for the bearer of all the sage's brilliant teaching was to perish in Scotland, killed at the side of his father at **Flodden.** He was clever. He was brave. He could not read a word, Erasmus says with affection, unless his nose touched the book. He had his tomb, too, made in Bruges. (D. D.)

Schlaffdruncke: RONDO, 9; PAWN, 1: See **Baltic drinking.**

Seals: See **Coquet seals; Great Seal; *Lion sans vilainie*.**

Semple family: HN: A name known in the west of Scotland since the thirteenth century, Semple is supposed to derive from one of the many French places named St Pol, such as St Pol de Léon in Brittany. About 1317 Robert Semple witnessed a donation by Walter the High Steward to the monks of Paisley. After Robert Semple married Marjorie Bruce, the family made their seat, as Stewart vassals, at Elliotstoun Tower by Lochwinnoch, Renfrewshire, until they moved in about 1493 to Castle Semple nearby. By the turn of the century they also had a large residence (a 'house and inn') in central **Edinburgh**, in the Friars' Wynd leading from the High Street down to the Cowgate and **Blackfriars** monastery. Another branch of the family was given land at Strathaven by John, Earl of Carrick, confirmed by Robert II (King of Scotland 1371–1390) in 1373.

Under the Stewarts, the main branch of the Semple family were hereditary bailies of the **regality** of Paisley and also sheriffs of Renfrewshire, which then included an offshoot in Ratho and Bathgate not far from **Linlithgow.** As seneschals and bailiffs under the High Stewards of Scotland, their arms were marked, as those of stewards tended to be (cf. Stewart and **Anselm Adorne***) by a *cheveron chequé.* John Semple, the fourth Lord of Elliotstoun, was knighted in 1430 and died in 1440. His successor, Sir Robert Semple of Elliotstoun, was followed, after a long life, by Sir William, who was in possession of Elliotstoun by 1474. William's son Thomas Semple married Elizabeth **Ross of Hawkhead** (of the family of the poet-jouster of **Blackness**) and fought on the King's side in the ultimate battle of Sauchieburn, where Semple, as well as **James III**,* lost his life. It was a pattern to be repeated, tragically, at the battle of **Flodden** against the English in 1513, where Thomas's only son John, Steward of Scotland, was killed. He did however leave two sons, one of them by Margaret, daughter of the hereditary seneschal **Sir Robert Colville** of

Ochiltree. From another branch, Henry Semple in 1489 obtained **remission** for the burning of Dumbarton during the rebellions against the early policies of **James IV**,* who had obtained the throne on opposing his father.

William, second Lord Semple, married the daughter of Arnot of Arnot (of the family of David **Arnot**) and also Marian Montgomery, granddaughter of **Archibald Douglas**, Earl of Argyll. William died in 1548 and was followed by Robert, third Lord Semple, whose sister Mary married Sir John Stirling of Keir.

Supremely loyal to the Stewart kings, the Semples were staunch guardians on other soils also. The name Semple in various forms appears from 1449 among the Scottish Archers* of Charles VII* of France, serving under Patrick Flockhart and then Thomas Halliday. A muster roll cites one such Semple as seigneur de la Cour de Colombières, but does not say whether the land was obtained through marriage or as a reward for service. Semples continue, serving under various commanders, through the rest of the fifteenth century and into the next.

Their connection with the leading characters of the novels is fictitious. It is purely by chance that Beltrees, a place picked for an imaginary tower, should prove to be the home of three generations of light-hearted rhymers descended from the family Semple.

The last, perpetrator of the unquoted epic 'The Blythsome Bridal', was a Francis Semple of Beltrees (*c.* 1605–*c.* 1680). Describing his armorial attributes, heraldry tells us that he 'carried as in Semple, but with a gilliflower for his difference'. (D. D.)

Sersanders, Anselm: RISING: (*fl.* until at least 1499) Nephew to **Anselm Adorne**,* Anselm Sersanders is known to posterity for the flood of business transactions which filled the latter part of his life, and made him one of the best-recorded merchant/dealers in Scotland. His work also suggests an early training in law, but it is not known why he left his parents' home in Ghent to join his fortunes to those of Anselm Adorne, or when or how he lost his politically active father or Adorne's sister, his mother. The character and fate of his mother, as depicted in the novels, is fictitious. There is no official record of brothers or sisters, but records in Scotland for later years suggest he had a sister, Katelijne Sersanders (See **Berecrofts**) and perhaps a daughter of the same name. He did appear to have a cousin, who may be the Jean Sersanders who lost his life in the troubles in Ghent in 1477.

Certainly, the families of Sersanders and of Adorne had traditional connections with the rulers of Flanders which may not always have commended them to the popular movements of the time. A Jean Sersanders, perhaps the same, was married to a descendant of a natural daughter of Louis de Nevers, Count of Flanders (*c.* 1304–1346). By 1270, the Adorne side of the family had settled in Bruges,* and when Anselm Sersanders's great-grandfather Pieter Adorne was in Paris with Janne Metteneye in 1386, buying gifts for the Joyous

Entry of Charles VI (King of France 1380–1422), he honoured the tomb of the same Count of Nevers. Pieter in the course of his life became Receiver-General of Flanders and Artois, and Hanse officials and others attended council meetings in his house, which was also famous for its feasts and lavish hospitality with music.

As did the Adornes, the Sersanders branch patronised artists. One of these, perhaps a great-aunt of Anselm, married into the well-known Ghent family of Borlut. In 1432 the artist Jan van Eyck* painted a Ghent altar-piece for the childless couple, Elizabeth Borlut and Joos Vijd of Ghent. (Anselm Adorne also bought the works of this artist.)

It is not known whether or not Anselm Sersanders accompanied his uncle on his visit to Scotland in 1468, and the account in UNICORN of his activities at this time is fictitious. In fact, the first trace of Anselm Sersanders in Scotland is in Perth Guildry Book three years later, which has an ambivalent entry for Anselm Adournes de Corthuy, Kt., burgess and guildsman, and 'Anselm his son'. This was the period of Adorne's 1471 visit to Scotland with his wife, when bringing back the King's sister **Princess Mary.** The following year, while still in Scotland, he was appointed Conservator of Scots Privileges in Bruges. Adorne did possess a son, Anselm Adorne, who had been a Knight of **Rhodes** from the age of seventeen, and seems to have died young. The records show no Knight Hospitaller of St John of that name living in Scotland, but Perth had several Ghent connections which would account for the interest of Sersanders, not least that of the **Carthusian** monastery. The novels predicate that, when Adorne returned to Bruges with his wife, and then proceeded to Poland, his nephew stayed to handle his business in Scotland. There is no evidence either way, and the expedition to **Iceland** is fictitious, as is the presence of Katelijne Sersanders, who was not as yet on record in Scotland.

After the death of **Charles, Duke of Burgundy,*** at Nancy, Adorne left Bruges for Scotland, and had arrived by July 1477. Sersanders may have been there already, but there is no trace of his name until the autumn of 1479, when Sallykin Adorne is pressed to pay John Brown ten pounds for a house he bought from him. (The name, discussed under **Anselm**, is one of several contorted versions, including Anselm Cessanders and Franskin Fersanders, in the contemporary records.) There is still no word of Katelijne Sersanders, although Brown is a name associated with the Crawford family, into which she married.

There next occurs a solid phalanx of seventeen claims at law for outstanding debts, successfully placed before the **Lords of Council in Civil Causes** by 'Franskin Fersanders', acting as procurator for one named foreign client. All the cases are dated 1480, the year in which Scotland and England went to war, and may represent business procedure as normally practised, whereby long-term debts were sustained as a form of **usury**, until put at risk by the hazards of war.

The first five cases were all heard on a single day, when the Council included the Bishops of Glasgow and Dunkeld and **John Stewart, Lord Darnley**, and the money owed ranged from one or two pounds to over twenty-five pounds Flemish money, a considerable sum. Most debtors had **Linlithgow** connections, one being a burgess and several having appeared in charters witnessed by Anselm Sersanders. One was William 'Fransch', possibly a kinsman of the John France, architect and burgess of Linlithgow whose tenement was to be owned one day by **Euphemia Adorne.** One had the Linlithgow-associated name of Amisfield, recalling Janet Amisfield, married to Archibald Crawford, son of William Crawford and father of Richard Crawford, who had died by 1498. One, Robert Doby, recalled the late William Doby, who paid rents from Peebles to the Hospital of St Leonard, of which **William Roger*** the musician was Master in 1469. And one, John Muir, may have been the man who, with William Crawford, acted as customars of Linlithgow that year.

The following month, the Acts of the Lords of Council dealt with a further twelve debtors, who were all directed to pay 'Franskin Fersanders' what was due to the same foreign client. Seven of the debtors were burgesses of Perth, and one of them, Alex Justice, may well have been the same Zander Gustis who in 1475 got into a fight in **Danzig** with a fellow Scot, William Watson. Two debtors were from St Andrews: John Ramsay and David Ireland, both of significant surnames. David Ireland was beholden to the sum of £2 18s. 6d. for a barrel of salmon.

The next flurry of legal activity occurs, understandably, on the heels of Anselm Adorne's murder in 1483, when the kingdom was still under threat from England and Albany. Adorne had confided his natural daughter 'Efemie' (Euphemia) to his nephew's care, and charged Sersanders, along with another who might be **Dr Andreas**, to see to the child, to whom he had willed his property in **Edinburgh** and elsewhere in Scotland.

The part, if any, played by Sersanders in the events surrounding the killing of Anselm Adorne is not known, and – discreet as his uncle – he seems to have taken no sides in the struggle between the King and his brother, or in the happenings at **Lauder Bridge.** Whatever he felt about the death of Adorne, Sersanders must have harboured no personal bitterness towards **James III**,* for he remained in Scotland, attending to his business and serving the King as his uncle had done. Evidence seems to show that he made proper provision for the child, and somewhere between the summer of 1483 and 1484, when he was given a gift of royal land, Sersanders was installed in his uncle's post as Captain of Linlithgow Palace, close to where Euphemia had property – an indication that James, also, wished to encourage Sersanders to stay.

Again, the court cases of March 1483, numbering under a dozen, indicate the business interests of 'Anselm Sersanders, poorter of Bruges' (i.e., merchant of special standing), who appeared again as procurator for the same family, appointed to collect outstanding debts, many of them for the delivery of salmon to Flemish customers. One of these, John of Ayton, was a burgess of **Haddington**, and might be the son of Mark Ayton, master in 1440 of the ship

Katherine of **Leith.** This legal action was less successful: none of those summoned appeared, and letters of distress on all their lands and goods had to be issued.

There follows a gap of nearly three years in the official records of that particular court, effectively obliterating any subsequent cases dealing with Sersanders, or indeed the effects of the death of his uncle. The last case on visible record involved a quarrel between two important members of the Edmonston family, one of great importance in Leith, and Anselm Sersanders, supported by Andreas Lepeldok (possibly Dr Andreas) and one John McCailzean, known because of his connection with Adorne's natural daughter. The reason for the dispute is unknown, except that it threatened actual bodily harm. The interval in the records was interrupted once, in late 1484, when Anselm Sersanders was found to have taken premature occupation of a piece of Linlithgow parkland, and was required to pay some back rent.

As the King's reign closed, there are glimpses of Sersanders going about his business. In 1486, he was confirmed in his royal Linlithgow land of Kincavil, 'so long as he remained in the King's service'. About the same time, he was involved in a herring deal at Damme (outside Bruges) with two Englishmen and Nicholas de May, of a well-known Bruges family. In 1487 'Anselm Sersanders, Captain of the palace of Linlithgow' was one of the witnesses to a royal charter involving the church of Linlithgow, along with other familiar names, such as that of John France.

Immediately after the battle of Sauchieburn in 1488, in which the King was killed, changes were made in the name of his young son, now **James IV**,* who had opposed him. Anselm Sersanders was relieved of his post as Captain of Linlithgow Palace, but also received in compensation (through the new Controller, **William Knollys***) the huge sum of £115 for arrears in service pay, and lost rents.

From 1488 until his last mention in Scottish archives, in 1498, Anselm Sersanders continued to lead, by all accounts, his customary life as a dealer and trader. Acting for Euphemia Adorne, he was presumably responsible for the repossession of her **tenements** in Linlithgow about the time of his departure from the palace. In October of that year, he failed to attend a summons by John McCailzie (or McCailzean) and his wife Janet Brice in his capacity as Euphemia's guardian. Nothing more is heard of the case, which might have had to do with his change of lodging, or temporary loss of income. The accounts for the burgh of Linlithgow for the year 1491–1492 were rendered at Edinburgh by Anselm Sersanders, as one of Linlithgow's four bailies. In 1494 he went to law to obtain £6 10s. Scots owing him from Sir Alexander Cunningham of Polmaise (who had a holding in Linlithgow) for the purchase of two ells of satin cramoisy. In 1496 he was one of those who witnessed a Linlithgow charter.

By 1499, Efemie Adorne was dead, and her cousin Anselm Sersanders may have decided, duty done, to return to Flanders, or he may have chosen to remain, and die in Scotland. There are no records to show either way. His last appearance, on 10 July 1498, once more before the Lords of Council in Civil Causes, successfully compelled Laurence Bertram, dwelling in Leith, to pay him five pounds of the usual money of Flanders owing to one Martine Pwys, spouse of the late Martin Pwys, porter of Lille, for whom Sersanders was procurator.

Thus, fittingly, is the final glimpse also of the mystery which runs all through these records.

Anselm Sersanders does not seem to have married. The **Katelijne Sersanders**, presumed his sister, who appears in Scotland, married to Robert Crawford of Berecrofts, and with substantial property in Edinburgh and Leith, is not involved in any litigation or property records which mention Anselm Sersanders, nor do they ever witness charters together in the records that have survived. They may have shared daily activities, interests, even houses, but nothing has come down.

What has emerged instead is the mysterious figure of the Flemish individual for whom Anselm Sersanders acted in Scotland. His name appears once, unconnected with Sersanders, when in 1479, John of Redpath is ordered by the Lords of Council to pay a four-pound debt in money of Flanders to Martin Pwllis, porter of Rijsel (Lille, the old capital of French Flanders, west of Ghent). Next, the man appears the following year, with Anselm Sersanders as his procurator, in the batch of seventeen cases settled in June 1480, all to be paid in Flemish money. There, the creditor is described as M'tin Pins. In the next batch, in July, he is called Martin Pwis or Pwyss.

Three years later, there is a change. The salmon debts of 1483 are payable to Anselm Sersanders, poorter of Bruges, as procurator for Martyna, spouse of the late Martin Pius, *and Katrine, the said Anselm's daughter.* Then there is nothing until the final entry for 1498, which affirms that he represents Martine Pwys, spouse of the late Martin Pwys, poorter of Lille.

It is always possible, but not likely, that Katrine is the Katelijne Sersanders who married Robert Crawford of Berecrofts. The lack of corroboration, the dates, the odd repetition of Martin and Martina for the parents, the chaotic surname do not inspire trust. First, who was Martin? It was known as a surname in Scotland. In the late 1440s a George Martin was famous in Scotland and Flanders as factor for Bishop Kennedy* of St Andrews, and a friend of Jacques Metteneye and hence of Anselm Adorne. By 1490, Archbishop **William Scheves** of St Andrews had a chancellor called Andrew Martin, perhaps the Andreas Martin who went to university with John Ireland, Henry Ramsay and Peter Monypenny, all surnames known to Sersanders. In 1507 a Hugh Martyn, merchant of **Veere**, was licensed to trade with Aberdeen, possibly the same as Hugo Martyn, Controller at Linlithgow in 1491, when Sersanders was bailie. Used as a Christian name, but later, there was a Martin of Tournai in 1495 buying white wool at Bergen ap Zoom for George Towris, using the *Gilbert of Edmonston.* Three years later, the same Martin was buying wood by shipload from William Todrik, husband of **Princess Margaret**'s daughter.

Lastly, and perhaps most attractively, there was a Marjorie Martin married to Henry, brother of the **Thomas Swift** who became Conservator of Scots Privileges within a matter of days after Adorne's death. Henry Swift died by 1471, and Elizabeth Swift their daughter married an Edmonston, by whom she had one son, John, but died herself before 1475. The Sersanders quarrel with Edmonston was possibly therefore a family dispute.

If Marjorie married a second time after 1471, and settled in Lille, she would be young enough to have a daughter to Sersanders, or to foster his daughter. In 1455, when Berwick-upon-Tweed* was still in English possession, the lands of Todrik were in the Scottish King's hands because of the death of a William Purwas. This was a member of an old Berwickshire family, vassals of the Earls of March, and several served the King in the 1470s, buying and tailoring cloth among other things. In 1500 Thomas Purves and the Swift family lived in the same wynd in Edinburgh.

The fate of Martyna and Katrine is unknown. But to confuse the issue still further, it should be noted that in the year 1540, rent for a house and land at **Torphichen** in Scotland was paid to the Knight of St John by a Marion Pwyss. The surname may represent Powys, the name of land owned by the Abbey of Culross. The connection with the Knights does, however, have echoes of a 1493 dispute with the Knights of St John over Haddington land held by Marion Martin, heir to the late John Martin. The novels propose a romance between Martin's wife and Sersanders in Berwick. It is one of a hundred possibilities. (D. D.)

Sersanders, Katelijne: See **Berecrofts.**

Sforzando: See ***Rallentando . . . Sforzando.***

Shamanism: RONDO 19; CASTLE II, 9: Practised by Mongol tribes of Russia, such as the Buryats and the Kalmyks amongst others, it is a primitive religion in which the priest or shaman communes directly with the spirits, often in a trancelike state. Shamanism was also widely practised in Hungary, surviving for centuries after Christianisation as an underground faith. The healing aspect of shamanism involves chanting, relying as it does on a belief in sonic therapy: both the nervous system and the organs of the body respond to sounds, which can therefore lower blood pressure and stop bleeding. Shamen would use the *buben*, a tambourine, to produce the rhythmic sounds. The quality of the sound itself was important and credited as responsible for the physiological improvements in the patient's condition.

Shaw, Sir James, of Sauchie: GEMINI: (*fl.* until at least 1508) The surname seems to derive from a place-name in the western lowlands of Scotland. In

1294 a charter by James Seneschal (Steward/Stewart) of Scotland to the church of Paisley was witnessed by a William of Shaw, so Norman ancestry is very possible.

Sir James Shaw, whose control of Stirling Castle was to influence the life of **Margaret of Denmark**, Queen of Scotland, as well as her husband **James III*** and their sons, was the grandson of a Sir James Shaw of Greenock who made his fortune by marrying Mary of Annand, co-heiress of Sauchie, land which lay in the west, as part of the old **barony** of Luss, **Colquhoun** and the Garioch. The other half of the estate went to Mary's sister, who married into the rumbustious family of Browns of Colston (Linlithgow), **Leith**, Ratho and Berwick-upon-Tweed,* one of whose seafaring members was to do business with **Anselm Sersanders**, and to be executed eventually for treason. Before 1440, Sauchie Tower, near Alva in Clackmannan, was built by the elder Sir James.

While the Shaws of Sauchie went on to operate mainly in the Stirling, Angus and Fife areas of central and east Scotland, they had a presence still in the south-west. In 1449 John of Shaw, royal squire, was witness to a Haliburton charter concerning the barony of Tranent. In 1459 James II's* Queen, Mary of Gueldres, acquired some land in Kirkcudbright from John Shaw of Alyth, in exchange for some land of hers in Balerno, near **Edinburgh.** Thirty years later Quintin Shaw, son of John, exchanged land with John, **Earl of Lennox.** Covering often the same areas, the families of Shaw, **Crawford** and **Semple** frequently appear in the same charters, either as allies or over some wrangle. In 1468 the wife of David Crichton of Cranston-Riddell was a Shaw, and in 1477 Elizabeth Shaw was the wife of John, heir to the Stewarts of Dalswinton, Dumfries.

The immediate predecessors of Queen Margaret's future Stirling officer come into view in 1467, when James Shaw of Sauchie witnessed a **Newbattle** charter concerning lead-mining rights in the lordship of Crawford-Lindsay. The following year, James witnessed a charter for George, Lord Haliburton, whose son married Elena Shaw. In 1471, John Shaw was a member of the embassy that visited Denmark following Parliament's ratification of the adjustments to the dowry of the new Queen. Between 1471 and 1473 a number of charters were witnessed by John Shaw of Sauchie. These included, in 1471 (with Michael Balfour), a royal charter concerning the land of Mary of Gueldres, and also the charter by which Andrew Charteris obtained the barony of **Cuthilgurdy.** In 1472, John Shaw witnessed the presentation to **Anselm Adorne*** of the lands of Teling and Polgavy forfeited by Robert Lord **Boyd.***

John Shaw ceased to appear as an official witness after June 1473, when the future King **James IV*** was born, and Sir James Shaw of Sauchie appears within the next year as Governor of the Prince and Keeper of Stirling Castle. In 1474, Sir James was one of the envoys who signed the contract in Edinburgh for the marriage of his young charge to the English King's daughter

Cecilia. He was further entrusted that year with pursuing, with others, compensation for the loss of Bishop Kennedy's* barge the ***St Salvator.***

He was also prominent in local Scottish affairs. In that same year, Sir James was appointed by the sheriff of Forfar to deal with the escheat and **remission** of the culprits in the drama at Forfar sheriff court that ended in the killing of **Thomas Preston**, a kinsman of the **Preston family** of **Craigmillar**, Edinburgh.

Outside their positions as members of Queen Margaret's household, James Shaw and **Robert Colville**, her original steward, worked together as their descendants were to do. In 1475 they were successfully sued by a John Crawford – the first of several clashes between Ayrshire Crawfords and Shaws – for withholding more than seventeen pounds due to a Walter Galbraith. In 1483 the Abbot of Lindores took them both to court for damages owing to the nonfulfilment of an indenture by the mason John Merlion.

As guardian of young James and Keeper of Stirling Castle, Shaw continued to keep closely in touch with both the King and the Queen and their growing young family. Their second son, James, Marquis of Ormond, was born in March 1476, and presently put into the care of the future Lord High Treasurer George Shaw, Abbot of Paisley, and Sir James's younger brother. In 1478 the Queen was given official custody of the heir. The last son, John, was born two years later (1479/1480), during the outbreak of the English war, and from 1480 onwards, the Queen appeared to keep to the security of Stirling with all her sons.

The safety of Stirling became of paramount importance in 1482, when **Richard, Duke of Gloucester**, brought an English army north to Scotland, accompanied by the King's renegade brother, **Alexander, Duke of Albany.*** If any defensive building took place at that time at the castle, the names of Merlion and **Thomas Cochrane**, who lost his life during the invasion, would seem likely to be involved. Certainly, Shaw did not leave his post at Stirling, although he must have been party to the planning by the high officers of state which resulted in the Duke of Albany abandoning Gloucester, who turned back, and coming to Stirling to interview the Queen and young James.

There followed the face-saving exercise to release the King from Edinburgh Castle, where he had been taken by his own people to prevent a disastrous defeat in the field. Presumably it was Shaw, with the Queen, who had to prepare the nine-year-old prince for the encounter with an uncle who may have seemed gallant and adventurous to a small child, but was now a potential usurper. Better than most, Shaw must have been able to gauge and influence the mood of the Queen and her son, and convey the situation to the high officers.

The threat from Albany had vanished by the end of 1484, and the deaths of King **Edward IV*** and then of Richard III of England brought the reign of Henry VII (1485–1509) and the prospect of settled peace between Scotland and England. Within Scotland, the Queen had died in 1486, leaving behind her a turmoil of cross-loyalties which perhaps explained an attempt by the King, the following year, to propose her canonisation. This was followed by an answering rumour from dissidents that the Queen had been poisoned with the consent of the King. All this reflected a growing resentment, especially among the **Home** family, against some aspects of the King's rule. At the same time, the royal advisers were aging, and less able to deal with an increasingly difficult man.

When the King made his young second son Duke of Ross in January 1488, overlooking the elder, it may have been a routine decision, or it may have indicated that he did not trust his heir, nearly fifteen, and indoctrinated by his late mother's men, with that territory. A few days later, in February 1488, with Shaw's sanction, the heir to the throne detached himself from his father's method of ruling and joined the band of the disaffected, which would eventually include **Colin Campbell**, Earl of Argyll, the Master of **Darnley** and the Bishops of Glasgow and Dunkeld.

Where the Prince stayed, and whether he was accompanied by Shaw or other members of the Queen's household, is unclear. One suspect account claims that Shaw was persuaded to hold Stirling Castle for the Prince against the King; another has the young Prince operate at first from **Linlithgow** Palace, in which case he had either the support or the neutrality of its Captain, Anselm Sersanders, who lost his captaincy but not the new King's favour later that year. At **Blackness**, the port of Linlithgow, the captain of the castle, **Sir John Ross of Hawkhead**, was to remain loyal to **James III.***

When, presently, the Prince and some of his supporters did elect to stay at Stirling Castle, the household there is not named. The late Queen's constable **Malcolm McClery** and Chancellor **Andrew Stewart, Lord Avandale**, had reached or were about to reach the end of their lives. Robert Colville the steward, if present, would not live long after the death of James III, but would be well rewarded in the new reign. The support of Sir James Shaw would be recognised also.

That there was, suddenly, a new reign was evidently an accident. From the beginning, the intention was that James III should abdicate, not lose his life. When negotiations failed, and a small, disorganised battle occurred, it still seemed likely that the King would survive. In fact, only two men, apart from the King, are known to have died.

In 1489 King James IV appointed James Shaw of Sauchie and John Shaw, his son, the custody of Stirling Castle for life, 'as the late Queen had it'. The mother of Sir James's sons was a Home, which might or might not have predisposed him against the late King. As soon as the King came to the throne, James also honoured the Abbot of Paisley, Shaw's brother. Paisley became a burgh of barony, 'as a mark of the King's singular love for the abbot, who had educated and nourished his brother James, Duke of Ross'. (John, Lord **Semple**, held the office of bailary of Paisley.) In 1488 the King also exonerated

John Shaw, the Keeper of the castle of Dunbar, which had early been taken by the rebels, and he received some forfeited land.

Despite his lifetime's appointment, Sir James Shaw gave up his captaincy of Stirling in 1490 to the King's chancellor Alexander Home, perhaps kin to Shaw's wife, and Home also became custodian of James IV's youngest brother, John, Earl of Mar. The accounts for that year also solemnly mark the return of a one-pound loan made by Sir James to the King, and there are entries for riding clothes and other garments presented to James Shaw, among other King's men. Shaw is still described as the King's familiar in 1507, when he is ceded Perthshire lands by James, Lord Haliburton, in a charter witnessed by Alexander Jardine of Applegarth. In 1508, Sir James and his wife and Alexander, one of his sons, received tack of a mill and other property at Tillicoultry.

This is the last direct mention of James Shaw. Sauchie was a divided inheritance, part of which lay with the family of Colquhoun of Luss, and was held by 1480 by Elizabeth **Dunbar**, lady of Luss, the widow of Sir John Colquhoun. In 1482 her son Humphrey paid fifty pounds to redeem Sauchie lands after Sir James Shaw's son, John Shaw of Alyth, had misguidedly carried off and married Janet, the daughter of Matthew Forrester, Provost of Stirling. It did not prevent him from becoming, in 1483, the procurator for Queen Margaret, whose son was in his father's care, or from being treated responsibly in time to come.

Indeed, men of Sir James Shaw's family and his name continued to proliferate, especially in the *familia* of the royal household. George Shaw, Abbot of Paisley, held the post of Lord High Treasurer until 1497, following **William Knollys*** and **Henry Arnot.** The next Abbot of Paisley was George's nephew, Robert Shaw. A Master John Shaw was vicar of Rothesay church, and, in 1525, Robert Shaw was Bishop of Moray.

Others maintained the tradition of personal service. In the last years of the century Master Alexander Shaw, possibly the son of Sir James, quartered the country from Aberdeen to Dumbarton, collecting and carrying money, buying riding gowns, gloves and other clothes for the King and performing or initiating such useful tasks as fitting a cupboard in the Treasure-house. He or another Alexander Shaw 'of the **Chapel Royal**' served as procurator to Abbot Robert Shaw.

In 1504, Richard Shaw was one of the King's sheriffs. His kinship to the main line is not clear, nor is that of the future sheriff Sir Harry Shaw, who appears all through the 1490s receiving money on behalf of the King for similar services, and in 1494 was paid for six bonnets and four taffeta tippets provided 'against Yule'. In the same year the King presented garments to Harry Shaw, James Shaw and Shaw, Master Cook, as well as to Robert Colville and others. In 1497, the King gave Harry land in Strathearn, and he received more Perthshire land with the King's gratitude in 1502. He was dead by 1511, when his land of Kilbride went to William Edmonstone of Duntreath, probably the son of Janet Shaw, and nephew of Harry.

Elena Shaw, who had married Archibald, son and heir of George, Lord Haliburton, later proceeded, as the widowed Lady of Dirleton, to take as second husband 'Lang Patrick of Pollart', the kenspeckle Patrick Home of Polwarth who had lands in the Borders, Edinburgh and Menteith, and was Keeper of the Castle of Banff. She owned a **tenement** in the Canongate, Edinburgh. Home died before 1506, and the regression of the Banff land fell to Alexander Innes, who had married the sister of **Euphemia Dunbar**, a cousin of Sir John Colquhoun's wife, who held part of Sauchie. The arrangement also involved Robert Colville of Hilton, Cleish.

Thomas Shaw, whose name surfaces after his death in a Linlithgow charter witnessed in 1487 by Anselm Sersanders, must have been the kinsman, if not the father, of one of the most spectacular Shaws of the new reign. Thomas Shaw appears in 1496 as a witness with Anselm Sersanders in another Linlithgow charter. In 1497, Thomas Shaw, Master Cook, is given the ward of the lands and rents of any heirs of the late John **Fleming** of Boghall: the next year Thomas has land formerly belonging to Andrew Crawford in Bonnington, where Thomas is shown in 1505 as having coal-bearing property supplying twenty chalders of coal for the palace of Linlithgow. Two years later, for service to the King, he is given more land and the benefit of the marriage of the late owner's daughter.

Thomas seems likely to have been the brother of Sir Harry and Janet, the wife of Archibald Edmonstone. Master Cook, as with 'carpenter', 'usher' and 'mason', was a job description whose limits today are unknown. But whatever his place in the Shaw family, he seems to have continued the tradition of personal commitment which – with perhaps far slighter cause – led to the maligning of other friends of an earlier King. (D. D.)

She who loves peril, into peril shall she fall: GEMINI, 16: Based on Proverbs 22:5 ('*Qui caret laqueis securus est*', or 'He that is aware of the snares shall be secure') and Ecclesiastes 10:8 ('*Qui amat periculum incidet in illud*', or 'He that loveth danger shall perish in it'). A thirteenth-century Guide for Anchoresses amalgamates the two to admonish its feminine readers in the form quoted in the novel. (D. D.)

Shiten shepherd and the clene shepe: CHECKMATE, V, 9: From the General Prologue to *The Canterbury Tales* by Geoffrey Chaucer (*c.* 1343–1400), describing the Clerk and relating how a parson should set a good example to his flock:

> And shame it is, if a prest take keep,
> A shiten shepherde and a clene sheep.
> Wel oughte a preest ensample [example] for to yive [give],
> By his clennesse, how that his sheep sholde lyve.

Shore, Jane: CHECKMATE, IV, 4: **Edward IV**'s lover, brought low and disgraced by his brother Richard III (**Duke of Gloucester**) and forced to do penance in the street, dressed only in her kirtle and with a taper in her hand, of which Sir Thomas More* said in his *History of Richard III*:

> In which she went in countenance and pace demure so womanly; and albeit she was out of all array save her kyrtle only, yet went she so fair and lovely, namelye, while the wondering of the people caste a comly rud in her chekes (of which she before had most misse) that her great shame wan her much praise among those that were more amorous of her body, then curious of her soule. And many good folke also, that hated her living, and glad wer to se sin corrected, yet pittied thei more her penance than rejoiced therin, when thei considred that the protector procured it more of a corrupt intent, than any virtuous affection.

Sic peril lies in paramours: KINGS, I, 5: From the poem attributed to Mersar from *c.* 1500, 'Allace! so Sobir is the Micht' which warns women against the less than honourable conduct of a potential lover:

Allace! So sobir [steady] is the micht [strength]
Of wemen for to mak debait [endure]
In contrair menis [men's] subtell slicht [sleight],
Quhilk [which] ar fulfillit with dissait [deceit];
With tressone so intoxicait
Ar mennis mouthis at all houris,
Quhome [whom] in to trest [trust] no woman wait [knows].
Sic perrell [peril] lyis in paramouris [lovers].

Sum sweris that he luvis so weill
That he will de [die] without remeid,
Bot gife that he hir freindschip feill
That garris [compels] him sic languor leid;
And thocht he haif no doubt of speid [success],
Yit will he sich [sigh] and schaw grit schouris [show great paroxysms of pain],
As he wald sterfe [die] in to that steid [place].
Sic perrell lyis in paramouris.

Athis [oaths] to sweir and giftis to hecht [promise]
Moir than he hes thretty [thirty] fold,
And for hir honour for to fecht [fight]
Quhill that his blude be cumin cold;
Bot fra scho [but for her] to his will is yold [has yielded],
Adew, fairweill thir somer flouris;

All grows [turns into] in glas that semit gold.
Sic perrell lyis in paramouris.

Than turnis he his saill annone
And passis to ane uthir port.
Thocht scho be nevir so wobegone,
Hir cairis cauld ar his confort.
Heirfoir I pray in termys schort,
Chryst keip thir birdis bricht in bowris
Fra [from] fals luvaris and thair resort.
Sic perrell lyis in paramouris.

Siege-machine: RONDO, 22: Not everything worked, even in the most expensive of battle camps. **Charles, Duke of Burgundy**,* besieging Neuss (July 1474–June 1475), was charmed by a Castilian nobleman into accepting a novel plan for a siege-engine made like a crane. Twenty feet long, it could hold three hundred men, and was supposed to roll up to the town and take its walls by assault, using a sixty-foot ladder as a bridge. At the same time, the carpenters of Campobasso and Galeotto, the Duke's Italian mercenaries, set to work on another idea: a splendid castle on twenty-four wheels, called a 'chat'. Unfortunately, when the time came to put them both into action, the wheels of the chat broke, and the crane slowly sank into the sand. At this point, it came to the Duke that the siege was about to last a very long time. (D. D.)

***Sifr*:** UNICORN, 37: Cypher, signifying zero, or nothing. In a number system based on a place-value notation, 'empty spaces' naturally occur. The West is indebted to the Arabs for the symbol to write in this empty place; they themselves obtained it from India and passed it on to European mathematicians towards the end of the Middle Ages. Hindu literature gives evidence that the zero may have been known before the birth of Christ, but no inscription has been found with such a symbol before the ninth century. The zero has also been found in Babylonian cuneiform.

SIMPSON, David: SCORPIONS (fl. 1463) Nothing is known of his life before he entered the Royal Guard of Scottish Archers of Charles VII* of France in 1459, where his name often appears as David de Salmeton. There he found **Andrew Wodman**, who had already served for three years, and Roland Cressant, who had joined the previous year. The captain of the guard was Patrick Flockart. In 1463 or early 1464, Wodman was dismissed for killing Cressant, and Simpson was also put out 'because he had become leprous'. No details are known. As for Simpson, the diagnostic skills for leprosy were not generally great, and the word could be attached to any unsightly condition of the skin, however temporary. One could imagine that in this band of magnificent Archers, on daily duty next to the King, such a state might not be tolerated. It is assumed that 'leprosy' was a convenient excuse for a man to leave the service without reproach.

Simpson's later career is matter of conjecture, and nothing is known of his appearance, his nature or any relationships he might have had. His travels as described in the novels are invented, as is the company he appeared to serve, but he might well have become involved in trade, as did many of the surname of Simpson in Scotland. Several of the families of the period belonged to Aberdeen, where there was a David Symson in 1448, and a David or Davy Symson in 1462, at a time when the Archer of the same name was still in France. In 1475, a Master Andrew Simpson, vicar, represented Church interests in an Aberdeen case where the laymen included the Prince **John of Mar, William Scheves**, Adam of Crawford and another Simpson, this time David.

In Fife, a Thomas Simpson was Receiver in 1463, and in 1470, a man of the same name was Constable of Falkland Palace. A son of Thomas Simpson, William Simpson of Lathrisk, Fife, was shield-bearer to King **James III**,* and had a wife Elizabeth who bore the famous Edinburgh merchant name of **Cant.** A Canongate **tenement** belonging to William Simpson *pelliparius* (skinner) was mentioned in 1467 together with William's daughter Margaret Simpson.

William Simpson was also the name of a Scottish trader in **Danzig** in the 1470s. And in 1482, William Simpson was a member of the group of men who garrisoned **Edinburgh** Castle following the return of the King from **Lauder Bridge. John Stewart, Lord Darnley**, had many links with soldiers serving in France.

Between 1448 and 1467 there were several Simpsons – Alexander, Andrew, James, John and Patrick – on the rolls of St Andrews University. Others who chose a career in the royal guard of France included John Simpson, who served in 1460 with Patrick Haliburton and George Ramsay and Thomas Spens, and Peter Simpson (or Pierre Semessan) who was one of the company of a hundred Scots Archers who fought in the Italian wars of the 1490s.

In a population so small, it is a fair guess that some of these families were connected with David Simpson the archer, but the lines of descent can only be guessed at. (D. D.)

Sinai, Mount:* UNICORN: The romantic connection between **Edinburgh** and the monastery of St Catherine's,* Mount Sinai, had begun in the fourteenth century, with the import of holy oil for the **Sinclair family.** It reappeared in 1471 when **Anselm Adorne*** brought King **James III*** his son's account of their pilgrimage there. In 1520, fifty years after that, a monk from Mount Sinai arrived one June day in Edinburgh to recruit well-wishers and raise funds for the monastery, dangerously placed as it was west of Cairo, and surrounded by non-Christian countries. The shrine at Sinai dated back to the sixth century and contained (and contains) the tomb of the legendary St Catherine of Alexandria (d. *c.* early fourth century), honoured in St Giles,*

Edinburgh, by an altar which had been there in the time of King David II (ruled 1329–1371).

Confusingly, in 1461 another Catherine (*c.* 1347–1380), daughter of a Sienese dyer, had been canonised. Though revered and politically influential in her time, Catherine of Sienna was not latterly prominent until William Caxton's* *Lyf of Saynt Katherin of Senis* was published after his death in 1491 by Wynken de Worde (d. 1535). Edinburgh took note. A chapel to St John the Baptist had been founded about 1511 by a **Holyrood** canon, John **Crawford** on land partly feued from a burgess, John **Cant**, on the Burgh Muir outside the city walls. Soon after, a Priory of Dominican nuns dedicated to St Catherine of Sienna was established by the widowed Lady Seton in 1517 on land acquired from John Crawford, which included the use of his chapel. It drew funds from the Napiers at Merchiston. During its short orthodox life, which ended at the Reformation, the Priory was known as the convent of Sciennes, or Sheens (KNIGHTS, III, 17). Its nuns appeared to patronise and revere the holy well, and to pray at the shrine in St Giles. Documentation, equally liberal, displays a splendid Edinburgh insouciance over which Catherine was which, and whether it mattered.

Into this stepped Neophitus, commissary and monk from Mount Sinai, authorised to collect alms and recruit the devout (men and women) to a Confraternity of St Catherine, sanctioned by Innocent VIII (Pope 1484–1492). The fee of one-third of a golden sovereign (and other donations) would care for the fabric of the monastery of the glorious virgin martyr, and sustain the Abbot and monks, and the pilgrims who thronged there. Spiritual privileges and indulgences were assured, including the right to establish an altar to St Catherine and an alms box in any suitable church.

How many Scots were enrolled is not known, but particulars do exist for one such, filled into a pre-printed form which Neophitus had clearly brought with him from Rome. The name of the devotee was Richard Maitland, and the form he signed in Edinburgh still exists, dated 26 June 1520. The Anglo-Norman family of Maitland was well known, having settled in Berwickshire in the twelfth century, their original keep being Thirlestane. By the fifteenth century they were connected with the **Cistercian** Priory in **Haddington**, and there was a Sir Richard Maitland, Lord Lethington, born at Lethington near Haddington in 1496, son of Sir William Maitland (killed at **Flodden**) and Martha, daughter of George, Lord Seton.

Sir Richard Maitland, who lived to be ninety, was a scholarly lawyer and writer, educated at St Andrews and Paris, who served King James V* and was Lord Privy Seal after his death to the Queen Regent Mary de Guise* and to her daughter Mary Queen of Scots,* although by Queen Mary's return to Scotland (on which he wrote a poem) Sir Richard was blind. He preferred all his life to stay uncommitted in political matters. His dispositions were not always successful, and for a time the family lost their possessions of Lethington, although he died high in the favour of Queen Mary's son, James VI and

I (ruled 1567–1625). He is best remembered for his treasured collection of early Scots poems, some of them his own. Of his seven children, William, the eldest (1528–1573), was the famous Secretary of State who served Mary of Guise and her daughter, and won the approbation of Elizabeth I, Queen of England 1558–1603, who called him 'the flower of wits of Scotland'. William married the daughter of Malcolm, third Lord **Fleming.**

Sir Richard's second son, John (born *c.* 1545) became Lord Chancellor of Scotland and First Baron Maitland of Thirlestane. By his marriage to Jean, daughter and heiress to James, fourth Lord Fleming, John had a son of his own name, who became the second Lord Maitland and First Earl of Lauderdale. The names of Richard Maitland of Lethington and a John Maitland appear in a charter of 1533 favourable to the convent of St Catherine of Sienna by Edinburgh, and involving the hospice of St Laurence by Haddington. The family of Seton, Sir Richard's mother, were in closest association with that convent. If, as seems likely, those who supported one St Catherine also tended to support the other, this distinguished statesman and poet may well be the Richard who subscribed to the Confraternity so far away.

In 1507, when Sir Richard Maitland of Lethington was eleven, King **James IV*** conferred on Henry **van Borselen** of Veere the lordship of Lauderdale, in gratitude for his good offices over Scots trade. The previous King had done the same for the late Paul, Henry van Borselen's father. One might conjecture that the Maitland familiarity with Mount Sinai owed something to traders and consuls such as these and their predecessor Adorne, who were members of confraternities like the **Dry Tree** in Bruges, and attended and even financed annual masses for St Catherine of Alexandria and Sinai. (D. D.)

SINCLAIR family: UNICORN: Originally from St Clair in Normandy, the Sinclairs are described by their admiring eighteenth-century biographer Father Hay as being descended from the family of William the Conqueror. Fair of face and yellow of hair, the first to cross from French shores was known, he says, as *'The Seemly Sinclair'*.

Historians now believe the family to have been vassals of the Morevilles, the Anglo-Norman family which founded Dryburgh Abbey and held great possessions in Scotland under King David I (ruled 1124–1153). During that reign, the Sinclairs are found in the **barony** of **Roslin**, outside **Edinburgh.** Henry de St Clair received the lands of Herdmanston in East Lothian from Hugh de Moreville the Constable, who died in 1189. To this, the Sinclairs added lands in Stirlingshire at Gartane, later known as Garden-Sinclair, and at Cousland, beside **Newbattle** Abbey, which they had supported from earliest times, along with the hospice of **Soutra.**

Under King Alexander II (ruled 1214–1249), Cousland became a heritable barony, and Sir William Sinclair followed a Mowbray as sheriff of Edinburgh, **Linlithgow** and **Haddington.** By 1279 Sir William was guardian both of the heir to the throne and Edinburgh Castle, and received the Baxter lands of

Inverleith, within modern Edinburgh, which had once belonged to Ailif, baker to King William the Lion (ruled 1165–1214). Sir William sat in Parliament, and took part in various royal missions. Captured when the castle of Dunbar surrendered during the English wars, he was imprisoned in England, but later escaped, to die in the first year of the fourteenth century.

His second son William became a fighting Bishop of Dunkeld, repulsing the English in Fife in 1317. Although admired by Robert the Bruce (ruled 1306–1329), the Bishop in 1332 was to crown Edward Balliol, the rival to Bruce's son David II (ruled 1329–1371) and to attend Balliol's first Parliament.

The Bishop's elder brother Henry Sinclair swore fealty to the English King, but later joined his father Sir William against him, and fought for Bruce at the battle of Bannockburn in 1314. Henry's son, Sir William Sinclair of Roslin, was one of those who set off to carry Bruce's heart, in a little coffer of gold, to the Holy Land after his death in 1329. Waylaid by Saracens, he was killed in Andalusia, Spain, in 1330.

Prior to that, he had acquired the Temple lands of Gorton, by Preston. He was also the hero of another gallant, pious story. Saved from a royal hunting predicament by a prayer to St Catherine, Sir William built a chapel to the saint just outside Edinburgh, and sent a priest overseas to her tomb for the famous oil dispensed from her bones. Returning, the priest spilled the oil close to Liberton, a few miles from the centre of Edinburgh, causing a spring to emerge, upon which floated (and floats) a perpetual coat of black oil, now named St Catherine's oil. Although later linked with another St Catherine, the older legend suggests that this oil came from St Catherine's monastery at the foot of **Mount Sinai.** The spring was known by 1505 as the Oly (or Oyly) Well, and deserved its reputation for wonderful properties, being rich in crude paraffin, an excellent treatment for ills of the skin.

Sir William had married a daughter of Malise of Strathearn, as a result of which, after some trouble, William's eldest son Henry in 1379 secured an inheritance of part of Caithness and all of Malise's earldom of Orkney, which was held under the Norwegian Crown. The earldom of Caithness itself had been resigned to the Scots Crown in 1375. Hence Henry Sinclair became Prince of Orkney, and in 1384 Robert Sinclair became the first of a wholly Scottish succession of Bishops of Orkney.

Henry was the seafaring Earl. According to different accounts, he encountered the Venetian captain Niccolò **Zeno** shipwrecked on the Faroe Islands, and appointed Zeno to lead his fleet with his brother Antonio. After conquests in the Faroes and Shetland and the death of Niccolò, Antonio sailed with Sinclair far to the west to a place which might have been Greenland, perhaps on the way to Nova Scotia. There Sinclair remained, exploring the coast for some time after Zeno's return, after which the fleet returned before winter.

Henry married a Haliburton of Dirleton and was followed by another adventurous Henry, Second Earl of Orkney and Admiral of Scotland. It was while in this Henry's care that the young Prince, soon to be James I (ruled

1406–1437) was captured by an armed English vessel when sailing for safety to France (in the Danzig ship *Maryenknyght*) in 1406. James was kept in England for eighteen years, but Henry was freed in 1407, to return several times for the purpose of trade or official missions. He married Egidia or Giles Douglas, the tall and formidable daughter of a **Black Douglas** and the Princess Egidia, a daughter of King Robert II (ruled 1371–1390). As a result Henry Sinclair acquired the lordship of Nithsdale and the wardenship of the three Border Marches between Whithorn and Berwick-upon-Tweed.* He also fought abroad, spending some months in the service of John the Fearless, Duke of Burgundy 1404–1419, with whom Scotland had strong trading links.

His only son William (called 'the Prodigious') became the great Third Earl of Orkney, the first Earl of Caithness, and Chancellor of Scotland (after Lord **Crichton**); his long life did not end until 1480. He visited Scandinavia to claim his hereditary earldom of Orkney, held for him during his minority by Bishop Tulloch. This was finally confirmed in 1434, although he had to travel once more in 1446 to swear allegiance to the then Danish King, and promise to hold for him the castle of Kirkwall which his Sinclair forebears had built. The Earl acquired from the Bishop of Orkney the patronage in Kirkwall of St Duthac's chapel, a saint already esteemed in Haddington, Edinburgh, Whithorn and Tain. Before that, as High Admiral of Scotland, he had commanded the fleet which took the Princess Margaret to her marriage with the Dauphin of France (see **James II's sisters**).

Now created Lord Sinclair, William began the building of his new **collegiate church** of **Roslin Chapel**, and extended his castle, erected on the riverside rocks directly below. He also lavished care on a library, which his grandson Henry was to continue, and commissioned translations from Sir Gilbert Haye, a former chamberlain to Charles VII* of France. Working at Roslin before 1456, Haye translated into Scots two chivalric French treatises, one on the *Law of Armys* and the other, also translated by Caxton,* on the *Ordre of Knycht-hede*. Haye later worked for Lord Erskine.

Aside from his cultural pursuits, William was active in helping King James II* to crush the power of the Black Douglases. The Earl himself supervised the carriage of 'the great bombard' from Edinburgh Castle to Threave. Then, in 1455, he exchanged his Nithsdale lands for the recovered earldom of Caithness, and the following year, Roslin was erected into a burgh of barony, with a Cross, and Saturday markets, and annual fairs on the day of Saints Simon and Jude. At the same time, there were signs that the period of favour was ceasing. The King was then renewing his private plans to wrench from Norway the mastery of Orkney and Shetland, the Northern Isles – a scheme which Sinclair, as hereditary Earl and a vassal of Norway, must have resisted. He lost the Chancellorship and lapsed from public life until the King's sudden death in 1460, from a burst gun, at the age of twenty-nine. This did not prevent William from keeping extreme state in his personal life, both at

Roslin and at the great house he occupied in Blackfriars' Wynd, one of the steep streets which still run down to the Cowgate in Edinburgh.

William Sinclair was one of the Regents for the new eight-year-old King, **James III**,* but no longer Chancellor under the Queen Dowager, Mary of Gueldres,* who was at this time spending six hundred pounds on the building of a new fortified castle at Ravenscraig, on the south coast of Fife. As the King's advisers renewed the campaign to recover the Northern Isles, William excused himself twice from leaving Scotland to swear allegiance for Orkney to **Christian IV**, King of Denmark, Norway and Sweden. In turn, Christian complained to James III, not for the first time, about rampaging incidents involving the Earl and his son and officials owing allegiance to Norway.

At home, Lord Sinclair also abstained from supporting the ambitions of the **Boyd** family, and was probably less than gratified by the marriage of Thomas Boyd to the **Princess Mary**, whom one of his own daughters, Elizabeth (Betha in the novels) was helping to train at Stirling in 1462, at the end of the Queen Dowager's life. William Sinclair appeared once or twice more in Parliament, and was named for a mission in England. His part in public affairs, however, altered permanently when he was asked to give up the earldom of Orkney to the King, who (with Boyd support) had solved the Northern Isles problem by offering to marry the daughter of Christian, to whom Scotland already owed money over the Western Isles (see **Orkney dowry**).

By the new agreement of 1468, this debt was remitted, and Christian instead pledged his lands and rights in Orkney to Scotland for fifty thousand florins as part of his daughter's total dowry of sixty thousand florins of the Rhine. The following year, having failed to raise all the missing ten thousand, Christian pledged Shetland to make up the rest. This covered only the rights of the Norwegian Crown. Nevertheless, very soon afterwards, James III personally took over the lucrative earldom of Orkney and castle of Kirkwall, which stayed with the Crown, administered locally by the Bishops of Orkney. So also, in fact, did all the lands, rights and revenues appertaining to the Norwegian Crown in both Orkney and Shetland, since the Scots blandly rejected all consequent Danish offers to redeem them.

The apparent loser in this was William Sinclair, but there were compensations. The Boyds immediately fell from power. William had been given the earldom of Caithness. Now he received the late Dowager's new castle of Ravenscraig with adjacent lands; an annual pension which rose to four hundred marks; assurance that his revenues would be sent to him wherever he lived; exemption, if he pleased, from all public duties, including Parliaments and embassies for life; and quittance of any debts claimed by Denmark. All this was in addition to his other mainland possessions, and large tracts of land he had recently picked up in Orkney which were neither royal nor comital, and from which he was consequently still entitled to draw rents.

This William Sinclair, last Earl of Orkney, died between 1479 and 1480.

One of his sisters married George Dunbar, Earl of March, who was forfeited for the faults of his father and died by 1463, ending three hundred years of his line. Dunbar's daughter **Euphemia Dunbar**, Sinclair's niece, is proposed as the mother of **Anselm Adorne**'s* natural daughter **Euphemia.** Another sister married a Douglas and had a daughter (another niece to Lord Sinclair) who became the wife of Robert, Lord **Fleming.**

William Sinclair himself had something like nineteen children by two marriages, and one known illegitimate son, Sir David of Sumburgh, who had a distinguished career in the north, which was probably the home of his mother. William Sinclair's first wife, his mother's cousin, was a Douglas and produced a son nicknamed William the Waster and four daughters, one of whom, Catherine, was to marry the King's brother **Alexander, Duke of Albany.*** That marriage produced two sons and was followed in 1478 by an expedient divorce on the grounds of propinquity, which bastardised Catherine's children, including the daughter she was then carrying, who was to grow up to marry Sir Patrick Hamilton of Kincavil, one of **James, Lord Hamilton**'s illegitimate sons.

Lord Sinclair's second wife was Marjorie Sutherland, descended from King Robert the Bruce and daughter of the extremely wealthy (and prolific) Alexander of Dunbeath, Master of Sutherland. The sons from the second marriage included William, Earl of Caithness, justiciar and Chamberlain, and Sir Oliver Sinclair of Roslin. Among the daughters was Elizabeth Sinclair, governess, attendant and protectress of the Princess Mary, and the recipient of regular royal payments through **Haddington** Priory from at least 1471, when Mary's young sister **Princess Margaret** was being reared there. Elizabeth Sinclair married Patrick Dunbar of Blantyre and Cumnock, and was widowed by 1463. She had three daughters of whom one, Euphemia, was heiress to the barony of Cumnock and married another Dunbar, the son of Isabelle Sutherland and Alexander Dunbar of Westfield, Elgin.

Through her aunt's marriage to George, Earl of March, Elizabeth ('Betha') was first cousin to Euphemia Dunbar, who was also paid for her services over the same period at Haddington Priory, and who (see above) is promulgated in the novels as the mother of Anselm Adorne's daughter.

Before Lord Sinclair died, his property was relegated among his older sons, and later adjustments were made in 1481 between Oliver and his half-brother the Waster, whose home was at Newburgh, Aberdeenshire, and who may have been less feeble-minded and pointlessly extravagant than was implied by the 1482 label of *incompos mentis et fatuus.* From Oliver, the Waster obtained Dysart and Ravenscraig Castle in Fife, and Cousland in Lothian, while Oliver retained the Roslin, Pentland, Morton and Stirlingshire lands. The Caithness title stayed with the family from Lord Sinclair's second marriage.

This elaborate and successful rearrangement was probably the brainchild of the Waster's son Henry, born of his marriage in 1458 to the daughter of

George, Earl of Rothes. Henry (associated fictitiously in the novels with the episode of the wine-ship) was in fact in the Orkney Islands in 1480, and, young as he was, handled much of the business there for his family. Through his mother, he was first cousin to the Earl of Rothes,* who married – and divorced – **Princess Margaret**'s illegitimate daughter by 1520. Henry married Margaret Hepburn, and left a son, William Sinclair, who became the fourth Lord Sinclair, dying in 1570. Like his grandfather, Henry collected books. The royal poem *The King is Quair* (see Hast thou no mind of love? Where is thy make?*) was copied for him by James Grey, and at his suggestion, a translation of Virgil's *Aeneid* was begun by Gavin Douglas, who called Henry the 'fader of bukis'.

Henry himself was killed at **Flodden**, in 1513. At his side died his uncle, William, Earl of Caithness, son of Earl William's second marriage. Earl William's brother Sir Oliver Sinclair (nicknamed Nowie in the novels) controlled Roslin, and the half-built chapel which was never completed to the grandiose plan which had once perhaps seemed necessary.

There is no proof that – as envisaged in the novels – **Thomas Cochrane** worked on the chapel, or that Anselm Adorne was ever present there. There were however, a number of clues which appear to link the masons and craftsmen working on the many Scottish construction schemes of the time. Bishop Kennedy* had been commissioning work in St Andrews, and Abbot **Archibald Crawford** in **Holyrood**, Edinburgh. Bishop **Thomas Spens**, building in Aberdeen, is shown in mischievous effigy in Roslin. John Cochrane, presumably a relative of Thomas, was working – as were Merlion and Andrew Lisouris – on Sinclair's Ravenscraig Castle, a fortified building, such as Thomas Cochrane was to deal with as Constable of Kildrummy in the north. Thomas held land in Cousland, beside Newbattle, under the Sinclairs. He must at least have been acquainted with the community of wilful, vigorous craftsmen which had settled by the chapel in Roslin, and have taken an interest in their work.

By several wives – a Borthwick, a Livingstone and perhaps a Haldane – Sir Oliver had four sons, one of whom, William, continued in Roslin. The oldest, Sir Oliver Sinclair of Pitcairn, was to blight his family name, deservedly or not, through the tale of his vainglorious appearance in 1542 as a royal favourite at the head of a halfhearted Scots army making a reciprocal raid into England. In an episode uncannily like the action sixty years earlier at **Lauder Bridge**, the Scots who mistrusted Sinclair stopped to argue, and an English force commanded by Dacre took the chance to attack. The Scottish band, about ten thousand in all, scattered in disarray across the treacherous ground of Solway Moss, with the loss of what were said to be one thousand prisoners, among whom were the lords Maxwell, Grey, Oliphant and Fleming; **Home** of Ayton; and the Masters of Erskine and Rothes. The death of James V* followed immediately, leaving the seven-day-old Mary Queen of Scots* on the throne.

Some of the brothers and sisters of Oliver Sinclair the elder (Nowie) also had careers of note. His brother John followed **Prosper de Camulio*** as Bishop of Caithness. A sister, Eleanor, became the second wife of James III's half-uncle, John, **Earl of Atholl.** Her daughter Anne, by marrying the Third **Earl of Lennox**, became the mother of Matthew, Fourth Earl of Lennox,* who married Margaret Douglas* and became the father of the future Lord Darnley, Queen Mary's consort. Elizabeth (Betha) married Patrick Dunbar as noted, and their sister Mariota married a Carruthers and was perhaps the mother of the Mariota Sinclair who became wet nurse to a child of **James IV**.*

The royal association persisted throughout, with allegiance to the fifteenth-century Queens – Mary of Gueldres* and **Margaret of Denmark** – as well as the Kings. In 1465 James III confirmed Earl William's gift of Garden-Sinclair in Stirlingshire to his squire **Malcolm McClery**, Constable of the castle of Stirling, and attorney to the Queen, and hence one of the magic circle of **Prestons** and Sinclairs who stood behind the throne, sometimes for centuries. (D. D.)

Sir Guy: KINGS, III, 3: A ballad telling the romantic life of Sir Guy of Warwick, popular as a children's song. Thirty-four verses of four lines each deal with Sir Guy's brave exploits such as killing dragons, a giant and a giant boar, before retiring as a hermit.

Sois tolérant à l'égard des caprices d'un vieux: RONDO, 20: 'Allow an old man his whims'.

Soldiers' Song: See ***Or a-t-il bien son temps perdu.***

Sorceror-Hedin: LIONS, 29: Appears in **Njall's** saga as an evil force of pagan times who, as **Iceland** was embracing Christianity, attempts to kill the Christian missionary Thangbrand:

> A man called Sorceror-Hedin lived at Kerlingardale. The heathens there hired him to put Thangbrand and his followers to death. He went up on to Arnarstakk Heath and held a great sacrifice there. While Thangbrand was riding westwards, the ground suddenly burst open under his horse. Thangbrand leapt off the horse and reached safety on the brink of the chasm, but the horse and all the gear were swallowed up in the earth and never seen again. Then Thangbrand praised God.

Sorcerer-Hedin was subsequently slain by Thangbrand's Icelandic warrior-companion, Gudleif.

Soutra: GEMINI, 17: Seventeen miles south of Edinburgh, and said to have been founded in 1164 by Malcolm IV (King of Scotland 1153–1165), but probably dating from before this time, Soutra was a lodging house and hospital for travellers, pilgrims and soldiers, run by the **Augustinians** on the main north–south thoroughfare, the old Roman road known as the King's Highway. The army of Edward II (King of England 1307–1327) camped here on the way to the battle of Bannockburn in 1314. In addition to the strategic importance for the military, it served many functions, including the provision of alms for the poor, a legal sanctuary and a place of hospitality, but interest in the hospice lies principally in its specialised treatment of the sick and wounded. The site measured seven hundred square metres, including infirmary accommodation and a physic garden, and is considered to be the largest hospital north of York. Foundations of the original church, drains, ditches and other structures are buried underneath later medieval buildings and recent archaeological research has unearthed the surgical wards, where major operations such as amputations were performed; the patients were anaesthetised with opium and hemlock, and wounds were treated with analgesic ointments containing opium and lard. Disinfectant ointments laced with arsenic have also been found, as has hemp. Blood-letting pits revealed the product of an estimated fifteen hundred operations, and the remains of stunted stillborn infants combined with the discovery of ergot fungus and juniper berries, both used in the medieval period to bring on uterine contractions, indicate that abortions were carried out at the site. Mass graves show the monks cared for victims of anthrax, plague, typhus, typhoid and smallpox.

Inadequate hygiene in the preparation of food and problems with its preservation would have caused our ancestors many stomach problems, including the pain and discomfort of parasitic worms. Finds of Tormentil pollen at Soutra would suggest that the plant may have been administered on a regular basis as a treatment for worms and diarrhoea. The astringent herb still features in more modern herbal recipes alongside galangal, marshmallow root and ginger to give relief from the latter condition.

SPENS, Thomas: GEMINI (*c.* 1415–1480) Bishop of Aberdeen from 1459 until 1480 when, after a career of unstinting work for his country and its young royals, he is said to have died of a broken heart over the final rupture of the peace between England and Scotland, which he had worked all his life to maintain.

Thomas Spens was the third son of John de Spens of Glen Douglas and Lathallan and the daughter of Sir John Wemyss of Reres, the ancestor of the Earls of Wemyss. He was born about 1415, and by 1445, as Archdeacon of Moray, was sent to escort the Princesses Joanna and Eleanor (see **James II's sisters**), to the French Court after the death of their mother, Joan Beaufort. He became in due course Provost of the **collegiate church** of Lincluden, Archdeacon of Galloway and a protonotary to the apostolic see, as well as a councillor of James II.*

In 1449 he stayed for some time at the French Court, welcomed by King Charles VII* (the Scottish King's uncle by marriage), and involved in diplomatic missions for the French King, as well as the negotiations for the marriages of the two Scottish Princesses, to whom he must have become something of a father figure by now. Back in Scotland, he contrived, probably without too much difficulty, to persuade King James to agree with France in supporting the Lancastrian cause in the current English civil war. After all, the King's mother, Joan Beaufort, had been the granddaughter of John of Gaunt, Duke of Lancaster (1340–1399), and hence second cousin of Henry VI, the Lancastrian claimant to the English throne (King of England 1422–1461; 1470–1471).

Spens became Bishop of Galloway in 1450, which connected him with the thriving trade of Kirkcudbright, where William of Edmonston handled customs and keeper duties at the port and at Threave Castle. Kirkcudbright was also a place with Genoese associations: sharing the customs duties with John of Moray was Lazar Lommellini* of Genoa, whose brother in Bruges* was a colleague of **Anselm Adorne**'s.*

At the start of the 1450s, Spens was one of the commissioners who negotiated a treaty of peace with England at Newcastle. Throughout his life, he would be sent to England many times more, fighting to renew and refresh the same peace. Several years later, he was in France with the French King when the betrothal of the Princess Annabella to Louis, Count of Geneva, was broken off. The bridegroom's father, it is said, 'begged to be excused from using force to make the lady depart from the country since, having nourished her so long, he would not have the heart to do it'. The Bishop brought the poor girl home to Scotland in 1458, where she was married to George Gordon, Master of Huntly, who for that purpose hurriedly dissolved his betrothal to Elizabeth **Dunbar**, Countess of Moray and future Lady of Luss.

When Annabella's sister-in-law, Queen Mary of Gueldres,* founded **Trinity Chapel** in **Edinburgh**, Thomas Spens was one of the witnesses, and perhaps the Queen's inspiration, since he maintained a connection there which resulted, years later, in his founding of a hospital for the poor at the foot of nearby Leith Wynd in 1479, for twelve poor men, endowed with land and rents to the sum of £120 Scots, further increased by a chapel dedicated to St Paul. Spens was buried in Trinity Church. His interest in building is further evinced by his lavish improvements to St Machar's Cathedral, accomplished during his next tenure as Bishop of Aberdeen. His effigy in **Roslin Chapel**, outside Edinburgh, may indicate an interest in the masonwork there – or even the use of the same masons.

After the death of James II, Spens's next care was to be the Princesses' nephew, James II's son, the young **Alexander, Duke of Albany.*** There was a preliminary incident. True or not, the story goes (told by an early historian) that the Bishop's Lancastrian sympathies so angered the Yorkist King **Edward IV*** that English pirates chased his ship, when carrying him on a trade mission in Burgundy, and he was wrecked off the Dutch coast. Succoured and fêted by Burgundy, he recovered the English King's favour by warning him of an assassination conspiracy brewing among exiles in Bruges. The King, delighted, thereupon presented the Bishop with an annual allowance of a thousand rose nobles.

Then the Queen Dowager, Mary of Gueldres, died at the end of 1463, leaving an eleven-year-old son who was now King **James III**,* and another, Alexander, aged nine, who had been for three years overseas at the court of the Burgundian relations of his mother and aunt. Bishop Kennedy,* the King's cousin, had taken him there, and Bishop Spens was asked to bring him back in the early part of 1464.

On the way home, despite sailing under safe conduct, the Bishop's two ships were attacked and taken by five English warships 'on their way south from Ultima Thule' – presumably **Iceland.** The Bishop was put in chains, and the young Prince carried to London. Both were eventually freed, but the suspicion remained that they had been considered as possible hostages during the current peace talks, or were to be used to wean Scotland from Lancaster. Neither the Bishop nor the Prince was allowed to go home until the summer of the following year.

None of this stopped Spens's peace-making efforts, which were to continue until the end of his life. Adviser to the English and French, as well as his own King, he encouraged the famous meeting near **Amiens** between Edward IV and the French King, **Louis XI*** in 1475 that averted the threat of a renewed English–French war. At home, he held major offices and attended Parliament conscientiously as one of its lords. He was one of the **Lords Auditor of Causes and Complaints.** He attended fifty-two meetings of the **Lords of Council in Civil Causes**, and in the records of the **Great Seal**, his signature appears over four hundred times. When Pope Sixtus IV* elevated St Andrews into a metropolitan see, Bishop Spens was allowed to exempt his diocese from the rule of the new Archbishop for his lifetime. His last diplomatic act, as he approached sixty, was to negotiate the engagement of the infant Prince James to the English King's daughter **Cecilia.**

There are traces of other interests. With King James III, the Bishop negotiated the building in Aberdeen of a home for **Observatine Friars**, colonised from Edinburgh in 1471.

He was concerned with the Order of St John.* In his twenties, as Thomas Spens, he visited England on the Order's business in 1439 in the company of the Prior of the Order, Friar Andrew Meldrum, and a Thomas Brown. An Adam Spens was a Brother of the same Order in 1483, as well as being Procurator to the Bishop of Galloway. **William Knollys**,* Preceptor of the Order in Scotland, had accompanied the Bishop to England on at least one of his early peace missions, and was to be his executor when he died. Knollys claimed the patronage of the chapel of St Paul, associated with the Leith Wynd hospital in 1495. There were other links with the Knights Hospitaller. During the Bishop's lifetime, a Cristine de Spens was married to Walter Lichton, of the family of a previous Preceptor. In 1490 a man with land in Fife, Alexander

Spens of Pittencrieff, was married to Elizabeth Monypenny, and by 1490 was bailie of the Order of St John in Fife with, later, a son in the Order.

It makes it seem very likely that Thomas Spens knew Anselm Adorne, the Bruges burgomaster and Conservator of Scots Privileges in Scotland, initially through Bishop Kennedy and trading connections in Bruges and latterly through Adorne's visits to Scotland, including his final five years, when he became Captain and Governor of the Palace of **Linlithgow.** Between 1477 and 1478, a Thomas Spens held ferme of the herbage and meadows and place of the Palace of Linlithgow at ten pounds a year, 'which he relinquished at the Feast of St Martin to Anselm Adorne'. There was an Edinburgh burgess of the same name, so the identification is not secure, but still possible. In the same way, when Adorne's two sons in due course became prebendaries of Aberdeen Cathedral, it is hard to know whether Bishop Blackadder or Bishop Spens might have arranged it beforehand.

He died on 15 April 1480, just a few months after Albany had fled Scotland for France, to return one day with an English army. The scenes involving Thomas Spens in the novels are fictitious, but the cause of his death is probably not (GEMINI, 28). He knew the children of the royal family through two generations, and it must have been hard to see his hard-won peace fail, as the wise counsel of his colleagues and his own became swamped by the erratic natures of the King, and the young Alexander he had protected in London. (D. D.)

Spindle of Necessity, The: RONDO, 44: From the myth of the soldier called Er, in *The Republic* of Plato (*c.* 428–347 BC). This tells how, after seven days of rest, souls return to their next life on earth. A journey of five days takes them to the Spindle of Necessity, a pure pillar of light formed like a simple hand-spindle used to make yarn. Instead of one whorl, the Celestial Spindle has a set of eight nested bowls, their rims forming circles representing planets or stars. On each of these rings stands a siren who sings as the great whorl revolves. The eight voices, each tuned to a different note, blend to make up the concords of a scale. Seated with them are the Fates, the daughters of Necessity, to whom the souls now apply to choose their own lives. Having done so, they drink of the waters of Lethe and, remembering nothing, pass on, like shooting stars, to their birth. (D. D.)

Spondaic rhythm: GEMINI, 4: A melody in the Hypophrygian mode in spondaic rhythm was famously employed by Pythagoras (6th c. BC) on occasion to soothe and sober a violent youth. He himself went to sleep lulled by odes, and woke to songs meant to invigorate. Music was used to calm **Hugo van der Goes**, when seized by frenzy in his monastic retreat (GEMINI, 25). Music was thought to induce a harmonious resonance between soul and body. Songs in the Phrygian mode, on the other hand, were believed to incite violence. See also **Music make[s] men mad.** (D. D.)

SQUARCIAFICO, Oberto: RONDO: (*fl.* 1474) Treasurer for Genoa at Caffa. The behaviour of the Squarciafico family, in proving the 'beastly' nature of the Tartars in Mingrelia, is related in **Josaphat Barbaro**'s account of his travels, revealing more about the manner and behaviour of the Genoese than of the Tartar:

> And they arr beastly people. For proof whereof, being in Vathi (where one Azolin Sqoarciafigo, a genowaie, arrived in companie of a panderia of Turks that went thither with us from Constantinople), there was a yonge woman stode in her doore unto whom this Genowaie saied SURINA PATRO NI COCON? Which is, mistress, is the good man within? Meaning her husbande. She answered Archilimisi, that is, to witt, he woll come anon. Whereupon he swapped her on the lippes and shewed her unto me, saieng, beholde what faire teethe she hath; and so shewd me her breast and touched her teates, which she suffered without moving. Afterwardes, we entred into her house, and sate us down, and this Azolin fayneng to have vermin about him beckened on her to serche him; which she did verie diligentlie and chastely. This mean while, the good man came in, and my companion put his hande in his purse, and saied PATRON TETARI SICA, which is as much to saie as, mister, hast thou any mooney? Whereunto he made a countenance that he had none about him: and so he took him a fewe aspres, with the which he went straight to bye some vittails. Within a while after, we went through the towne to sporte us, and this Genowaie did every wheare after the maner of that countrey what pleased him without reproche of any man, whereby it may appeare weather they be beastly people or no, and therefore the Genowaie that practise in those parts use for a proverbe to saie Thou art a Mongrello, whan they arr disposed to saie thou art a foole.

Staple: HN; LC: A burgh port where merchants of a particular nation paid lower duties on the goods they imported and exported, and were granted special privileges, in return for which they were supposed to use only that particular port. If relations between the merchants and the port deteriorated, a new port could be chosen instead, as **Veere**, for example, replaced Bruges* as the Scottish Staple.

***Sterner* versus the *Psitticher*:** UNICORN, 22: The stars and the parrots, names of two rival knightly societies belonging to Basle.

STEWART, Alexander: See **Albany, Alexander, Duke of.**

STEWART, Andrew: GEMINI: James III's youngest half-uncle, bishop-elect of Moray at the time of the crisis at **Lauder Bridge.** He was one of the King's temporary jailors. He also took the Archbishopric of St Andrews from **William**

Scheves, but to pay for his promotion to the office, he and his brothers needed money which had been raised from foreign bankers, using the burgh of **Edinburgh** and its revenues as security. For their underwriting of the loan as much as for their assistance in supporting the King during the siege, Edinburgh was granted certain privileges, including the confirmation of the town's property and the right to hold its own sheriff courts (see **Blue Blanket**).

Stewart was obliged to return the office of the following year, as Scheves claimed he was placed under duress to resign. Following the King's return to full authority, Stewart was banished to his see of Moray.

STEWART, Andrew: See **Avandale, Andrew Stewart, Lord.**

STEWART, Drew: See **Avandale, Andrew Stewart, Lord.**

STEWART, John, Second Duke of Albany: See **Albany, John Stewart, Second Duke of.**

STEWART, James, of Auchterhouse, Earl of Buchan: See **Buchan, Earl of.**

STEWART, John, of Balveny, Earl of Atholl: See **Atholl, Earl of.**

STEWART, John, Earl of Mar: See **Mar, John of.**

STEWART, Sir John: See **Darnley, John Stewart, Lord.**

STEWART, Margaret: See **Margaret, Princess.**

STEWART, Mary: See **Mary, Princess.**

Stockfish: LIONS, 20: Salted and dried cod, sometimes referred to as 'the commodius stokfysshe'. There have been as many as ten cod wars since the Middle Ages, the majority of fifteenth- and sixteenth-century conflicts stemming from Denmark's attempts to control **Iceland**'s trade and government. Icelanders feared permanent settlements by the English and the **Hanseatic League** undermining their social, political and economic systems. Twentieth-century cod wars have been a reaction to Iceland's expansion of territorial fishing boundaries.

There was a small verse extant in 1435:

> Of Yseland to wryte is lytill nede
> Save of stok fische . . . unto the costes colde.

Storax: SCORPIONS, 32: See **Rhodes.**

Stupor Mundi: LIONS, 6: 'The Wonder of the World'. One of the magnificent titles of Frederick II, Holy Roman Emperor 1215–1250. The word '*Stupor*' has several meanings.

Success, that implacable foeman of virtue: RONDO, 7: The words of clergyman, scholar and learned classical writer John of Salisbury (*fl.* 1120–1180), upbraiding the courtiers of Henry II (King of England 1154–1189) in his book *Policraticus*. He continues:

> [Success] applauds its devotees only to harm them, and with its ill-starred prosperity escorts them on their joyous way to bring about their ultimate fall by first pledging them in cups of sweet wine and, when they are intoxicated thereby, mixing into the draught deadly poison or something conceivably worse. The more brilliant the success, the denser the clouds that gather around their dazzled eyes. As the darkness thickens truth vanishes, virtue withers with severed roots, and a crop of vices sprouts. (D. D.)

Suis ici!: LIONS, 5: 'Here I am!'

Suspendit gaudium: See **Delay . . .**

SWIFT, Thomas: UNICORN: (d. by 1501) On 29 January 1483, six days after the assassination of **Anselm Adorne**,* Adorne's post of Conservator of the Privileges of the Scottish Nation in the Low Parts of Burgundy was given to the King's familiar servant, Thomas Swift.

Adorne had been a burgess of Bruges.* Swift was a Scottish resident, of a family of **Edinburgh** merchants dating back to the time of James I (King of Scotland 1406–1437), who in 1427 gave John Swift, burgess, a **tenement** near the Cross on the south side of the High Street, Edinburgh. Swift's Close, now World's End Close at the lower end of the High Street, may mark his house. In the year 1505 Robert Crawford of **Berecrofts** and Katherine Sersanders, his spouse, were drawing rents from lands and tenements in the Canongate next to the house occupied by John Swift.

Like the Adornes, the Swifts knew a lot about gold. The first known John Swift, dead by 1475, had three sons, of whom one was Thomas, the future Conservator. Another, Sir Walter, was a chaplain who served the Abbot of **Holyrood, Archibald Crawford**, by storing his treasure. The third, Henry Swift, married a Marjorie Martin – perhaps a relation of Bishop Kennedy's* factor – and had one daughter, Elizabeth, dead by 1475, who married into the Edmonston family of merchants who did business with Adorne's nephew, **Anselm Sersanders.** Elizabeth had one son, John Edmonston, to whom his great-uncle, the chaplain Walter, was guardian, and who married Janet Brown, daughter and heiress of Alexander Brown, probably the same who sailed the trading ship the *James* for **Thomas Yare.**

In 1439 the father John Swift acquired through King James II* a tenement at the east gate of St Giles* cemetery sold by Edinburgh burgess Robert Lauder for the very large sum of four hundred pounds. James Grey, son of the late William Grey, goldsmith, had resigned from the property. Two years later, the house was in use as the King's mint, for which John Swift received rent.

John Swift, witnessing a charter of 1447, does so in the company of mint warden Thomas de Cranston, and the master moneyer, John of Dalrymple. By 1477 the late John Swift's land was part of a small, wealthy colony of solid houses whose owners included William Inglis, Robert Bell, **William Goldsmith** and the late Henry Goldsmith, and the land of the monastery of **Melrose.** 'Wille Goldsmith called Halfpenny Man' was one of the master moneyers of **James III**,* and supposedly involved with the hated **Black Money.** In 1473, he is also described as a gun founder, and under the distorted name of lorimer/lonnard, he might even be identified in the fanciful list of the King's favourites later set upon at **Lauder Bridge.** By 1495 the late John Swift's neighbours included **Henry Cant**, the late William Napier, and the late Alexander Napier of Merchiston. Sir Alex Napier, Provost of Edinburgh, had been one of the searchers of the port and houses of **Leith:** the group which had the duty of preventing illicit exports of gold and silver.

Thomas Swift, son of John, fell heir to all this fortunate heritage. An Edinburgh burgess by 1459, he also had land in Stirling, which he gave up by 1464, and which might be connected with another mint-house run by one Robert Hacket. The year before, Thomas had been allotted hall, chamber and kirkyard cellars next to St Giles in the High Street for his business. One of his neighbours was connected with the Edinburgh Skinners' Guild (see guild*), and one was from a shipmaster's family. Thomas Swift dealt in wool, and presumably fells and skins also. By 1482 he was a bailie, and allowed certain customs concessions. The customar was Thomas Yare, and the concessions were modelled on those once afforded 'Thomas Moffat'. It is probably relevant that a future Conservator of the **Staple** in 1517 at Bergen ap Zoom was a John Moffat.

Thomas Swift's housing evidently expanded with his business. Records of 1501 after his death mention a great mansion of Thomas Swift's on the north side of the High Street, and another land on the south, 'now of Jonet Swift'. His brothers were not far away. Henry lived to the west of St Mary's Wynd, at the foot of the High Street, having land, walls and a garden close to William **Lamb**; to John Redpath, again of a goldsmith dynasty; and to Robert **Preston**, vicar of Linton, by Preston, whose land, garden and croft in the High Riggs eventually belonged to James Ross, Temple bailie in Edinburgh of **William Knollys.***

Walter Swift, the Holyrood chaplain, lived in the Canongate, next to a tenement which paid revenues in 1499 to Gilbert Edmonston of Leith, whose ship of the same name was heavily used by the merchant Andrew Haliburton, and whose wife was Elizabeth Crawford. The chaplain had two illegitimate daughters, Margaret and Jonet, who both died unmarried, leaving their inheritance in dispute. This included property owned by the daughters in Bell's Wynd (perhaps the house of Robert Bell, their grandfather's neighbour), and occupied by one Henry Purves. After a claim, through a marriage connection, by William Sinclair, the joint fortune of Thomas and Walter Swift went to Archibald, one of the Edmonstons.

The death of Sir Walter himself, by 1497, created a far deeper anxiety. In common with other owners of secure houses, Abbot Archibald Crawford of Holyrood used his Abbey as a storage place for the Church's valuables, and for those of others which fell to his care, particularly during his period of office as Treasurer. Some of these he had shared for safe-keeping with his chaplain. Accordingly, when Walter Swift died, it was the task of Robert Bellenden, the next Abbot of Holyrood, with the help of the young King **James IV**,* to recover from the chaplain's surviving heirs (i.e., his two natural daughters) the total of 1,000 English gold nobles, 1,700 *demis* of gold, and other sums of gold and silver deposited with Sir Walter before Abbot Archibald's death in 1483. The witnesses to this decree, whose results are unknown, were John Halkerston, notary, and John Reid, under the better known pen-name of John Reid of Stobo (see **This officer but dout is callit Deid**).

Thomas Swift replaced Adorne as Conservator until his death in 1501, with both Andrew Haliburton and Paul **van Borselen** to assist him. For a year or two the post was held by John Francis or French (see **Linlithgow**). By 1510, the new Conservator was Henry van Borselen, bailie of Veere, son of the late Paul, followed by his son and his grandson. Parallel with the Dutch Conservators there operated the Scots, in the person of John Moffat from 1517, to be followed by Alexander Muir, and then another John Moffat in 1529.

Given that the administration of Flanders and the Flemish ports were in a state of flux, Swift was, as a practical businessman with a lively trade with Flanders and a certain grasp of the bullion situation, a good choice as Adorne's successor. Adorne was an expert on finance, and his active interest is illustrated by his possession of the famous tiled house at **Blackness**, once the responsibility of Alan Landells, of a famous master moneyers' family, who recovered land in Blackness in 1502.

The records on Swift indicate that he was commercially and probably domestically involved with Adorne's family, and it is certain that Adorne and Swift knew one another well, although the premise that Swift gave them the use of his house is purely supposition. The fast appointment was perhaps an act of diplomacy, in that it offered an excuse for an immediate mission to Bruges, to explain and excuse Adorne's death. What is very clear is that there is much more to know than is evident. (D. D.)

Swiss Horns: RONDO, 43: The 'bull' of Uri and the 'cow' of Unterwalden were the terrifying battle horns of the Swiss Confederation, a loose association of something like eight free cantons. The horns were employed in the series of conflicts that led up to the battle at Nancy in which **Charles, Duke of Burgundy,*** lost his life in 1477.

T

Tais-toi!: GEMINI, 42: 'Be quiet!'

Takk! Takk fyri!: LIONS, 21: Faroese for 'I thank you'.

Tarasque: LIONS, 2: Tarascon is a beautiful castle of René of Anjou* which lies on the River Rhône in the south of France. For a long time, the region of Provence was terrorised by the monstrous dragon Tarasque which periodically emerged from the river to devour human beings and devastate the country with its terrible tail. It was tamed by St Martha, the domesticated sister of Mary and Lazarus. Arriving in Marseilles, the saint, legend says, sprinkled the monster with holy water and led it meekly bound by her girdle to Arles, where it was slaughtered. In time, the dragon became one of the legendary monsters of France, to be seen on the wagons of **Mystery Plays**, belching fire, along with the Graoulli of Metz and the Doudou of Mans.

St Martha herself ended her life in Provence, and her relics were found in Tarascon soon after the discovery of those of her sister. Martha was laid in a magnificent chapel there, her head encased in a rich golden reliquary supplied by King **Louis XI*** of France. As the sister of Mary she appears in the Gospels in the tale of the raising of Lazarus who, with his sisters, was thought to have evangelised Provence. Martha is the patron of housewives, and is generally shown with a ladle, a broom or a bunch of keys. Also a dragon. (D. D.)

Tartars: See **Golden Horde, Tartar khanate of the; Mengli-Girey.**

Taverns in Rome: LIONS, 16: There were fifteen taverns in the centre of fifteenth-century Rome, and in 1455 the oldest of the great inns on the Campo de' Fiori went by the names of the Cow, the Angel, the Bell, the Crown and the Sun. The Albergo del Sole in the via del Biscione outlasted them all. Flemish taverns, which were also places of business, might sell only wine, or ale, or beer, or several varieties of drink. Gambling was a favourite pastime in Florence in places such as the Piazza de San Andrea, where wine was sold. The Inn of the Lion was a favourite tavern in 1433. In the same town, as an unpleasant joke, the prison cell in the bell-tower was called the *Alberghettino*, the Little Inn. Cosimo de' Medici* was held there in 1433. There were some

Scottish inns. When Bishop Robert Blackadder visited Venice in 1508, he stayed in the lodging Ca' Frizier. (D. D.)

tellement quellement: GEMINI, 16: Willy-nilly; 'somehow'.

Tenements: See ***Tigh a' Nicol.***

Tête-Dieu!: UNICORN, 34: 'God's head!' Favourite oaths of the early French Kings were memorised by their courtiers, and somebody even made up a rhyme:

Quand la Pasque-Dieu! décéda
Par le Jour-Dieu! luy succéda
Le Diable m'emporte! s'en tint près
Foy de Gentilhomme! vint après.

When the risen God! went to his Maker [Louis XI]
By God's Own Day! followed on [Charles VIII]
Devil take me! came later [Louis XII]
Until Word of a Gentleman! came along [Francis I].

Teutonic Knights: RONDO, 1: Their full title was the Order of the Hospital of the Blessed Virgin Mary of the German House of Jerusalem. The Teutonic knights were a crusading force reconstituted as a chivalric order in 1198, following the failure of the Third Crusade and the fall of Jerusalem in 1187. Their members were mostly friars, drawn from the German nobility; they acted as a hired mercenary force in Europe against the infidel, joined periodically by chivalric and mercenary knights from Western Europe. In Poland they were known as 'the Black Crusaders', because they wore black crosses on their white mantles. They came into the Baltic in the early thirteenth century: unable to cope with the raids of his neighbours, the pagan Prussians, in 1226 Konrad, Prince of Masovia, invited the Order to conquer and Christianise these northern tribes. The tribes were successfully subdued and, with the Knights' encouragement, Prussia was dominated by German culture and inhabitants. In return for their missionary work, the Knights were given their own territory at Chelmno, or Kulm.

The Order established a Teutonic State, which, between 1230 and 1283, expanded beyond conquered Prussia to the mouth of the **Vistula**, aiming at mastery over Pomerania. This the Knights accomplished in 1308; they held it until 1454, building up a network of towns, some from scratch, like **Thorn.** The importance of trade led the Order to ally itself with the **Hanseatic League** from the very beginning. Run by Grand Masters, Knights and Gentry, the combination of diplomacy, armed force and large financial resources made it a force to be reckoned with. When Poland and Lithuania united under the recently baptised Jogaila (Jagiello), the Order's original *raison d'être* – fighting the eastern infidel – no longer applied, but they clung to their territories, their German colonies and their trade empire. The battle of Grunwald near Tannenberg in 1410 saw the **Jagiellonian** army of Lithuania and Poland defeating the Order, killing the Master and half of the Knights and taking fourteen thousand prisoners. The Order split from the Hanseatic League after the Hanse towns sued for a separate peace with Poland-Lithuania.

Relations rapidly worsened between the Order and the Hanse towns, particularly as the Knights engaged in trade themselves, imposing a monopoly on grain exports, denying merchants access to the sea and profiting themselves. They were desperately short of funds in the early part of the fifteenth century, because of war and having to pay for mercenaries, hence the recourse to trade, especially in grain.

In 1454 the Thirteen Years War broke out between the Knights and the cities of eastern Pomerania (**Danzig**, Thorn and Elbing) who had formed the Prussian League and were supported by the Jagiellonian monarchy. It was ended by the Peace of Thorn in 1466, which freed the towns from the influence of the Knights. Wars lessened their territorial hold in the Baltic, but their power was not removed totally from the coast until 1525, when the Order was secularised and the Knights forced to disband.

Thames shout: LIONS, 25: In early times a 'shout', meaning a skiff, was also spelled 'schout' (Dutch, *schuiten*) and was ideal for internal waterways. When **Thomas Yare**'s tombstone (GEMINI, 1) was bought in Bruges and shipped to Scotland in the *Eagle*, there was an accounting for the cost of the packing, the porter fee, the Bruges tolls and the hire of a shout to the Fair. (D. D.)

The *abboccamento*. The *impalmamento*. The *ductio* . . . : RONDO, 41: One way of ratifying an agreement was to shake hands (*impalmare*), and another was a kiss on the lips (*abboccamento*). In Florence, it was part of the ceremonial of wedding when, say, a girl was sixteen and unmarried, and her despairing parents called in a professional mediator. Done properly, all the formalities of the wedding and the consummation could take place in one day. The mediator made a short speech about the terms of the contract at the *impalmare* ceremony in his house, hands were shaken, and part of the dowry was obtained from the public bank of the Monte and handed to the groom, who supplied a receipt. The *ductio* was the walk that led to the bridal chamber. See **Consanguinity.** (D. D.)

***The Art and Craft to Know Well to Dye*:** See **Pynson.**

The beards of women, the roots of stones . . . : LIONS, 22: A list of the items making up the cord that shackled the great wolf Fenrir, a monster of Northern

European mythology. Offspring of the cunning god Loki, Fenrir grew up in Asgard, the realm of the gods, but became so huge and so terrible that only the god Tyr dared to feed him. When all attempts to bind him had failed, the dwarves forged this silklike cord made of strange and unlikely components. Confident of his power to break it, Fenrir agreed to be trussed, provided one of the gods set a hand in his jaws at the same time. Tyr offered to do so; the rope held; and Fenrir, furious, bit off the hand. (D. D.)

The birds of hell shall devour them with bitter breath . . . : QUEENS, IV, 4: Deuteronomy 32:24, 33, as quoted by Geoffrey Chaucer (*c.* 1343–1400) in 'The Parson's Tale' from his *Canterbury Tales:*

> For God saith thus by Moses:
> 'They shul been wasted with hunger, and the briddes of helle shul devoren hem with bitter deeth, and the galle of the dragon shal been hire drynke, and the venym of the dragon hire morsels.'

The catoptric flour of parrots and poesy: LIONS, 6: A punning reference to the flower of poesy, and the distorting mirror and flour of Philip the Good, Duke of Burgundy's* palace of Hesdin. (D. D.)

The cyrugyens ought also to be debonayr, amyable and to have pytye of their pacyents: LIONS, 18; KINGS, III, 2: From William Caxton's* *The Game and Playe of the Chesse.*

Th'erratic starres heark'ning harmony: KINGS, II, 1: From *Troilus and Criseyde,* Geoffrey Chaucer's longest complete poem, written in the second half of the 1380s. Book V describes Earth from the perspective of Heaven, hearing the music of the spheres and witnessing the folly of mankind:

> The wrath, as I bigan yow for to seye,
> Of Troilus the Grekis boughten deere.
> For thousandes his hondes maden deye,
> As he that was withouten any peere,
> Save Ector, in his tyme, as I kan heere.
> But weilawey, save only Goddes wille!
> Despitously hym slough the fierse Achille.
>
> And whan that he was slayn in this manere,
> His lighte goost ful blisfully is went
> Up to the holughnesse of the eighthe spere,
> In convers letyng everich element;
> And ther he saugh, with ful avysement,
> The erratik sterres, herkenyng armonye
> With sownes ful of hevenyssh melodie.

And downe from thennes faste he gan avyse
This litel spot of erthe, that with the se
Embraced is, and fully gan despise
This wrecched world, and held al vanite
To respect of the pleyn felicite
That is in hevene above; and at the laste,
Ther he was slayn, his lokyng down he caste.

And in hymself he lough right at the wo
Of hem that wepten for his deth so faste;
And dampned al oure werk that foloweth so
The blynde lust, the which that may nat laste,
And sholden al oure herte on heven caste.
And forth he wente, shortly for to telle,
Ther as Mercurye sorted him to dwelle . . .

The face of a hoore and the tongue of a serpent: CHECKMATE, IV, 3: Richard Eden's* preface to the reader in *The First Three English Books on America 1511–1555:*

> Who hath given thee the face of a hoore and tongue of a serpent withowt shame to speake venemous woordes in secreates ageynst the annoynted of God. Hath not the pocke of thy licentiousnesse bruste furt in maner to thyne owne destruction . . .

The hombull bee . . .: CHECKMATE V, 10: The following is the whole verse:

The sowe sat on hye benke and harpyd Robyn Howd
The fox fydylyd, the raton rybybyd, the larke noty withall
The hombull bee hendyll the hornepype,
for ham fyngers wer small.

The Kyng of Fraunce spared none . . . But sent for hem everychone: CHECKMATE, I, 1: From the Middle English verse romance of 1,035 lines, *Emaré*, written in the mid-fourteenth century: the King of France calls upon his lords to help him fight the Saracen menace. The King of Galys (Galicia) goes to his King's bidding, leaving his pregnant wife behind with a loyal steward.

The pumpkin gives birth, and the fence has the trouble: UNICORN, 17: A Moroccan proverb invented, one imagines, by a person suffering from feckless friends. Another sample is rather more bracing: If you are a peg, endure the knocking; if you are a mallet, strike. (D. D.)

The Queen got a new hat from five murders: See **Remissions.**

The shepherd clutch thee fast: the wolves are many: PAWN, 22: Fragment of a thirteenth-century *ghâzel* by Jelal-ud-Din (1207/8–1273/4*) (see Ottoman poetry*):

> Or good or ill the brother be, indeed he
> Upon a long and toilsome road will lead thee.
> The shepherd clutch thee fast, the wolves are many;
> O my black lamb, O my black lambkin, heed me!
> And be thou Turk, or be thou Greek, or Persian,
> The tongue of those the tongueless learn, I rede thee!

The soul is a widow who has lost her husband: GEMINI, 16: Searching for Christian symbolism in the biblical Song of Songs, the medieval church contemplated the idea of Christ as a king, wooing the individual soul. In this instance, a fourteenth-century friar, addressing women committed to virginity, uses the imagery to propose the soul as the bride of Jesus Christ, who has lost Christ her husband through sin. It continues: 'Similarly, he is fatherless who has through his sin lost the father of heaven'.

The Sun and I alone know the boy is beautiful: SCALES, 19: In the novel, a scathing quotation from a man whose friendship for another is being questioned. The original lines were inscribed on a Greek pot of classical times, decorated with a picture of a nude, handsome boy and his lover. (D. D.)

Theiked with skaillie: LIONS, 10: Scots, meaning roofed with a superior quality of blue slate, as opposed to the more usual thatch.

These serpents slay men, and they eat them weeping: KINGS, II, 1: The crocodile, described in chapter thirty-one of *The Travels of Sir John Mandeville*. See Mandeville.*

This officer but dout is callit Deid . . . : GEMINI, 18: From the poem 'The Thrie Priests of Peblis' (Peebles) by John Reid of Stobo (*c.* 1430–1505), royal clerk and poet.

Thorn: RONDO, 6: Toruń, in Pomerania (Poland), founded in 1231 by the **Teutonic Knights**, and inhabited initially by German immigrants, but granted a large degree of self-determination and many privileges by the Order. In 1410, when the Hanse towns stood against the Order, retribution was so harsh as to alienate the burghers and merchants from the Knights, cleaving apart the **Hanseatic League** and the Teutonic Order. The subsequent Thirteen Years War saw the Danzigers rally their ships against the Order, the struggle for

Pomerania being as much a test of who could control the sea as the land. The Treaty of Thorn in 1466 freed the town from the Knights and it came under Polish control. The town was the birthplace of the astronomer **Copernicus.**

Thracian Wizard: RONDO, 27: A byname for Orpheus,* legendary poet, musician and husband of Eurydice. Clement of Alexandria (150–*c.* 215), an early Christian, despised the Thracian Wizard, and preferred to attribute his powers to Jesus. (D. D.)

Thread of the mistar: CASTLE, III, 3: An instrument used in the Ottoman Empire to rule paper. The mistar is made of stout card and threads are attached to it to mark the space between the lines. When paper is pressed on top of the mistar, the thread leaves a series of impressions.

Three sausages on a spike: UNICORN, 22: Jousting crest of Marx Walther of Augsburg, as illustrated in his Tournament Book. These books, compiled for sixteenth-century noblemen, were especially popular in Germany, where artists like Lucas Cranach the Elder might be employed by an Elector of Saxony to record his triumphs in the field. From these, we know the diversity of helms worn at tournaments, which might include a wolf, an eagle, a maiden, a boar, an otter, a goose, a jester's cap, a curled feather or bells. Walther himself seems to have been an excellent jouster who, although well-enough born to compete at the highest level, did not take himself or others too seriously. His Book shows him cheerfully falling off his horse in a civic joust of 1518, and on another occasion taking part in a Shrovetide tournament, surrounded by men in fools' clothing. Lastly, there is a magnificent painting of him (without the three sausages) riding into the lists at Nuremberg with a small boy in striped hose and a feathered hat perched on his great levelled lance. (D. D.)

Thundering Poison: LIONS, 37: An Arab nick-name for a tenth-century doctor.

Tiens! Tiens! Comme c'est gars bachique!: LIONS, 19: Said of a child: 'My word, what a handful this is!' The speaker continues: '*Va-t-en, tu l'verras*' ('off with you, and you'll see it').

Tigh a' Nicol: GEMINI, 29: 'Nicol's house', rendered in Gaelic, referring to the hero of the *House of Niccolò* series. The same fictitious **Canongate** house was, in more portentous times, referred to as the *Casa di Niccolò*, with the same meaning. It eventually became, sensibly, the Floory Land; or the Land of de Fleury.

Land, in Scottish towns, often did not mean terrain, but was the term for a large building of several storeys, usually shared among different occupants. Today, its more usual name is a tenement. Then – the reverse of today – the word tenement represented a plot of land. Accordingly, a tenant of the Abbot of **Holyrood** might be granted a tenement (land) with no land (building) on it, or share a land (building) with no rights to the tenement (plot) on which it was built. They understood it all perfectly. (D. D.)

Tiphaine: LIONS, 2: (d. 1458) Tiphaine la Magnine was a nurse. Her home was in Saumur on the River Loire, and she came to the castle of Angers to care for Marie, daughter of Louis II (1377–1417), King of Sicily, Duke of Anjou, Count of Provence. When the next child, René of Anjou,* was born in 1409, Tiphaine tended him through all his childhood, as in age he was to care for her. When she came to die, René commissioned the *atelier* Poncet, father and son, who had designed his own tomb, to build one for her in the nave of the church of Notre-Dame de Nantilly, by Saumur. It showed Tiphaine with two babies swaddled in fleur-de-lis, one on each arm: himself and Marie as infants. The epitaph, in its spontaneity and its fondness, could have been dashed off by no one but René, poet, artist and King:

Ci gist la nourrice Thiephaine	Here lies the nurse Tiphaine
La Magine, qui ot grant paine	la Magine, who with great devotion
A nourrir de let, en enfance,	nourished at her breast
Marie d'Anjou, royne de France,	Marie of Anjou, Queen of France,
And après, son frère René,	and then her brother René,
Duc d'Anjou, et depuis nommé,	Duke of Anjou, then and now
Comme encore est, roy de Sicile,	King of Sicily,
Qui a voullu en ceste ville,	who has desired, in this town,
Pour grant amour de nourreture,	to mark the deep love he feels for her
Faire faire la sépulture	to have made a tomb
De la nourrice dessusdicte,	for the one named above,
Qui à Dieu rendit l'âme quiete,	who has given up her quiet soul to God
Pour avoir grâce et tout déduit,	to attain expiation and grace,
Mille cccc cinquante et huit,	in the year 1458
Ou mois de mars, XIIIe jour.	on the 13th day of March.
Je vous prye tous, par bonne amour,	I ask you all, of your goodness and love,
Affin qu'elle ait ung pou du vostre	that she may have your support.
Donnez luy ugne patesnostre.	Bequeath to her one Paternoster.

The tomb was destroyed during the French Revolution. (D. D.)

To horse, to horse, my royal liege: KINGS, II, 3: When pronounced without a drunken slur, the verse is recognisably from *Hardyknute*, a ballad which relates the battle of Largs in 1263 when the forces of Alexander III (ruled 1249–1286) repelled the invading army of Haakon IV, King of Norway, from the coast of Ayrshire. The poem relates how Hardyknute, the valiant knight who resides at nearby Fairly Castle, is called upon by his king:

The king of Norse in summer tyde,
Puff'd up with pow'r and might,
Landed in fair Scotland the isle
With mony a hardy knight.
The tydings to our good Scots king
Came, as he sat at dine,
With noble chiefs in brave aray,
Drinking the blood-red wine.

'To horse, to horse, my royal liege,
Your faes [foes] stand on the strand,
Full twenty thousand glittering spears
The king of Norse commands'.
'Bring me my steed Mage dapple gray',
Our good king rose and cry'd,
A trustier beast in a' the land
A Scots king nevir try'd.

'Go, little page, tell Hardyknute,
That lives on hill sae hie,
To draw his sword, the dread of faes,
And haste and follow me'.
The little page flew swift as dart
Flung by his master's arm,
'Come down, come down, lord Hardyknute,
And rid your king from harm'.

The fragment of the ballad which exists, although considered in many anthologies to be genuine, appears in fact to have been written by Lady Wardlaw (1677–*c.* 1727), second daughter of Sir Charles Halket of Pitfirrane, a gentleman of Fife. It was first published in 1719, and not doubted as genuine until 1755 when Thomas Percy (1729–1811) in his *Reliques* (1765) exposed it as a modern piece.

Tohorsh, tohorsh, maroyaleesh: See **To horse, to horse, my royal liege.**

Tolbooth: GEMINI, 37: The tradesmen and merchants occupying this building are listed in records of **Edinburgh** dated 1480–1481, which gives the name, individual rooms rented and the cost to the merchants. It includes mention of Isobell Williamsoun, occupying the sixth booth on the north side of the building, and her rent of four pounds per annum, the same as that of Andro Bertram in the same part of the building, compared with the less illustrious Hector Meldrum, in the 'littil sellar' of the bellhouse, under the stair. His rent was twenty-four shillings. Next to him, Robert Gray paid twenty shillings, and also under the stair was 'The fleschehous sett for four pounds'. **Henry Cant**, in the loft, paid forty shillings. In 1482 the description of the booths and their occupants lets us know that Andro and Isobell stay put and their rent is the same, but Hector Meldrum is now paying twenty shillings for the 'pentis under the bellhous stair'; there is no mention of Robert Gray, his skinner's booth and the loft is now let to Henry **Preston.**

Toleta planks: RONDO, 4: A common early sanitary arrangement in **monasteries** and houses of chivalric orders was a latrine block made of cubicles fitted with pierced wooden boards over a stream. The Venetian word for a plank was *toleta* (hence 'toilet'). The washhouse was called a *lavatorium.* In the Scottish castle of Stirling, the latrines were equipped with hay from a neighbourhood croft.

It seems likely, to add a Victorian footnote, that the discreet guidebook lists of *lieux d'aisance* (places in which to relieve oneself) may be the source of the polite modern loo. (D. D.)

Ton papa est en retour: LIONS, 45: 'Your father is home!'

Torphichen: See **William Knollys.***

Tournesol: LIONS, 17: Sunflowers, whose seeds provided a rich oil, good for simulating blood on the stage when fermented with urine.

Towarzysz: RONDO, 4: 'Comrade', used in the military to indicate equality amongst the Polish nobility.

Trinity Chapel: LIONS, 14: The **collegiate church** at the bottom of the southern slopes of Calton Hill in **Edinburgh.** Holy Trinity was founded by **James III**'s* mother, Mary of Gueldres, in 1460, under the direction of John **Halkerston** as master of works, and costing almost £1,100 to build in the first three years alone (see Edward Bonkle*). Aside from **Holyrood**, it was considered to be one of the finest examples of gothic architecture in Edinburgh. Its elegant simplicity contrasts with the contemporary choir of **Roslin.** After the death of Mary of Gueldres, the church was never completed; only the choir and transepts were complete by 1488. What remained of the church was dismantled in the nineteenth century and eventually rebuilt. The reconstructed choir now stands at the foot of Chalmer's Close on the north side of the High Street.

Trotula, Dame, of Salerno: SCORPIONS, 42: Queen of eleventh-century midwives, Dame Trotula was a woman of noble family who is believed to have written and taught on obstetrics and hygiene at the famous Italian medical school of Salerno. Largely theoretical in tone, her writing contains no actual instruction on, for example, how to deliver a baby. In the fourteenth and fifteenth century women doctors did, however, practise in Salerno. Among medical tips from the school come the following (a seventeenth-century translation):

Do not sleep in the afternoon, if there is an R in the month.

Drink sage-water with wine to avoid sea-sickness.

Wine, women, baths, by art or nature warm,
Used or abused, do men much good or harm.

And finally: Water-drinkers never make good verses.

The medical school of Montpellier, in the south of France, also famous by the twelfth century, reached its peak in the sixteenth, when it too specialised in obstetrics and also in dissection of, for example 'a handsome courtesan who had died in childbirth'. As later happened in grave-robbing Edinburgh, corpses were dug up from their graves in the cloister and dissected in a friendly doctor's house. The school supplied the court with physicians, and sent its graduates as far as Cracow in Poland. Among those who supplied it with books was the printer Macé Bonhomme of Lyons (CHECKMATE, I, 6). (D. D.)

True to the hand, the tongue, the loins: UNICORN, 37: A pronouncement of the Bektashi* dervishes, meaning (sardonically in this case) 'saved from lust'.

Tubal: LIONS, 2; 28: Tubal, sometimes known as Tubal-Cain, appears in the Old Testament as the descendant of the fratricide Cain, son of Adam, and the brother of Magog. In Genesis, he is described as 'the instructor of every artificer of brass and iron', and hence in medieval **Mystery Plays** (see **Nails**) he is associated with smithies. He is eventually ranked with Gog, the evil Prince opposed to the kingdom of God. An early Icelandic interpretation of the Bible held that Nibal, brother of Tubal-Cain, invented harmony as a protest against the dissonant clangs of the smithy. From the same source came the belief that boys were born crying in A, and girls in E. (D. D.)

Tutto e fritto: UNICORN, 19: 'All is undone'.

Twa young quines: GEMINI, 26: Scots dialect for 'two young lassies'. Still to be heard in Aberdeenshire.

Two Romes have fallen . . . : CASTLE, I, 3: See **Ivan III.**

U

Ultima Thule: See **Iceland.**

Un méchant, oui. 'Suis alloui: LIONS, 19: 'Naughty, yes!' 'I'm starving!' (the last in the dialect of Blois).

Union charnelle: See ***Virginité voluntaire***.

Univiva, unicuba et virginia: UNICORN, 41: Description of a virtuous woman: one who has spent her life faithful to only one man, lying only in his bed (that is, refusing to remarry). Such a woman was, of course, an object of praise to the religious.

Uri and Unterwalden: See **Swiss horns.**

Uspensky Cathedral: RONDO, 34: See **Fioravanti, Rudolfo.**

Usury: HN: The prohibition in many societies against usury was more than an attempt to stamp out the bad practice of lending money at a high rate of interest or taking financial advantage of a debtor who was then completely in your thrall; it was to forbid any loan at all which resulted in a profit. Making money by racking up interest over the time it was lent was considered contrary to the laws of God: time belongs to God, not to man, so man cannot sell time at a profit. According to Deuteronomy 23:19–20, you should not charge interest to your brother. This the Christian Church took to refer to your fellow Christian, hence it allowed interest to be charged in the case of 'strangers', i.e., Muslims.

The exception to the Church's injunction against usury was the lending of money if there was risk involved in the enterprise or investment. This naturally included trade; one's ship may not return to port at all, let alone with a lucrative cargo. Similarly, Bills of Exchange allowed the merchant to pay for commerce from one country to another without necessitating the actual and immediate transfer of bullion or cash. As the money markets rose and fell, a profit could not be guaranteed in advance, therefore interest could be included in the calculation. Interest also applied to loans to princes in times of war, although a wise bank would do its best to ensure its officials were not over-generous or over-ambitious in the terms and amounts they were willing to risk to such loans (see Tommaso Portinari*). See also Pawnbroking.*

UZUM HASAN:* RAM: (*c.* 1408–1478) The life of the Chief of the White Sheep tribe is substantially covered in Volume I. For his continuing struggle against the Ottoman Turks, see under **Ludovico de Severi da Bologna; Zacco, King of Cyprus**; and **Zeno family.** Caterino Zeno was elected to be Venetian ambassador to his court in 1471 (the previous two elected candidates having turned down the honour) and he was followed in the role by **Ambrogio Contarini** and **Josaphat Barbaro.** All urged Uzum to commit his forces to war against the Ottoman Empire, but internal rebellion forced him to delay. Mistakenly informed of his father's death, Uzum's son Orgalu Mahumeth took the town of Shiraz. Uzum was quick to put down the rebellion, and Orgalu was imprisoned and executed. However, any hopes the West had that Uzum might help against the Turk ended with Uzum's last illness. He became very sick whilst in Tabriz in 1477, and died the following Epiphany. He left four sons, three by one mother and one by his Christian wife Theodora. The night of his death, the three sons strangled their twenty-year-old half-brother and divided their father's estate between them. The second brother, Yacoob, then caused his elder to be slain, and he remained as King, ruling until 1490, but after his death the White Sheep were torn apart by internal conflict and ceased to be a threat to their more powerful neighbours.

V

Väinämöinen to Vipunen: PAWN, 24: See **I shall sink my anvil further into the flesh of your heart; I shall install my forge in a deeper place.**

VAN BORSELEN family: RISING: From their strategic position on the island of Walcheren in the Low Countries, the van Borselen family of shipowners and ducal advisers formed a consistently energetic and capable clan who influenced, not least through their marriages, a good deal of the political and trading history of their times.

Their base, created by themselves, was the small port of Veere, once called Campveere, after the ferry which crossed from there to Campen. Close beside this was the modest trading centre of Middleburg, which as early as 1323 contained a Scottish community. Unlike Bruges* and the rest of Flanders, which had a wide mercantile reach, Holland and Zeeland were to develop their trade chiefly with Scotland. Veere also had physical advantages. It was close to the sea, and ships could unload in safety, although not in great numbers. Because of its high quay, merchants' cellars were not flooded. Also, the 'road' or sea inlet at hand was sheltered and offered a clear passage to the open sea, free of rocks and seldom frozen.

The original overlords of Zeeland, and hence of Veere and of Middleburg, were the Counts of Flanders, under whom the Counts of Holland held fief. The possession of Zeeland, and the van Borselen hold upon Veere, was a matter of constant dispute, and the owners of Veere were not always successful. In 1292, Guy de Dampierre, Count of Flanders 1278–1305 gave Zeeland controversially to his son, Guy of Namur. At the same time the precious fourteen-year-old John, son of Florence V of Holland (ruled 1256–1296) and grandson of Edward I of England (ruled 1272–1307) acquired (on English advice) a new tutor: 'that strenuous, prudent and handsome knight, Wolfaert of Borselen'. It was not a wise move. In the ensuing controversy, Wolfaert was killed on the orders of John of Avesnes, Count of Hainault, next heir to Holland after young John. Then John himself was poisoned and died (1299). In spite of the efforts of Wolfaert's brothers, the intruder Guy settled in Veere and then won the other trading centre of Middleburg, held against him by a son of William, next Count of Hainault and Holland (ruled 1304–1337).

The dynasty, however, survived. In 1423 a Philip van Borselen was steward to Philip the Good, Duke of Burgundy.* And a decade after that, another van Borselen added to the family's fame by contriving to marry in 1432 Jacqueline, Countess of Holland. The fortunate groom was Franck (Frans) van Borselen, Count of Ostrevant, seigneur of Veere, Governor of Holland, and he received ducal permission for the union in return for recognising Duke Philip as overlord of Holland and Zeeland.

The next lord of Veere was Henry van Borselen (1405–1470), Governor of Holland, and Knight of the Golden Fleece (as was Franck). In 1429, Henry of Veere married Joanne van Halewyn from an illustrious Flemish family. It was their son, the sixth Wolfaert van Borselen (1430–1487), who was to become in 1444 the very young husband of the fifteen-year-old **Princess Mary**, one of the six daughters of James I, King of Scotland (1406–1437) and his Queen, Joan Beaufort of England (d. 1445). The marriage took place in the castle of Sandenburg, Veere, and Wolfaert did not travel to Scotland. About the same time, by another impressive contract, an Adrian van Borselen became the husband of Anne, one of Duke Philip's natural daughters.

Trading links between Scotland and the Low Countries were by now very strong, and were being sealed by other illustrious marriages. In 1449, the Duke of Burgundy permitted the marriage of his cousin Mary of Gueldres* to the Scottish King James II,* brother of the Princess Mary, lady of Veere. In this case, Count Henry, Wolfaert's father, travelled to Scotland for the wedding, and left immediately afterwards for a pilgrimage to Rome. A year later, in 1451, Wolfaert's son Charles was born, with **Charles**, the future **Duke of Burgundy**,* as his godfather, but the boy died, aged thirteen, soon after beginning his studies at Louvain University.* Louis, Dauphin of France (the future **Louis XI***), who also studied at Louvain, was accompanied by Wolfaert van Borselen when he returned to France for his coronation, and must have known the van Borselens well, although the developing rift between France and Burgundy must have disappointed any hopes of a friendship with both.

In 1455 Wolfaert's sister Margaret married the powerful Louis de Bruges, seigneur of Gruuthuse,* future Lieutenant-General to the Duke of Burgundy in Holland, Zeeland and Frisia. Five years later, Mary of Gueldres, Queen of Scotland, confided to the Duke and her family her son Alexander, aged six, the future **Duke of Albany**.* The boy remained in the Low Countries for four years, leaving for Scotland in 1464, the year his cousin Charles died, and just after the death of his own mother, the Queen.

A few years later the Princess Mary, Wolfaert van Borselen's Scots wife, was dead, and Wolfaert had to surrender his privileged title of Earl of Buchan. In fact, the honour was to pass to the King of Scotland's half-brother **James Stewart**, who, visiting Calais only a few years before, had met Henry, Count of Veere, where he was known simply as 'the brother of my lady of Buchan'. Henry himself was not only lord of Veere but also comte de Grandpré, an area in Champagne east of Rheims.

A widower with no legitimate heir (but one very able son Paul, outside marriage), Wolfaert van Borselen looked for his second wife to the great ducal tribe of the **Bourbons**, as Alexander, Duke of Albany, was to do twelve years later. Charlotte de Bourbon, whom Wolfaert married in 1468, was the youngest daughter of Louis de Bourbon, comte de Montpensier et Clermont, third son of John I, Duke of Bourbon (1410–1434), whose lineage went back to Duke Philip's own father. Duke Philip's bastard brother, Louis de Bourbon, was provost of St Peter's, Lille. And a very young Anna, elder daughter of this marriage of Wolfaert's, was in 1478 to marry Philip, whose father was the late Duke Philip's own famous son, the Bastard Anthony. So Anna became lady of Veere, and wife to Philip of Burgundy, Knight of the Golden Fleece, lord of Beveren, Governor of Artois, Admiral of Flanders and Chamberlain of **Maximilian I** King of the Romans. The Bastard's other son, cleverly placed in France, was showered with favours by King Louis, and none of the Bastard Anthony's French lands was destined for Anna's husband. In 1503, in a second marriage, she was to become the wife of Louis of Montfort.

By 1478, the year of Anna's marriage, her father Wolfaert had lost both his second wife and Henry his father. Of Wolfaert's five children by Charlotte, four daughters including Anna were to survive. Count Henry seemed, through his long active life, to remain the prime mover in the family, seizing the political, maritime and military opportunities, and arranging these advantageous marriages. It was Count Henry who founded a religious foundation in 1462, and who went to war in 1467 against Liège, Wolfaert beside him. Wolfaert also fought the following year. When, in 1470, Edward of York (**Edward IV***) fled from England to shelter with Louis de Gruuthuse and his van Borselen wife, it was Henry van Borselen, as Burgundian Admiral, who supplied the ship *Antony* on which Edward returned. It must have been one of the last acts of his life.

Throughout this period, the fortunes of Veere and of Middleburg shifted according to the power of the times. Bruges, with its flourishing foreign merchant colonies, had long had main claim to the **Staple** which handled foreign trade, although this moved periodically in response to current threats or disputes. The main agent serving the Scots in the Low Countries was often a resident Scot, such as Stephen Angus, who was both Scots Conservator and clerk of the **Hanseatic League** in 1466, and probably belonged to the family Bonkle.* The most powerful single appointment of this time was that of **Anselm Adorne*** of Bruges, who formed a close relationship with King **James III*** of Scotland and acted as his consul in the Low Countries from 1472 to 1476.

The post fell into several different hands in the turmoil which followed the death of Duke Charles in the battle of Nancy, 1477, and was largely held by Scots with strong trading connections with Bruges. Sometimes the position seemed to be shared by several at once, and sometimes separate appointments were made for specific areas. It is unsurprising, then, to find Wolfaert van Borselen's descendants prominent among Scottish consuls. Adorne and **Andrew Wodman**, who shared the post until 1483, were succeeded by

Thomas Swift, and then by two men, the well-known Scots trader Andrew Haliburton, and Paul van Borselen, Wolfaert's natural son. In 1501, the Staple moved back to Middleburg, and the Conservator was guaranteed an annual salary, provided he resided there, 'with his wife, children and household'. A John France followed after Haliburton had died, and before the Scottish Staple once more moved, officially, in 1506 to Veere. The English Merchant Adventurers had already moved their Staple to **Antwerp**, hitherto largely a fishing and farming community.

In 1509, the Scottish King **James IV*** was in touch with the bailie of Veere over the goods of James Mackeson of **Leith**, a Haliburton associate. By 1510 Henry van Borselen, bailie of Veere, was named as the next Scottish Conservator. Prior to that, in an Edinburgh charter dated 12 December 1507, King James ceded to Henry van Borselen, knight, son of Paul van Borselen, knight, for singular favour and good service to humanity and to merchants working and sailing abroad, the lordship of Lauderdale, Berwickshire, 'as given by King James III to Henry's father, the late Paul van Borselen'. The annual fee for the lordship was a single red rose, brought to Lauder.

In 1508, Henry van Borselen made a gift of Flemish horses to the Scots King. When he died, he was followed by another Henry van Borselen, and then by Philip, who died in 1547, and was the last Conservator to be described as 'from Holland'. Other consuls appointed in the same period included John Moffat, who was Conservator about 1517, possibly at Bergen ap Zoom, to which the Staple had moved in 1495. Moffat had been an agent of Haliburton, and his family in Scotland had lived next to Robin Crawford of **Berecrofts.** John received a yearly pension and 'use of the white house', and dying in 1526 was followed by his son Erasmus.

Another Conservator, appointed in 1522 by James V,* was an Alexander Muir, whose successor was expected to be his nephew, Jasper Crawford. Muir's appointment was notified to Odulf of Burgundy, lord of Veere, whose mother was Anna, Wolfaert van Borselen's daughter. Anna, lady of Veere, was painted by Jan Grossart about 1525, when he was in the service of Odulf of Burgundy, and her likeness, magically refined, was used by the same artist to portray the Virgin in a picture of the Virgin and Child presently in the Metropolitan Museum of Art in New York.

By 1553, in the catalogue of Conservators, one George Gordon had been dismissed, and a James Henderson or Henrisoun appointed, giving way to a George Hacket. (The Crawfords and Henrisouns were intermarried, and lived next to the Moffats in Edinburgh.) After about 1541, Staple towns provided houses for the Conservator in which Scottish merchants could lodge, as the family Metteneye had done in Bruges. By 1600 the name of Crawford had appeared again – a Patrick and a James Crawford, both at Veere.

The novels therefore reflect the real customs of the time, including the Crawford and van Borselen links, although the character of Florence van Borselen, 'half brother of Count Henry', is fictitious, as are his two daughters.

The records for the illegitimate Paul van Borselen mention Henry his son, but do not name his wife, and her identification in the novels is imaginary. (D. D.)

VAN DER GOES, Hugo: SCALES: (*c.* 1440–1482). Flemish painter, probably born in Ghent, and Dean of the Guild* of Painters in Ghent 1473–1475. The Portinari* Altar-piece is said to be his masterpiece; the altar-piece in **Trinity Chapel**, featuring **James III,*** **Margaret of Denmark** and Edward Bonkle,* is also his work. He was involved in helping paint the decorations for the marriage of **Charles, Duke of Burgundy,*** to **Margaret of York** in 1468, and work in and for the town of Bruges* probably brought him into contact with Portinari and with **Hans Memling.**

His illness and mental decline were chronicled by Gaspar Ofhuys from Tournai, a novitiate at the same time that Hugo became a monk in the Red Cloister (Soignes Monastery) near Brussels in the autumn of 1475, probably just after completing the Portinari Altar-piece. Joining as a *frater conversus*, van der Goes, a celebrity of his day, was given privileges above the other monks. He continued to paint and received visitors, including among them the future Emperor **Maximilian I**, but his illness began to manifest itself in 1481. Suffering from suicidal thoughts and confused speech (and probably dependent upon alcohol), he was unable to work and made even more depressed and anxious at the thought of his unfinished commissions. The Prior tried playing music to him (as the harp had soothed Saul; see also **Spondaic rhythm**); van der Goes briefly recovered his sanity, but died shortly after. See also **Justus of Ghent.**

Veere: See **Van Borselen.**

Vessel of death: LIONS, 17: A poignant phrase to describe a father whose heir has predeceased him.

Victory, a great national: See **Flodden.**

***Virginité voluntaire*:** LIONS, 17: 'Self-imposed chastity', and *union charnelle* ('physical intercourse') are presented as opposing conditions in the text of a **Mystery Play.** The first was applied to the marriage of Mary and Joseph.

Vishnevetsky: CASTLE: A famous Ukrainian clan, the 'Lords of Cherry Village'. An early member of the family appears fictitiously in RONDO, but its most famous son was Dymitr Wiśniowiecki (d. 1563), half-Ruthenian, half-Romanian, who founded the first Cossack *sich* (military camp) at Chortyca on the Dnieper. He was captured by the Turks and executed in Istanbul for piracy. The name, in the form of Vishnevetsky, appears in the annals of Ivan the Terrible, Tsar of Russia,* as the famous Cossack leader nick-named Baida, who figures, with his ballad, in CASTLE. (D. D.)

Vistula: RONDO, 4: Over six hundred miles long, the River Vistula runs through the heart of the Polish countryside from Cracow to **Danzig** on the coast. As all of the main tributaries of the river were navigable it was the ideal means of transporting heavy and bulky items that would not be economically feasible to take by land routes. Fifteenth-century improvements in agricultural production allowed the export of surplus grain, an increasingly lucrative trade for the Polish nobility and the many intermediaries who transported rye and wheat to the coast.

To transport the grain many different forms of craft were employed, the most important being *szkuta*, massive shallow rafts made from whole timbers, surmounted by a square silo containing the grain with a lean-to shelter for the crew. The rafts were often chained together to form a convoy, propelled by the current of the river, aided by the crew punting and by rigging a large square sail. The raft was guided by the steersman (*sternik*), who steered with a large oar from the stern. A skilled master boatman (*rotman*) would hire himself out to navigate the often dangerous fast-flowing river. On arrival in Danzig, the rafts would be broken up and sold for timber.

It made sense to get the grain to Danzig as early in the season as was possible. Grain producers from the far south would send their grain as far north as they could in the autumn, and as soon as the thaw had begun the following spring, arrange for the grain to come to Danzig. It provided a perfect opportunity for the landlocked aristocracy of the interior to see something of the greater part of their country, including the wealth and decadence of Danzig. Sebastian Fabian Klonowic wrote a poem about his journey to the coast on the swollen river (1596). Dangers included hitting underwater logs, *wilki* ('wolves'); or becoming snagged in the moorings of a floating water mill, called *bździeły* ('farters') because of the characteristic noise they made. The final danger was hitting the great wooden boom when they arrived at Danzig.

***Vivit, et est vitae nescius ipse suae*:** QUEENS, 1, 6: 'He's alive, but doesn't know it'.

W

Walking quadrilles in the street like the sodomitical partridge: LIONS, 7: The phrase comes from the knight of unorthodox tastes who bore a picture of 'the supposedly sodomitical partridge' as a charge in his arms. The reason for this claim for the bird is not entirely clear, nor the type of partridge involved, unless it be the red-legged or French variety. To walk quadrilles was to swagger, hand on hip. (D. D.)

Wallace tharwith has tane him on the croune . . . : GEMINI, 17: A quote from **Blind Harry**'s ***The Wallace***, Book III.

Wallace, The: GEMINI, 17: It has been argued that the unpopularity of the 1474 peace with England and the betrothal of Prince James to **Cecilia** was the impetus for the vituperative piece of anti-English propaganda that is Blind Harry's poem of about 12,000 lines in heroic couplets. It tells the tale of the Scottish patriot who rose against Edward I, King of England (1271–1307). William Wallace (*c.* 1270–1305) won against the English at Stirling in 1297 but was defeated by Edward at Falkirk the following year. Edward conquered Scotland once more and Wallace was taken south and executed in London in 1305. Scotland united under Robert the Bruce (ruled 1306–1329), defeating Edward II (ruled 1307–1327) at the battle of Bannockburn in 1314. For a work of the late-fifteenth century, the propaganda value was tremendous. Its rabid anti-English standpoint and the gruesome scenes of slaying made it a popular vehicle for those who wished to maintain hostility across the border. Northern Earls, such as **David Lindsay**, Earl of Crawford, and Colin Campbell, **Earl of Argyll**, supported peace with England, as did merchants and traders who had profited from peace to go about their business free from piracy and English attack. Those families who were against peace (and England) were concentrated in the south and allied to **Alexander, Duke of Albany**.* Harry was provided with source material for his epic by **Sir James Liddell of Halkerston**, Albany's steward, and Wallace of Craigie, killed by Albany's guns at Dunbar (see **Sir John Colquhoun of Luss**).

Wally Gowdy: KINGS, I, 5: 'Jewel': Scots term of endearment. For more along the same lines, such as 'huny soppis', 'tyrlie myrlie' and 'crowdie mowdie', see the poem, 'In Secreit Place this Hyndir Nycht' by William Dunbar (*c.* 1460–1520).

Waszmość: RONDO, 10: See **Etiquette: language.**

Watermarks: LIONS, 19: Coded watermarks on paper were early used for a number of subversive purposes, such as symbols of gnostic amulets in southern France. Not being readily visible, they could equally be used to embarrass an innocent party.

Weans and wames: LIONS, 19: Children and tummies (Scots). 'Speug' (pronounced spyugg), a fond name for a child, is the Scots word for sparrow. The Ukrainian term *Yunitsa*, meaning heifer, carries, for adults, the same kind of personal endearment.

Westmann Islands: LIONS, 20: An archipelago comprising some fifteen small islands, twelve kilometers off the southern coast of **Iceland**. The natural harbour of Heimaey and the fertile fishing grounds nearby where the fish spawn drew fishermen from as far south as the east coast of England in the fifteenth century, seeking cod, ling, hake, pollack and salmon. To arrive before the cod spawned, ships had to sail early in the year; the season was short for cod, but the journey was long. They would bring enough supplies with them to fish for the whole season, whether the **Hanseatic League** wanted them there or not. See **Stockfish**.

Where are you going, pretty fair maid . . . : PAWN, 22; 23: A line from a poem. Washing the face in water in which strawberry leaves had been soaked was said to be good for the complexion.

'Where were you going, fair maid', said he,
'With your pale face and your yellow hair?'
'Going to the well, sweet sir', she said,
'for strawberry leaves make maidens fair'.

'Shall I go with you, fair maid', said he,
'with your pale face and your yellow hair?'
'Do if you wish, sweet sir', she said,
'for strawberry leaves make maidens fair'.

'How if I lay you on the ground,
with your pale face and your yellow hair?'
'I'll get up again, sweet sir', she said,
'for strawberry leaves make maidens fair'.

'How if I get you with child,
with your pale face and your yellow hair?'
'Then I will bear him, sweet sir', she said,
'for strawberry leaves make maidens fair'.

'Whom will you find to father your child,
with your pale face and your yellow hair?'
'You'll be his father, fair sir,' she said,
'for strawberry leaves make maidens fair'. . . .

Where hast thou hung the carlish knight?: CHECKMATE, I, 5: See **He's twice the size of common men.**

Whitekirk: GEMINI, 49: Four miles south-east of **North Berwick** Priory on the east coast of Scotland, the lands and parish church of Whitekirk, then called Hamer, were conferred by David I (King of Scotland 1124–1153) on the canons of **Holyrood, Edinburgh**. By the fourteenth century, a well had appeared nearby, reputed to have powers of miraculous healing, and by 1413 pilgrims were visiting the *alba ecclesia* at the supposed rate of fifteen thousand a year, bringing lucrative offerings and requiring special hostels to house them. The church was pillaged by the English during the invasion of 1356, and the image of Our Lady despoiled of its jewels: legend tells how one of the robbers was fatally injured by a falling crucifix, and how their ship later sank in a storm. Saved from a less apposite storm in 1435, the future Pope Pius II,* then Aeneas Silvio Piccolomini, walked barefoot to the shrine at Whitekirk, and later had his damaged feet treated by the Duke of Milan's famous physician, Giammatteo Ferrari of Grado. A few years later, in 1438, the year after her husband had been assassinated, the Dowager Queen of James I used the shrine at Whitekirk as a pretext to escape with her son to the safety of Stirling, while pretending to sail south on pilgrimage.

King **James IV*** visited Whitekirk several times, but about 1540 the pilgrims' quarters were demolished by leave of James V* to build a castle for Oliver, the son of Sir Oliver **Sinclair** of **Roslin**. The west end of the seventeenth-century tithe barn may incorporate part of Sinclair's tower, which was attacked by the English in 1544 and again in 1548. No trace remains of the well.

The church itself has undergone several changes, and the present version is a restoration of the fifteenth-century building which was burned down by suffragettes in 1914. This was and is cruciform, with a square three-storey tower and a fine south-western vaulted porch entered through a pointed archway. Above the unusual east window is a panel bearing the arms of **Archibald Crawford**, Abbot of Holyrood from 1450 to 1483. As with all substantial religious buildings, it provided a seemly place for secular meetings on higher issues involving diplomacy, the law and the state. It was a meeting-place for the court of **regality** of Broughton, another of the responsibilities of the Abbots of Holyrood. In 1493 Abbot Robert and the bailie of the regality dealt in open court with a case involving a local man, Patrick Scougal. Ten years earlier, Flemish records suggest that Whitekirk was the place allotted for a meeting of reconciliation between **Alexander, Duke of Albany**,* then at Dunbar Castle seven miles to the south, and representatives of his brother **James III**.* This occasioned the death at North Berwick of **Anselm Adorne**.* (D. D.)

WHITELAW, Archibald: UNICORN: (*c.* 1420–1498) Scholar, humanist, diplomat, Archibald Whitelaw was picked by King James II* of Scotland to tutor his heir, and thereafter, for thirty-one years, served as secretary of state to King **James III*** and his son and successor.

The lands after which he was named are in southern Scotland, near the border with England. Whitelaw was sent to the University of St Andrews, where he graduated in arts in 1439, a time when the teaching staff was just parting with two leading conciliarists, John Athilmer and James Ogilvie, supporters of the fated non-Roman Pope Felix V (Antipope 1439–1449) in the famous schism between rival pontiffs which was to last for another ten years. Like the conciliarists, Whitelaw elected to enter the University of Cologne, after which he taught at both Cologne and St Andrews until into his middle years.

This substantial teaching career, the constant exercise and perfecting of his Latin, the building of a great classical library qualified him for the highest kind of specialised advancement. His royal service began in or before 1460, when he was chosen to tutor the royal heir, but was also employed by the King as a secret envoy to Richard of York (1411–1460) during the English civil war between Yorkists and Lancastrians. Later that same year, King James II met his death by an exploding cannon; but Whitelaw was retained by the child Prince's mother, Mary of Gueldres.

In 1461, the first Parliament of the new reign was attended by the new Chancellor, **Andrew Stewart, Lord Avandale**. Bishop Kennedy* and the **Earl of Argyll** joined the Queen Dowager in a Council of Regency. And between 1461 and 1462, Archibald Whitelaw was appointed Clerk Register.

By 1462, Whitelaw was Archdeacon of Moray, where he would be followed by Archibald Knollys. In 1467 he became subchanter of Moray, a position once held by **Thomas Spens**, and later to fall to John Ireland. The same year, Archibald Whitelaw became dean of the **collegiate church** of Dunbar, and in 1468 Archdeacon of Glasgow, where he would later hold the post of subdean. His chief clerical appointment, which he held for nearly thirty years, was that of Archdeacon of Lothian, where one of his predecessors was a man with a career like his own: William Turnbull, another humanist and royal secretary who became Bishop of Glasgow and went on to found the university there.

In the last years of the lives of Kennedy and the Dowager, Whitelaw was part of the inner cabal that was forming about the young King. In 1462, he served as an **exchequer** auditor with Argyll and Avandale, and as Master Secretary Whitelaw he accompanied them, and the Bishop and **John Stewart, Lord Darnley**, on the three-month progress made by the twelve-year-old King in 1464. When the **Boyds** launched their attempt to control the King, they failed to shake the authority of the royal officers, including Whitelaw, who weathered the fall of the Boyds and the departure of the King's sister **Princess Mary**. When she returned in 1471 with **Anselm Adorne**,* Whitelaw had been in Alnwick at a meeting between Scots and English commissioners, ostensibly to settle matters of dispute on the Borders, but actually to test the position of Scotland and France. The King, his charge, was now married to **Margaret of Denmark**, and soon to have his own son. It was Whitelaw as royal secretary who helped to draw up a treaty of marriage between the infant prince and the King of England's daughter **Cecilia**.

In the fraught days before the King's brother **Alexander, Duke of Albany**,* brought an English army to Scotland in 1482, Whitelaw was the appointed substitute for Archbishop **William Scheves** in the deliberations of the Lords of the Articles (a committee of Parliament). When the army arrived and the King was imprisoned, Whitelaw continued as part of the temporary government, whereas his colleagues withdrew until the moment for negotiation arrived. Once the English army had gone, Whitelaw again held his place in the chaotic administration formed to satisfy Albany, while the others once more remained apart. When Albany finally left, government resumed with Whitelaw still in the position of Secretary. Only Avandale, returning, was no longer Chancellor, the appointment being eventually given to Argyll.

During the King's final years, Whitelaw continued to sit as one of the Lords of Council, and to act as co-ordinator between the legislators of the kingdom. In 1484, he accompanied the embassy, led by the Earl of Argyll, which met the new English King, Richard III (see **Richard, Duke of Gloucester**) at Nottingham Castle, to discuss a truce and a new Anglo-Scottish alliance. While there, Whitelaw delivered a speech, interlarded with classical quotations, paying tribute to the martial prowess of Richard and praising the glories of peace. Although perhaps oppressive to its hearers, it represents the first known example of Scots-Latin oratory of the time. Two years later, Whitelaw accompanied Bishop Elphinstone to England to continue the truce with Richard's successor, the Tudor King Henry VII (ruled 1485–1509). When national unrest reached its climax in 1488, Whitelaw remained out of the field, continuing to handle **Great Seal** charters in Edinburgh up to a fortnight before the battle at which the King was killed. Afterwards, he returned to his office, carrying his experience and the continuity of royal government to the youth who was now King, as he had once served his grandfather, and attending his coronation in Scone. He was with the King at Stirling during the revolt which involved Dumbarton Castle.

Whitelaw worked for five years as royal secretary for **James IV**,* sitting as a **Lord Auditor of Causes and Complaints** with Argyll, who was again Chancellor. He was not the King's tutor, but no doubt gave something to his first, formative years. At Christmas 1493 he retired, just before James turned twenty-one. He had an estate, perhaps in the Lothians. One of his last acts was to make a donation to St Kentigern's altar in the church of Currie, from High Street land possessed by the Edinburgh burgess Adam Halkerston. It perhaps argued a fondness for Glasgow.

Only the facts of Whitelaw's career survive, and nothing of the man, barring what remains of his impressive collection of books – a Horace, a Lucan, a Sallust, a commentary on the speeches of Cicero – some of them annotated in his own hand. Nothing is known of his family (or if he wore spectacles). What he thought of Albany cannot be guessed, although he must have understood him to a degree, given his knowledge of youth, and what advice Bishop Kennedy offered. The fact that Albany allowed him to stay through the ultimate crisis suggests that he saw the Secretary as useful. Certainly, he carried the Signet. But in addition, perhaps James's tutor and secretary still represented a figure of early authority: someone to be respected and feared, in spite of his wearisome learning.

There is nothing to show, either, how Whitelaw regarded **John of Mar**, or the two Princesses, or the Queen, who was so young and so different from the experienced Mary of Gueldres. He seems to have taken no part in papal missions. His achievement was to add his skills as a teacher and his knowledge of classical balance to the more worldly experience of Avandale, of Argyll and of Scheves, and so help devise, through thirty turbulent years, the strategies that would best benefit the young in his charge. (D. D.)

Whither are you going, pretty fair maid . . . ?: KNIGHTS, III, 10: See **Where are you going, pretty fair maid . . .**

Whoever is unsupported by the Mystery of Love . . . : RONDO, 6: The high-principled preamble to the Acts of Horodło (1413). The combined armies of Poland and the Grand Duchy of Lithuania triumphed over the **Teutonic Knights** at the battle of Grunwald in 1410, and the Acts were intended to strengthen their opposition to their common foe. Poland's lords and Lithuania's boyars were united into a joint estate by these Acts signed at Horodło (a town on the Bug River, near the border between Lithuania and Poland). The **Jagiellonian dynasty** of Lithuania ruled as Kings of Poland, while the Grand Duke of Lithuania was elected by the nobles of Poland and Lithuania, in order to maintain the Duchy's political sovereignty.

This quotation from the Acts is continued in RONDO, 44.

Whoever shall cast love aside, shall lose everything: RONDO, 44: See **Whoever is unsupported by the Mystery of Love . . .**

Wiśniowiecki: RONDO: See **Vishnevetsky**.

WODMAN, Andrew: UNICORN: (*fl.* 1470s) Little is known of his life, apart from his service in France from 1456, when he became an Archer of the King of France's bodyguard. By 1459 he was one of the forty-eight Archers serving under Patrick Flockart with fellow Archers Roland Cressant and **David Simpson**, whose background is similarly unrecorded. The event which ended his service appears on the record for 1 February 1464, which states that Andro Wodman had been dismissed from the guard for the killing of Roland Cressant. At the same time, David Simpson left 'on the grounds of leprosy'.

The killing has never been explained, and no amount of research has produced a connection between Cressant and Wodman, far less the trace of a vendetta. Yet a drunken quarrel that went too far would not seem to warrant such punishment, especially after so many years' service. Perhaps Roland Cressant was more important than he seemed – the name could have been a version of Concressault, a French-Scottish title, or it could reflect a link with René of Savoy, who much favoured his pursuivant, Croissant – a name commemorating René's Order du Croissant, recently suppressed for political reasons by the Pope. There is no proof either way. The reasons assigned to the death in the novel are fictitious. There are no hard facts to demonstrate Andrew Wodman's subsequent career, but research into the families of that name in Scotland produced a man called Andrew Wodman who by 1476 had won a place close to King James as his familiar esquire, and who was appointed that year to succeed **Anselm Adorne*** as Conservator of Scots Privileges in Bruges. The change was probably a matter of Scottish policy, and seems to have lasted only so long as Adorne was in disfavour in Bruges.* Some time after Adorne left Bruges to settle finally in Scotland, the position seems to have been restored to him, and he remained Conservator until his death, when the post passed to another, not Wodman.

The family of Wodman seemed to belong to Aberdeen, where there was an Andrew Wodman in 1402, about the same time that a Nicholas Wodman was a burgess. Another burgess, Thomas Wodman, was prominent in Aberdeen at the end of the century, when he was several times dunned, along with others, for dues from the salmon trade, required to repair the church of Aberdeen. Salmon exports involve other countries, and there were Wodmans in England, one being arrested in 1461 by the sheriff of Lincoln, and one William, a squire, taken for treason in 1440 when the Duchess of Gloucester was arrested for treason and witchcraft.

The best-recorded Scottish Wodman of Andrew's time was John, who entered the church and became in time Prior of May, Abbot of Jedburgh and Bishop of Ross. John Wodman had a career of some turbulence: in the course of a papal dispute over his claim to the Priory of Restinneth in the see of St Andrews, he is described as 'an alleged canon of the **Augustinian** Order'. In August 1481, William Elphinstone was appointed to the bishopric of Ross, but he was not consecrated as Bishop because the terms of his appointment made it clear that the incumbent was responsible for the debts of his predecessor. The former incumbent was John Wodman, who had died owing nine hundred ducats to the Papal Camera. Although the novels describe John and Andrew as brothers, the relationship between the two is unknown. Certainly, John was in frequent contact with Bruges, as was common with holders of church offices with annates to transmit to Rome.

The Bruges firm of Paolo Bociardo exchanged bills with the Medici bankers of Venice.* John Wodman's favoured Bruges intermediary was one Peter Bogart, possibly of the same family, who was a papal scriptor, notary, interpreter and agent of the **Duke of Burgundy**. Peter Bogart, possibly the same man, was at that time Archdeacon of St Salvator, Bruges, a position held as a rule by the future Chancellors of Flanders. For ten years from 1472 a Pierre Bogard held a position in the church of St Pierre of Lille. With such connections, Andrew Wodman would have been well qualified to follow Adorne as a Conservator in Scotland. By 1541 a churchman called Dominus Andrew Wodman witnessed a Hamilton charter at **Linlithgow**. (D. D.)

Woe now to the chickens, woe to the blind lion: LIONS, 48: From a motet by French prelate, music theorist, poet and composer Philippe de Vitry (1291–1361): *Ve pullis mox, ve ceco leoni.* The blind lion is Philip IV (the Fair), King of France 1285–1314; and the fox of the warning is Enguerran de Marigny, his wily chief counsellor. (D. D.)

Wood, Sir Andrew: GEMINI: (c. 1460–1540) Born in Largo in Fife, from whence he took his title, Wood spent most of his adult life trading from **Leith** with his ships the *Yellow Caravel* and the *Flower* and owned property in the south-west corner of north Leith; a sycamore tree or plane tree grew in his garden. A loyal captain to three generations of Stewart monarchs, Wood became prominent when Anglo-Scottish relations were at a low ebb. When the English began to attack the Scots by sea in 1480, **John, Lord Howard**, seized eight ships at Leith, Kinghorn and Pittenweem, and burned **Blackness**, but was harried by Wood, who received his knighthood and lands in Largo from **James III*** as thanks and recompense for the losses he suffered on land and at sea. In 1488, when James III fought his rebel nobility at Sauchieburn, Wood's ships cruised up and down the Forth, removing the wounded from the battlefield. Under **James IV*** he maintained his position of favour and was made captain of the King's famous flagship, the *Great Michael*, built at Newhaven, near Leith, and launched in 1512. Following the disaster of **Flodden**, Wood was amongst those in the Scottish embassy sent to France in 1515 to encourage **John Stewart, Second Duke of Albany**, to come to Scotland as Regent. The *Great Michael* was later sold to Francis I* of France for forty thousand francs. After over forty years of service, Wood was described as a gentleman of the household in the reign of James V* in 1526.

Wound Man: LIONS, 40: The hand-coloured woodcut called *The Wound Man* appeared in 1517 in a Field Book of wound surgery which was based on a manuscript a century older. The picture showed the stoical figure of a man displaying every variety of wound, sore, abscess and injury that a physician might hope to meet in a lifetime. The equivalent model on another level was Disease Man, upon whom might be discerned the symptoms of pox, impetigo, mania, running eyes, foul breath and heart disease. In that order. (D. D.)

Wrestling with ghosts, after the matter of the Antabatae: CHECKMATE, I, 4: (For details on the antabatae [gladiators], see Volume 1.) The exact quotation comes from a letter sent to Sir Thomas More (1478–1535) by Cuthbert, Bishop of London, in 1528. In the letter More is given licence to keep and read heretical books, so that he may confound any Wycliffite or Lutheran arguments and strengthen the Catholic religion:

> And in order that you should not be wrestling with ghosts, after the manner of the Antabatae, ignorant of what you are fighting against, I am sending you their mad incantations in our tongue along with some of Luther's books, whence those monstrous ideas have sprung. When you have studied them closely you will understand more easily in what hiding places these twisting serpents lurk, and by what quibbles they seek to slip away when they have been caught. For it is a great step towards victory if you can spy out the enemy's plans, read his thoughts thoroughly and anticipate his aims. For if you set yourself to refute something which they will say they never meant, all your labour will be in vain.

Wubbit: GEMINI, 4: More commonly 'wabbit': a mildly derisive Scots term for the weak, limp or exhausted. To 'dwine', in Scots, is picturesquely to swoon.

Y

YARE, Thomas: GEMINI: 'Thom of Yare' was an exceptionally astute royal merchant, one of whose jobs was to supply luxury goods to two Kings, **James III*** and **James IV*** of Scotland. More than that, he was a merchant in both **Edinburgh** and Berwick-upon-Tweed,* at a time when the latter was about to be lost for the last time, to the English.

It is likely that Yare was a native of Berwick. England and Scotland were at peace in 1471, when he was a burgess and customs officer for wool cloth in Edinburgh. In Berwick-upon-Tweed over the years he performed similar duties involving customs and land-letting rights, and in 1474, James III gave him possession of William Hall's **tenement** there. By 1477, when another clutch of tenements was being distributed to key men in the kingdom's administration, Thomas Yare was both chamberlain and bailie of Berwick, and acted as controller of customs along with **Walter Bertram**, a future Provost of Edinburgh. His fellow residents, in addition to Bertram, included **William Scheves**, the future Archbishop of St Andrews; **Sir John Colquhoun of Luss**; Alexander Inglis, the Clerk Register, and the Browns, merchants of Couston, as well as the great houses of the Abbey of **Melrose**, and of the Abbot of **Newbattle** Abbey. One of the last glimpses of Yare's transactions there, before the town changed hands, is a trip he took for the King, riding to Berwick to acquire the King's wine, for which he was paid expenses of three pounds. The loss of the direct Berwick wine trade must have made **Thomas Preston**'s shipload of English wine especially welcome.

When trading by sea, Yare shared the cost of the shipping with others, as was usual. In 1473 he had a year's permit for the *James*, with sixteen mariners and Alexander Brown as their master. He also used the *Mary* when trading to England, and once had to go to law to recover his two-hundred-pound cargo of salmon and other fish, illegally seized from him off Flamborough Head by an English ship under a master from Whitby. Yare's attorney, Archibald Todrik, was an Edinburgh burgess and trader himself, sailing the *Margaret* from Leith in 1469 with William Todrik as master – almost certainly the same who married **Princess Margaret**'s illegitimate daughter.

There are many records, from 1473 onwards, of the splendid purchases Thomas Yare made for the King. Most were of cloth. They included three ells of English russet (at thirty-five shillings an ell) for a gown; sixteen shillings' worth of tartar to line the sleeves of a cloth-of-gold gown, and satin sleeve-linings for another; velvet for a foot mantle, broadcloth for a head sheet, and velvet to cover the King's porteous (portable breviary). Yare supplied James Brown, the saddler, with silk for the King's harness at four shillings an ounce. There were quantities of purple and tawny silk camlet, sometimes nine ells at a time, if the King was dressing up for foreign envoys. Yare bought him a chasuble for his closet.

He also served the Queen. She bought from him scarlet cloth for a petticoat, damask for a gown, blue silk camlet and velvet for kirtles, satin for the lining of collars, and black double tartar to line gowns. But the heavy expenditure came at Yule, when it was the custom for both the King and the Queen to present gifts, usually gowns, to their servants, such as that given to the King's physician and astrologer **Dr Andreas**.

By the gifts, it was possible to tell who was in favour, or whose friendship the King hoped to rely on. In 1474, 'my lord Prince's nurse' (presumably Agnes **Preston**, nurse of the future James IV, born in March 1473) was given over four pounds' worth of English russet for a gown, and James Haldane of the King's chamber got three ells of green for a side-gown. Master Thomas Pottinger also got russet, but Herbert Balfour did rather less well. There was a certain more practical expenditure on velour for the King's henchmen's doublets. One summer (1473), 'the King's little lutar' was given lining material and small graith, which could be applied to many things, but was probably horse harness.

Thomas Yare also fixed soft furnishings and much else for visiting potentates or their envoys. In an age where there were no hotels, and the King's lodgings were not fit for guests, monarchs pressed both the Church and well-doing house-owners to put up state visitors, as was done in London for the Muscovite ambassador Nepeja (CASTLE III, 6). When English envoys came to Edinburgh in 1474, Thom of Yare, now called the King's seneschal, saw that they were accommodated at the Bishop of Dunkeld's great lodging in the Cowgate, at a cost of £240 to the King, plus an extra £100 to himself for the expenses of envoys at the **monastery of Blackfriars**.

By the 1490s, Yare was entertaining important visitors in his own house. For one night of 'Hollanders', number unspecified, he invoiced the King for three pounds, and earned another twelve the following year for housing an envoy from **Maximilian I** of Austria. And about the same time, Yare made up a kist (chest) full of doublets and jackets of cloth of gold to be sent with an embassy to the King of Denmark, the uncle of James IV. Some of these tasks Yare may have shared with the Lord High Treasurer (in earlier years, **Archibald Crawford**, Abbot of Holyrood) within whose remit such work later more clearly fell. Much is unknown, since from 1474 until James III was killed in 1488, the records are lost.

In 1480, Thom of Yare became Treasurer of the burgh of Edinburgh, and ten years later was one of its bailies. He was one of the burgh's team of fish-pricers, who saw to the strict control of the sale of burgh fish during Lent. In 1482, he does not appear, either as a villain or a possible victim, in the events which led to the hanging of **Thomas Cochrane** at **Lauder Bridge**. In fact, he was probably philosophical about the impending loss of Berwick-upon-Tweed, and had long since made his dispositions. He did, however, play a role in the complicated strategy of that year which prevented King James from going to war by returning him to detention in Edinburgh Castle, from which he was presently gallantly freed by his burgh officers. This band, which included Thomas Yare, also numbered men from the shipping families of **Cant**, Todrik, **Crawford**, Crammy, Bonkle* and Richardson, now all happily operating out of Leith.

His home in Edinburgh, on the north side of the High Street, seems to have been close to that of Robert Knollys, one of the natural sons of **William Knollys**,* the Preceptor of Torphichen, whose family name occurs once or twice in the same documents as Yare's. The Preceptors of the Order of St John* had some affinity with the handling of money, a past family, Livingstone, having provided both a Preceptor and an Officer of the Mint, and William Knollys himself holding the position of Lord High Treasurer in the course of both reigns.

The doyenne of Yare's hospitable residence, his wife Margaret, was a **Home**. Her place in that important family is not certain, but Thomas appears as a witness in a 1492 charter which allotted property in Duns, Berwickshire, to the King's squire John Home, son of George Home of Ayton. The marriage confirms Yare's importance. His wife was also an asset in her own right. In 1495 the merchant George of Touris, sailing on the *Gilbert of Edmonston* (a name well known to **Anselm Sersanders**), sold to a Bruges man some ells of Thomas Yare's wife's cloth.

A 'yare' is an enclosure of stake-nets in which fish are caught as the tide ebbs. The family's fortunes were accordingly linked in all likelihood to Berwick fishing. Tom Yare's personal characteristics are conjecture, including the famed Berwick impediment ('wharring') in his speech. His extended family can be guessed at, but not confirmed. Friar John Yare, guardian of the once-sumptuous Friary Church of the Franciscans at Haddington, was possibly a brother. The friary, interestingly, had an altar to St Duthac, also celebrated in Tain (see **Princess Margaret**). There were Yares in Stirlingshire, such as Margaret Yare, widow of Thomas Adamson, and Sir John Yare, chaplain of the altar of St Michael in 1472. Also possibly connected were Yares further west, in the **Lennox** area, one of whom, John, dying a bastard without heirs, had his land given in 1476 to one of **Queen Margaret**'s high officials, **Malcolm McClery**. The man never appears in the history books, but in Scotland in the last quarter of the fifteenth century, there can have been few people as well known as Thom Yare. (D. D.)

Yci creve Judas par le ventre et les trippes saillent dehors: LIONS, 2: 'Now bursts the belly of Judas, and forth gush his tripes with his soul'. A gory excerpt from a French **Mystery Play** based on the *Passion* of Arnoul Gréban, 1452. (Very difficult to simulate, but they managed.) (D. D.)

Yo lo siento: KNIGHTS, II, 2: 'I am sorry'.

Yoles: LIONS, 21: Small, handy vessels which were common in Orkney, and could be built in three or four days of communal work. Wood was imported to Shetland from Norway as early as the Viking period, since indigenous timber was not available. Ness yoles had three thwarts and three pairs of oars, and were about twenty-one feet long, with five and a half feet midships. They were **clinker built**, and carried a single square sail. (D. D.)

You have come until the grisly land of mirknes: KINGS, II, 1: In the poem 'The Broad and Narrow Way' from *The Prick of Conscience* by the English mystical writer Richard Rolle of Hanpole (*c.* 1300–1349):

This world es the way and passage
Thurgh whilk [which] lyes our pilgrimage
By this way by-hoves us al gang,
Bot be war we ga noght wrang;
For in this world liggis twa ways
Als men may fynd that tham assays
The tane es way of the dede calde [called],
The tother es way of lyfe to halde
The way of dede semes large and eesy
And that may lede us ouer-lightly,
Un-til the grysly land of mirknes
Thar sorow and pyn ever-mare es.
The way of lyfe semes narow and harde
That ledes us til our contré-warde

That es the kyngdom of heven bright
Whare we sal won ay [dwell always] in goddes sight
And goddes awen [God's own] sons than be calde
If we the way of lyfe here halde.

You know we've cornered the paper: See **Watermarks**.

Yunitsa: CASTLE, III, 11: See **Weans and wames**.

Z

ZACCO, King of Cyprus:* SCORPIONS: (*c.* 1440–1473) After finally wresting the island of Cyprus from the grasping hands of his half-sister Carlotta,* the beautiful Zacco, James II of Lusignan, King of Cyprus, played out the rest of his short life in a state of furious defiance against the increasing domination of Venice.* Caught between the Ottoman threat from Constantinople and the demands of the Mameluke* Sultan of Egypt, he was forced to make a political marriage. His first choice was **Zoe**, the Byzantine Emperor's niece, but she was given instead to **Ivan III** of Muscovy (and became the grandmother of Ivan the Terrible*). In her place, Zacco married and had shipped to him later another Imperial candidate: Catherine,* the stout eighteen-year-old half-Byzantine daughter of Marco Corner,* of an old and rich Venetian family with a palace in Venice, and valuable cane-sugar land at Episkopi on the south coast of Cyprus. Each marriage brought with it a stake in the future of Constantinople, and a claim, were it to be recovered, to the imperial throne.

Unfortunately, the Turks were not only in possession of Constantinople; they were menacing Europe, Cyprus included. When making his marriage by proxy in 1468, Zacco had expected to acquire the protection of Venice, and a call on her troops and her armour on Crete. He relied on being included if (in the interests of trade) Venice were to make peace with the Turk. He was disappointed. Peace moves did not include Cyprus. And if Venice deployed arms and help, it was to those areas where it best served her interests. Worse, she interfered with Zacco's own rule in Cyprus.

Despite the efforts of Zacco's noseless, powerful mother, Marietta of Patras, his relations with his own courtiers were turbulent, and his unpredictable behaviour invited plots. He favoured Catalans, whom Venice mistrusted (one of them had promulgated the Muscovite marriage). On the credit side, he made intimate friends with some Venetians – in particular his Queen's cousin Marco Bembo, and her father's brother Andrea Corner,* the Auditor of Cyprus. Andrea, with land, wine concessions and the family sugar plantations to draw upon (he repaid loans in sugar), was a rich merchant long established in Cyprus. At one point, Zacco turned violently against him for reasons unknown, unless he thought him involved in the unexpected death of Zacco's much-loved little daughter Charlotte, aged twelve, who had been contracted to marry Sor de Naves, the Sicilian Constable of Cyprus. In time, however, Zacco was to renew the friendship, restoring to Andrea all his confiscated villages, taking him to his heart and publicly referring to him with affectionate respect as 'our father', '*notre père*'. And the instant his Venetian Queen came to Cyprus in 1472, Zacco made her pregnant.

Eight months later, in July 1473, the King was dead, taken ill when on a hunt with his courtiers and those same two Venetians; and claimed within nine days by an ailment supposed to be dysentery. Because Corner and Bembo would at first admit no one to his sickroom, the rumour spread that the Venetians had poisoned the King. Either they wanted to control Cyprus themselves, it was said, or they were acting for Venice, which disapproved, for example, of Zacco's negotiations with the Persian prince **Uzum Hasan**.* Eventually, the other magnates forced their way to the dying King's bedside. Among them was the Venetian Captain-General Pietro Mocenigo, soon to be Doge (and soon also to die – in 1476 – worn out by his ten Turkish concubines).

This was the time when the papal and Venetian fleets were at sea in an attempt to keep Karamania out of Ottoman hands, and Uzum Hasan (for whom **Ludovico de Severi da Bologna*** would be speaking at Trèves in September) was about to suffer a defeat at Terjan (August 1473) which would end all these hopes. Venice had attempted, too late, to send artillery and other munitions to help. That April Zacco, caught between the powerful demands of the Sultan of Cairo and the other predators all around (wolves, he called them), had been forced to deny the harbour at Famagusta* to an incoming shipment of arms, lest by angering Cairo, also greedy for guns, he would find himself defenceless if Uzum failed to hold back the Turk. The Venetian envoys, shuttling between the Signoria and Tabriz, knew the dangers. **Caterino Zeno** (married to Violante of Naxos,* and hence Queen Catherine's uncle by marriage) had attended Uzum since 1471. Another, **Josaphat Barbaro**, on his way to replace Zeno in Persia, had been delayed in Karamania and Cyprus since the arms ships arrived, and was there when Zacco fell ill. Barbaro remained after his death as an observer for Venice, sending his reports by fast trireme from Famagusta. He attended, with Mocenigo, the baptism of James, the son Zacco never saw, born seven weeks after he died, and destined to live for less than a year.

Zacco's will, made on his deathbed, named among his executors Andrea Corner and Rizzo di Marino, his Sicilian Chamberlain. His heir was to be the Queen's child, not then born, or failing that, successively his three illegitimate children. These were the little son he called Tzenios (Eugène or Genio), 'who was adored not only by men', someone wrote, 'but by the very stones of the island'. Next came his younger son Jean or Janus, and finally his surviving daughter Charlotte or Charla or Zarla, who was the oldest, aged six. The King also spoke of a great treasure, painfully gathered, and asked that his galley slaves should be freed, and his political prisoners. This last was done, but the treasure, rumoured to be six thousand ducats, was never found. Controversy followed Zacco even in death: he was buried in dishonour, one report says, since for his sins there was not enough wax in Cyprus to make the funeral candles.

Wild and brave, cruel and charming, James II of Lusignan left a strange legacy which has provoked admiration and horror, exasperation and dismay. He spent his life fighting. Of what he did in other ways for his island, only a little is known for certain. He founded an academy for the sons of noblemen in Nicosia,* and provided for salaried teachers. He is said to have tried to tackle trade, justice, coinage. He is known to have made fierce efforts to remedy the locust pest. He did a great deal also that was oppressive, wrongheaded and passionate. It is unlikely that he would ever have changed.

His mother outlived him by thirty years. Terrified of further insurrection, the Venetians bundled her out of the island in 1477, along with her three illegitimate grandchildren. She and the two princes and Charla were taken by Antonio Loredano to a convent in Venice and kept there for a year, secure against the efforts of Naples to seize and marry ten-year-old Charla, as Zacco had wanted, to Alfonso, the natural son of King Ferrante of Naples.* In 1478, the three children and their grandmother were taken to Padua, where the Princes were well treated and given a tutor, but allowed to leave the castle only under strong guard. They lived there for twenty-two years, and Marietta and her granddaughter died there. Charla went quickly, after only two years, but Zacco's strong mother survived until 1503, and was buried with Charla in a tomb in the church of St Augustine, Padua. It is no longer there.

Grown into fine, upstanding men, the two Princes both managed to marry (against their captors' intention) and made several bids for freedom, but had varying success in the marketplace. As potential rulers of Cyprus they were welcomed by some opponents of Venice, while others attempted to kill them. Disappointingly, the Emperor **Maximilian I**, who occupied Padua in 1509, showed no interest in helping them to a throne, and especially none in underwriting their keep. Cairo was less interested now, and even **Rhodes** failed (in fact the Grand Master of the Knights of St John* eventually had to agree that the Grand Commanderie at Kolossi* in Cyprus should be made hereditary to the family Corner).

A visit to Rome was more profitable and for a while, about 1520, both princes were being supported, unsurprisingly, by revenues drawn from the alum* at Tolfa. Haled (by Venice) back to Padua yet again, both made their final escape, but with differing consequences. Eugène, once Zacco's darling Tzenios, went to Turkey for help to take Cyprus, and was killed there. Janus applied again to the Emperor, who did not treat him well. In 1530 he left and surrendered himself to the Venetian officials in Bologna. Taken back to Venetian territory, he remained there until he died, an old man, in Padua in 1553.

In Cyprus, Zacco's Queen also had to leave, in the end, to escape dangerous suitors. When word of her husband's death reached him, the Sultan of

Cairo (Qayt Bey*) sent a gold robe, and demanded payment of three years' arrears of tribute, or twenty-four thousand gold ducats. He also allied himself in due course with Zacco's half-sister Queen Carlotta to foster the marriage designs of King Ferrante. (When Charla died, he decided to marry his son to Queen Catherine.) Until the final demise of the Cairo Mamelukes, they never ceased to demand tribute, and generally to get it; while exerting themselves now and then to urge Turkey to try for the island.

Gradually, after Zacco's death, Cyprus lapsed into the form of a Venetian colony. At the time, the Venetian fleet, hovering in protection, tried and failed to deliver arms to Uzum, and went to winter at Modon. Within Cyprus, the Queen's dear Venetian friends hovered at her side under Andrea Corner, despised for his languor and cowardice by an impatient Josaphat Barbaro, who was to be there until the following February (1474). With Corner were his nephews Marco Bembo and George Contarini. Barbaro himself was protected by the master gunner Thomas of Imolo, who had been sent to Cyprus at the same time as Barbaro with a hundred picked bombardiers. (Some of the artillery and munitions, originally worth over four thousand ducats, would end up in Crete, and some would be taken back to the arsenal in Venice.)

The opposite party, and much the stronger internally, comprised the powerful Sicilians and Catalans chosen by Zacco, and led by men like his Sicilian chamberlain, Sir Rizzo di Marino, who preferred the King of Naples to Venice. Strife between the two factions led to the assassination by Catalans of a handful of Venetians at the end of 1473. Among them were Andrea Corner and Marco Bembo, and Gabriel Gentile, the late King's physician, all distrusted since Zacco's suspicious death. Rizzo di Marino and some of the other Catalan conspirators fled. The other ringleaders were hanged by Mocenigo. A few months after the rising, the Queen's infant died of malaria, and the Queen's father Marco Corner was appointed to move in and help manage the loose cannon that Cyprus had become.

He was unpopular, overbearing, critical (probably rightly) of the neglect and disrespect surrounding his daughter, and was not helped by the tempestuous arrival of Fiorenza of Naxos, his wife, who, far from comforting her child, expressed herself appalled by the Queen's mindless extravagance. Catherine was also suspected (she was not very bright) of showing an interest in marriage with Alfonso of Naples, who had reappeared as a threat to Venetian sovereignty. It was decided, in the most courteous way, to get rid of her. In 1489 she agreed to an abdication, and the dear daughter of the Signoria left Cyprus in a blaze of rather unflattering public joy. It was the year in which Josaphat Barbaro sat on the tribune in Venice which decreed the death of Sir Rizzo di Marino, Zacco's councillor, captured and indicted sixteen years after he caused the death of the Queen's uncle and cousin.

Catherine possessed a large income, a royal suite of eighty, and the determination to spend the rest of her life in feasting, music and dance at a miniature court designed for pleasure, where she need have no duties at all. An estate was found for her in Asolo, a day's ride north of Venice. There, she occupied a palace in the town, and built herself a summer house called Le Barco on the Treviso plain, not far from the Bosco del Montello and its nearby **Carthusian** monastery where **Anselm Adorne**,* nearly twenty years earlier, had visited the grave of his uncle.

Queen Catherine became a social success. Poets extolled her. Unusually, in the Veneto, she and her ladies eschewed personal artifice, preferring complexions adorned only by Nature, although they were expensively dressed. In time, the Queen took to moving about, staying at Venice, or the palace she acquired at Murano, and having her portrait painted by Gentile Bellini (*c.* 1429–1507) when she was in her late forties. It is thought to be the best likeness of the several that were made, of which only copies remain. It shows a solid woman with a heavy, discontented face and a chest strung with jewellery. She died in 1510.

Within Cyprus, the new Venetian administration strove against incompetence and chicanery and the unpalatable truth that no one of any stature wanted to live on the depleted island. The threat from Cairo, the threat from Naples, the threat from Constantinople overshadowed all the following years: as early as 1478 Antony Erizzo (brother of Paul, killed in the atrocities that followed Negroponte), was occupied with **Ambrogio Contarini** in arming Cypriot ships against the old fear of an attack on Famagusta by the forces of Genoa, stirred up by Prosper Adorno against a Venetian alliance. When Sultan Mehmet II* died in 1481, the internal disruption over the succession offered some respite. It was not until the time of Selim I and Suleiman the Magnificent,* his successor, that Venice managed a truce that was to give Cyprus a long-lasting peace.

The island of Venus was to have a brave history, but the Lusignan magic had gone. 'The luxury of France, the softness of Syria, the subtlety and cunning of Greece' ('*fasticus gallicus, syra mollities, graecae blanditiae ac fraudes*' [UNICORN, 42]) was how one dispassionate writer defined it. Another was gentler:

> Love hath an island
> And I would be there;
> Love hath an island
> And nurtureth there
> For men the Delights,
> the beguilers of care,
> Cyprus, Love's island;
> And I would be there.
> (Eurpides, *c.* 480–406 BC, *The Bacchae*, 11.)
> (D. D.)

ZENO, Caterino: See **Zeno family**.

ZENO family: SCORPIONS: A great patrician Venetian family. Marino Zeno was made Venetian ruler of Constantinople in 1209, and in 1242, Renier Zeno became Doge of Venice.* In 1366 Carlo Zeno, canon of Patras, excelled himself in defending the castle of Patras (later home to the mother of **Zacco, King of Cyprus***) against the widow of the then King of Cyprus and her son. It was said he learned all the quirks of Greek warfare while fighting there and against Turkish pirates. After some criticism of Zeno's activities in the cause of his patron, the Archbishop Angelo Acciajuoli* of Patras, Zeno lost his canonry but ended as bailie of Achaia, and assistant to the Archbishop his friend. In 1379, under Doge Andrea Contarini, the Venetian hero Carlo Zeno engaged Piero Doria and the Genoese fleet and relieved the blockade of Chioggia. The revelation that he, with other Venetian nobles, had been receiving bribes from dissident Padua was less well received.

Sixteen years after that, in the best-known seafaring exploit of the family, Antonio Zeno captained the fleet of Henry **Sinclair**, Earl of Orkney, on its initial voyage to explore the West Atlantic. The details are sufficiently confused to have kept historians arguing for years. One version says that the adventure began in the north of Scotland, in the Faroe Islands, where Zeno's brother Niccolò had been wrecked, and was saved by Sinclair, come to seize his new inheritance in the North. Niccolò then helped the Earl conquer the Faroes and later the Shetland Isles. When Niccolò died, Antonio sailed with Sinclair's fleet to test a fisherman's story of a golden land in the west discovered during a storm. Delayed by fog, they eventually made a landing, perhaps in Greenland, and Antonio went further still, but was sent home with the main fleet before winter set in. Describing his journey, which may have reached Nova Scotia, Antonio is supposed to have told how he saw burning pitch running into the sea at the foot of a mountain – possibly Stellarta. Claims have also been made that exotic plants found on this voyage are reproduced in the richly carved interior of **Roslin Chapel**, beside the Sinclairs' castle outside **Edinburgh**; but the interpretation is not beyond doubt.

In 1437, the Venetian merchant Michele Zeno was commissioned by Pope Eugenius IV (1431–1447) to raise money to bring to Florence the Emperor of Constantinople (John VIII Paleologus, ruled 1421–1448), Cardinal Bessarion* and the Patriarch of Constantinople, Joseph II, to discuss rapport between the Eastern and Western Christian churches at the Council of Ferrara–Florence. As papal agent, Zeno cared for the Greeks when they broke their voyage at Venice, and supplied the Emperor and the Patriarch with six hundred and four hundred florins apiece for the expense of their suites.

The following year, the Venetian admiral against Milan was Pietro Zeno: an earlier energetic Zeno of the same name had been made Baron of the island of Andros, and was employed by Venice in all her difficult negotiations in the Levant. His death in 1437 led to friction, when his widow was imprisoned by the young Duke Andrea's uncles, and forced to agree to the marriage of their nephew to her small daughter, with Andros as her dowry. In 1453,

Marco Zeno was captain of the Flanders galleys at Sluys, and the Cardinal Battista Zeno was nephew of the Venetian Pope Paul II,* who died in 1471.

Caterino Zeno,* Venetian envoy and husband of one of the Princesses of Naxos,* passed a life of indefatigable diplomacy on behalf of the Signoria, greatly aided by the Eastern connections of his wife Violante, who was a niece of the Christian Theodora, one of the wives of **Uzum Hasan*** of Persia. Passing to Uzum via Rhodes in 1471, Zeno remained at the Prince's court at Tabriz over the winter and was successful in persuading the prince to refuse the overtures of friendship from Sultan **Mehmet II*** of Turkey, and to undertake to attack Turkey himself, given sufficient support from the West. Early victories followed, but his forces were routed at the battle of Terjan in 1473, which left the Turks in a strong position. In this, Venice had so far lagged behind, but seemed about to redeem herself by dispatching two further envoys to Persia, **Josaphat Barbaro** and **Ambrogio Contarini**, to continue discussions, and allow Zeno to return. This he did, but was forced to hide in Caffa from the Genoese, and ran short of money until his servant Martin said that he would auction himself as a slave to enable his master to escape (RONDO, 17). Martin was indeed auctioned, but was not left in Caffa forever; the Republic of Venice paid his ransom and guaranteed him a pension for life. Zeno visited Rome and Naples, and reached Venice finally in 1474 – to find his masters deep in negotiations, initiated by the Sultan's stepmother, for a cease-fire with Turkey.

By 1478 the chief of the White Sheep and his Christian wife were both dead, and two of their daughters fled to Aleppo, then on to Damascus. As for the assiduous Zeno, his line was to continue through Pietro, his only known son, whose own son, another Caterino Zeno, appears in 1512 as a young merchant trading in Damascus, visiting Uzum Hasan's daughters. There is no proof that Caterino had other children, although the *House of Niccolò* novels provide him with at least one fictitious bastard; a daughter well placed to continue into the period of the *Lymond Chronicles*. (D. D.)

Zero: See ***Sifr***.

Zielone Świątki: RONDO, 8: Traditional Polish Whitsuntide celebration, regarded as the festival for farmers and shepherds. A festival of similarly pagan origin continued to be celebrated in Poland long after Christianity was adopted, in the countryside each June, when bonfires were lit in honour of the Son, and of Love. This was one of the few occasions when the nobility would mix freely with the peasants rather than holding a separate celebration.

'Zione: LIONS, 12: Short for Venetian *Attenzione!* ('Mind out!')

ZOE PALAEOLOGINA: CASTLE II, 8; LIONS, 16: (d. 1503) Niece of Constantine XI, the last Byzantine Emperor (1448–1453), (and grandmother of Ivan the Terrible*), Zoe at twelve was called beautiful. The attribution remained until she fell under the gaze of the Italian humanist poet Luigi Pulci (1432–1484) in Rome, just before her marriage to the Grand Prince **Ivan III** of Moscow.

> I wish to describe [Pulci wrote to his friend Lorenzo de Medici*] this mountain of fat we have just seen. We entered the chamber of this *giovedì grasso* of a woman, seated in pomp (and there was, I assure you, plenty of wherewithal upon which to sit), with two great bowls on her chest, a fearsome chin, a pair of cheeks like a sow's and a neck sunk in rings. Her two eyes were of a size to make four, with such eyebrows, and such pillows of fat that the Pô itself isn't better banked up. Nor should you imagine she had the legs of a Giulio the Lean. I have never seen anything as unhealthy, as flabby, as ridiculous as this bizarre *befana* [witch]. Afterwards, I dreamed all night long about mountains of butter and bundles of bread rolls and suet.

To make matters worse, Pulci and his companions were offered no food or wine, but were expected to chat through the entire evening audience, with a brother of Zoe's to interpret. One of Pulci's starving companions was more humane than he was. 'Benedetto [wrote Pulci] rhapsodised over the lady's small mouth, and observed that she spat quite deliciously'.

Zoe was one of four children of the despot Thomas of the Morea,* who died in 1465, just five years after he had fled with Zoe and her two brothers to the safety of Rome and Pope Pius II.* In Rome, Zoe was confided to a fellow-countryman, Bessarion* of Trebizond, Cardinal of Nicaea, who trained her wisely in Latin speech and beliefs, without which the Pope, now Paul II,* might have withdrawn his protection. She early entered the marriage market. Her own claim to the blood of Byzantium gave her considerable status as a potential bride (and claimant to Constantinople), and one of her first suitors was **Zacco, King of Cyprus**, who married instead Catherine Corner,* great-granddaughter of Emperor John IV of the Byzantine Empire of Trebizond. Next, an alliance with the court of Mantua failed because of Zoe's lack of a dowry. When the Russian marriage finally materialised in 1472 (despite the Grand Prince having been sent Zoe's portrait), it seemed to offer advantages to both sides. Ivan would acquire a personal interest in repelling the Turks who held Constantinople, and might be encouraged by his new wife towards the resolution of Greek and Latin beliefs so long urged by the West.

Whatever the West might have hoped, Zoe shed her Latin beliefs as soon as she stepped out of Rome. The new Pope, Sixtus IV* (whose own secretary was a son of George of Trebizond), had sent with her the Genoese Antonio Bonumbre, Bishop of Accia, but he was not well received, the Muscovites finding themselves shocked by his scarlet robes, his fancy mitre and gloves and, above all, by the Cross which he tried to have carried before him.

He lasted eleven weeks in Moscow, and failed to convert anyone from the Russian Orthodox faith. Religious disputations were thoughtfully staged but the Bishop's performance was poor, since – as he complained – all his books were at home. Nor did he receive the promised support from his fellow Italian Gian-Battista della Volpe, who had brokered the wedding as Ivan's ambassador, and led the bridal procession from Rome. Volpe, already established as Ivan's mint-master, had long since discreetly changed to the Russian faith. For a while, the Pope believed that he was to be recognised as the legitimate successor to St Peter in Russia; then hope gradually died. Bonumbre, who left Moscow in January 1473, immediately vanished from record, and is assumed to have died before 1480.

Meanwhile Zoe settled down, ponderously, to recreate Byzantium in Moscovy in other ways. She was the Grand Duke Ivan's second wife. In the household were the Dowager Grand Princess Maria, the mother of Ivan, his unreliable brothers Andrew and Boris, and another Ivan, her husband's son by his first wife Maria, daughter of Prince Boris of Tver. Whether or not she deserved Pulci's description, the Grand Duchess was not a lady who required to be pitied. She could even influence Ivan, who was tall, thin, handsome, but so hostile to women, reported one bemused guest, that they fainted on meeting him. It was supposedly Zoe, conscious of her own family's fall, who shamed Ivan into shaking off Mongol vassaldom ('I have married a slave of the Tartars!' she cried), and after a fortuitous dream, swept the Tartar tribute house out of the Kremlin and built a votive church in its place (which they could not enter).

Matured into a formidable and high-handed strategist, she was resented by the Court. Ivan, reinventing himself, with the approval of Venice, as Byzantine Emperor and successor to the earlier Caesars, adopted the black two-headed eagle and the hat, with its vibrating spirals, of Vladimir Monomach. Momentous decisions required to be sanctioned by Ivan's *duma*, but others were placed in the hands of Ivan's state secretaries. Any trace of the old, easy patriarchal fashion of rule became subject to rigid Byzantine etiquette: Ivan distanced himself from his own boyars, and by contrast Zoe flouted custom and opened the *terems*, the women's quarters, to the world, giving audiences to foreigners and dispatching messengers to the West.

Some of what she did was successful. The Italian Renaissance came early to Hungary and Russia because their rulers saw themselves as the representatives of classical Rome. The architect and military engineer **Rudolfo Fioravanti** accepted an invitation by **Mathias Corvinus** of Hungary, but moved to Moscow in 1474, where Zoe, protegée of his late patron Bessarion, must have fostered his work, intent as she was on re-creating a Byzantine–Roman tradition of magnificence, with the court of Milan as one exemplar. She treated the Venetian **Ambrogio Contarini** to an excessively gracious audience when he came to Moscow (as did the Latin Patriarch **Ludovico de Severi da Bologna***) after the fall of the Genoese colony of Caffa in 1475. In fact, her affability was exceeded only by that of the Grand Duke, who banqueted the suffering Contarini, and then pressed upon him a vast cup of hydromel, which etiquette required should be drunk in one draught. He managed a quarter.

As was necessary to protect her position, Zoe herself was fervently Orthodox in religion, rushing to pray at the tomb of St Sergius in the Troitsa monastery when she lost a newly born child. Later, she was known to dislike the diplomatic marriage of her daughter Helen in 1495 to a Catholic. (This was Aleksander Jagiello, Grand Duke of Lithuania and soon to be King of Poland, educated as a humanist by **Callimachus**. See **Casimir IV.**)

The crisis in Zoe's own life occurred when her ambitions for her eldest son Gabriel, born in 1478, were thwarted by the Grand Prince her husband, who chose to crown as his successor his young grandson Dmitri, whose father (son of Ivan's first wife) had died in 1490 (poisoned, it was rumoured, by Zoe). After a period of threats, accusations and counter-accusations, and the deaths of a few boyars and women suspected of witchcraft, the situation reversed itself. The young Dmitri was disgraced in his turn, and Zoe reinstated, assured that her son Gabriel (now called Vasily) was to be anointed with the tincture of gladness and rule as Vasily III Ivanovich, Grand Prince of Moscow.

Zoe died before Ivan her husband, having inspired some at least of the conquests made in his name, which altered the frontiers of Muscovy, and set it on the course to be followed by her son and Ivan her grandson, who merited so much more than her husband the nickname of '*Grozny*', or 'Terrible'. Zoe would have been proud of him, one feels.

The rest of Zoe's family had a feebler destiny. Her older sister Catherine, widow of King Stephen of Bosnia, lived in modest exile in Rome at the charge of the Pope. Of her two brothers, so carefully educated by Bessarion, one, Manuel, turned coat and became an inadequate pensioner of Sultan **Mehmet II**. Of his sons, one died a Christian but childless, and one was forcibly circumcised and enrolled in the Sultan's army, leaving no trace thereafter. Andrew, the remaining brother of Zoe, enjoyed for a while the generosity of Sixtus IV, his regular pension and the rent-free possession of a magnificent palace in the Campo Marzo. Later Pontiffs showed less understanding, and his credit fell with his status, none of it helped by a misguided marriage which produced one unimpressive son.

Now short of income, Andrew made two trips to Moscow, both suspiciously brief and reputedly leaving Zoe the poorer. The first was in 1480, when Sixtus died, and the next ten years later. A year after that, in 1491, Andrew applied for a pension to France, and in 1494 sold to Charles VIII (King of France 1483–1498), for a yearly 4,300 gold ducats, his rights to the Empires of Trebizond and Constantinople, and his interests in Serbia. As it turned out, he had also sold the same rights to Spain. He was dead by 1502, leaving his son Constantine a simple captain in the pontifical guard with no future. The rights, in any case, had never been renounced by Zoe. (D. D.)

Zot!: LIONS 12: 'Fool!' In Dutch proverbs it equated with *stultus*, and was particularly applied to Brabanters.

Bibliography

This bibliography indicates the sources for the *Companions*, Volumes I and II, and those used in the research for the novels themselves. Primary sources are listed first, followed by other firsthand accounts from the fifteenth and sixteenth centuries: ambassadors, pilgrims etc. This is followed by a select bibliography of secondary sources, divided into Scottish history; general; literature, etc.; and the visual arts. I stress that this is not an exhaustive list of all source material for the period, nor does it include sources not consulted for the novels or the *Companions*.

The editions or dates of publication refer to the version consulted, not necessarily the most recent imprint. Publishers' details have generally been omitted, but the date and location of publication have been retained to indicate the age of the source. Similarly, where the imprint is other than that of a major publishing house, such as a small or academic press, the details have been given (where possible) to aid the tracing of the sources. Occasionally the location or exact date of publication could not be ascertained. Rather than omit the item altogether, a few sources are listed with partial details. Where a series of volumes has been published over a number of years, only the start date of publication or that appropriate to a particular volume is given.

PRIMARY SOURCES

Printed Primary Sources of (Predominantly) Scottish History

Acta Dominorum 1501–1502/3, transcribed by J. A. Crawford, ed. James A. Clyde (Stair Society, Edinburgh, 1943).

Acts of the Lords Auditor of Causes and Complaints, ed. T. Thomson (Edinburgh, 1839).

Acts of the Lords of Council in Civil Causes (Acta Dominorum Concilii), ed. T. Thomson, vol. i, 1478–1495 (Edinburgh, 1839).

Acts of the Lords of Council in Civil Causes (Acta Dominorum Concilii), eds George Neilson & Henry Paton, vol. ii, 1496–1501 (Edinburgh, 1918).

Acts of the Lords of Council in Public Affairs, Scotland 1501–1554: Selections from Acta Dominorum Concilii, ed. R. K. Hannay (Edinburgh, 1932).

Acts of the Parliaments of Scotland, ed. T. Thomson & C. Innes, vol. ii, 1424–1567 (Edinburgh, 1814–1875).

Acts of the Privy Council of England 1547–1552; Oct. 1552–Dec. 1554.

Apostolic Camera and Scottish Benefices 1418–1488, ed. A. I. Cameron (Oxford, 1934).

Calendar of Border Papers 1560–1594, ed. J. Bain (Edinburgh, 1894), 2 vols.

Calendar of Close Rolls, vol. ii, 1468–1476 (London, 1953).

Calendar of Documents Relating to Scotland, ed. J. Bain, vols. iii & iv, to 1509 (Edinburgh, 1881–1888).

Calendar of English State Papers Relating to Scotland, 1509–1589, ed. John Thorpe Markham (London, 1858).

Calendar of Entries in the Papal Registers Relating to Great Britain and Ireland, vols. covering the period 1447–1492 (HMSO, 1915).

Calendar of Patent Rolls (England), vol. i, 1461–1467, vol. ii, 1467–1477 (London, 1897–1900); 1476–1485 (London, 1901).

Calendar of Scottish Supplications to Rome 1428–1432, ed. A. I. Dunlop & Ian B. Cowan (Scottish History Society, Edinburgh, 1970).

Calendar of Writs Preserved at Yester House 1166–1503, eds C. C. H. Harvey & J. Macleod (Scottish Record Society, 1930).

Carte Monialum de Northberwic, ed. Cosmo Innes (Edinburgh, 1847).

Charters and Other Documents Relating to the Royal Burgh of Stirling, 1124–1705, ed. R. Renwick (Glasgow, 1884).

Charters, Writs and Public Documents of the Royal Burgh of Dundee 1292–1880, ed. W. Hay (Dundee, 1880).

Chartulary of the Abbey of Lindores, 1195–1479, ed. J. Dowden (Scottish History Society, 1903).

Compota Thesauriorum Regum Scotorum (Accounts of the Lord High Treasurer of Scotland), ed. Thomas Dickson, vol. i, 1473–1498 (Edinburgh, 1877).

Compota Thesauriorum Regum Scotorum, ed. Sir James Balfour Paul, vols. for 1500–1504 & 1548–1552 (Edinburgh, 1877).

Criminal Trials in Scotland from 1488 to 1624, ed. R. Pitcairn (Edinburgh, 1833).

Early Records of the University of St Andrews 1413–1579 (Scottish History Society, 1926).

English Historical Documents 1485–1558, ed. C. H. Williams (London, 1967).

Exchequer Rolls of Scotland, vols. v–x, 1437–1496, ed. George Burnett (Edinburgh, 1880–1887).

Extracts from the Council Register of the Burgh of Aberdeen (Spalding Club, 1844–1848).

Extracts from the Records of the Burgh of Edinburgh 1403–1513 (Scottish Burgh Records Society, 1869–1892).

Fasti Ecclesiae Scoticanae Medii Aevi ad annum 1638, D. E. R. Watt (Scottish Record Society, Edinburgh, 1969).

Foreign Correspondence of Marie de Lorraine, ed. Marguerite Wood, Balcarres Papers 1548–1557 (Scottish History Society, 1923).

Ledger of Andrew Halyburton 1492–1503, ed. C. Innes (Edinburgh, 1867).

Letter of James III to Duke of Burgundy (Scottish History Society, Miscellany, vol. viii).

Letters of James the Fourth 1505–1513, eds. R. K. Hannay & R. L. Mackie, 3rd series, vol. xlv (Scottish History Society, 1953).

Origines Parochiales Scotiae (Bannatyne Club, 1851–1855).

Papers Relative to the Royal Guard of Scottish Archers in France, ed. Alexander Macdonald (Maitland Club, Edinburgh, 1835).

Perth Guildry Book, 1452–1601, ed. Marion L. Stavert (Scottish Record Society, 1993).

Protocol Book of Dominus Thomas Johnsoun, 1528–1578, eds J. Beveridge *et al.* (Scottish Record Society, 1920).

Protocol Book of James Young 1485–1515, ed. Gordon Donaldson (Scottish Record Society, 1952).

Protocol Book of John Foular 1501–1528, eds W. Macleod & M. Wood (Scottish Record Society 1930–1953).

Register of Burgesses of the Burgh of Aberdeen 1399–1631 (The Miscellany of the New Spalding Club, 1890–1908).

Register of the Privy Council of Scotland, ed. J. H. Burton (Edinburgh, 1877–1970), 8 vols.

Registrum Cartarum Ecclesie Sancti Egidii de Edinburgh, ed. David Laing (Bannatyne Club, Edinburgh 1859).

Registrum Magni Sigilli Regum Scotorum (Register of the Great Seal of Scotland), 1424–1513, ed. J. Balfour Paul (HM General Register House, Edinburgh, 1882).

Registrum Sancte Marie de Neubotle 1140–1528, vol. xciii (Bannatyne Club, Edinburgh, 1849).

Registrum Secreti Sigilli Regum Scotorum (Register of the Privy Seal of Scotland), 1488–1529, ed. M. Livingstone (Edinburgh, 1908).

Rental Book of the Cistercian Abbey of Coupar-Angus, ed. Revd Charles Rogers, vol. i (Grampian Club, London, 1879).

Rental Book of the Diocese of Glasgow, 1509–1570, ed. J. Bain (1875).

Report on the English Border in the Days of Henry VIII, Sir Robert Bowes, vol. iv (Reprints of Rare Tracts, Newcastle, 1849).

Roll of Edinburgh Burgesses and Guild-Brethren 1406–1700, ed. C. B. B. Watson (Scottish Record Society, 1929).

Rotuli Scaccarii Regum Scotorum (The Exchequer Rolls of Scotland), 1548–1552, ed. John Stewart *et al.*

Scottish Correspondence of Mary of Lorraine 1543–1558, ed. Annie M. Cameron (Scottish History Society, Edinburgh, 1927).

Scottish Historical Documents, ed. George Donaldson (Edinburgh, 1970).

Scottish Nation in the University of Orleans 1336–1538, The, ed. John Kirkpatrick (Scottish History Society, Miscellany, vol. ii).

Selections from the Records of the Regality of Montrose 1547–1706, ed. Charles S. Romanes (Scottish History Society, Edinburgh, 1914), 3 vols.

Chronicles and Contemporary Accounts

Boece, Hector, *Hector Boece's Chronicles of Scotland*, tr. into Scots by John Bellenden, 1540 (Scottish Text Society, n.d.).

Bower, Walter, *Scotichronicon*, ed. D. E. R. Watt (Aberdeen, 1987).

Buchanan, George, *The History of Scotland*, tr. from Latin by James Aikman (Glasgow, 1827), 4 vols.

Diurnal of Occurents: A Diurnal of Remarkable Occurents that have passed within the country of Scotland, since the death of James the Fourth till the year 1575 (Bannatyne and Maitland Clubs, 1833).

Herries, Lord, *Historical Memoirs of the Reign of Mary Queen of Scots*, ed. Robert Pitcairn (Abbotsford Club, Edinburgh, 1836).

Kirkaldy, Sir William, *Memoirs and Adventures of Sir William Kirkaldy* (Edinburgh, 1849).

Leslie, John, *Historie of Scotland* (1577), tr. from Latin by James Dalrymple, ed. E. G. Cody & William Murison, vol. ii (Scottish Text Society, Edinburgh, 1888).

Pitscottie, Robert Lindesay of, *The Historie and Cronicles of Scotland*, vols. i–iii (Scottish Text Society, Edinburgh, 1899–1911).

Rymer, Thomas, *Foedora* (Farnborough, 1967).

Steuart, A. Francis, *Memoirs of Sir John Melville 1535–1617* (London, 1929).

Wyntoun, Andrew, *Original Chronicle of Andrew of Wyntoun*, ed. F. J. Armours (Scottish Text Society, Edinburgh, 1904).

Printed Primary Sources of Bruges History

Gilliodts-van Severen, L., *Cartulaire de l'ancien consulat d'Espagne à Bruges 1280–1771* (Bruges, 1901).

Gilliodts-van Severen, L., *Cartulaire de l'Ancienne Estaple de Bruges* (Bruges, 1904).

Gilliodts-van Severen, L., *Cartulaire de l'ancien grand Tonlieu de Bruges* (Bruges, 1908).

Gilliodts-van Severen, L., *Inventaire des Archives de Bruges: Section I: Inventaire des Chartes par L. Gilliodts-van Severen* (Bruges, 1876).

Contemporary Memoirs, Dispatches and Travelogues

Anselm Adorne's Pilgrimage to the Holy Land

Coste, M. E. de la, tr., *Anselm Adorne, sire de Corthuy, Pèlerin de Terre Sainte* (Brussels, 1855).

'Épigraphiques des Anciens Pèlerins', *Bulletin de la Société Royale de Géographie d'Egypte, tome* XIX.

Itinéraire d'Anselme Adorno en Terre Sainte: 1470–1471, eds J. Heers & G. de Groër (Paris, 1978).

Limbourg-Stirum, Comte, 'Anselme Adournes, or a Bruges Traveller in the Fifteenth Century', *Messager des Sciences Historiques: Archives des Arts et de la Bibliographie de Belgique, tome* XLIX (Ghent, 1881).

Storme, Albert, 'Le Voyage d'Anselm Adornes en Terre Sainte–Notes on the "Itinéraire" by Heers and Groër', *LA* 31 (1981).

General

Allen, W. E. D., *Russian Embassies to the Georgian Kings, 1589–1605* (Hakluyt Society, 1970; reprinted 1972).

Balbi de Carregio, Francisco, *The Siege of Malta, 1565*, tr. by Ernle Bradford (London, 1965).

Barbaro, Josafa & Contarini, Ambrogio, *Travels to Tana and Persia by Josafa Barbaro and Ambrogio Contarini*, tr. by William Thomas (Hakluyt Society, London, 1873).

Beatis, Antonio, de, *The Travel Journal of Antonio de Beatis (Germany, Switzerland, the Low Countries, France & Italy 1517–1518)*, tr. by J. R. Hale & J. M. A. Lindon, ed. J. R. Hale (London, 1979).

Bellon, Pierre, *Petri Bellonii Cenomani 1546–1549* (1589).

Bisticci, Vespasiano da, *Lives of Illustrious Men of the Fifteenth Century* (London, 1926).

Brantôme, Pierre de Bourdeille, *Memoirs de Pierre de Bourdeille, seigneur de Brântome* (d. 1614), 14 vols.

Brézé, Louis de, Grand Sénéschal de Normandie, *Les Chassés de François 1er & la Chasse sous les Valois par le Comte Hector de la Ferrière*, Libraire de la Société des Bibliophiles Français (Paris, 1869).

Bruce, John, ed., *Historie of the arrivall of Edward IV in England, and the finall recouerye of his kingdomes from Henry VI* (Camden Society, London, 1838).

Cadamosto, *The Voyages of Cadamosto*, tr. & ed. by G. R. Crone (Hakluyt Society, London, 1937).

Camugliano, Ginevra Niccolini di, *The Chronicles of a Florentine Family 1200–1470* (London, 1933; reprinted 1936).

Cellini, Benvenuto, *Memoirs*.

Chesneau, Jean, *Le Voyage de M. d'Aramon (Recueil de Voyages et de Documents pour servir a l'Histoire de la Geographie XIIIe–XVIe Siècles,* vol. viii) (Paris, 1887).

Collis, Louise, *Memoirs of a Medieval Woman: Margery Kempe* (London 1964; reprinted 1983).

Comines, Philip de, *The Memoirs of Philip de Comines* (including *The Scandalous Chronicle, or Secret History of Louis XI* by Jean de Troyes), ed. Andrew R. Scoble (London, 1855), 2 vols.

Dee, John, *The Private Diary of Dr Dee,* ed. James Orchard Halliwell.

Early Voyages and travels to Russia and Persia by Anthony Jenkins and Others, ed. Morgan & Coote (Hakluyt Society, 1885).

Eden, Richard, *The First Three English Books on America 1511–1555: Compiled by Richard Eden from Writings and Maps of Pietro Martire of Anghiera (1455–1526), Sebastian Munster (1489–1552) and Sebastian Cabot (1471–1557),* ed. Edward Arber F.S.A. (Birmingham, 1885).

Europeans in West Africa 1450–1560 (Hakluyt Society).

Evliya, Chelebi, *Travels of Evliya Efendi,* tr. by Joseph von Hammer (London, 1850).

Fabri, Felix, *Wanderings in the Holy Land,* tr. by Aubrey Stewart (London, 1892–1893).

Fosse, Eustace de La, 'Voyage à la Côte Occidentale d'Afrique, en Portugal et en Espagne 1479–1480', *Revue Hispanique* (1897).

Grey, Charles, Esq., ed., *A Narrative of Italian Travels in Persia in the Fifteenth and Sixteenth Centuries* (Hakluyt Society, London, 1873).

Gyllii, Petri, *De Topographia Constantinopoleos* (1562).

Harff, Arnold von, *The Pilgrimage of Arnold von Harff, 1496–1499,* tr. & ed. by Malcolm Letts (Hakluyt Society, London, 1946).

Harleian Collection of Voyages, vol. i (1745).

Herberstein, Sigismund von, *Notes Upon Russia,* tr. by R. H. Major (Hakluyt Society, 1851), 2 vols.

Ibn Battuta, *Travels of Ibn Battuta,* tr. & ed. by H. A. R. Gibb, vol. ii (Hakluyt Society, Cambridge, 1962).

Joinville, Jean de & Villerhardouin, Geoffrey de, *Chronicles of the Crusades,* tr. by Margaret Shaw (London, 1963).

Lettres de Louis XI, Roi de France, eds J. Vaesen & Etienne Charavay (Paris, 1883–1909).

Machyn, Henry, *Diary of Henry Machyn of London, 1550–1563* (Camden Society, London, 1848).

Marche, Olivier de la, *Mémoires* (Paris, 1883), 4 vols.

Moryson, Fynes, Gent, *An Itinerary* (London, 1617).

Nicolai, Nicolas de, extracts from *Navigantium atque Itinerantium Bibliotheca: Collection of Voyages and Travels by John Harris*, book iii, ch. 12 (London, 1705).

Pallis, Alexander, *In the Days of the Janissaries* (1951).

Pitti, Buonaccorso, *Two Memoirs of Renaissance Florence: The Diaries of Buonaccorso Pitti and Gregorio Dati*, tr. by Julia Martines, ed. Gene Brucker (New York & London, 1967).

Pius II, Pope, *Memoirs of a Renaissance Pope*, tr. by F. A. Gragg (London, 1960).

Platter, Felix, *Beloved Son Felix: The Journal of Felix Platter*, tr. by Seán Jennett (London, 1961).

Polo, Marco, *The Travels of Marco Polo*, tr. by Ronald Latham (London, 1972).

Purchas, Samuel, *Hakluytus Posthumus, or Purchas his Pilgrimes*, vol. viii (Glasgow, 1905).

Thevet, André, *Cosmographie de Levant* (Geneva, 1985, facsimile of the 1554 original).

Tafur, Pero, *Travels and Adventures 1435–1439*, tr. & ed. by Malcolm Letts (London, 1926).

Tully, Richard, Esq., *Narrative of a Ten Years' Residence at Tripoli in Africa* (London, 1817).

Wilton, Arthur, Lord Grey of, *A Commentary of the Services and Charges of William, Lord Grey of Wilton, K. G., by his son Arthur, Lord Grey of Wilton*, ed. Sir Philip de Malpas & Grey Egerton (Camden Society, London, 1847).

Ambassadorial Dispatches and State Papers

At this period, a few courts were wealthy enough to place resident ambassadors, for the first time, in foreign countries. Their dispatches are a mine of contemporary information, covering domestic and political events over the known world. Spanning many editors and volumes, these various archives have been consulted by Dorothy Dunnett up to the end of 1558. They include the items listed below:

Calendar of State Papers and Manuscripts Existing in the Archives and Collections of Milan, ed. A. B. Hinds, vol. i, 1385–1616 (London, 1912).

Calendar of State Papers and Manuscripts, Relating to English Affairs, Existing in the Archives and Collections of Venice and Other Libraries of Northern Italy, ed. R. Brown, vol. i, 1202–1509 (Lozndon, 1864).

Dépêches des Ambassadeurs milanais en France sous Louis XI et François Sforza 1461–1466, ed. B. de Mandrot, vols. i–iv (Paris, 1916).

Dispatches of Milanese Ambassadors in France and Burgundy 1450–1483, vols. i & ii, tr. & ed. by Paul M. Kendall & Vincent Ilardi (Ohio, 1970–1971); vol. iii, tr. by F. J. Fata, ed. Vincent Ilardi (Illinois, 1981).

English Calendar of State Papers (Domestic).

English Calendar of State Papers (Foreign).

English Calendar of State Papers (Ireland).

English Calendar of State Papers (Scotland).

Spanish Calendar of State Papers.

Venetian Calendar of State Affairs.

SECONDARY SOURCES

Scotland

Angus, William, *Ettrick and Yarrow* (Selkirk, 1894).

Archeological and Historical Collections Relating to the County of Renfrew, vol. i, Lochwinnoch (Paisley, 1885).

Bateson, Donald, *Scottish Coins* (Shire, 1987).

Baxter, J. H., 'The Marriage of James II', *Scottish Historical Review*, vol. xxv (1947–1948).

Baxter, J. H., 'Scottish Students at Louvain University 1425–1484', *Scottish Historical Review*, vol. xxv (1947–1948).

Beaugué, Jean de, *Histoire de la Guerre d'Écosse pendant les campagnes 1548 et 1549*, ed. Joseph Bain (Maitland Club, Edinburgh, 1830).

Beckett, W. N., 'The Perth Charterhouse before 1500', *Analecta Cartusiana*, no. 128 (Salzburg, 1988).

Bingham, Caroline, *James V: King of Scots* (London, 1971).

Brady, W. M., *The Episcopal Succession in England, Scotland and Ireland 1400–1875* (Rome, 1876–1877), 3 vols.

Brown, J. M., ed., *Scottish Society in the Fifteenth Century* (London, 1977).

Brown, P. Hume, *George Buchanan: Humanist and Reformer* (Edinburgh, 1890).

Brown, P. Hume, *History of Scotland* (Cambridge, 1902), 3 vols.

Brown, P. Hume, *John Knox* (London, 1895).

Bryce, William Moir, *Mary Stuart's Voyage to France in 1548* (Edinburgh, 1907).

Bryce, William Moir, *The Scottish Grey Friars* (Edinburgh, 1909), 2 vols.

Burnett, Charles J., 'The Development of the Royal Arms to 1603', *Journal of the Heraldry Society of Scotland*, vol. i (1977).

Burns, Revd Charles, *The Golden Rose and the Blessed Sword: Papal Gifts to Scottish Monarchs* (Glasgow, 1970).

Burns, Revd Charles, 'Papal Gifts to Scottish Monarchs: the Golden Rose and the Blessed Sword', *The Innes Review*, vol. xx (1969).

Burns, J. H., *Scottish Churchmen at the Council of Basle* (Glasgow, 1962).

Burton, John Hill, *The History of Scotland* (Edinburgh, 1876), 8 vols.

Calderwood, David, *History of the Kirk in Scotland 1575–1650* (Edinburgh, 1672).

Calman, Denis, RN, 'Some Notes on the Order in Scotland', *Annales de L'Ordre Souverain Militaire de Malte* (Avril/Juin 1964).

Cant, Ronald G., *College of St Salvator* (Edinburgh, 1950).

Carrick, J. C., *The Abbey of St Mary, Newbottle* (Edinburgh, 1908).

Chalmers, George, *Mary Queen of Scots*, vol. i (London, 1818).

Chandler, S. B., 'An Italian Life of Margaret, Queen of James III', *Scottish Historical Review*, vol. xxxii (1953).

City of Edinburgh, *Royal Commission of Ancient Monuments of Scotland* (HMSO, 1951).

Cochran-Patrick, Robert William, *Early Records Relating to Mining in Scotland* (Edinburgh, 1878).

Cockran-Patrick, Robert William, *Medieval Scotland* (Glasgow, 1892).

Cockran-Patrick, Robert William, *Records of the Coinage of Scotland from the Earliest Period to the Union*, vol. i (Edinburgh, 1876).

Cockburn, James H., *The Medieval Bishops of Dunblane and their Church* (Edinburgh, 1959).

Counties of Midlothian and West Lothian, *Report of the Royal Commission of Historic Monuments and Constructions of Scotland* (HMSO, 1929).

County of East Lothian, *Report of the Royal Commission of Historic Monuments and Constructions of Scotland* (HMSO, 1924).

County of Stirlingshire, *Inventory of the Ancient Monuments by the Royal Commission on the Ancient and Historical Monuments of Scotland* (HMSO, 1963).

Cowan, E. J. & McDonald R. A., eds, *Alba: Celtic Scotland in the Medieval Era* (East Linton, 2000).

Cowan, Ian & Easson, David, *Medieval Religious Houses in Scotland* (London, 1957).

Cowan, Ian B. & Shaw, Duncan, eds, *Renaissance and Reformation in Scotland* (Edinburgh, 1983).

Cowan, Ian B., Mackay, P. H. R. & Macquarrie, Alan, *The Knights of St John of Jerusalem in Scotland* (Edinburgh, 1983).

Cowan, Samuel, *The Ancient Capital of Scotland: the Story of Perth* (London, 1904), 2 vols.

Cruden, Stewart, *Scottish Abbeys* (HMSO, Edinburgh, 1960).

Cunningham, Andrew S., *Mining in Mid and East Lothian: A History from Earliest Times* (Edinburgh, 1925).

Cunningham, Andrew S., *Culross, Past and Present* (Leven, 1910).

Davidson, John & Gray, Alexander, *The Scottish Staple at Veere* (London, 1909).

Dilworth, Mark, 'Coldingham Priory and the Reformation', *The Innes Review*, vol. xxiii (1972).

Dilworth, Mark, *Scottish Monasteries in the Late Middle Ages* (Edinburgh University Press, 1995).

Donaldson, Gordon, *All the Queen's Men* (London, 1983).

Donaldson, Gordon, *Northern Commonwealth, Scotland and Norway* (Edinburgh, 1990).

Donaldson, Gordon, *The Auld Alliance: The Franco-Scottish Connection* (Edinburgh, 1985).

Dowden, John, *The Bishops of Scotland* (Glasgow, 1912).

Dunlop, Annie, *Scots Abroad in the Fifteenth Century* (London, 1942).

Dunlop, Annie, *The Life and Times of James Kennedy, Bishop of St Andrews* (Edinburgh, 1950).

Dunbar, John G., *The Historic Architecture of Scotland* (London, 1966).

Durkan, John, 'The Beginnings of Humanism in Scotland', *The Innes Review*, vol. iv (1953–1954).

Durkan, John, 'The Cultural Background in Sixteenth-Century Scotland', *The Innes Review*, vol. x (1959).

Durkan, John, 'The Observantine Franciscan Province in Scotland', *The Innes Review*, vol. xxxv (1984–1985).

Eddington, Alex, *Castles and Historic Homes of the Borders* (1926).

'Extracts from Scottish Students' Accounts of the Marriage of Mary Queen of Scots', *The Library, A Quarterly Review of Bibliography*, 4th series, vol. xii (1932).

Fawcett, Richard, *Scottish Abbeys and Priories* (Edinburgh, 1994).

Fawcett, Richard, *The Architectural History of Scotland* (Edinburgh, 1994).

Ferguson, Revd John, *Ecclesia Antiqua or the History of an Ancient Church (St Michael's, Linlithgow)* (Edinburgh, 1905).

Ferguson, John, *Linlithgow Palace, Its History and Tradition* (Edinburgh, 1910).

Fischer, T. A., *Scots in Eastern and Western Prussia* (Edinburgh, 1903).

Fischer, T. A., *The Scots in Germany* (Edinburgh, 1902).

Fittis, Robert Scott, *Ecclesiastical Annals of Perth* (Perth, 1885).

Fleming, D. Hay, *Reformation in Scotland* (London, 1910).

Fleming, John Arnold, *The Four Maries* (Glasgow, 1951).

Flemish-Scottish Connections (pub. for exhibition of the Foundation Flanders-Scotland 2002, Brussels).

Forbes-Leith, William, *Scots Men at Arms and Life-Guards in France* (Edinburgh, 1882), 2 vols.

Fraser, Alex of Philorth, *The Frasers of Philorth* (Edinburgh, 1879), 3 vols.

Fraser, W., *The Lennox* (Edinburgh, 1874).

Grant, I. F., *Social and Economic Development of Scotland before 1603* (Edinburgh, 1930).

Grant, James, *Old and New Edinburgh* (Edinburgh, 1880), 3 vols.

Grant, Will, *Tweeddale* (Edinburgh, 1948).

Gray, W. Forbes, *A Short History of Haddington* (Edinburgh, 1944).

Guthrie, Douglas, *King James IV of Scotland: His Influence on Medicine & Science* (1947).

Hallex, A. W. C., 'Northern Notes and Queries: Abstract of the Protocol Book of the Burgh of Stirling', *Scottish Antiquary*, vols. x & xi (1896).

Hamilton Papers 1548–1549, ed. J. Bain (Edinburgh, 1890–1892).

Hannay, R. K., *The Early History of the Scottish Signet* (Edinburgh, 1936).

Hannay, R. K., *The Scottish Crown and the Papacy 1424–1560* (The Historic Association of Scotland in Edinburgh, n.d.).

Harris, Stuart, *The Place Names of Edinburgh* (Edinburgh, 1996).

Hendrie, William F., *Linlithgow* (Edinburgh, 1989).

Herkless, Joan & Hannay, R. K., *The Archbishops of St Andrews* (Edinburgh, 1907).

Holmes, Nicholas, *Scottish Coins* (Edinburgh, 1998).

Hunter, William, *Biggar and the House of Fleming* (Edinburgh, 1862).

Hutchinson, A. F., *The Lake of Menteith* (Stirling, 1899).

Keith, Robert, *Historical Catalogue of Scottish Bishops to 1688* (Edinburgh, 1824).

Keith, Bishop Robert, *The History of the Affairs of the Church and State of Scotland 1568* (Spottiswoode Society, Edinburgh, 1844), 3 vols.

Labanoff, Prince, *Letters de Marie Stuart*, vol. i (Paris, 1859).

Lee, Maurice du Pont, *James Stewart, Earl of Moray* (New York, 1953).

Lees, J. Cameron, *St Giles* (Edinburgh, 1889).

Liber Conventus S. Katherine Senensis (Sciennes) Proper Edinburgum (Abbotsford Club, Edinburgh, 1841).

Lynch, M., Spearman, M. & Stell, G., *The Scottish Medieval Town* (Edinburgh, 1988).

Lythe, S. G. E., *The Economy of Scotland 1550–1625* (Edinburgh, 1960).

Macdougall, Norman, *James III: A Political Study* (Edinburgh, 1982).

Macdougall, Norman, *James IV* (Edinburgh, 1989).

Macdougall, Norman, 'The Struggle for Coldingham Priory', *The Innes Review*, vol. xxiii (1972).

Macfarlane, Leslie, 'The Primacy of the Scottish Church, 1472–1521', *The Innes Review*, vol. xx (1969).

Macfarlane, Leslie, *William Elphinstone and the Kingdom of Scotland 1431–1514* (Aberdeen, 1985).

Macgibbon, David & Ross, Thomas, *The Castellated and Domestic Architecture of Scotland* (Edinburgh, 1887–1892), 5 vols.

McGladdery, Christine, *James II* (Edinburgh, 1990).

McKean, Charles, 'The House of Pitsligo', *Society of Antiquaries of Scotland*, vol. cxxi (1991).

Mackerlie, E. M. H., *Mary of Guise Lorraine* (London, 1931).

Mackie, R. L., *King James IV of Scotland, a Brief Survey of His Life and Times* (Edinburgh, 1958).

MacQuarrie, Alan, 'Anselm Adornes of Bruges', *The Innes Review*, vol. xxxiii (1982).

MacQuarrie, Alan, *Scotland and the Crusades 1095–1560* (Edinburgh, 1985).

McRoberts, David, 'Scottish Pilgrims in the Holy Land', *The Innes Review*, vol. xx (1969).

Maitland Club, *Miscellaneous Papers, Principally Illustrative of Events in the Reign of Queen Mary and King James VI*, ed. William J. Duncan (Glasgow, 1834).

Malden, John, 'Anselm Adorne and the Two Collars', *Journal of the Heraldry Society of Scotland*, vol. x (1988).

Marshall, James Scott, *The Life and Times of Leith* (Edinburgh, 1986).

Marwick, Sir James D., *The History of the Collegiate Church and Hospital of the Holy Trinity* (Edinburgh, 1911).

Mason, Roger & Macdougall, Norman, eds, *People and Power in Scotland: Essays in Honour of T. C. Smout* (Edinburgh, 1992).

Mathieson, William Law, *Politics and Religion* (Glasgow, 1902).

Metcalfe, William, *A History of Paisley, 600–1908* (Paisley, 1909).

Mignet, M., *Histoire de Marie Stuart* (Paris, 1851).

Miller, James, *The Lamp of Lothian, The History of Haddington* (Haddington, 1900).

Milne, R., ed., *The Blackfriars of Perth* (Edinburgh, 1893).

Mitchell, R. J., 'Scottish Law Students in Italy in Later Middle Ages', *Juridical Review*, vol. xlix (1937).

Moncreiffe of That Ilk, Sir Iain, *The Highland Clans,* with photographs by David Hicks (London, 1967).

Mowat, Sue, *The Port of Leith: Its History and its People* (Edinburgh, 1994).

Murray, Joan, 'The Black Money of James III', *British Archaeological Reports,* vol. xlv (1977).

Naismith, R. J., *The Story of Scotland's Towns* (Edinburgh, 1989).

Nicholl, John, *Worshipful Company of Ironmongers* (London, 1851).

Nicholson, Ranald, *Scotland: the Later Middle Ages, 1286–1513* (Edinburgh, 1974).

Nicolay, Nicolas de, *The Life and Death of James V, and the Navigation of That King Round Scotland,* tr. from the French, 1612 (Edinburgh, 1819), 2 vols.

Pryde, George S., 'The Scottish Burghs', *Scottish Historical Review,* vol. xxviii (1949).

Rae, Thomas, *The Administration of Scottish Frontiers 1513–1603* (Edinburgh, 1966).

Reid, W. Stanford, *Skipper from Leith: History of Robert Barton* (Philadelphia, 1962).

Riddell, John & Laing, David, 'Historical Notices of the Family of King James I of Scotland', *Proceedings of the Society of Antiquaries of Scotland,* vol. iii, part 1 (1857–1858).

Robertson, J. D., *A Handbook to the Coinage of Scotland* (Chicago, 1968).

Rogers, Charles, *History of the Chapel Royal of Scotland* (Edinburgh, 1882).

Rooseboom, Matthijs P., *The Scottish Staple in the Netherlands* (The Hague, 1910).

Ruble, Le Baron Alphonse de, *La Première Jeunesse de Marie Stuart* (Paris, 1891).

Scotland, A. W., Taylor, A. J. & Park, W. G., *The Streets of Edinburgh* (Edinburgh, 1984).

Simpson, Grant G., ed., *Scotland and Scandinavia 800–1800* (Edinburgh, 1990).

Simpson, Grant G., ed., *The Scottish Soldier Abroad* (Edinburgh, 1992).

Sitwell, William, *The Border From a Soldier's Point of View* (Newcastle upon Tyne, 1927).

Skelton, John, *Maitland of Lethington and the Scotland of Mary Stuart* (Edinburgh, 1894).

Smith, John, *A Handbook and Directory of Old Scottish Clockmakers* (Edinburgh, 1903).

Smout, T. C., *Scotland and Europe 1200–1850* (Edinburgh, 1986).

Spalding Club, *Illustrations of the Topography and Antiquities of Aberdeen and Banffshire,* vol. iii (Spalding Club, Aberdeen, 1847).

Spottiswoode Miscellany, ed. James Maidment, vol. ii (Edinburgh, 1844).

Stoddart, Jane T., *The Girlhood of Mary, Queen of Scots* (London, 1908).

Strickland, Agnes, *Life of Mary, Queen of Scots* (London, 1873).

Strickland, Agnes, *Lives of Queens of Scotland and English Princesses*, vol. ii (Edinburgh, 1850).

Stringer, K. J., ed., *Essays on the Nobility of Medieval Scotland* (Edinburgh, 1985).

Stuart, Marie W., *The Scot Who Was a Frenchman* (London, 1940).

Teulet, A., *Papiers d'État Relatifs à l'Histoire de l'Écosse*, vol. i (Bannatyne Club, Paris, 1851).

Thomson, Andrew, *Coldingham Parish and Priory* (Galashiels, 1908).

Thomson, J. A. F., 'Some New Light on the Elevation of Patrick Graham', *Scottish Historical Review*, vol. xl (1961).

Tytler, Patrick Fraser, *The History of Scotland* (Edinburgh, 1828; reprinted Kent, 1872), 4 vols.

Warrack, John, *Domestic Life in Scotland 1488–1688* (London, 1920).

Weber, Bernard Clarke, *The Youth of Mary Queen of Scots* (Philadelphia, 1941).

West, John F., *Faroe: The Emergence of a Nation* (London, 1972).

Whittington, G. & Whyte, I. D., *An Historical Geography of Scotland* (London, 1983).

Wilkes, Margaret, *The Scot and His Maps* (Motherwell, 1991).

Wilson, James, *Annals of Hawick 1214–1814* (Edinburgh, 1850).

Wormald, Jenny, *Lords and Men in Scotland: Bonds of Manrent 1442–1603* (Edinburgh, 1985).

Wright, Gordon, *The Royal Mile, Edinburgh* (Edinburgh, 1979; reprinted 1990).

Yeoman, Peter, *Medieval Scotland: an Archaeological Perspective* (London, 1995).

General

Acton, Harold, *The Pazzi Conspiracy* (London, 1979).

Ady, C. M., *A History of Milan under the Sforza* (London, 1907).

Ady, C. M., *The Bentivoglio of Bologna: a Study in Despotism* (London, 1937).

Agapeyeff, Alexander D', *Codes and Ciphers* (London, c. 1939).

Alef, Gustave, *Rulers and Nobles in Fifteenth-Century Muscovy* (London, 1983).

Allen, John W., *A History of Political Thought in the Sixteenth Century* (London, 1928).

Ancient Laws of Ireland: Senchus Mor (Commissioners for Publishing the Ancient Laws and Institutes of Ireland, Dublin, 1865).

Andalusi, Sa'id ibn Ahmad al-, *Science in the Medieval World* (University of Texas Press, Austin, Texas, 1991).

Apsley, Lady, *Bridleways Through History* (London, 1936).

Arano, Luisa Cogliati, *The Medieval Health Handbook*, tr. & adapted by Oscar Ratti & Adele Westbrook (New York, 1976).

Argenti, Philip P., *The Occupation of Chios by the Genoese and Their Administration of the Island, 1346–1566* (Cambridge, 1958), 3 vols.

Armstrong, Charles A. J., *England, France and Burgundy in the Fifteenth Century* (Hambledon Press, London, 1983).

Ashmole, Elias, *Institutes, Laws and Ceremonies of the Order of the Garter* (London, 1963).

Aston, Margaret, *The Fifteenth Century* (London, 1968).

Atiya, Aziz S., *Crusade, Commerce and Culture* (Indiana & London, 1962).

Aubigny, *Ville d'Aubigny* (Franco-Scottish Festival, Aubigny, 1931).

Ayalon, David, *Gunpowder and Firearms in the Mamluk Kingdom* (London, 1956).

Babinger, Franz, *Mehmet the Conqueror and His Time*, tr. by William Hickman (Princeton University Press, 1975).

Bacon, James, *The Life and Times of Francis the First, King of France* (London, 1829).

Bagwell, Richard, *Ireland under the Tudors*, vol. i (London, 1885).

Balance, Selina, 'The Byzantine Churches of Trebizond', *Anatolian Studies* (*c.* 1958).

Balzac, Honoré de, *About Catherine de Medici*, tr. by Clara Bell (London, 1910).

Barbé, Louis, *Margaret of Scotland and the Dauphin Louis* (London, 1917).

Barber, Richard & Barker, Juliet, *Tournaments* (Woodbridge, 1989).

Baron, Hans, 'Franciscan Poverty and Civic Wealth in Humanist Thought', *Speculum*, vol. xiii (1938).

Barraclough, Geoffrey, *The Medieval Papacy* (London, reprinted 1979).

Batiffol, Louis, *Century of the Renaissance* (London, 1916).

Bayard, Tania, *Sweet Herbs and Sundry Flowers* (Metropolitan Museum of Art, New York, 1985).

Beaucourt, G. Du Fresne de, *Histoire de Charles VII*, vol. vi (Paris, 1881–1891).

Bedford, Revd W. K. R., *Malta and the Knights Hospitallers* (London, 1894).

Bedford, Revd W. K. R., *Regulations of the Old Hospital of Knights of St John at Valetta* (Edinburgh, 1882).

Bedford, Revd W. K. R., *The Order of the Hospital of St John of Jerusalem* (London, 1902).

Bell, Christopher, *Portugal and the Quest for the Indies* (London, 1974).

Bell, Rudolph, *Holy Anorexia* (Chicago, 1985).

Beltz, George Frederick, *Memorials of the Most Noble Order of the Garter* (London, 1841).

Bennett, Henry S., *The Pastons and Their England* (Cambridge, 1922).

Besant, Sir Walter, *London in the Time of the Tudors* (London, 1904).

Binder, Pearl, *Muffs and Morals* (London, 1953).

Birge, John K., *The Bektashi Order of Dervishes* (London, 1937).

Bishop, W. J., *Early History of Surgery* (London, 1960).

Black, William G., *Folk Medicine* (London, 1883).

Blake, John W., *European Beginnings in West Africa 1454–1578* (London, 1937).

Blackmore, Howard L., *Hunting Weapons* (London, 1971).

Bouillé, René de, *Histoire des Ducs de Guise* (Paris, 1849).

Bourassin, Emmanuel, *Philippe le Bon: le grand lion des Flandres* (Paris, *c*. 1983).

Bovill, E. W., *Golden Trade of the Moors* (London, 1958).

Bradbury, Jim, *The Medieval Archer* (Woodbridge, 1985).

Bradford, Ernle, *Southward the Caravels: The Story of Henry the Navigator* (London, 1961).

Bradford, Ernle, *The Great Siege* (London, 1961).

Bradford, Ernle, *The Shield and the Sword: The Knights of St John* (London, 1972).

Brandon, Michael, *Hunting and Shooting from Earliest Times* (London, 1971).

Braudel, Fernand, *The Mediterranean and the Mediterranean World of Philip II* (France, 1949; London, 1972).

Braudel, Fernand, *The Perspective of the World* (Civilization and Capitalism, vol. iii) (France, 1979; London, 1985).

Braudel, Fernand, *The Structures of Everyday Life* (Civilization and Capitalism, vol. i) (France, 1979; London, 1981).

Braudel, Fernand, *The Wheels of Commerce* (Civilization and Capitalism, vol. ii) (France, 1979; London, 1985).

Breul de, *Antiquités de Paris* (1612).

Brion, Marcel, *Catherine Cornaro, Reine de Chypre* (Paris, 1945).

British Library, *The Benedictines in Britain* (BL Series no. 3, 1980).

British Library, *William Caxton* (British Museum Publication to accompany a quincentennial exhibition, for the British Library, London, 1976).

Broderick, Alan Houghton, *Parts of Barbary* (London, 1944).

Broderick, Alan Houghton, *Touraine* (London, 1948).

Brosset, M., *Histoire de la Géorgie* (St Petersburg, 1856).

Brucker, Gene, *The Society of Renaissance Florence* (New York & London, 1971).

Bryer, Anthony, 'Greeks and Turcomens – The Pontic Exception', *Dumbarton Oaks Papers*, no. 29 (Dumbarton Oaks Center for Byzantine Studies, 1975).

Bullard, Melissa Meriam, *Filippo Strozzi and the Medici* (Cambridge, 1980).

Burckhardt, Jacob, *Civilization of the Renaissance in Italy* (London, 1929; reprinted New York, 1958).

Burgon, John William, *Life and Times of Sir Thomas Gresham* (London, 1839).

Burke, Edmund, *The History of Archery* (London, 1958).

Burton, Richard F., *The Book of the Sword* (1884; revised reprint, New York, 1987).

Burton, Sir Richard, *Ultima Thule; or, A Summer in Iceland* (London, 1875), 2 vols.

Burwash, Dorothy, *English Merchant Shipping 1460–1540* (Toronto, 1947).

Butler, Lionel, *The Siege of Rhodes, 1480* (Order of St John, Historical Pamphlets no. 11, London, 1980).

Bynum, Caroline Walker, *Holy Feast and Holy Fast: The Religious Significance of Food to Medieval Women* (London, 1987).

Cambridge Economic History of Europe, eds M. M. Postan & E. E. Rich, vols. ii & iii (Cambridge, 1952).

Cambridge Modern History, vol. ii: *Reformation* (Cambridge, 1902).

Carden, Robert Walter, *The City of Genoa* (London, 1908).

Carson, Patricia, *The Fair Face of Flanders* (Ghent, 1969; reprinted 1974).

Carus-Wilson, E. M., *Medieval Merchant Adventurers* (London, 1954).

Cattaneo, Elene Chiavari della Volta, *Adorno/Adornes* (Associazione Nobiliare della Liguria, 1997).

Cavaliero, Roderick, *The Last of the Crusades* (London, 1960).

Chambers, David S., *The Imperial Age of Venice, 1380–1580* (London, 1970).

Christian Orient (pub. for British Library Exhibition, London, 1978).

Cimber L. & Danjou F., *Archives Curieuses de l'Histoire de France* (Paris, 1835).

Cipolla, Carlo M., *Clocks and Culture 1300–1700* (London, 1967).

Clarke, Peter B., *West Africa and Islam* (London, 1982).

Clephan, R. C., *The Tournament: Its Periods and Phases* (London, 1919).

Clifford, Henry, *The Life of Jane Dormer, Duchess of Feria* (London, 1887).

Clowes, G. S. Laird, *Sailing Ships, Their History and Development* (London, 1932).

Cohen, R., *Knights of Malta 1523–1798* (London, 1920).

Coignet, Clarisse, *Francis the First and His Times*, tr. by Fanny Tivemlow (London, 1888).

Cola, Giuseppe, *I Monti della Tolfa nella Storia* (Tolfa, 1984).

Comrie, John D., A *History of Scottish Medicine to 1860* (London, 1927; 2nd edn. 1932).

Concannon, Dale, *Golf* (Stroud, 1999).

Contamini, Philippe, *War in the Middle Ages*, tr. by Michael Jones (Paris, 1980).

Cope, Christopher, *Phoenix Frustrated: The Lost Kingdom of Burgundy* (London, 1986).

Copeman, W. S. C., *Doctors and Diseases of Tudor Times* (London, 1960).

Cosman, Madeline Pelmer, *Fabulous Feasts* (1989).

Cotter, Charles H., *Astronomical & Mathematical Foundations of Geography* (London, 1966).

Cox, E. H. M., *History of Gardening in Scotland* (London, 1935).

Cox, Eugene L., *The Green Count of Savoy* (Princeton, 1967).

Cox, H. A., *London in the Sixteenth Century* ('Old London Illustrated', 3rd edn. 1922).

Cox, N., *The Gentleman's Recreation*, intro. by James Wentworth Day (London, 1686).

Coxe, William, *History of the House of Austria* (London, 1895).

Currey, Edward Hamilton, *Sea Wolves of the Mediterranean* (London, 1910).

Curtis, Edmund, A *History of Ireland* (London, 1936).

Dallaway, James, *Constantinople, Ancient and Modern* (London, 1797).

Darmesteter, A. & Hatzfeld, Adolphe, *Le Seizième Siècle en France* (Paris, 1928).

Darwin, Tess, *The Scots Herbal* (Edinburgh, 1996).

Davidson, H. R. Ellis, *Gods and Myths of Northern Europe* (London, 1964; reprinted 1976).

Davies, Norman, *God's Playground: A History of Poland* (Oxford, 1981), 2 vols.

Davies, R. R., ed., *The British Isles (1100–1500)* (Edinburgh, 1988).

Davis, Ralph, *The Rise of the Atlantic Economies* (London, 1973).

Dawson, Warren R., A *Leechbook, or Collection of Medical Recipes, of the Fifteenth Century* (London, 1934).

Deacon, Richard, *John Dee* (London, 1968).

Deer, Noel Fielding, *The History of Sugar*, vols. i & ii (London, 1949–1950).

Delumeau, Jean, *L'Alun de Rome, XVe–XIXe Siècle* (Paris, 1962).

Dennistoun, James, *Memoirs of the Dukes of Urbino*, with notes by Edward Hutton, vols. i–iii (London, 1851; 1909 edn.).

Dollinger, Philippe, *The German Hanse*, tr. by D. Ault & H. Steinberg (London, 1970).

Dorigato, Atillia, *Murano Glass Museum* (Milan, 1986).

Duby, Georges, *The Knight, the Lady and the Priest: The Making of Modern Marriage in Medieval France*, tr. by Barbara Bray (London, 1985).

Duclos, A., *Bruges, Histoire et Souvenirs* (Bruges, 1910).

Dufayard, Charles, *Histoire de Savoie* (Paris, 1922).

Duffy, Eamon, *Saints and Sinners: A History of the Popes* (Yale, 1997).

Dunbar, C. F., 'The Bank of Venice', *Quarterly Journal of Economics*, vol. vi (1892).

Dutton, Ralph, *The Châteaux of France* (London, 1957).

Dyke, Paul Van, *Catherine de Medici* (London, 1923).

Ehrle, Francesco, *Roma, Prima di Sistro V* (Rome, 1908).

Elias, Norbert, *The History of Manners*, tr. by Edmund Jephcott (Oxford, 1978; reprinted 1983).

Elliot, Frances, *Old Court Life in France* (London, 1873).

Ellis, Edgar Severn, *Ancient Anodynes* (London, 1946).

England, Sylvia Lennis, *The Massacre of Saint Bartholomew* (London, 1938).

Erlanger, Philippe, *Diane de Poitiers* (Paris, 1955).

Evans, Joan, *Magical Jewels of the Middle Ages and the Renaissance* (Oxford, 1926).

Fallmerayer, Jac. Ph., *Geschichte des Kaiserthums von Trapezunt* (Munich, 1827).

Fennell, J. L. I., *Ivan the Great of Moscow* (London, 1961).

Ferguson, John, *English Diplomacy, 1422–1461* (Oxford, 1972).

Ferrari, Henri Maxime, *Une Chaire de Médicin au XVe Siècle, Un Professeur à l'Université de Pavie de 1432 à 1472* (Paris, 1899).

Feuillerat, Albert, *Documents Relating to the Revels at Court in the Time of King Edward VI and Queen Mary* (London, 1914).

Finlay, George, *Medieval Greece and the Empire of Trebizond* (*A History of Greece, 146 BC–1864*, vol. iv) (Oxford, 1877).

Finot, Jules, 'Etude sur les relations commerciales entre la Flandre et Gênes au Moyen Âge', *Annales du Comité Flamand de France, tome* XVIII (1906–1907).

Finot, Jules, 'Le Commerce de l'Alun dans les Pays Bas', *Bulletin Historique et Philologique* (1902).

Fisher, Sir Godfrey, *Barbary Legend: War, Trade and Piracy in North Africa 1415–1830* (Oxford, 1957).

Forbes, C. S., Commander, RN, *Iceland, its Volcanoes, Geysers, and Glaciers* (London, 1860).

Foss, Michael, *Chivalry* (London, 1975).

Frérérix, Pierre, *La Mort de Charles le Téméraire, 5 janvier 1477* (Paris, 1966).

Gabrieli, Francesco, *Arab Historians of the Crusades*, tr. by E. J. Costello (London, 1969).

Gade, John A., *The Hanseatic Control of Norwegian Commerce During the Late Middle Ages* (Leiden, 1957).

Galey, John, *Sinai and the Monastery of St Catherine* (Massada, 1979).

Gébelin, François, *Châteaux de la Loire* (1964).

Geddes, Olive M., *A Swing Through Time: Golf in Scotland 1457–1743* (Edinburgh, 1992).

Gies, Frances, *The Knight in History* (London, 1986).

Gilbert, Felix, *The Pope, His Banker and Venice* (Harvard University Press, 1980).

Gill, Joseph, *The Council of Florence* (Cambridge, 1959).

Gilliat-Smith, Ernest, *Bruges* (1909).

Giuseppi, Montague S., 'Alien Merchants in England in the Fifteenth Century', *Transactions of the Royal Historical Society.*

Glorieux, P., 'Un Chanoine de St Pierre de Lille, Jean Adornes', *Bulletin du Comité Flamand de France, tome* XVIII (1971).

Godefroy, Theodore, *Le Ceremonial françois* (Paris, 1649).

Gordon, Major Lawrence Lee, *British Orders and Awards* (Stafford, 1959; revised 1968).

Grant, Sir Francis J., *A Manual of Heraldry* (Edinburgh, reprinted 1962).

Gravière, E. Jurien de la, *Les Derniers Jours de la Marine à Rames* (c. 1890).

Gregory, Heather, 'Filippo Strozzi and Medicean Politics', *Renaissance Quarterly*, vol. xxxviii (1985).

Grunzweig, A., ed., *Correspondance de la filiale de Bruges des Medici* (Brussels, 1931).

Grunzweig, A., *Philippe le Bon et Constantinople* (University of Brussels, 1953).

Guérard, Albert, *Life and Death of an Ideal: France in the Classical Age* (London, 1929; reprinted 1957).

Gutkind, Curt S., *Cosimo de' Medici, Pater Patriae, 1389–1464* (Oxford, 1938).

Hackett, Francis, *Francis the First* (London, 1934).

Haggard, Andrew C. P., *Two Great Rivals: Francis I & Charles V and the Women Who Influenced Them* (London, 1910).

Hale, J. R., ed., *Renaissance Venice* (London, 1973).

Hale, J. R., *Florence and the Medici: The Pattern of Control* (London, 1977).

Hale, J. R., *Renaissance Europe 1480–1520* (Oxford, 2000).

Hale, J. R., *Renaissance War Studies* (London, c. 1983).

Hall, Margaret Wilslaw, 'Early Bankers in Genoese Notarial Records', *Economic History Review*, vol. vi (1935–1936).

Hamel, Frank, *Dauphines of France* (London, 1909).

Hare, Charles E., *The Language of Field Sports* (Country Life, New York & Glasgow, 1949).

Harington, Sir John, tr., *The School of Salernum, Regimen sanitatis Salerni* (Salerno, 1959).

Hart, G. M., *Three Famous Occultists.*

Harvey, John, *Medieval Gardens* (London, 1981; reprinted 1990).

Harvey, John, *The Plantaganets 1154–1485* (revised edn. 1981).

Hautcoeur, E., *Cartulaire de l'Église Collégiale de St Pierre de Lille* (Paris, 1894), 2 vols.

Hautcouer, E., *Histoire de l'Église Collégiale et du Chapitre de St Pierre de Lille* (Paris, 1897), 3 vols.

Hay, Denys, *Europe in the Fourteenth and Fifteenth Centuries* (London, 1966; reprinted 1980).

Hayes, John, ed., *The Genius of Arab Civilization* (New York, 3rd edn. 1992).

Head, Constance, 'Pope Pius and the Wars of the Roses', *Archivum Historiae Pontificial*, vol. viii (1970).

Heers, Jacques, *Genoa nel Quattrocento* (Paris, 1971; Italian edn. 1984).

Henderson, Helen W., *Dianne de Poytiers* (London, 1928).

Héritier, Jean, *Catherine de Medici*, tr. by Charlotte Haldane (London, 1963).

Herval, René, *Dieppe* (Caen, 1947).

Herval, René, *Histoire de Rouen* (Rouen, 1947).

Heulard, Arthur, *Villegagnon (1510–1572)* (Paris, 1897).

Heyd, W., *Histoire du Commerce du Levant au Moyen Âge*, tr. by Furcy Reynaud, vol. ii (Amsterdam, 1959), 8 vols.

Hibbert, Christopher, *The Rise and Fall of the House of Medici* (London, 1974).

Hill, Sir George, A *History of Cyprus*, vol. ii & iii (Cambridge, 1940–1952), 8 vols.

Hindley, Geoffrey, *England in the Age of Caxton* (London, 1979).

Hingley, Ronald, *The Tsars, Russian Autocrats* (London, 1968).

Historical Manuscripts Commission, *The Manuscripts of Lord de L'Isle and Dudley at Penshurst Place*, vol. i (1925).

Hogan, Edmund, *The Irish Wolfdog* (Dublin, 1897).

Holmes, George A., 'Florentine Merchants in England', *Economic History Review*, 2nd series, vol. xiii (1960).

Holmes, George A., *The Later Middle Ages* (Edinburgh, 1962).

Hook, Judith, *Lorenzo de' Medici: An Historical Biography* (London, 1984).

Hook, Judith, *Siena, a City and Its History* (London, 1979).

Hügel, Baron Friedrich von, *The Mystical Element of Religion as Studied in St Catherine of Genoa and Her Friends* (London, 1908), 2 vols.

Humble, Richard, *Warfare in the Middle Ages* (Mallard Press, USA, 1989).

Hurton, William, *A Voyage from Leith to Lapland* (London, 1851), 2 vols.

Hussey, J. M., *The Orthodox Church of the Byzantine Empire* (Oxford, 1986).

Hutton, Alfred, *Old Sword Play* (London, 1892).

Hutton, Alfred, *The Sword and the Centuries* (London, 1901).

Hutton, William Holden, *Constantinople* (London, 1900).

Hyde, J. K., *Society and Politics in Medieval Italy 1000–1350* (London, 1973).

Ianziti, Gary, 'Giovanni Simonetta, Secretary to the Sforzas', *Renaissance Quarterly*, (winter 1981).

Ilardi, Vincent, 'Eyeglasses and Concave Lenses in C.15th Florence and Milan', *Renaissance Quarterly* (autumn 1976).

Inalcik, Halil, 'Mehmet the Conqueror and His Time', *Speculum*, vol. xxxv.

Iongh, Jane de, *Mary of Hungary* (London, 1959).

Jacobs, E. F., *The Fifteenth Century, 1399–1485* (Oxford, 1993).

Jena, Carl-Zeiss-Siftung, A *Spectacle of Spectacles* (catalogue of exhibition in the National Museums of Scotland, 1988–1989).

Jenkins, Rhys, 'The Alum Trade in the Fifteenth and Sixteenth Century', *Collected Papers* (Newcomen Society, Cambridge, 1936).

Jenkinson, Wilberforce, *Royal and Bishops' Palaces in Old London* (London & New York, 1921).

Jordan, W. K., *Edward VI: The Threshold of Power* (London, 1968).

José, Marie, *Amadeus VIII – Le Duc qui devint Pape* (Paris, 1962).

José, Marie, *La Maison de Savoie* (Paris, 1956).

Joyce, P. W., *A Social History of Ancient Ireland* (London, 1902).

Kaeuper, Richard, *Bankers to the Crown: The Riccardi of Lucca* (Princeton University Press, 1973).

Kaeuper, Richard, 'The Frescobaldi of Florence and the English Crown', *Studies in Medieval and Renaissance History*, ed. William M. Bowsky, vol. x (Lincoln, Nebraska, 1973).

Keen, Maurice, *Chivalry* (Yale, 1984).

Keen, Maurice, *The Laws of War in the Late Middle Ages* (London, 1965).

Kendall, Paul Murray, *Louis XI* (London, 1971).

Kent, Dale, 'The Florentine Reggimento in the 15th Century', *Renaissance Quarterly*, (winter 1975).

Kent, Francis William, *Household and Lineage in Renaissance Florence* (Princeton, c. 1977).

King, E. J., *Grand Priory of the Order of the Hospital of St John of Jerusalem in England* (London, 1924).

Kirk, John Foster, *History of Charles the Bold* (London, 1863–1868), 3 vols.

Kirkman, Finlay, *Selections from Unpublished Manuscripts in the College of Arms and British Museum Illustrating the Reign of Queen Mary*, ed. Joseph Stevenson (Glasgow, 1837).

Knowles, David, *The Evolution of Medieval Thought* (London, 1988).

Kourennoff, Paul M. & George, George St, tr. & ed. *Russian Folk Medicine* (London, 1970).

Kozny, Leon, *The Baltic Policy of the Teutonic Order* (London, 1936).

Krekić, B., *Dubrovnik (Raguse) et le Levant au Moyen Âge* (Paris, 1961).

Labarge, Margaret Wade, *Medieval Travellers, the Rich and Restless* (London, 1982).

Lane, Frederic C., *Andrea Barbarigo, Merchant of Venice 1418–1449* (Baltimore, 1944).

Lane, Frederic C., 'Venetian Naval Architecture c. 1550', *Mariner's Mirror (Journal of the Society for Nautical Research)*, vol. xx, (Cambridge University Press, 1934).

Lane, Frederic C., *Venetian Ships and Shipbuilders of the Renaissance* (Baltimore, 1934).

Lane, Frederic C., *Venice and History* (Baltimore, 1966).

Langlois, E. H., *Description Historique des Maisons de Rouen* (Paris, 1821).

Larking, L. B., *The Knights Hospitaller in England* (Camden Society, London, 1857).

Larner, John, *Culture and Society in Italy 1290–1420* (London, 1971).

Latrie, L. de Mas, *Histoire de Chypre* (Paris, 1855).

Leggett, William F., *Story of Silk* (New York, 1949).

Lemonnier, Henri, *Histoire de France, tome* V.

Lettenhove, Baron H. Kervyn de, *La Toison d'Or* (Brussels, 1907).

Letts, Malcolm, *Bruges and Its Past* (Bruges, 1924).

Lewis, Bernard, *The Muslim Discovery of Europe* (New York, 1982).

Lewis, Bernard, *The Jews of Islam* (Princeton, 1984).

Lewis, D. B. Wyndham, *The Soul of Marshall Gilles de Raiz.*

Lienau, Otto, *Das Grosse Kraweel der Peter von Danzig, 1462–1475* (Danzig, 1943).

Livermore, H. V., *History of Portugal* (Cambridge, 1947).

Lloyd, T. H., *England and the German Hanse 1157–1611* (Cambridge, 1991).

Loades, D. M., *Two Tudor Conspiracies* (Cambridge, 1965).

Lockley, R. M., *Puffins* (London, 1953).

Loisel, G., *Histoire des Ménageries de l'Antiquité à Nos Jours* (Museum d'Histoire Nationale, Paris, 1912).

Longworth, Philip, *The Cossacks* (London, 1969; reprinted 1971).

Lopez, Roberto, 'Aux Origines du Capitalisme Génois', *Annales d'Histoire Economique et Sociale* (*c.* 1937).

Lubimenko, Inna, *Les Relations Commerciales et Politiques d'Angleterre avec la Russie avant Pierre le Grand* (Paris, 1933).

Luke, Sir Harry, *Cyprus* (London, *c.* 1957).

Luke, Sir Harry, *Malta* (London, 1949; 2nd edn. 1960).

Lybyer, A. H., 'Influence of the Rise of the Ottoman Turks upon the Routes of Oriental Trade', *American Historical Association.*

Lybyer, A. H., 'The Ottoman Turks and the Route of Oriental Trade', *English Historical Review*, vol. cxx (October 1915).

Lynch, H. F. B., *Armenia: Travel and Studies* (London, 1901).

Maalouf, Amin, *The Crusades Through Arab Eyes*, tr. by Jon Rothschild (London, 1984).

McFarlane, Kenneth B., *England in the Fifteenth Century* (London, 1981).

MacKay, Angus, *Spain in the Middle Ages 1000–1500* (London, 1977).

Mackie, J. D., *The Earliest Tudors 1485–1558* (Oxford, 1994).

MacLeish, Andrew, ed., *In the Medieval Monastery* (Minnesota, 1988).

MacPherson, H. H., *The Hare* (London, 1896).

Malleson, G. B., *Studies from Genoese History* (London, 1875).

Mallett, Michael, *The Borgias* (London, 1971).

Mallett, Michael, *The Florentine Galleys in the Fifteenth Century* (Oxford, 1967).

Mallett, Michael, *Mercenaries and Their Masters* (London, 1974).

Marche, Albert Lecoy de la, *Le Roi René* (Paris, 1875), 2 vols.

Markham, Sir Clements R., *King Edward VI* (London, 1907).

Martin, Jane, *Medieval Russia 980–1584* (Cambridge, 1995).

Martines, Lauro, *The Social World of the Florentine Humanists 1390–1460* (London, 1963).

Mattingly, Garrett, *Renaissance Diplomacy* (New York, 1955).

Maxwell, Constantia, *Irish History from Contemporary Sources 1509–1610* (London, 1923).

Mayes, Stanley, *An Organ for the Sultan* (Putnam, 1956).

Mead, W. E., *The English Medieval Feast* (London, 1931; reprinted 1967).

Merriman, Roger B., *Suleiman the Magnificent, 1520–1566* (Cambridge, Mass., 1944).

Michaud, Joseph François & Poujoulat, Jean, *Memoires à l'histoire de France XIIIe–XVIIIe Siècles*, vol. ix (Paris, 1836).

Michel, Albin, *La Vie du Chameau* (1938).

Michel, Francisque, *Les Écossais en France, Les Français en Écosse* (London, 1862).

Mijatovich, Chedomil, *Constantine, the Last Emperor of the Greeks* (London, 1892).

Miller, William, *The Latins in the Levant 1204–1566* (London, 1908).

Miller, William, *Trebizond, the Last Greek Empire* (London, 1926).

Milligen, Alex von, *Byzantine Constantinople* (London, 1899).

Mitchell, R. J., 'Scottish Law Students in Italy in Later Middle Ages', *Juridical Review*, vol. xlix (1937).

Mitchell, R. J., *The Laurels and The Tiara: Pope Pius II* (London, 1962).

Mitchell, R. J., *The Spring Voyage: The Jerusalem Pilgrimage in 1458* (London, 1964).

Molho, Anthony, *Florentine Public Finances in the Early Renaissance* (Cambridge, Mass., 1971).

Montfaucon, *Les Monumens de la Monarchi François* (Paris, 1732).

Montifaud, Marc de, *Les Triomphes de l'Abbaye des Conards* (Paris, 1874).

Moorman, John, *A History of the Franciscan Order from its Origins to 1517* (Clarendon Press, Oxford, 1968).

Morgan, J., *A Complete History of (Barbary) Algiers* (1737).

Moynihan, Elizabeth B., *Paradise as a Garden in Persia and Mughal India* (London, 1980).

Muir, Dorothy, *A History of Milan under the Visconti* (London, 1924).

Muir, Sir William, *The Mameluke or Slave Dynasty of Egypt 1260–1517* (London, 1896).

Myers, A. R., *England in the Late Middle Ages* (London, 1952).

Neale, J. E., *Age of Catherine de Medici* (London, 1943).

Neale, John M., *History of the Holy Eastern Church: The Patriarch of Antioch* (London, 1851).

Obolensky, Dmitri, *The Byzantine Commonwealth, 500–1453* (1st British edn. 1971; reprinted 1974).

Oman, Sir Charles, *A History of the Art of War in the 16th Century* (London, 1937).

Oppenheim, M., *A History of the Administration of the Royal Navy and of Merchant Shipping*, vol. i (London, 1896).

Origo, Iris, 'The Domestic Enemy – The Eastern Slaves in Tuscany in the Fourteenth and Fifteen Centuries', *Speculum*, vol. xxx (July 1955).

Origo, Iris, *The Merchant of Prato: Francesco di Marco Datini* (London, 1957).

Orliac, Jehanne d', *Francis I, Prince of the Renaissance* (Philadelphia & London, 1932).

Orliac, Jehanne d', *The Moon Mistress, Diane de Poitiers* (London, 1931).

Ostrogorsky, George, *History of the Byzantine State*, tr. by Joan Hussey (Oxford, 1956; reprinted 1980).

Packard, Francis R., *Life and Times of Amboise Paré* (London, 1922).

Paganel, Camille, *Histoire de Scanderbeg* (Paris, 1855).

Paget, Stephen, *Ambroise Paré and His Times* (New York, 1897).

Pardoe, Julia, *The Court and Reign of Francis I* (London, 1887).

Parker, Derek & Julia, *A History of Astrology* (London, 1983).

Partner, Peter, *The Papal State under Martin V* (London, 1958).

Partner, Peter, *The Pope's Men* (Oxford, 1990).

Pastor, Dr Ludwig Friedrich August von, *The History of the Popes*, ed. Frederick Ignatius Antrobus, vols. ii–iv (London, 1891–1894).

Pattie, T. S., *Astrology as Illustrated in the Collections of the British Library and the British Museum* (London, 1980).

Pennick, J., *De Jeruzalemkerk te Brugge* (Bruges, reprinted 1986).

Penrose, Boies, *Travel and Discovery in the Renaissance 1420–1620* (New York, 1975).

Penzer, N. M., *The Harem* (London, 1936; reprinted 1965).

Pierling, Fr, *Itinéraires Russes en Orient* (Geneva, 1889).

Pierling, Fr, *La Russie et la Saint Siège*, vol. i (Paris, 1896; reproduced 1967).

Pierling, Fr, *La Russie et l'Orient* (1891).

Pilon, Edmund, *Fontainebleau* (London, 1933).

Pirenne, Henri, 'L'Instruction des Marchands au Moyen Âge', *Annales d'Histoire Economique et Sociale* (1929).

Plat, Sir Hugh, *Delight for Ladies.*

Playfair, Lt-Col. R. L., *The Scourge of Christendom* (London, 1884).

Poleggi, Ennio & Cerini, Paolo, *La Città nella storia d'Italia* (Italy, 1981).

Pollak, Kurt, *The Healers: the Doctor, Then and Now* (Nelson, 1968).

Pollock, Walter Herries, *Fencing* (London, 1893).

Poole, Stanley Lane, *Barbary Corsairs* (London, 1890).

Porter, G. R., *A Treatise on the Origin of Silk Manufacture* (1831).

Porter, Whitworth, *The Knights of Malta* (London, 3rd edn. 1884).

Postan, M. M., 'Credit in Medieval Trade', *Economic History Review*, vol. i (1928).

Postan, M. M., *Medieval Trade and Finance* (London, 1973).

Postan, M. M., *The Medieval Economy and Society* (London, 1981).

Pottinger, David T., *The French Book Trade in the Ancien Régime 1500–1791* (Cambridge, Mass., 1958).

Pouncey, Carolyn, tr. & ed., *The Domostroi: Rules for Russian Households in the Time of Ivan the Terrible* (New York, 1994).

Powell, George H., *Duelling Stories* (from the French of Brantôme) (London, 1904).

Power, Eileen & Postan, M. M., *Studies in English Trade in the Fifteenth Century* (London, 1933).

Power, Eileen, *The Wool Trade in English Medieval History* (London, 1941).

Praet, Jules van, *Louis de Bruges, Seigneur de la Gruthuyse* (Paris, 1831).

Praet, Jules van, *Notice sur Colard Manson* (Paris, 1829).

Preliminary Report on the Excavation in the Hippodrome of Constantinople, 1927 (1928).

Prescott, H. F. M., *Jerusalem Journey: Pilgrimage to the Holy Land in the Fifteenth Century* (London, 1954).

Prescott, H. F. M., *Once to Sinai: The Further Pilgrimage of Friar Felix Fabri* (London, 1957).

Prescott, W. H., *History of the Reign of Philip II* (London, 1906).

Prevenier, Walter & Blockmans, Wim, *The Burgundian Netherlands* (Cambridge, 1986).

Previté-Orton, Charles William, *The Shorter Cambridge Medieval History*, vol. ii (Cambridge, 1952).

Prichard, A. H. Cooper, *A History of the Grand Duchy of Luxembourg* (1950).

Przezdziecki, Count Renaud, *Diplomatic Ventures and Adventures* (London, 1953).

Pullan, Brian, *Rich and Poor in Renaissance Venice* (Oxford, 1971).

Putnam, Ruth, *Charles the Bold, Last Duke of Burgundy, 1433–1477* (New York & London, 1908).

Rabind, M. H. L., *Le Monastère de Saint-Catherine, Mount Sinaï: Souvenirs.*

Rady, Martyn, *The Tsars, Russia, Poland and the Ukraine 1462–1725* (London, 1990).

Rashdall, Hastings, *Universities of Europe in the Middle Ages* (Oxford, 1936).

Raynaldo, Odoric, *Annales Ecclesiastici, tome* X, 1454–1480 (Luca, 1753).

Redway, W. F., Penson, J. H., Halecki, O. & Dyboski, R. eds., *The Cambridge History of Poland* (Cambridge, 1950).

Richard, J., *Croisés, Missionaires et Voyageurs: les perspectives orientales du monde latin médiéval* (London, 1983).

Richard, J., 'La Papauté et les Missions d'Orient au Moyen Âge', *Collection de l'École Française de Rome,* xxxiii (1977).

Richards, Richard D., *The Early History of Banking in England* (London, 1929).

Richey, A. G., *A Short History of the Irish People* (Dublin, 1887).

Robertson, Joseph, 'The First Russian Embassy to England', *Archeological Journal,* vol. xiii (1856).

Robinson, Wilfrid C., *Bruges* (Bruges, 1899).

Robson, Ralph, *The English Highland Clans: Tudor Responses to a Mediaeval Problem* (Edinburgh, 1989).

Roeder, Ralph, *Catherine de' Medici and the Lost Revolution* (London, 1937).

Röhl, John C. G., Warren, Martin & Hunt, David, *Purple Secret: Genes, 'Madness' and the Royal Houses of Europe* (London, 1998).

Romier, Lucien, *Le Royaume de Catherine de Medici* (Paris, 1922).

Roncière, Charles de la, 'La Découverte de L'Afrique au Moyen Âge', *Mémoires de la Société Royale de Géographie d'Egypte,* (Cairo, 1924).

Roover, Florence Edler de, 'Andrea Banchi: Florentine Silk Manufacturer and Merchant in the Fifteenth Century', *Studies in Medieval and Renaissance History,* vol. ii (1960).

Roover, Florence Edler de, 'Early Examples of Marine Insurance', *Journal of Economic History,* vol. v (1945).

Roover, Raymond de, *Money, Banking and Credit in Mediaeval Bruges* (Cambridge, Mass., 1948).

Roover, Raymond de, *The Medici Bank* (New York, 1948).

Ross, Charles, *Edward IV* (London, 1974).

Ross, Charles, *The Wars of the Roses: A Concise History* (London, 1976).

Rowe, Vivian, *Royal Châteaux in Paris.*

Rowse, A. L. *Bosworth Field and the Wars of the Roses* (London, 1966).

Ruddock, A. A., *Italian Merchants and Shipping in Southampton 1270–1600* (Southampton, 1951).

Ruddock, A. A., 'Method of Handling the Cargoes of Medieval Merchant Galleys', *Economic History Review* (1944).

Runciman, Steven, *A History of the Crusades,* (London, 1951; reprinted 1981), 3 vols.

Runciman, Sir Steven, *The Fall of Constantinople, 1453* (Cambridge, 1965).

Runciman, Steven, *The Great Church in Captivity: A Study of the Patriarchate of Constantinople* (Cambridge, 1968).

Runciman, Steven, *The Medieval Manichee* (Cambridge University Press, 1947).

Ryan, Lawrence V., *Roger Ascham* (London & Stanford, California, 1963).

Saad, Elias N., *A Social History of Timbuktu 1400–1900* (Cambridge, 1983).

St Benedict's Rule for Monasteries, tr. by Leonard J. Doyle (Minnesota, 1948).

Saint-Priest, M. le comte de, *Mémoires sur l'Ambassade de France en Turquie* (Paris, 1877).

Sass, Lorna J., *To the King's Taste: Richard II's Book of Feasts and Recipes* (London, 1976).

Saural, Henri, *Histoire et Rescherches des Antiquités de la Ville de Paris* (Paris, 1724).

Schelle, Klaus, *Charles le Téméraire* (Paris, 1979).

Schermerhorn, Elizabeth W., *On the Trail of the Eight-Pointed Cross* (New York, 1940).

Schevill, Ferdinand, *The Medici* (New York, 1949).

Scofield, Cora, *The Life and Reign of Edward IV* (London, 1923), 2 vols.

Sedall, Revd Henry, *Malta, Past and Present* (London, 1870).

Seely, Grace Hart, *Diane the Huntress* (London, 1936).

Segel, Harold B., *Renaissance Culture in Poland: The Rise of Humanism, 1473–1543* (Ithaca & London, 1989).

Setton, Kenneth M., *The Papacy and the Levant 1204–1571* (Philadelphia, 1976).

Severi, Angelo Bargallesi, 'Nuovi Documenti su Fr. Lodovico da Bologna al Secolo Lodovico Severi, Nunzio Apostolico in Orienti, 1455–1457', *Archivum Franciscanorum Historicum, tome* LXIX (Collegio S. Bonaventura, Rome, 1976).

Shahar, Shulamith, *The Fourth Estate: A History of Women in the Middle Ages* (London, 1983).

Sharman, Tim, *Poland* (London, 1988).

Shaw, Stanford J., *History of the Ottoman Empire and Modern Turkey*, vol. i (Cambridge, 1977).

Sheehan, Michael M., 'Choice of Marriage Partner in the Middle Ages', *Studies in Medieval and Renaissance History*, new series, vol. i (1978).

Sherrard, Philip, *Constantinople: Iconography of a Sacred City* (London, 1965).

Sichel, Edith, *Catherine de Medici and the French Reformation* (London, 1905).

Simpson, Helen, *Spanish Marriage* (London, 1933).

Singer, Charles, *The Earliest Chemical Industry* (Folio Society, London, 1948), 2 vols.

Smith, G. Rex, *Medieval Muslim Horsemanship* (London, 1979).

Spufford, Peter, *Monetary Problems and Policies in the Burgundian Netherlands 1433–1496* (Leiden, 1970).

Studi in Onore di Armando Sapori (Milan, 1957), 2 vols.

Taaffe, John, *The History of the Holy, Military, Sovereign Order of St John of Jerusalem*, vol. iii (London, 1852).

Taylor, E. G. R., *Tudor Geography 1485–1583* (London, 1930).

Thierry, Adrien, *Diane de Poitiers* (Paris, 1955).

Thuasne, L., *Gentile Bellini et Sultan Mohammed II: Notes sur le séjour du Peintre vénitien à Constantinople 1479–1480* (Paris, 1888).

Tilley, Arthur, *Modern France* (Cambridge, 1922).

Tobin, Stephen, *The Cistercians* (London, 1995).

Tough, D. L. W., *The Last Years of a Frontier: a History of the Borders During the Reign of Elizabeth* (Oxford, 1928).

Tourneur, Victor, 'Les Origines de l'Ordre de la Toison d'Or', *Bulletin de l'Académie Royale de Belgique* (1956).

Trexler, Richard C., *Public Life in Renaissance Florence* (London, 1980).

Trexler, Richard C., 'The Magi Enter Florence: The Ubriachi of Florence and Venice', *Studies in Medieval and Renaissance History*, new series, vol. i (1978).

Trollope, T. A., *The Girlhood of Catherine de Medici* (London, 1856).

Tuohy, Thomas, *Herculean Ferrara: Ercole d'Este, 1471–1505, and the Invention of a Ducal Capital* (Cambridge, 1996).

Turk, Anthony, *Crown and Nobility 1272–1461: Political Conflict in Late Medieval England* (London, 1985).

Turner, E. S., *Court of St James's* (London, 1959).

Turner, E. S., *Taking the Cure* (London, 1967).

Twiss, Sir Travers, *Black Book of the Admiralty (Liber Niger Admiralitatis)* (1871).

Ure, John, *Henry the Navigator* (London, 1977).

Usher, Abbott Payson, 'Origins of Banking: The Primitive Bank of Deposit 1200–1600', *Economic History Review*, vol. iv (1934).

Vale, M. G. A., *Charles VII* (London, 1974).

Varillas, Antoine, *The Secret History of the House of Medici*, tr. by Ferrand Spence (London, 1685).

Vasiliev, A., *The Goths in the Crimea* (Cambridge, Mass., 1936).

Vast, Henri, *Le Cardinal Bessarion* (Paris, 1878).

Vaughan, Richard, *Philip the Good: The Apogee of Burgundy* (Harlow, 1970).

Vernadsky, George & Karpovich, Michael, *Russia at the Dawn of the Modern Age (History of Russia*, vol. iv) (Yale, 1944).

Vertot, M. l'Abbé de, *Histoire des Chevaliers Hospitaliers de St Jean de Jérusalem* (Paris, 1727; tr. into English 1770).

Vincenes, Emile, *Histoire de Gênes, tome* II (1842).

Wadding, Luke, *Annales Minorum seu Trium Ordinum a S. Francisco Institutorum, tome* XIII (Rome, 1735).

Waley, Daniel, *Later Medieval Europe from St Louis to Luther* (London, 1964).

Walsh, James T., *Medieval Medicine* (London, 1920).

Walsh, Richard J., 'Charles the Bold and the Crusade', *Journal of Medieval History*, vol. iii (1977).

Watanabe, Morimichi, 'Humanism in the Tyrol', *Journal of Medieval and Renaissance Studies*, vol. iv (summer 1974).

Watson, Francis, *The Life and Times of Catherine de Medici* (London, 1934).

Watt, William & Cachia, Pierre, *A History of Islamic Spain* (Edinburgh, 1965).

Weightman, Christine, *Margaret of York, Duchess of Burgundy 1446–1503* (Gloucester, 1989).

Weiss, Robert, *The Renaissance Discovery of Classical Antiquity* (Oxford, 1969).

Wernham, R. B., *Before the Armada* (London, 1966).

Werveke, Hans van, *Gand* (Brussels, 1946).

White, Beatrice, *Mary Tudor* (London, 1935).

Wiesener, Louis, *La Jeunesse d'Elisabeth* (1879).

Willan, T. S., *Muscovy Merchants of 1555* (Manchester, 1953).

Williams, Hugh Noel, *Henri II, His Court and Times* (London, 1910).

Wilson, Francesca, *Muscovy: Russia Through Foreign Eyes, 1553–1900* (London, 1970).

Wilson, Philip, *The Beginnings of Modern Ireland.*

Wise, Terence, Hook, Richard & Walker, William, *Medieval Heraldry*, Men-at-Arms Series (London, 1980; reprinted 1992).

Wolffe, Bertram P., *Henry VI* (London, 1981).

Wortman, Richard S., *Scanarios of Power: Myth and Ceremony in Russian Monarchy* (Princeton, 1995).

Zamoyski, Adam, *The Polish Way* (London, 1987).

Zambrini, ed., *Il libro della cucina del Secolo XIV* (1863).

Zippel, G., 'L'Allume di Tolfa', *Archivo della r Societa di Storia Patra,* vol. xxx (1907).

Literature, Drama, Music, Civic Ritual, Religious and Astrological Texts

Ancrene wisse: Guide for Anchoresses, tr. by Hugh White (London, 1993).

Annals of the Kingdom of Ireland by the Four Masters, ed., John O'Donovan (1851), 7 vols.

Barbour, John, *The Bruce*, ed. Matthew P. McDiarmid & James A. C. Stevenson (Scottish Text Society, Edinburgh, 1981).

Bareste, Eugene, *Nostradamus* (Paris, 1840).

Bawcutt, Priscilla, 'A Medieval Scottish Elegy and its French Original', *Scottish Literary Journal* (May 1988).

Blades, William, *The Life and Typography of William Caxton, England's First Printer, with Evidence of his Typographical Connection with Colard Mansion, the Printer at Bruges* (London, 1861), 2 vols.

Blake, N. F., *Caxton, England's First Publisher* (London, 1976).

Brown, Edward Granville, *Persian Literature in Modern Times* (Cambridge, 1909).

Bullett, Gerald, ed., *Silver Poets of the 16th Century* (London, 1947; reprinted 1970).

Burton, Robert, *The Anatomy of Melancholy*, ed. Holbrook Jackson (London, 1932).

Buuren, Catherine van, ed., *The Buke of the Chess,* Middle Scots version of the 13th Century *Ludus Scaccorum* of Jacobus de Cessolis (Scottish Text Society, Edinburgh, 1997).

Callimachi Experientis, *Carmina* (poetry of Philippi Bonaccorsi), intro. by Gioacchino Paparelli (Naples, 1981).

Cawley, A. C., ed., *Everyman and Medieval Miracle Plays* (London, 1986).

Caxton, William, *The Book of Curtesye. Printed at Westminster by William Caxton about the year 1477* (Cambridge, 1907).

Cheetham, Erika, *Prophecies of Nostradamus* (pub. by Neville Spearman, Great Britain, 1973; reprinted 1975).

Cohen, Gustave, *Le Livre de Conduite du Régisseur et le Compte des Dépenses pour le Mystère de la Passion joué à Mons en 1501* (Paris, 1925).

Craik, Henry, *English Prose Selections*, vol. i (1893).

Cross, T. & Slover, C. eds., *Ancient Irish Tales* (Dublin, 1969).

Dante, Alighieri, *The Divine Comedy: Hell*, tr. by Dorothy L. Sayers (London, 1988).

Dunbar, William, *Poems*, ed. John Small (Edinburgh, 1893), 3 vols.

Everyman (London, 1930).

Fitzgibbon, H. Macaulay, ed., *Early English Poetry* (London, 1887).

Frank, Grace, *Medieval French Drama* (Oxford, 1954).

Gaston III ('Phoebus'), *The Master of Game*, tr. with interpolations by Edward, Second Duke of York, 1413 (1904 edn.).

Gibb, E. J. W., *A History of Ottoman Poetry*, vols. i–iii (Glasgow, 1931), 8 vols.

Harris, Clement A. & Hargreave, Mary, *Story of British Music and the Earlier French Musicians* (London & New York, 1919).

Henderson, T. F., *Scottish Vernacular Poetry* (Edinburgh, 1910).

Henebry, Richard, *Handbook of Irish Music* (London & Cork, 1928).

Henry, Derrick, *The Listener's Guide to Medieval and Renaissance Music* (Poole, 1983).

Hoppin, Richard H., ed., *Medieval Music* (New York, 1978).

Hrafnkel's Saga and Other Stories, tr. & ed. by Hermann Pálsson (London, 1971; reprinted 1976).

Jackson, Kenneth, tr., *A Celtic Miscellany* (London, 1951; reprinted 1971 & 1975).

James, Jamie, *Music of the Spheres* (London, 1993).

Jamieson, John, ed., *Wallace: The Life and Acts of Sir William Wallace by Henry the Minstrel* (Glasgow, 1869).

Knight, Alan E., 'The Image of the City in the Processional Theatre of Lille', *Research Opportunities in Renaissance Drama*, vol. xxx (1988).

Konigsen, Elie, *L'Espace théâtral médiéval* (Paris, 1975).

Kristjánsson, Jónas, *Icelandic Manuscripts, Sagas, History and Art*, tr. Jeffrey Cosser (Reykjavik, 1993).

Kritzeck, James, *An Anthology of Islamic Literature: From the Rise of Islam to Modern Times* (London, 1964).

Laing, David, *Early Popular Poetry of Scotland* (London, 1895), 2 vols.

Lane, Edward William, *An Arabic–English Lexicon* (London, 1863; reprinted 1984), 2 vols.

Lilly, William, *Christian Astrology* (London, 1647).

Lindsay, Sir David, *Poetical Works*, ed. David Laing (Edinburgh, 1871), 3 vols.

Lyall, Roderick J., 'Two of Dunbar's Makars, James Affleck and Sir John the Ross', *The Innes Review*, vol. xxvii (1976).

McDiarmid, Matthew P., ed., *Hary's Wallace* (Scottish Text Society, 1967–1969).

MacQueen, John, *Robert Henryson* (Oxford, 1967).

Mandeville, Sir John, *Travels*, ed. M. C. Seymour (Oxford, 1967).

Martorell, Joanot, *Tirant lo Blanc*, tr. David H. Rosenthal (London 1984; reprinted 1985).

Merval, Louis de, *L'Entrée de Henri II, Roi de France à Rouen, Octobre 1550* (Societé des Bibliophiles Normands, Rouen, 1868).

Mills, Maldwyn, ed., *Six Middle English Romances* (London, 1973).

Moura, Jean & Louvet, Paul, *La Vie de Nostradamus* (Paris, 1930).

Muir, Edward, *Civil Ritual in Renaissance Venice* (Princeton, 1981).

Nettle, Reginald, *Seven Centuries of Popular Song* (London, 1956).

Nizam al-Mulk, *The Book of Government, or, Rules for Kings*, tr. by Hubert Darke (London, 1978).

Njal's Saga, tr. by Magnus Magnusson and Hermann Pálsson (London, 1960; reprinted 1975).

Oliver, John W. & Smith J. C., *A Scots Anthology* (Edinburgh, 1949).

Partridge, A. C., *The Language of Renaissance Poetry* (London, 1971).

Percy, Thomas, *Reliques of Ancient English Poetry* (Edinburgh, 1858), 3 vols.

Purser, John, *Scotland's Music* (Mainstream & BBC Scotland, Edinburgh, 1992).

Qur-an, the Holy, tr. by Maulvi Muhammed Ali.

Robb, Stewart, *Prophecies of Nostradamus* (New York, 1961).

Robbins, Rossell Hope, *Secular Lyrics of the XIV and XV Centuries* (Oxford, 2nd edn., 1955).

Robinson, F. N., ed., *The Complete Works of Geoffrey Chaucer* (Oxford, 1985).

Ross, D. James, *Musick Fyne: Robert Carver and the Art of Music in Sixteenth Century Scotland* (Edinburgh, 1993).

Ross, J., ed., *The Book of Scottish Poems, with Memoirs of the Author* (Edinburgh, 1949).

Rose, Martial, ed., *Wakefield Mystery Plays* (London, 1961).

Runnalls, Graham A., *Études sur les Mystères* (Paris, 1998).

Runnalls, Graham A., 'Le Mystère de la Passion à Amboise au Moyen Âge: Représentations théâtrales et texte', *Le Moyen Français, tome* XXVI (Editions CERES, Montréal, 1991).

Scott, Tom, *Late Medieval Scots Poetry* (London, 1967).

Snorri Sturluson, 'The Story of Harald the Hard-redy' from the *Heimskringla (The Saga Library*, vol. iii), eds William Morris & Eiríkr Magnússon (London, 1895).

Spiers, John, *Medieval English Poetry* (London, 1957; reprinted 1971).

Sternhod, T. & Hopkins, I., eds, *The Whole Booke of Psalmes Collected into English Metre* (John Crespin, Geneva, 1569).

Stevens, Martin, *Four Middle English Mystery Cycles* (Princeton, *c.* 1987).

Strohm, Reinhard, *Music in Late Medieval Bruges* (Oxford, 1990).

Strong, Roy, *Splendour at Court* (London, 1973).

Tusser, Thomas, *Five Hundred Points on Husbandry* (1557) (London, 1931).

Ward, Charles A., *Oracles of Nostradamus* (London, 1891).

Welsford, Enid, *The Court Masque* (Cambridge, 1927).

Yeats, W. B., ed., *Irish Fairy and Folk Tales* (London, 1893).

The Visual Arts and Costume

Angelis, Rita de, *Botticelli: the Complete Paintings*, tr. by Jane Carroll (Italy, 1979; London, 1980).

Angels, Nobles and Unicorns: Art and Patronage in Medieval Scotland (pub. for exhibition by the National Museum of Antiquities of Scotland, Edinburgh, 1982).

Arnould, Alain & Massing, Jean Michel, *Splendours of Flanders: Late Medieval Art in Cambridge Collections* (Cambridge, 1993).

Avery, Charles, *Florentine Renaissance Sculpture* (London 1970; reprinted 1982).

Baldass, Ludwig, *Van Eyck* (London, 1952).

Basing, Patricia, *Trades and Crafts in Medieval Manuscripts* (London, 1990).

Bauman, Guy, *Early Flemish Portraits 1425–1526* (Bulletin pub. by Metropolitan Museum of Art, New York, 1986).

Beckwith, John, *The Art of Constantinople* 330–1453 (London, 1961; reprinted 1968).

Bennett, Bonnie A. & Wilkins, David G., *Donatello* (Oxford, 1984).

Benzi, Fabio, *Sisto IV, Renovator Urbis Architettura a Roma, 1471–1484* (Rome, 1990).

Bialostocki, Jan, *Les Musées de la Pologne*, (Brussels, 1966).

Bisthoven, A. Janssens de, Baes-Dondeyne, M. & Vos, D. de, *De Vlaamse Primitieven* (Brussels, 1981).

Brookes, John, *Gardens of Paradise: History and Design of the Great Islamic Gardens* (New York, 1987).

Brown, Patricia Fortini, *Venetian Narrative Painting in the Age of Carpaccio* (Yale, 1988).

Campbell, Ian, 'A Romanesque Revival and the Early Renaissance in Scotland', *Journal of the Society of Architectural Historians*, 54:3 (September, 1995).

Campbell, Lorne, 'Edward Bonkil, A Scottish Patron of Hugo van der Goes', *Burlington Magazine*, cxxvi (1984).

Campbell, Lorne, 'Edward Bonkil and Hugo van der Goes', *Burlington Magazine*, cxliii (March 2001).

Campbell, Lorne, 'Notes on Netherlandish Pictures in the Veneto in the 15th and 16th Centuries', *Burlington Magazine* (August 1981).

Campbell, Lorne, *Renaissance Portraits* (Yale, 1990).

Cherry, John, *Goldsmiths* (Toronto, 1992).

Cole, Alan S., *Ornament in European Silks* (London, 1899).

Cole, Alison, *Art of the Renaissance Courts: Virtue and Magnificence* (London, 1995).

Destrée, Joseph, *Hugo van der Goes* (Brussels, 1914).

Dhanens, Elizabeth, *Van Eyck* (New York, n.d.).

Ettinghausen, Richard & Yarshater, Ehsan, *Highlights of Persian Art* (Colorado, 1979).

Garas, Klára, *Italian Renaissance Portraits*, tr. by Lili Halápy (Budapest, 1974).

Hale, J. R., ed., *A Concise Encyclopaedia of the Italian Renaissance* (London, 1981).

Hamilton, G. H., *Art and Architecture of Russia* (London, 1954).

Hand, John O. & Wolff, Martha, *Early Netherlandish Painting in the National Gallery, Washington* (Washington, 1986).

Hennessy, John Pope & Christensen, Keith, *Secular Painting in Fifteenth Century Tuscany* (Metropolitan Museum of Art, New York, 1980).

Herald, Jacqueline, *Renaissance Dress in Italy, 1400–1500* (London, 1981).

Houston, Mary G., *Ancient Greek, Roman and Byzantine Costume and Decoration* (London, 1931; reprinted 1977).

Islamic Painting (Metropolitan Museum of Art, New York, 1978).

Johnson, Arthur W., *Bookbinding* (London, 1978).

Kaufmann, Thomas Da Costa, *Court, Cloister & City: The Art and Culture of Central Europe, 1450–1899* (London, 1995).

Knox, Brian, *The Architecture of Poland* (London, 1971).

Letts, Rosa M., *Florentine Art Treasures* (London, n.d., *c.* 1981).

Letts, Rosa M., *The Renaissance* (Cambridge, 1981).

Levenson, Jay A., *Circa 1492* (pub. for quincetenary exhibition on Columbus at National Gallery of Art, Washington, USA, 1992).

Levey, Michael, *The World of Ottoman Art* (London, 1975).

Luca, Andrea, *Giovanni della Robbia* (Gaeta Bertelà, Florence, n.d.).

Macmillan, Duncan, *Scottish Art 1460–1990* (Edinburgh, 1989).

McRobert, David, 'Notes on Scoto-Flemish Artistic Contacts', *The Innes Review*, vol. x (1959).

Mantegna, Andrea (pub. for exhibition by Royal Academy of Arts, London & Metropolitan Museum of Art, New York, 1992).

Marshall, Rosalind & Dalgleish, G. R., *The Art of Jewellery in Scotland* (in conjunction with Scottish National Portrait Gallery Exhibition, Edinburgh, 1991).

Mawdsley, William N. H., *A History of Legal Dress in Europe to the End of the Eighteenth Century* (Oxford, 1963).

Mayer, L. A., *Mamluk Costume: A Survey* (Geneva, 1952).

Metin, A., *Turkish Miniature Painting* (Ankara, 1974).

Millon, Henry, ed., *The Renaissance from Brunelleschi to Michelangelo: The Representation of Architecture* (London, 1994).

Munman, Robert, 'Optical Corrections in the Sculpture of Donatello', *Transactions of the American Philosophical Society*, vol. lxxv, part 2 (1985).

Murray, Peter & Murray, Linda, *The Art of the Renaissance* (London, 1963; reprinted 1978).

Olivari, Mariolina, *Giovanni Bellini* (Italy, 1990; New York, 1991).

Oman, Charles, *English Silver in the Kremlin 1557–1563* (London, 1971).

Percival, MacIver, *Chats on Old Jewellery and Trinkets* (London, 1912).

Piponnier, Françoise, *Costume et vie sociale: la cour d'Anjou XIVᵉ–XVᵉ siècle* (Paris, 1970).

Quicherat, J., *Histoire de Costume en France* (Paris, 1875).

Renaissance: Six Essays, The (pub. by the Metropolitan Museum of Art, New York, 1953; republished by Harper & Row, 1962).

Renaissance in Italy and Spain, The (Metropolitan Museum of Art, New York, 1987).

Renaissance in the North, The (Metropolitan Museum of Art, New York, 1987).

Rice, David Talbot, *Byzantine Art* (Oxford, 1935; reprinted London, 1968).

Rice, David Talbot, *Islamic Art* (London, 1965; reprinted 1984).

Rice, David Talbot, *The Church of Haghia Sophia at Trebizond* (Edinburgh, 1968).

Rice, Tamara Talbot, *Concise History of Russian Art* (London, 1963).

Rice, Tamara Talbot, *Russian Art* (London, 1949).

Richardson, J. S., *The Mediaeval Stone Carver in Scotland* (Edinburgh, 1964).

Robin, Françoise, *La cour d'Anjou–Provence: la vie artistique sous le règne de René* (Picard, 1985).

Roover, Florence Edler de, 'A Prize of War: a Painting of 15th-century Merchants', *Bulletin of the Business Historical Society* (New York, n.d.).

Roudaut, Jean & Perocco, Guido, *Tout l'Oeuvre Peint de Carpaccio* (Milan, 1967; Paris, 1981).

Scott, Margaret, *The Fourteenth and Fifteenth Centuries: a Visual History of Costume* (London, 1986).

Seidel, Linda, *Jan van Eyck's Arnolfini Portrait* (Cambridge, 1993).

Steer, John, *A Concise History of Venetian Painting* (London, 1970).

Swaan, Wim, *Art and Architecture of the Late Middle Ages* (London, 1982).

Thompson, Colin & Campbell, Lorne, *Hugo van der Goes and the Trinity Panels in Edinburgh* (Glasgow, 1974).

Thornton, Peter, *The Italian Renaissance Interior 1400–1600* (London, 1991).

Titley, Norah M., *Sports and Pastimes in Turkish, Persian and Mughal Paintings* (London, 1979).

Unterkircher, Franz, *King René's Book of Love*, tr. by Sophie Wilkins (New York, 1975; reprinted 1980).

Végh, Jánds, *Fifteenth-Century Netherlandish Painting* (Budapest, 1977).

Vasari, Giorgio, *Lives of Painters, Sculptors and Architects, 1550* (London, 1996, from English tr., first pub. 1912).

Vecellio, Cesare, *Vecellio's Renaissance Costume Book* (New York, 1977).

Vos, Dirk de, *Hans Memling – Complete Works* (London, 1994).

Vos, Dirk de, *Hans Memling Exhibition, Bruges, 1994: Catalogue & Essays*, tr. by T. Atkins & Marcus Cumberledge (Bruges, 1994).

Welch, Stuart Cary, *Royal Persian Manuscripts* (London, 1976).

Wilcox, R. Turner, *The Mode in Costume* (New York, 1948).

Wolf, Robert E. & Millen, Ronald, *Renaissance and Mannerist Art* (Germany & London, 1968).

Yarwood, Doreen, *The Encyclopaedia of World Costume* (London, 1978).

Zuffi, Stefano, *Giovanni Bellini*, tr. Richard Sadleir (Milan, 1991).

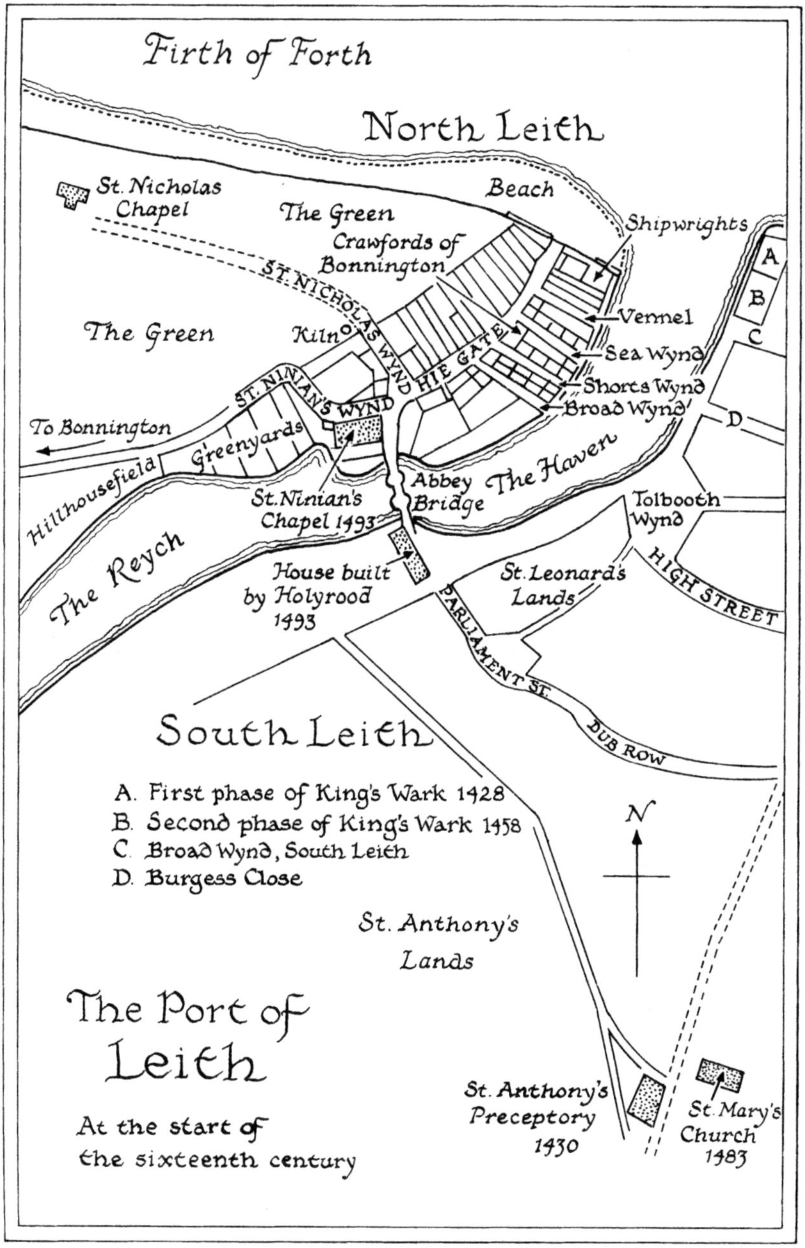
Firth of Forth
North Leith
St. Nicholas Chapel
The Green
Beach
Crawfords of Bonnington
Shipwrights
A
B
C
D
ST. NICHOLAS WYND
Vennel
The Green
Kiln
HIE GATE
Sea Wynd
Shorts Wynd
Broad Wynd
ST. NINIAN'S WYND
To Bonnington
Greenyards
Hillhousefield
The Haven
Abbey Bridge
St. Ninian's Chapel 1493
Tolbooth Wynd
The Reych
House built by Holyrood 1493
St. Leonard's Lands
HIGH STREET
PARLIAMENT ST.
DUB ROW
South Leith
A. First phase of King's Wark 1428
B. Second phase of King's Wark 1458
C. Broad Wynd, South Leith
D. Burgess Close
N
St. Anthony's Lands
The Port of Leith
At the start of the sixteenth century
St. Anthony's Preceptory 1430
St. Mary's Church 1483

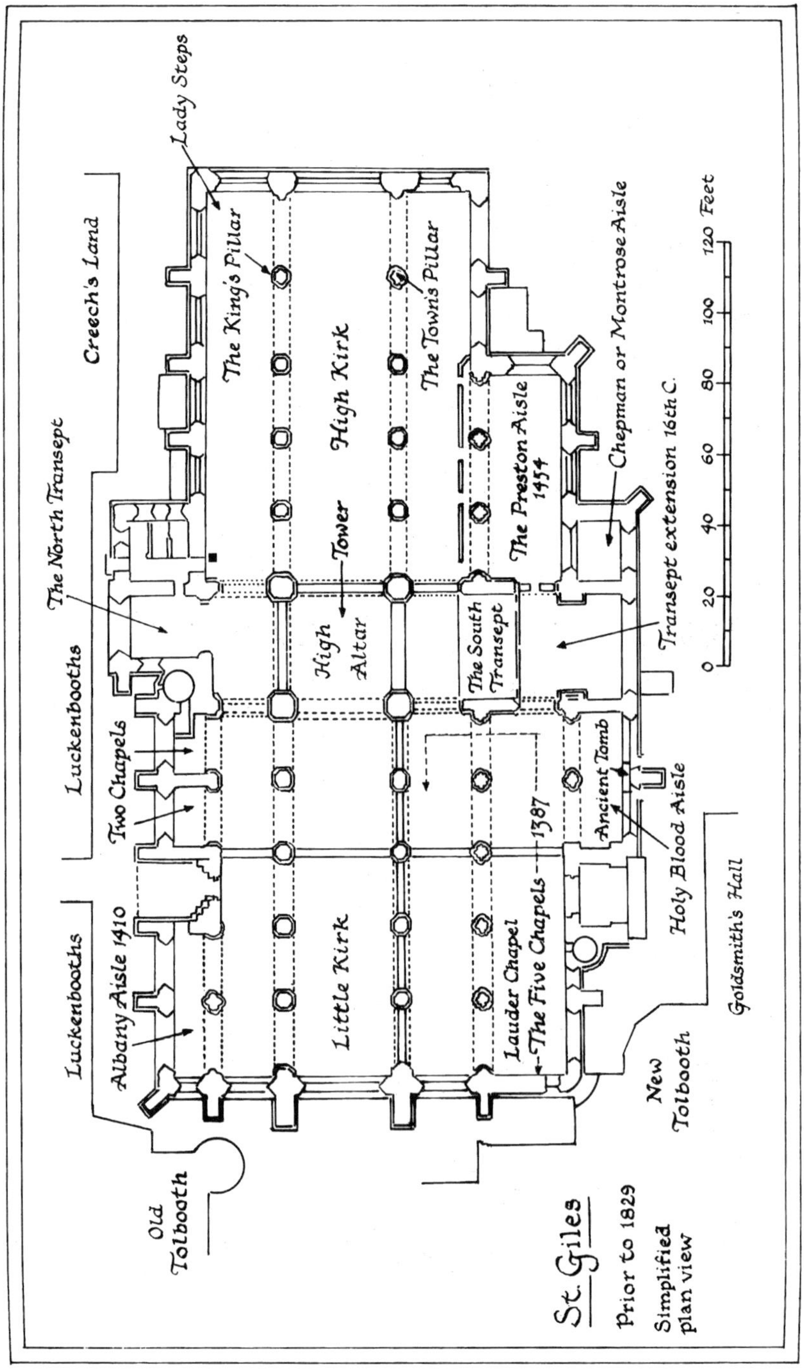
St. Giles
Prior to 1829
Simplified plan view
Lady Steps
Creech's Land
The King's Pillar
High Kirk
The Town's Pillar
Chepman or Montrose Aisle
120 Feet
100
80
60
40
20
0
The Preston Aisle 1454
Transept extension 16th C.
The North Transept
Tower
High Altar
The South Transept
Luckenbooths
Two Chapels
Ancient Tomb
Holy Blood Aisle
1387
Goldsmith's Hall
Luckenbooths
Albany Aisle 1410
Little Kirk
Lauder Chapel
The Five Chapels
New Tolbooth
Old Tolbooth

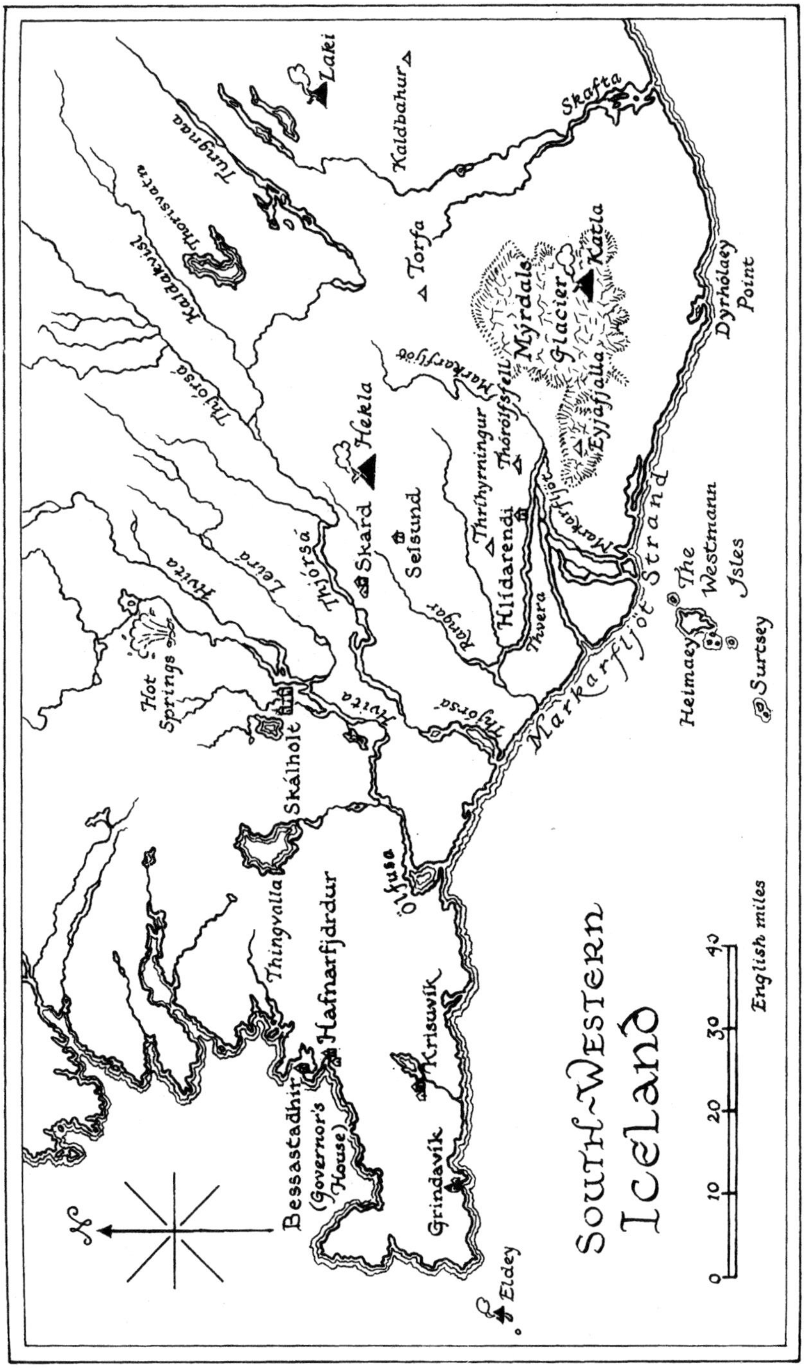
South-Western
Iceland
Laki
Kaldbakur
Skafta
Tungnaa
Thorisvatn
Kaldakvisl
Torfa
Katla
Myrdals
Glacier
Dyrhólaey
Point
Markarfljót
Thjórsá
Hekla
Eyjafjalla
Thórólfsfell
Thríhyrningur
Skard
Selsund
Hlidarendi
Rangar
Thvera
Markarfljót
Strand
The
Westmann
Isles
Heimaey
Surtsey
Hvitá
Leira
Hot
Springs
Skálholt
Ölfusa
Thingvalla
Hafnarfjördur
Bessastadhir
(Governor's
House)
Krisuvík
Grindavík
Eldey
0 10 20 30 40
English miles

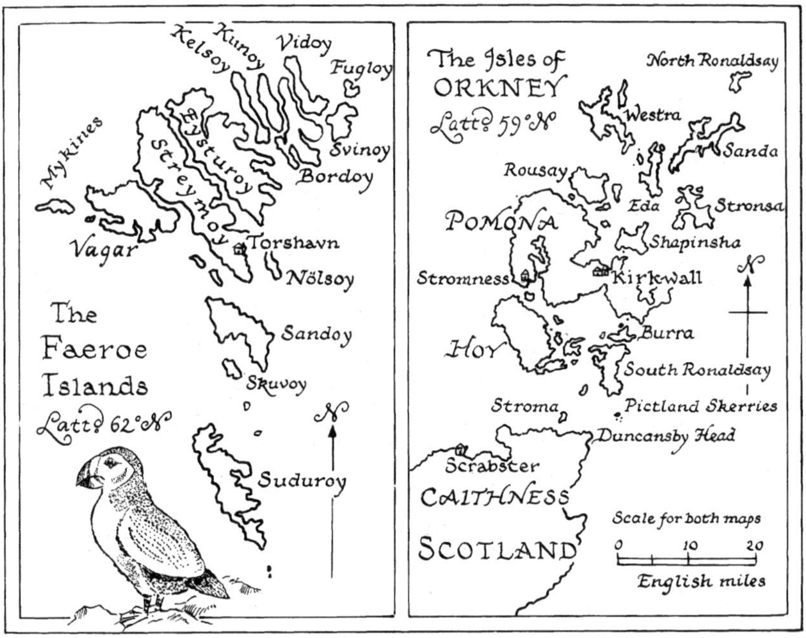
Kunoy
Kelsoy
Vidoy
Fugloy
Mykines
Eysturoy
Streymoy
Svinoy
Bordoy
Vagar
Torshavn
Nölsoy
The Faeroe Islands
Latt. 62° N
Sandoy
Skuvoy
N
Suduroy
The Isles of ORKNEY
Latt. 59° N
North Ronaldsay
Westra
Sanda
Rousay
Eda
Stronsa
POMONA
Shapinsha
Stromness
Kirkwall
N
HOY
Burra
South Ronaldsay
Stroma
Pictland Skerries
Duncansby Head
Scrabster
CAITHNESS
SCOTLAND
Scale for both maps
0
10
20
English miles

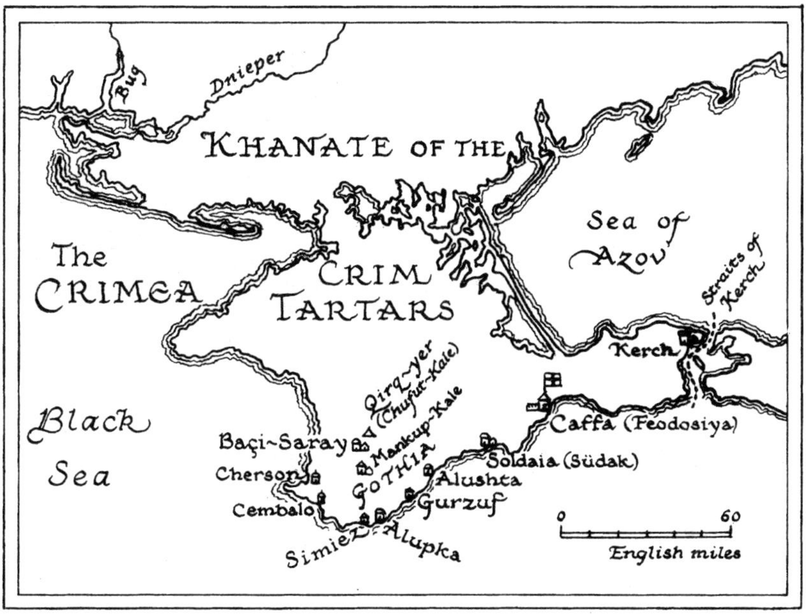
Bug
Dnieper
KHANATE OF THE
CRIM
TARTARS
The
CRIMEA
Sea of
Azov
Straits of
Kerch
Kerch
Black
Sea
Qirq-yer
(Chufut-Kale)
Mankup-Kale
Baçi-Saray
Cherson
Cembalo
GOTHIA
Caffa (Feodosiya)
Soldaia (Südak)
Alushta
Gurzuf
Simiez
Alupka
0
60
English miles

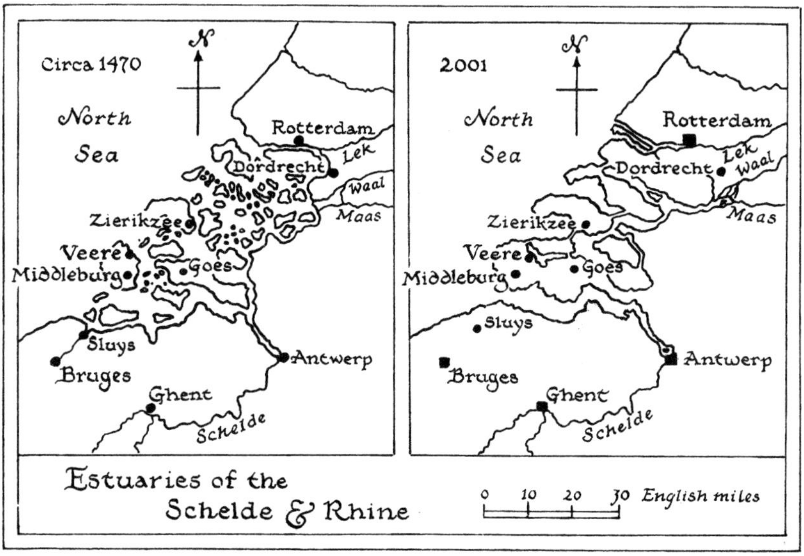
Circa 1470
N
North
Sea
Rotterdam
Lek
Dordrecht
Waal
Maas
Zierikzee
Veere
Middleburg
Goes
Sluys
Bruges
Ghent
Antwerp
Schelde
2001
N
North
Sea
Rotterdam
Lek
Dordrecht
Waal
Maas
Zierikzee
Veere
Middleburg
Goes
Sluys
Bruges
Ghent
Antwerp
Schelde
Estuaries of the
Schelde & Rhine
0 10 20 30 English miles

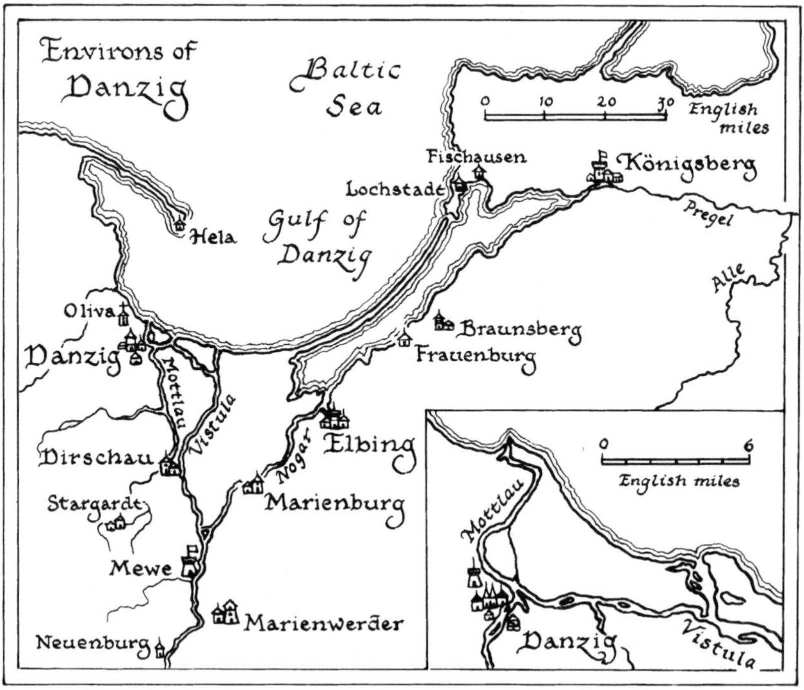
Environs of Danzig
Baltic Sea
0 10 20 30 English miles
Fischausen
Königsberg
Lochstade
Pregel
Hela
Gulf of Danzig
Alle
Oliva
Braunsberg
Danzig
Frauenburg
Mottlau
Vistula
Elbing
Nogat
Dirschau
Marienburg
Stargardt
Mewe
Marienwerder
Neuenburg
0 6
English miles
Mottlau
Danzig
Vistula

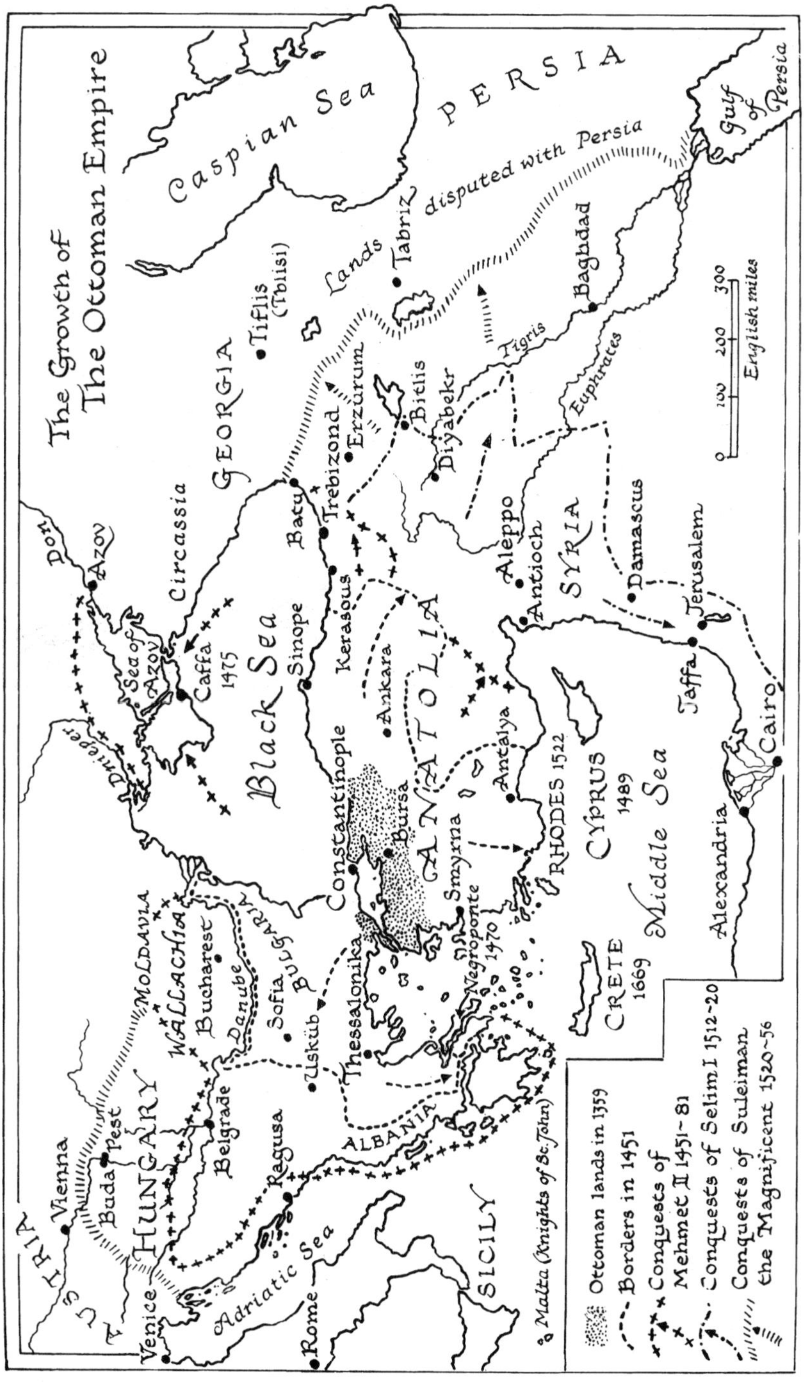
The Growth of
The Ottoman Empire
Caspian Sea
PERSIA
Lands disputed with Persia
Gulf of Persia
Tabriz
Tiflis (Tbilisi)
GEORGIA
Circassia
Don
Azov
Sea of Azov
Caffa 1475
Black Sea
Batu
Trebizond
Erzurum
Bitlis
Diyabekr
Tigris
Baghdad
Euphrates
Aleppo
Antioch
SYRIA
Damascus
Jerusalem
Jaffa
Cairo
Alexandria
Sinope
Kerasous
Ankara
ANATOLIA
Constantinople
Bursa
Smyrna
Antalya
RHODES 1522
CYPRUS 1489
Middle Sea
CRETE 1669
Negroponte 1470
Thessalonika
Üsküb
Sofia
BULGARIA
Danube
Bucharest
WALLACHIA
MOLDAVIA
Dniepr
Belgrade
HUNGARY
Buda Pest
Vienna
AUSTRIA
Venice
Ragusa
ALBANIA
Adriatic Sea
Rome
SICILY
Malta (Knights of St. John)
0 100 200 300
English miles
Ottoman lands in 1359
Borders in 1451
Conquests of Mehmet II 1451–81
Conquests of Selim I 1512–20
Conquests of Suleiman the Magnificent 1520–56

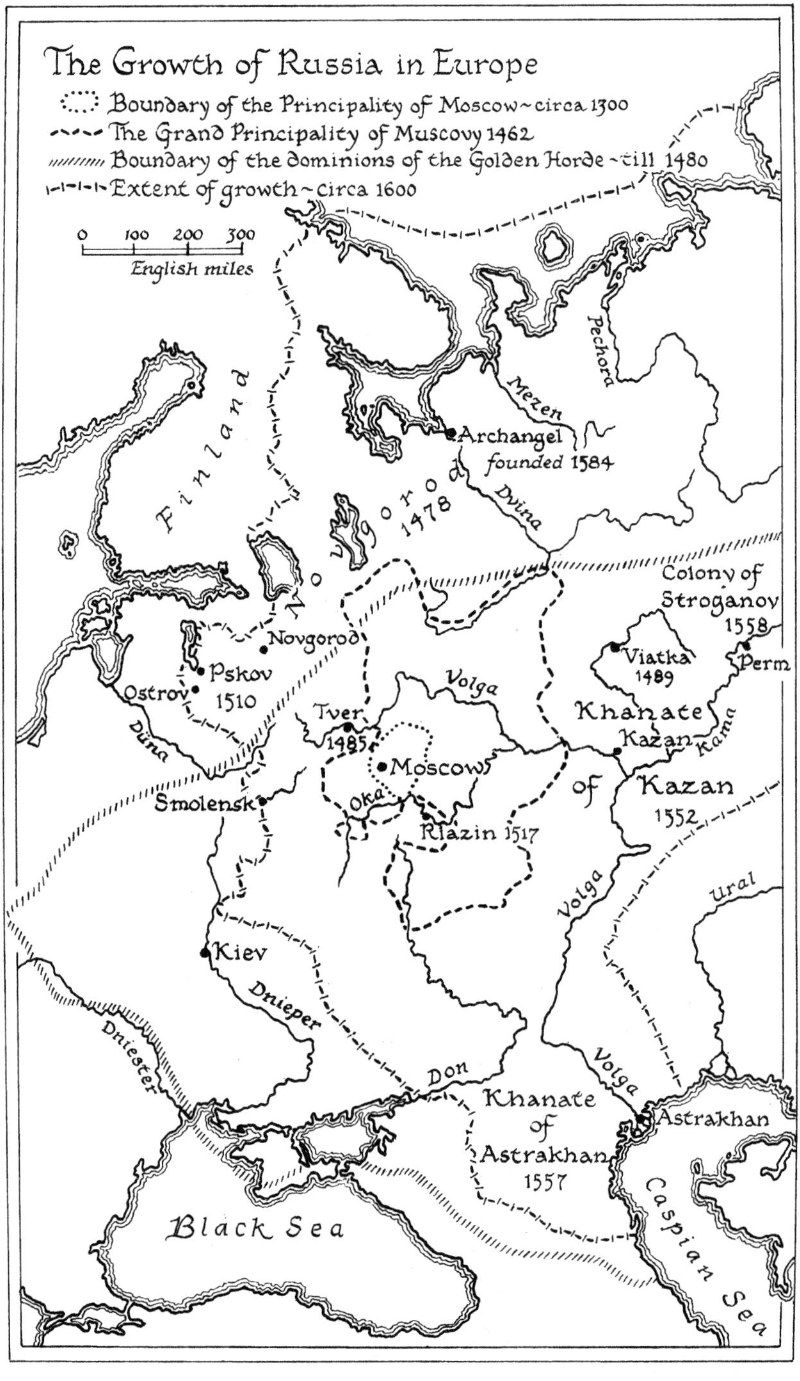
The Growth of Russia in Europe
Boundary of the Principality of Moscow ~ circa 1300
The Grand Principality of Muscovy 1462
Boundary of the dominions of the Golden Horde ~ till 1480
Extent of growth ~ circa 1600
0 100 200 300
English miles
Finland
Novgorod 1478
Archangel
founded 1584
Mezen
Pechora
Dvina
Colony of Stroganov 1558
Viatka 1489
Perm
Novgorod
Pskov 1510
Ostrov
Düna
Tver 1485
Volga
Khanate of Kazan 1552
Kazan
Kama
Moscow
Oka
Smolensk
Riazin 1517
Volga
Ural
Kiev
Dnieper
Dniester
Don
Khanate of Astrakhan 1557
Volga
Astrakhan
Caspian Sea
Black Sea

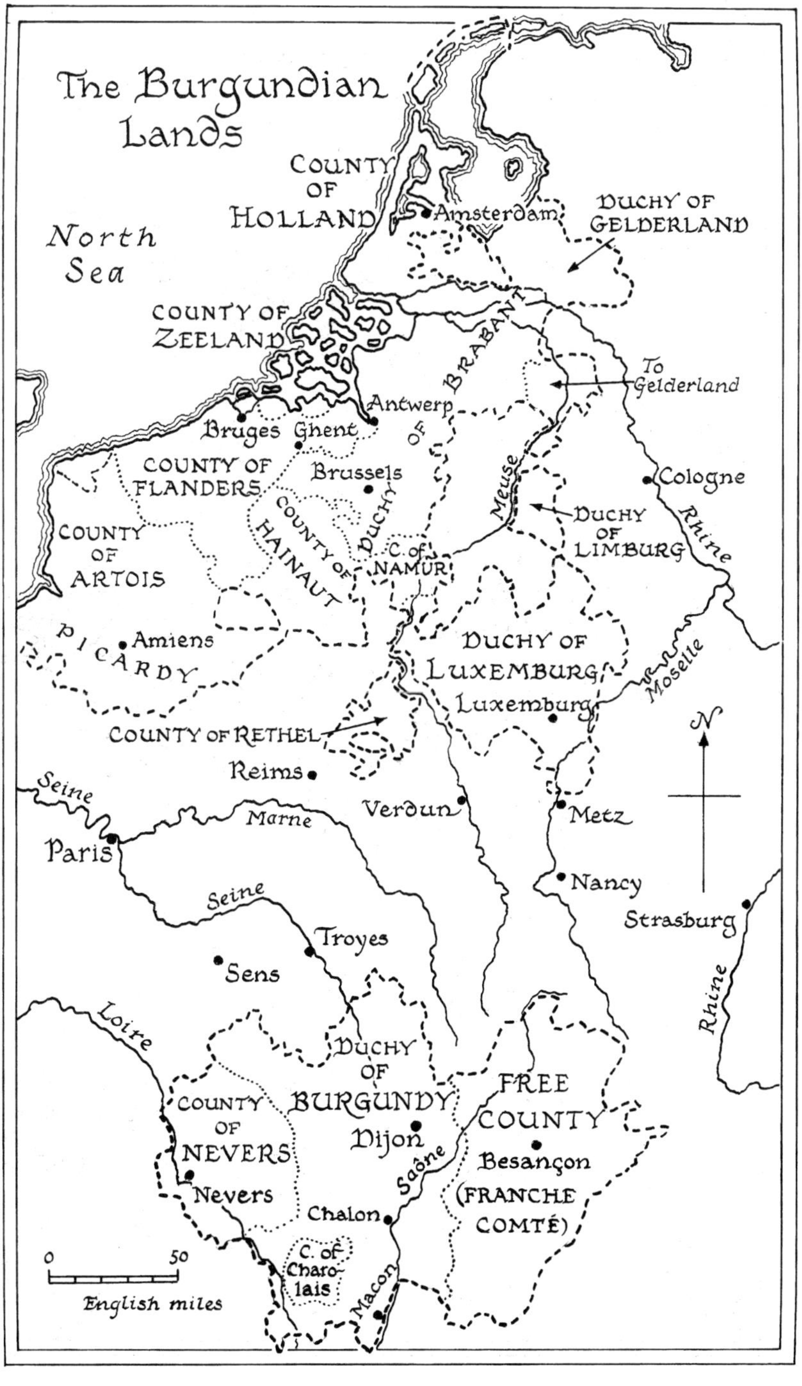
The Burgundian Lands
COUNTY OF HOLLAND
Amsterdam
DUCHY OF GELDERLAND
North Sea
COUNTY OF ZEELAND
BRABANT
To Gelderland
Antwerp
Bruges
Ghent
OF
COUNTY OF FLANDERS
Brussels
Cologne
Rhine
DUCHY
COUNTY OF HAINAUT
Meuse
DUCHY OF LIMBURG
COUNTY OF ARTOIS
C. of NAMUR
PICARDY
Amiens
DUCHY OF LUXEMBURG
Luxemburg
Moselle
COUNTY OF RETHEL
N
Reims
Seine
Verdun
Metz
Marne
Paris
Nancy
Seine
Strasburg
Troyes
Sens
Rhine
Loire
DUCHY OF BURGUNDY
FREE COUNTY
COUNTY OF NEVERS
Dijon
Besançon
(FRANCHE COMTÉ)
Saône
Nevers
Chalon
C. of Charolais
Macon
0
50
English miles

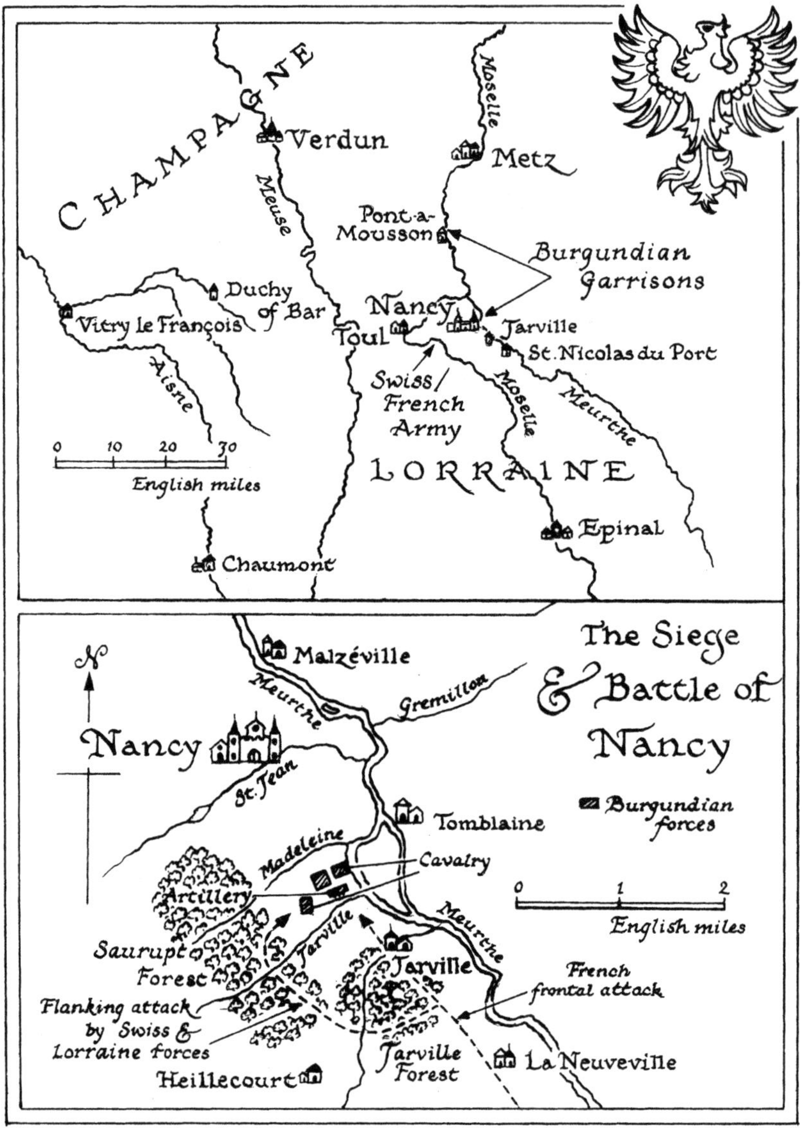
CHAMPAGNE
Verdun
Meuse
Moselle
Metz
Pont-a-Mousson
Burgundian Garrisons
Duchy of Bar
Vitry le François
Nancy
Toul
Jarville
St. Nicolas du Port
Aisne
Swiss/ French Army
Moselle
Meurthe
0 10 20 30
English miles
LORRAINE
Epinal
Chaumont
Malzéville
The Siege & Battle of Nancy
N
Meurthe
Gremillon
Nancy
St. Jean
Tomblaine
Burgundian forces
Madeleine
Cavalry
Artillery
0 1 2
English miles
Meurthe
Saurupt Forest
Jarville
Jarville
French frontal attack
Flanking attack by Swiss & Lorraine forces
Jarville Forest
La Neuveville
Heillecourt

Foreword to Family Trees

In addition to the royal families of early modern Europe, these genealogies give an impression of the complex links of kinship and loyalty that extend through the generations, so that readers may follow the families, such as the Strozzi and Lennox, who appear in the *House of Niccolò* and the *Lymond Chronicles.* They have been selectively compiled to draw attention to the historical figures prominent in both series, many of whom have entries in either Volume I or II of the *Companion.*

Dates of rule have been given for monarchs; for other characters only their date of death has been given.

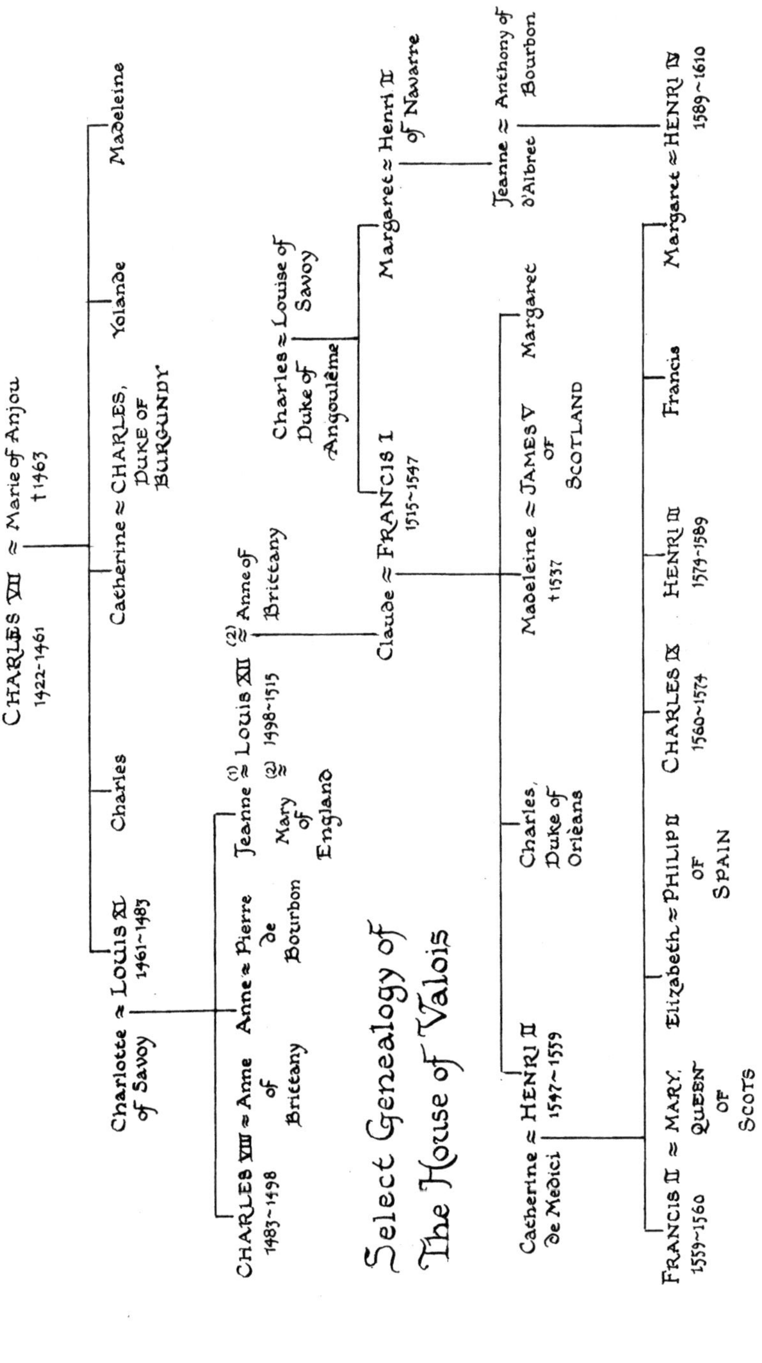
Select Genealogy of The House of Valois
CHARLES VII 1422-1461 ≈ Marie of Anjou †1463
Charlotte of Savoy ≈ LOUIS XI 1461-1483
Charles
Catherine ≈ CHARLES, DUKE OF BURGUNDY
Yolande
Madeleine
CHARLES VIII 1483-1498 ≈ Anne of Brittany
Anne ≈ Pierre de Bourbon
Jeanne (1) ≈ LOUIS XII 1498-1515 (2) ≈ Anne of Brittany
(2) ≈ Mary of England
Charles, Duke of Angoulême ≈ Louise of Savoy
Claude ≈ FRANCIS I 1515-1547
Margaret ≈ Henri II of Navarre
Catherine de Medici ≈ HENRI II 1547-1559
Charles, Duke of Orléans
Madeleine †1537 ≈ JAMES V OF SCOTLAND
Margaret
Jeanne d'Albret ≈ Anthony of Bourbon
FRANCIS II 1559-1560 ≈ MARY, QUEEN OF SCOTS
Elizabeth ≈ PHILIP II OF SPAIN
CHARLES IX 1560-1574
HENRI III 1574-1589
Francis
Margaret ≈ HENRI IV 1589-1610

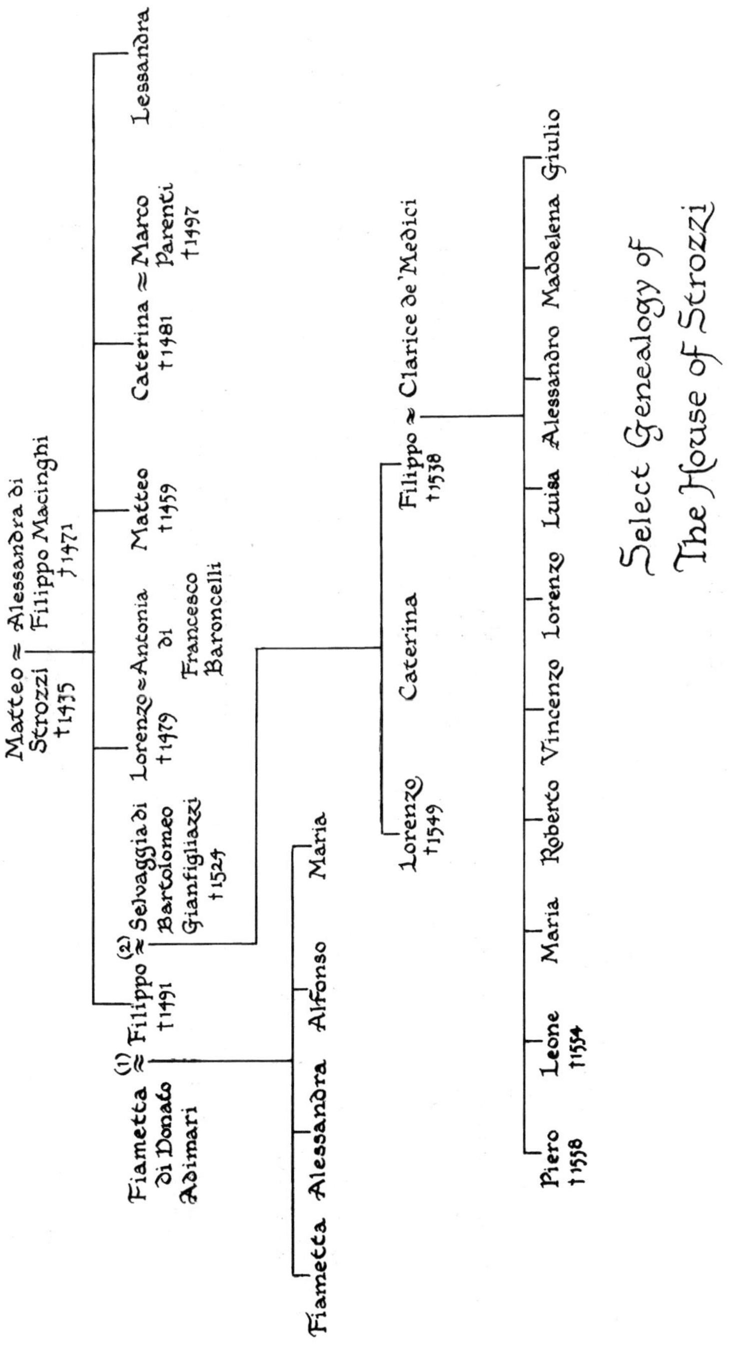
Select Genealogy of The House of Strozzi
Matteo Strozzi †1435 ≈ Alessandra di Filippo Macinghi †1471
Filippo †1491
Lorenzo †1479 ≈ Antonia di Francesco Baroncelli
Matteo †1459
Caterina †1481 ≈ Marco Parenti †1497
Lessandra
Fiametta di Donato Adimari (1) ≈ Filippo (2) ≈ Selvaggia di Bartolomeo Gianfigliazzi †1524
Fiametta
Alessandra
Alfonso
Maria
Lorenzo †1549
Caterina
Filippo †1538 ≈ Clarice de' Medici
Piero †1558
Leone †1554
Maria
Roberto
Vincenzo
Lorenzo
Luisa
Alessandro
Maddelena
Giulio

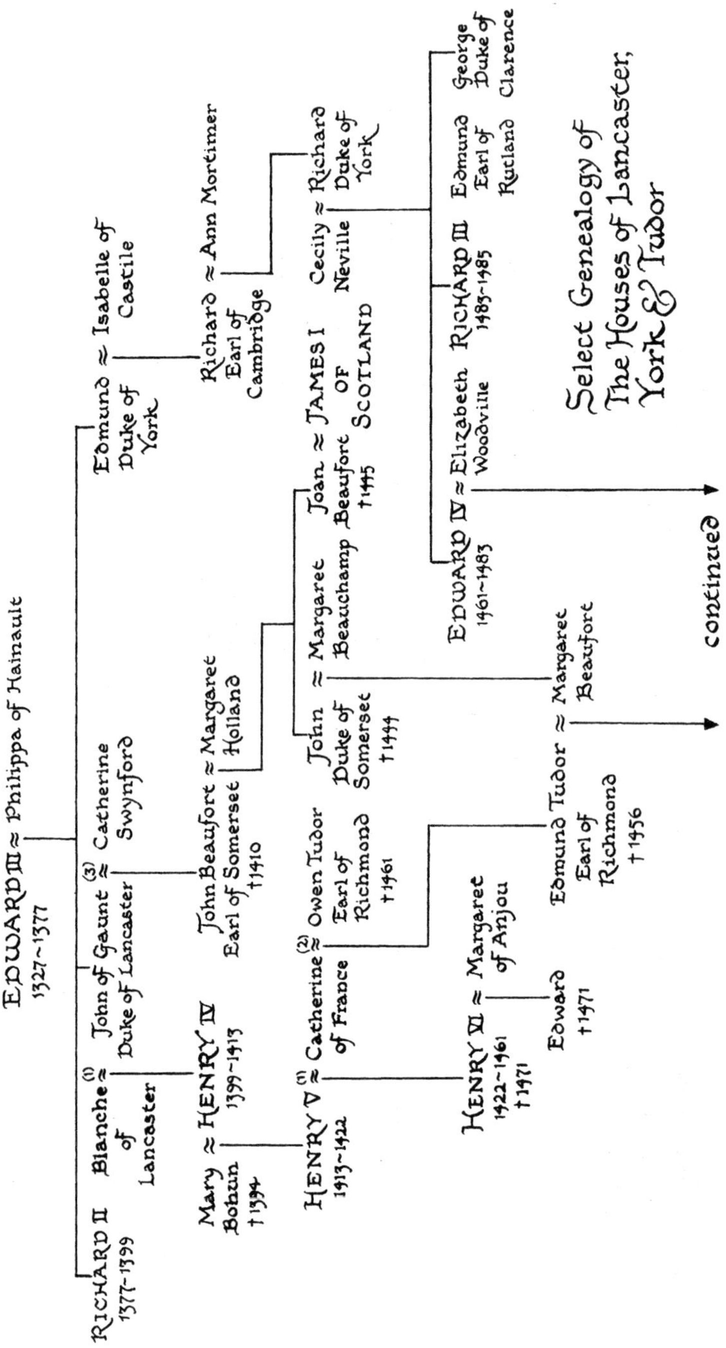
Select Genealogy of The Houses of Lancaster, York & Tudor
EDWARD III 1327~1377
Philippa of Hainault
RICHARD II 1377-1399
Blanche of Lancaster
(1)
John of Gaunt Duke of Lancaster
(3)
Catherine Swynford
Edmund Duke of York
Isabelle of Castile
Mary Bohun †1394
HENRY IV 1399-1413
John Beaufort Earl of Somerset †1410
Margaret Holland
Richard Earl of Cambridge
Ann Mortimer
HENRY V 1413-1422
(1)
Catherine of France
(2)
Owen Tudor Earl of Richmond †1461
John Duke of Somerset †1444
Margaret Beauchamp
Joan Beaufort †1445
JAMES I OF SCOTLAND
Cecily Neville
Richard Duke of York
HENRY VI 1422-1461 †1471
Margaret of Anjou
Edward †1471
Edmund Tudor Earl of Richmond †1456
Margaret Beaufort
EDWARD IV 1461-1483
Elizabeth Woodville
RICHARD III 1483-1485
Edmund Earl of Rutland
George Duke of Clarence
continued

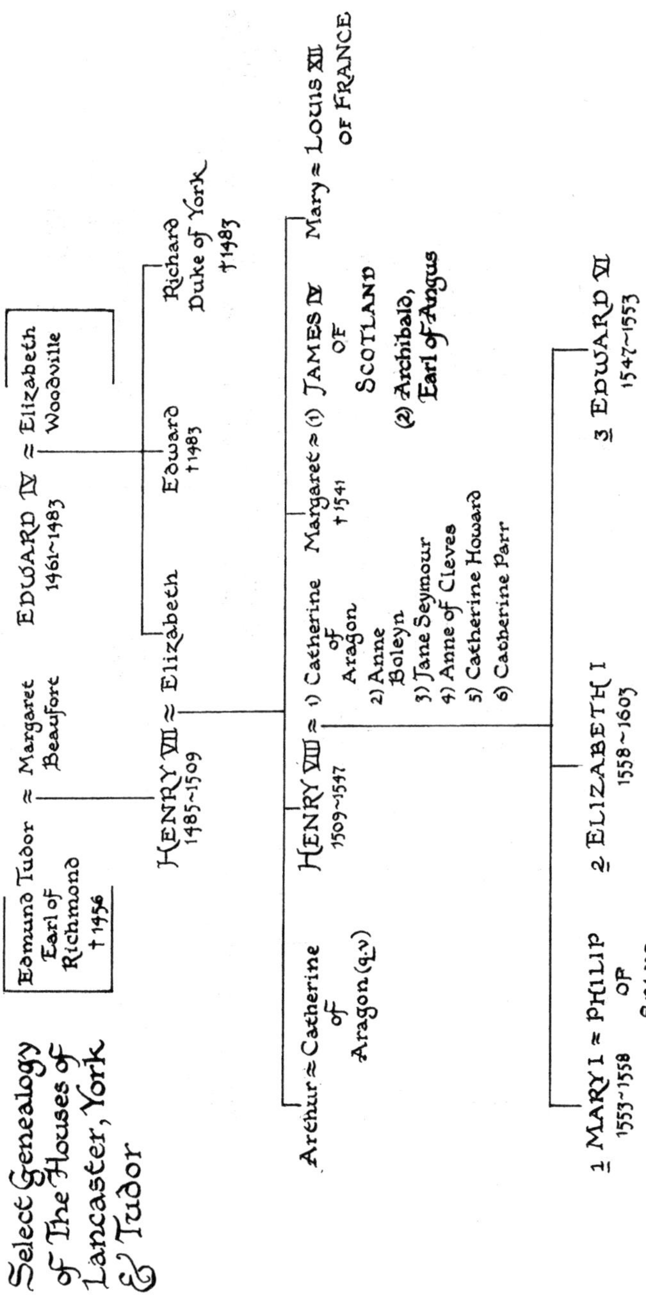
Select Genealogy of The Houses of Lancaster, York & Tudor
Edmund Tudor Earl of Richmond †1456
≈ Margaret Beaufort
EDWARD IV 1461~1483
≈ Elizabeth Woodville
HENRY VII 1485~1509
≈ Elizabeth
Edward †1483
Richard Duke of York †1483
Arthur ≈ Catherine of Aragon (q.v)
HENRY VIII 1509~1547
≈ 1) Catherine of Aragon
2) Anne Boleyn
3) Jane Seymour
4) Anne of Cleves
5) Catherine Howard
6) Catherine Parr
Margaret †1541
≈ (1) JAMES IV OF SCOTLAND
(2) Archibald, Earl of Angus
Mary ≈ LOUIS XII OF FRANCE
1 MARY I 1553~1558 ≈ PHILIP OF SPAIN
2 ELIZABETH I 1558~1603
3 EDWARD VI 1547~1553

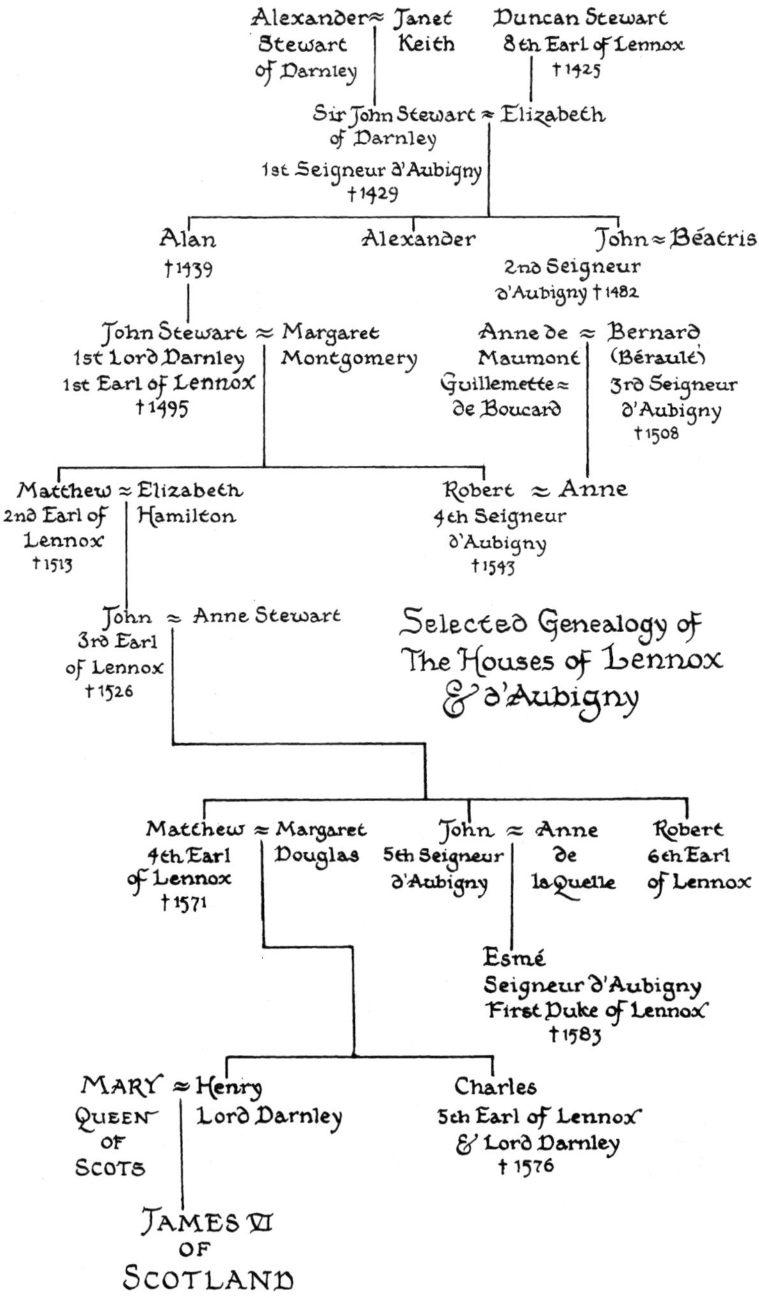
Alexander Stewart of Darnley ≈ Janet Keith
Duncan Stewart 8th Earl of Lennox †1425
Sir John Stewart of Darnley 1st Seigneur d'Aubigny †1429 ≈ Elizabeth
Alan †1439
Alexander
John ≈ Béatris
2nd Seigneur d'Aubigny †1482
John Stewart 1st Lord Darnley 1st Earl of Lennox †1495 ≈ Margaret Montgomery
Anne de Maumont ≈ Bernard (Bérault) 3rd Seigneur d'Aubigny †1508
Guillemette ≈ de Boucard
Matthew 2nd Earl of Lennox †1513 ≈ Elizabeth Hamilton
Robert 4th Seigneur d'Aubigny †1543 ≈ Anne
John 3rd Earl of Lennox †1526 ≈ Anne Stewart
Selected Genealogy of The Houses of Lennox & d'Aubigny
Matthew 4th Earl of Lennox †1571 ≈ Margaret Douglas
John 5th Seigneur d'Aubigny ≈ Anne de la Quelle
Robert 6th Earl of Lennox
Esmé Seigneur d'Aubigny First Duke of Lennox †1583
MARY QUEEN OF SCOTS ≈ Henry Lord Darnley
Charles 5th Earl of Lennox & Lord Darnley †1576
JAMES VI OF SCOTLAND

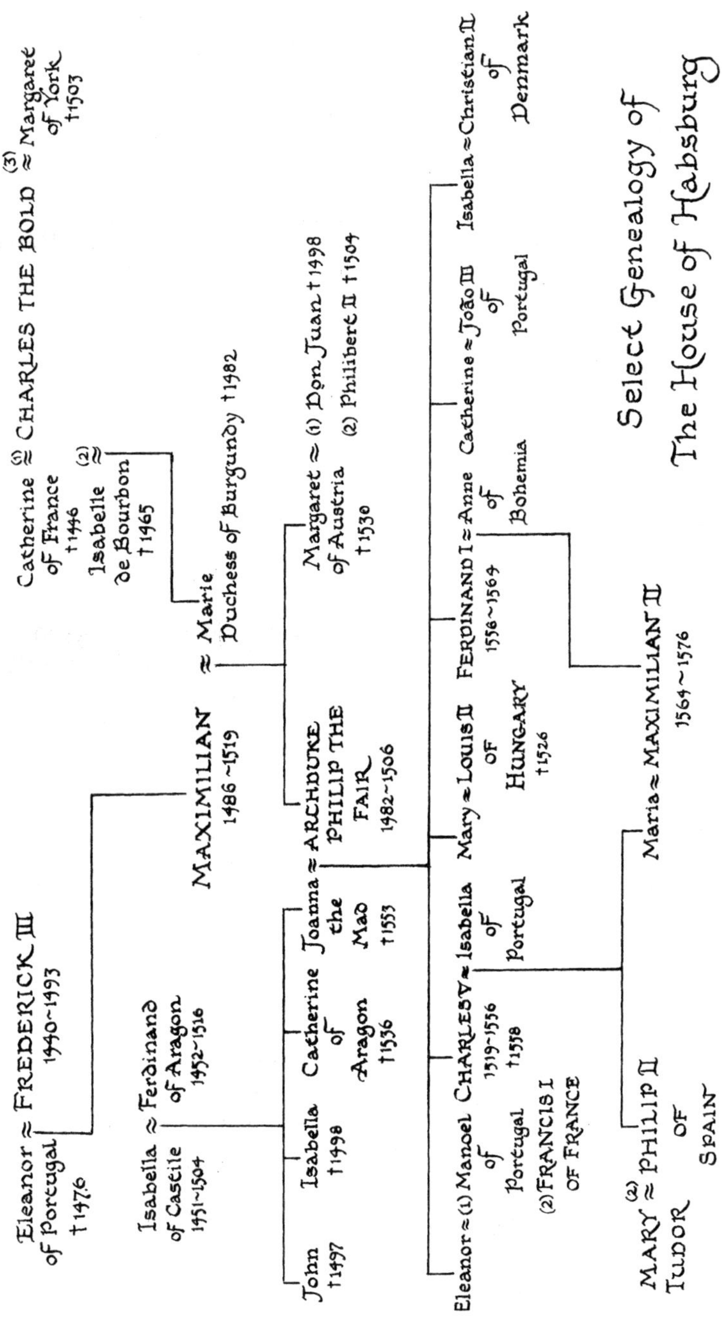
Select Genealogy of The House of Habsburg
Eleanor of Portugal †1476 ≈ FREDERICK III 1440–1493
Catherine of France †1446 (1) ≈ CHARLES THE BOLD (3) ≈ Margaret of York †1503
(2) ≈ Isabelle de Bourbon †1465
MAXIMILIAN 1486–1519 ≈ Marie Duchess of Burgundy †1482
Isabella of Castile 1451–1504 ≈ Ferdinand of Aragon 1452–1516
John †1497
Isabella †1498
Catherine of Aragon †1536
Joanna the Mad †1555 ≈ ARCHDUKE PHILIP THE FAIR 1482–1506
Margaret of Austria †1530 ≈ (1) Don Juan †1498 (2) Philibert II †1504
Eleanor ≈ (1) Manoel of Portugal (2) FRANCIS I OF FRANCE
CHARLES V 1519–1556 †1558 ≈ Isabella of Portugal
Mary ≈ Louis II of Hungary †1526
FERDINAND I 1556–1564 ≈ Anne of Bohemia
Catherine ≈ João III of Portugal
Isabella ≈ Christian II of Denmark
MARY TUDOR (2) ≈ PHILIP II OF SPAIN
Maria ≈ MAXIMILIAN II 1564–1576

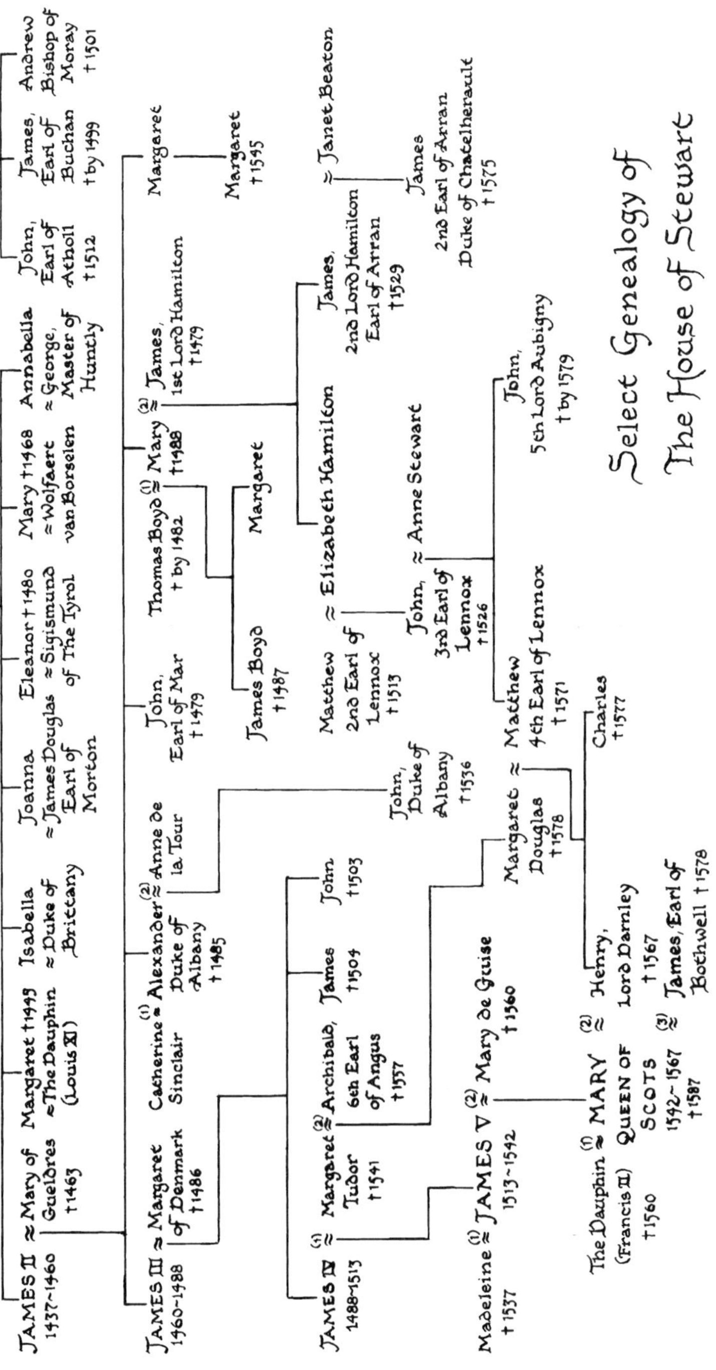
Select Genealogy of The House of Stewart
JAMES I 1406–1437
(1) ≈ Joan Beaufort †1445 (2) ≈ James Stewart 'The Black Knight of Lorne'
JAMES II 1437–1460 ≈ Mary of Gueldres †1463
Margaret †1445 ≈ The Dauphin (Louis XI)
Isabella ≈ Duke of Brittany
Joanna ≈ James Douglas Earl of Morton
Eleanor †1480 ≈ Sigismund of The Tyrol
Mary †1468 ≈ Wolfaert van Borselen
Annabella ≈ George, Master of Huntly
John, Earl of Atholl †1512
James, Earl of Buchan †by 1499
Andrew Bishop of Moray †1501
JAMES III 1460–1488 ≈ Margaret of Denmark †1486
Catherine Sinclair (1) ≈ Alexander (2) ≈ Anne de la Tour
Alexander Duke of Albany †1485
John, Earl of Mar †1479
Thomas Boyd †by 1482 (1) ≈ Mary †1488 (2) ≈ James, 1st Lord Hamilton †1479
Margaret
Margaret †1545
James Boyd †1487
Margaret
JAMES IV 1488–1513 (1) ≈ Margaret Tudor †1541 (2) ≈ Archibald, 6th Earl of Angus †1557
James †1504
John †1503
John, Duke of Albany †1536
Matthew 2nd Earl of Lennox †1513 ≈ Elizabeth Hamilton
James, 2nd Lord Hamilton Earl of Arran †1529 ≈ Janet Beaton
James 2nd Earl of Arran Duke of Chatelherault †1575
John, 3rd Earl of Lennox †1526 ≈ Anne Stewart
Matthew 4th Earl of Lennox †1571
John, 5th Lord Aubigny †by 1579
Madeleine †1537 (1) ≈ JAMES V 1513–1542 (2) ≈ Mary de Guise †1560
Margaret Douglas †1578 ≈ Matthew
Charles †1577
The Dauphin (Francis II) †1560 (1) ≈ MARY QUEEN OF SCOTS 1542–1567 †1587
(2) ≈ Henry, Lord Darnley †1567
(3) ≈ James, Earl of Bothwell †1578